Data Analysis Using SPSS

D. N. Sansanwal

SHIPRA

₹ 950; US$ 31.70
ISBN: 978-93-91978-38-9

First Published in India in 2023

Data Analysis Using SPSS

Published by:
SHIPRA PUBLICATIONS
LG 18-19, Pankaj Central Market
I.P. Ext., Patparganj, Delhi 110092, India
Tel.: +91 11 2223 5152/6152; 96500 28065
E-mail: info@shiprapublication.com
www.shiprapublication.com

Preface

The quality of life of human beings and animals depends to a large extent on the quality of research being conducted by different institutions of the country. It has been pointed out time and again by different people that the quality of research in India is too low. University Grants Commission (UGC) is trying to formulate regulation for improving quality of research in India. Both qualitative and quantitative researches have poor quality. Research being a process, there are many steps of research. One of the important steps is "Data Analysis". There are different techniques to analyse qualitative data as well as quantitative data. To facilitate the quantitative data analysis different software are available but majority of researchers do not know how to use these softwares. The purpose of writing this manual is to educate researchers in the use of Statistical Package for Social Sciences (SPSS). SPSS is most commonly used statistical package. Majority of institutes do not teach the use of SPSS. Keeping in mind the need of having a manual for using SPSS, the present manual is prepared.

Different parts of this manual have been read by many Research Fellows, Assistant Professors, Associate Professors, Professors and Deans of Faculties of different universities. Their suggestions have contributed a lot in improving this manual. I thankfully acknowledge their untiring support. I wish to express my gratitude to my wife Urmila, daughter Aditi, Son Ankur, granddaughter Aarya and Son-in-law Daniel Sequoyah Tuell who allowed me free time to write this manual. Last but not least I acknowledge the support of all those who directly or indirectly helped me in writing this manual.

I do acknowledge the support of Mr. D. Kumar and his team who readily agreed to publish this manual.

D.N.Sansanwal

Contents

Introduction

By now you must have understood steps of research. The steps of research are:

1. Identification of Problem
2. Formulation of Hypothesis
3. Data Collection
4. Data Analysis
5. Conclusion

In all types of research, Data Analysis is one of the steps of research. Data are qualitative as well as quantitative. You know that qualitative data can be converted into quantitative but not vice versa. There are different techniques to analyse qualitative data and quantitative data. Quantitative data are analysed with the help of statistical techniques. It can be analysed manually as well as with the help of software. Different available software are: Excel, SPSS (Statistical Package for Social Sciences), Stata (It is a symbolic abbreviation of the words Statistics & Data.), SAS (Statistical Analysis System), R (First letter of names of its two developers Ross Ihaka & Robert Gentleman), MATLAB (MATrix LABoratory), JMP (John's Macintosh Project), Python, etc.

In this manual, only the use of SPSS has being explained step by step. There are different versions of SPSS but this manual equips readers to use any version of SPSS.

Starting SPSS

1. Before start learning the use of SPSS, please load any version of SPSS in your computer / laptop. Now look at the following screen:

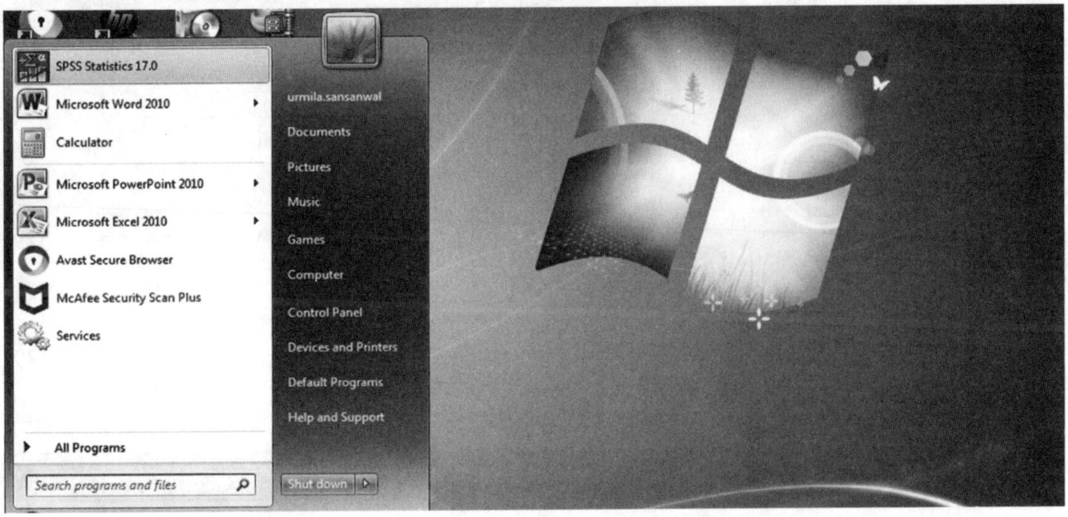

2. In the above screen you can see SPSS Statistics 17.0. Click at SPSS icon to get the following screen.

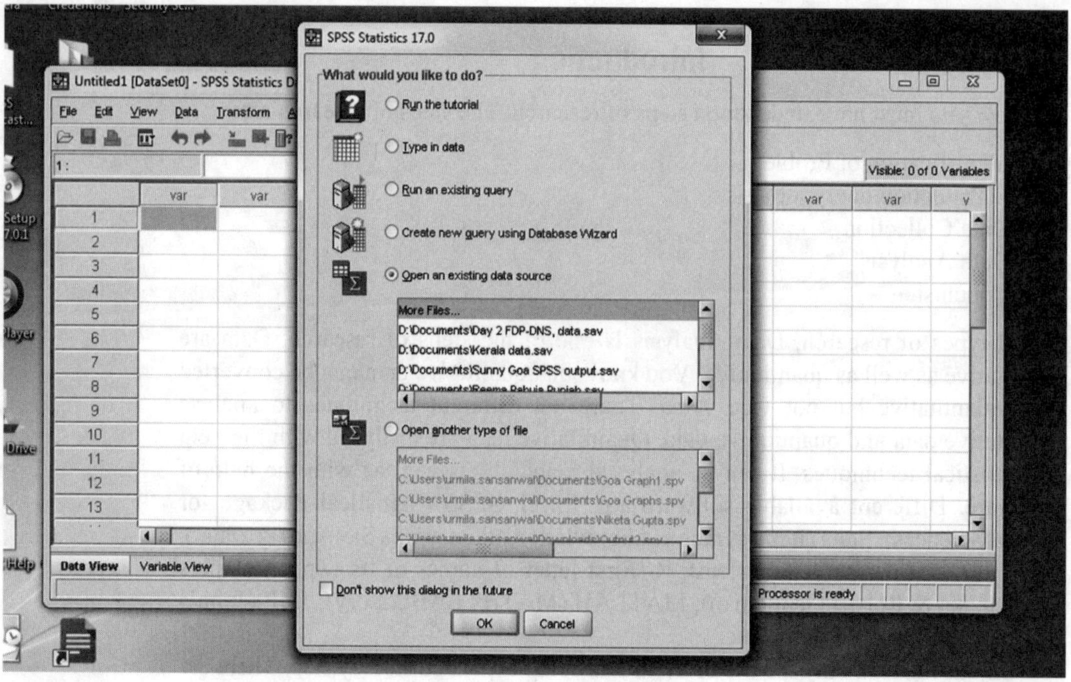

3. If data file is already there, you may use it otherwise you can enter the data. For entering the new data, click on "**Cancel**" tab to get the following screen.

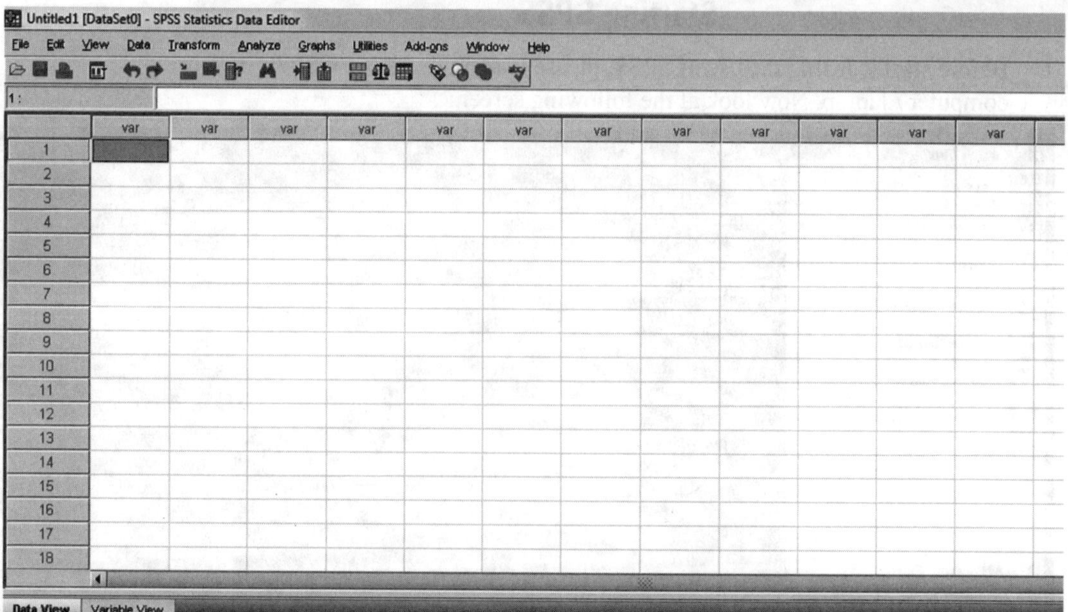

Preparation for Entering Data

"Var" stands for variable. In one column, one variable data is to be entered. In case you have six variables, you require six columns. If you have two variables, you need only two columns. The variable can be continuous or discontinuous. Irrespective of type of variable one needs to enter the information of one variable in one column.

Look at the bottom of SPSS screen you can see two **Data Editors: Data View and Variable View**.

4. For entering the data, click on the **"Variable View"** tab to get the following screen.

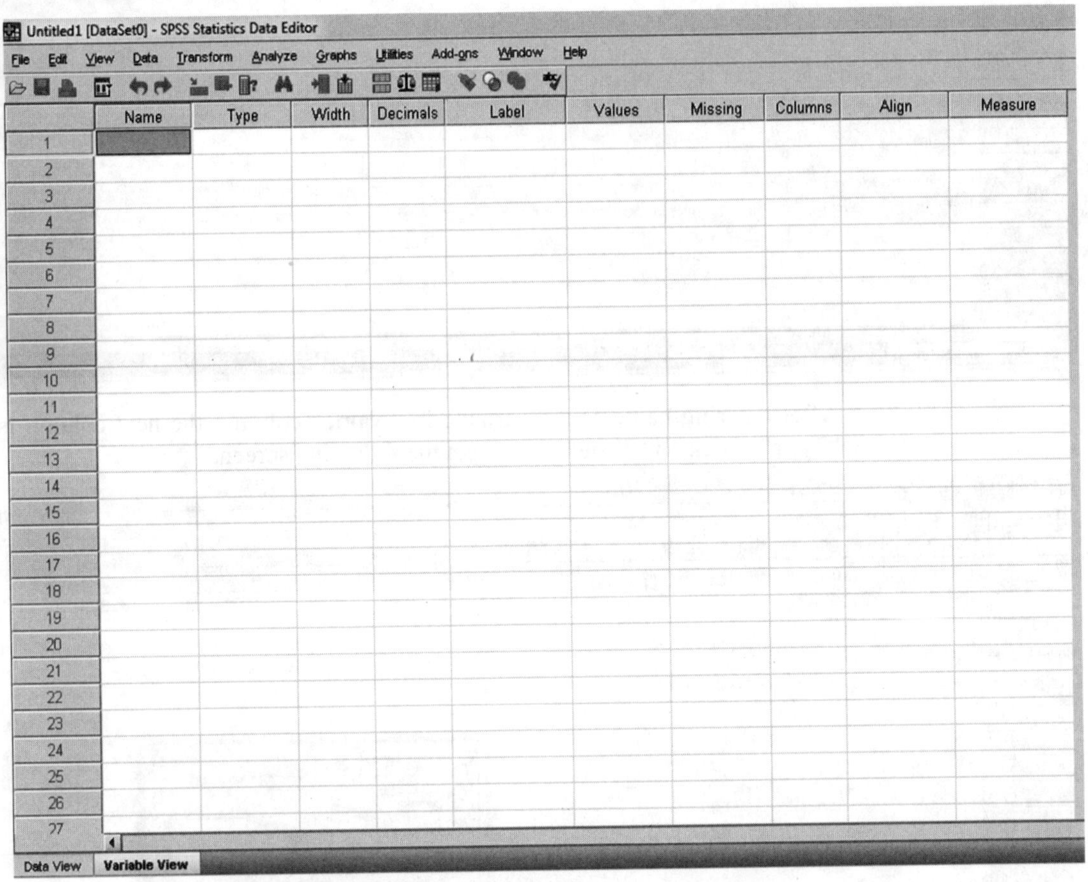

Suppose you want to enter data of variables: Gender, Residential Background, Types of School, Achievement in Physics, and Intelligence. Gender, Residential Background, and Types of School are discontinuous variables having different labels while Achievement in Physics and Intelligence are continuous variables.

5. Suppose you want to enter information about "**gender**". In the first column "**Name**" is written, so type "**gender**" under first column and click on "**Enter key**" to get the following Screen.

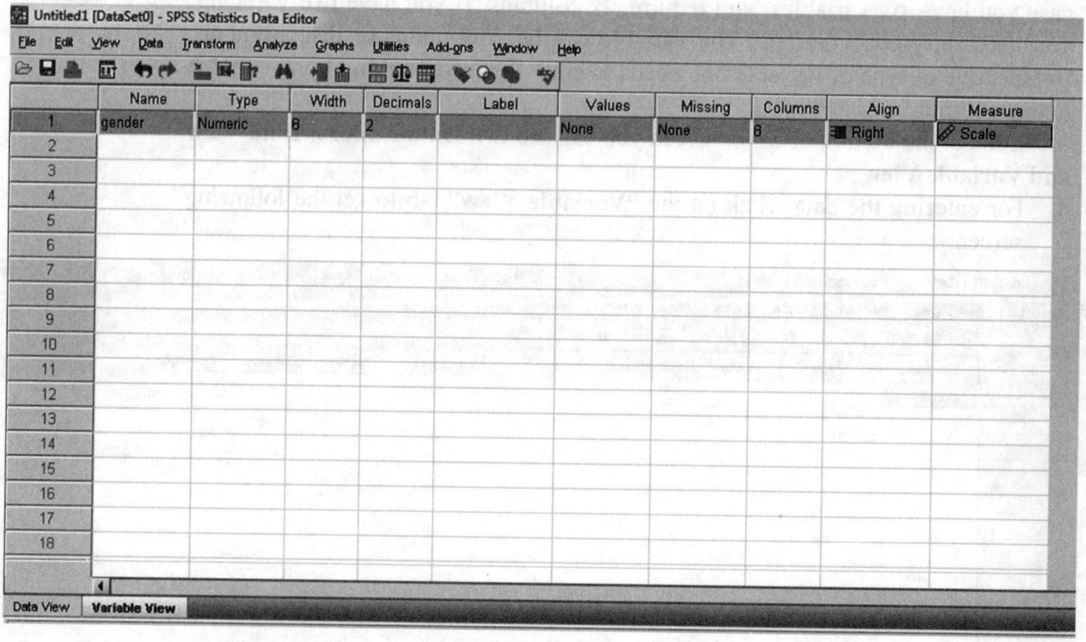

6. After entering name of the variable in "**Name**" column, the next column is "**Type**". Click on "**Type**" icon to get the following screen.

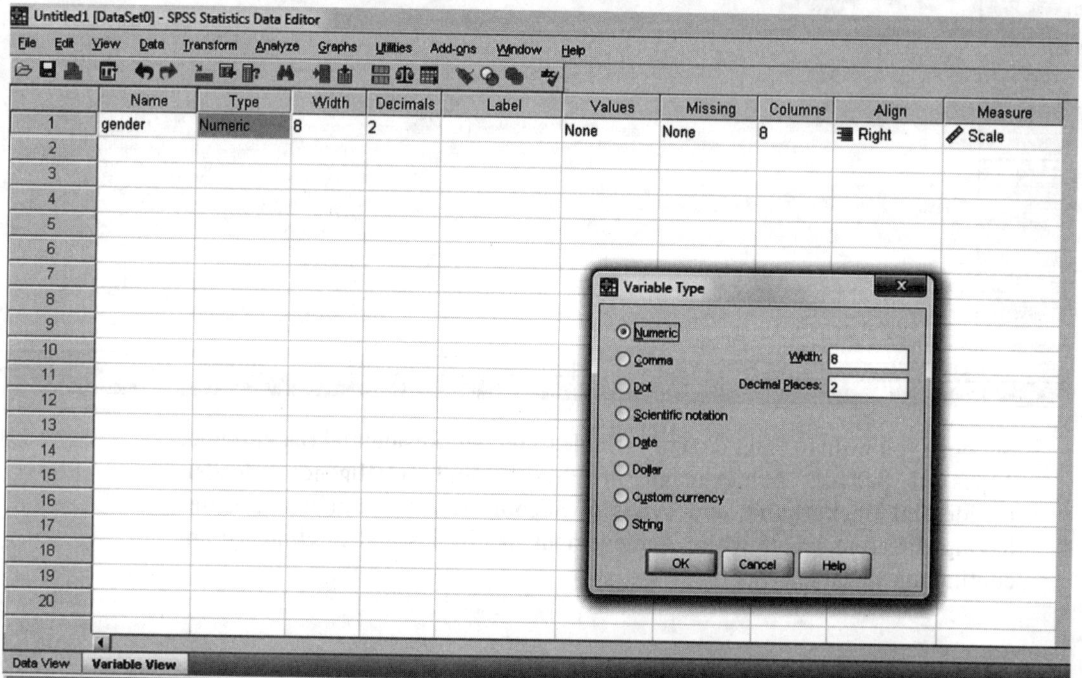

7. You can see that there are different options, such as, Numeric, Comma, Dot, Scientific Notation, Date, Dollar, Custom Currency, & String. In the above screen one can see that by default "**Numeric**" is active because most people use SPSS for analyzing Numeric data.

   If your data are "**String**", then select "**String**" and click on "**OK**" to get the following screen.

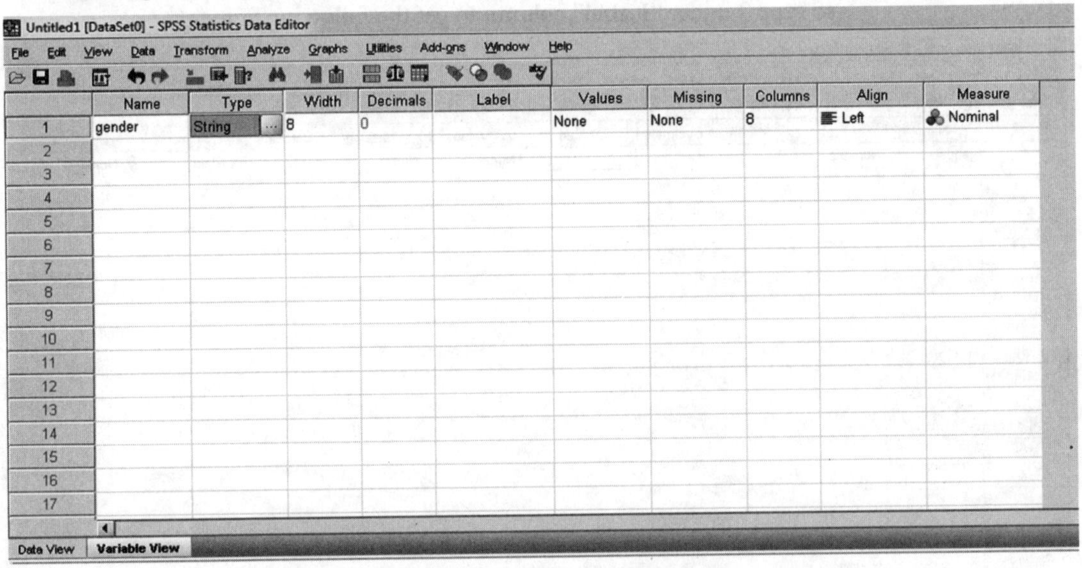

8. After "**Type**", next columns are "**Width**" & "**Decimals**". By default, "**Width**" size is 8 & "**Decimals**" are 2 so it can accommodate 8 digits number up to two decimals.

   "**Width**" & "**Decimals**" can be changed according to the size of number as shown in the following screen.

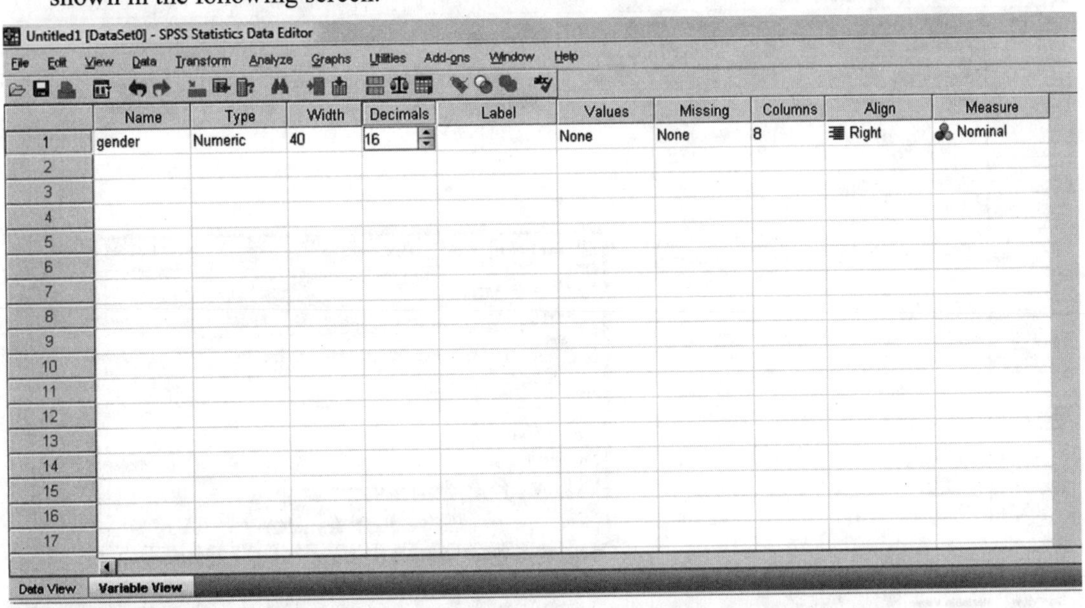

9. In the above screen, the maximum "**Width**" shown is 40 and maximum "**Decimals**" is 16. As per researcher's requirement, "**Width**" and "**Decimals**" can be decided but "**Width**" cannot be more than 40 and "**Decimals**" cannot be more than 16. If any researcher has quantitative data which does not fit in the above given limit, SPSS cannot be used for analyzing such data.

   After "**Decimals**", next column is "**Label**". There are two labels of "**gender**", so type 2 under "**Label**" column to get the following Screen.

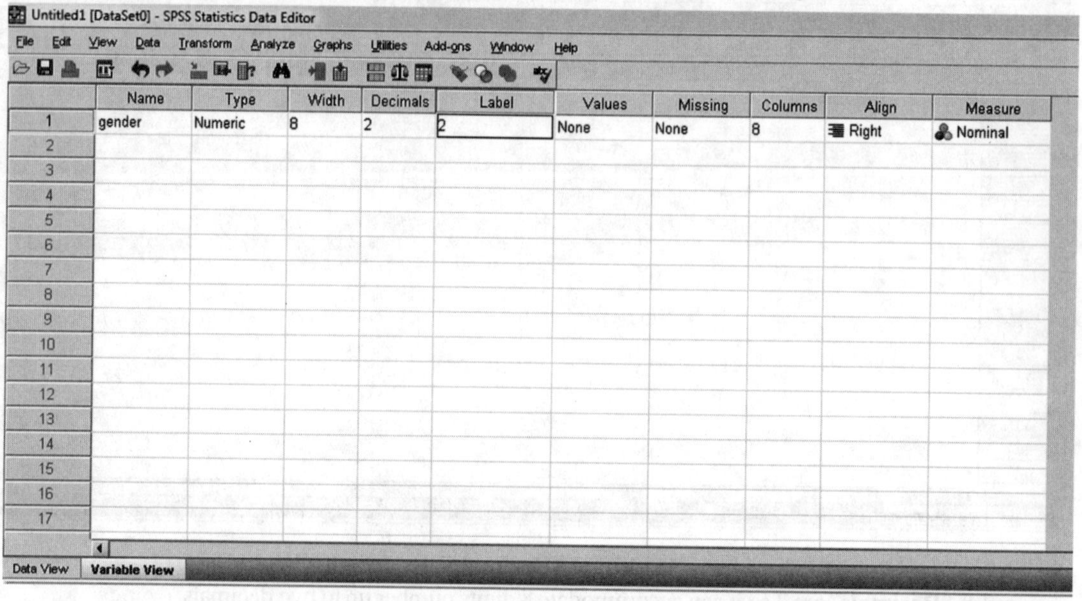

10. Next column is "**Value**", click on "**Value**" to get the following Screen.

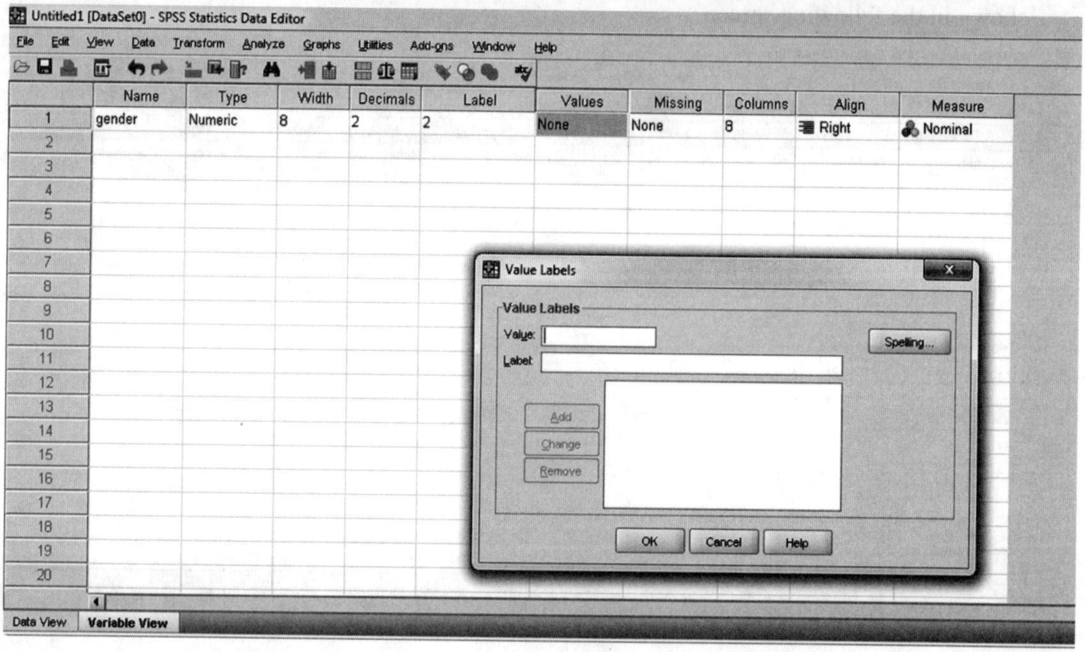

11. Now enter the information of "**Value**" and "**Label**". Gender has two labels, Male and Female. You may decide to enter any "**Label**" information first. Suppose you want to enter "**Male**" information first and is denoted by 1. Here 1 is not a number but a Code. Your mobile number is a code; and bank account number is also a code. If you wish you may use "0" code for Male.

    Under "**Value**", enter 1 and under "**Label**" type "**Male**" to get the following screen.

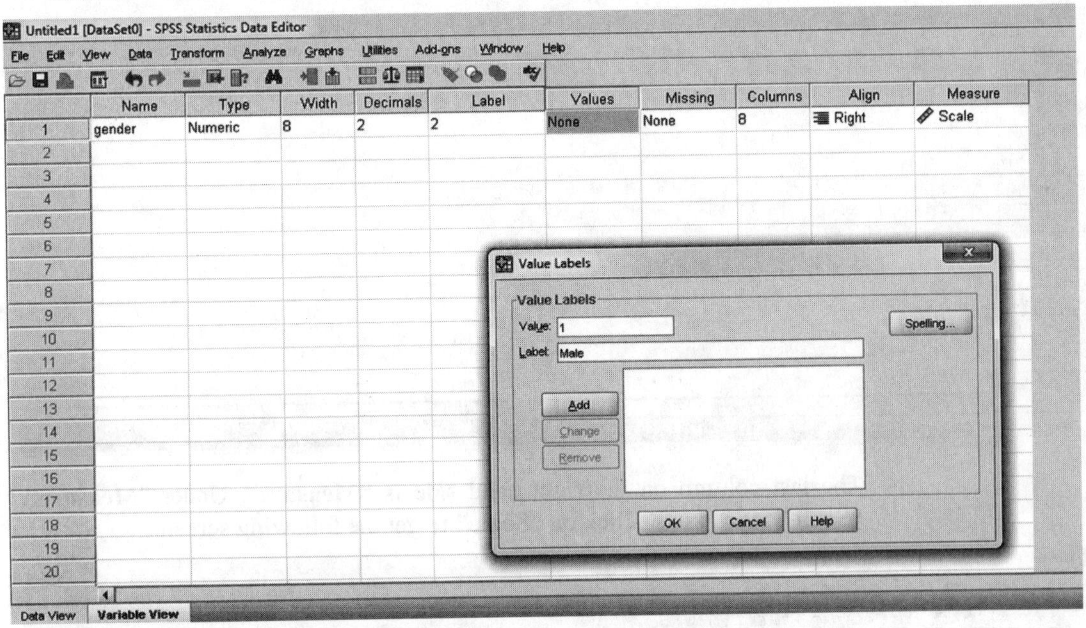

12. Click on **"Add"** and define another label to get the following screen.

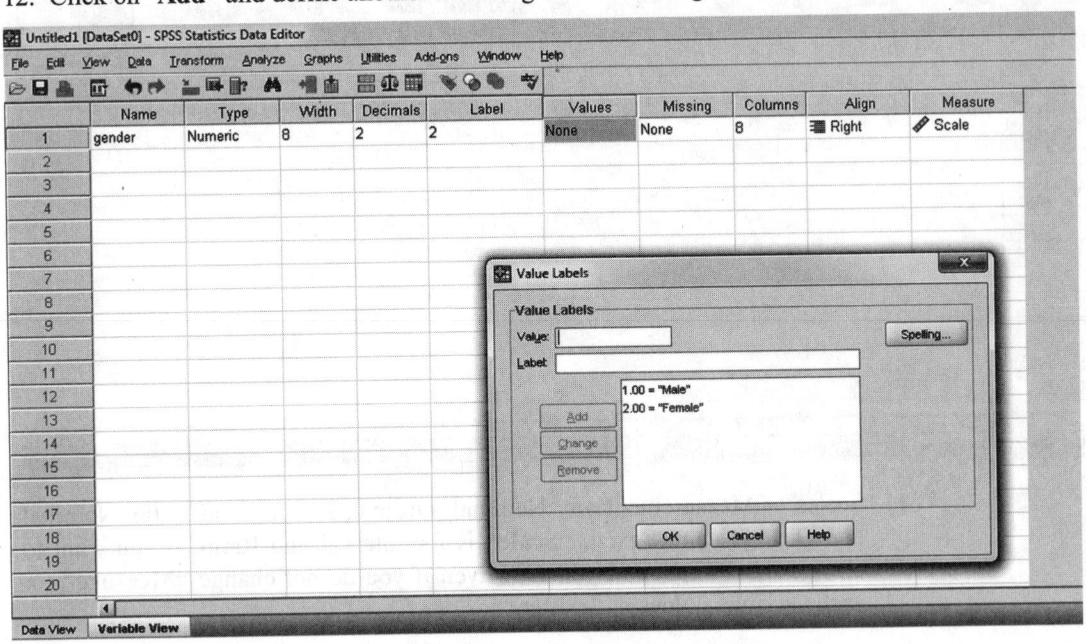

13. Click on **"OK"** to get the following screen:

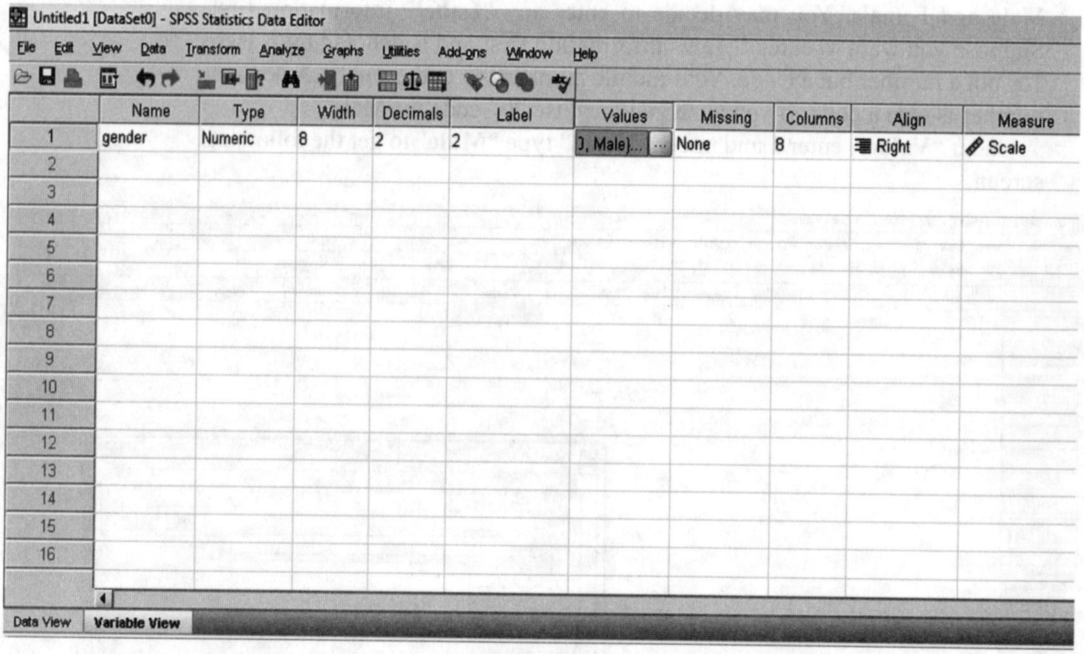

14. The last column on the right hand side is **"Measure"**. Under **"Measure"**, **"Scale"** icon exists. Click on **"Scale" to** get the following screen.

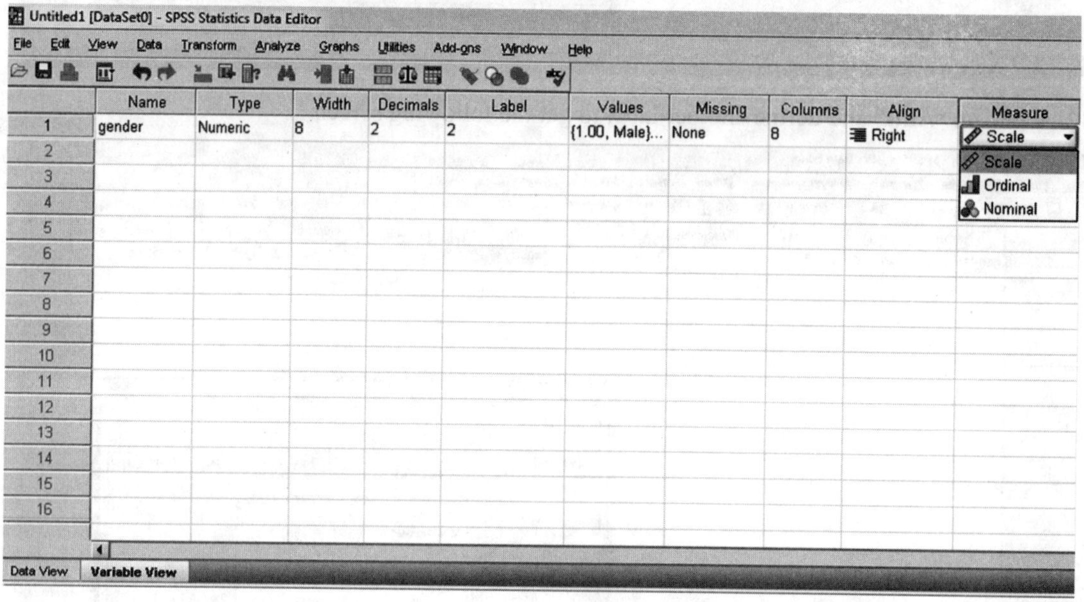

15. Scales of Measurement are: Nominal, Ordinal, Interval and Ratio. Nominal and Ordinal names exist. **"Scale"** is for Interval and Ratio. If you want to change the "**Measure**", you can. Even if you do not change **"Measure"** for each variable, it does not matter.

You know that **"Gender"** information is on Nominal Scale. Click on **"Nominal"** to get the following screen.

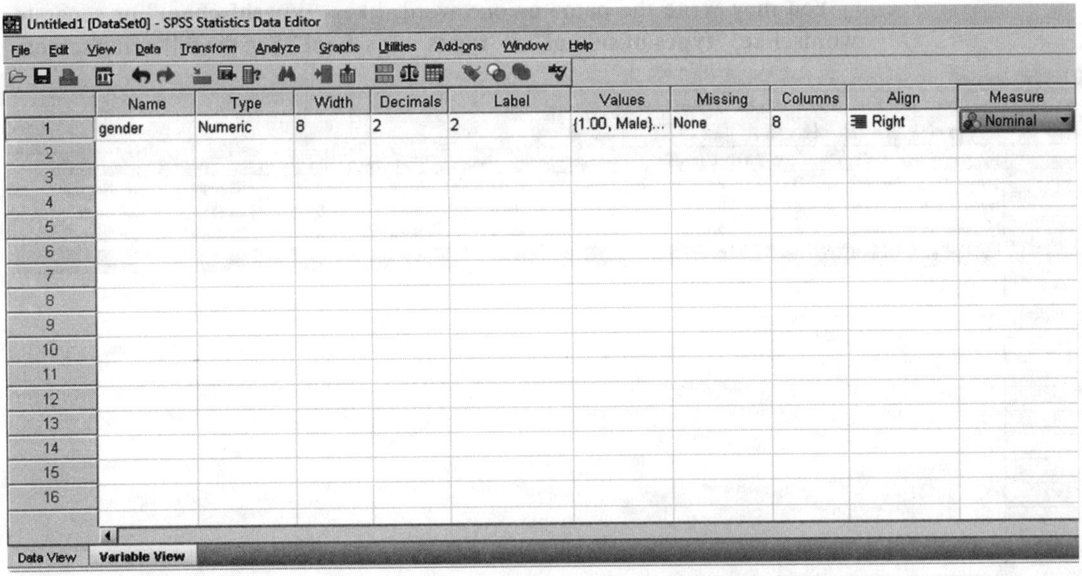

16. Also you have to enter data related to Residential Background, Types of School, Achievement in Physics, and Intelligence variables. The data of all variables must be entered. **The sequence of entering the data is not important.**

    Suppose now you want to enter the data of **"Types of School"**. Let us enter **"Types of School"** under **"Name"** column and click on **"Enter"** to get the following screen.

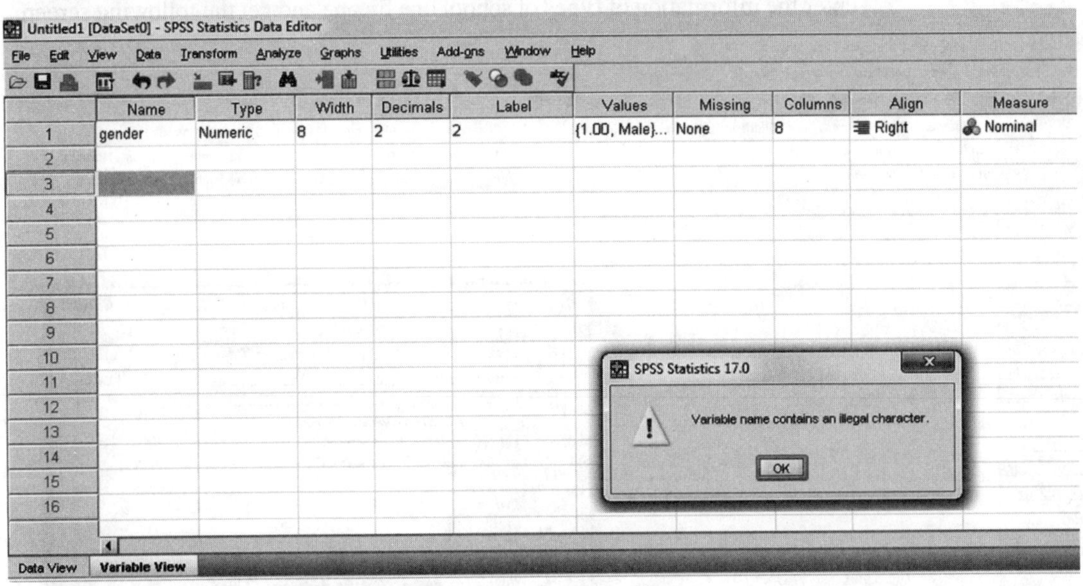

17. On the screen **"Variable name contains an illegal character"** appears because the gap was left between first & second words also second & third

words. Whenever variable name contains two or more words, **"gap"** should not be left between words.

You may write the name as one word, like, **"typesofschool"** or separate words, like, **"types.of.school"** or **"types_of_school"**. See the following screen.

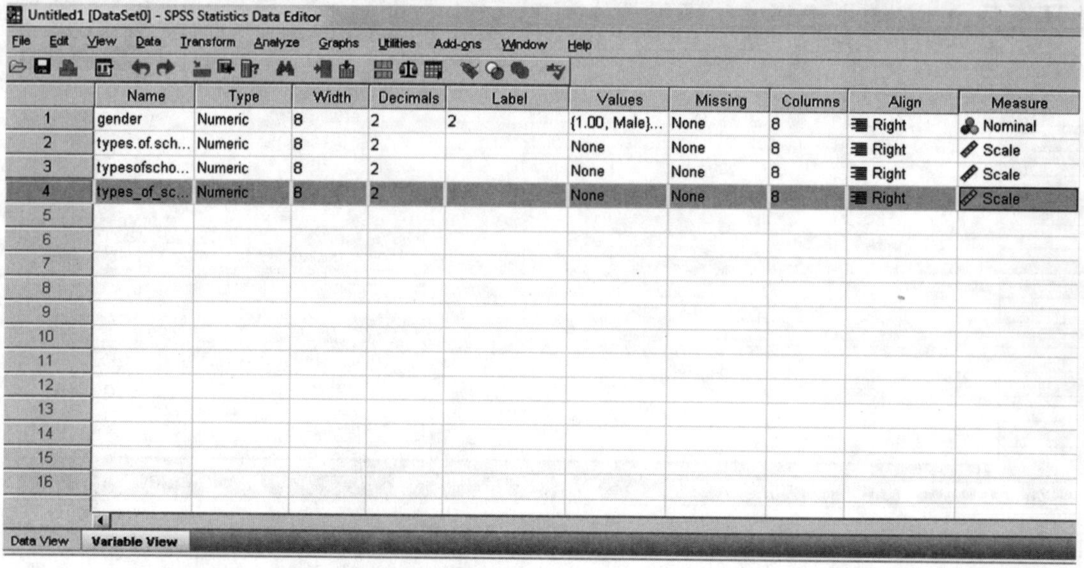

18. One should not enter the name of one variable in different formats. Choose anyone you like and proceed.

    There are three types of school. Under **"Label"** type 3. Click on **"Values"** to enter the information of types of school one by one and get the following screen.

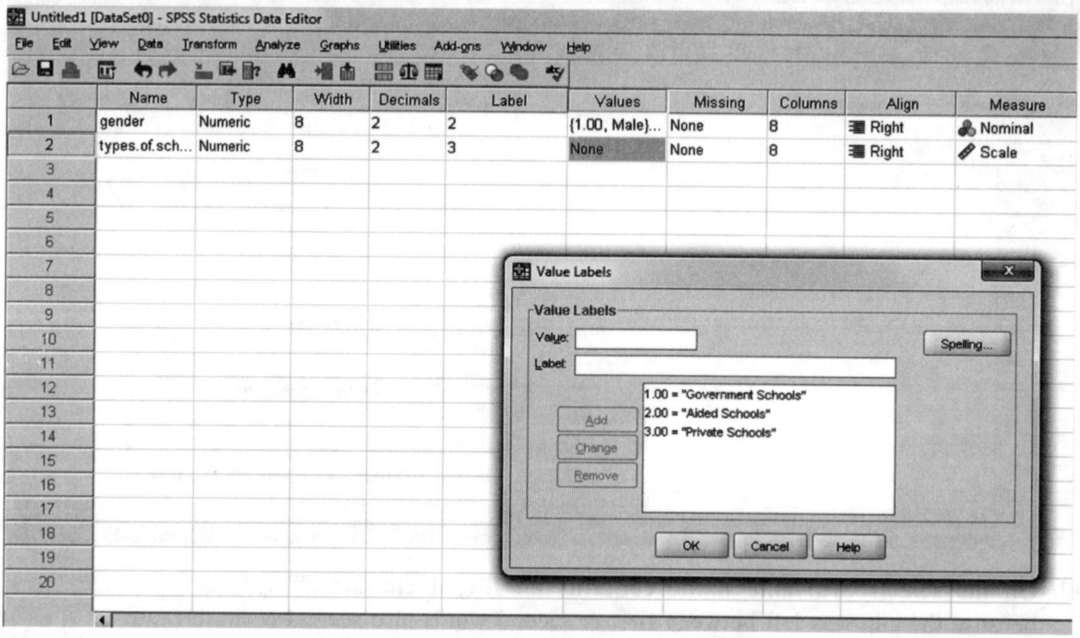

19. Click on **"OK"** to get the following screen.

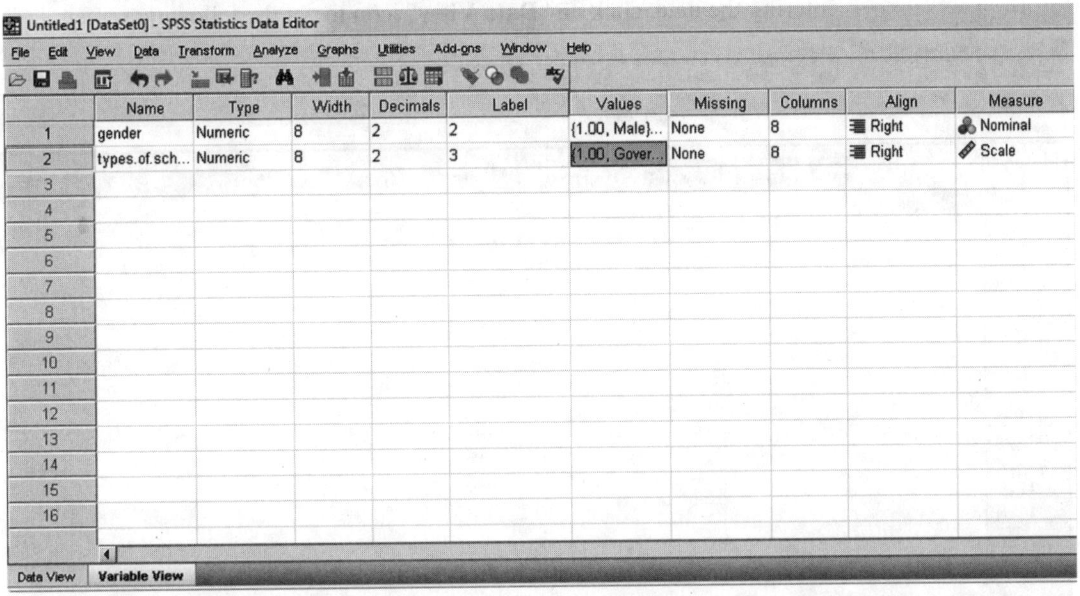

20. **"Scale"** of "**Types.of.school**" has not been changed. It will automatically take it to be Nominal Scale data.
 Enter the names of all remaining variables to get the following screen.

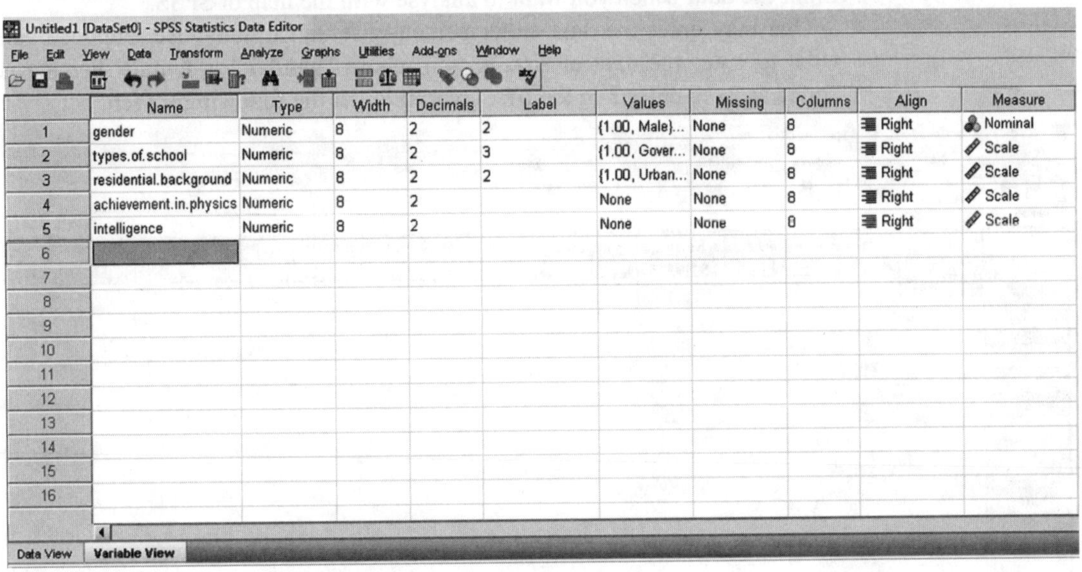

Data Entering

21. "**Achievement in Physics**", and "**Intelligence**" are continuous variables, so there is no need of label.

After entering the names of variables, now it time to enter the data. For entering the data, click on "**Data View**" icon to get the following screen.

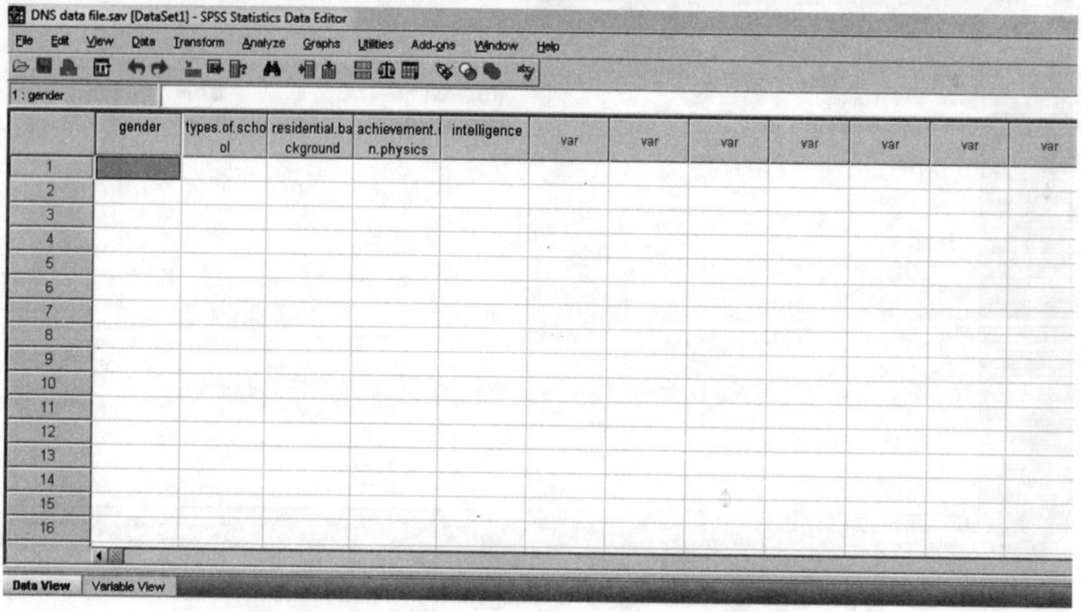

22. You may see that in each column one variable name appears as entered by you. Enter the data which you want to analyse with the help of SPSS.

    One may enter the data either person-wise or variable-wise. Suppose you want to enter the data of first person whose "**gender**" is female. Female is coded as **2**, so enter **2** in the first column to get the following screen.

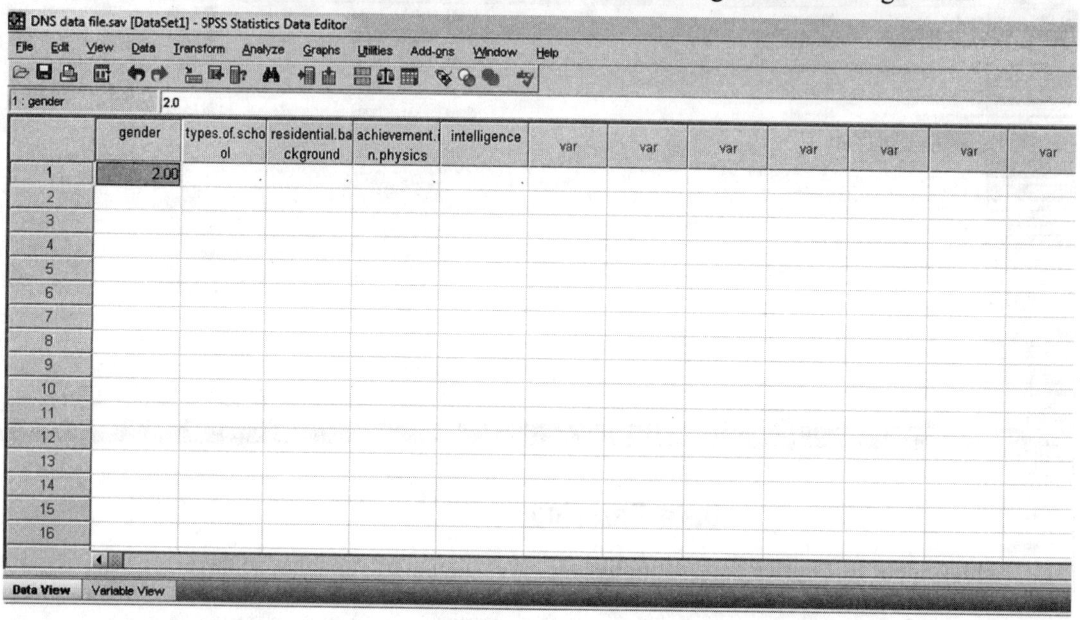

23. If this person belongs to Private School, then **types of school=3**. Enter this information in the second column to get the following screen.

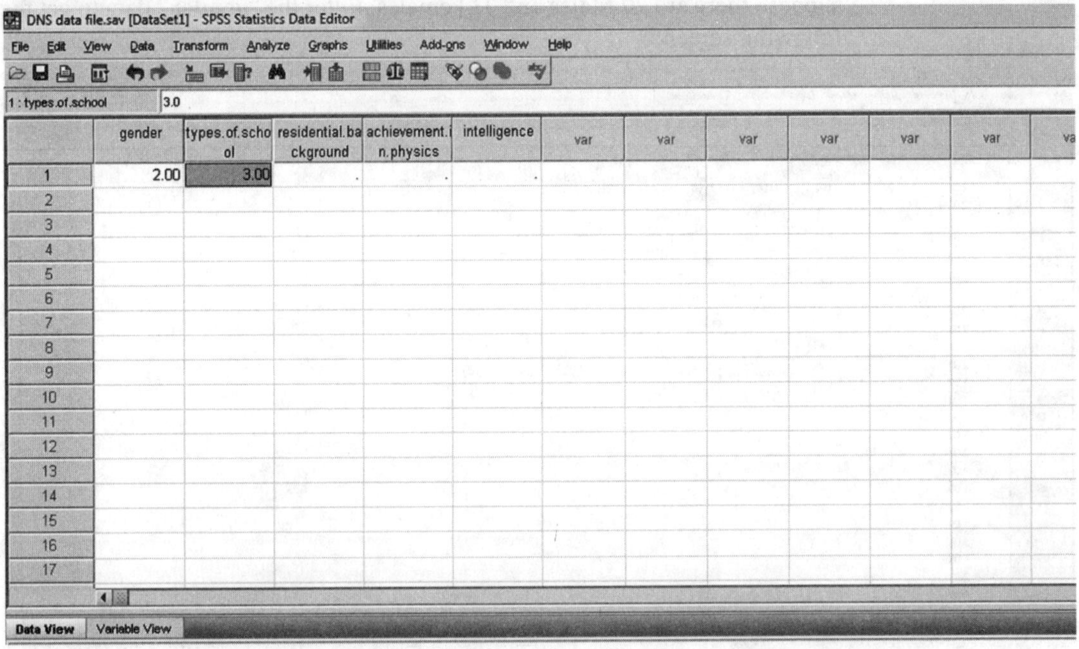

24. Suppose the person belongs to urban area, so **residential background=1**, suppose score in **achievement in physics is 28** and **intelligence score is 21**. Enter this data under appropriate columns to get the following screen.

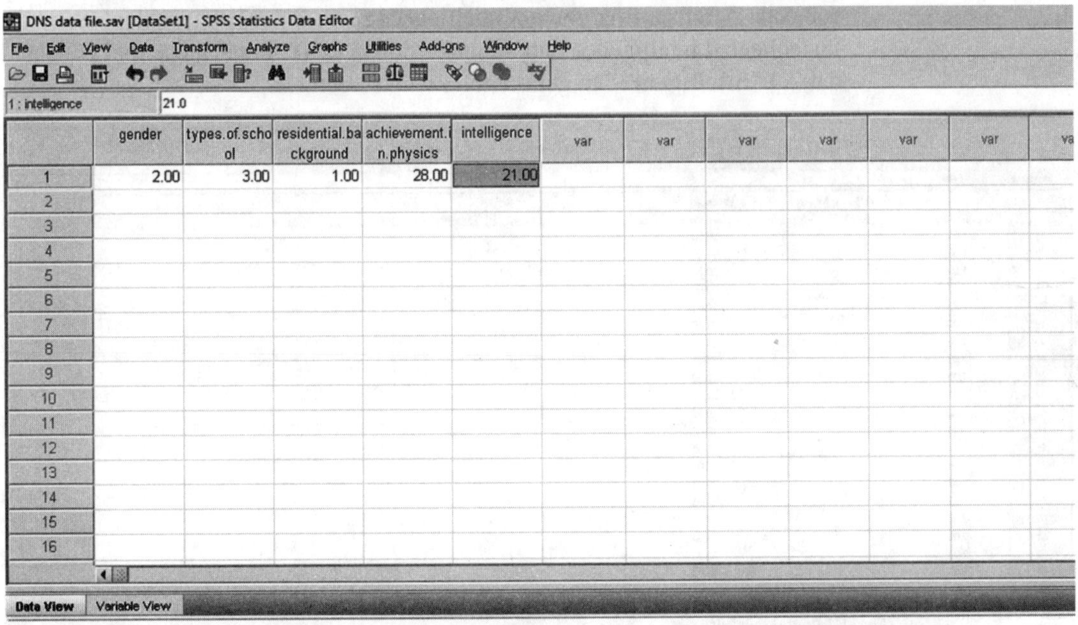

25. Now you may enter complete data as explained above. Alternatively you may enter complete data variable-wise. Suppose the sample size is 53. Out of 53, suppose there are 20 Males and 33 Females. Enter the "**gender**" data to get the following screen.

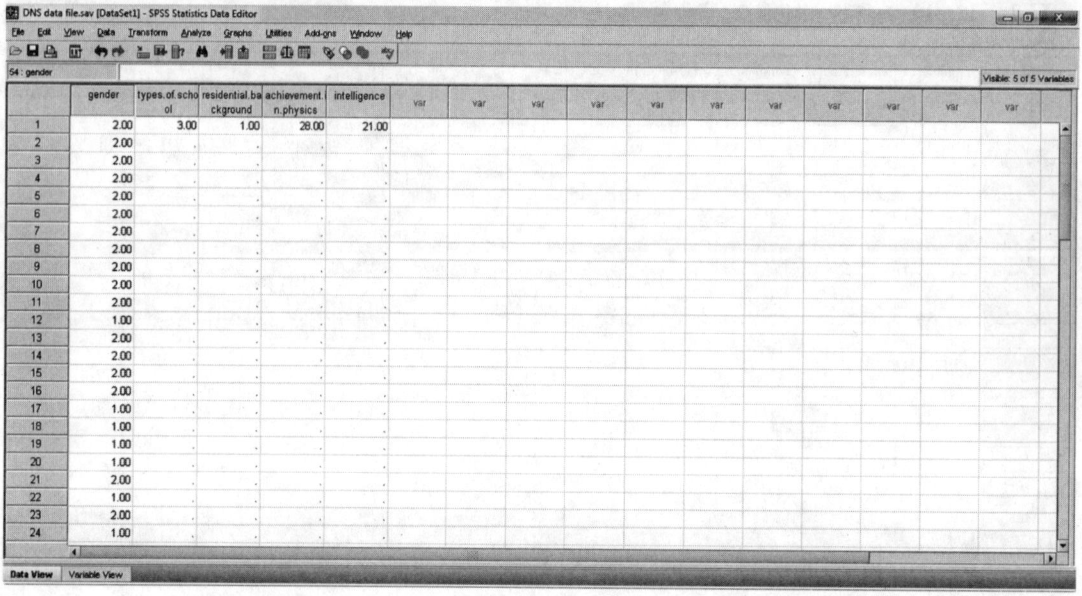

	gender	types.of.school	residential.background	achievement.in.physics	intelligence
1	2.00	3.00	1.00	28.00	21.00
2	2.00	.	.	.	.
3	2.00	.	.	.	.
4	2.00	.	.	.	.
5	2.00	.	.	.	.
6	2.00	.	.	.	.
7	2.00	.	.	.	.
8	2.00	.	.	.	.
9	2.00	.	.	.	.
10	2.00	.	.	.	.
11	2.00	.	.	.	.
12	1.00	.	.	.	.
13	2.00	.	.	.	.
14	2.00	.	.	.	.
15	2.00	.	.	.	.
16	2.00	.	.	.	.
17	1.00	.	.	.	.
18	1.00	.	.	.	.
19	1.00	.	.	.	.
20	1.00	.	.	.	.
21	2.00	.	.	.	.
22	1.00	.	.	.	.
23	2.00	.	.	.	.
24	1.00	.	.	.	.

26. After entering the gender information, next you may enter the data of any variable. Suppose you want to enter the data of "**intelligence**". You have already collected data by administering appropriate intelligence test on 53 subjects. After scoring you get intelligence score for each individual. Suppose the collected intelligence data ranges from 15 to 48. Enter the actual collected data of "**intelligence**" to get the following screen.

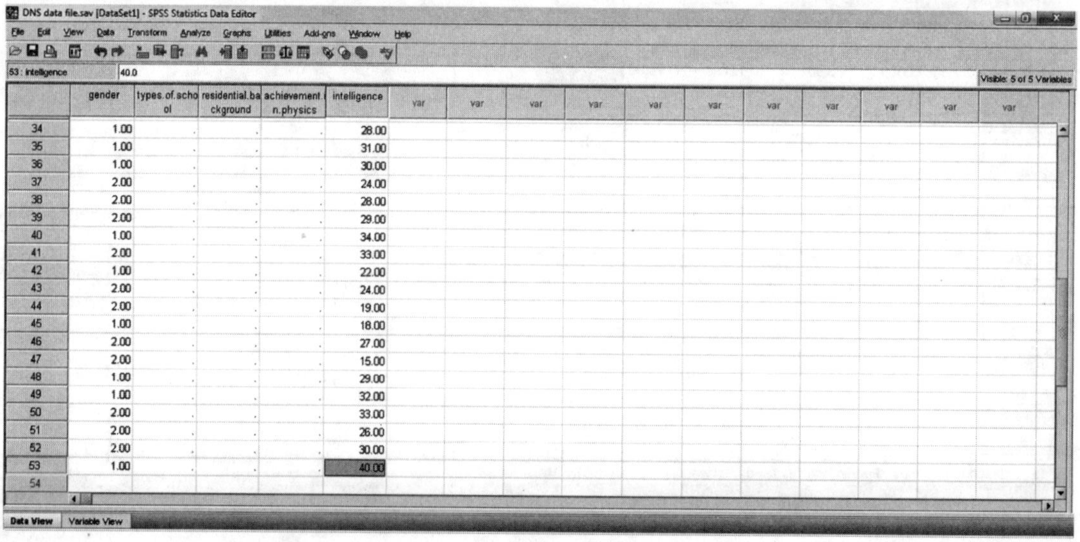

	gender	types.of.school	residential.background	achievement.in.physics	intelligence
34	1.00	.	.	.	28.00
35	1.00	.	.	.	31.00
36	1.00	.	.	.	30.00
37	2.00	.	.	.	24.00
38	2.00	.	.	.	28.00
39	2.00	.	.	.	29.00
40	1.00	.	.	.	34.00
41	2.00	.	.	.	33.00
42	1.00	.	.	.	22.00
43	2.00	.	.	.	24.00
44	2.00	.	.	.	19.00
45	1.00	.	.	.	18.00
46	2.00	.	.	.	27.00
47	2.00	.	.	.	15.00
48	1.00	.	.	.	29.00
49	1.00	.	.	.	32.00
50	2.00	.	.	.	33.00
51	2.00	.	.	.	26.00
52	2.00	.	.	.	30.00
53	1.00	.	.	.	40.00
54					

27. Enter the data of the remaining variables to get the following screen.

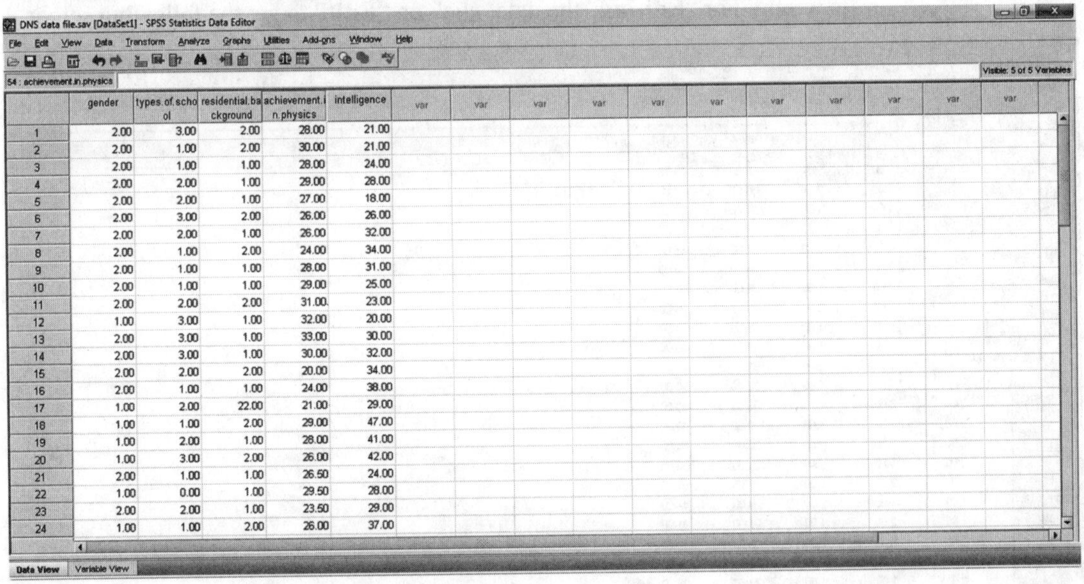

	gender	types.of.school	residential.background	achievement.in.physics	intelligence
1	2.00	3.00	2.00	28.00	21.00
2	2.00	1.00	2.00	30.00	21.00
3	2.00	1.00	1.00	28.00	24.00
4	2.00	2.00	1.00	29.00	28.00
5	2.00	2.00	1.00	27.00	18.00
6	2.00	3.00	2.00	26.00	26.00
7	2.00	2.00	1.00	26.00	32.00
8	2.00	1.00	2.00	24.00	34.00
9	2.00	1.00	1.00	28.00	31.00
10	2.00	1.00	1.00	29.00	25.00
11	2.00	2.00	2.00	31.00	23.00
12	1.00	3.00	1.00	32.00	20.00
13	2.00	3.00	1.00	33.00	30.00
14	2.00	3.00	1.00	30.00	32.00
15	2.00	2.00	2.00	20.00	34.00
16	2.00	1.00	1.00	24.00	38.00
17	1.00	2.00	22.00	21.00	29.00
18	1.00	1.00	2.00	29.00	47.00
19	1.00	2.00	1.00	28.00	41.00
20	1.00	3.00	2.00	26.00	42.00
21	2.00	1.00	1.00	26.50	24.00
22	1.00	0.00	1.00	29.50	28.00
23	2.00	2.00	1.00	23.50	29.00
24	1.00	1.00	2.00	26.00	37.00

Data Editing

28. Before proceeding further, one must make sure that data are entered correctly. Compare the entered data with the original data and in case of any discrepancy, correct the data.

    One may see, under **"types.of.school"** 0.00 appears against serial number 22. This is wrong entry. It should have been 2.00. Make correction to get the following screen.

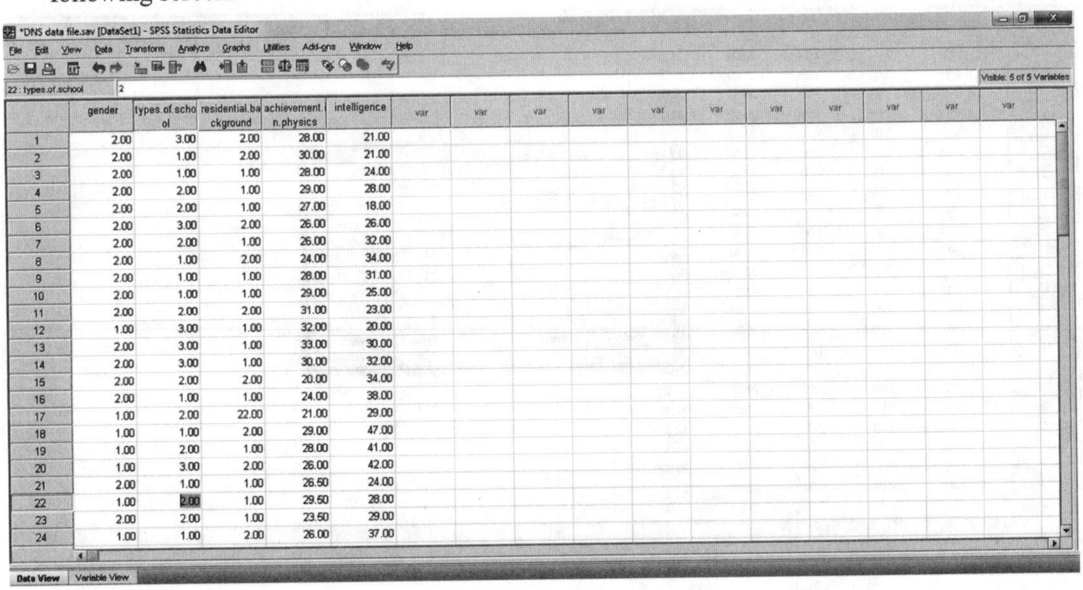

	gender	types.of.school	residential.background	achievement.in.physics	intelligence
1	2.00	3.00	2.00	28.00	21.00
2	2.00	1.00	2.00	30.00	21.00
3	2.00	1.00	1.00	28.00	24.00
4	2.00	2.00	1.00	29.00	28.00
5	2.00	2.00	1.00	27.00	18.00
6	2.00	3.00	2.00	26.00	26.00
7	2.00	2.00	1.00	26.00	32.00
8	2.00	1.00	2.00	24.00	34.00
9	2.00	1.00	1.00	28.00	31.00
10	2.00	1.00	1.00	29.00	25.00
11	2.00	2.00	2.00	31.00	23.00
12	1.00	3.00	1.00	32.00	20.00
13	2.00	3.00	1.00	33.00	30.00
14	2.00	3.00	1.00	30.00	32.00
15	2.00	2.00	2.00	20.00	34.00
16	2.00	1.00	1.00	24.00	38.00
17	1.00	2.00	22.00	21.00	29.00
18	1.00	1.00	2.00	29.00	47.00
19	1.00	2.00	1.00	28.00	41.00
20	1.00	3.00	2.00	26.00	42.00
21	2.00	1.00	1.00	26.50	24.00
22	1.00	2.00	1.00	29.50	28.00
23	2.00	2.00	1.00	23.50	29.00
24	1.00	1.00	2.00	26.00	37.00

29. Under "**residential.background**" at serial number 17, 22.00 is entered which is wrong. For "**Editing**" the data, click on "**Edit**" to get the following screen.

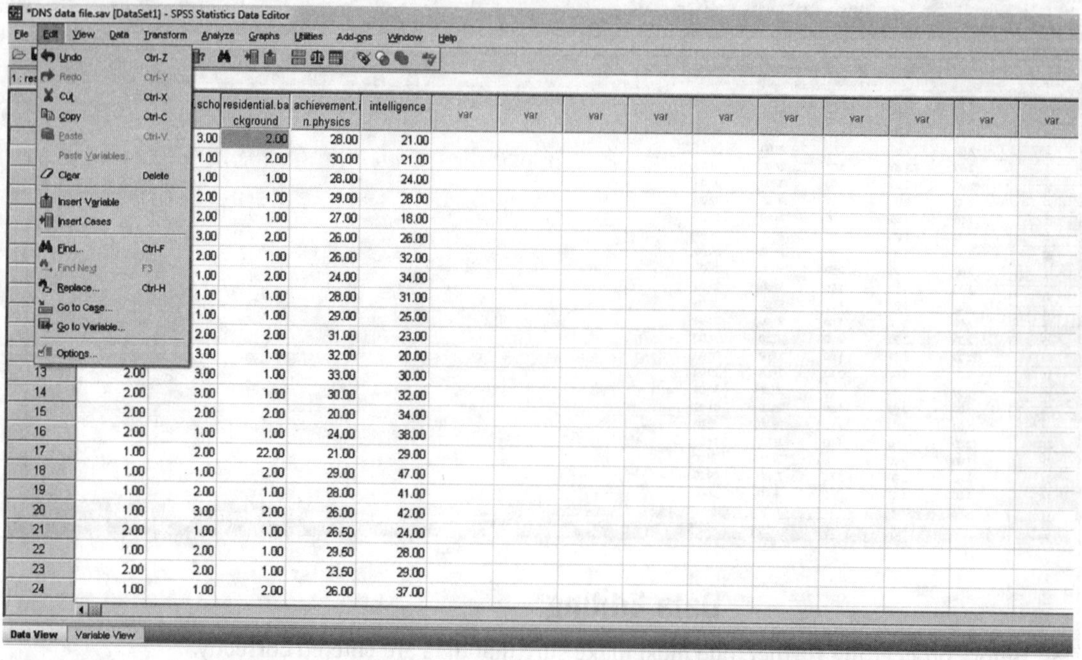

30. Click on "**Find**" to get "**Find and Replace-Data View**". Enter 22.00 which is to be replaced to get the following screen.

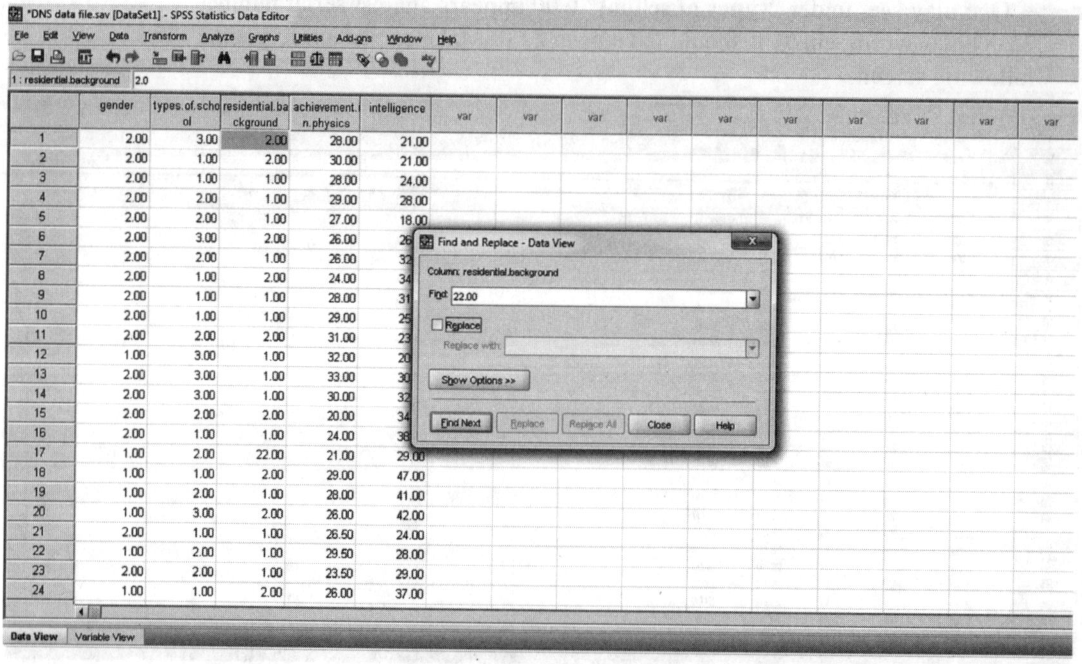

31. Click on "**Replace**" icon and put the number 2.00 under "**Replace with**" to get the following screen.

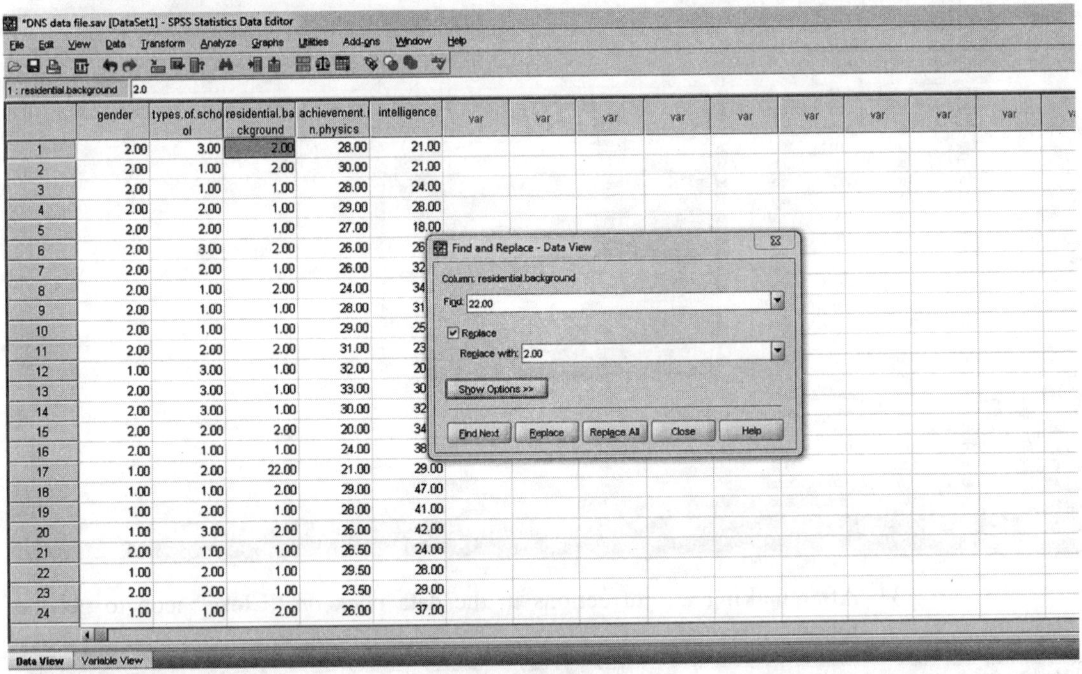

32. Click on "**Find Next**" icon to get the following screen.

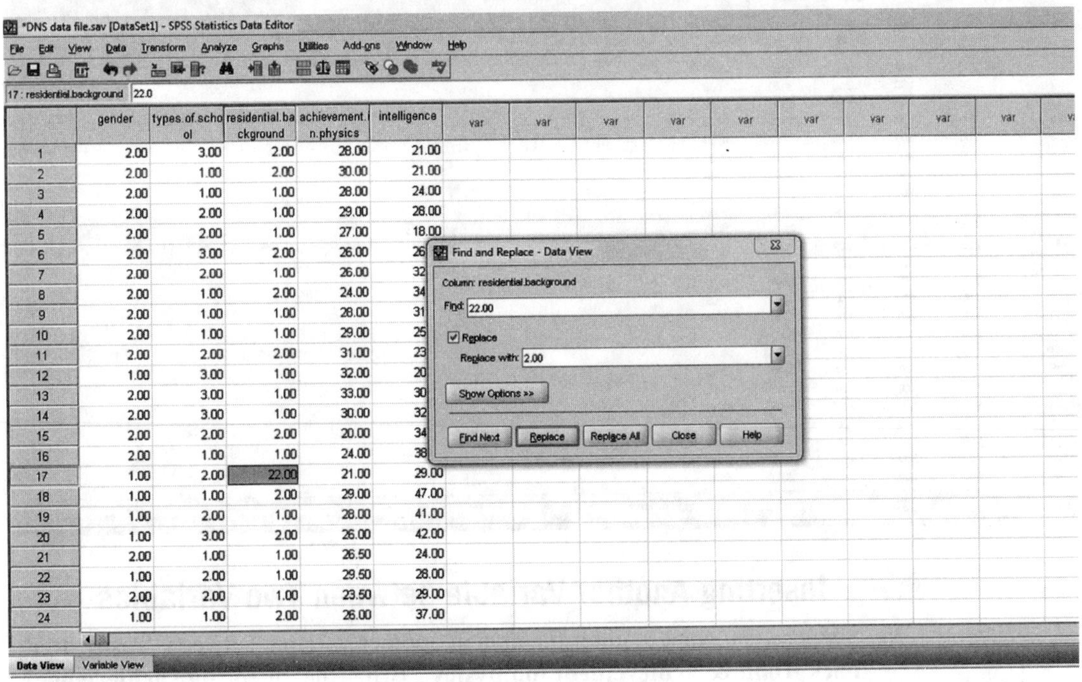

33. Click on "**Replace**" icon to get the following screen.

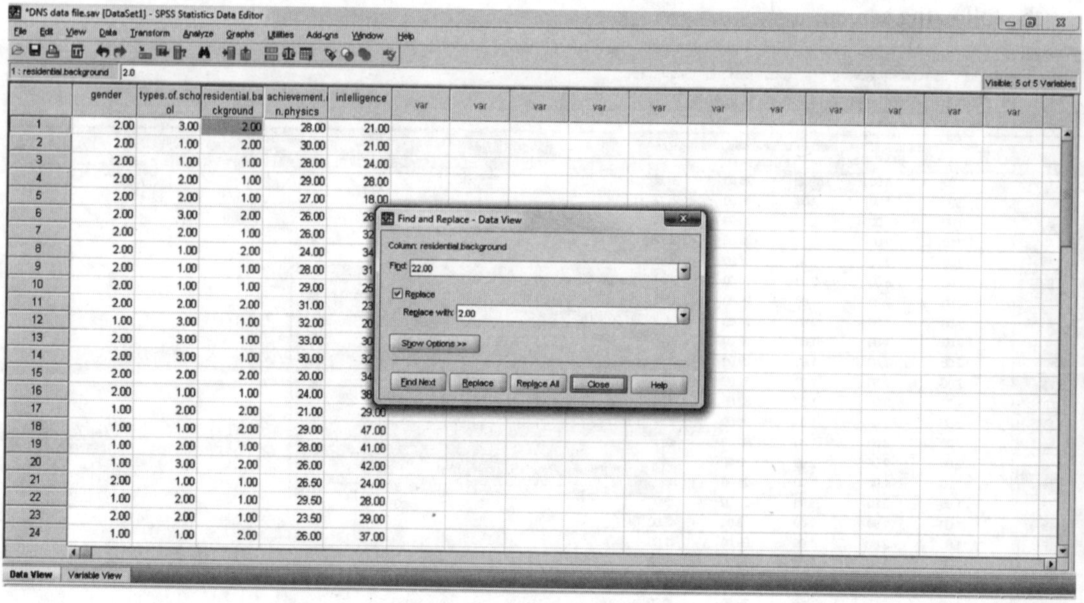

34. After making all corrections in the data click on "**Close**" icon to get the following screen.

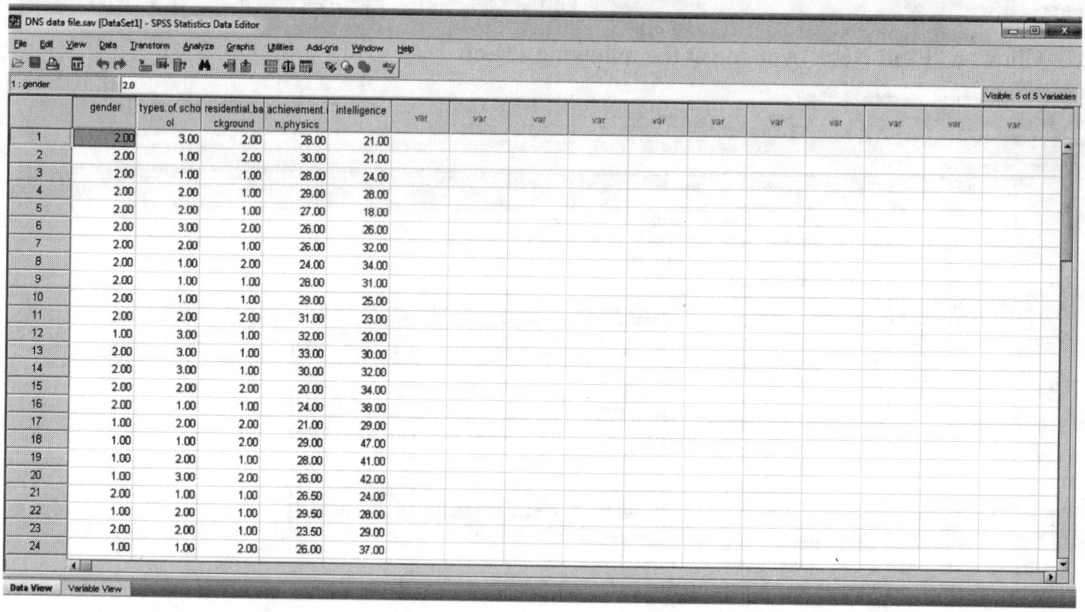

Inserting Another Variable between Two Variables

35. Suppose you want to enter the data of another variable between "**residential. backgrond** & **achievement.in.physics**". Bring the cursor on "**achievement.**

in.physics" column, click on "**Edit**" and bring the cursor on "**Insert Variable**" to get the following screen.

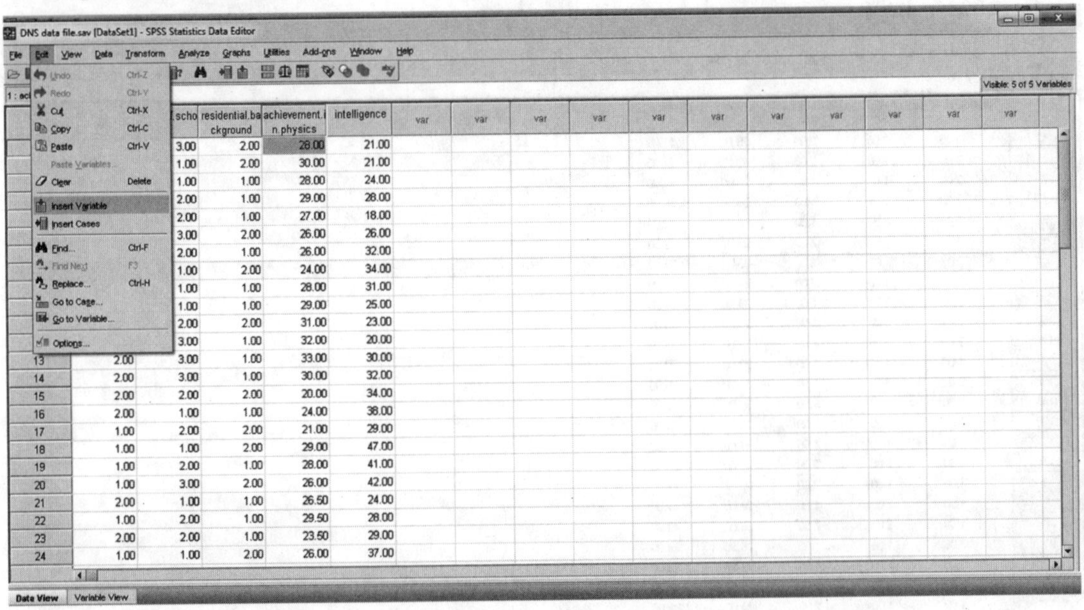

36. Click on "**Insert Variable**" to get the following screen.

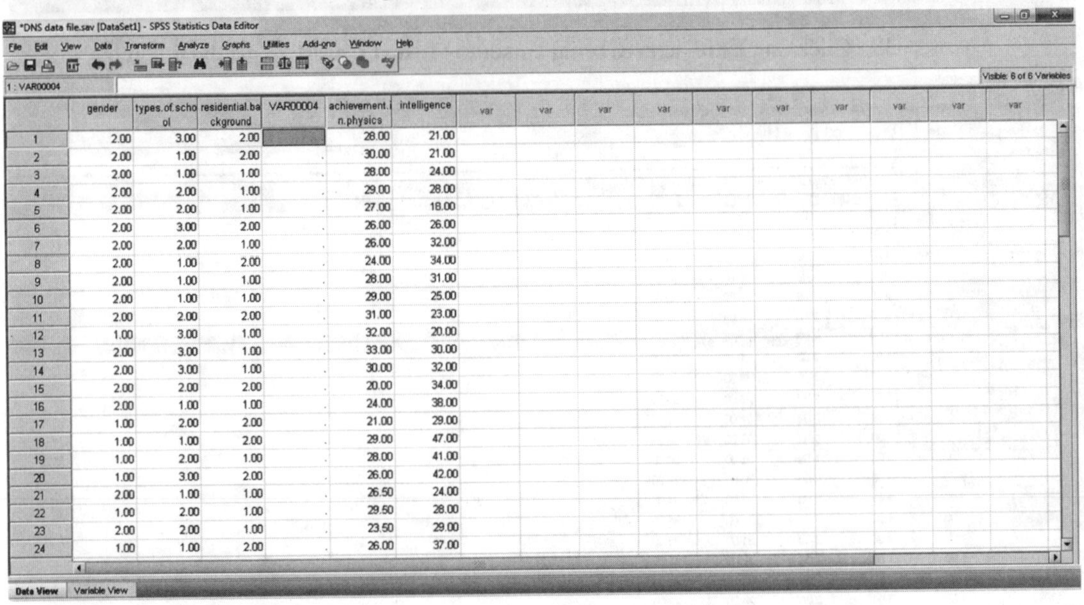

37. You have got one column for the variable which you wanted to insert between "**residential.background** and **achievement.in.physics**" variables. Click on "**Variable View**" to enter the name of variable and proceed further to enter the name of variable and its data.

Suppose you want to enter the data of one subject after serial number 6 as shown in the following screen.

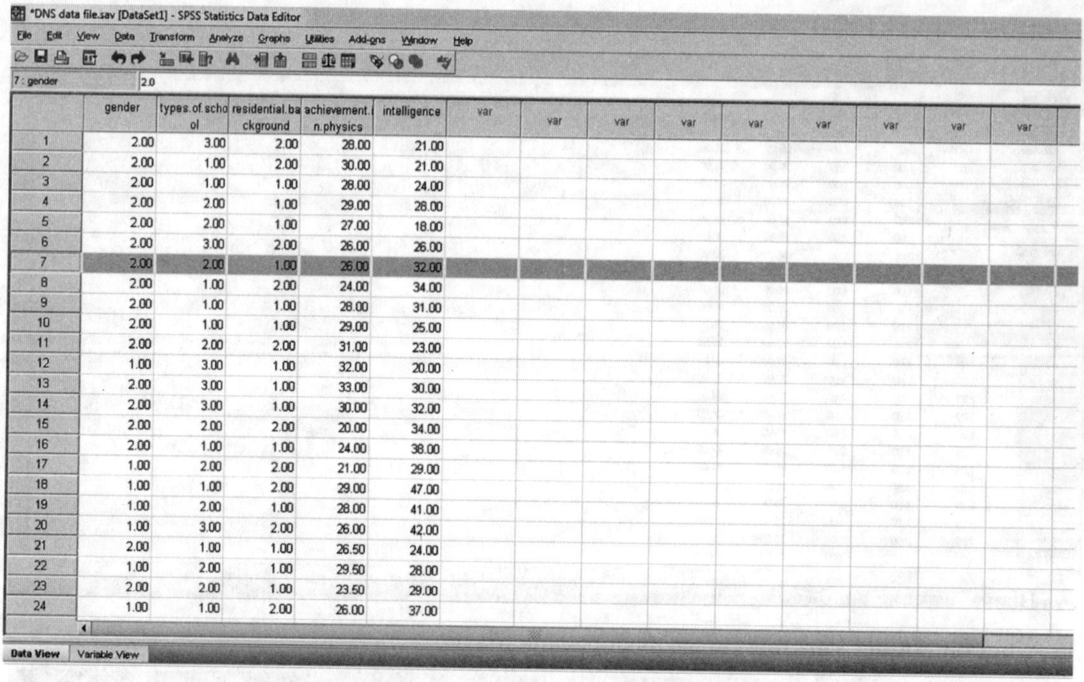

38. Click on "**Edit**" icon & bring curser to "**Insert Cases**" to get the following screen.

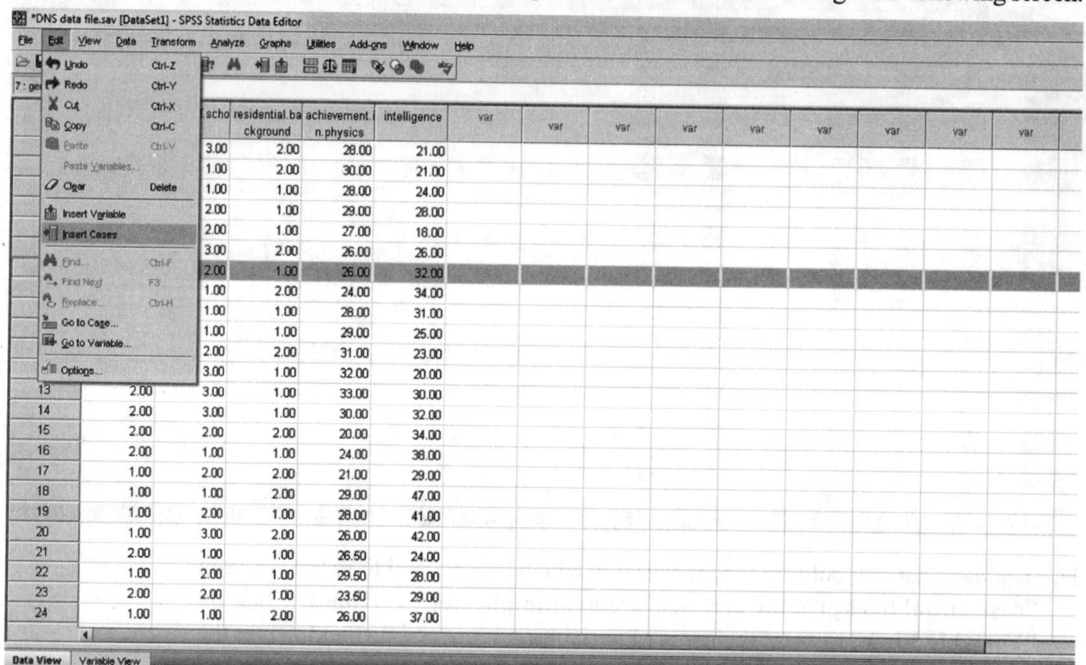

39. Click of "**Insert Cases**" to get the following screen.

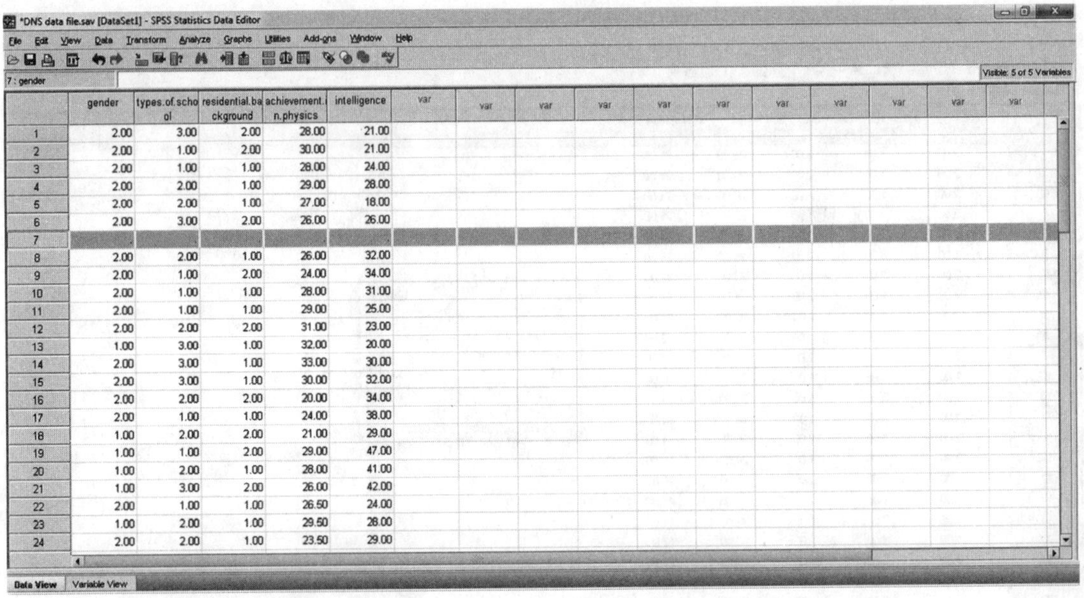

Blank row has been created for entering the data after serial number 6. Now you may enter the data.

Use of Edit

40. Click on "**Edit**" and bring curser to "**Go to Case**" to get the following screen.

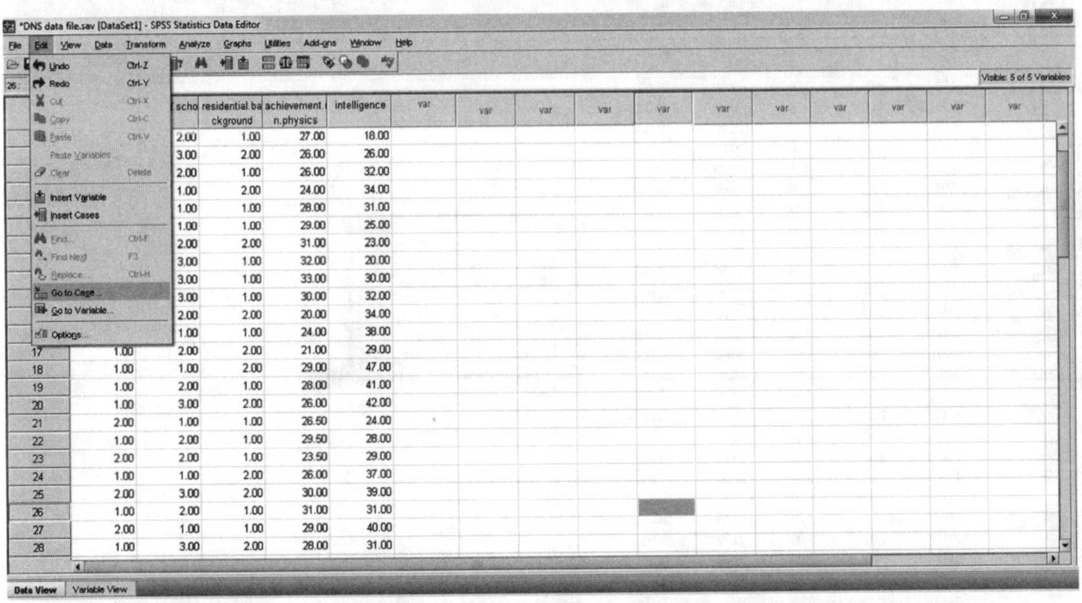

41. Click on "**Go to Case**" icon to get the following screen.

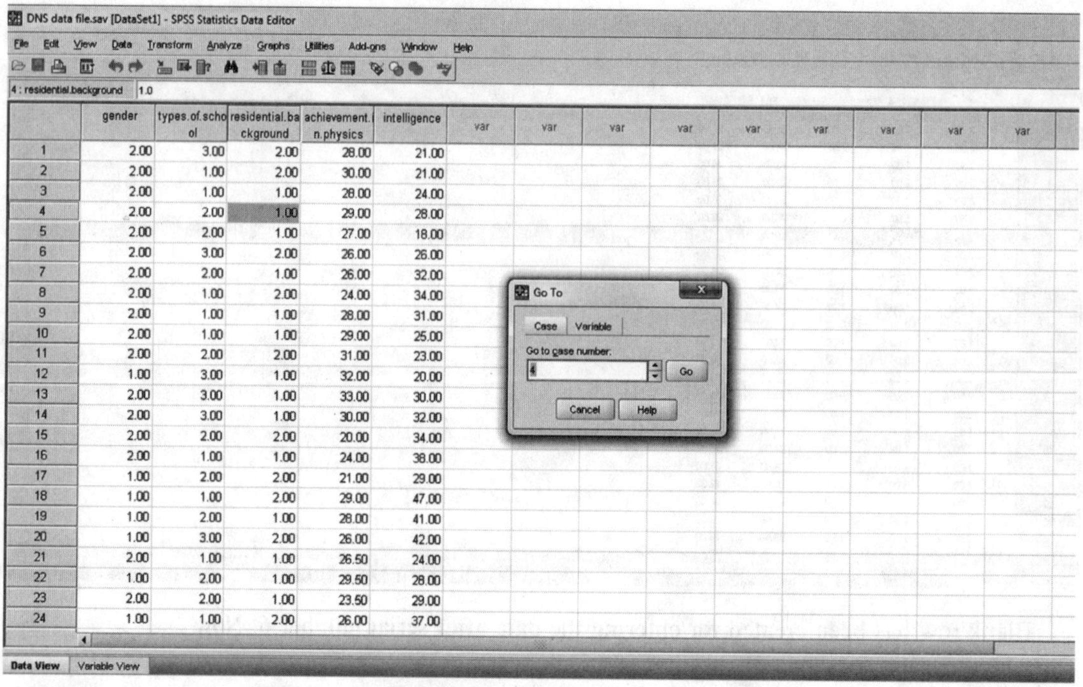

42. First click on "**Variable**" icon under "**Go To**" as shown in the following screen.

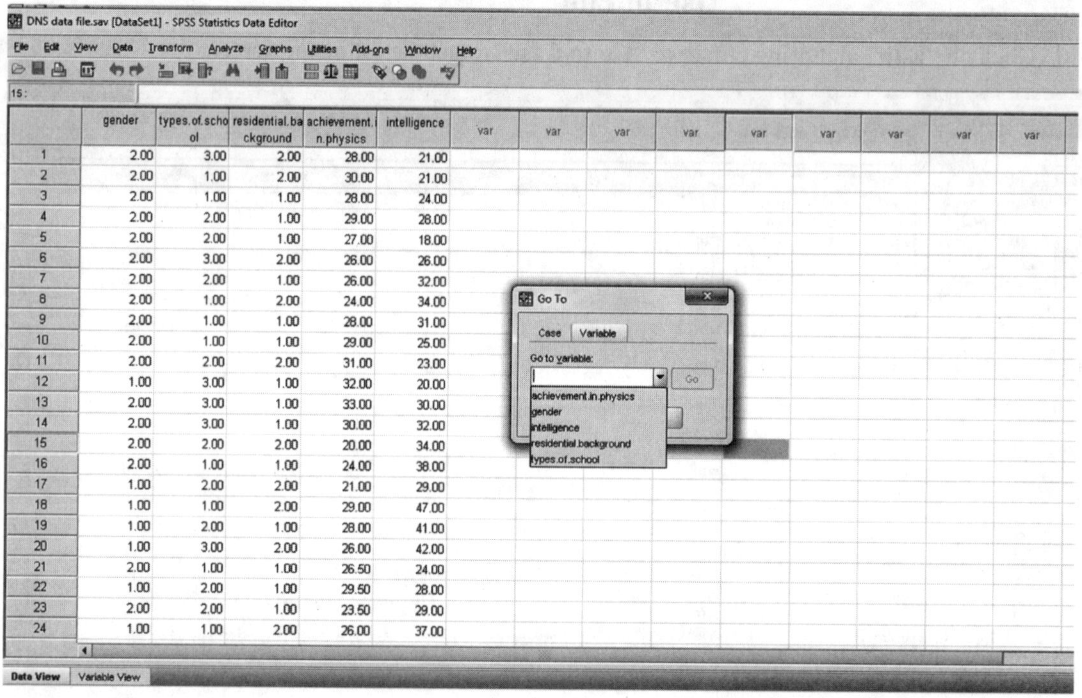

43. Since you want to edit "**intelligence**" variable data, bring curser on "**Intelligence**" and click to get the following screen.

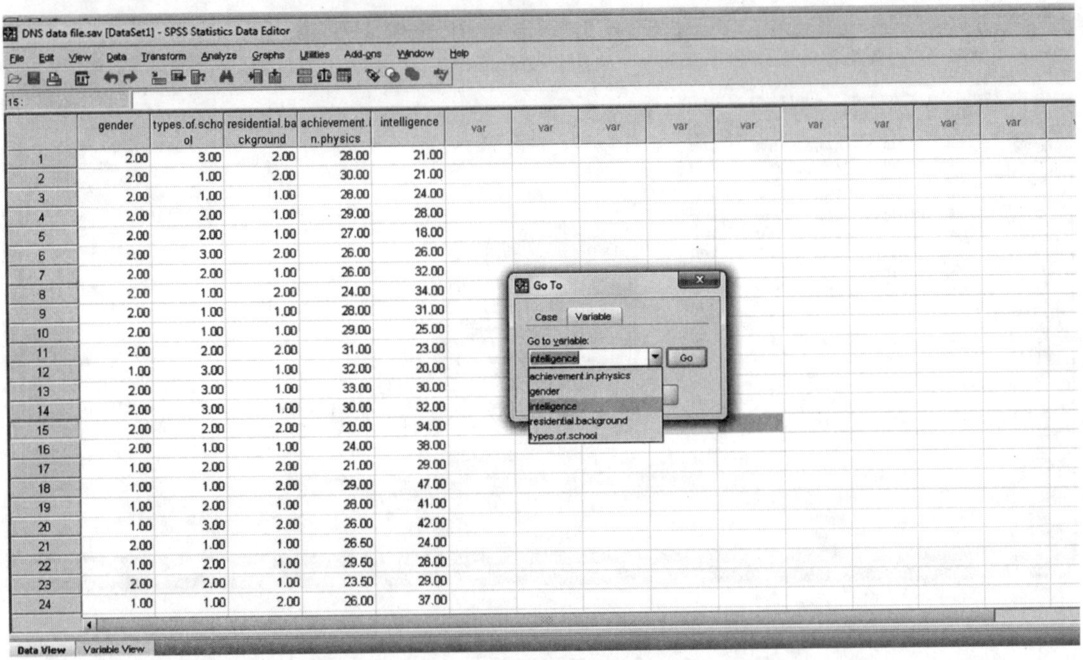

44. Suppose you want to Edit data of Intelligence at serial number 41, click on "**Case**" and enter "**41**" under "**Go to Case Number**" to get the following screen.

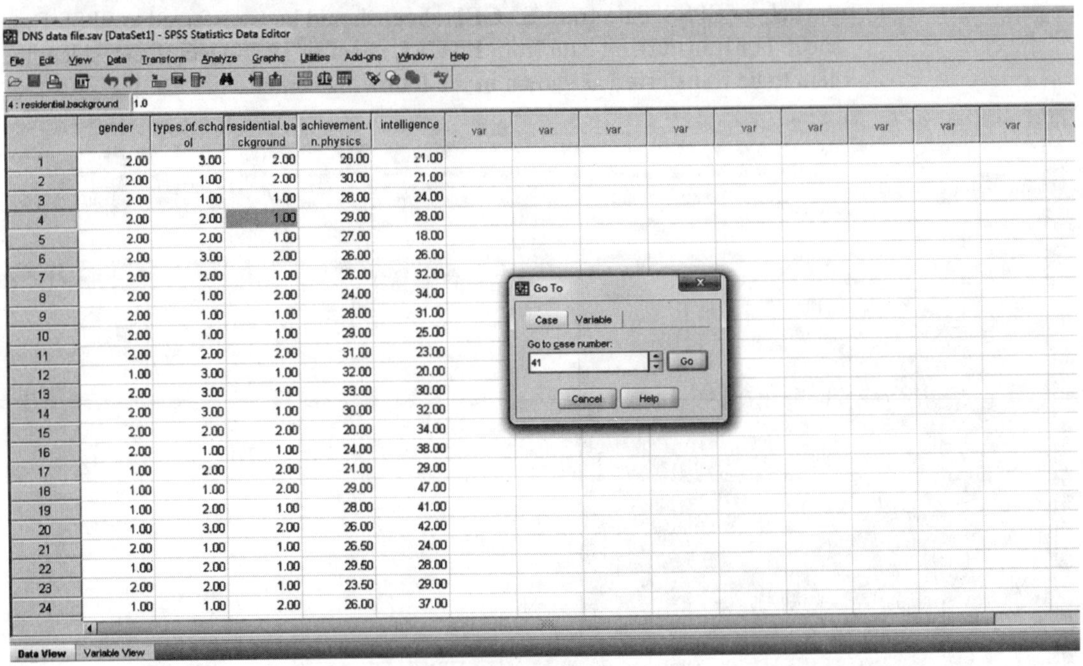

44. Now click on "**Go**" icon to go directly to "**intelligence**" score of "**Case**" 41 as shown in the following screen. Now make changes whatever you want.

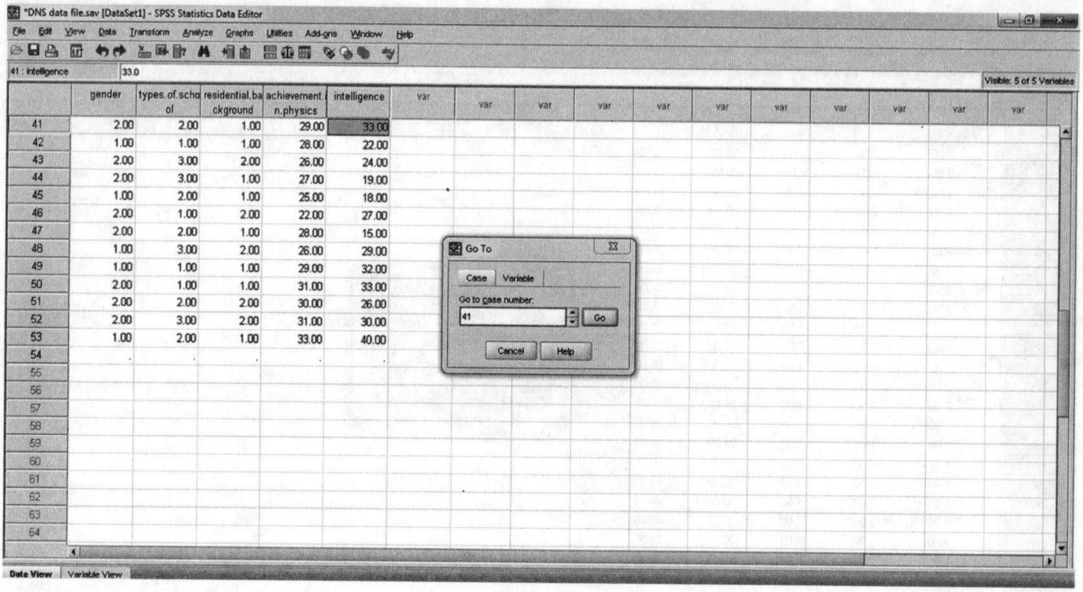

Transferring Data from EXCEL Sheet to SPSS

45. Many researchers enter the data in the **EXCEL sheet.** For analyzing data with the help of SPSS, data from **EXCEL sheet** should be transferred to SPSS Data sheet. For transferring data from **EXCEL sheet** to SPSS Data Sheet, select the data to be transferred as shown in the following screen.

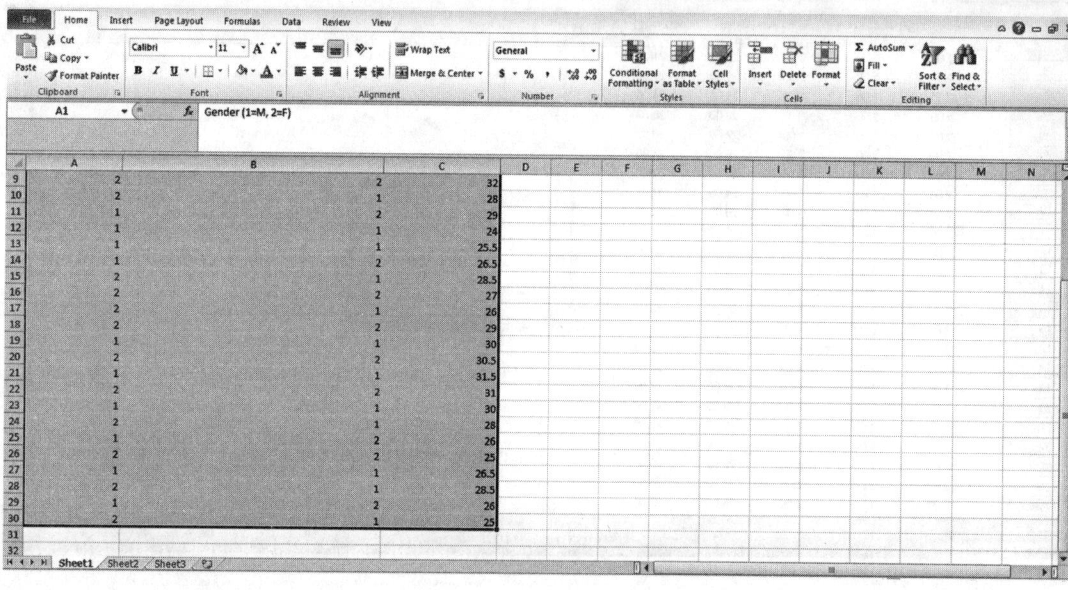

46. Open the blank SPSS Data sheet as shown below.

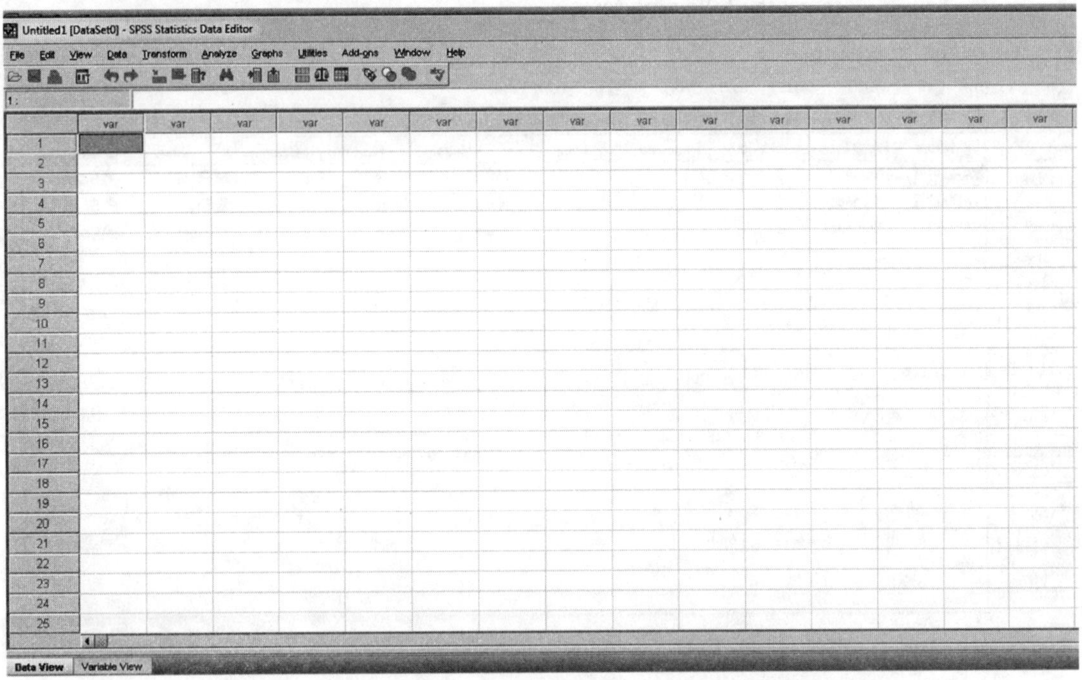

47. Copy the Data from the **EXCEL** sheet to the **SPSS** Data sheet as shown in the following screen.

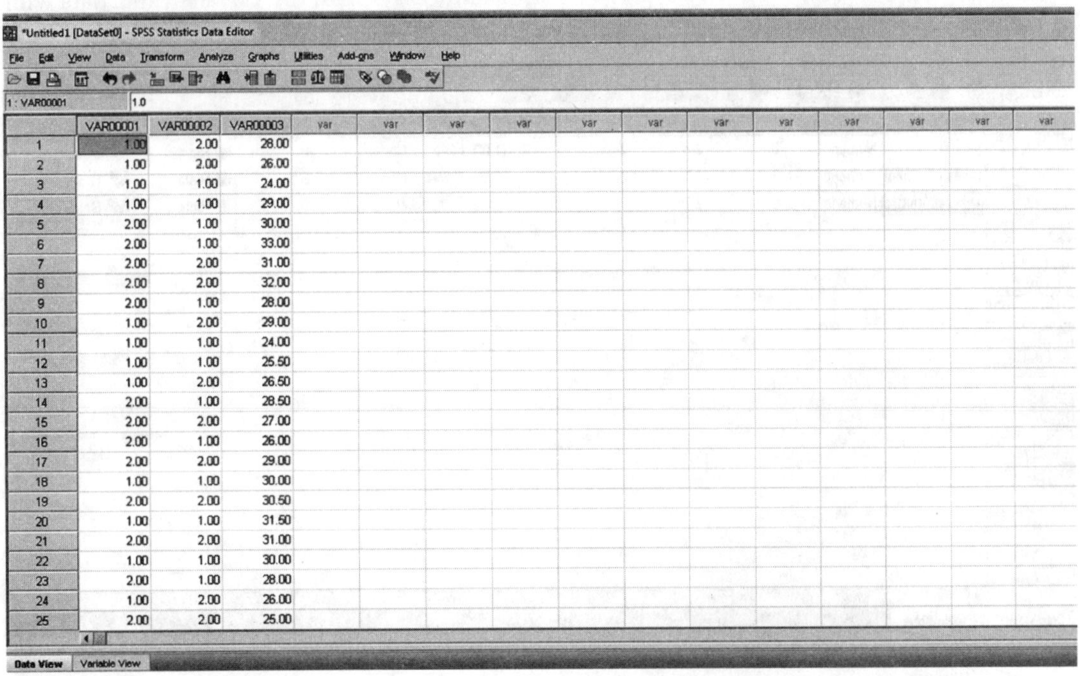

	VAR00001	VAR00002	VAR00003
1	1.00	2.00	28.00
2	1.00	2.00	26.00
3	1.00	1.00	24.00
4	1.00	1.00	29.00
5	2.00	1.00	30.00
6	2.00	1.00	33.00
7	2.00	2.00	31.00
8	2.00	2.00	32.00
9	2.00	1.00	28.00
10	1.00	2.00	29.00
11	1.00	1.00	24.00
12	1.00	1.00	25.50
13	1.00	2.00	26.50
14	2.00	1.00	28.50
15	2.00	2.00	27.00
16	2.00	1.00	26.00
17	2.00	2.00	29.00
18	1.00	1.00	30.00
19	2.00	2.00	30.50
20	1.00	1.00	31.50
21	2.00	2.00	31.00
22	1.00	1.00	30.00
23	2.00	1.00	28.00
24	1.00	2.00	26.00
25	2.00	2.00	25.00

48. For entering the name of variables and their labels, click on "**Variable View**" to get the following screen.

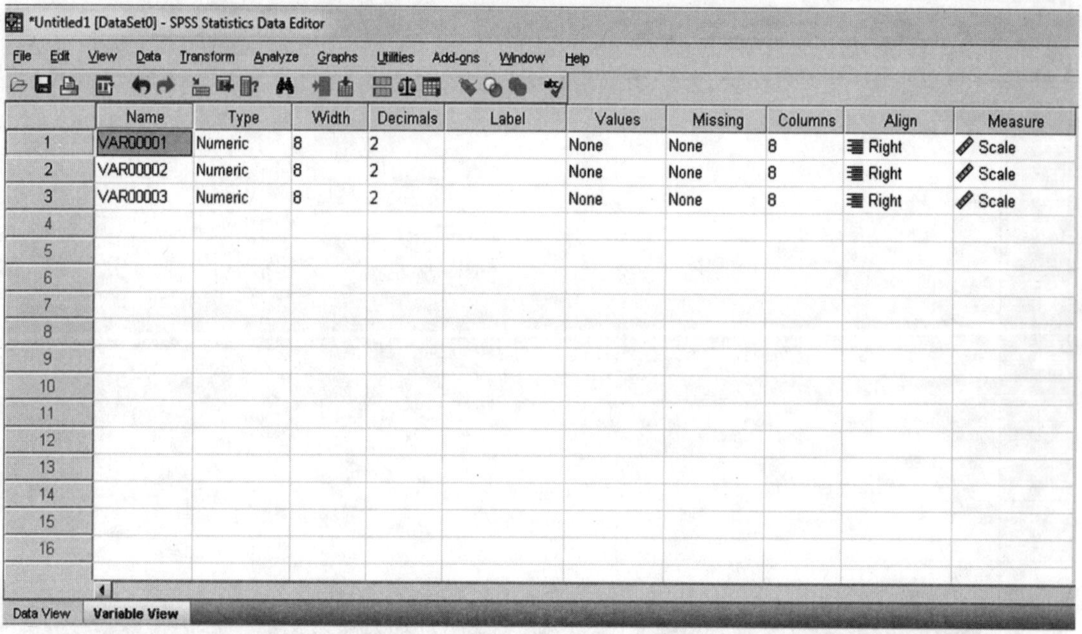

49. Now enter the "**Name**" and other information of variables "**Gender**", "**Types of School**" and "**Achievement in English**" to get the following screen.

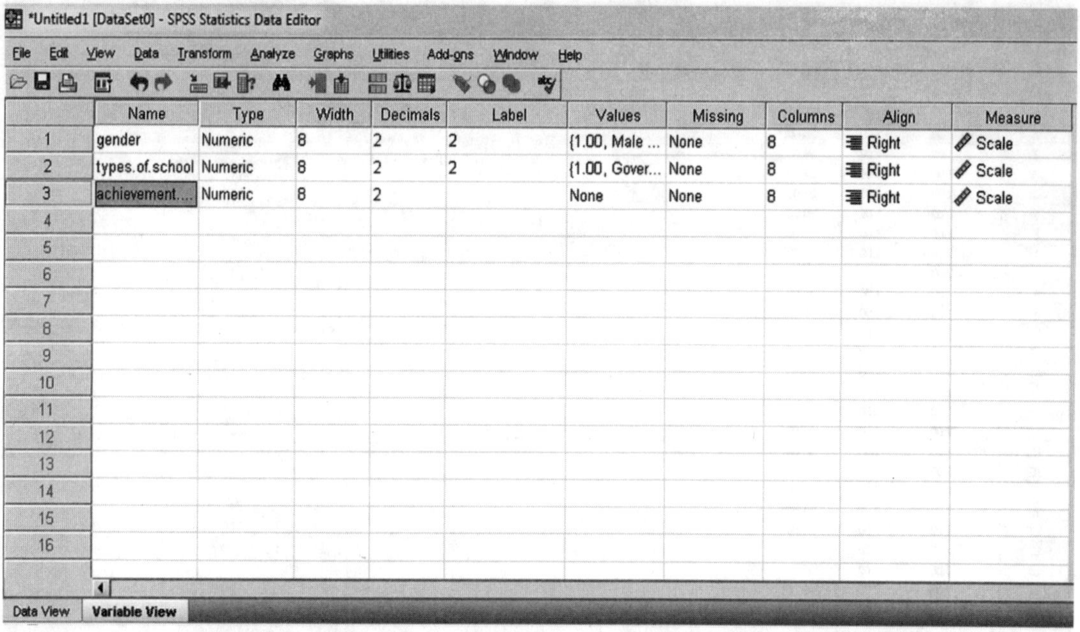

50. Click on "**Data**" icon to get the following screen.

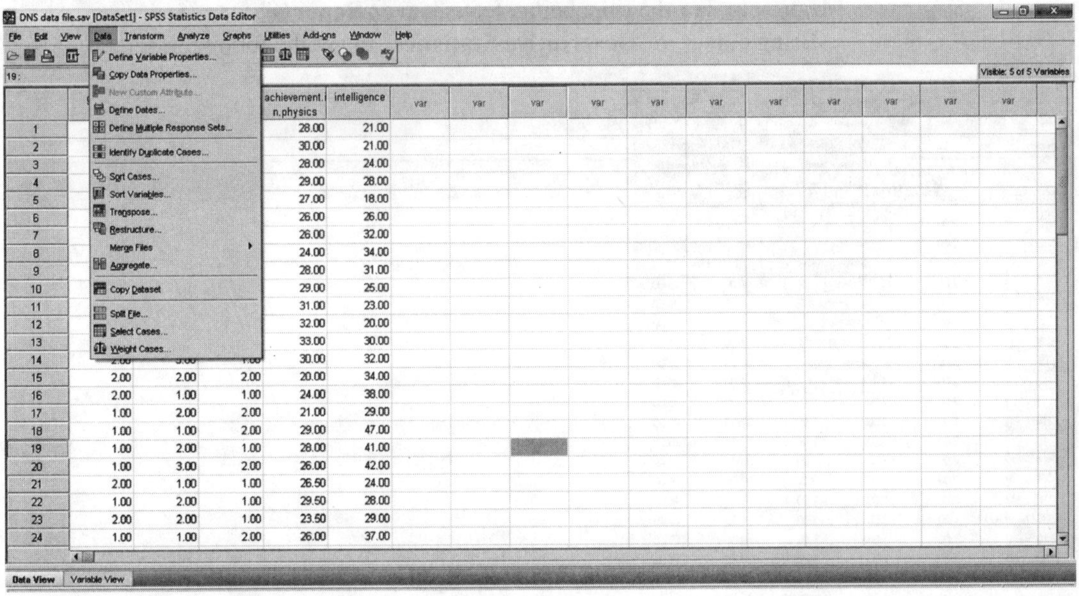

Different options are available under **"Data".** These are explained in appropriate frames of this manual.

Using Descriptive Statistics

51. Click on "**Analyse**" to get the following screen.

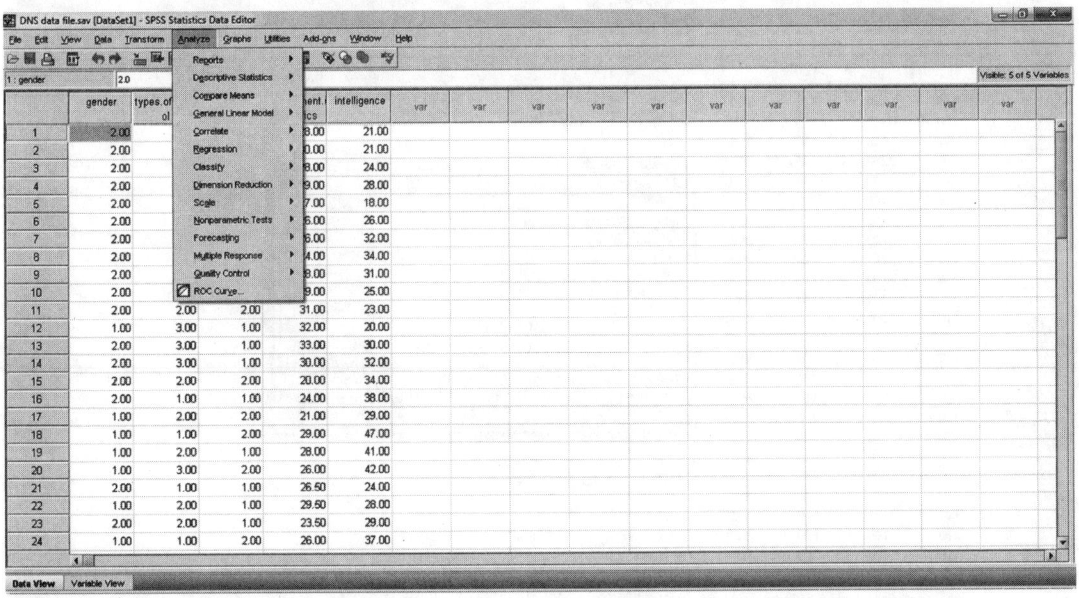

52. Different options available are: Reports, Descriptive Statistics, Compare Means, etc. For the time being, let us leave "**Reports**".

    Bring curser to "**Descriptive Statistics**" to get the following screen.

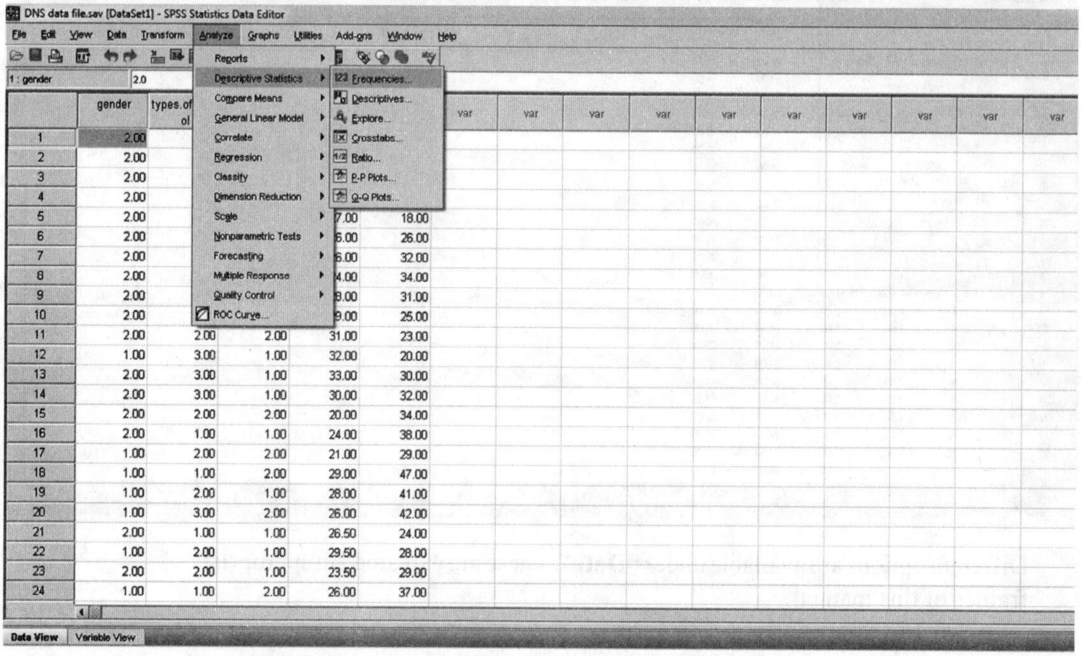

53. Click on "**Frequencies**" to get the following dialogue box.

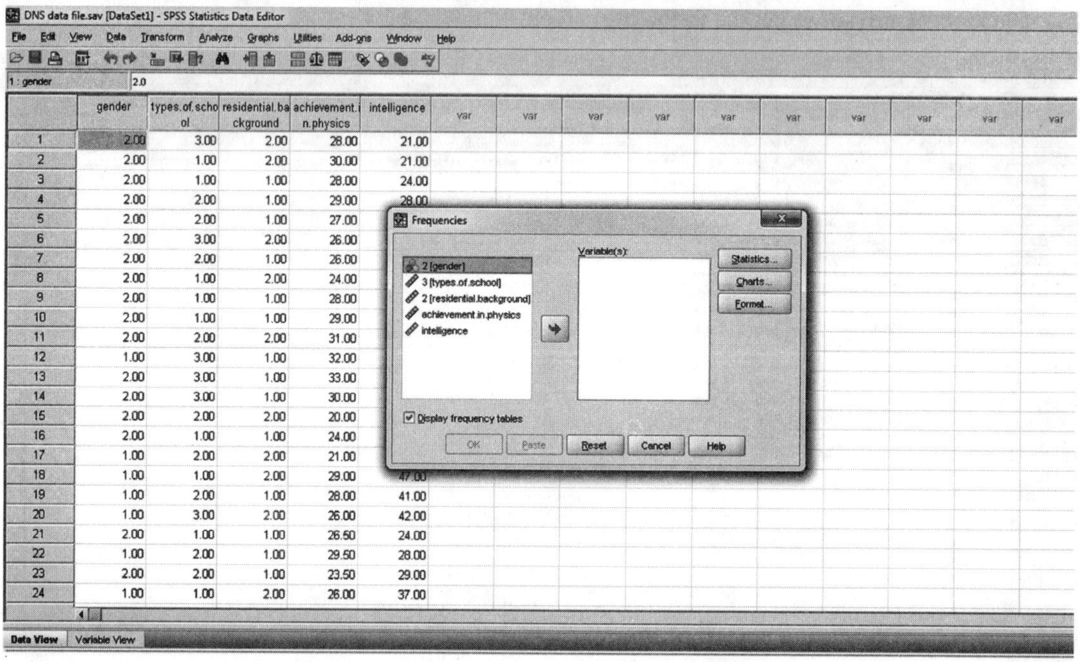

54. In order to find out number of observations for each level of discontinuous variables "**gender, types.of.school & residential.background**" select all these as shown in the following screen.

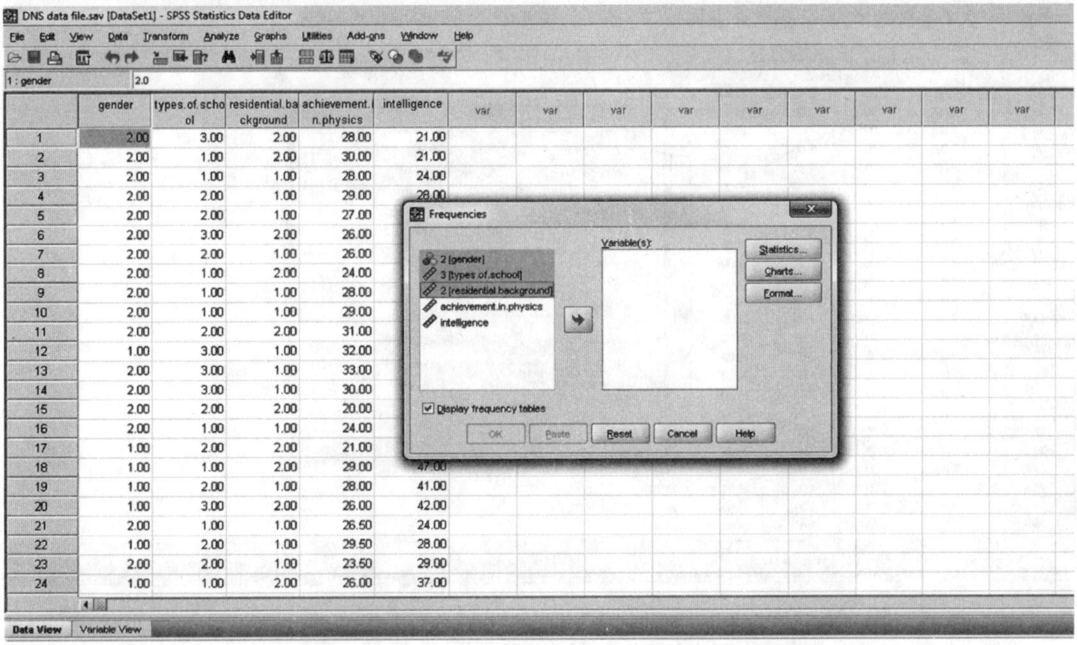

55. Shift these under "**Variable(s)**" dialogue box to get the following screen.

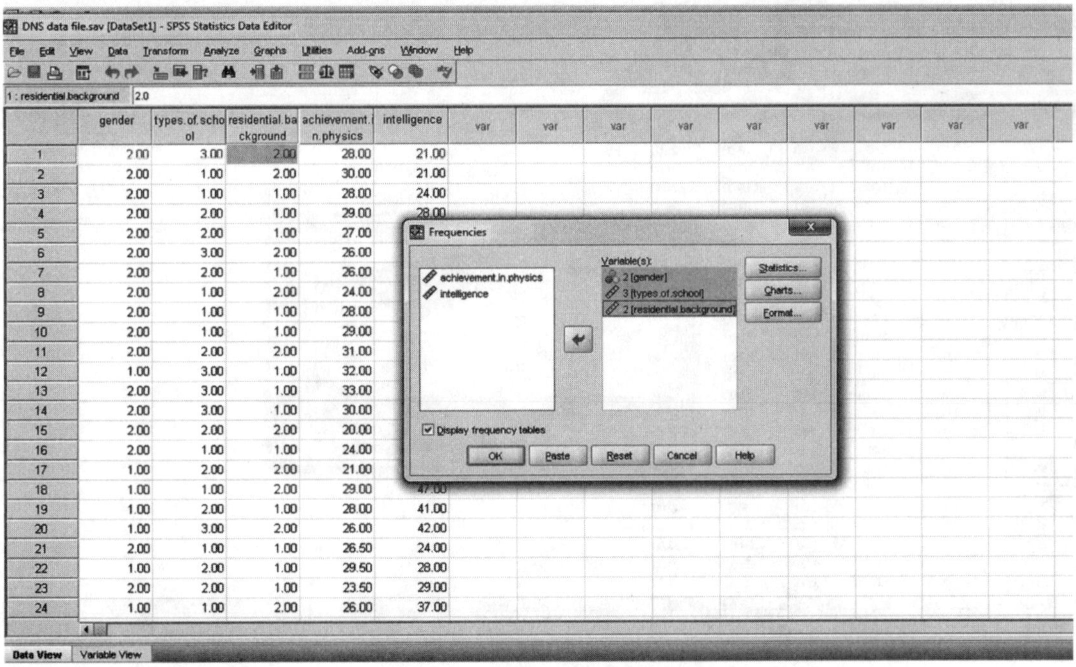

56. On the right hand side the three buttons are "**Statistics, Charts & Format**". Let us click on "**Statistics"** to get the following screen.

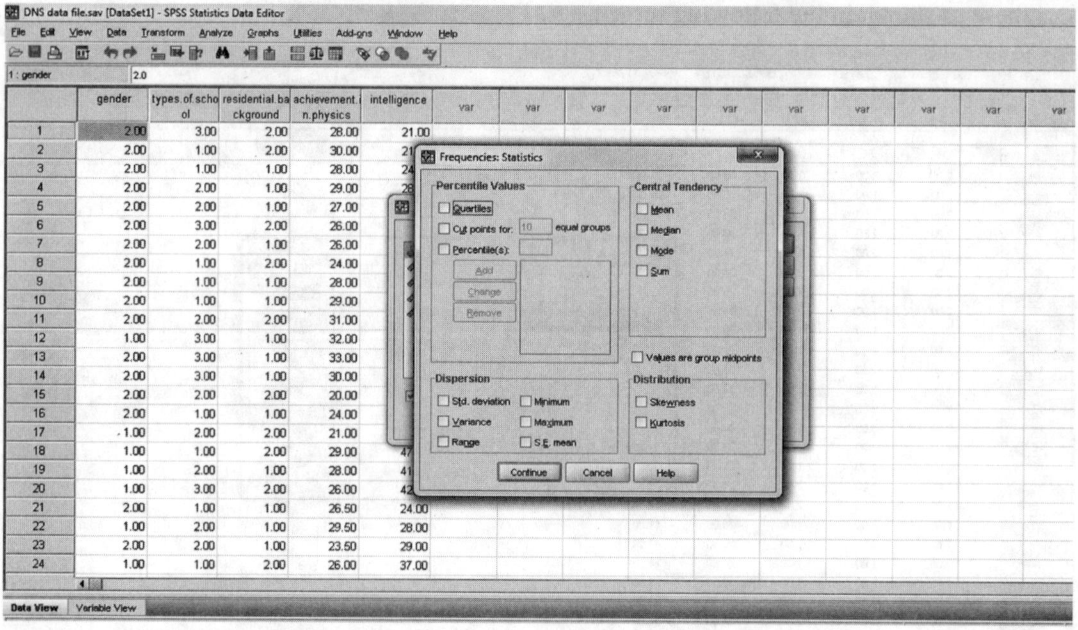

57. Many options are available. Depending of your requirement you may click on the option after that click on "**Continue**" icon. If you do not want to calculate anything, click on "**Continue**" icon to get the following screen.

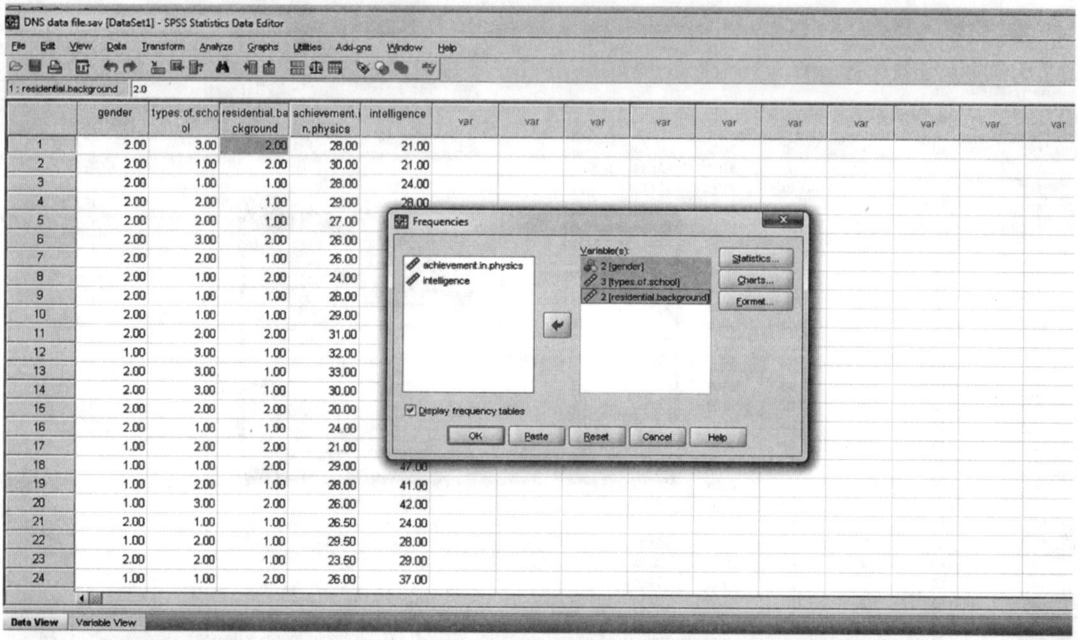

58. Click on "**OK**" to get the following output screen.

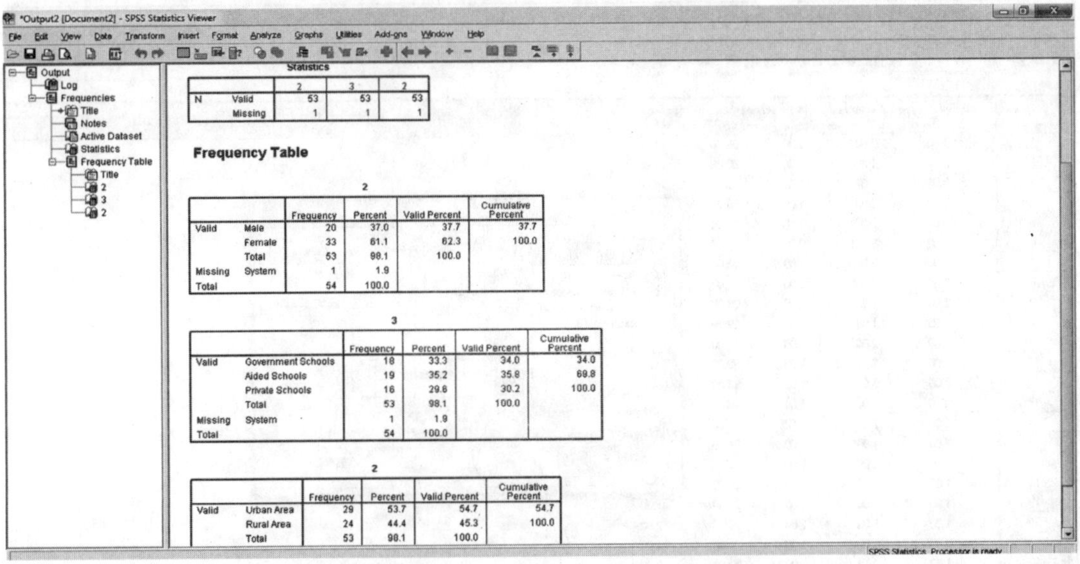

Checking Normal Distribution of Data

59. Normal Distribution of the Continuous Variable is one of the assumptions of Parametric Statistics. Different tests are available for checking the Normal Distribution of the continuous variable. These are Kolmogorov-Smirnov Test, Shapiro-Wilk Test, Q – Q Plot (Quartile – Quartile Plot), etc. Let us examine the Normal Distribution of Intelligence Data as given in Frame 57.

    Click on "**Analyse**" bring curser to "**Descriptive Statistics**" icon and finally to "**Explore**" icon to get the following screen.

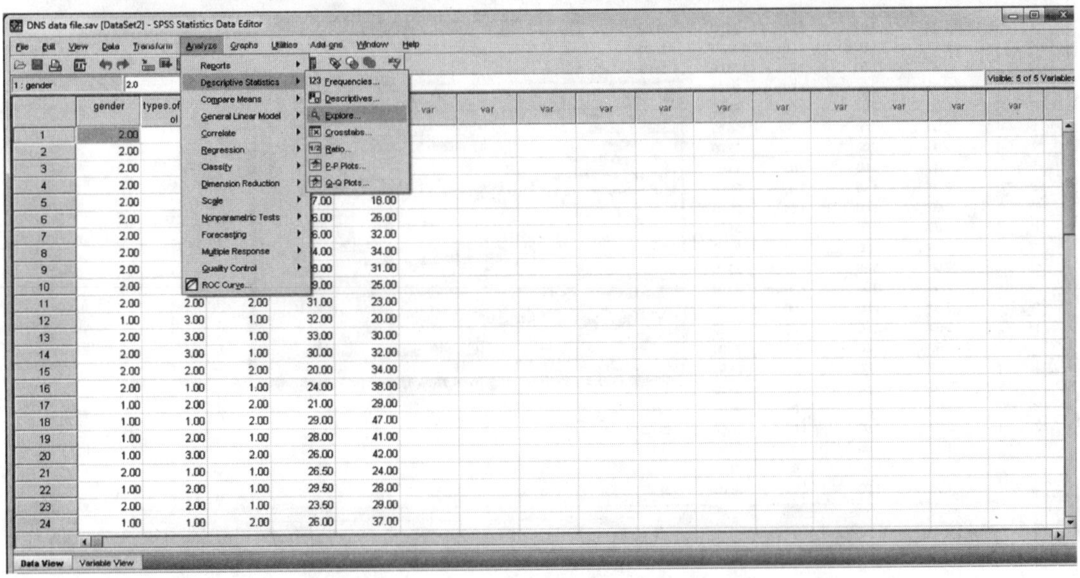

60. Click on "**Explore**" icon to get the following screen.

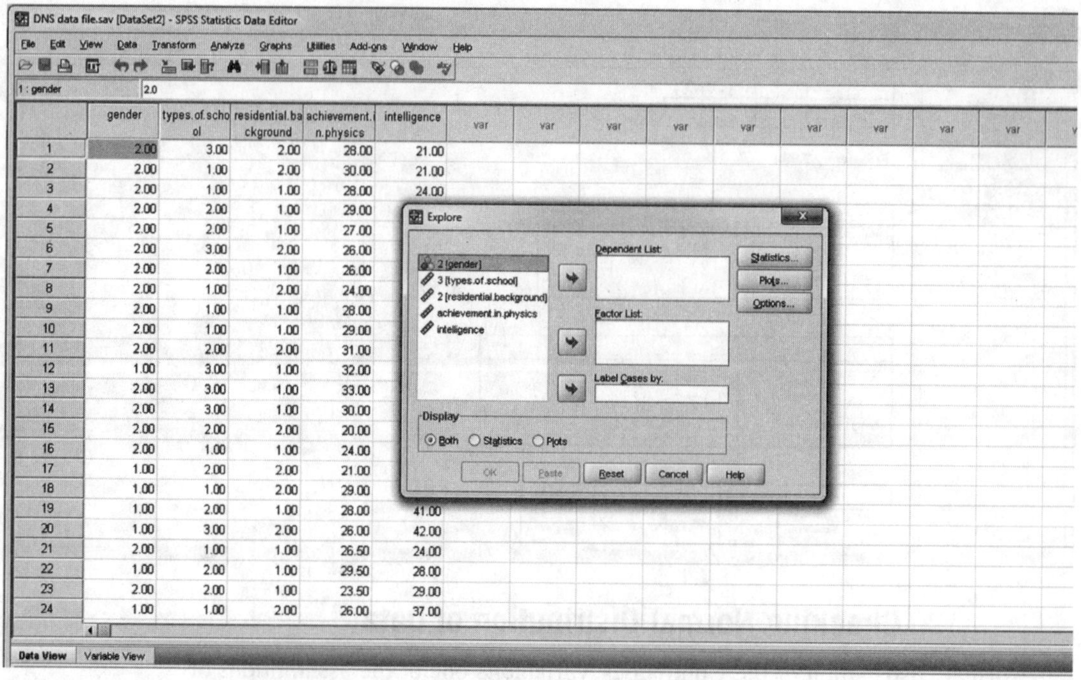

61. Shift "**Intelligence**" variable to the "**Dependent List**" slot to get the following screen.

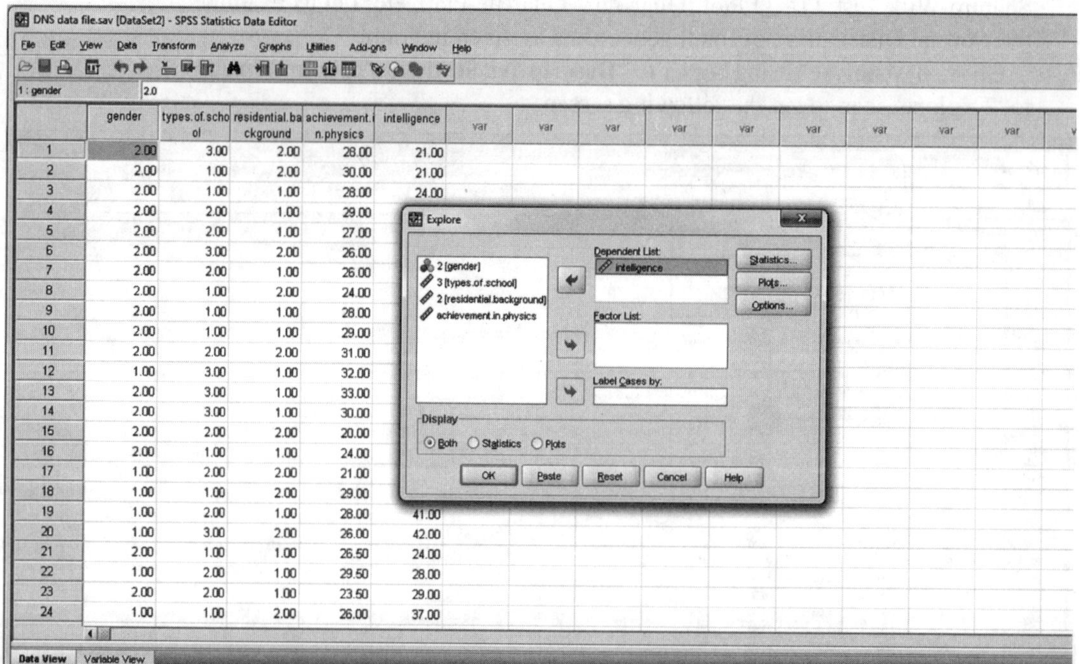

62. Click on "**Plots**" button to get the following screen.

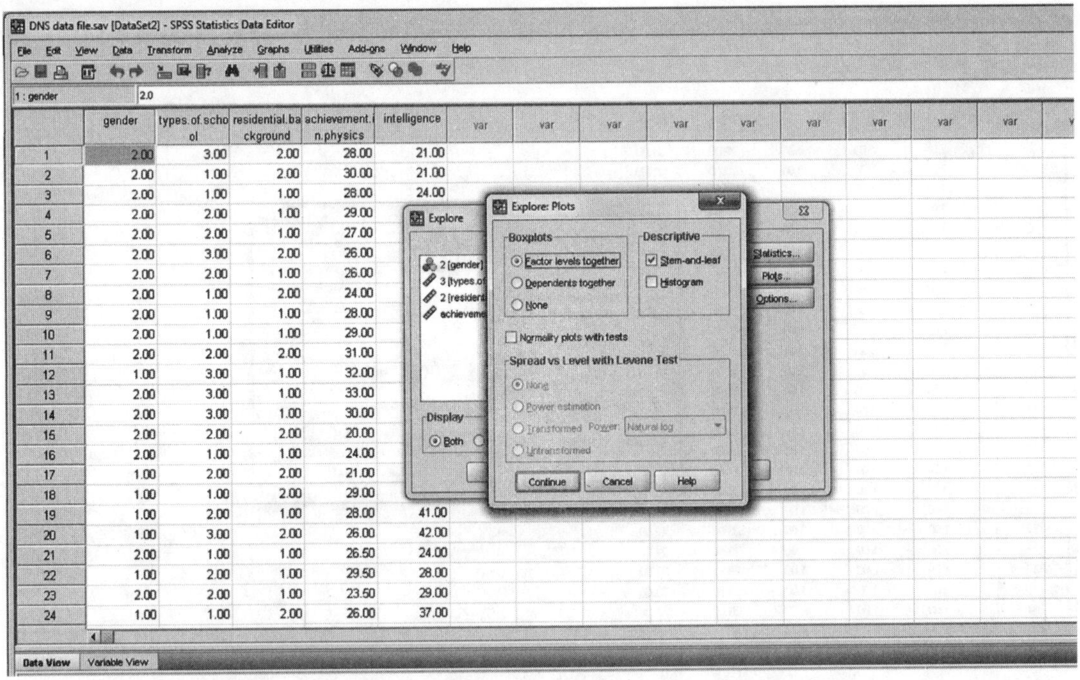

63. "**Factor levels together**" icon and "**Stem- and- Leaf**" icon are pre-highlighted. Now highlight "**Normality Plots with Tests**" to get the following screen.

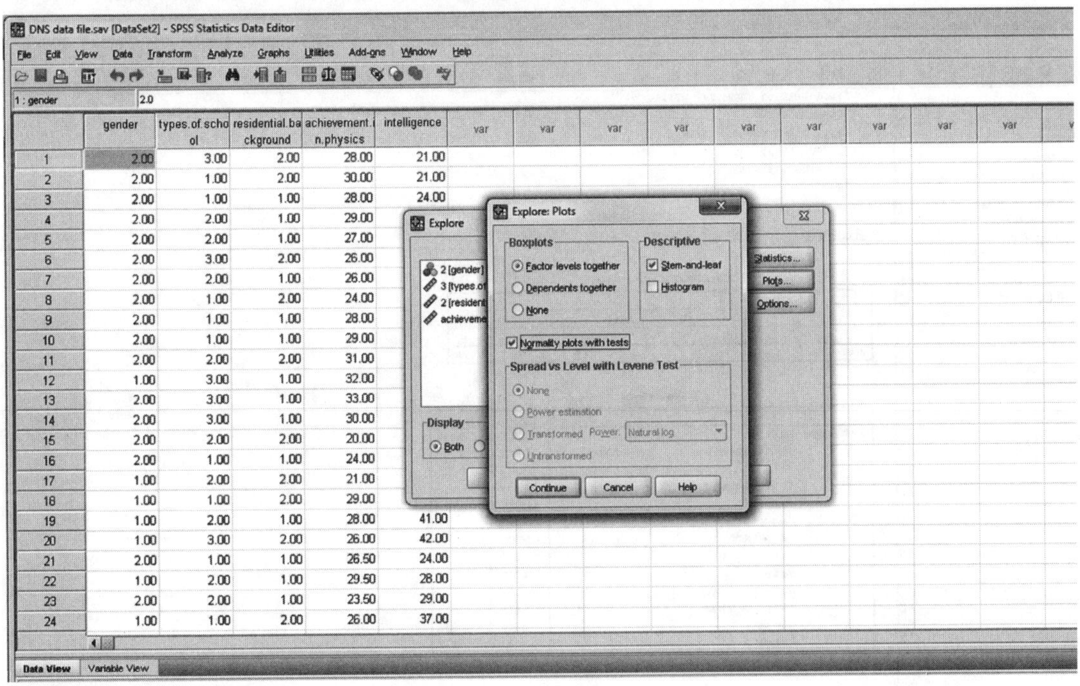

64. Click on "**Continue**" to get the following screen.

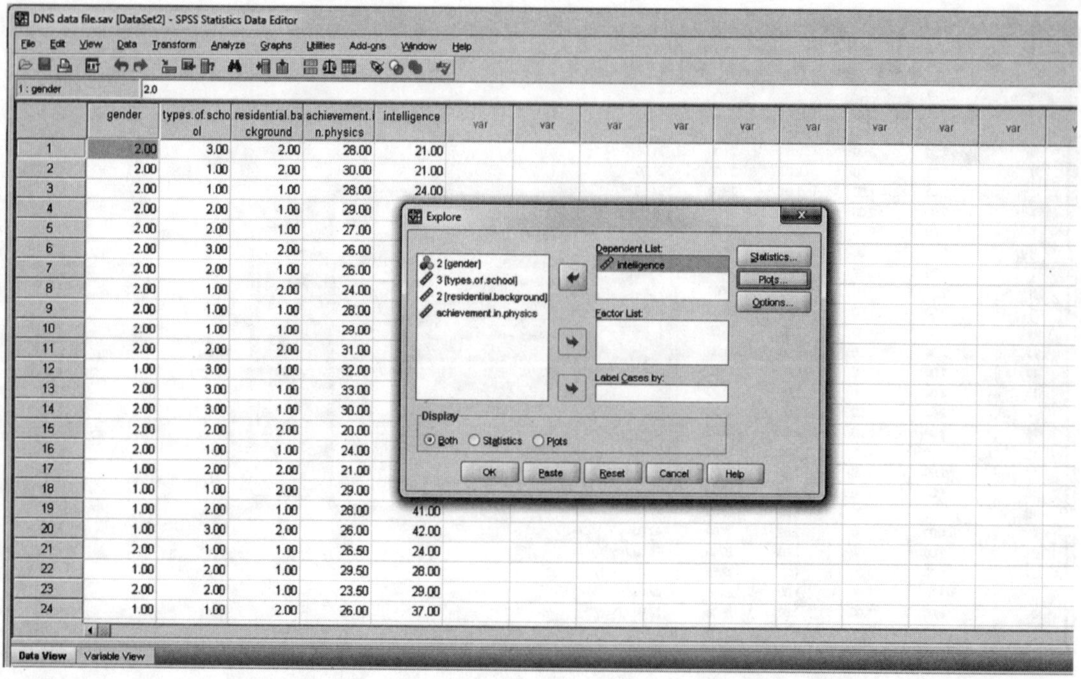

65. Click on "**OK**" icon to get the following outputs of normal distribution of Intelligence.

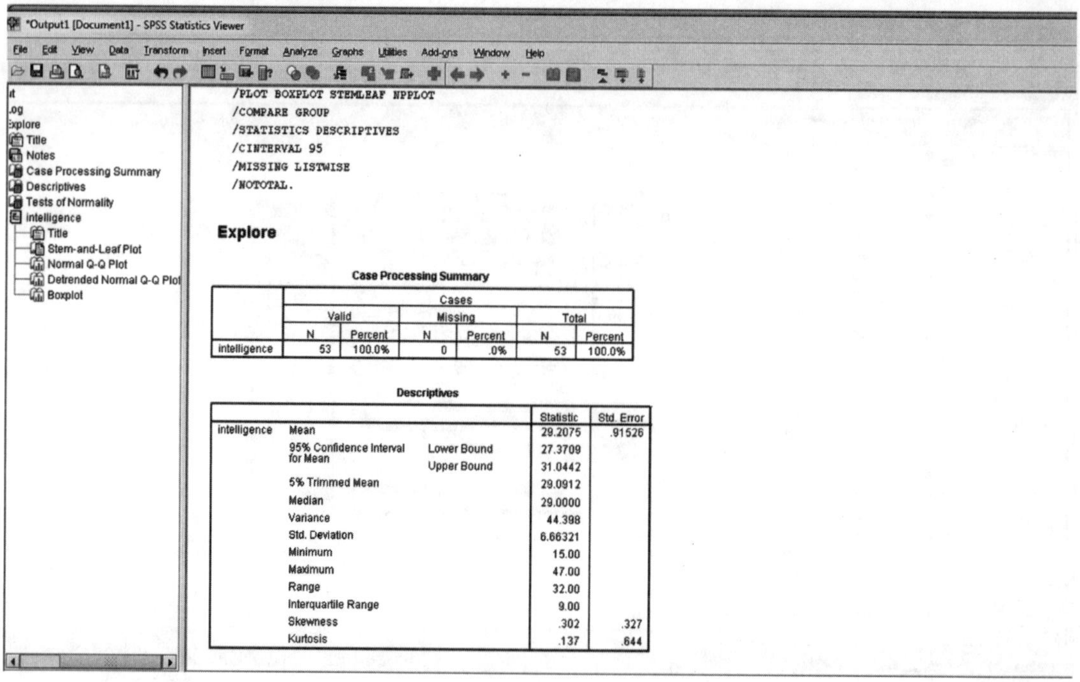

Case Processing Summary

	Cases					
	Valid		Missing		Total	
	N	Percent	N	Percent	N	Percent
intelligence	53	100.0%	0	.0%	53	100.0%

Descriptives

			Statistic	Std. Error
intelligence	Mean		29.2075	.91526
	95% Confidence Interval for Mean	Lower Bound	27.3709	
		Upper Bound	31.0442	
	5% Trimmed Mean		29.0912	
	Median		29.0000	
	Variance		44.398	
	Std. Deviation		6.66321	
	Minimum		15.00	
	Maximum		47.00	
	Range		32.00	
	Interquartile Range		9.00	
	Skewness		.302	.327
	Kurtosis		.137	.644

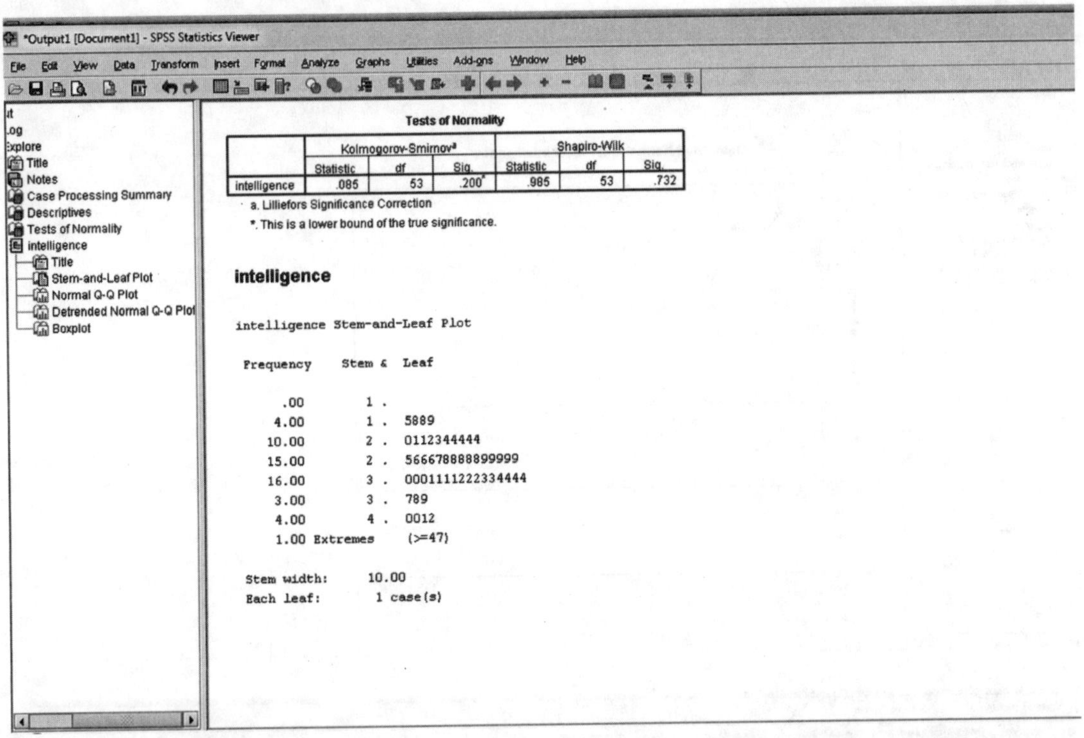

*Output1 [Document1] - SPSS Statistics Viewer

Tests of Normality

	Kolmogorov-Smirnov[a]			Shapiro-Wilk		
	Statistic	df	Sig.	Statistic	df	Sig.
intelligence	.085	53	.200*	.985	53	.732

a. Lilliefors Significance Correction

*. This is a lower bound of the true significance.

intelligence

```
intelligence Stem-and-Leaf Plot

 Frequency    Stem &  Leaf

      .00        1 .
     4.00        1 .  5889
    10.00        2 .  0112344444
    15.00        2 .  566678888899999
    16.00        3 .  0001111222334444
     3.00        3 .  789
     4.00        4 .  0012
     1.00 Extremes    (>=47)

 Stem width:      10.00
 Each leaf:        1 case(s)
```

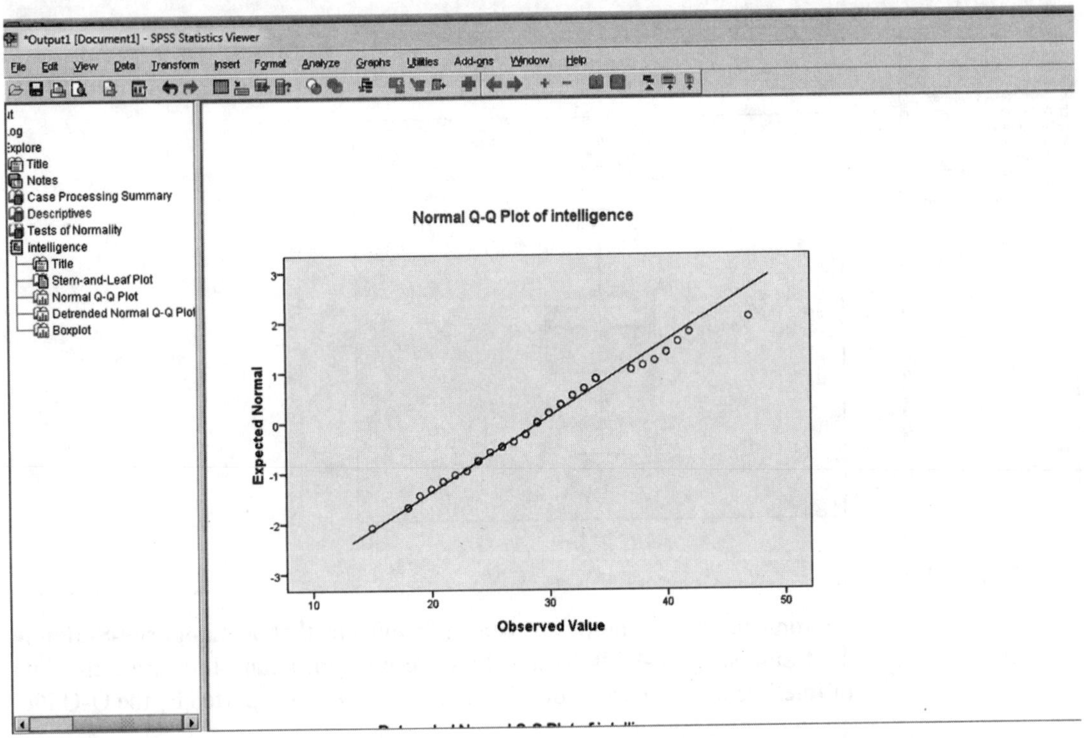

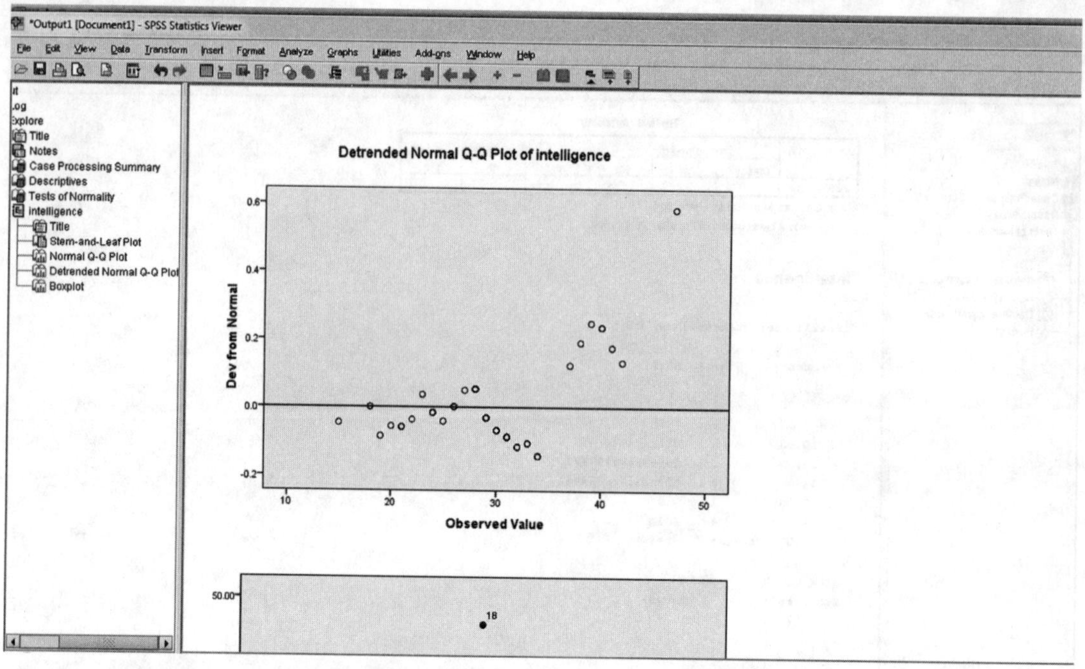

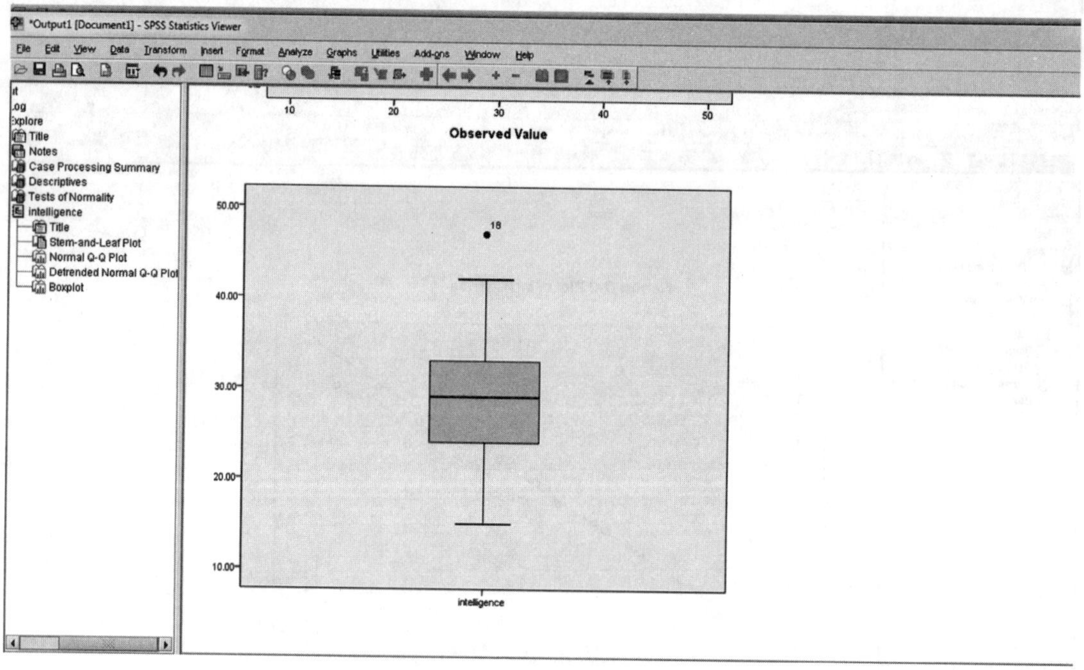

From the second output screen, it is evident that **Kolmogorov-Smirnov Test and Shapiro-Wilk Test values** are not significant. Indicating the data of Intelligence has normal distribution. It is further supported by the Q-Q Plot given in third output.

66. Let us test the normality of data of "**Achievement in Physics**" variable. Click on "**Analyse**" icon bring curser to "**Descriptive Statistics**" and finally on "**Explore**" to get the following screen.

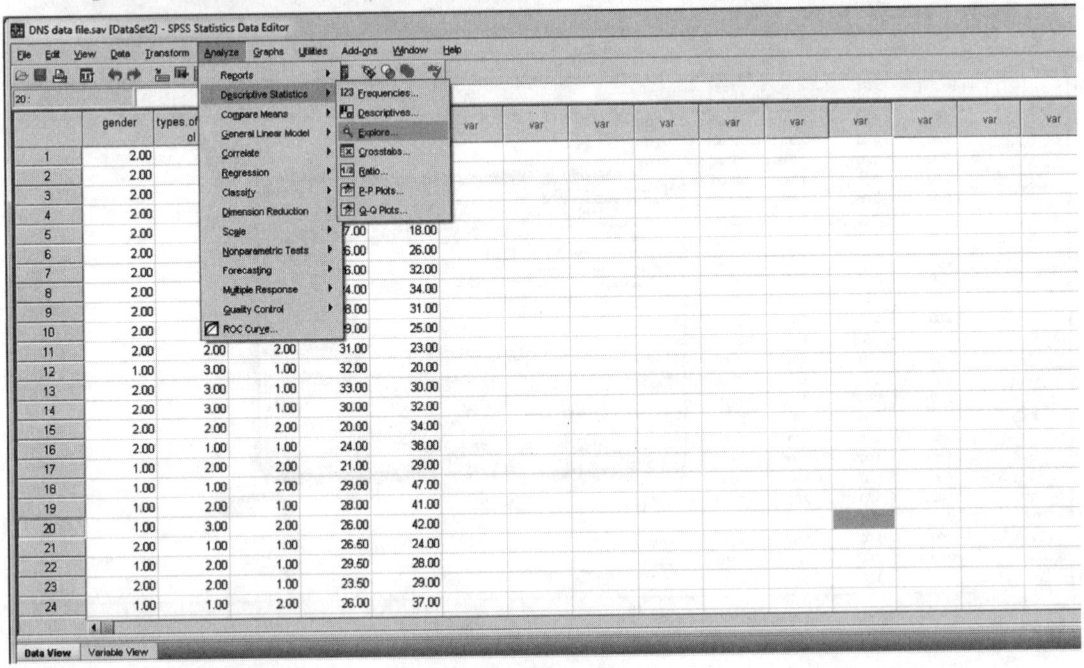

67. Click on "**Explore**" to get the following screen.

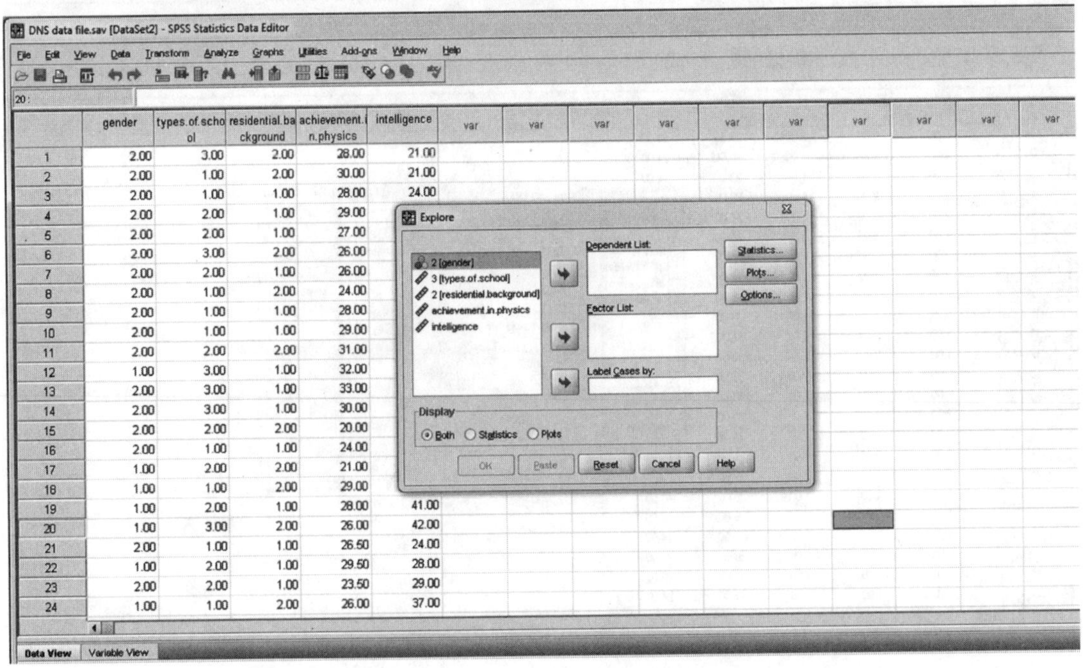

68. Shift "**Achievement in Physics**" variable to "**Dependent List**" dialogue box to get the following screen.

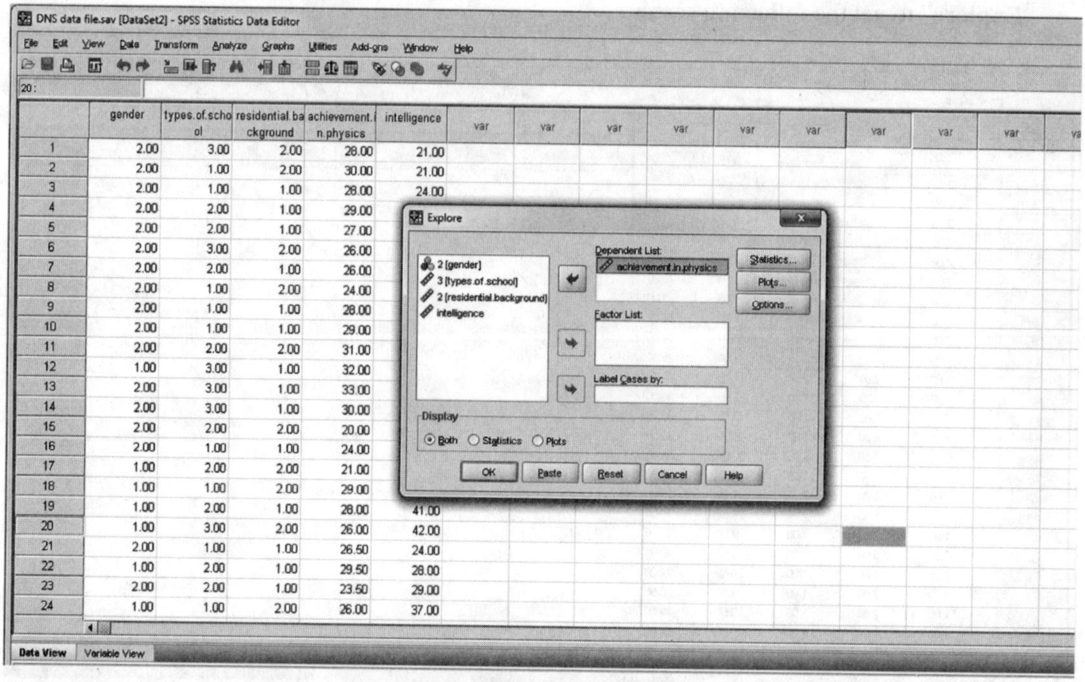

69. Click on "**Plots**" to get the following screen.

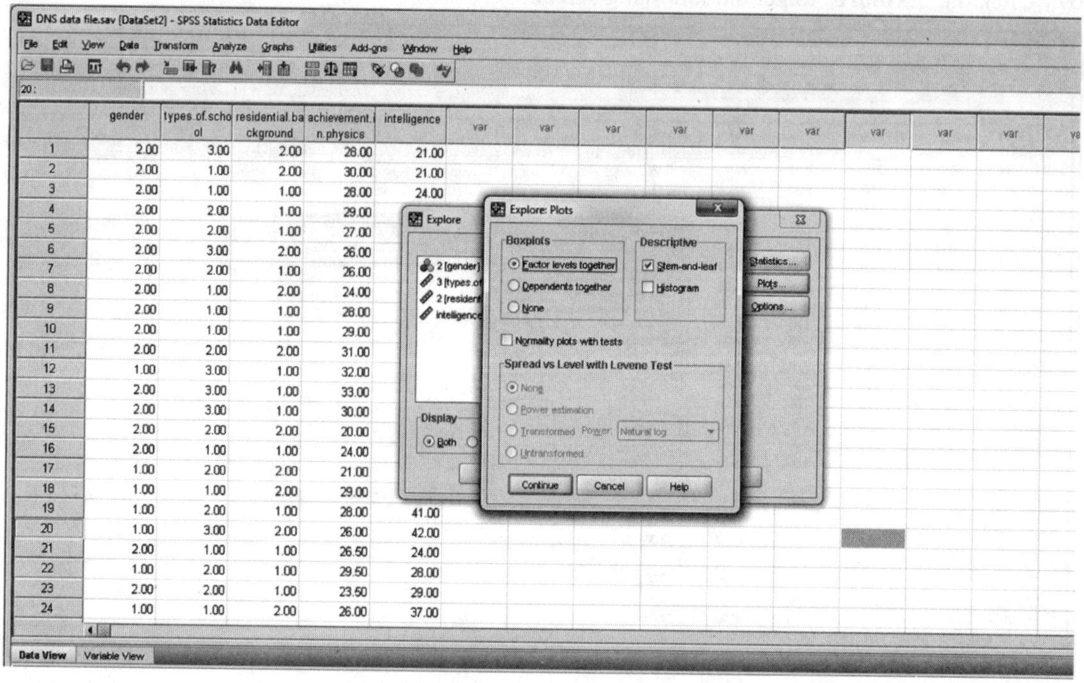

70. Highlight "**Normal Plots with Tests**" to get the following screen.

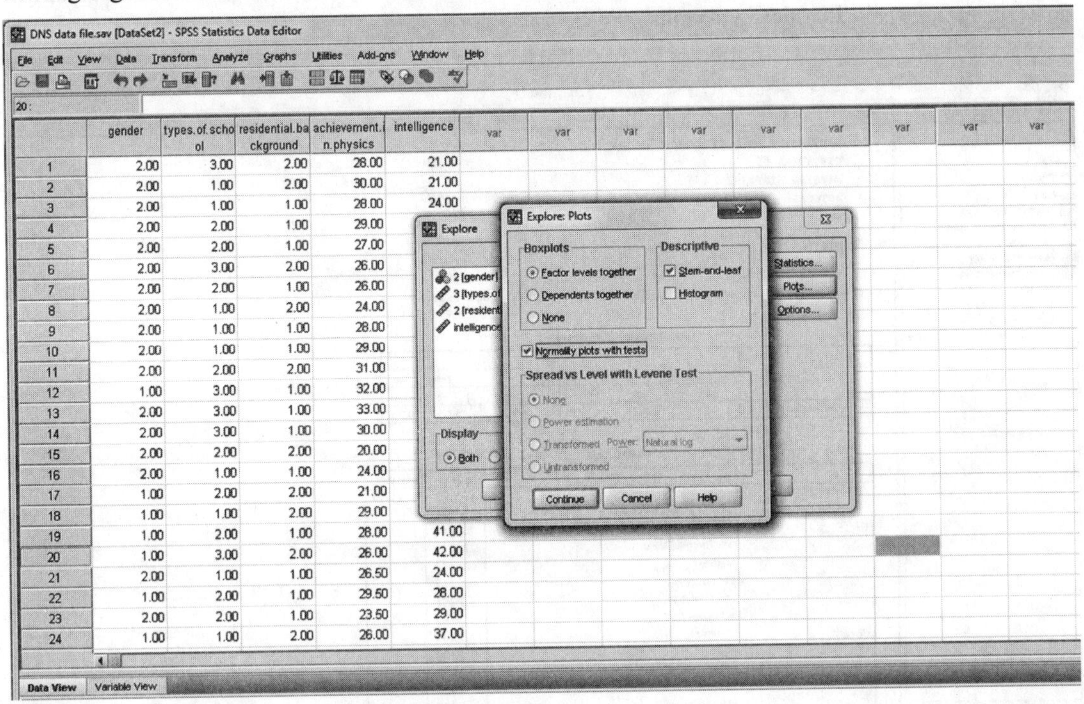

71. Click on "**Continue**" icon to get the following screen.

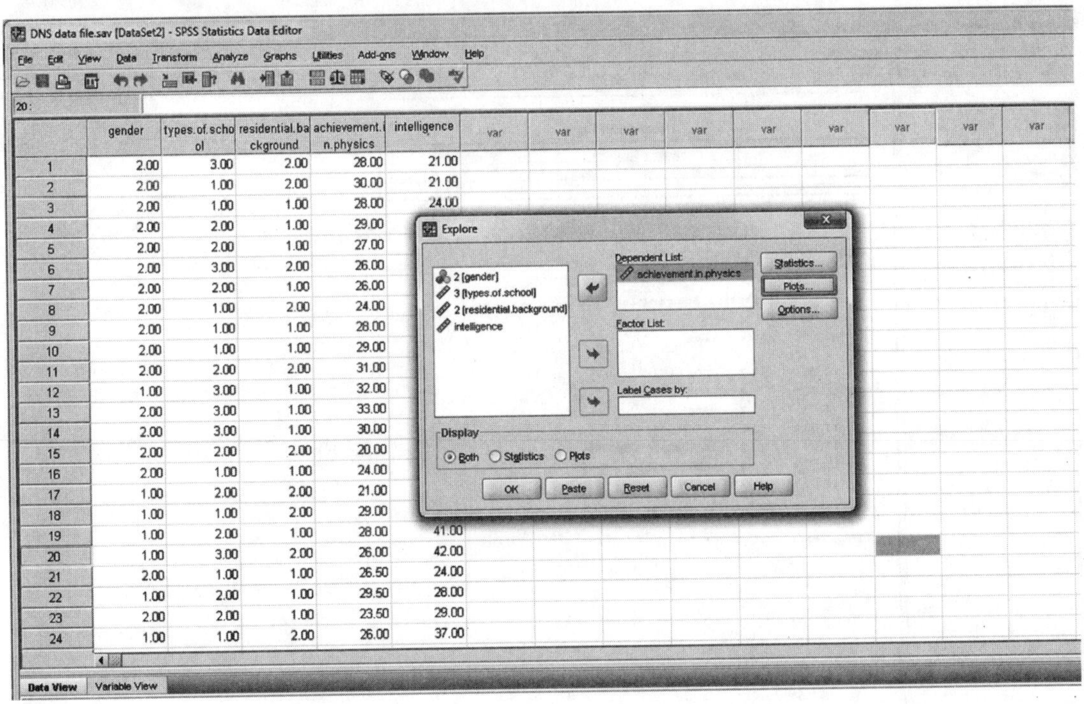

72. Click on "**OK**" to get the outputs of Normal Distribution of "**Achievement in Physics**" variable.

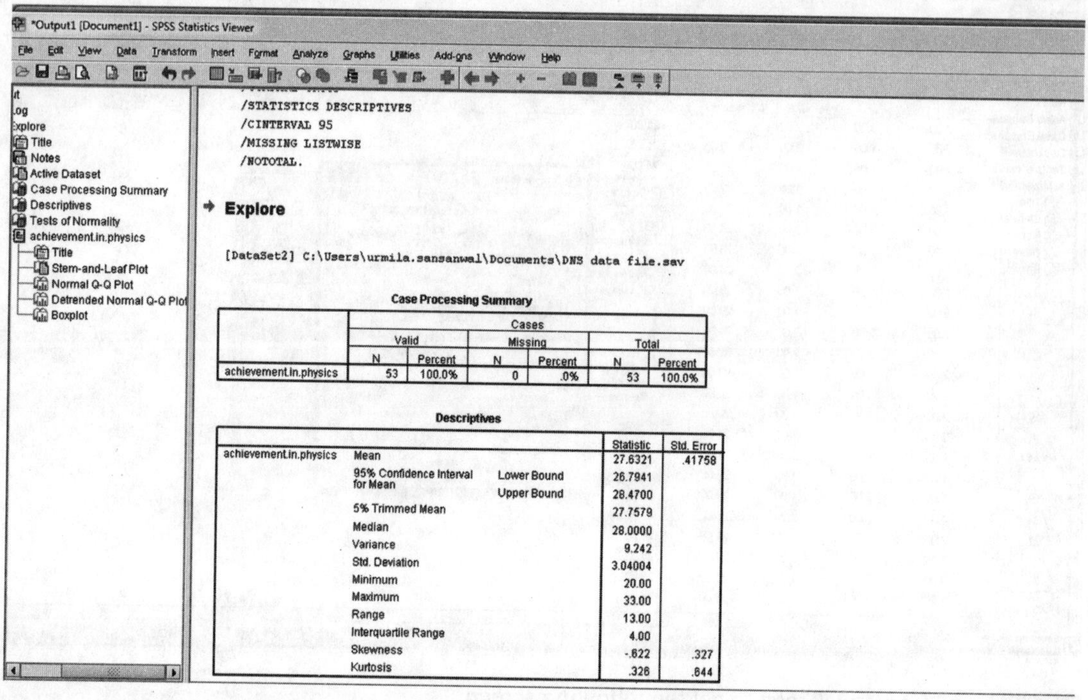


```
/STATISTICS DESCRIPTIVES
/CINTERVAL 95
/MISSING LISTWISE
/NOTOTAL.
```

Explore

[DataSet2] C:\Users\urmila.sansanwal\Documents\DNS data file.sav

Case Processing Summary

	Cases					
	Valid		Missing		Total	
	N	Percent	N	Percent	N	Percent
achievement.in.physics	53	100.0%	0	.0%	53	100.0%

Descriptives

			Statistic	Std. Error
achievement.in.physics	Mean		27.6321	.41758
	95% Confidence Interval for Mean	Lower Bound	26.7941	
		Upper Bound	28.4700	
	5% Trimmed Mean		27.7579	
	Median		28.0000	
	Variance		9.242	
	Std. Deviation		3.04004	
	Minimum		20.00	
	Maximum		33.00	
	Range		13.00	
	Interquartile Range		4.00	
	Skewness		-.622	.327
	Kurtosis		.326	.644

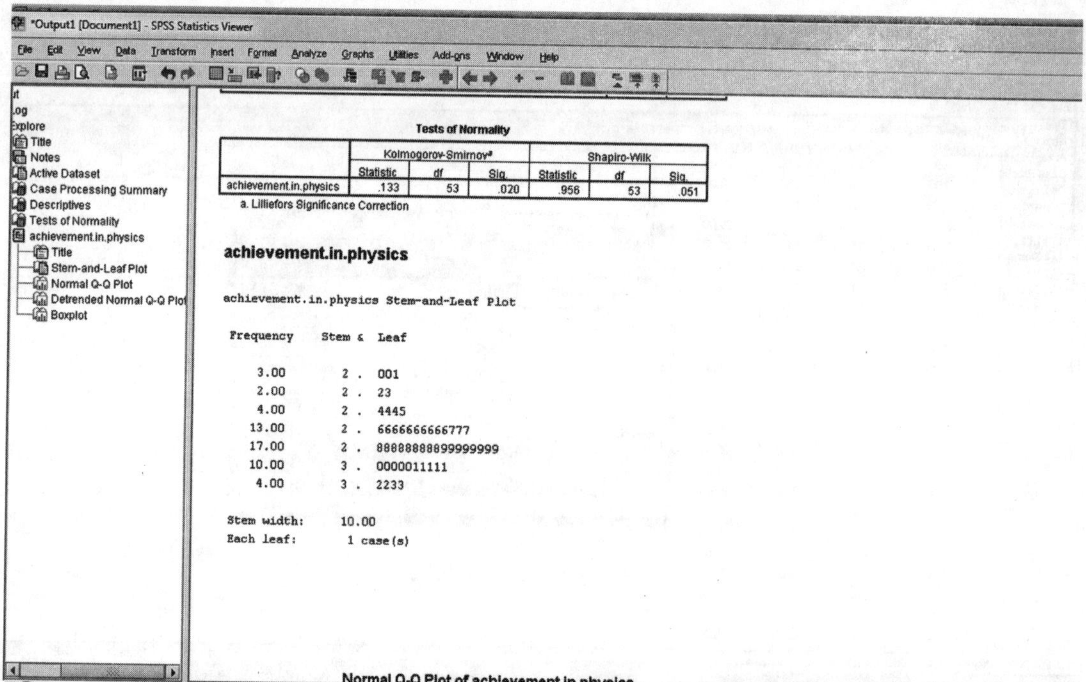

Tests of Normality

	Kolmogorov-Smirnov[a]			Shapiro-Wilk		
	Statistic	df	Sig.	Statistic	df	Sig.
achievement.in.physics	.133	53	.020	.956	53	.051

a. Lilliefors Significance Correction

achievement.in.physics

```
achievement.in.physics Stem-and-Leaf Plot

 Frequency    Stem &  Leaf

     3.00        2 .  001
     2.00        2 .  23
     4.00        2 .  4445
    13.00        2 .  6666666666777
    17.00        2 .  88888888899999999
    10.00        3 .  0000011111
     4.00        3 .  2233

 Stem width:      10.00
 Each leaf:        1 case(s)
```

Normal Q-Q Plot of achievement in physics

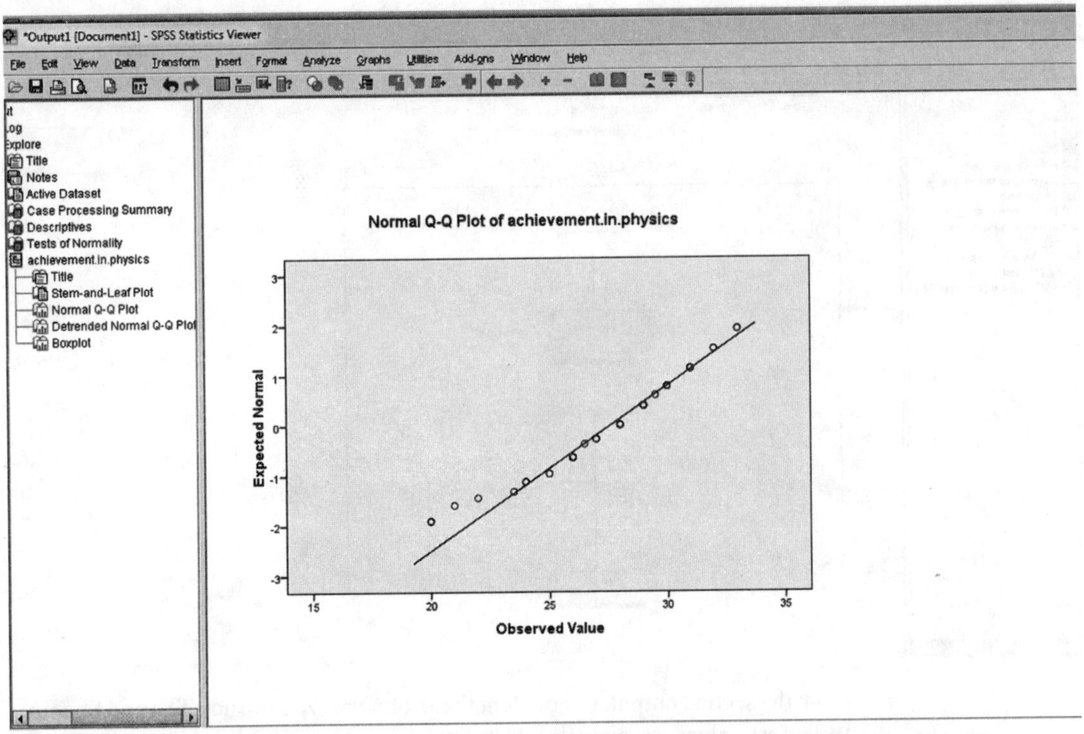
*Output1 [Document1] - SPSS Statistics Viewer
File Edit View Data Transform Insert Format Analyze Graphs Utilities Add-ons Window Help
Log
Explore
Title
Notes
Active Dataset
Case Processing Summary
Descriptives
Tests of Normality
achievement.in.physics
Title
Stem-and-Leaf Plot
Normal Q-Q Plot
Detrended Normal Q-Q Plot
Boxplot
Normal Q-Q Plot of achievement.in.physics
Expected Normal
Observed Value

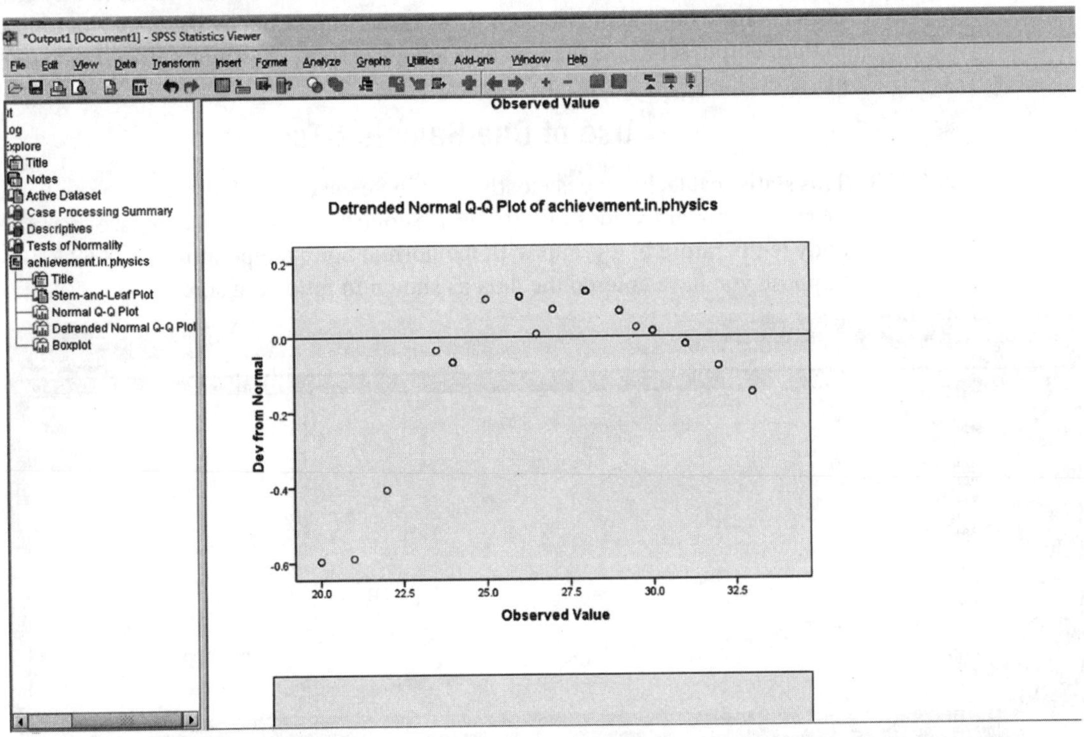
*Output1 [Document1] - SPSS Statistics Viewer
File Edit View Data Transform Insert Format Analyze Graphs Utilities Add-ons Window Help
Observed Value
Log
Explore
Title
Notes
Active Dataset
Case Processing Summary
Descriptives
Tests of Normality
achievement.in.physics
Title
Stem-and-Leaf Plot
Normal Q-Q Plot
Detrended Normal Q-Q Plot
Boxplot
Detrended Normal Q-Q Plot of achievement.in.physics
Dev from Normal
Observed Value

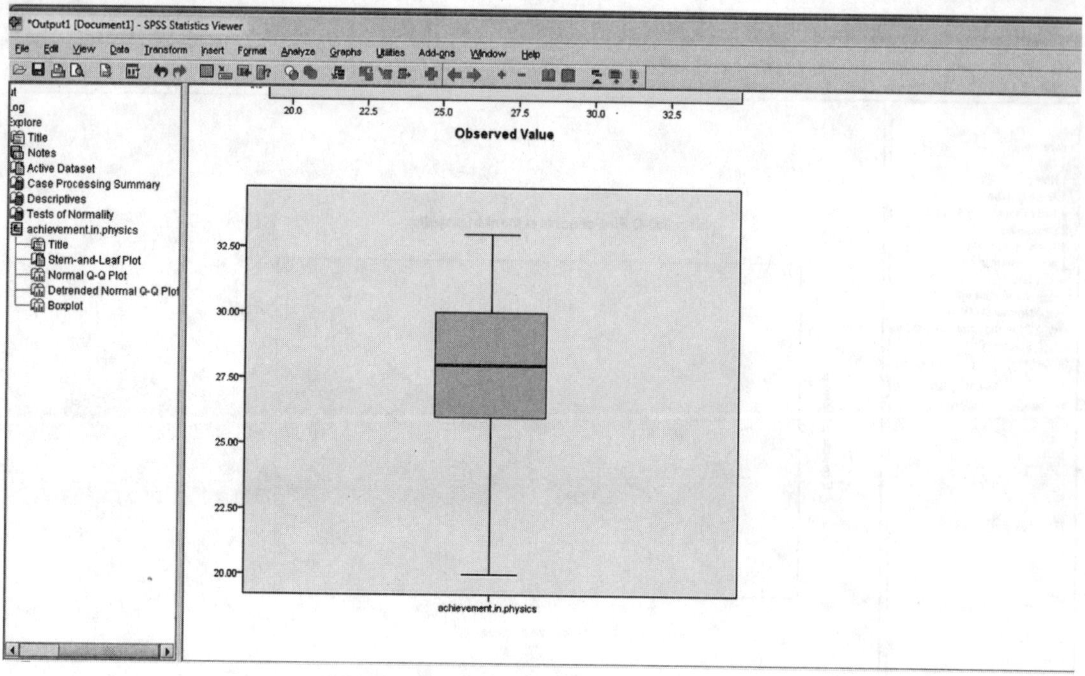

From the second output, it is evident that Kolmogorov-Smirnov Test and Shapiro-Wilk Test values are significant. Indicating the data of Achievement in Physics does not have normal distribution. It is further supported by the Q-Q Plot given in third output screen as many scores are away from the straight line.

Use of One Sample t-Test

73. This statistical technique is mostly used in Science and Medical Science where there are standard values of variables. Suppose you want to compare average body temperature of a group with the normal body temperature of 98.6° F. Suppose you have entered the data as shown in following screen.

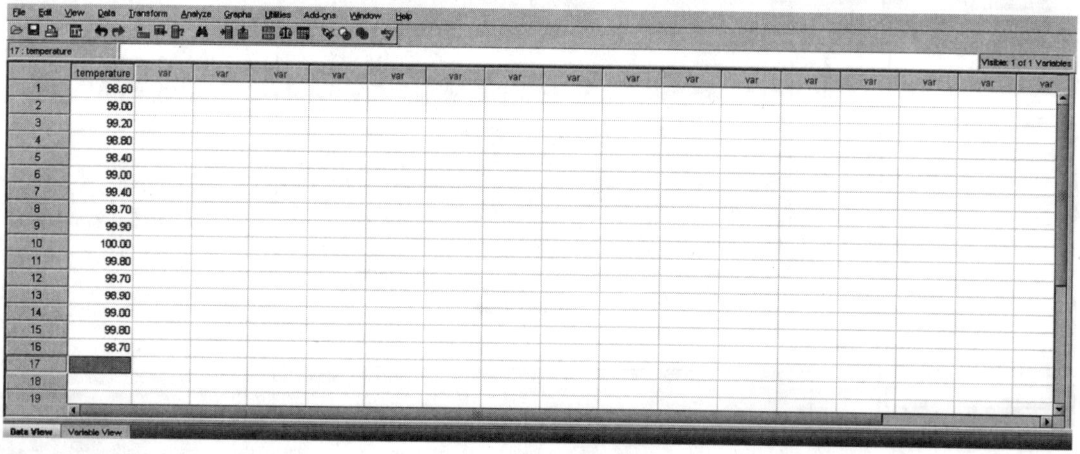

74. Click on "**Analyse**" and bring curser on "**Compare Means**" to get the following screen.

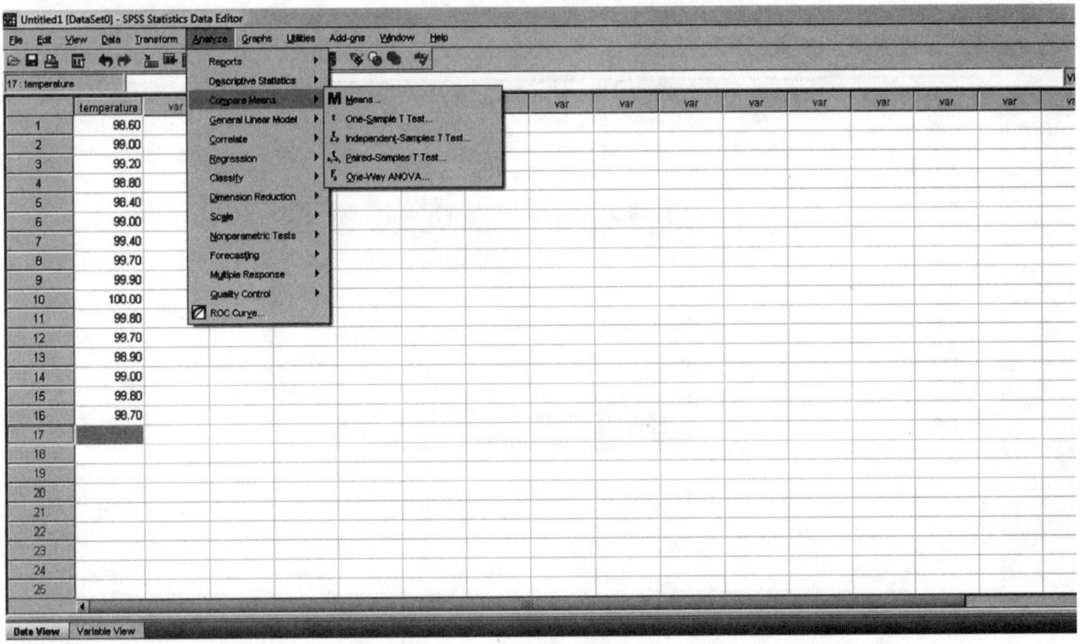

75. You want to analyse body temperature data with the help of "**One Sample t-Test**", bring curser on "**One Sample t-Test**" icon and click to get the following screen.

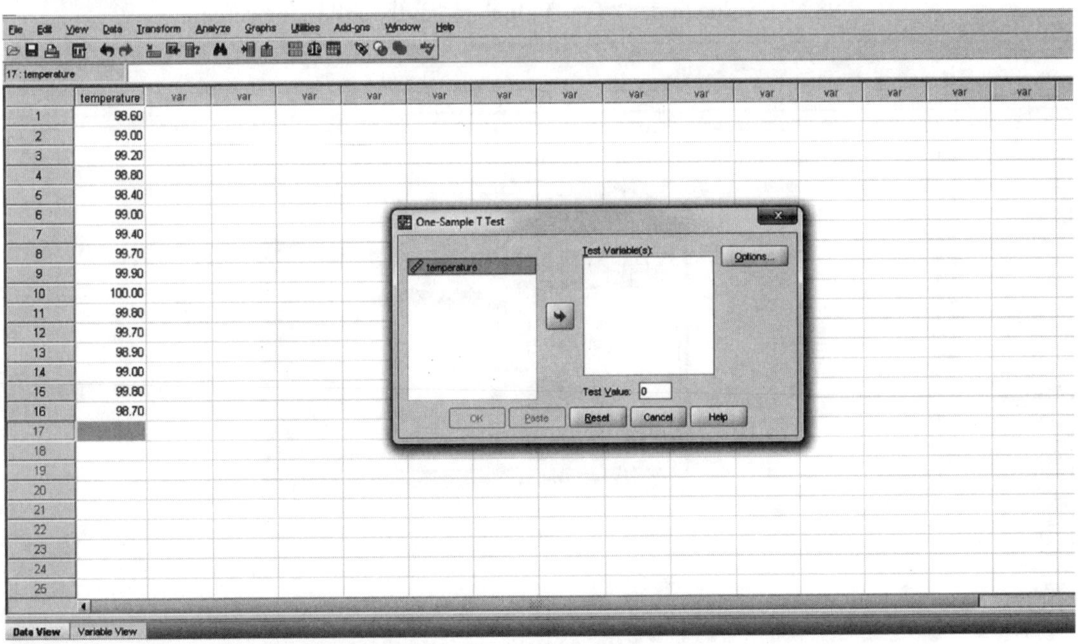

76. Shift "**Temperature**" variable from left hand side to right hand side dialogue box to get the following screen.

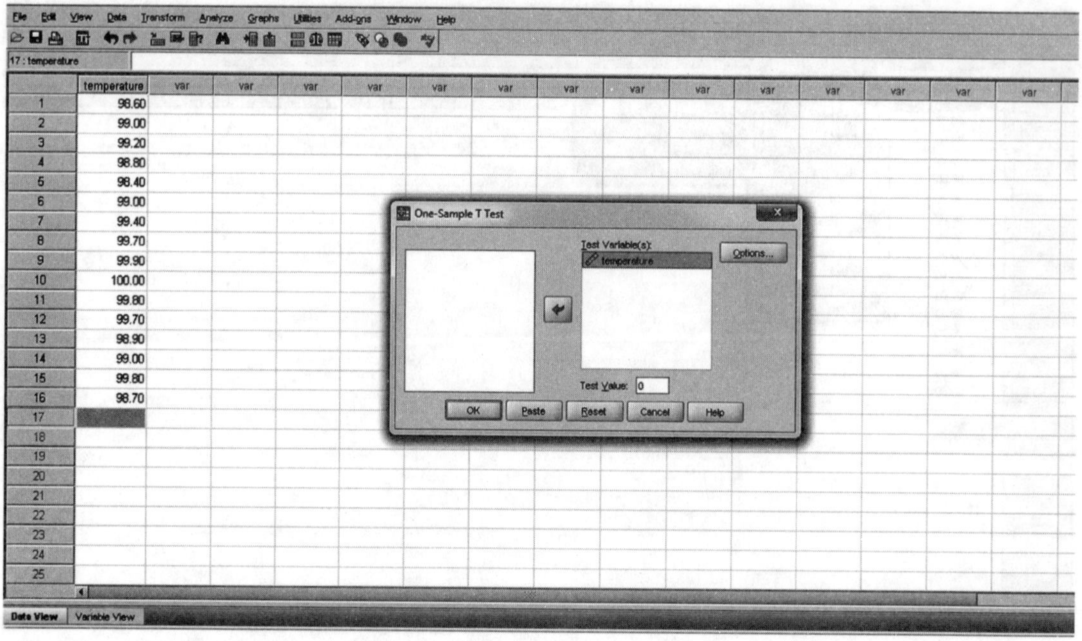

77. In the "**One Sample t-Test**" screen, you have to enter the "**Test Value**" against which you want to compare average body temperature of subjects. Suppose you want to compare with normal body temperature which is 98.6^{O} F. Enter 98.6^{O} F value under "**Test Value**" to get the following screen.

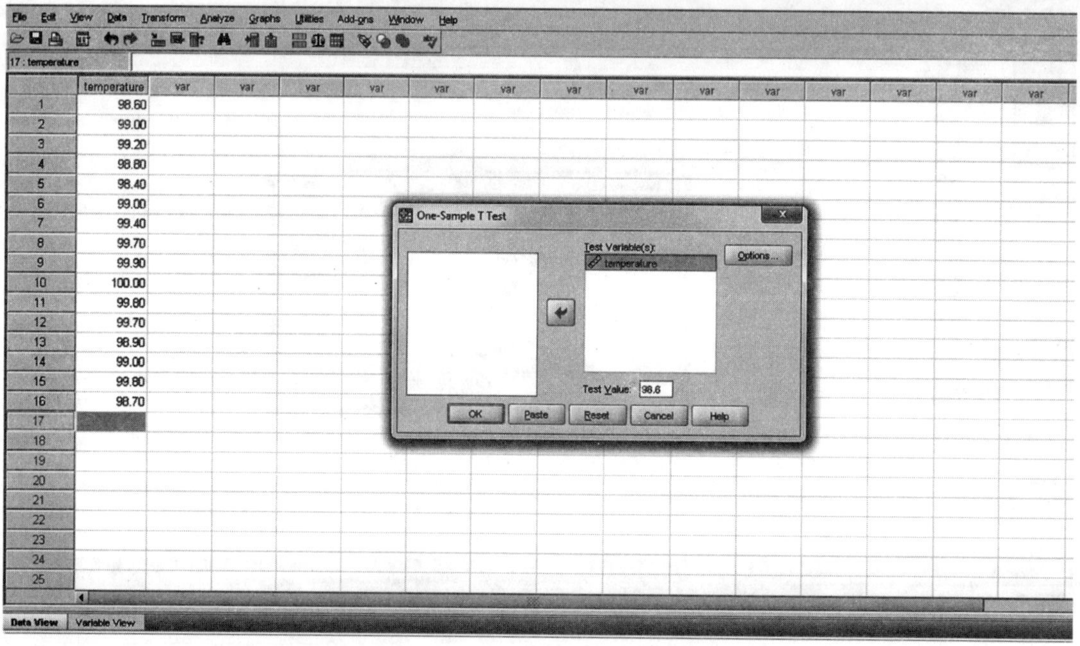

78. Click on "**Options**" icon to get the following screen.

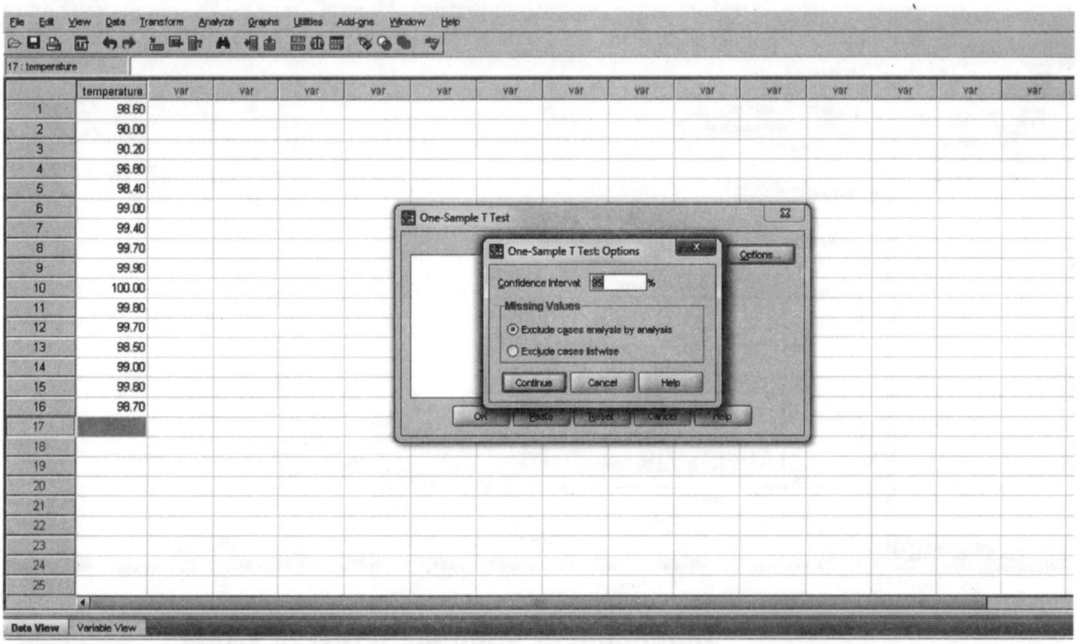

79. By default "**Confidence Interval**" is 95%. In case you want to change it to 99%, you may do so. If you do not want to change the "**Confidence Interval**", click on "**Continue**" icon to get the following screen.

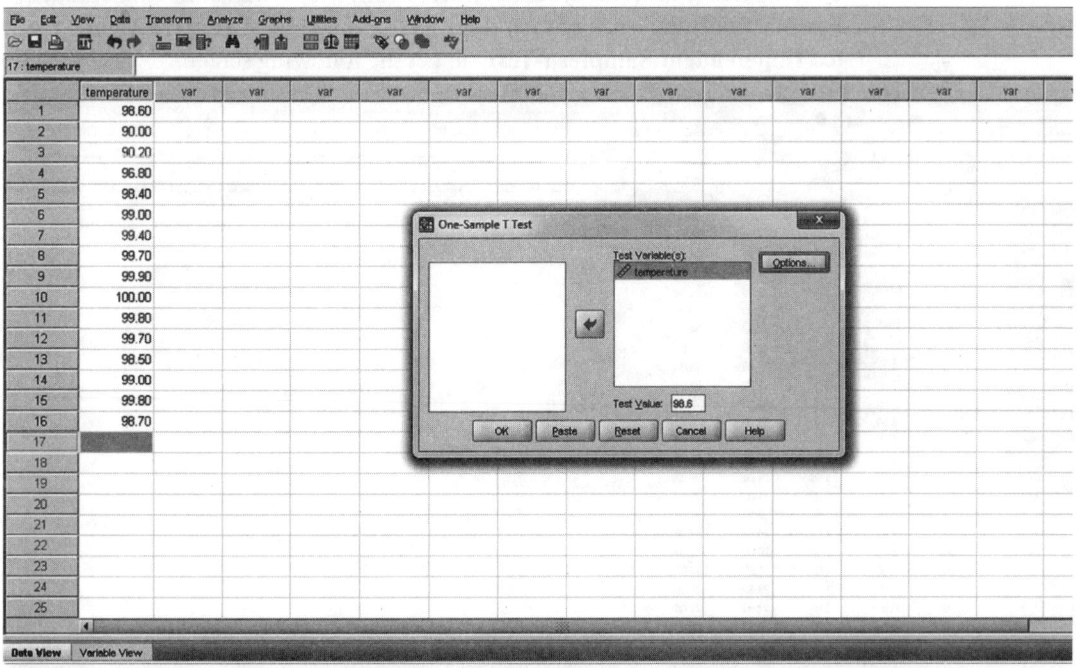

80. Click on "**OK**" icon to get the following outputs of One Sample t-Test.

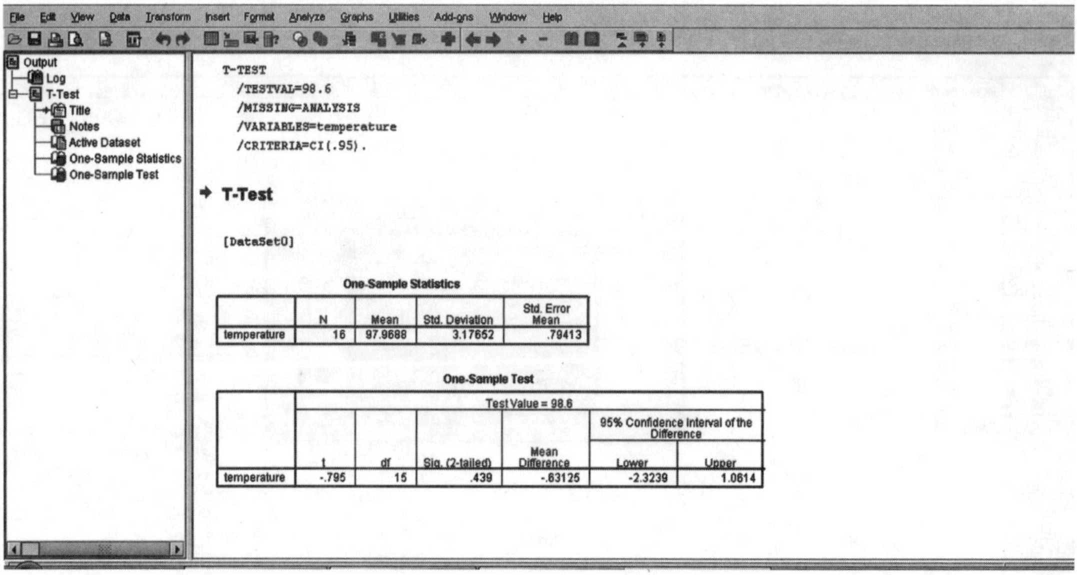

Independent Samples t-Test or t-Test

81. Next option under "**Compare Means**" icon is "**Independent Samples t-Test**". It's another name is "**t-Test**". Suppose the objective of research is:
To compare mean scores of Achievement in Physics of Male and Female students. For analyzing data click on "**Analyse**" bring curser to "**Compare Means**" then to "**Independent Samples t-Test**" to get the following screen.

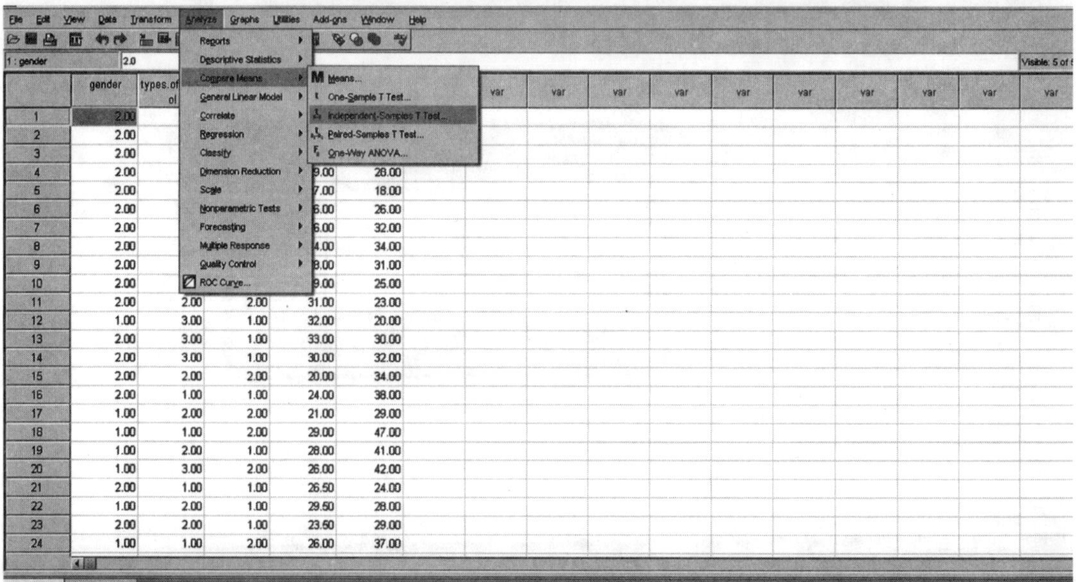

82. Click on "**Independent Samples t-Test**" to get the following screen.

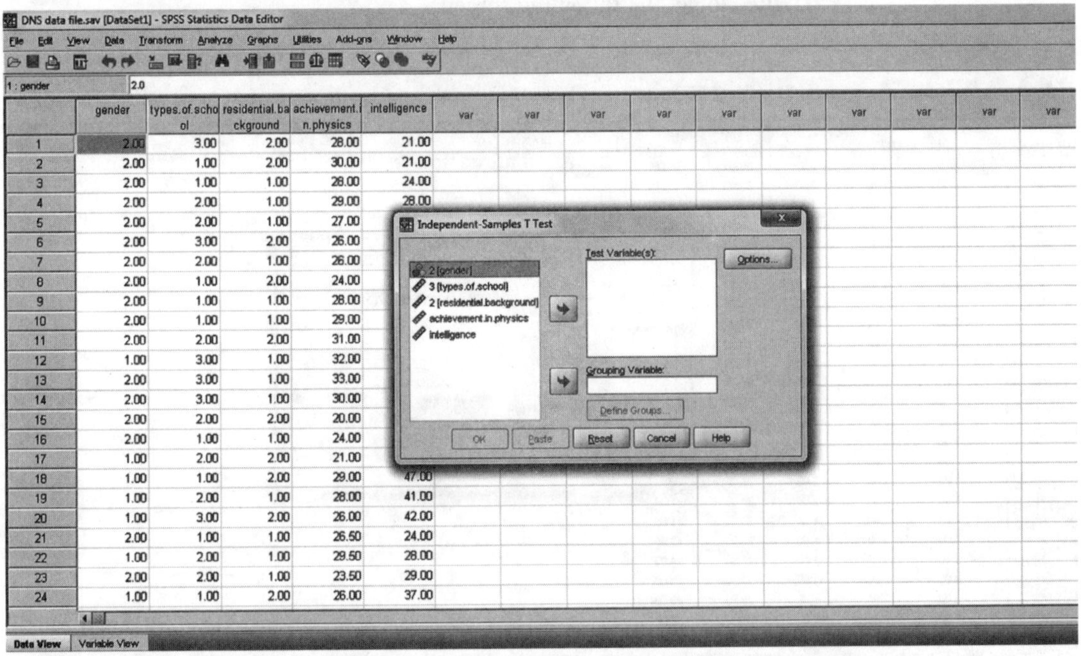

83. You want to compare mean scores of "**Achievement in Physics**". This is your "**Test Variable**". Shift "**Achievement in Physics**" to the "**Test Variable(s)**" dialogue box to get the following screen.

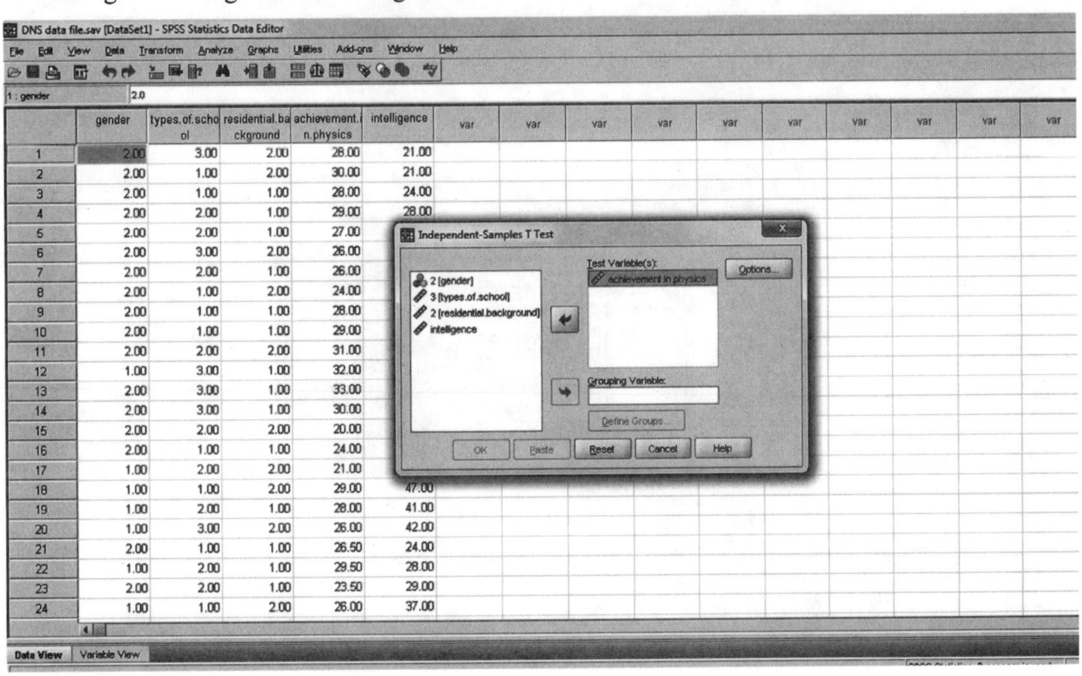

84. **"Gender"** is your **"Grouping Variable"**. Shift **"Gender"** to **"Grouping Variable"** to get the following screen.

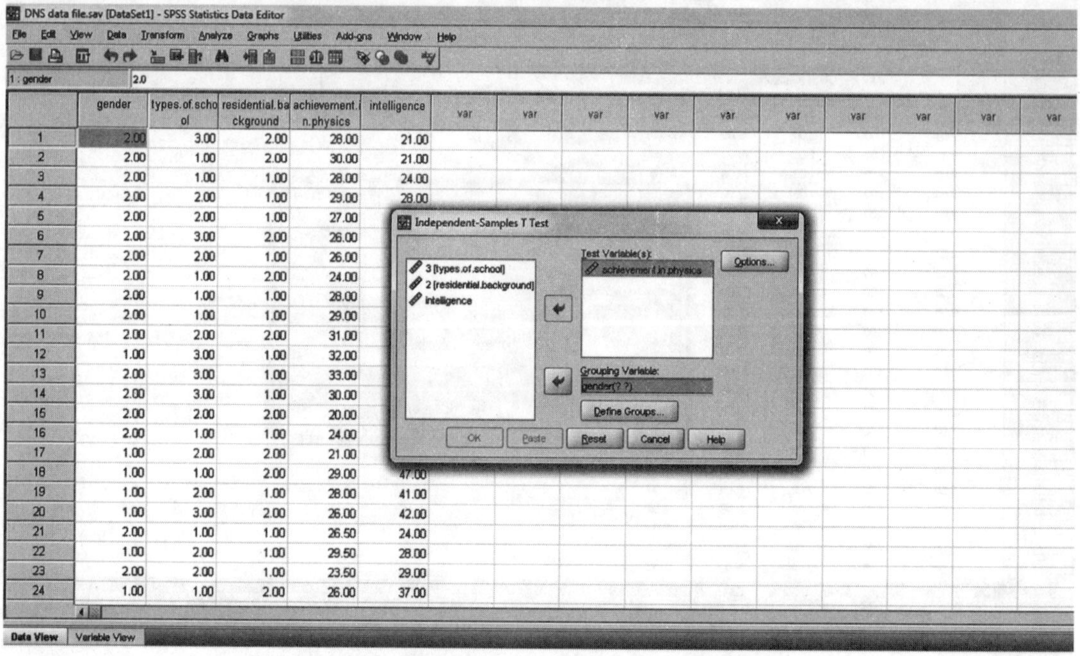

85. There are two question marks against **"gender"**. Click on **"Define Groups"** icon to get the following screen.

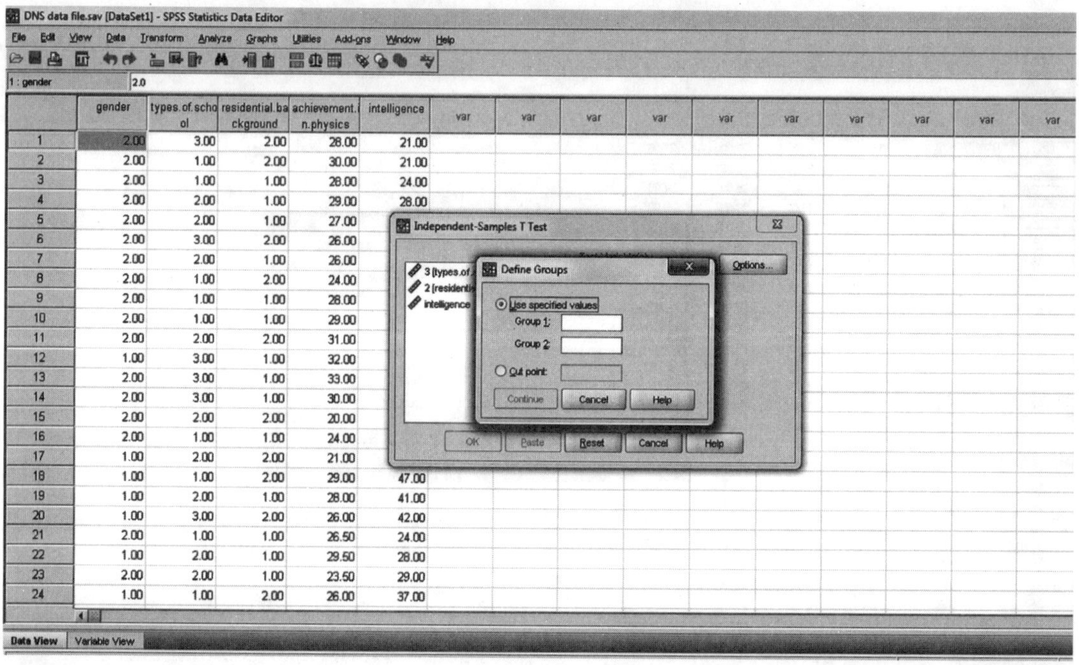

86. Male and Female are two levels of "**Gender**". Suppose Male is coded as "**1**" and Female as "**2**". Enter these two digits under "**Use Specified Value**" in any sequence you like to get the following screen.

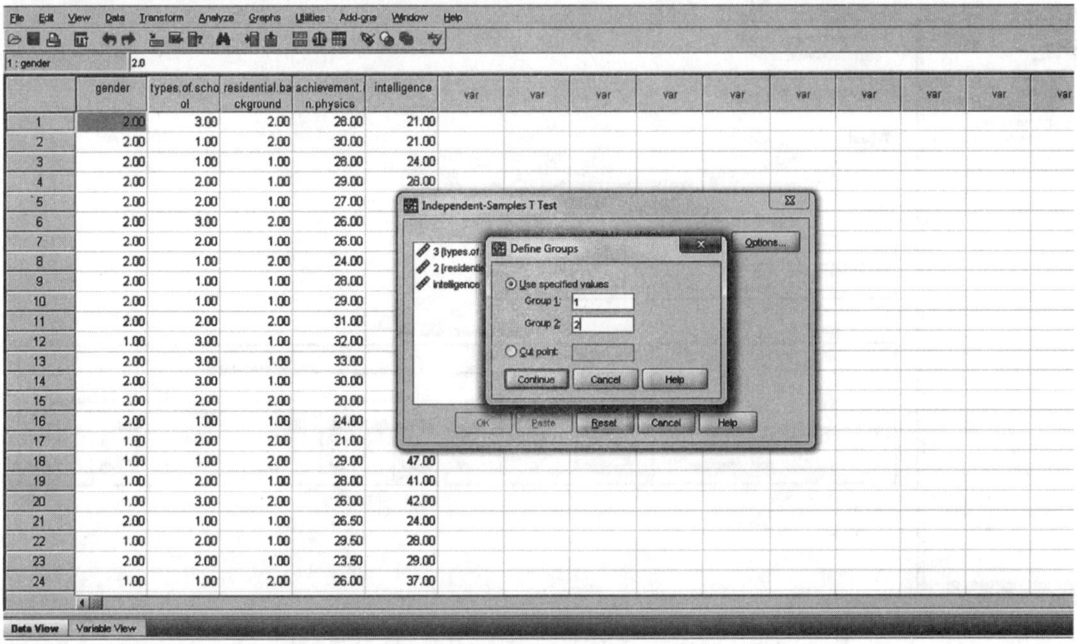

87. Now click on "**Continue**" icon to get the following screen.

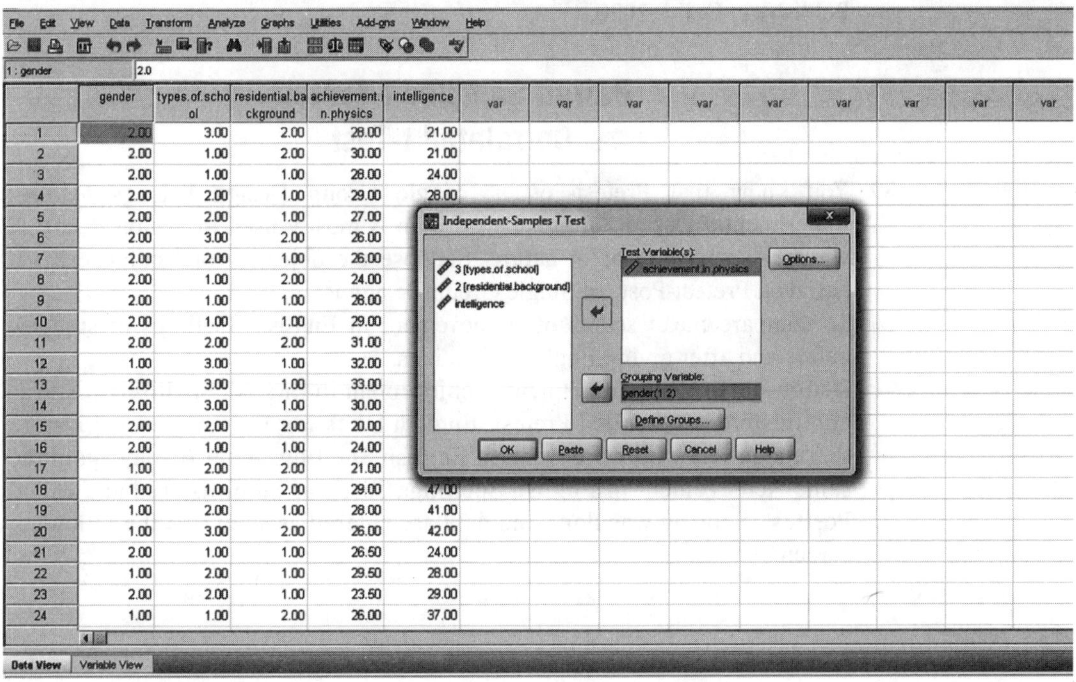

88. Click on "**OK**" to get the following outputs of Independent Samples t-Test.

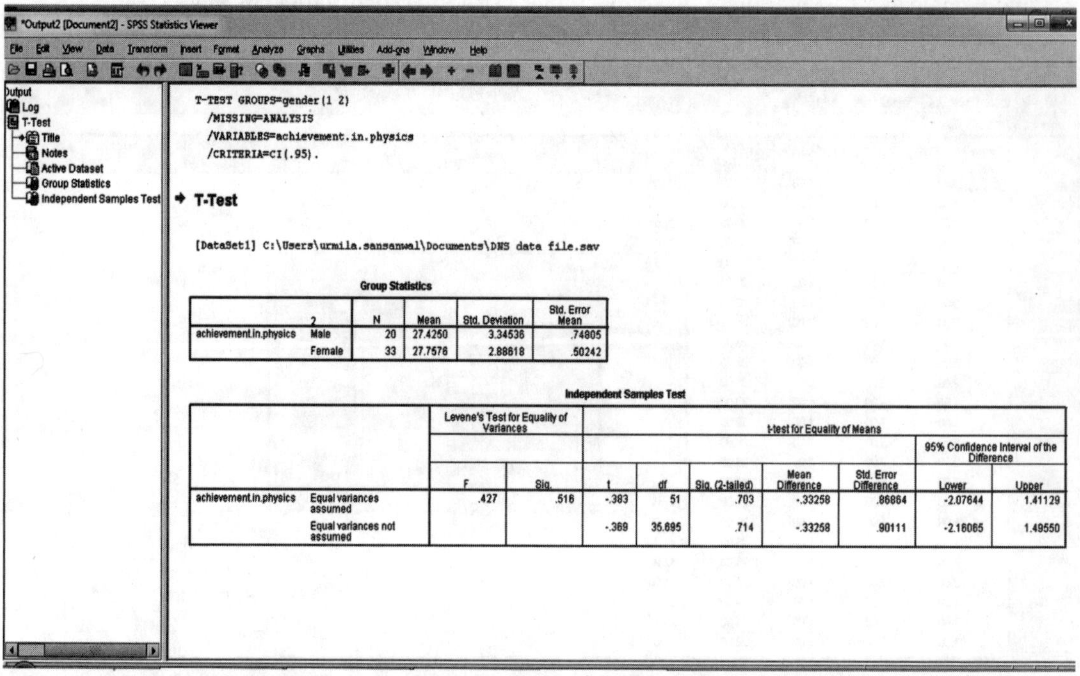

Group Statistics

	2	N	Mean	Std. Deviation	Std. Error Mean
achievement.in.physics	Male	20	27.4250	3.34536	.74805
	Female	33	27.7576	2.88818	.50242

Independent Samples Test

		Levene's Test for Equality of Variances		t-test for Equality of Means						
									95% Confidence Interval of the Difference	
		F	Sig.	t	df	Sig. (2-tailed)	Mean Difference	Std. Error Difference	Lower	Upper
achievement.in.physics	Equal variances assumed	.427	.516	-.383	51	.703	-.33258	.86864	-2.07644	1.41129
	Equal variances not assumed			-.369	35.695	.714	-.33258	.90111	-2.16065	1.49550

For interpretation of Independent Samples t-Test results, you may refer to book by D.N.Sansanwal, Research Methodology and Applied Statistic, Shipra Publishers, Delhi, 2020.

Paired Samples t-Test or Correlated t-Test

89. You know that Pretest-Posttest Single Group Design belongs to Pre-Experimental Design Group. This design is mostly used in Action Research which is experimental in nature. Suppose the objective of Action research based on Pretest-Posttest Single Group Design is:

To compare mean scores of Achievement in English Spellings of students before and after giving English Dictations.

Before starting the experiment, Achievement in English Spellings Test was administered and called Pretest. English Dictation for 6 days was given to those students who were weak in English Spelling. After 6th day again the same Achievement in English Spellings Test was administered and called Posttest. Scoring was done and data are entered as shown in the following screen.

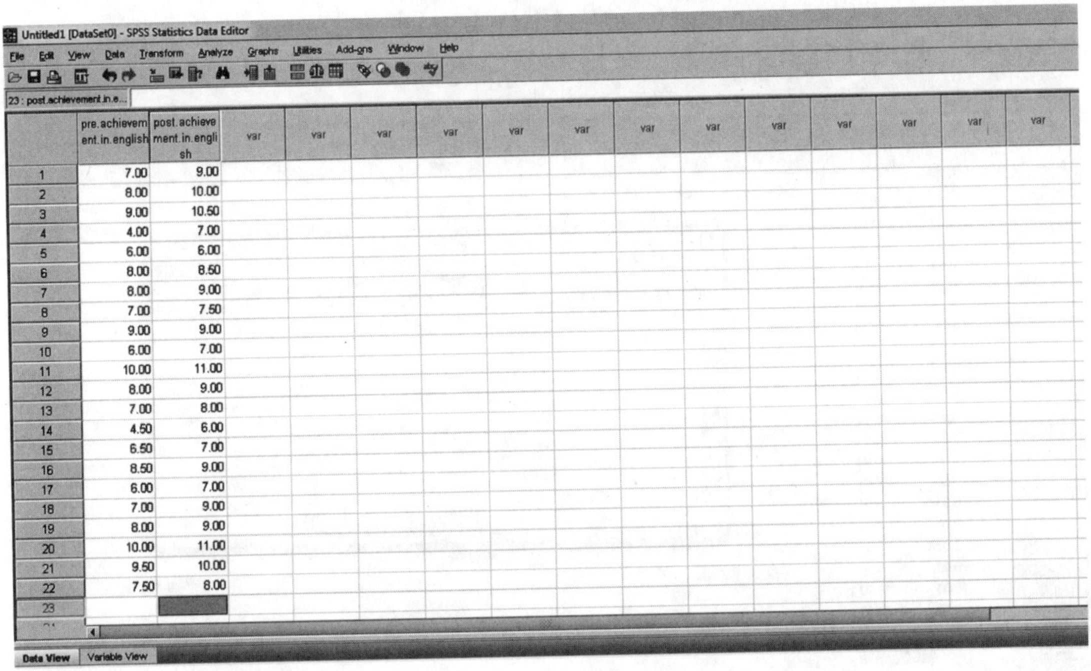

90. First click on "**Analyse**" bring curser on "**Compare Mean**" and finally on "**Paired Samples t-Test**" icon as shown in the following Screen.

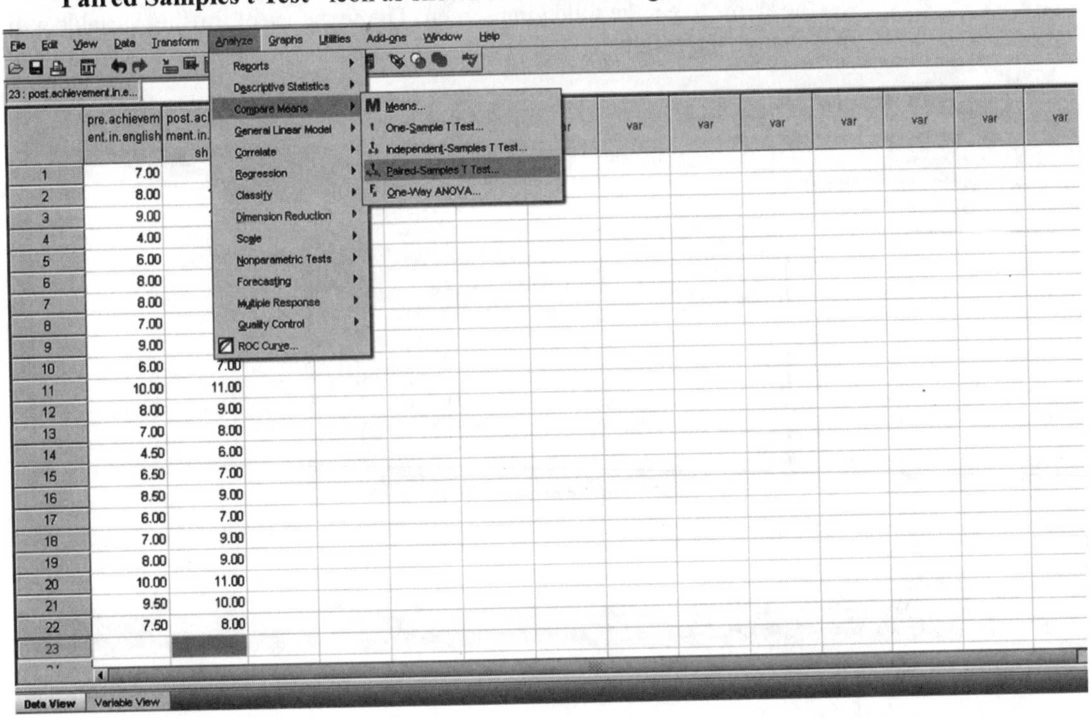

91. Click on "**Paired Samples t-Test**" to get the following screen.

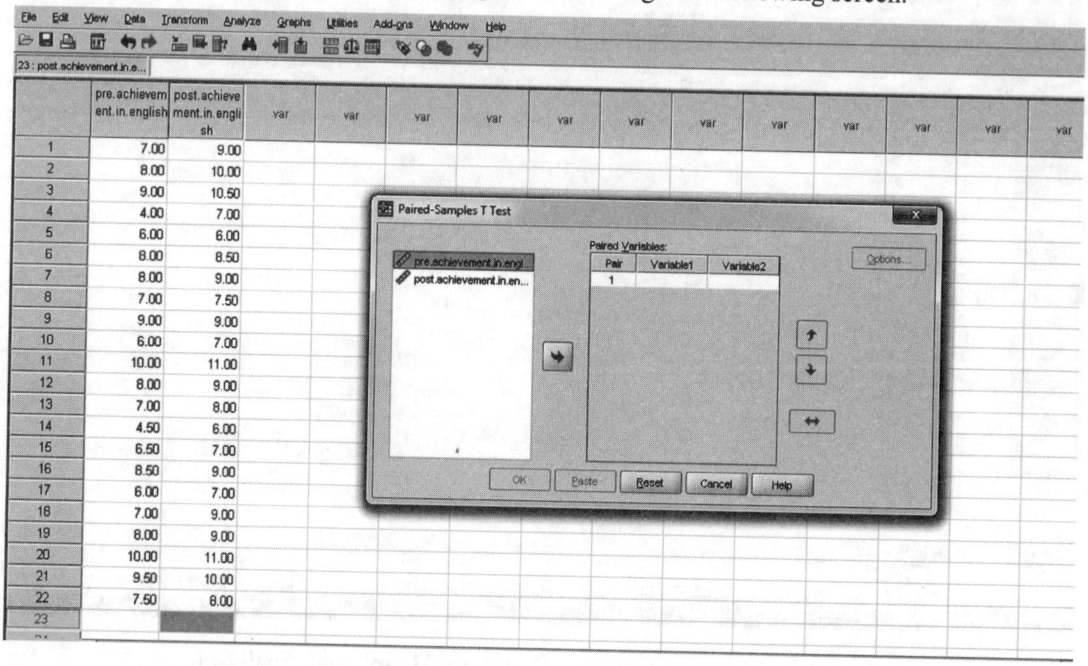

92. Shift each variable from left hand side to the right hand side dialogue box, click on the arrow to get the following screen. The sequence of shifting variable will not change the result.

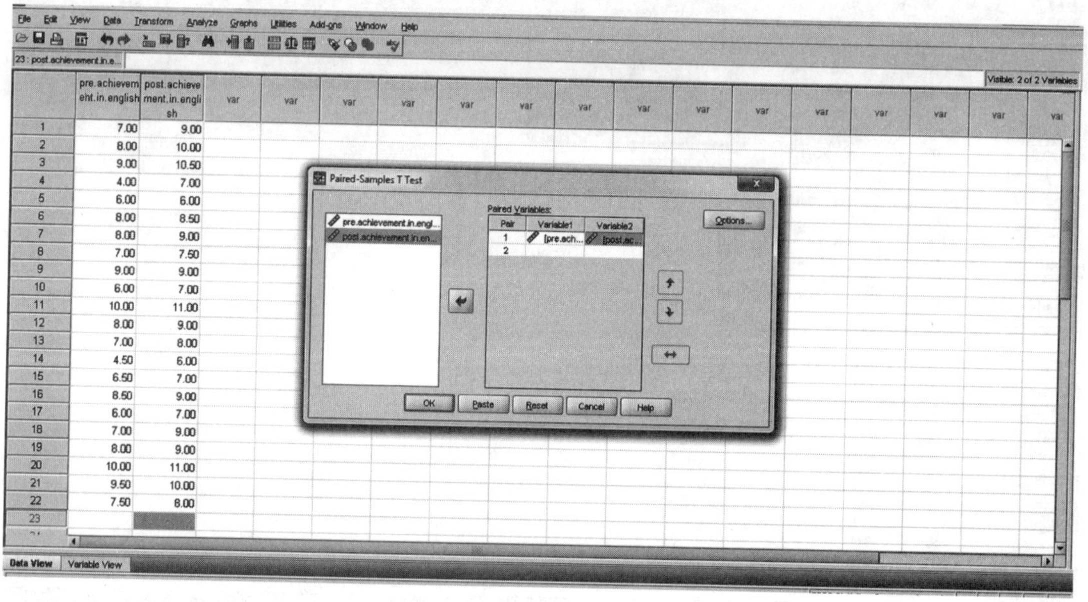

93. Click on "**OK**" icon to get the following outputs of Paired Samples t-Test.

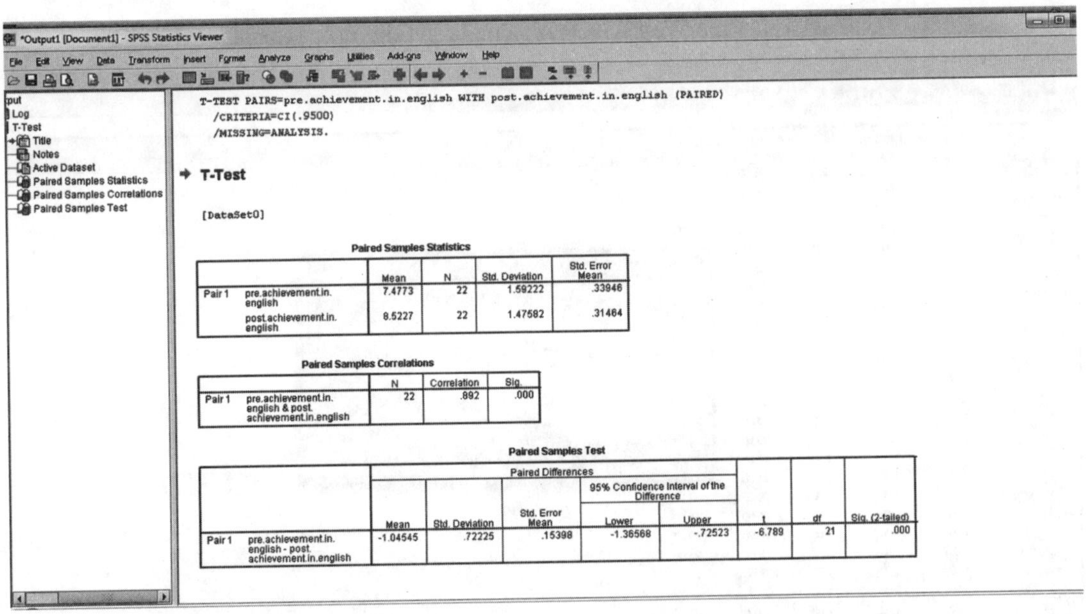

For interpretation of Paired Samples t-Test results, you may refer to book by D.N.Sansanwal, Research Methodology and Applied Statistic, Shipra Publishers, Delhi, 2020.

One Way Analysis of Variance (ANOVA)

94. If there is one discontinuous variable having two or more sub-groups and one continuous variable, the data can be analysed with the help of One Way ANOVA. Suppose the Objective of research is:

    To compare mean scores of Intelligence of students studying in Government, Aided and Private Schools.

    Click on "**Analyse**" bring curser on "**Compare Means**" and finally on "**One Way ANOVA**" icon to get the following screen.

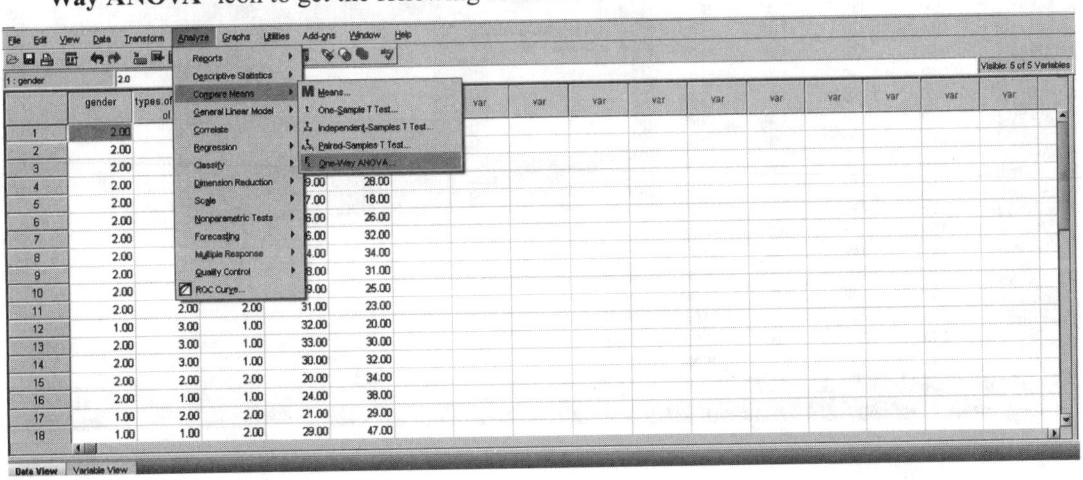

95. Click on "**One Way ANOVA**" icon to get the following screen.

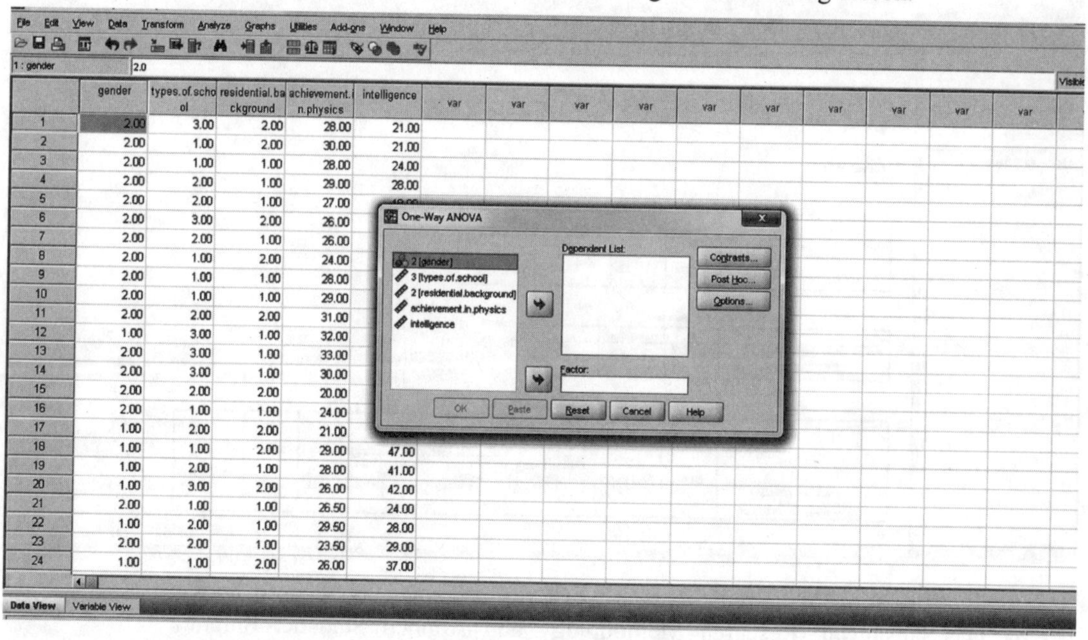

96. Shift "**Intelligence**" to the "**Dependent List**" dialogue box and "**Types of School**" to "**Factor**" to get the following screen.

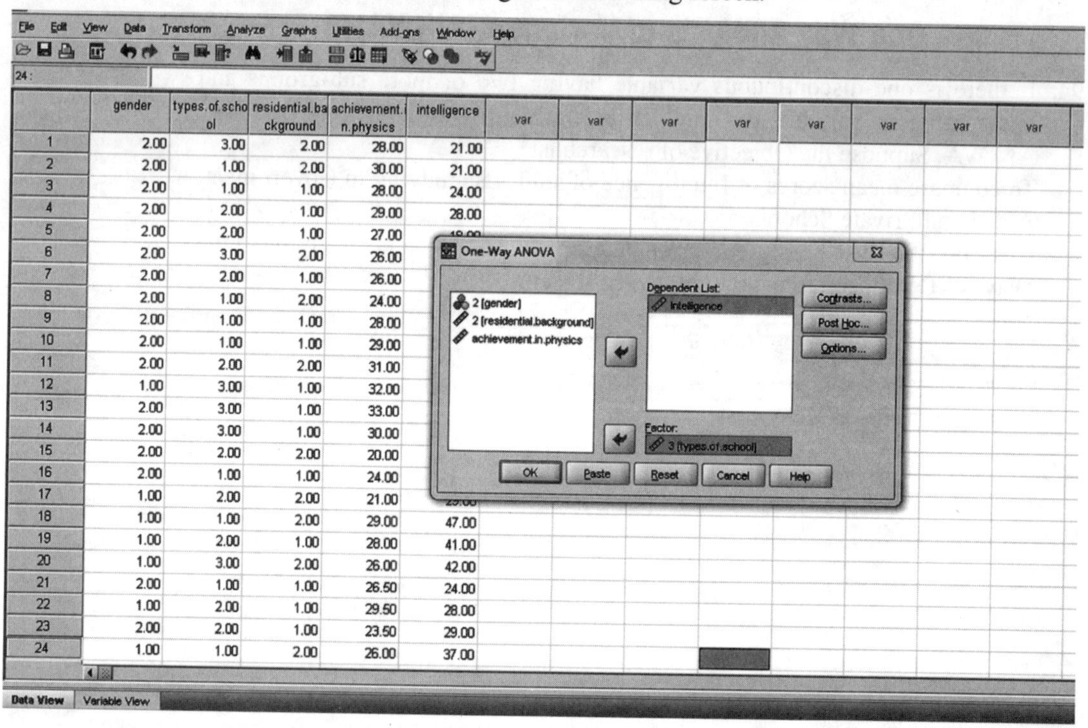

97. Click on "**Contrast**" to get the following screen.

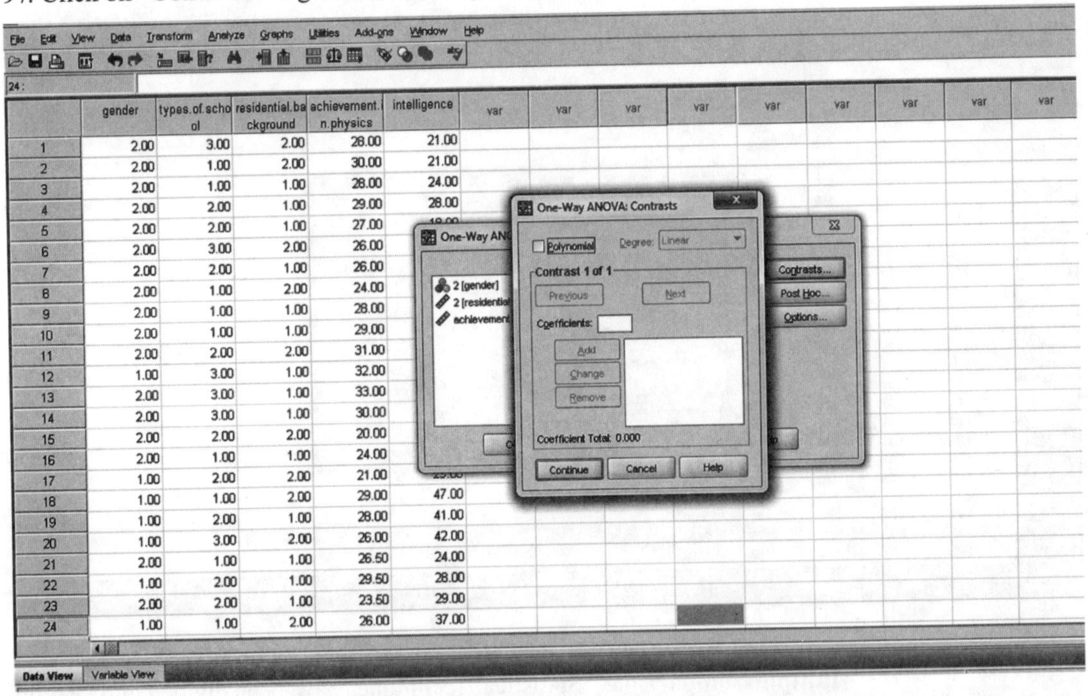

98. "**Contrast**" is to be used only for studying the Trend. For the present objective it is not to be used. So click on "**Continue**" to get the following screen.

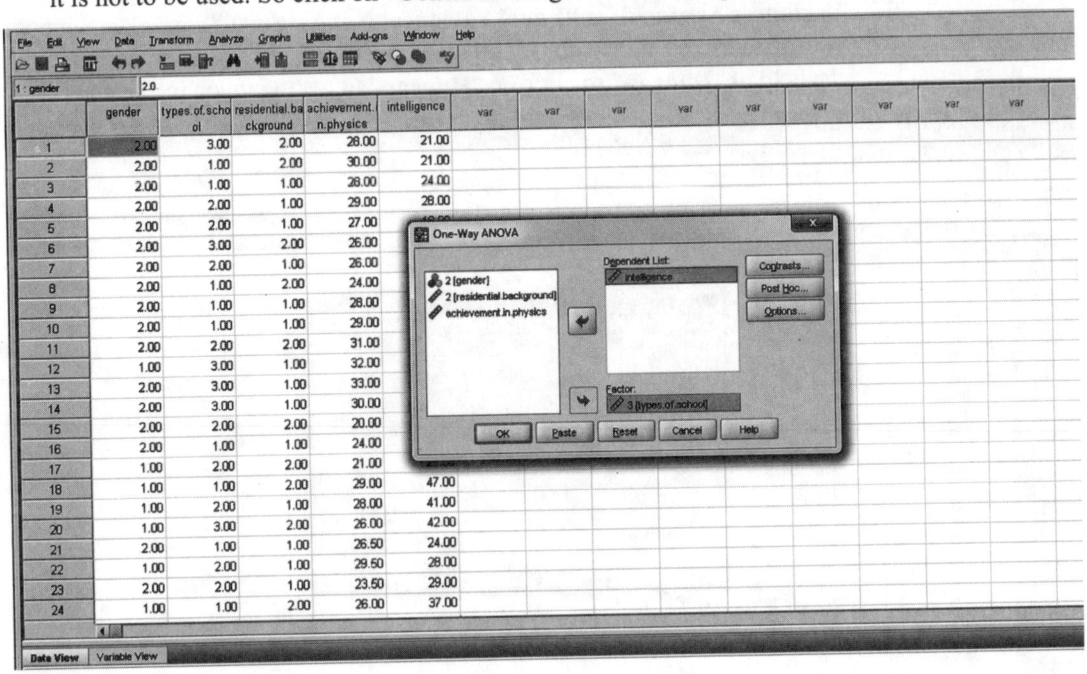

99. Click on "**Post Hoc**" to get the following screen.

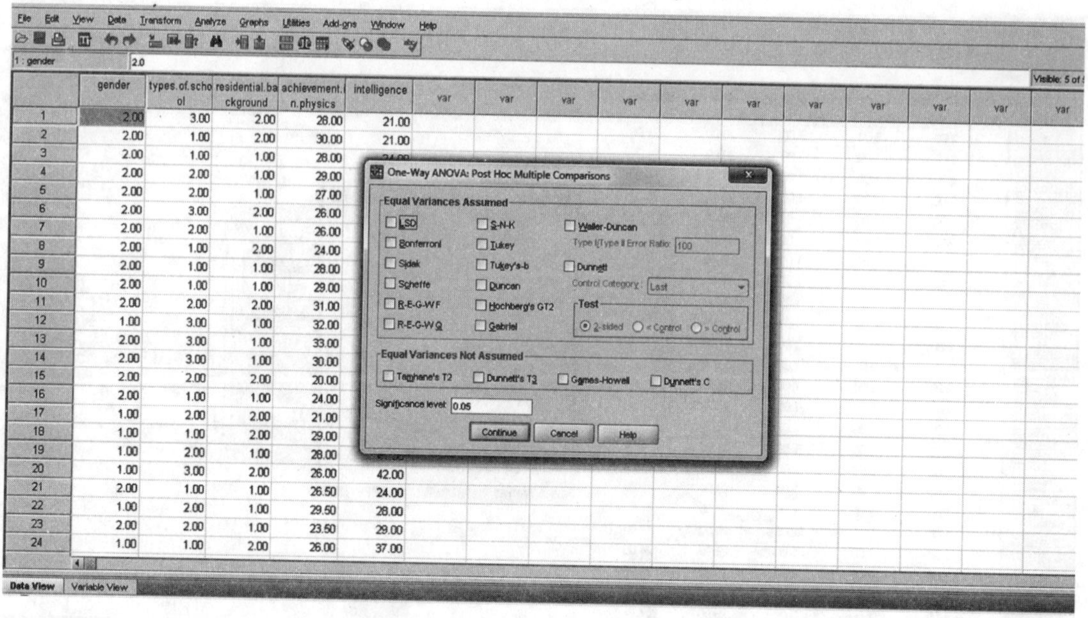

100. From "**One Way ANOVA: Post Hoc**" screen, you can observe that "**Post Hoc Multiple Comparisons**" Statistical Techniques have been divided into "**Equal Variances Assumed**" and "**Equal Variances Not Assumed**" groups. Before doing One Way ANOVA, you must find out whether the data satisfies "**Equal Variances Assumed**" or "**Equal Variances Not Assumed**" condition. Suppose your data satisfy the "**Equal Variances Assumed**" and want to analyse with the help of "**Duncan**" so click on "**Duncan**" to get the following screen.

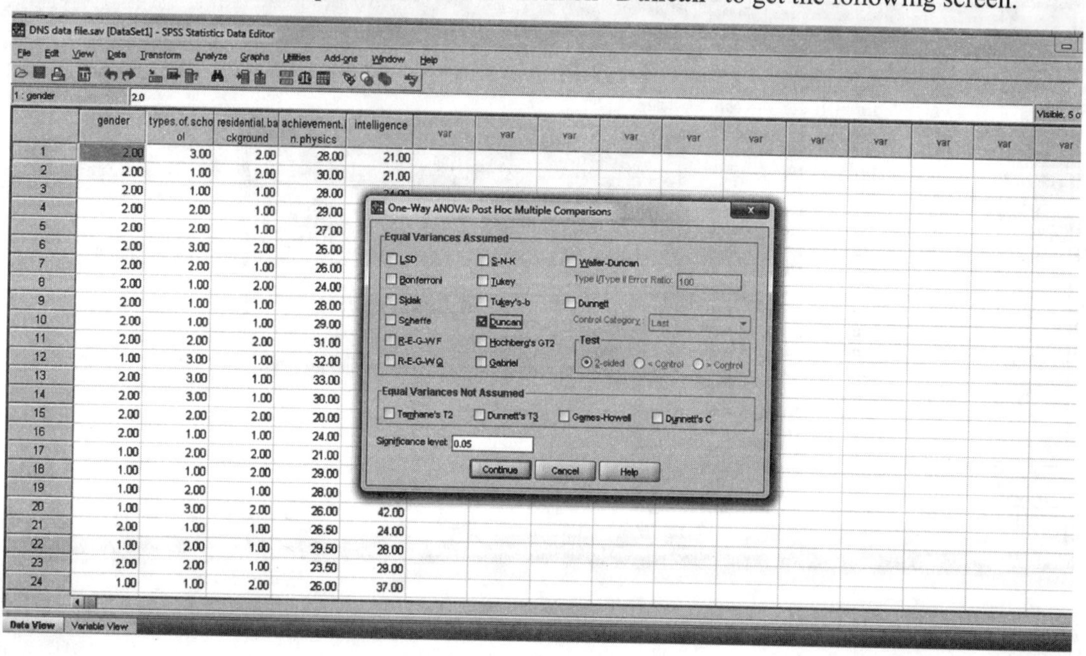

101. Click on "**Continue**" to get the following screen.

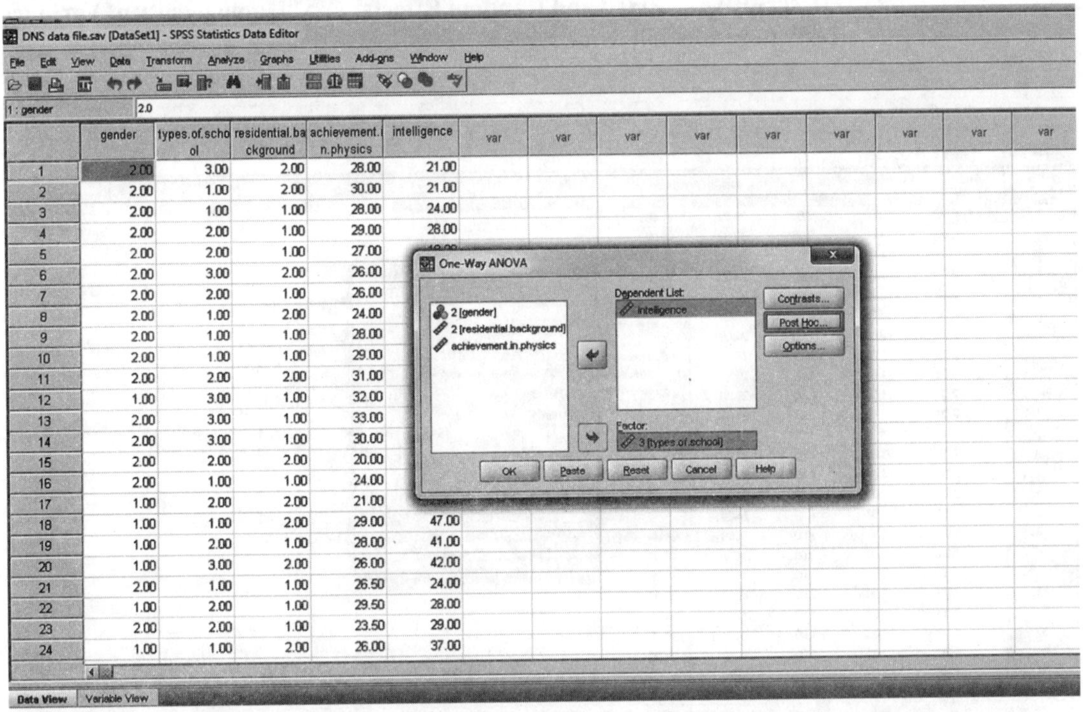

102. Click on "**Options**" to get the following screen.

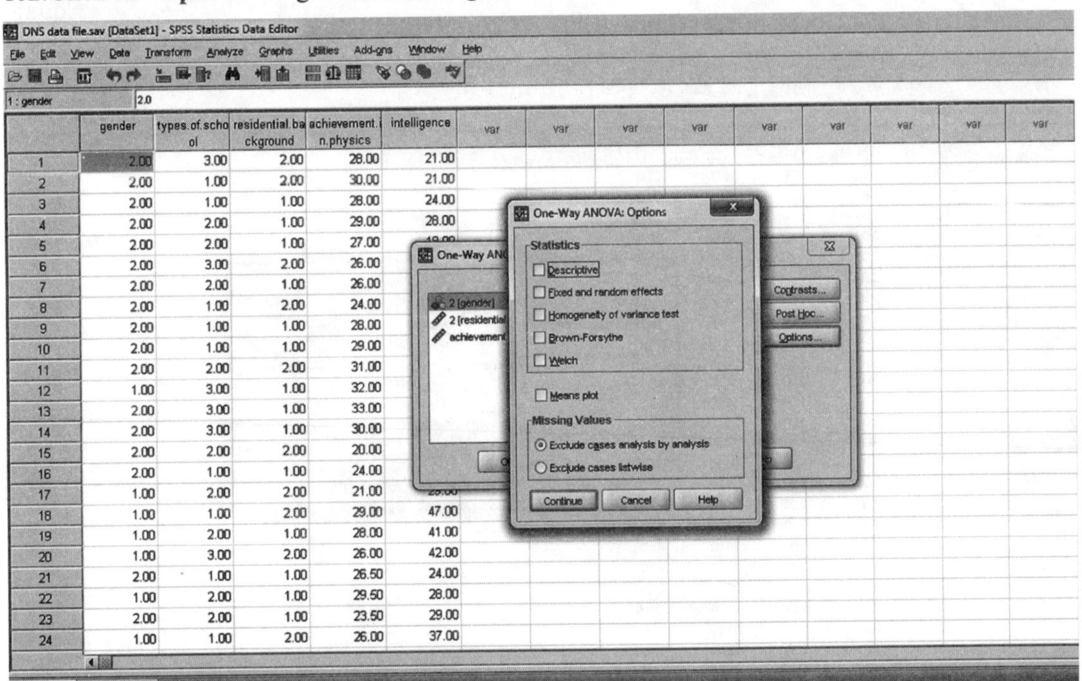

103. There are many "**Options**" under "**Statistics**". Under "**Statistics**", highlight "**Descriptive**", "**Fixed and Random Effects**" and "**Homogeneity of Variance Test**" to get the following screen.

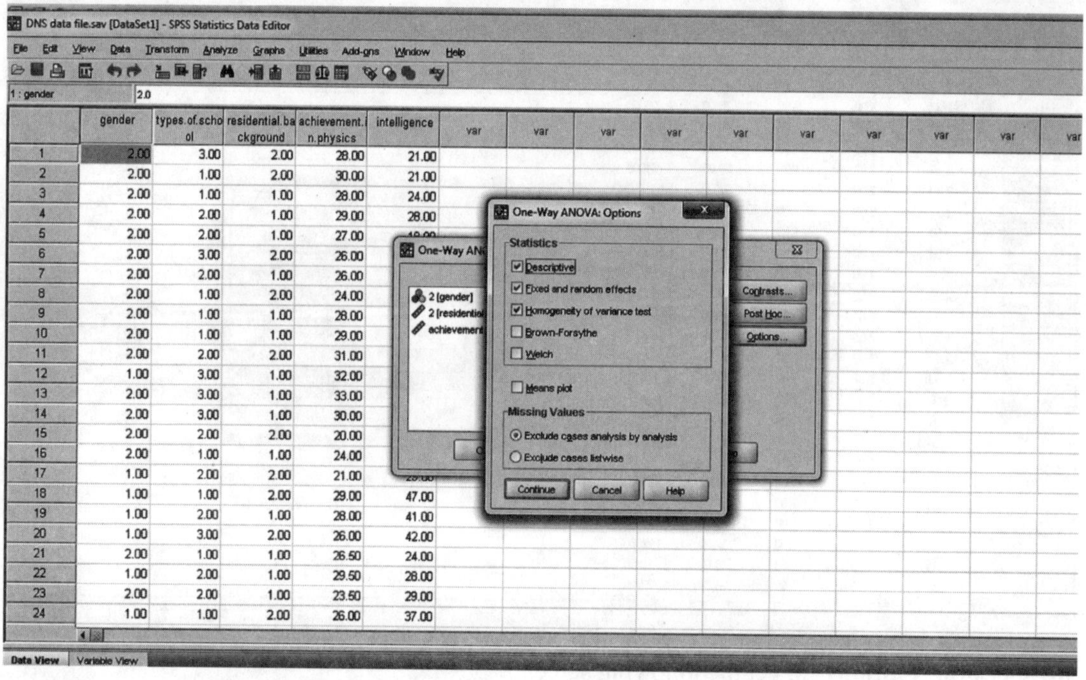

104. Click on "**Continue**" icon to get the following screen.

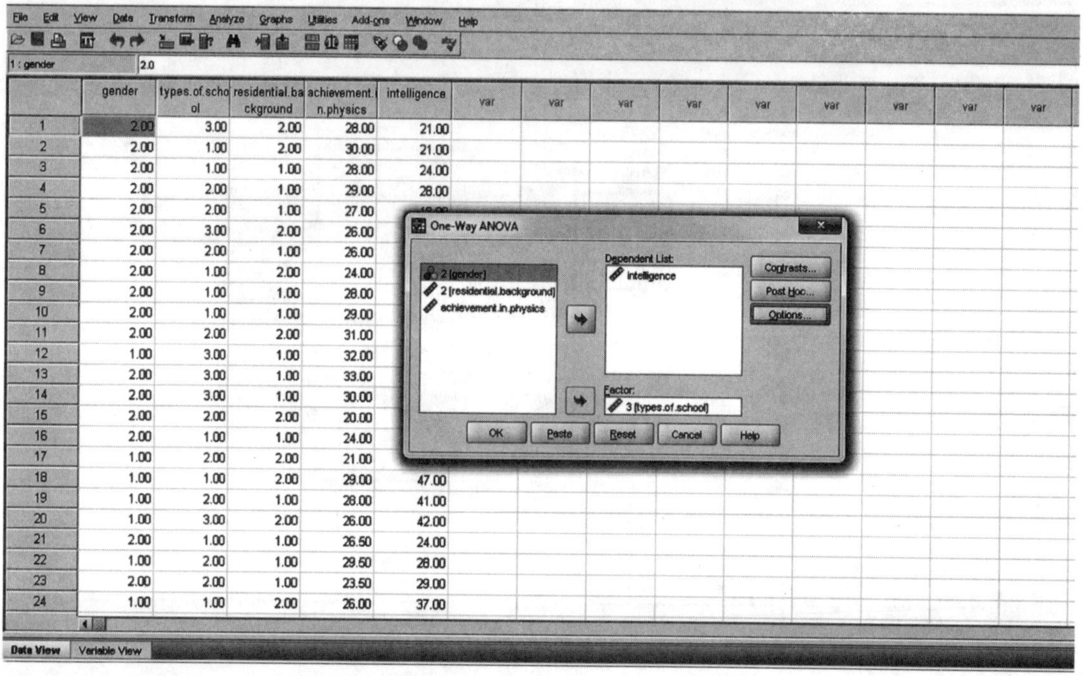

105. Click on "**OK**" to get the following outputs of One Way ANOVA.

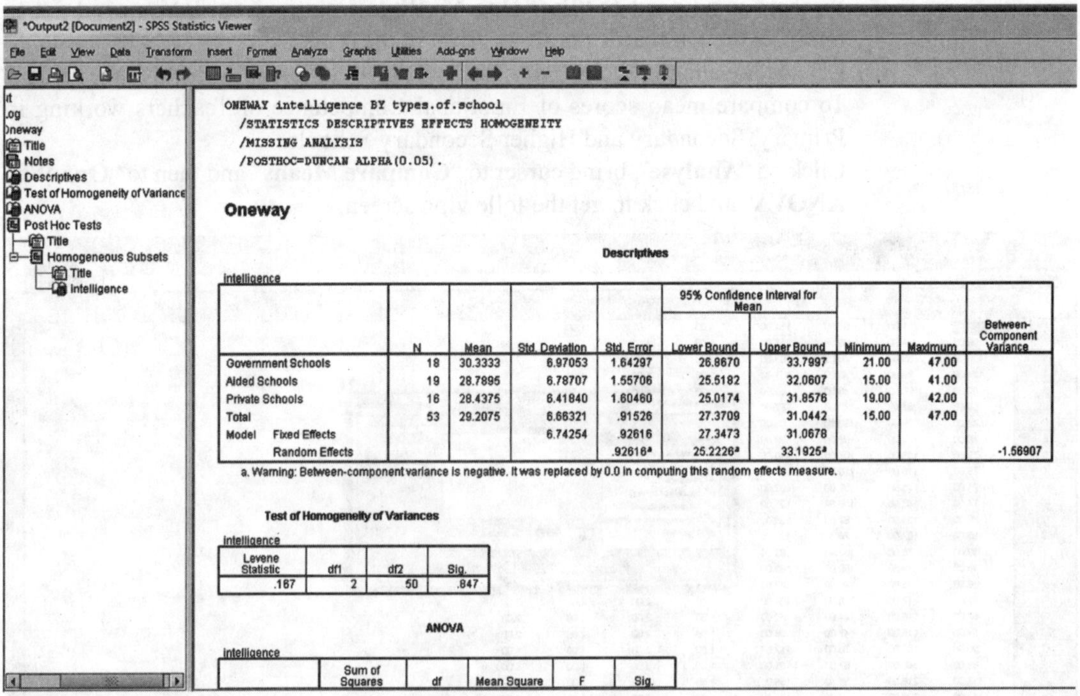

```
ONEWAY intelligence BY types.of.school
  /STATISTICS DESCRIPTIVES EFFECTS HOMOGENEITY
  /MISSING ANALYSIS
  /POSTHOC=DUNCAN ALPHA(0.05).
```

Oneway

Descriptives

intelligence

		N	Mean	Std. Deviation	Std. Error	95% Confidence Interval for Mean: Lower Bound	95% Confidence Interval for Mean: Upper Bound	Minimum	Maximum	Between-Component Variance
Government Schools		18	30.3333	6.97053	1.64297	26.8670	33.7997	21.00	47.00	
Aided Schools		19	28.7895	6.78707	1.55706	25.5182	32.0607	15.00	41.00	
Private Schools		16	28.4375	6.41840	1.60460	25.0174	31.8576	19.00	42.00	
Total		53	29.2075	6.66321	.91526	27.3709	31.0442	15.00	47.00	
Model	Fixed Effects			6.74254	.92616	27.3473	31.0678			
	Random Effects				.92616[a]	25.2226[a]	33.1925[a]			-1.56907

a. Warning: Between-component variance is negative. It was replaced by 0.0 in computing this random effects measure.

Test of Homogeneity of Variances

intelligence

Levene Statistic	df1	df2	Sig.
.167	2	50	.847

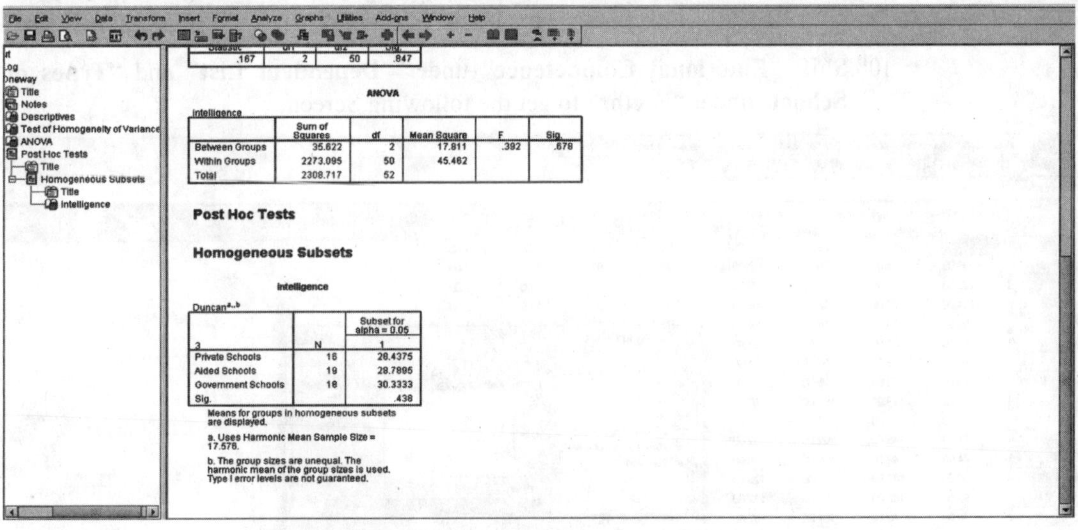

ANOVA

intelligence

	Sum of Squares	df	Mean Square	F	Sig.
Between Groups	35.622	2	17.811	.392	.678
Within Groups	2273.095	50	45.462		
Total	2308.717	52			

Post Hoc Tests

Homogeneous Subsets

intelligence

Duncan[a,b]

3	N	Subset for alpha = 0.05: 1
Private Schools	16	28.4375
Aided Schools	19	28.7895
Government Schools	18	30.3333
Sig.		.438

Means for groups in homogeneous subsets are displayed.

a. Uses Harmonic Mean Sample Size = 17.578.

b. The group sizes are unequal. The harmonic mean of the group sizes is used. Type I error levels are not guaranteed.

106. From the "**output**" given in the above frame, you can see the results of "**Descriptive**", "**Test of Homogeneity of Variance**" as well as "**ANOVA**". Under "**Test of Homogeneity of Variance**", Levens Statistic value is 0.167 which is not significant because the error is 84.7%. It reflects that the assumption of "**Homogeneity of Variance**" condition is satisfied.

Further F-Value is 0.392 which is not significant because the error is 67.8%. So there is no need of "**Post Hoc Multiple Comparisons**". You need not to interpret the **Duncan's result** as given in the output.

107. Let us take another Objective:

To compare mean scores of Emotional Competence of Teachers working in Primary, Secondary and Higher Secondary Schools.

Click on "**Analyse**", bring curser to "**Compare Means**" and then to "**One Way ANOVA**" and click to get the following screen.

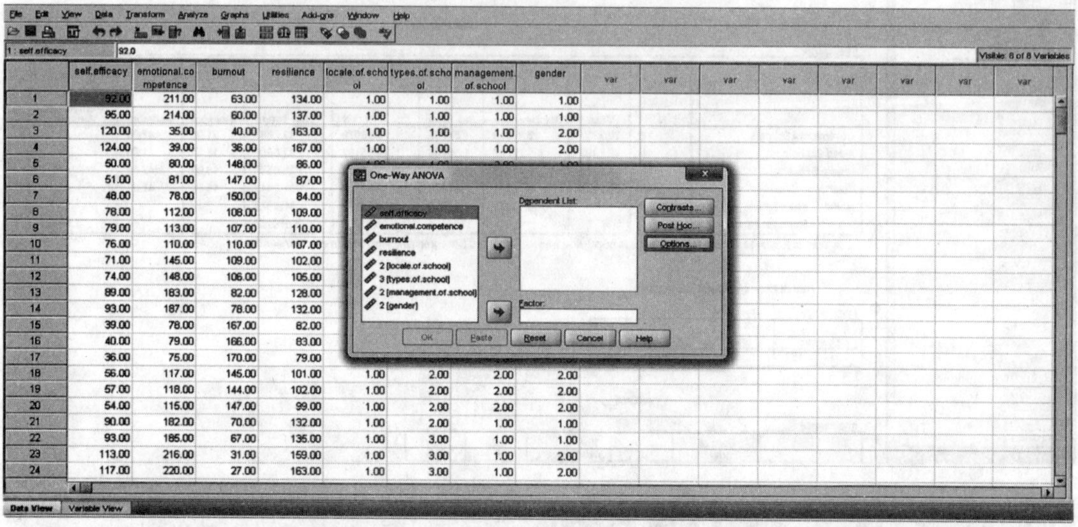

108. Shift "**Emotional Competence**" under "**Dependent List**" and "**Types of School**" under "**Factor**" to get the following Screen.

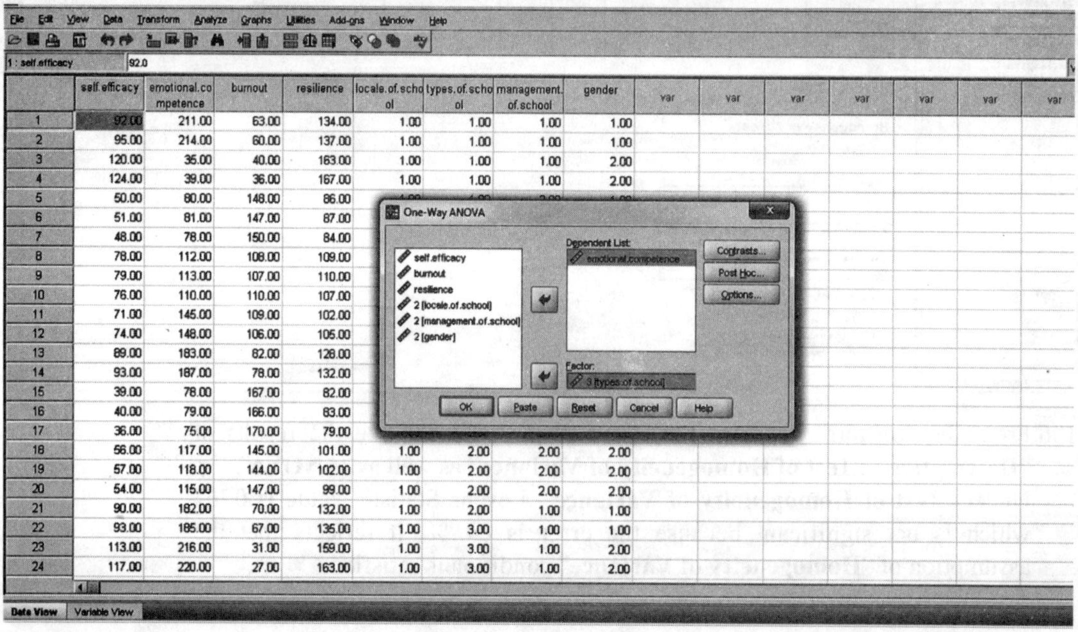

109. Click on "**Options**" to get the following screen.

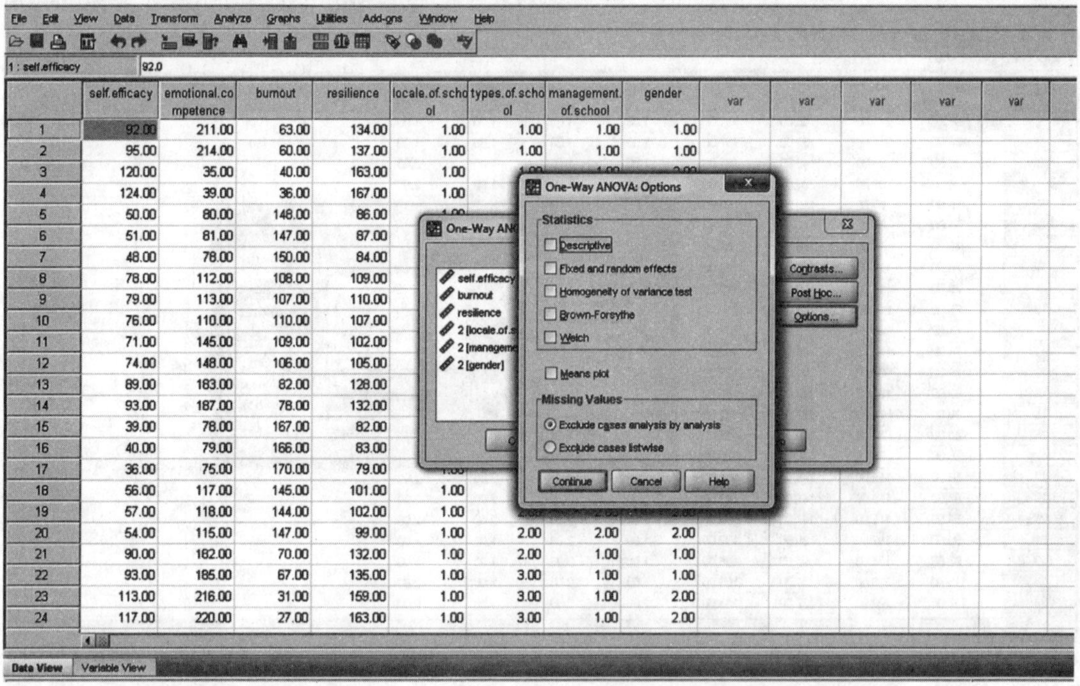

110. Highlight "**Descriptive**", "**Fixed and random effects**" and "**Homogeneity of Variance**" to get the following screen.

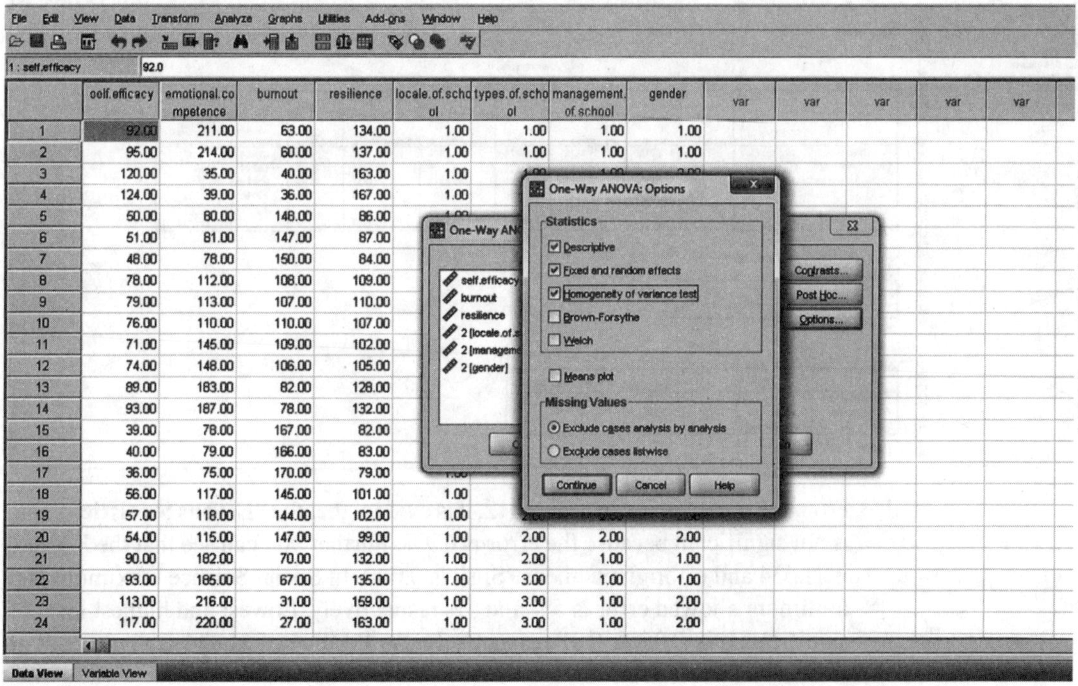

111. Click on "**Continue**" icon to get the following Screen.

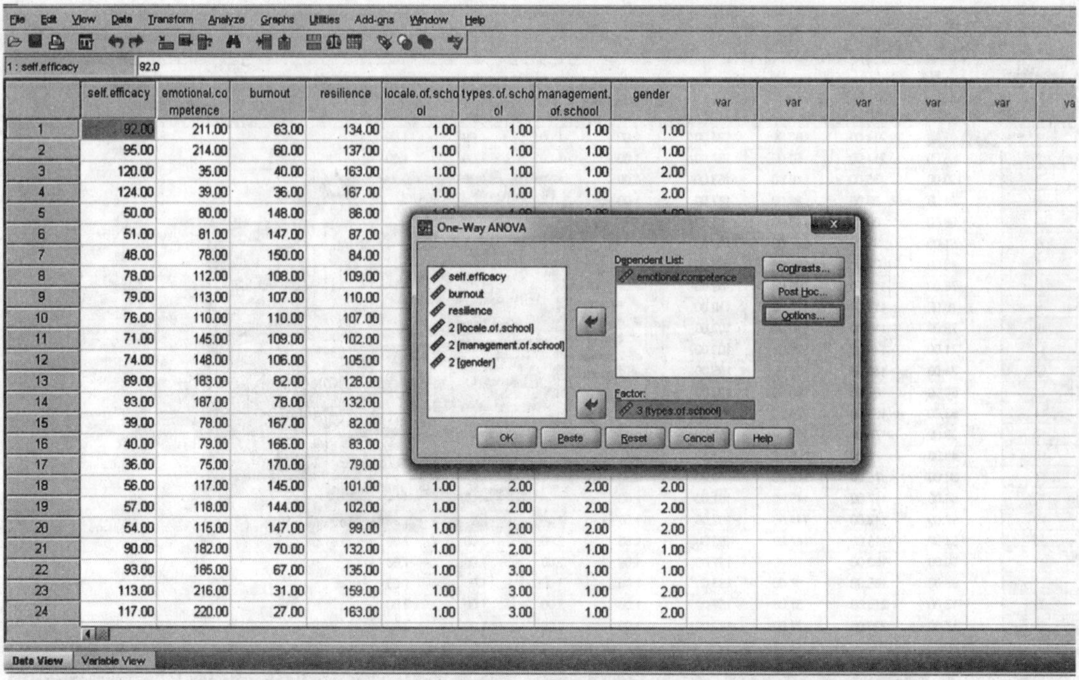

112. By clicking on "**OK**" icon to get the following outputs of One Way ANOVA.

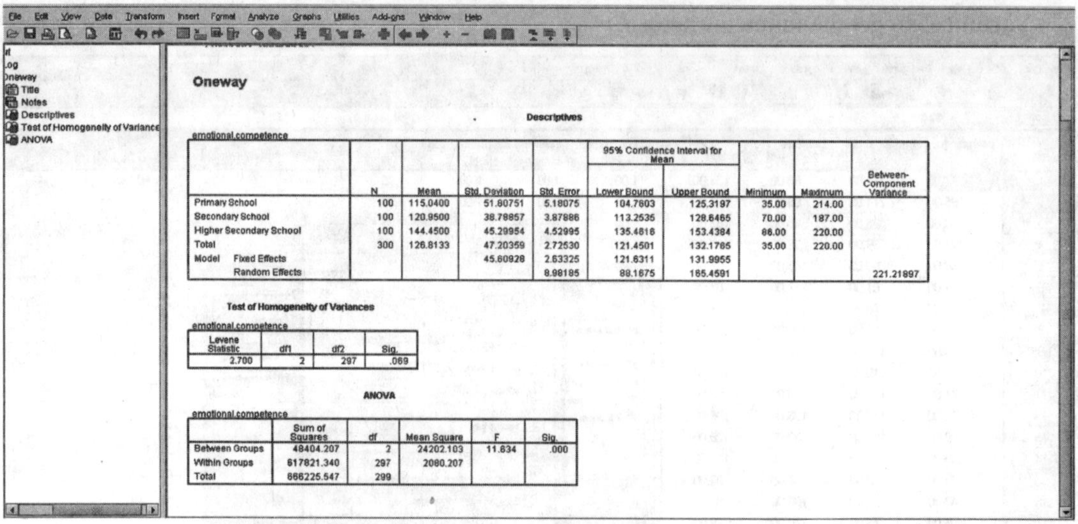

113. From the output given in Frame 112, it is evident that the "**Levens Statistic**" value is not significant because the error is 6.9%. Further you can see that the F-Value is 11.634 and error given under "**Sig.**" is 0.000. In Social Science maximum and minimum allowed error is 5% and 1% respectively. Lowest and highest level of significance is 0.05 & 0.01 respectively. So F-Value of 11.634 is significant at

0.01 level with df=2/299. In order to know teachers working in which Types of School have significantly higher Emotional competence, the data were further analysed with the help of "**Post Hoc Tests**". Since "**Homogeneity of Variance**" condition is satisfied, you can select appropriate Statistical Techniques listed under "**Homogeneity of Variance**". You may select more than one statistics but for interpretation, use any one that is appropriate in your case.

114. Let us highlight "**LSD**" & "**Duncan**" to get the following screen.

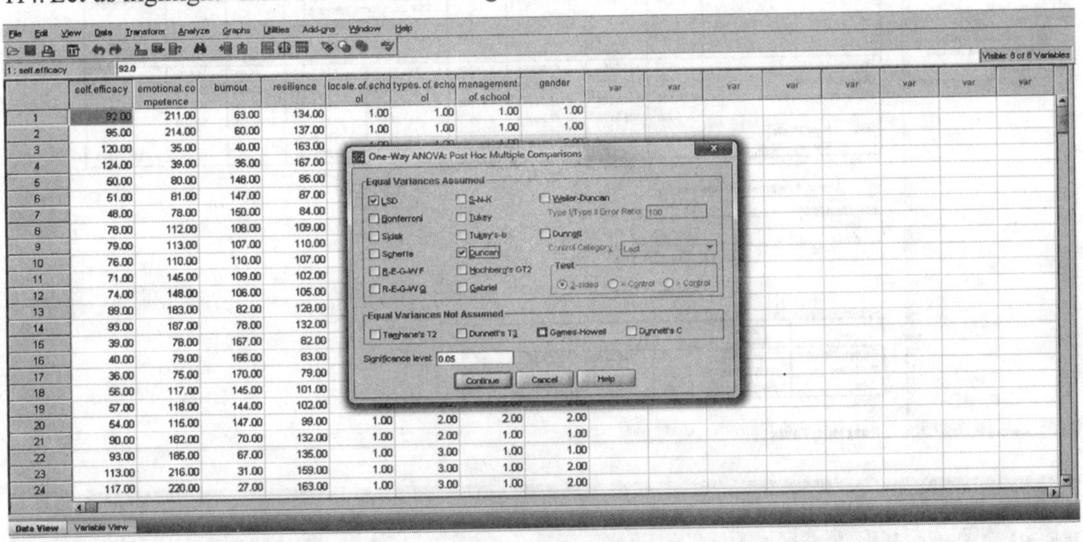

115. Click on "**Continue**" icon to get the following screen.

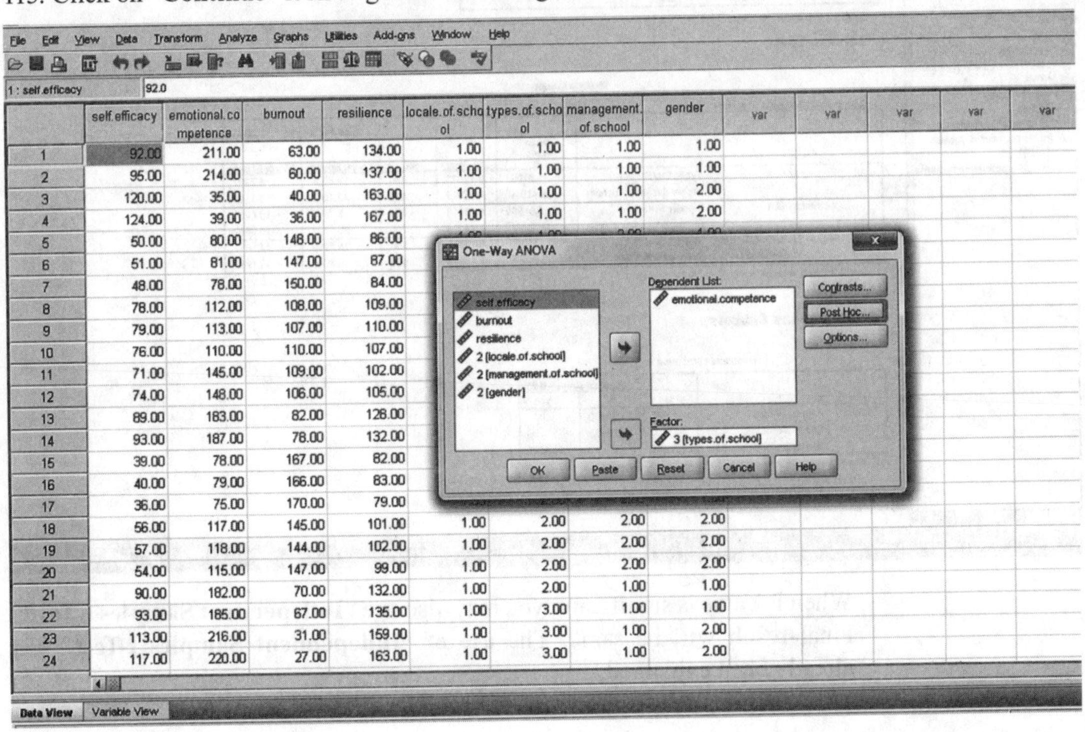

116. Click on "**OK**" icon to get the following outputs of One Way ANOVA.

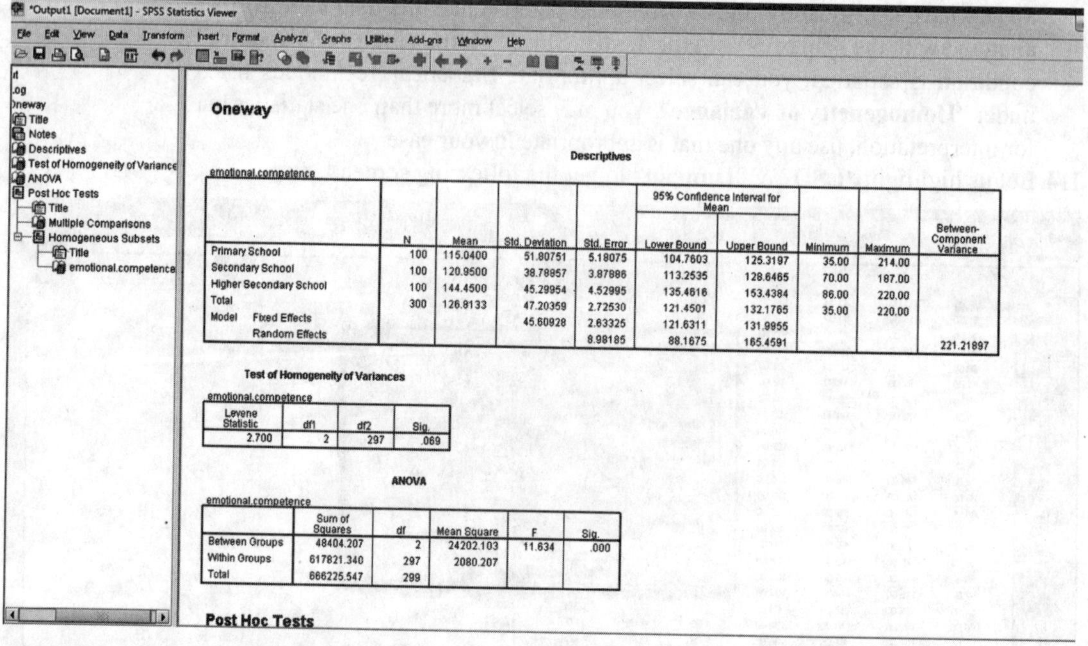

Oneway

Descriptives

emotional.competence

		N	Mean	Std. Deviation	Std. Error	95% Confidence Interval for Mean		Minimum	Maximum	Between-Component Variance
						Lower Bound	Upper Bound			
Primary School		100	115.0400	51.80751	5.18075	104.7603	125.3197	35.00	214.00	
Secondary School		100	120.9500	38.78857	3.87886	113.2535	128.6465	70.00	187.00	
Higher Secondary School		100	144.4500	45.29954	4.52995	135.4616	153.4384	86.00	220.00	
Total		300	126.8133	47.20359	2.72530	121.4501	132.1765	35.00	220.00	
Model	Fixed Effects			45.60928	2.63325	121.6311	131.9955			
	Random Effects				8.98185	88.1675	165.4591			221.21897

Test of Homogeneity of Variances

emotional.competence

Levene Statistic	df1	df2	Sig.
2.700	2	297	.069

ANOVA

emotional.competence

	Sum of Squares	df	Mean Square	F	Sig.
Between Groups	48404.207	2	24202.103	11.634	.000
Within Groups	617821.340	297	2080.207		
Total	666225.547	299			

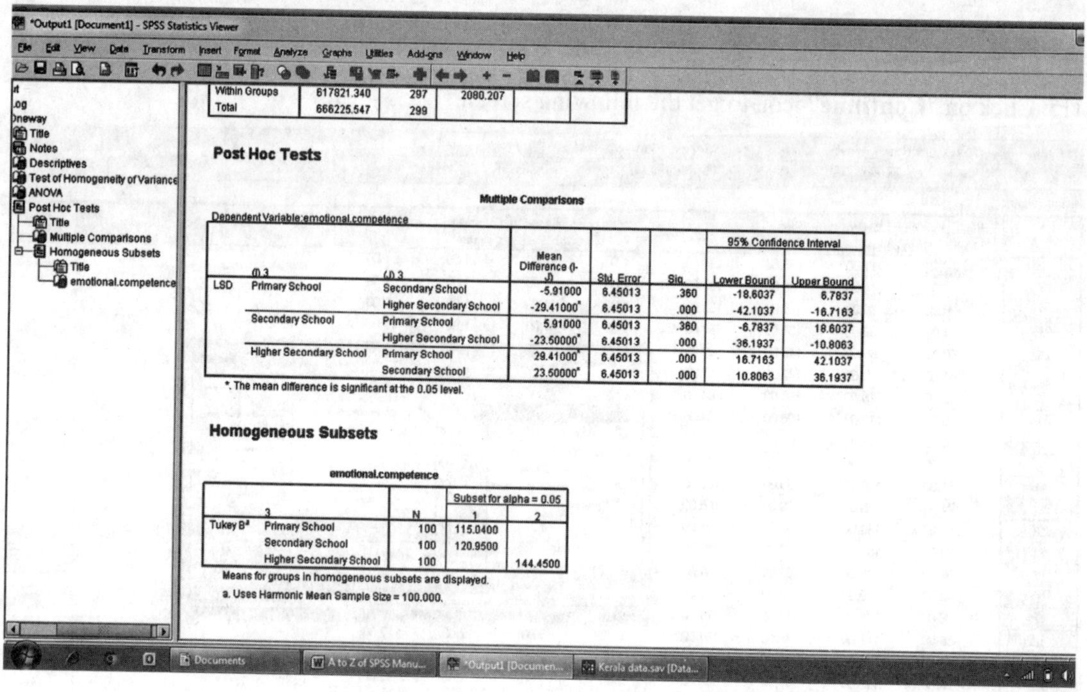

Post Hoc Tests

Multiple Comparisons

Dependent Variable:emotional.competence

	(I) 3	(J) 3	Mean Difference (I-J)	Std. Error	Sig.	95% Confidence Interval	
						Lower Bound	Upper Bound
LSD	Primary School	Secondary School	-5.91000	6.45013	.360	-18.6037	6.7837
		Higher Secondary School	-29.41000*	6.45013	.000	-42.1037	-16.7163
	Secondary School	Primary School	5.91000	6.45013	.360	-6.7837	18.6037
		Higher Secondary School	-23.50000*	6.45013	.000	-36.1937	-10.8063
	Higher Secondary School	Primary School	29.41000*	6.45013	.000	16.7163	42.1037
		Secondary School	23.50000*	6.45013	.000	10.8063	36.1937

*. The mean difference is significant at the 0.05 level.

Homogeneous Subsets

emotional.competence

	3	N	Subset for alpha = 0.05	
			1	2
Tukey B[a]	Primary School	100	115.0400	
	Secondary School	100	120.9500	
	Higher Secondary School	100		144.4500

Means for groups in homogeneous subsets are displayed.

a. Uses Harmonic Mean Sample Size = 100.000.

When F-Value is significant, you may also use "**Independent Samples t-Test**". Final result will be same. The use of "**Independent Samples t-Test**" has already been explained.

For interpretation of One Way ANOVA results, you may refer to book by D.N.Sansanwal, Research Methodology and Applied Statistic, Shipra Publishers, Delhi, 2020.

Two Way ANOVA

117. By now you must have understood the use of SPSS for analyzing data with the help of One Way ANOVA. It is to be used when there is One Discontinuous Variable having two or more labels or sub-groups and one continuous variable. If there are two Discontinuous Variables each having two or more labels or sub-groups and at least one Continuous variable, then Two Way ANOVA is to be used for analyzing the data. If each Discontinuous Variable has two levels, then you may also call it 2 X 2 Factorial Design ANOVA. Suppose one variable has three labels and another variable has two labels, it is called 3 X 2 Factorial Design ANOVA. In general, it is m x n Factorial Design ANOVA.

Let us consider the following Objective:

To study the influence of Gender, Types of School and their interaction on Achievement in Physics of students.

In this objective, "**Gender** and **Types of School**" are two discontinuous variables. There are two labels of "**Gender**" and three labels of "**Types of School**". So data are to be analysed with the help of Two Way ANOVA or 2 X 3 Factorial Design ANOVA.

Click on "**Analyse**" bring curser on "**General Linear Model**", and then on "**Univariate**" to get the following screen.

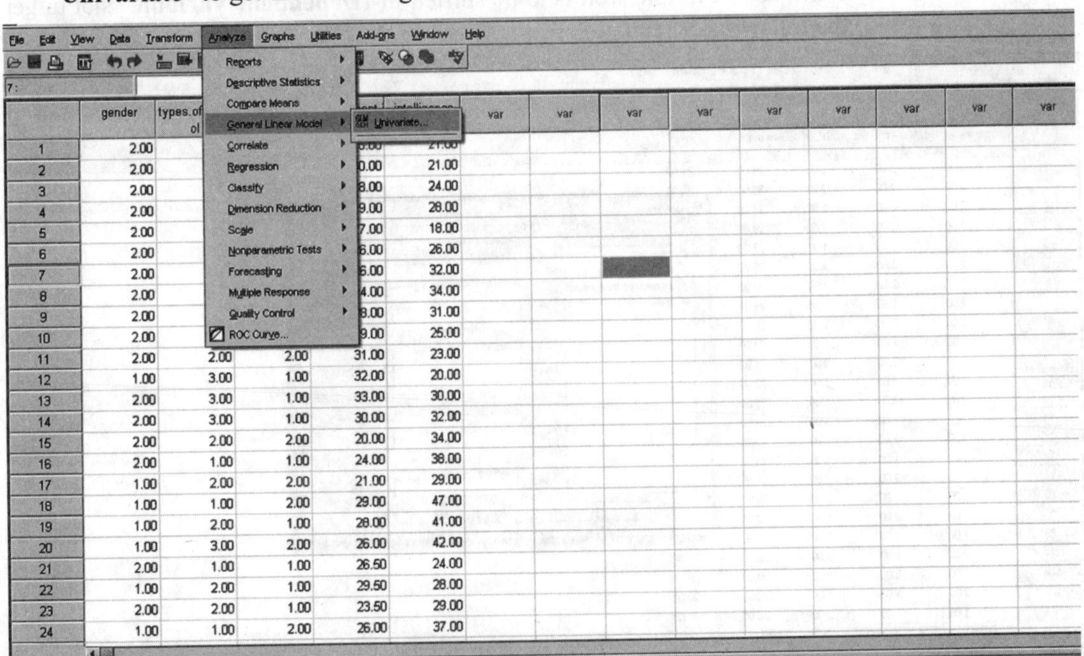

118. Click on "**Univariate**" icon to get the following screen.

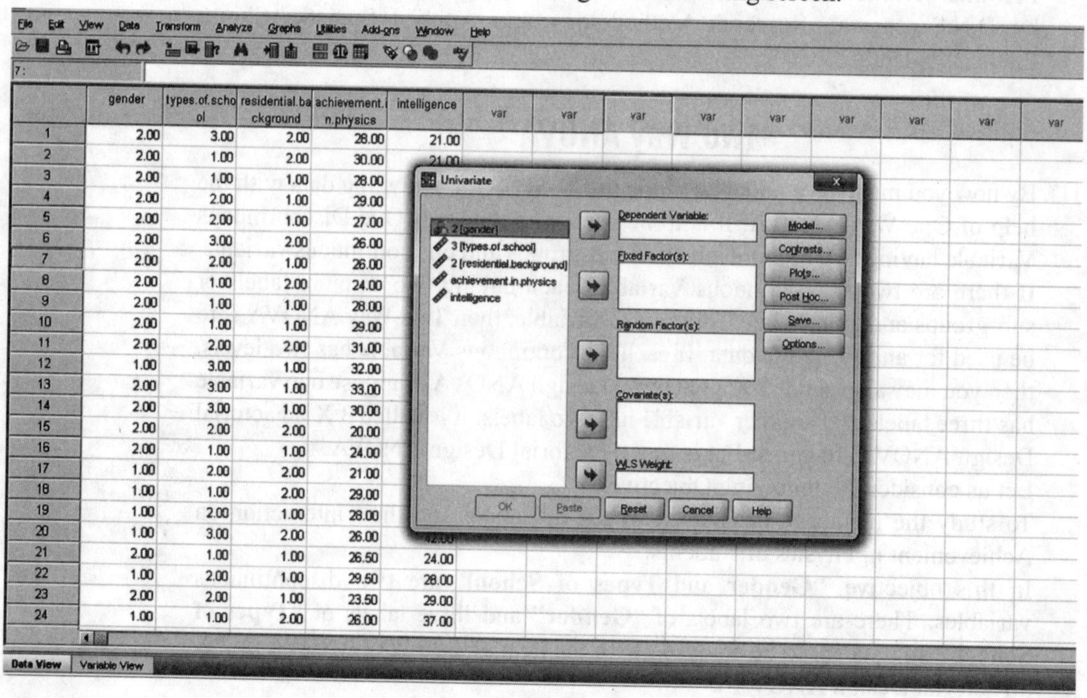

119. According to the objective mentioned in Frame 117, Achievement in Physics is continuous variable so it is to be shifted in "**Dependent Variable**" slot to get the following Screen.

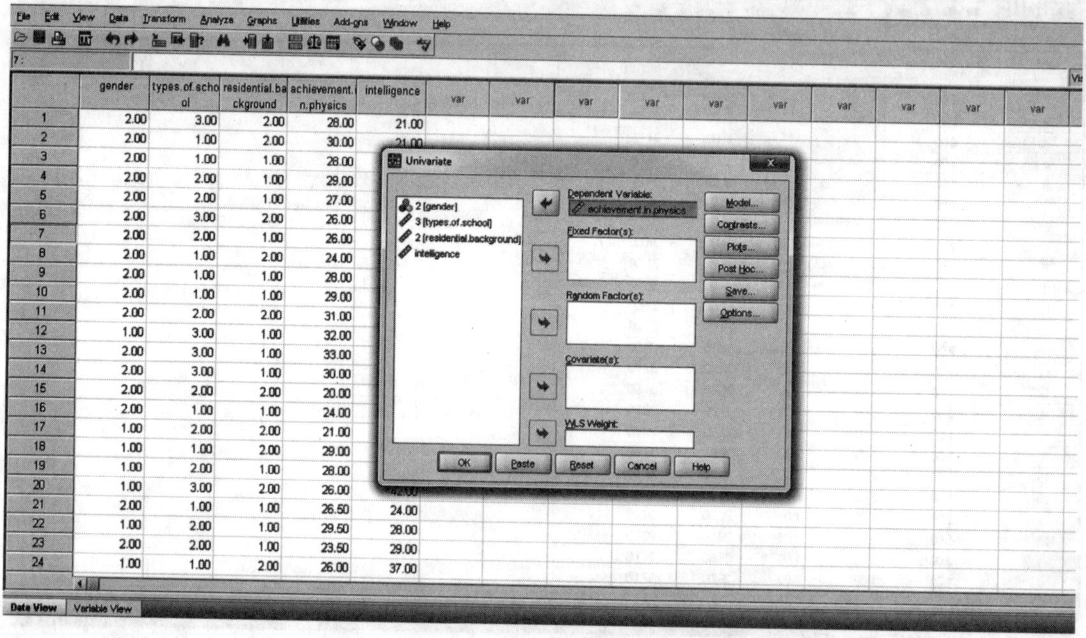

120. Further according to the objective mentioned in Frame 117, Gender and Types of School are the "**Fixed Variables**". Shift both these discontinuous variables under "**Fixed Variables**" slot to get the following screen.

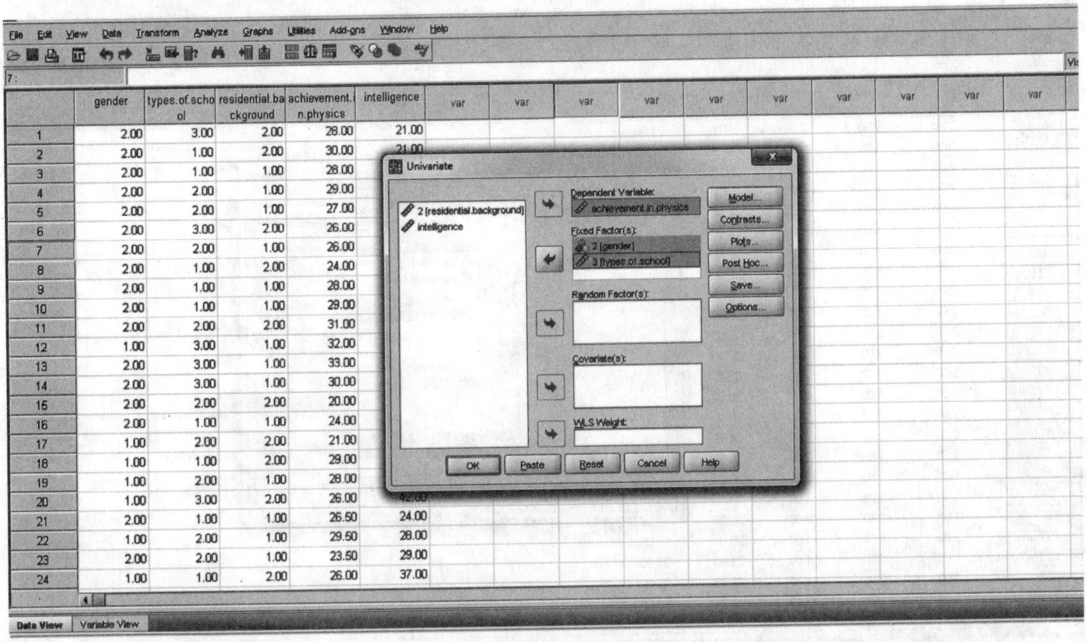

121. The six active icons are **"Model", "Contrast", "Plots", "Post Hoc", "Save", and "Options".** To understand each one of these, click on "**Model**" to get the following screen.

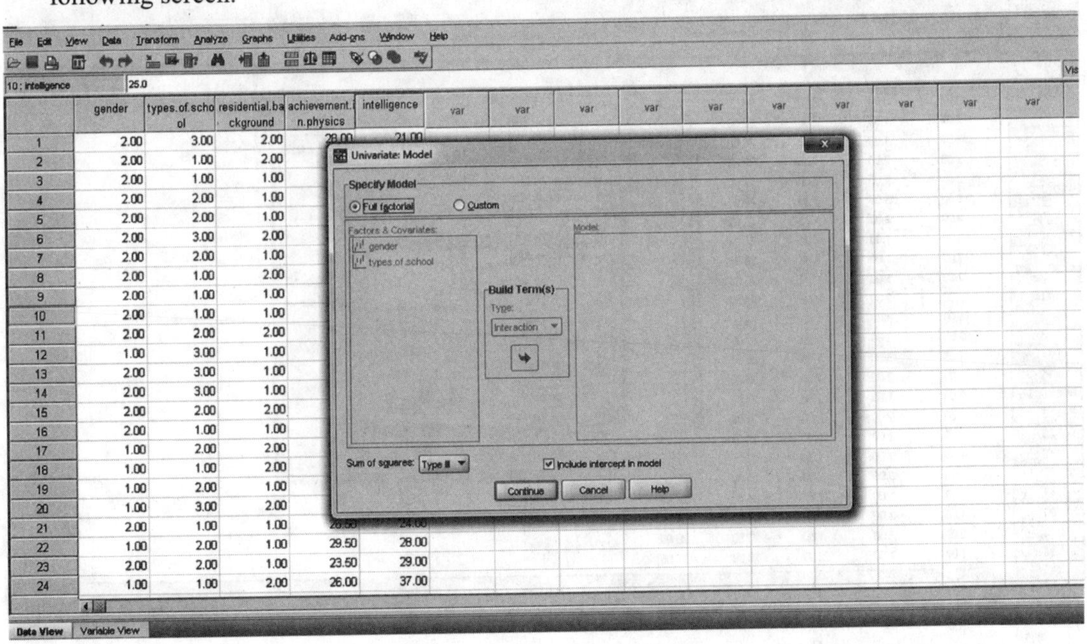

122. Under "**Specific Model**", two options are "**Full Factorial**" and "**Custom**". Normally researchers use "**Full Factorial**" option which is already highlighted, click on "**Continue**" to get the following screen.

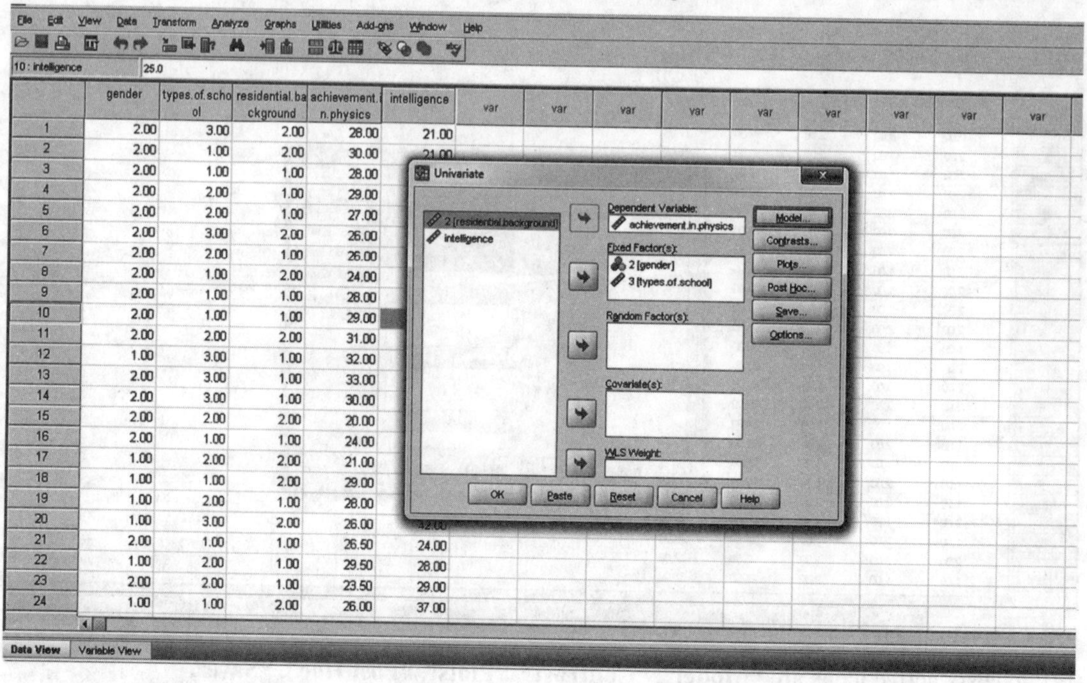

123. Click on "**Contrast**" to get the following screen.

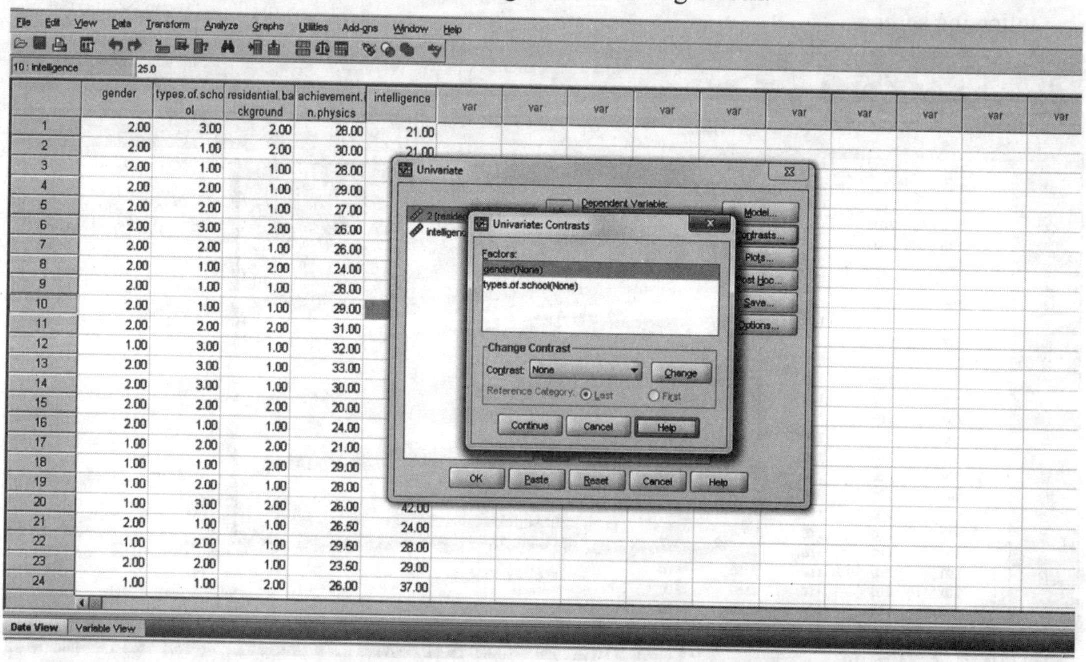

124. In case you do not want to change anything, click on "**Continue**" to get the following screen.

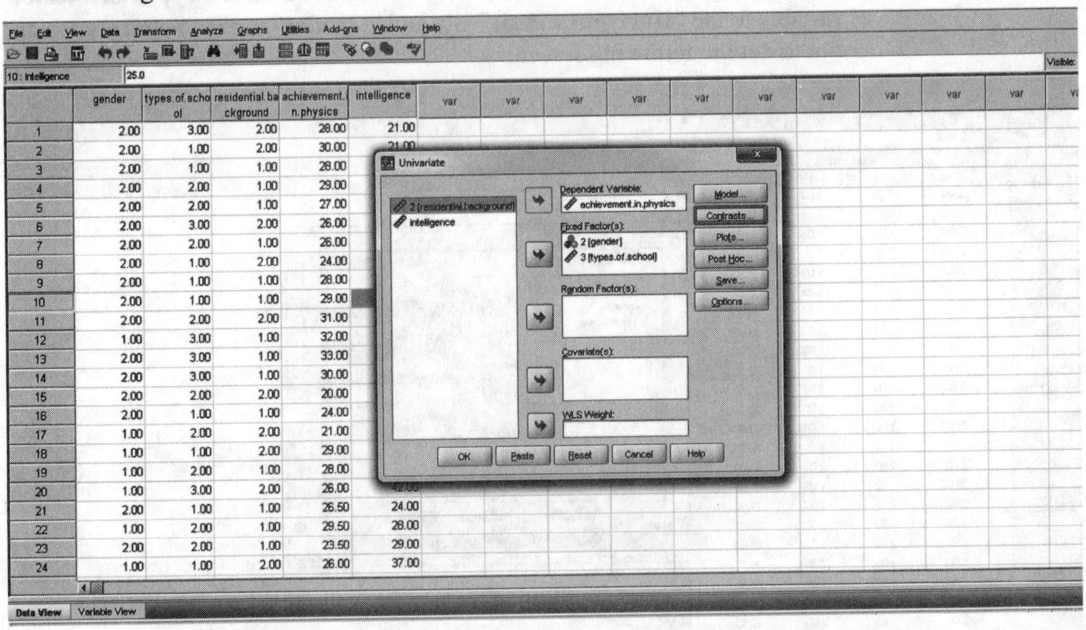

125. From the top, third icon is "**Plot**". "**Plot**" is useful for studying the influence of interaction between the given discontinuous variables on continuous variable. In this example, there are two discontinuous variables, namely, "**Gender** and **Types of School**". There might be interaction among "**Gender** and **Types of School**". Click on "**Plot**" to get the following screen.

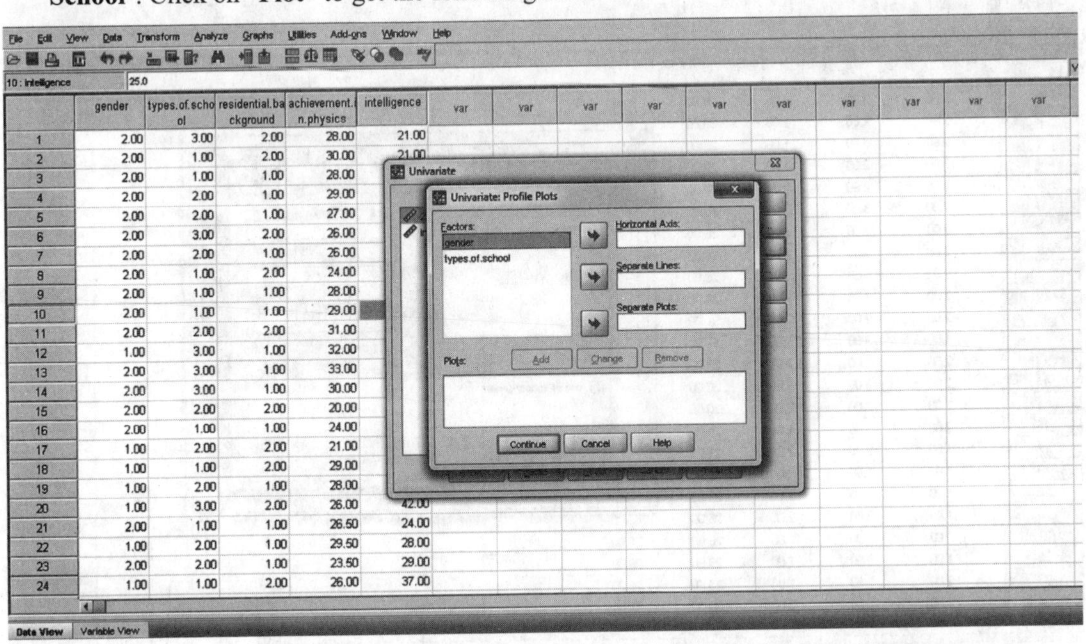

126. Shift any one variable to the "**Horizontal Axis**" slot and another variable to the "**Separate Lines**" slot. Suppose you decide to shift "**Types of School**" variable to the "**Horizontal Axis**" slot and "**Gender**" to the "**Separate Lines**" slot to get the following screen.

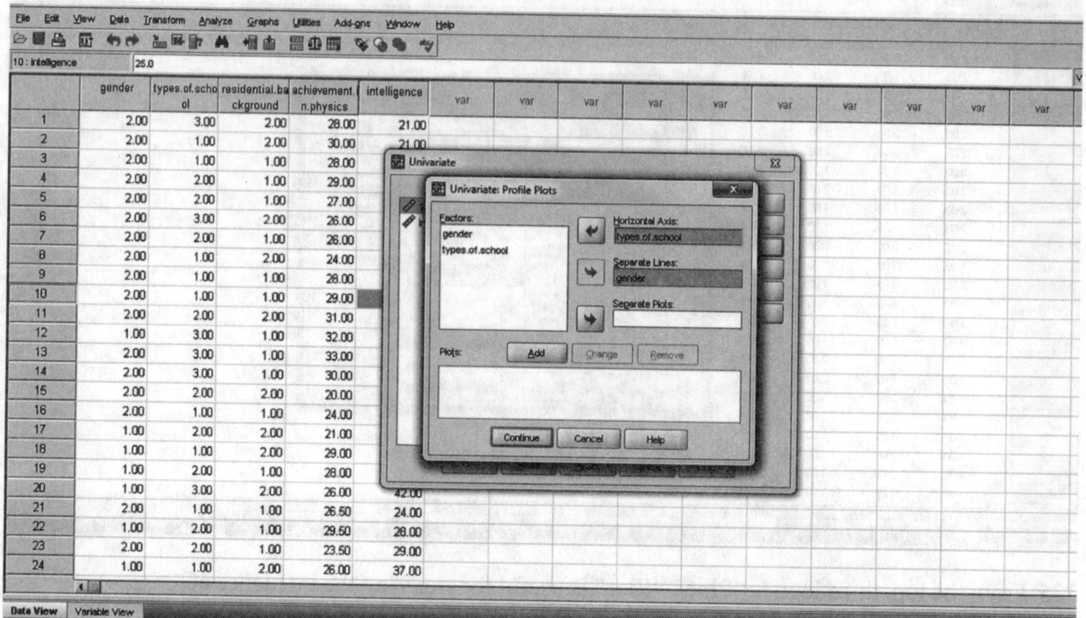

127. Click on "**Add**" to get the following screen.

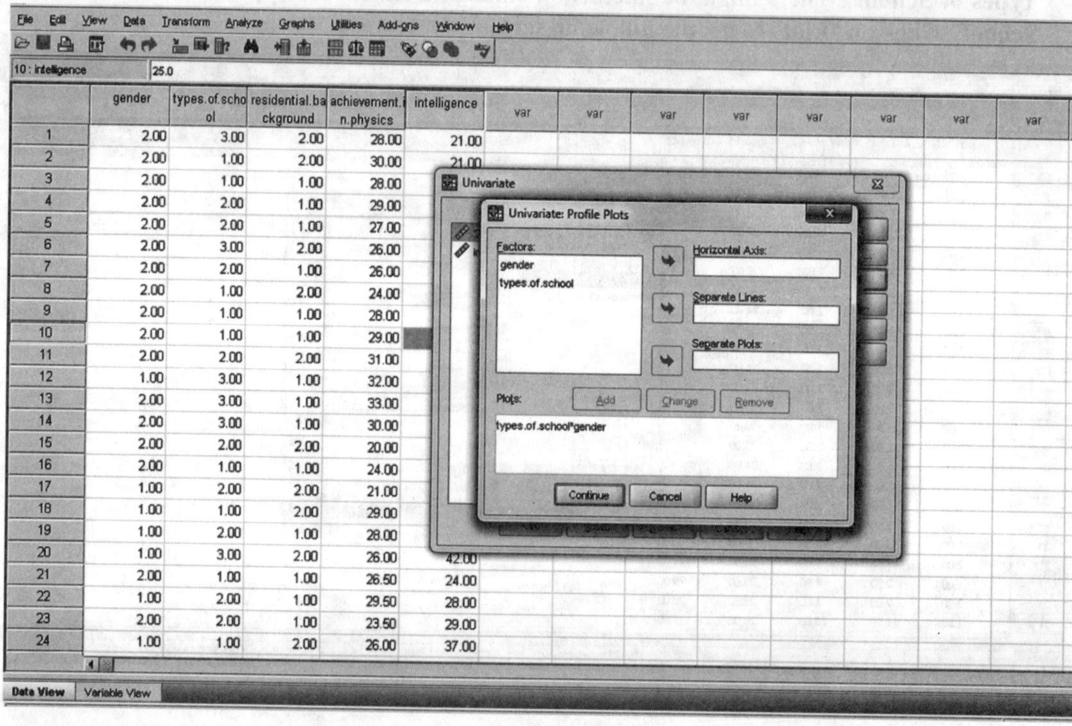

128. Click on "**Continue**" to get the following screen.

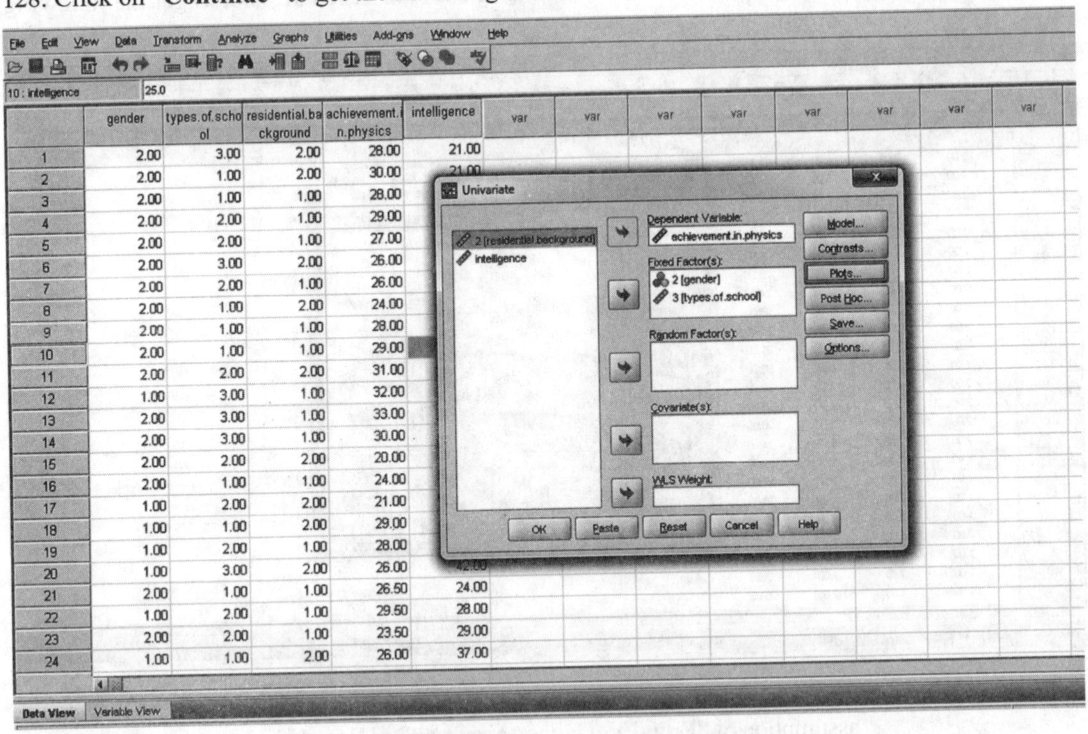

129. Next icon is "**Post Hoc**". You already know the use of "**Post Hoc**" icon. In this example, "**Post Hoc**" is to be used only for "**Types of School**" because there are three labels of it. Click on "**Post Hoc**" to get the following screen.

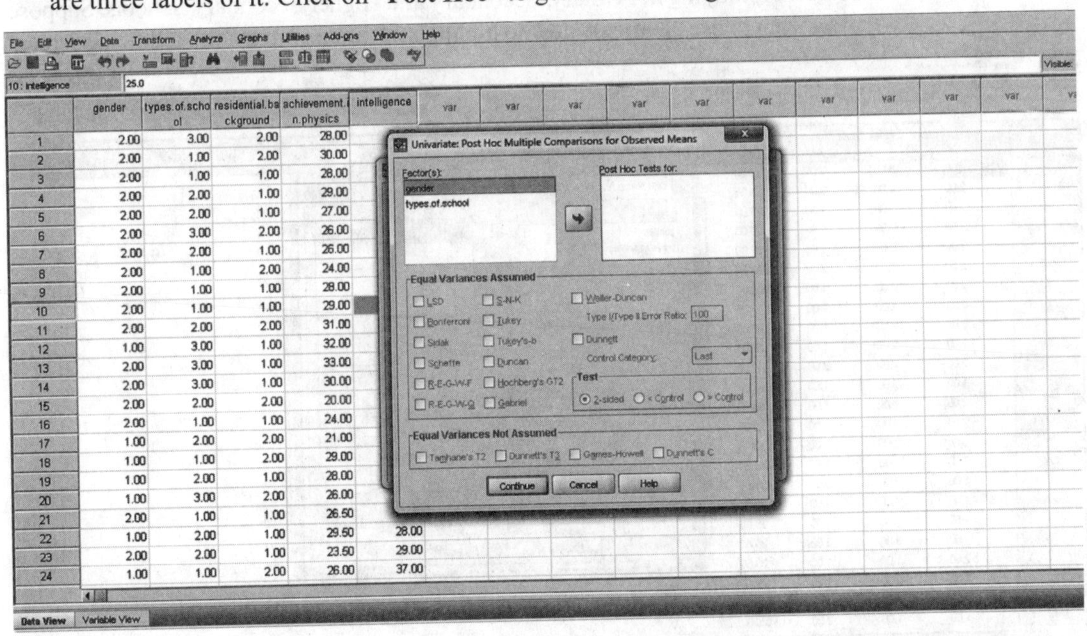

130. Shift **"Types of School"** to the **"Post Hoc Test For"** slot to get the following screen.

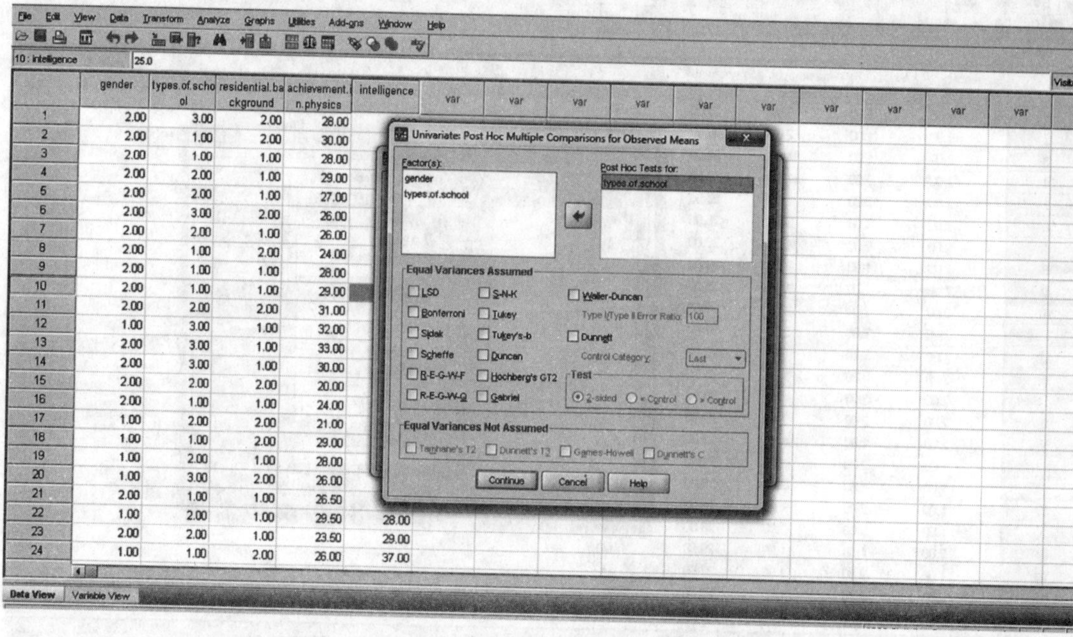

131. You know how to use **"Post Hoc Test"** depending upon whether your data satisfy the assumption of **"Equal Variances Assumed"** or **Equal Variances Not Assumed"**. In the present case **Equal Variances Assumed"** condition is satisfied. You may use relevant option for comparing mean scores of Achievement in Physics of students studying in Primary, Secondary and Higher Secondary Schools. Suppose you want to use **"Duncan"** test so highlight **"Duncan"** to get the following screen.

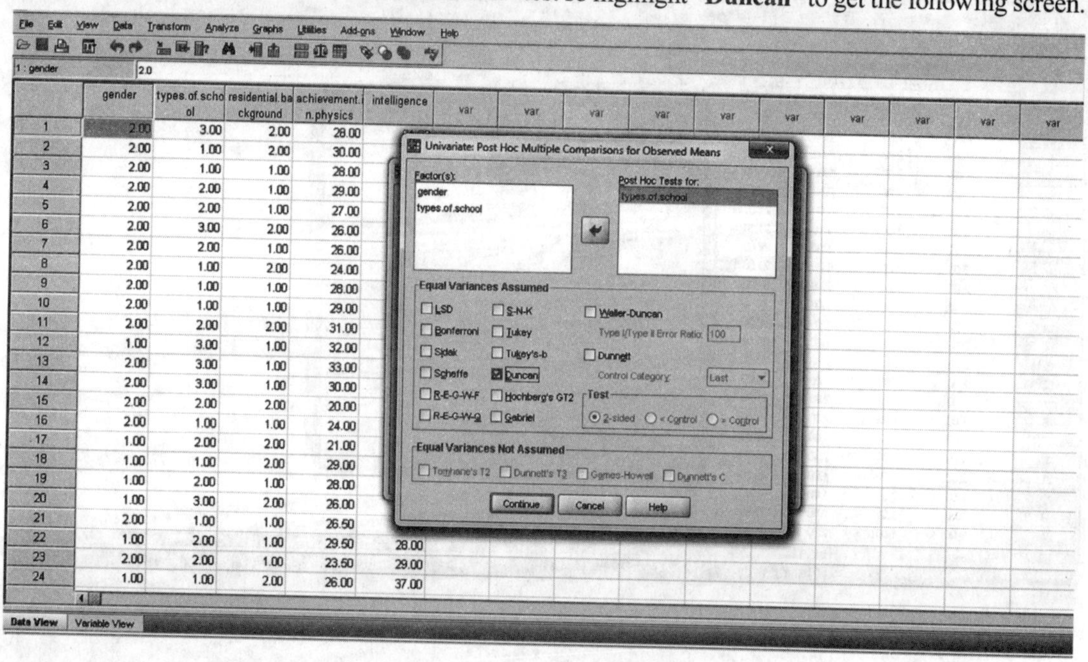

132. Click on "**Continue**" icon to get the following screen.

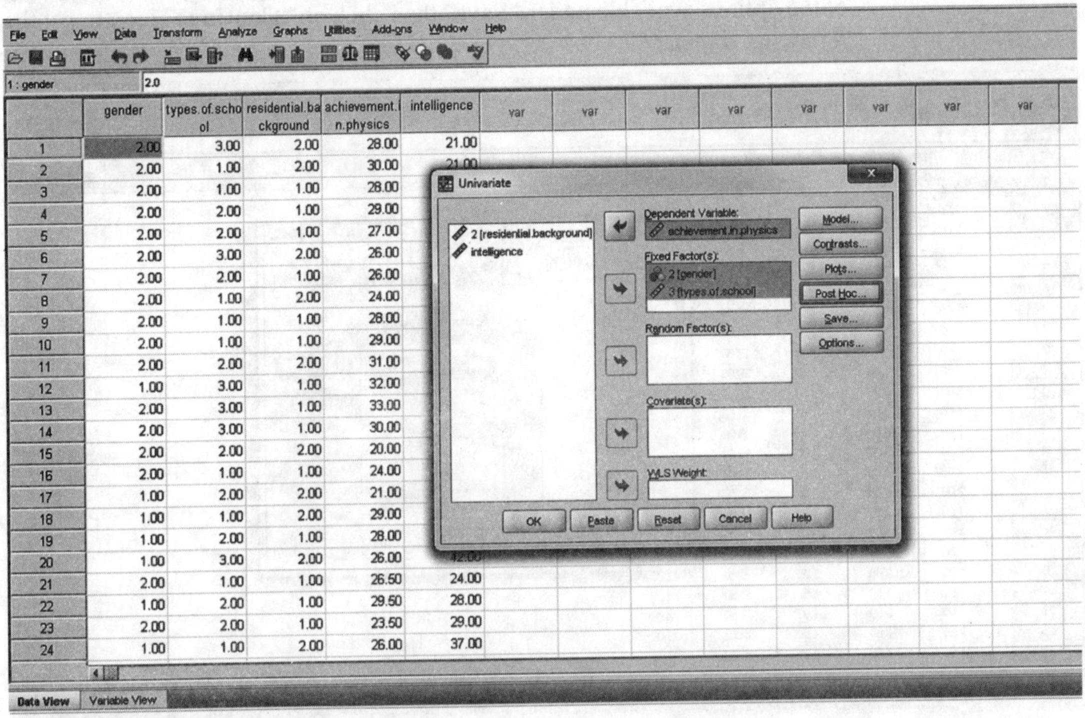

133. Next icon is "**Save**". Click on "**Save**" to get the following screen.

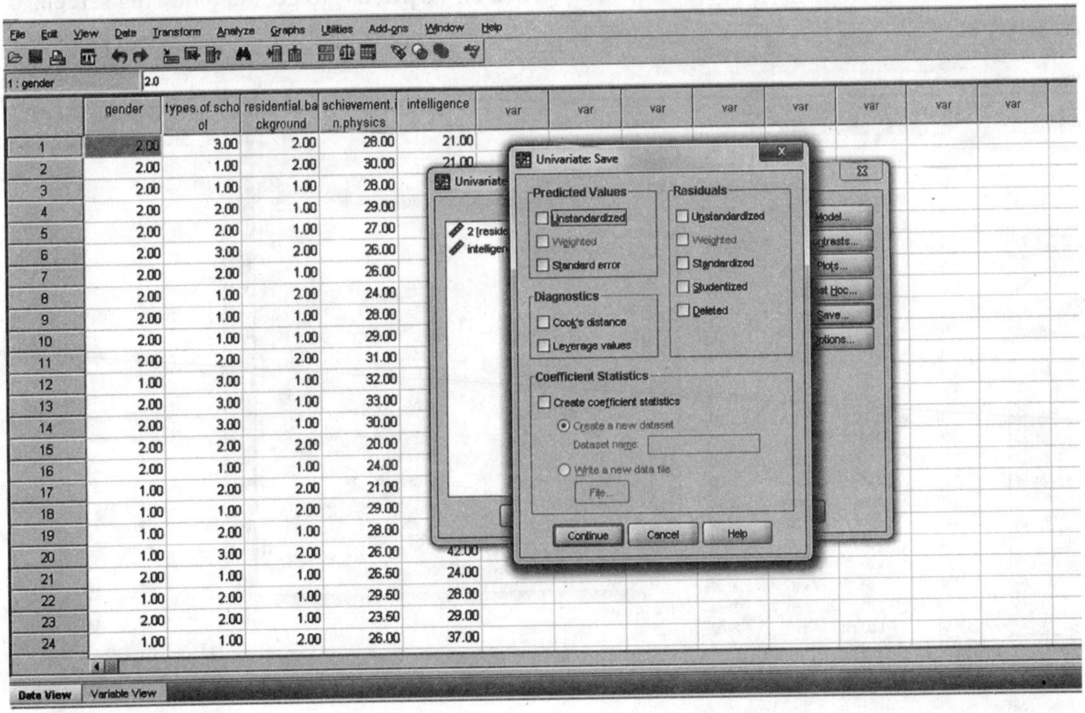

134. There are many options available under "**Save**". If you do not want to use any of the options available under "**Save**" then click on "**Continue**" icon to get the following screen.

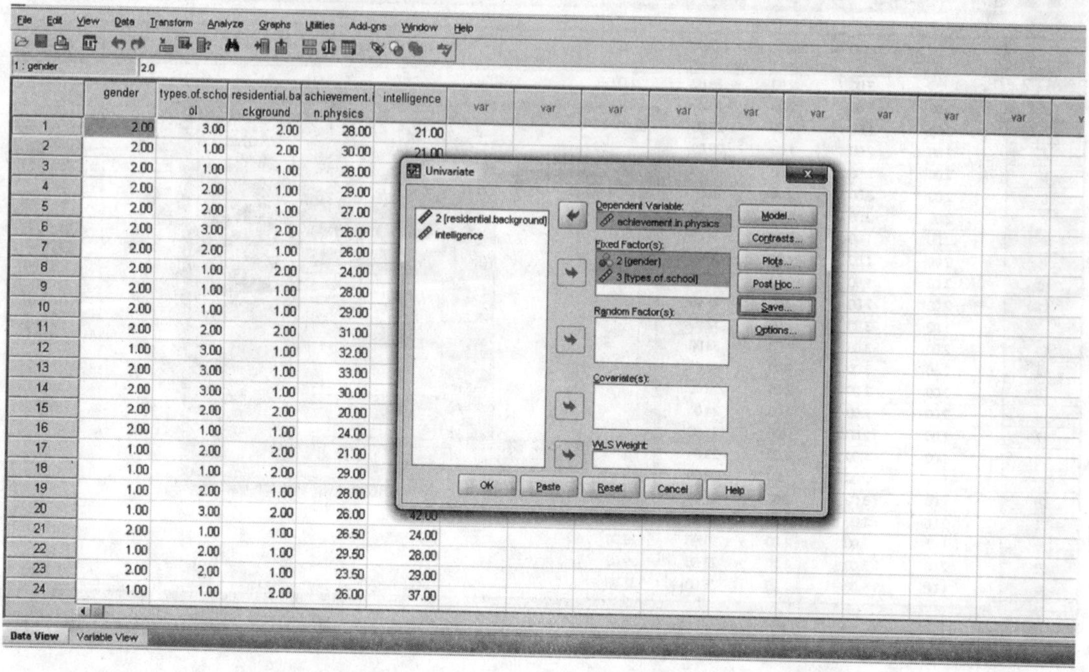

135. The last icon is "**Options**". Click on "**Options**" to get the following screen.

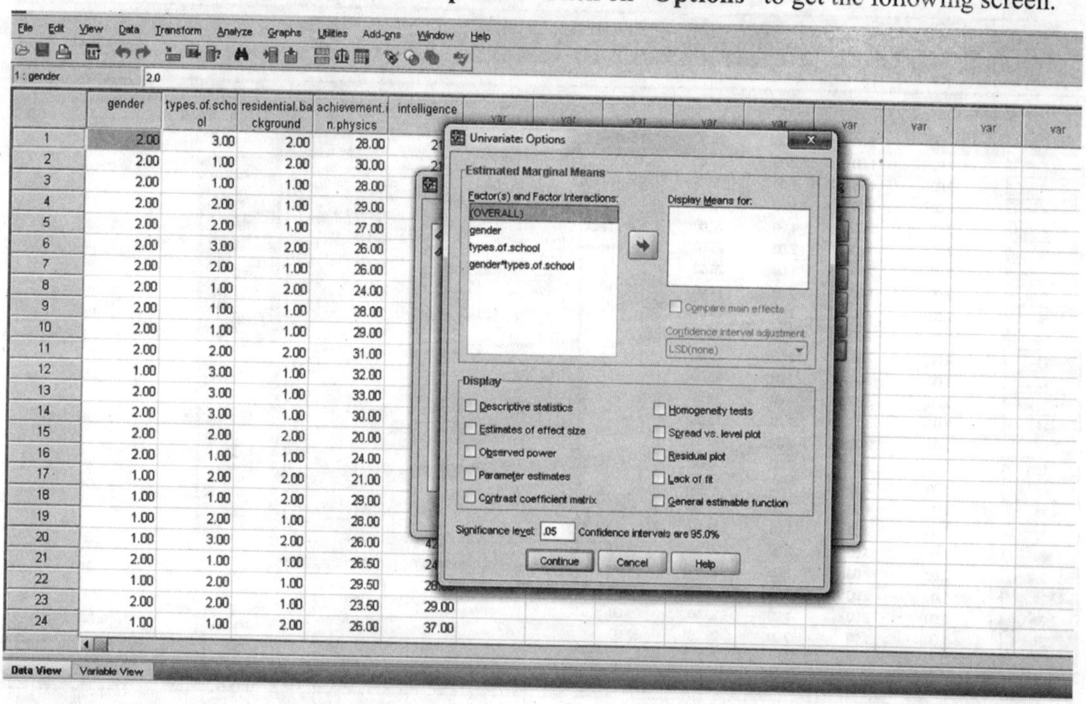

136. Shift all variables from left hand side dialogue box to right hand side dialogue box to get the following screen.

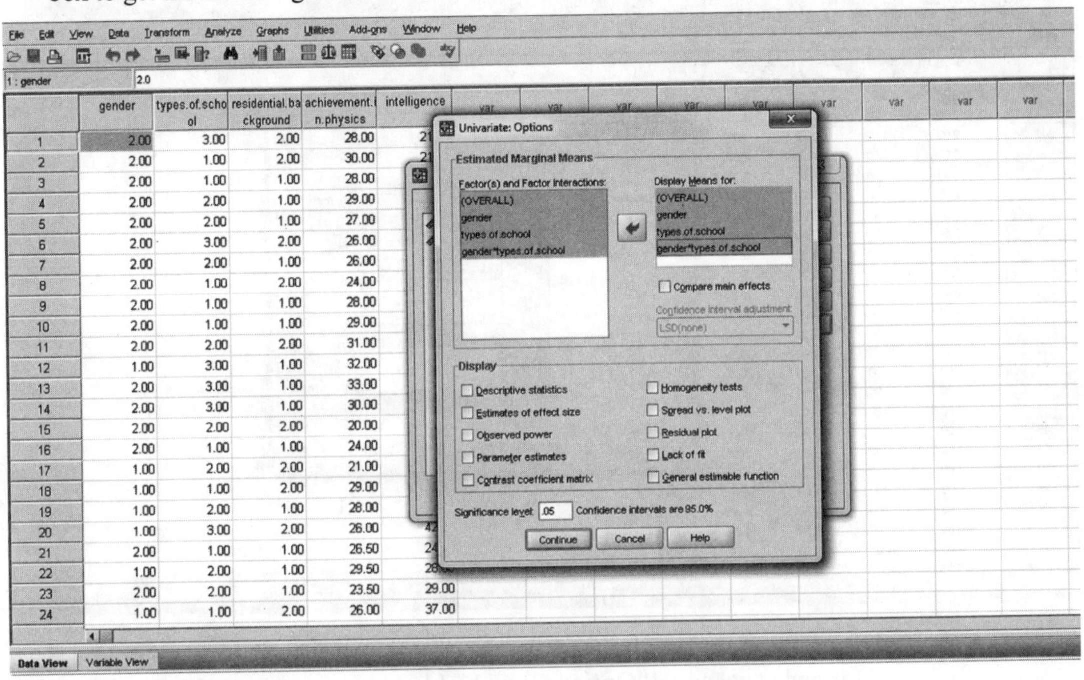

137. There are many options under "**Display**" icon. Suppose we want information related to "**Descriptive Statistics**", "**Homogeneity Test**" and "**Estimates of effect size**". Highlight all these icons to get the following screen.

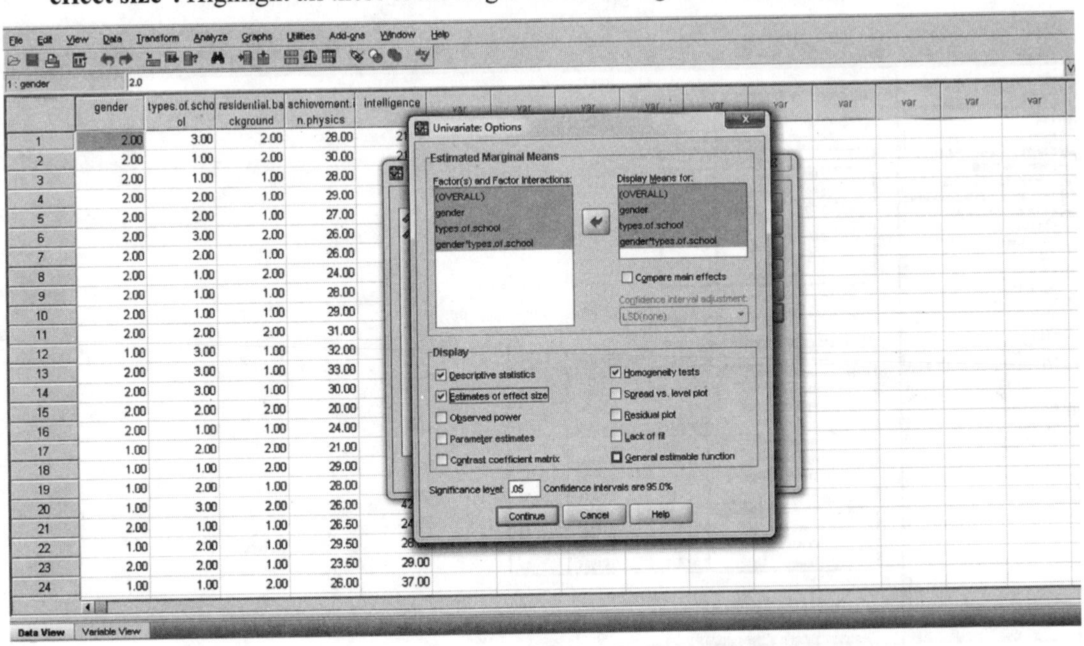

138. Click on "**Continue**" icon to get the following screen.

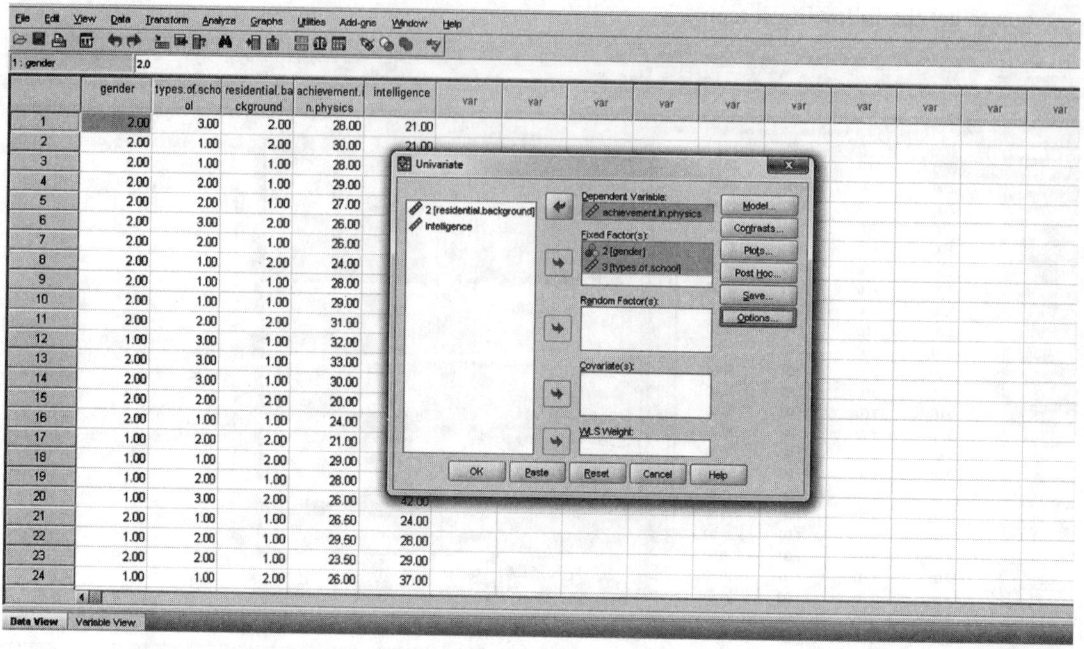

139. You must have understood the function of each available option. You have already clicked on "**Options**" and highlighted appropriate "**Options**". You have already highlighted "**Post Hoc**" Options and also entered variables under "**Plot**" options. Click on "**OK**" to get the following outputs of Two Way ANOVA.

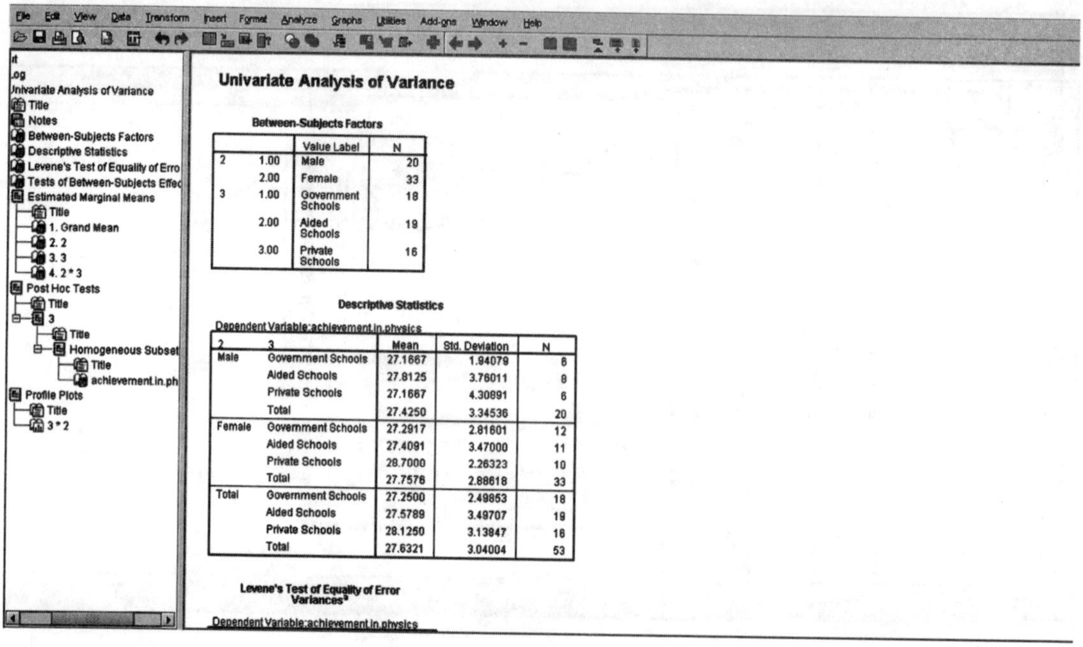

Between-Subjects Factors

		Value Label	N
2	1.00	Male	20
	2.00	Female	33
3	1.00	Government Schools	18
	2.00	Aided Schools	19
	3.00	Private Schools	16

Descriptive Statistics

Dependent Variable:achievement.in.physics

2	3	Mean	Std. Deviation	N
Male	Government Schools	27.1667	1.94079	6
	Aided Schools	27.8125	3.76011	8
	Private Schools	27.1667	4.30891	6
	Total	27.4250	3.34536	20
Female	Government Schools	27.2917	2.81601	12
	Aided Schools	27.4091	3.47000	11
	Private Schools	28.7000	2.26323	10
	Total	27.7576	2.88618	33
Total	Government Schools	27.2500	2.49853	18
	Aided Schools	27.5789	3.49707	19
	Private Schools	28.1250	3.13847	16
	Total	27.6321	3.04004	53

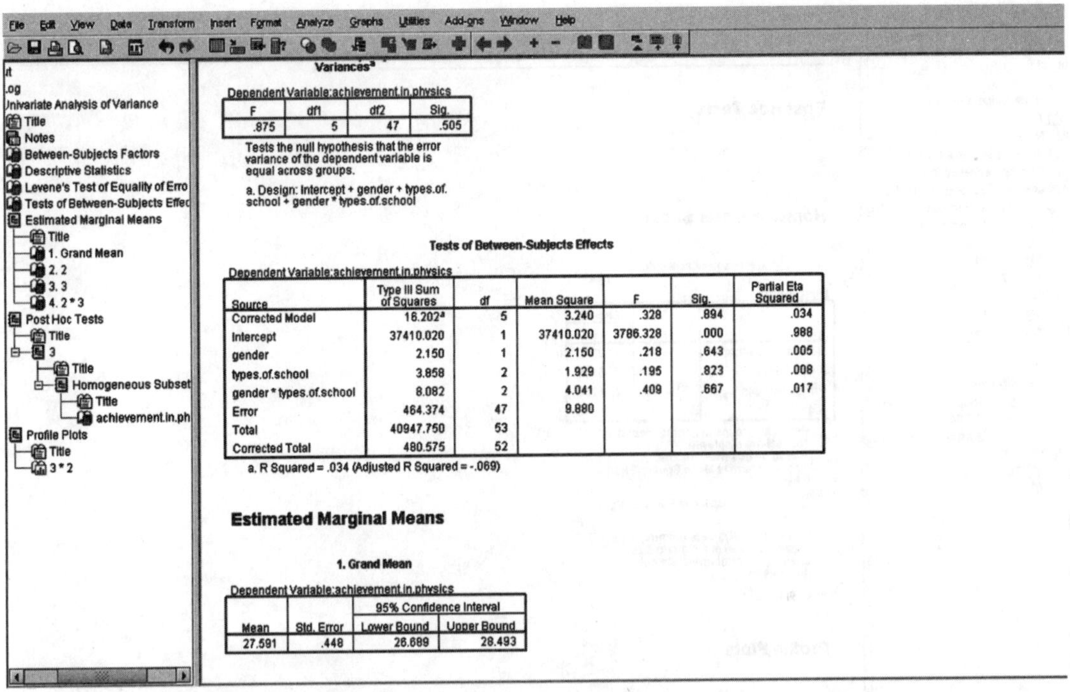

Variances[a]

Dependent Variable:achievement.in.physics

F	df1	df2	Sig.
.875	5	47	.505

Tests the null hypothesis that the error variance of the dependent variable is equal across groups.

a. Design: Intercept + gender + types.of.school + gender * types.of.school

Tests of Between-Subjects Effects

Dependent Variable:achievement.in.physics

Source	Type III Sum of Squares	df	Mean Square	F	Sig.	Partial Eta Squared
Corrected Model	16.202[a]	5	3.240	.328	.894	.034
Intercept	37410.020	1	37410.020	3786.328	.000	.988
gender	2.150	1	2.150	.218	.643	.005
types.of.school	3.858	2	1.929	.195	.823	.008
gender * types.of.school	8.082	2	4.041	.409	.667	.017
Error	464.374	47	9.880			
Total	40947.750	53				
Corrected Total	480.575	52				

a. R Squared = .034 (Adjusted R Squared = -.069)

Estimated Marginal Means

1. Grand Mean

Dependent Variable:achievement.in.physics

Mean	Std. Error	95% Confidence Interval	
		Lower Bound	Upper Bound
27.591	.448	26.689	28.493

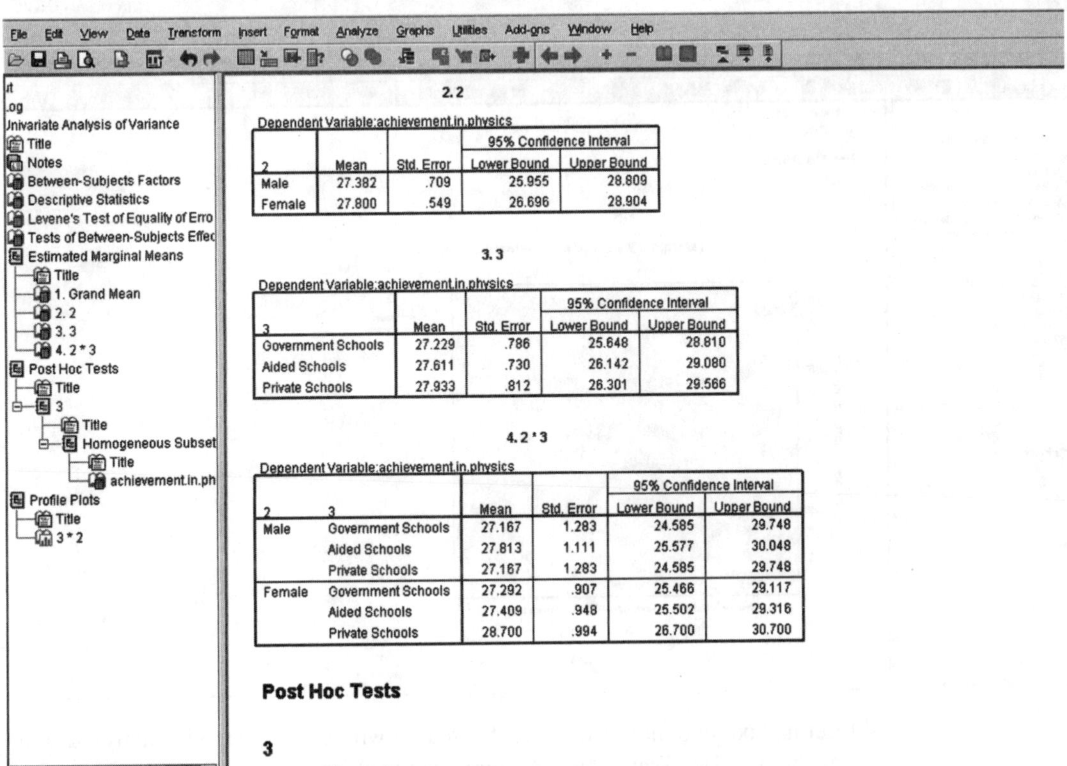

2. 2

Dependent Variable:achievement.in.physics

2	Mean	Std. Error	95% Confidence Interval	
			Lower Bound	Upper Bound
Male	27.382	.709	25.955	28.809
Female	27.800	.549	26.696	28.904

3. 3

Dependent Variable:achievement.in.physics

3	Mean	Std. Error	95% Confidence Interval	
			Lower Bound	Upper Bound
Government Schools	27.229	.786	25.648	28.810
Aided Schools	27.611	.730	26.142	29.080
Private Schools	27.933	.812	26.301	29.566

4. 2 * 3

Dependent Variable:achievement.in.physics

2	3	Mean	Std. Error	95% Confidence Interval	
				Lower Bound	Upper Bound
Male	Government Schools	27.167	1.283	24.585	29.748
	Aided Schools	27.813	1.111	25.577	30.048
	Private Schools	27.167	1.283	24.585	29.748
Female	Government Schools	27.292	.907	25.466	29.117
	Aided Schools	27.409	.948	25.502	29.316
	Private Schools	28.700	.994	26.700	30.700

Post Hoc Tests

3

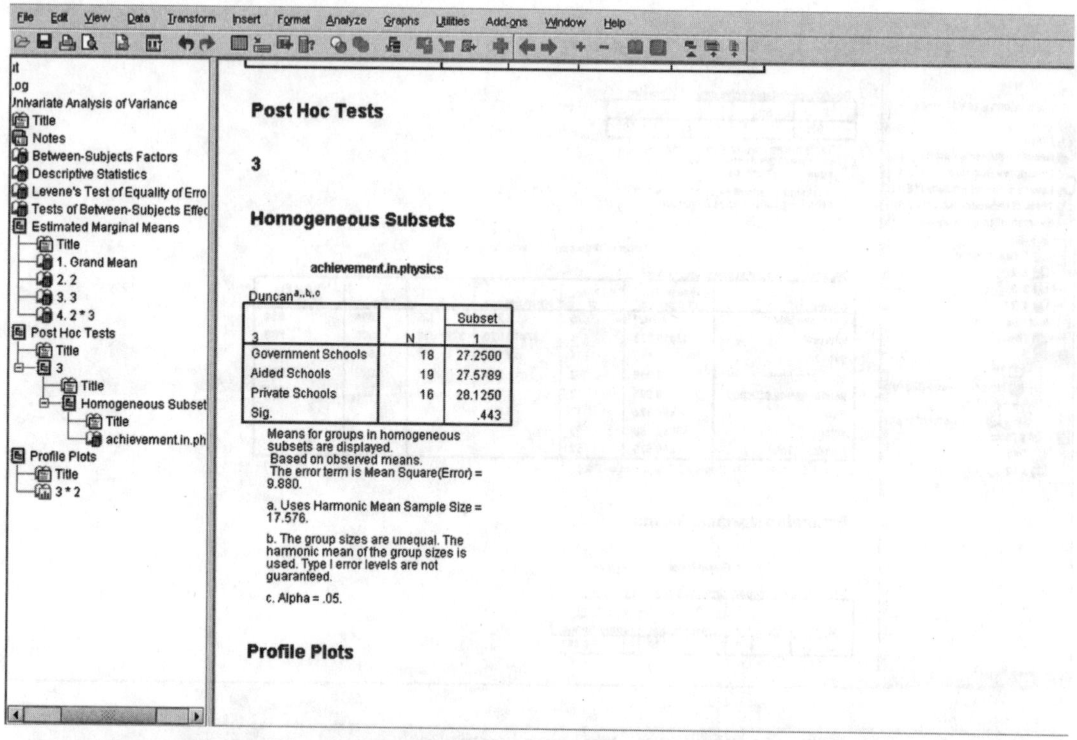

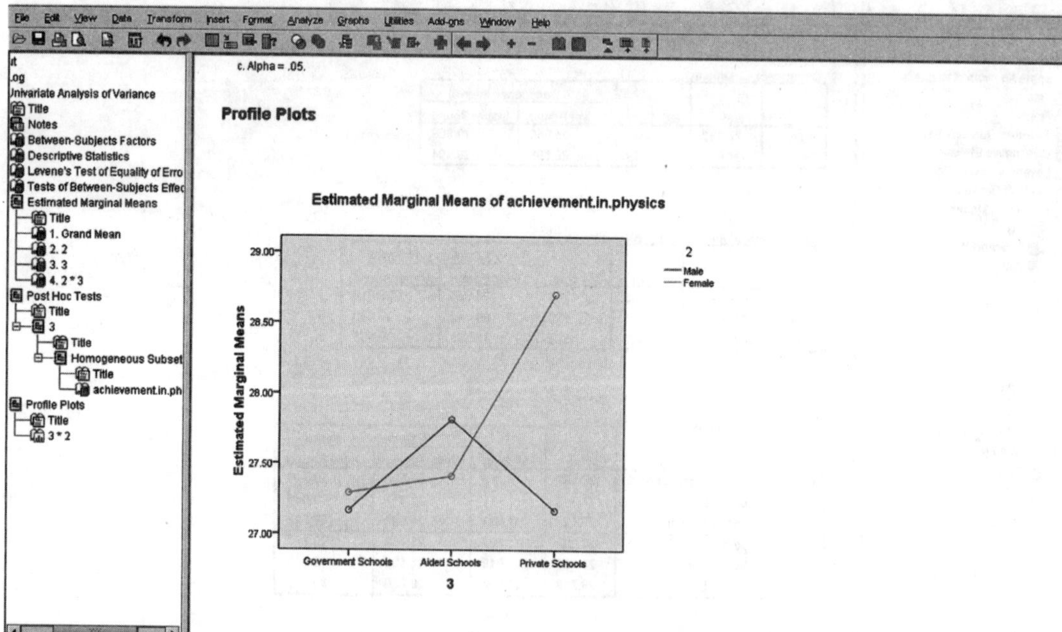

140. Let us take one more example of research where data are to be analysed with the help of Two Way ANOVA. Suppose the objective is:

To study the influence of Gender, Locale of School and their interaction on Emotional Competence of Teachers.

Click on "**Analyse**", then on "**General Linear Model**" and finally on "**Univariate**" icon to get the following screen.

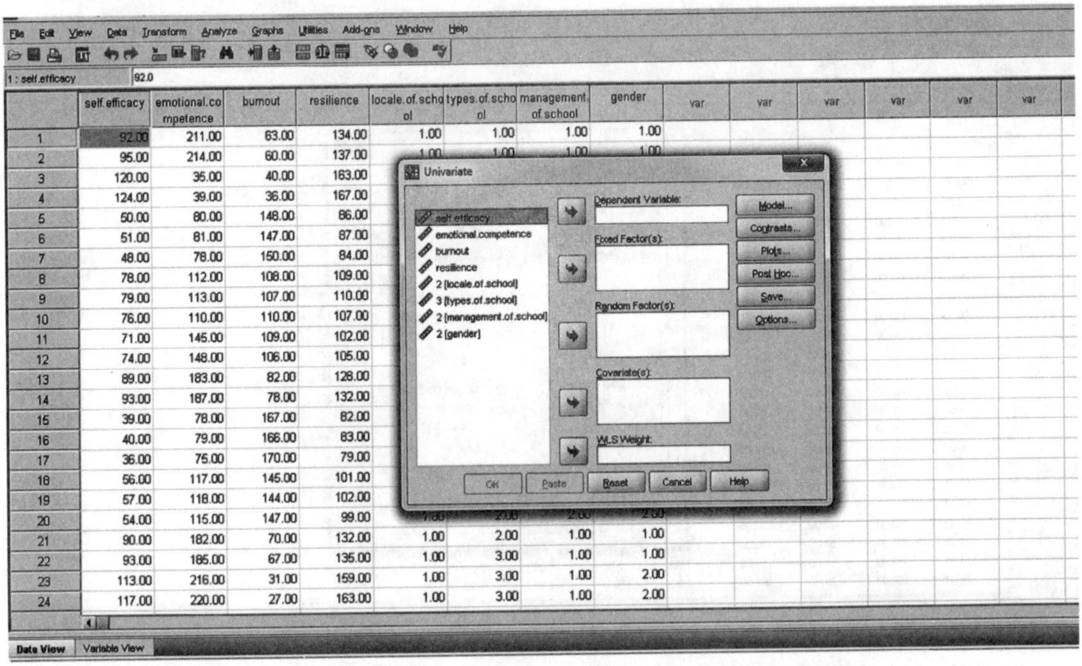

141. Shift "**Emotional Competence**" to "**Dependent Variable**" slot. Also shift "**Gender**" and "**Locale of School**" to "**Fixed Factors**" slot to get the following screen.

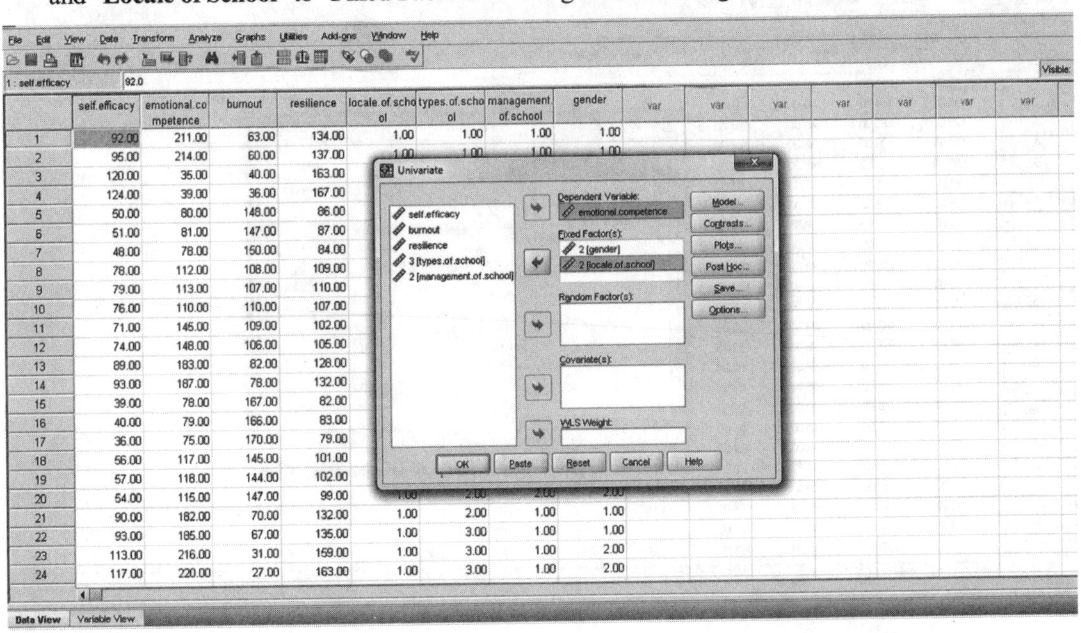

142. By clicking on "**Options**" shift all variables from left hand side dialogue box to right hand side dialogue box. Under "**Display**" options, also highlight "**Descriptive Statistics**", "**Homogeneity Tests**" and "**Estimates of effect size**" to get the following screen.

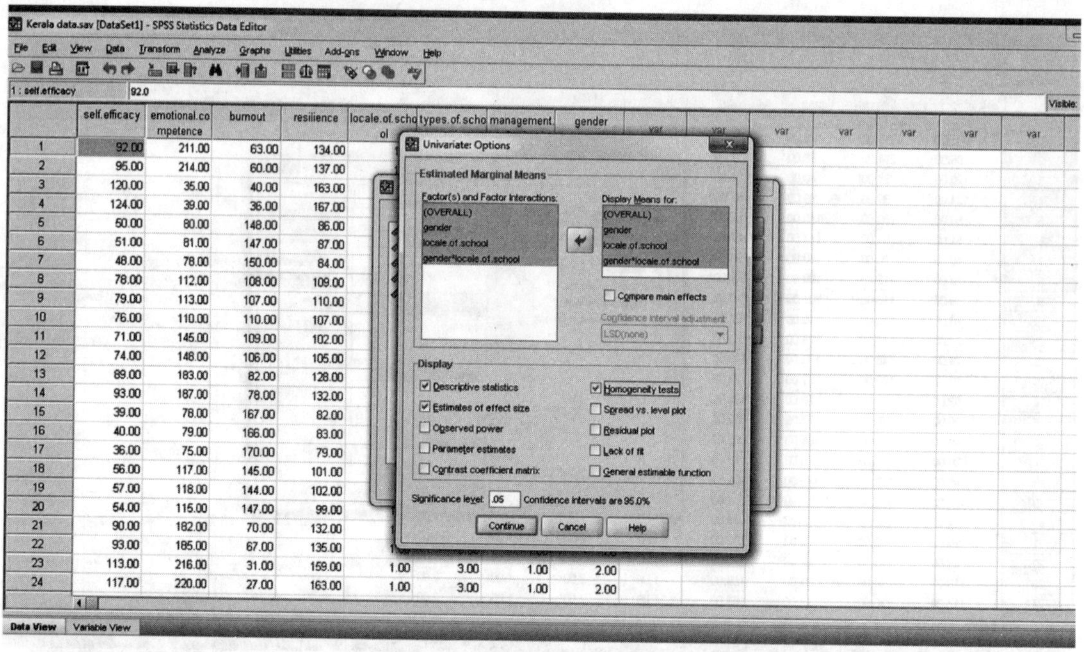

143. Click on "**Continue**" icon to get the following screen.

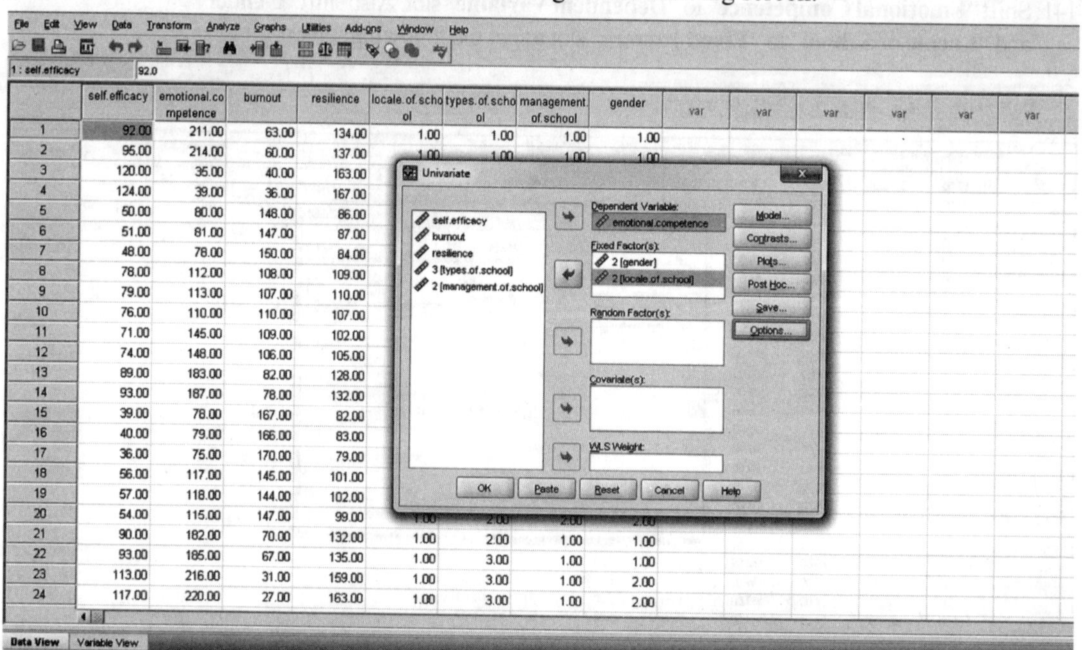

144. By clicking on "**Plots**" and shifting "**Locale of School**" under "**Horizontal Axis**" and "**Gender**" to "**Separate Lines**" and clicking on "**Add**" to get the following screen.

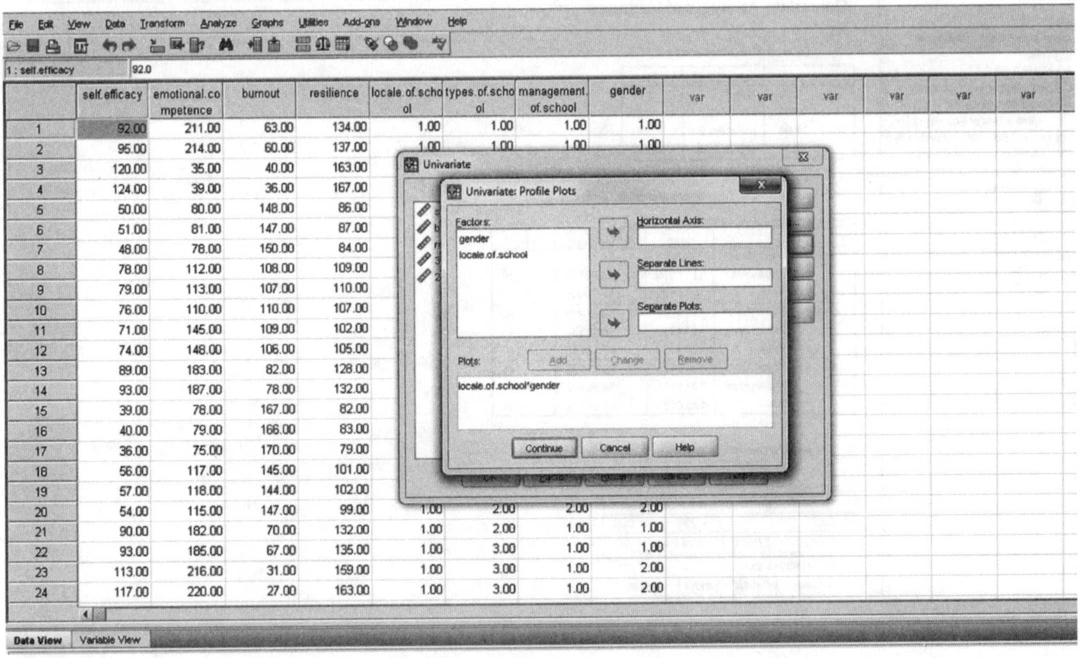

145. Click on "**Continue**" icon to get the following screen.

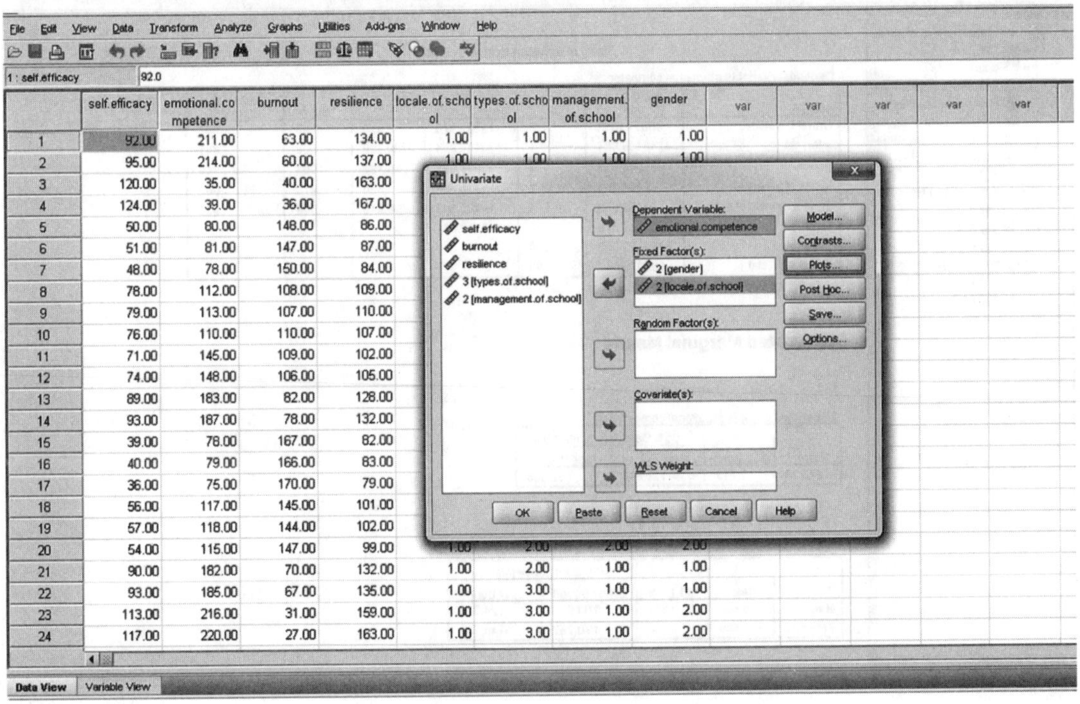

146. Click on "**OK**" to get the following outputs of Two Way ANOVA.

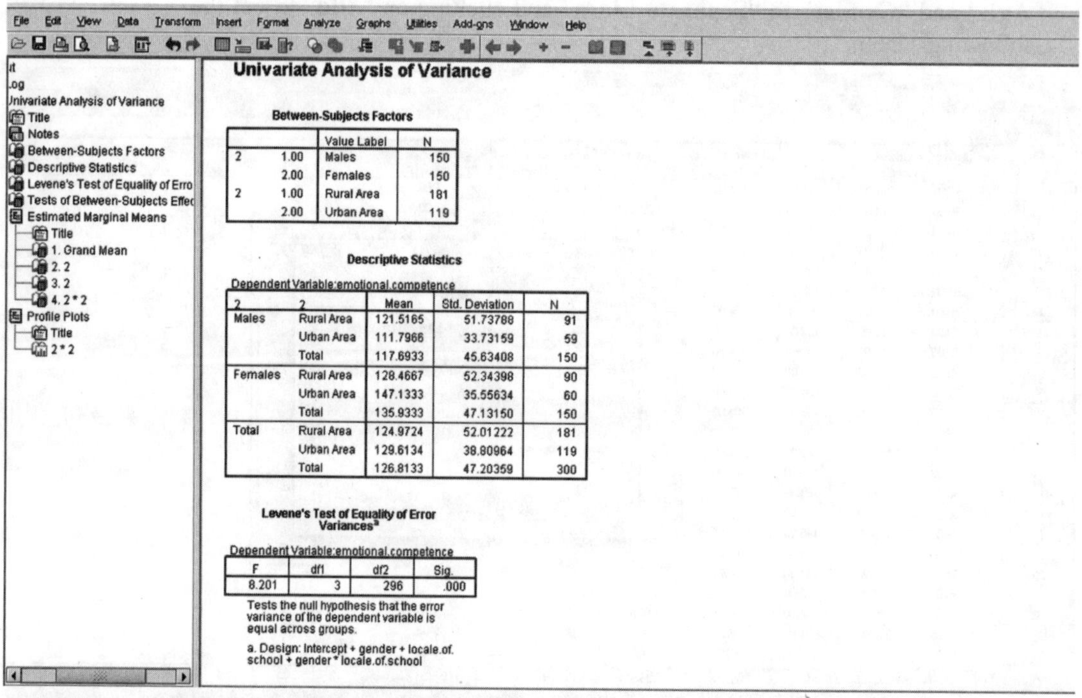

Univariate Analysis of Variance

Between-Subjects Factors

		Value Label	N
2	1.00	Males	150
	2.00	Females	150
2	1.00	Rural Area	181
	2.00	Urban Area	119

Descriptive Statistics

Dependent Variable:emotional.competence

2	2	Mean	Std. Deviation	N
Males	Rural Area	121.5165	51.73788	91
	Urban Area	111.7966	33.73159	59
	Total	117.6933	45.63408	150
Females	Rural Area	128.4667	52.34398	90
	Urban Area	147.1333	35.55634	60
	Total	135.9333	47.13150	150
Total	Rural Area	124.9724	52.01222	181
	Urban Area	129.6134	38.80964	119
	Total	126.8133	47.20359	300

Levene's Test of Equality of Error Variances[a]

Dependent Variable:emotional.competence

F	df1	df2	Sig.
8.201	3	296	.000

Tests the null hypothesis that the error variance of the dependent variable is equal across groups.

a. Design: Intercept + gender + locale.of.school + gender * locale.of.school

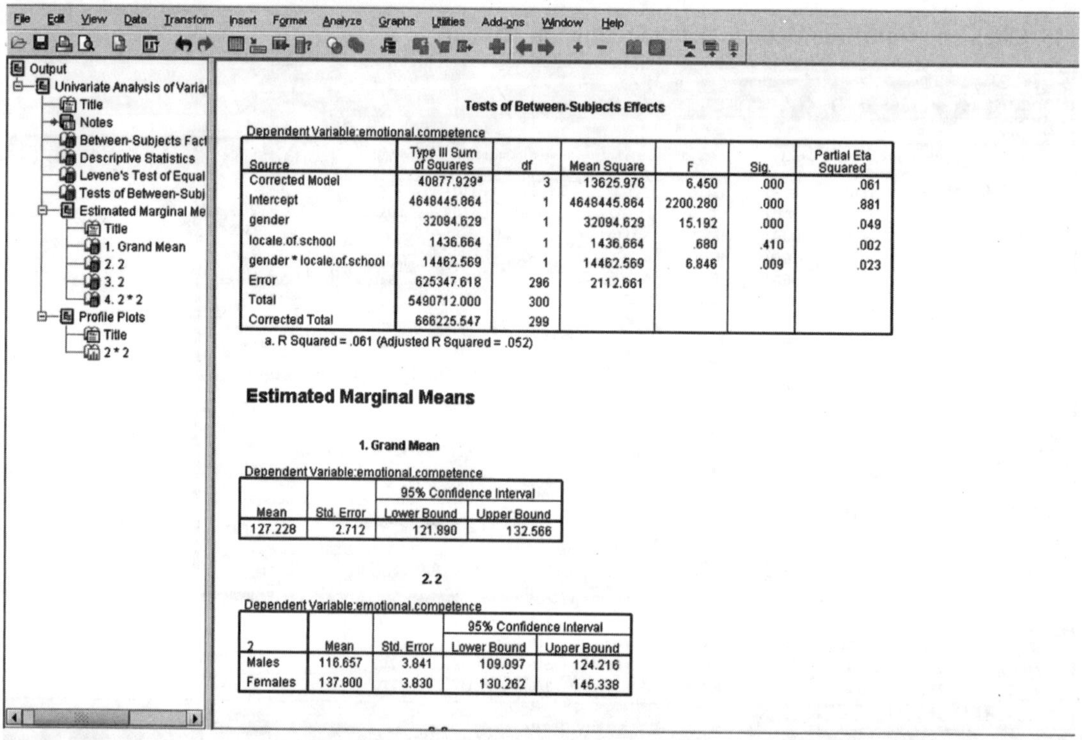

Tests of Between-Subjects Effects

Dependent Variable:emotional.competence

Source	Type III Sum of Squares	df	Mean Square	F	Sig.	Partial Eta Squared
Corrected Model	40877.929[a]	3	13625.976	6.450	.000	.061
Intercept	4648445.864	1	4648445.864	2200.280	.000	.881
gender	32094.629	1	32094.629	15.192	.000	.049
locale.of.school	1436.664	1	1436.664	.680	.410	.002
gender * locale.of.school	14462.569	1	14462.569	6.846	.009	.023
Error	625347.618	296	2112.661			
Total	5490712.000	300				
Corrected Total	666225.547	299				

a. R Squared = .061 (Adjusted R Squared = .052)

Estimated Marginal Means

1. Grand Mean

Dependent Variable:emotional.competence

Mean	Std. Error	95% Confidence Interval Lower Bound	95% Confidence Interval Upper Bound
127.228	2.712	121.890	132.566

2. 2

Dependent Variable:emotional.competence

2	Mean	Std. Error	95% Confidence Interval Lower Bound	95% Confidence Interval Upper Bound
Males	116.657	3.841	109.097	124.216
Females	137.800	3.830	130.262	145.338

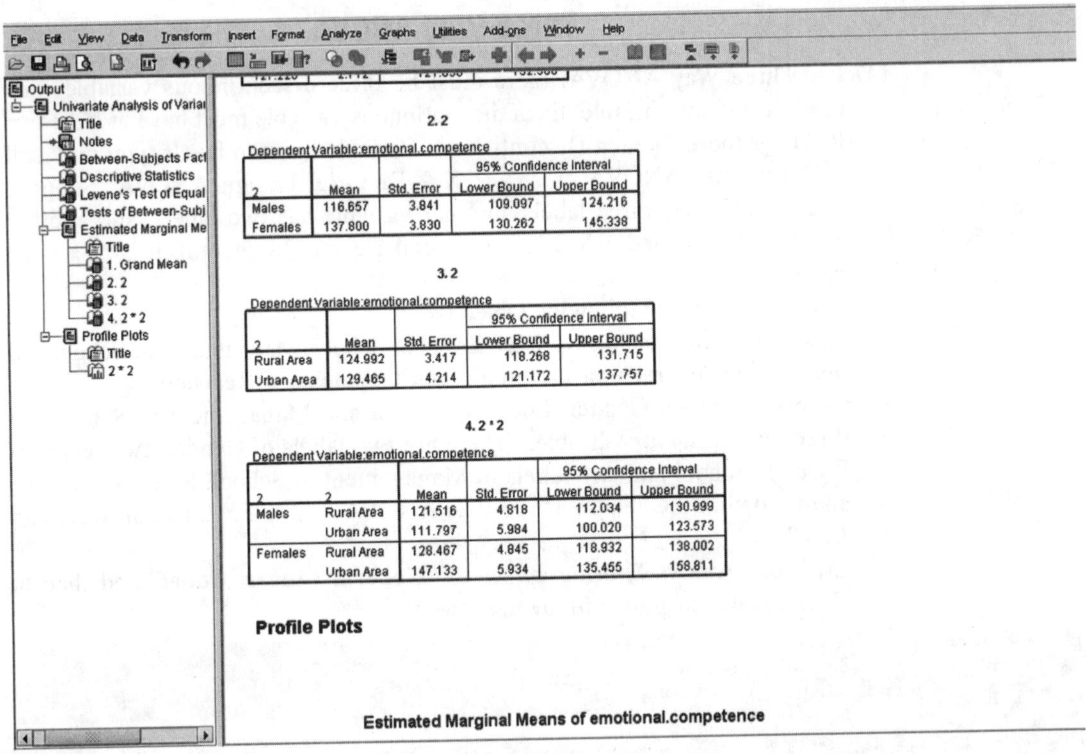

2.2

Dependent Variable:emotional.competence

2	Mean	Std. Error	95% Confidence Interval Lower Bound	Upper Bound
Males	116.657	3.841	109.097	124.216
Females	137.800	3.830	130.262	145.338

3.2

Dependent Variable:emotional.competence

2	Mean	Std. Error	95% Confidence Interval Lower Bound	Upper Bound
Rural Area	124.992	3.417	118.268	131.715
Urban Area	129.465	4.214	121.172	137.757

4.2 * 2

Dependent Variable:emotional.competence

2	2	Mean	Std. Error	95% Confidence Interval Lower Bound	Upper Bound
Males	Rural Area	121.516	4.818	112.034	130.999
	Urban Area	111.797	5.984	100.020	123.573
Females	Rural Area	128.467	4.845	118.932	138.002
	Urban Area	147.133	5.934	135.455	158.811

Profile Plots

Estimated Marginal Means of emotional.competence

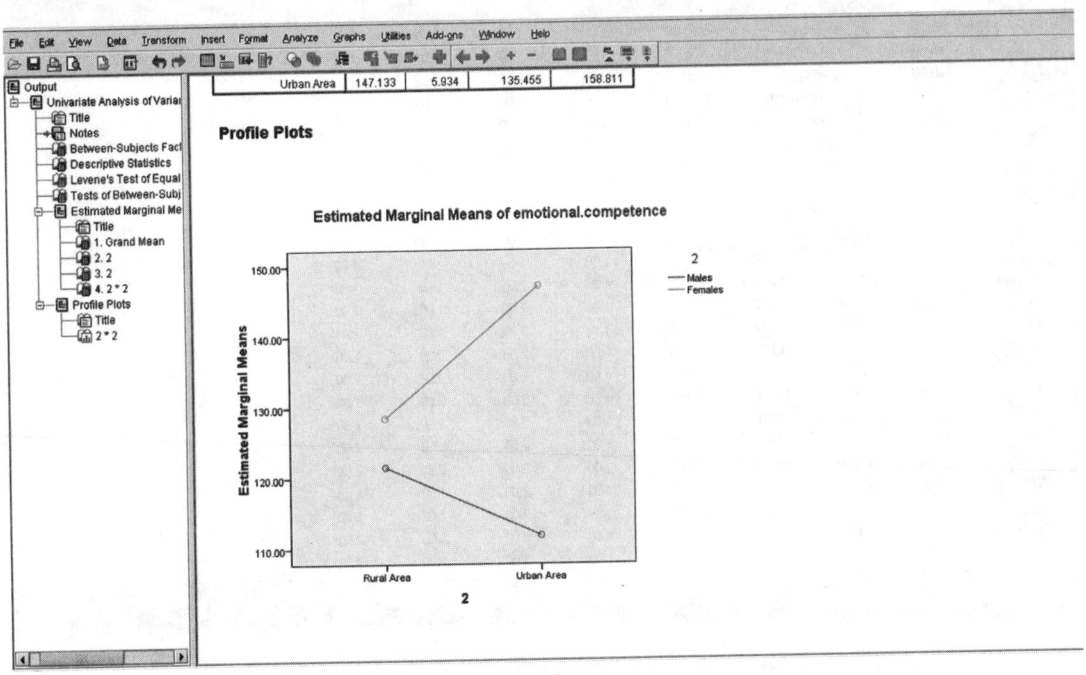

For interpretation of Two Way ANOVA results, you may refer to book by D.N.Sansanwal, Research Methodology and Applied Statistic, Shipra Publishers, Delhi, 2020.

Three Way ANOVA

147. For Three Way ANOVA, there must be three discontinuous variables and one continuous variable. Each discontinuous variable must have at least two labels or more. If each Discontinuous Variable has two levels, you may call it Three Way ANOVA or 2 X 2 X 2 Factorial Design ANOVA. Suppose one variable has three labels, another variable has two labels, and another 4 labels, it is called 3 X 2 X 4 Factorial Design. In general, it is m x n x l Factorial Design.

Let us consider the following Objective:

To study the influence of Gender, Local of School, Management of School and their various interactions on Emotional Competence of Teachers.

In this objective, Gender, Local of School and Management of School are three discontinuous variables. There are two labels of Gender, two levels of Local of School and two labels of Management of School. So data are to be analysed with the help of Three Way ANOVA or 2 X 2 X 2 Factorial Design ANOVA.

Click on "**Analyse**", bring curser to "**General Linear Model**" and then to "**Univariate**" to get the following screen.

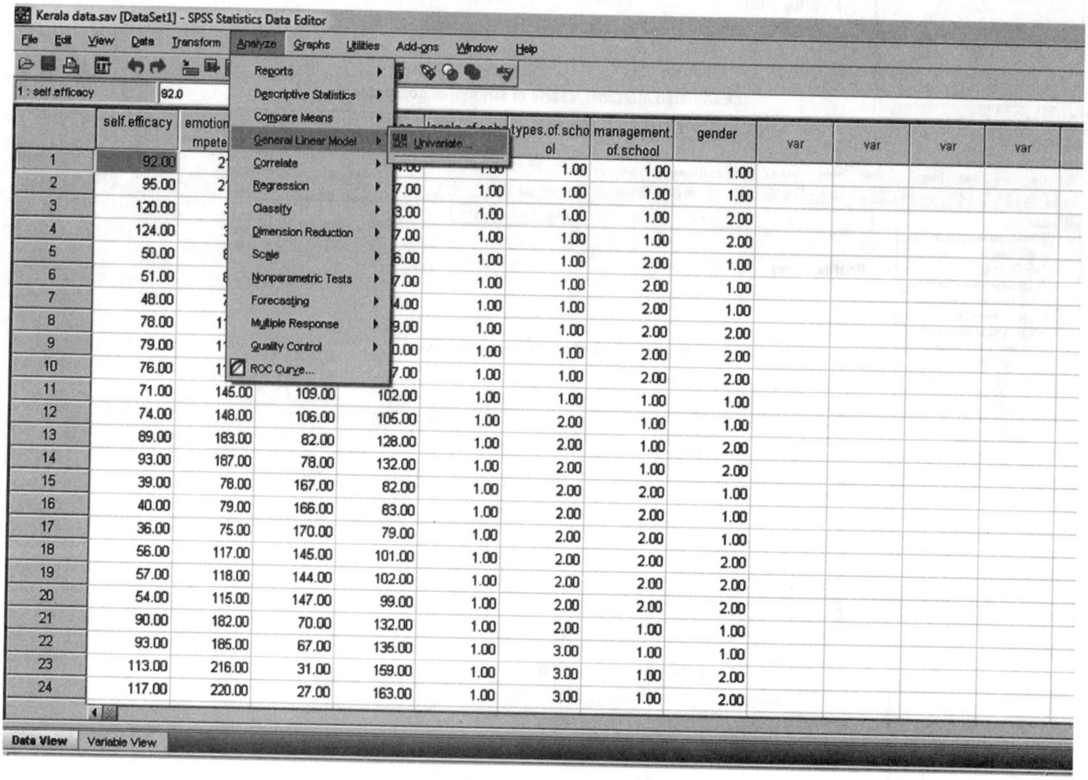

148. Click on "**Univariate**" to get the following screen.

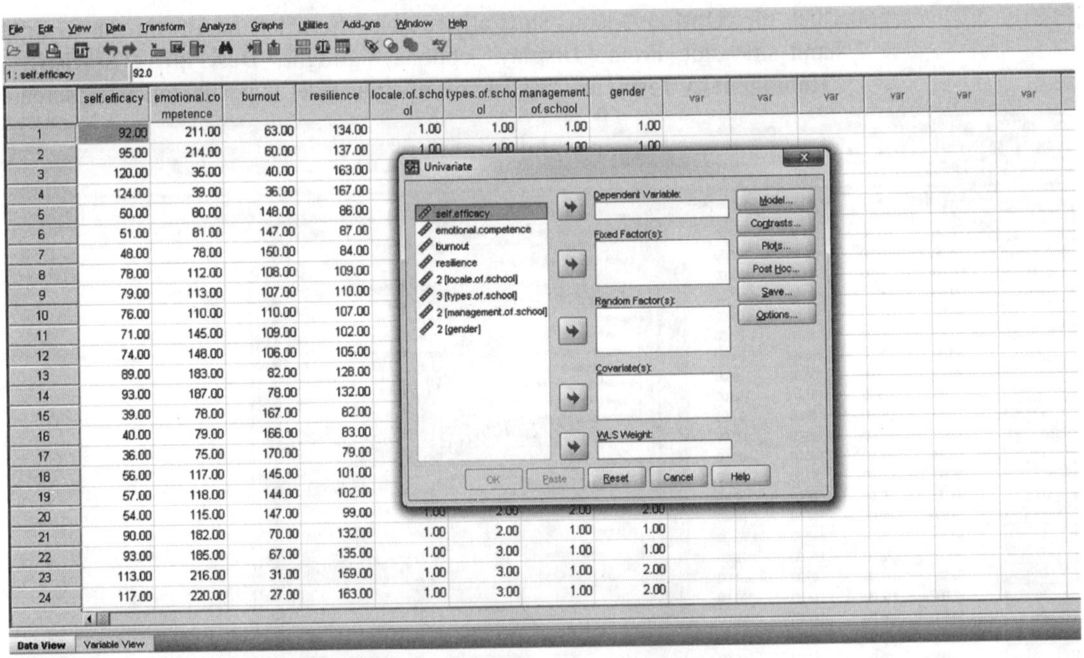

149. Shift "**Emotional Competence**" under "**Dependent Variable**" slot. Also shift "**Gender**", "**Locale of School**" and "**Management of School**" under "**Fixed Factor(s)**" box to get the following screen.

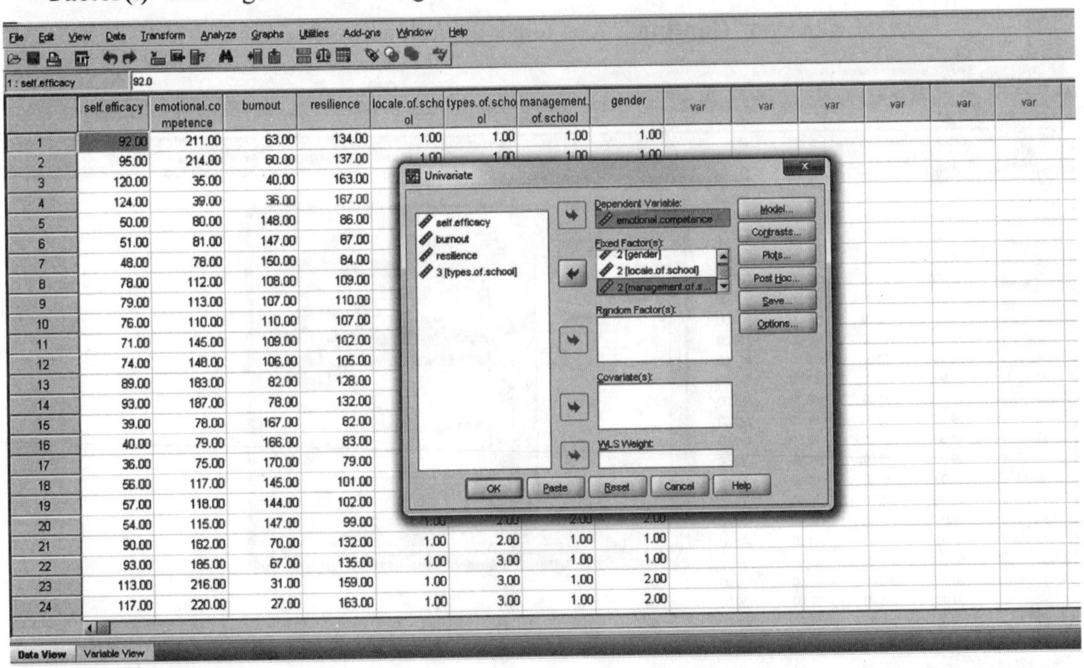

150. Click on "**Options**" icon. Shift all variables from left hand side slot to right hand side slot. From "**Display**" options highlight "**Descriptive Statistics**", "**Homogeneity Tests**" and "**Estimates of effect size**" to get the following screen.

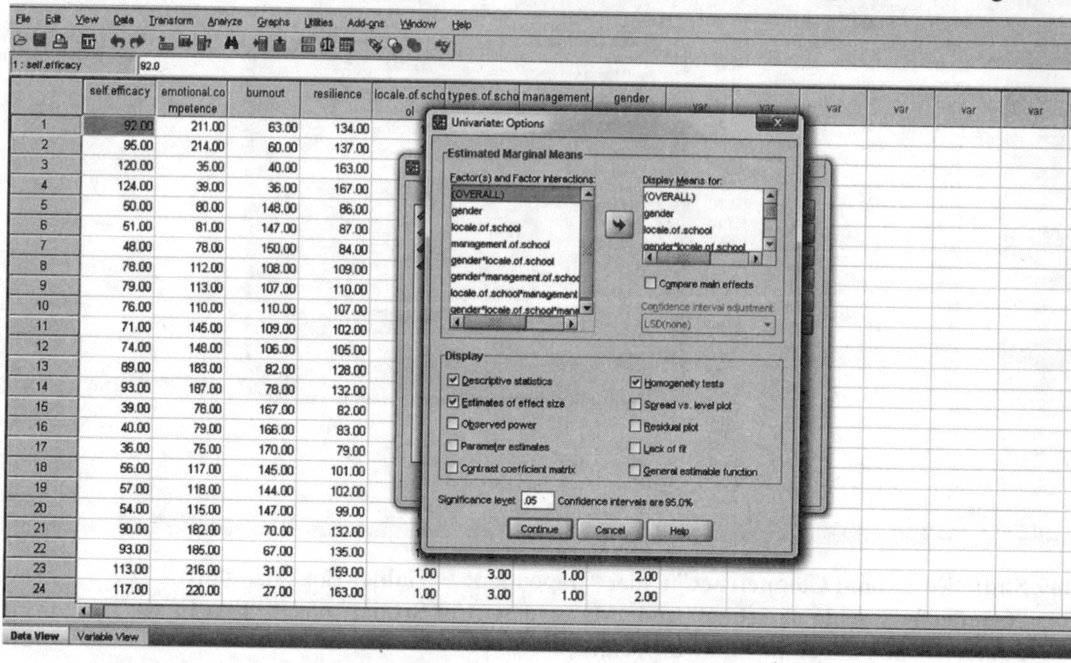

151. Click on "**Continue**" icon to get the following screen.

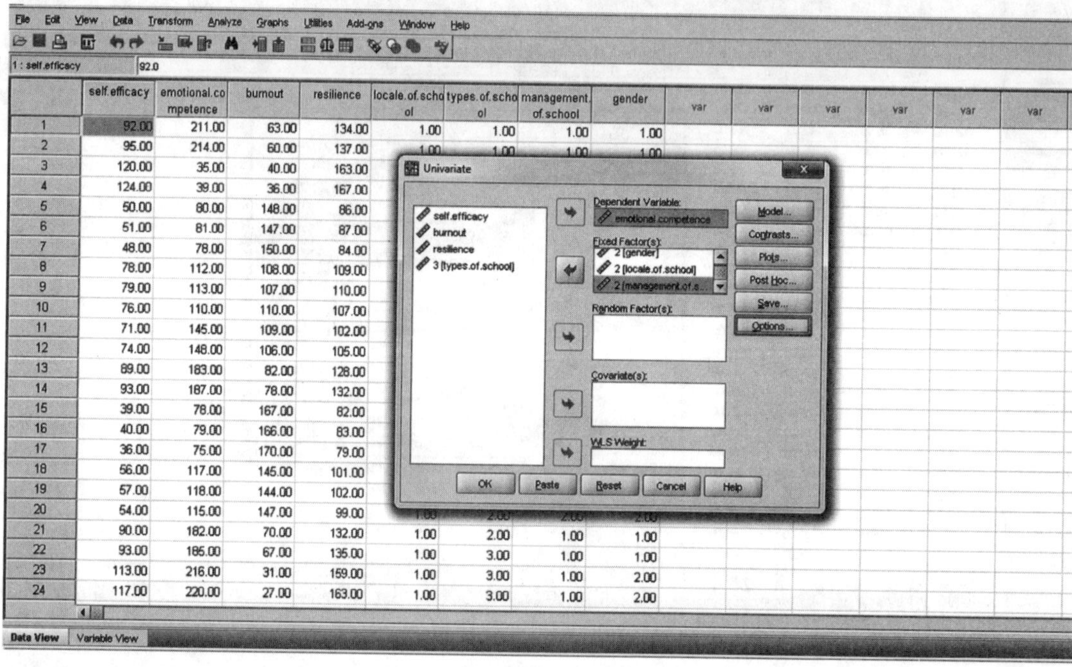

152. As there are two labels of each discontinuous variable, there is no need of any "**Post Hoc Test**". There might be interactions between and among discontinuous variables, so click on "**Plots**" to get the following screen.

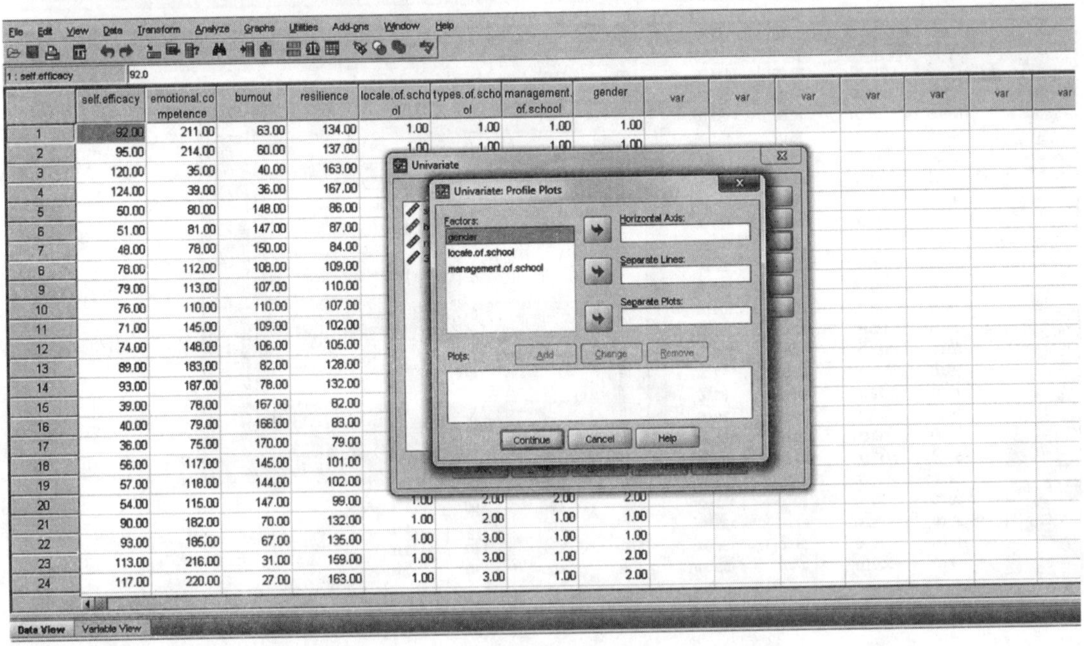

153. Shift "**Types of School**" variable to "**Horizontal Axis**" and "**Gender**" variable to "**Separate Lines**" to get the following screen. You may decide which variable is to be shifted to which slot.

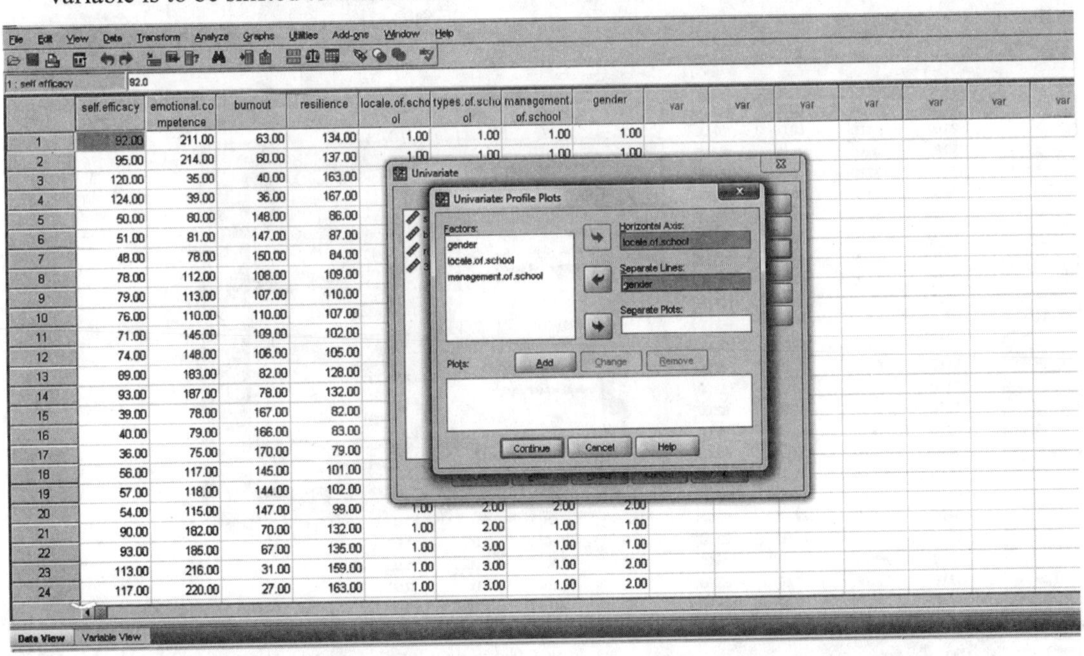

154. Click on "**Add**" icon to get the following screen.

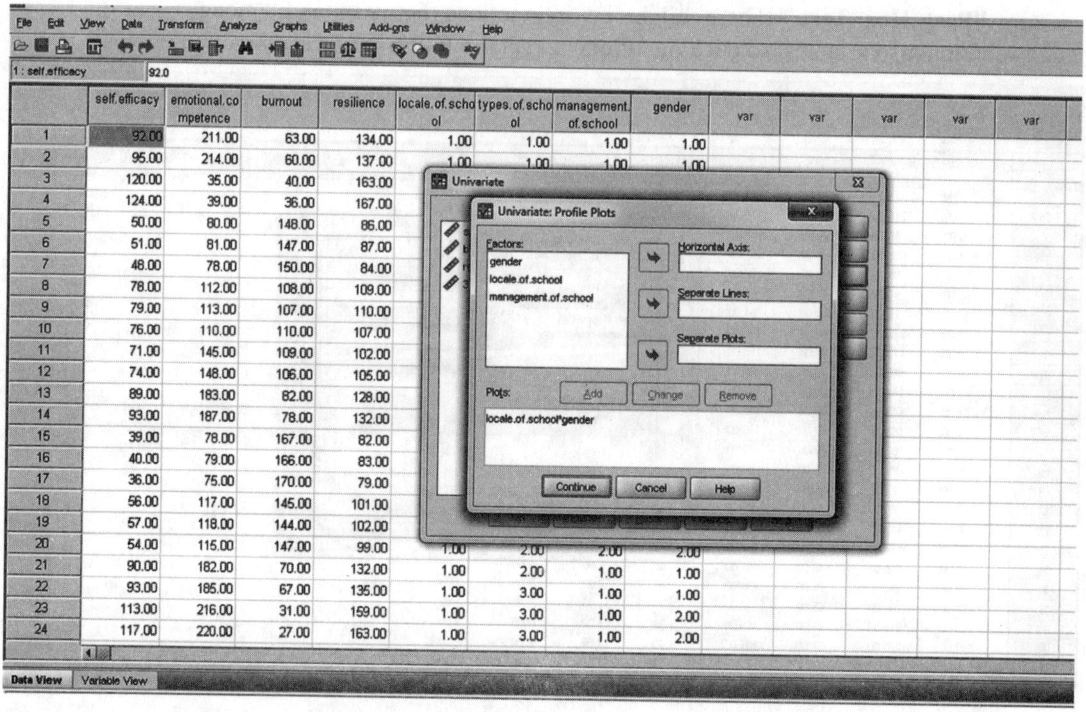

155. Shift "**Management School**" to "**Horizontal Axis**" and "**Gender**" to "**Separate Lines**" slots to get the following screen.

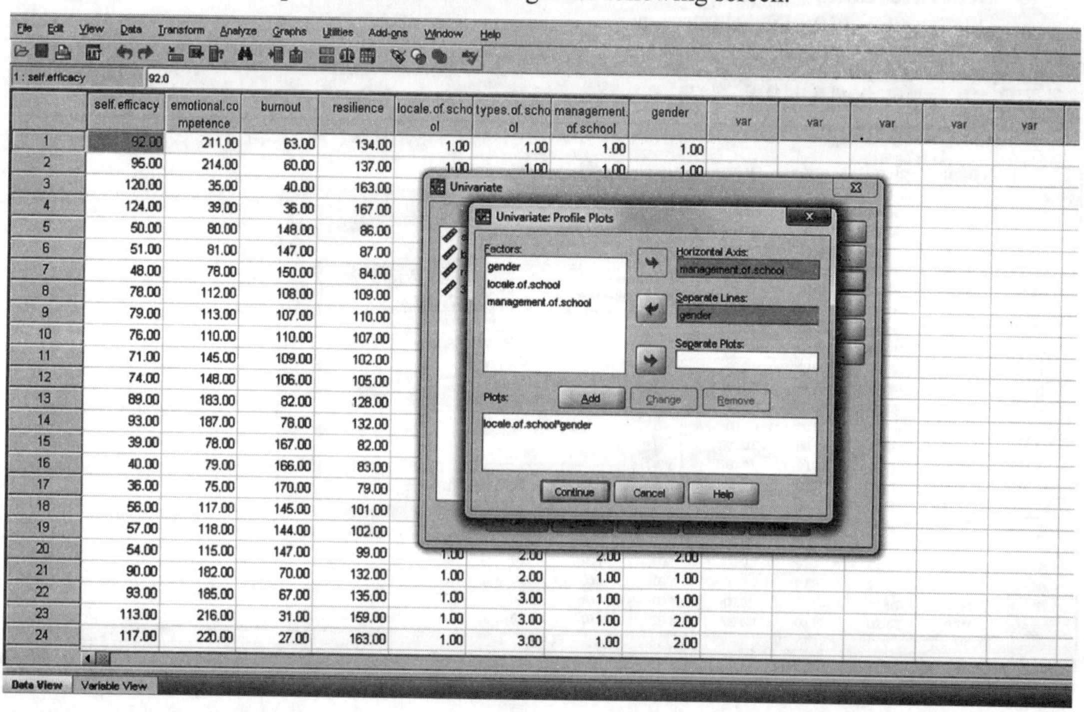

156. Click on "**Add**" to get the following screen.

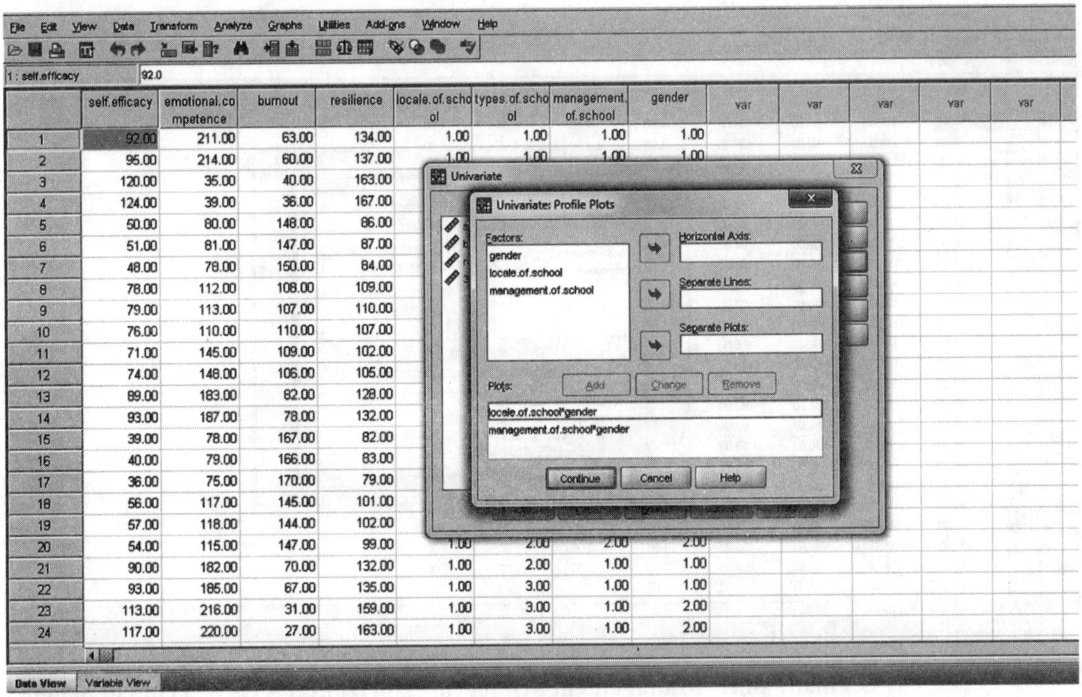

157. Shift "**Management School**" to "**Horizontal Axis**" and "**Types of School**" to "**Separate Lines**" slot to get the following screen.

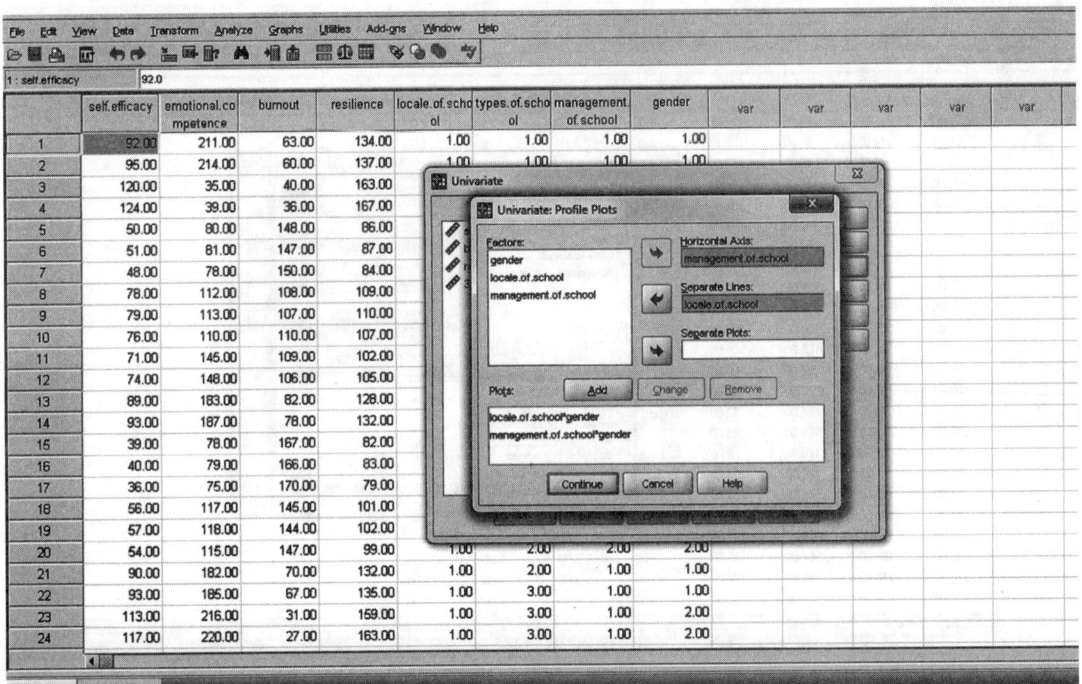

158. Click on "**Add**" to get the following screen.

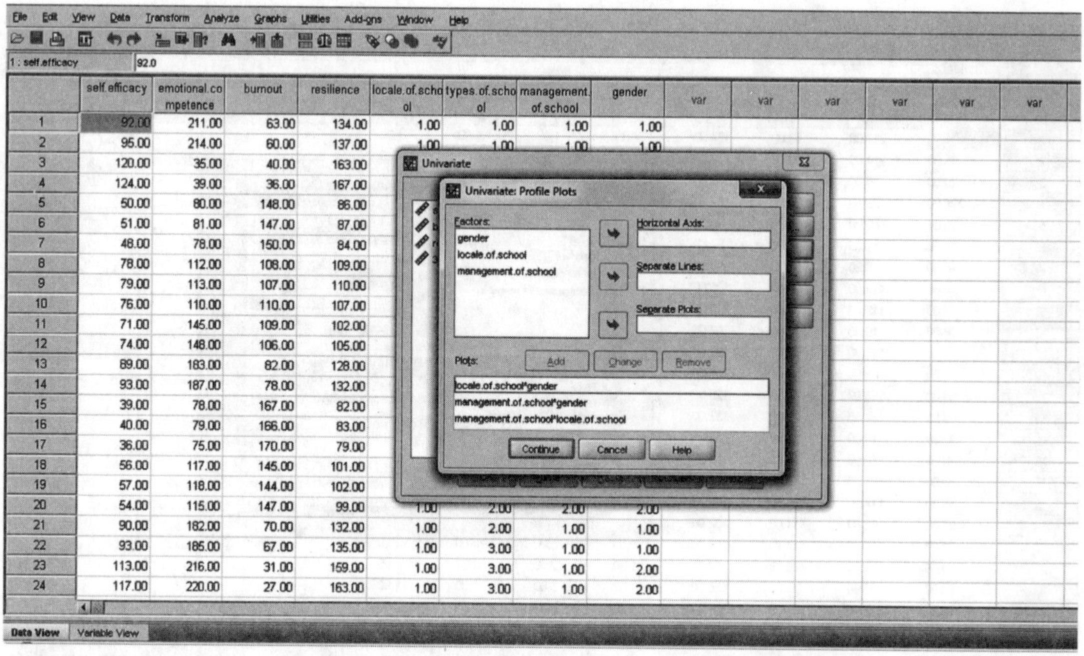

159. Finally shift "**Management School**" to "**Horizontal Axis**", "**Types of School**" to "**Separate Lines**" and "**Gender**" to "**Separate Plots**" slots to get the following screen.

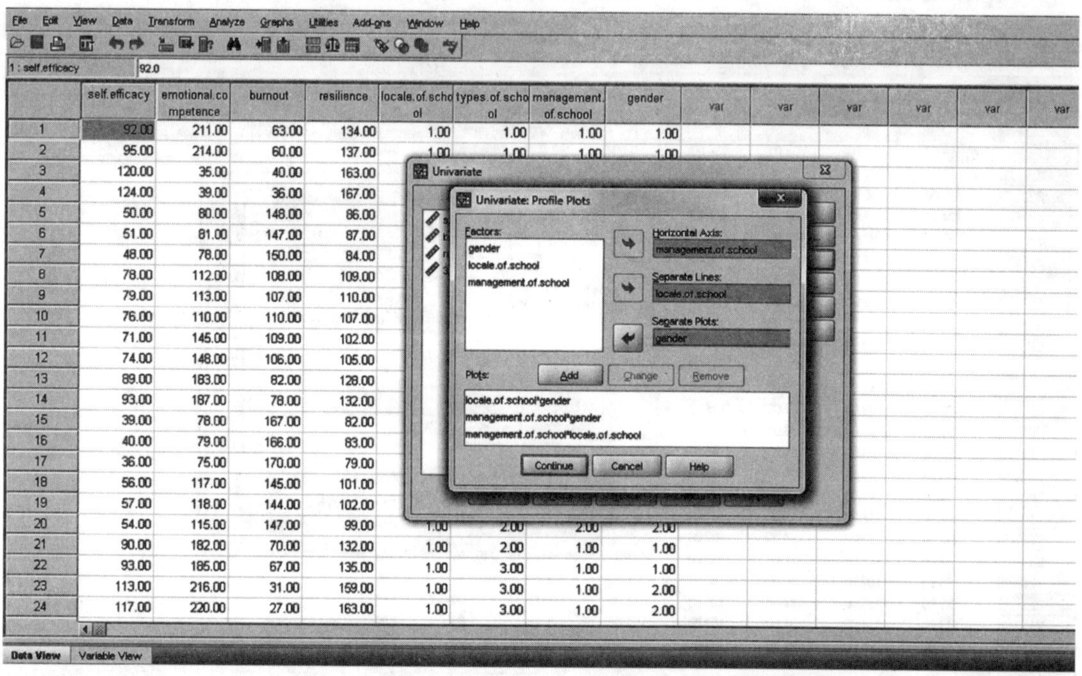

160. Click on "**Add**" to get the following screen.

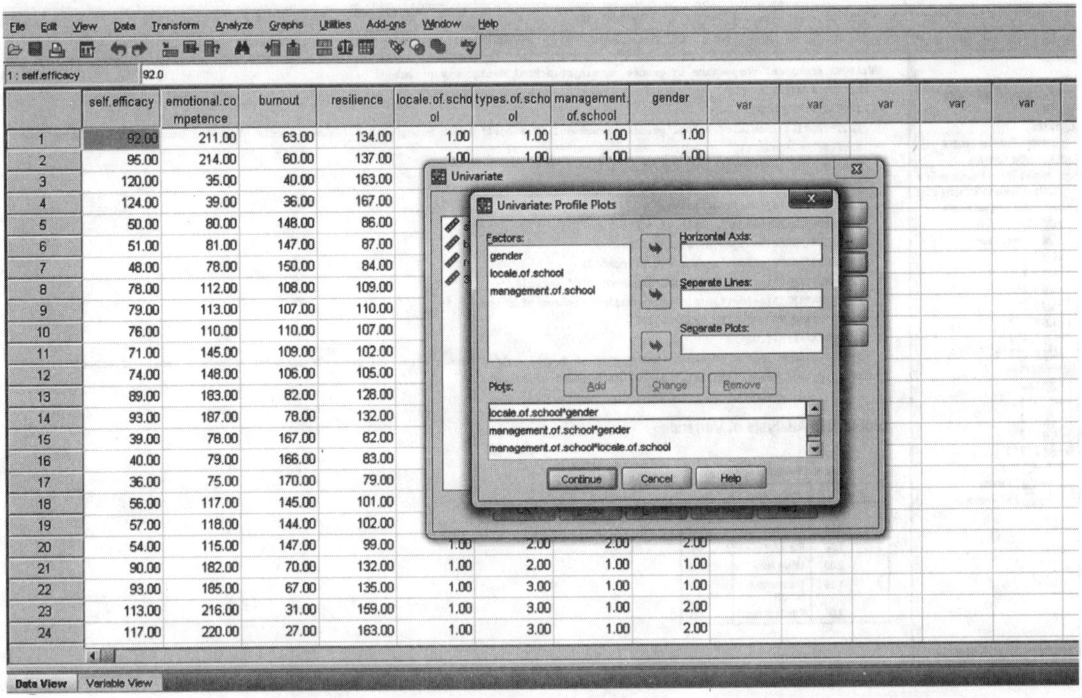

161. Click on "**Continue**" icon to get the following screen.

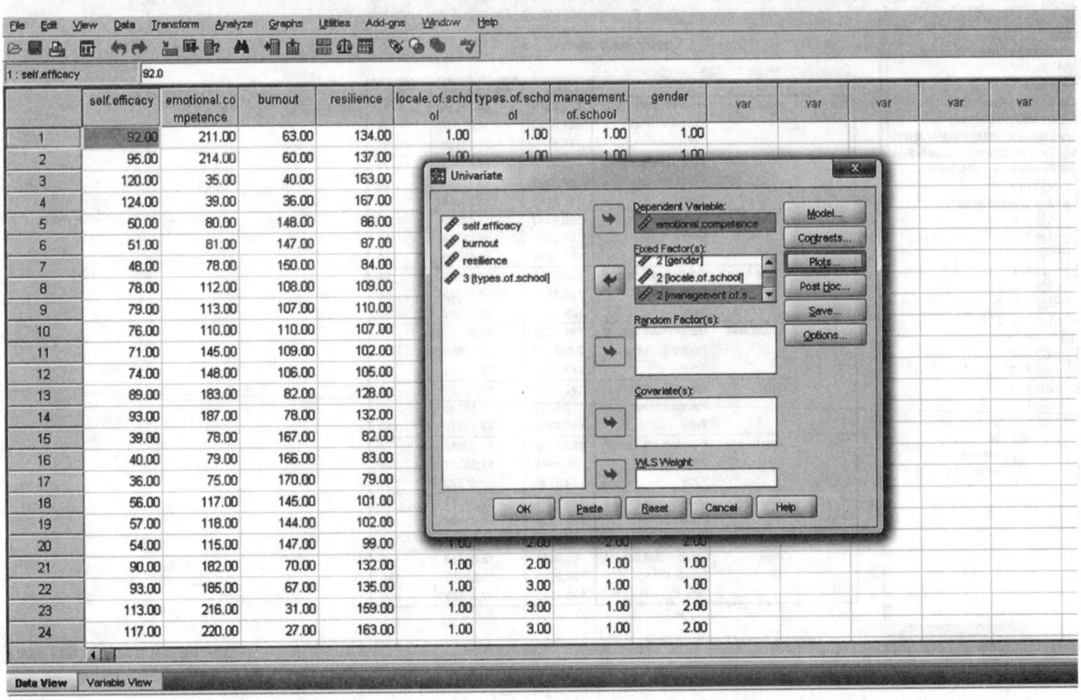

162. Click on "**OK**" to get the following outputs of Three Way ANOVA.

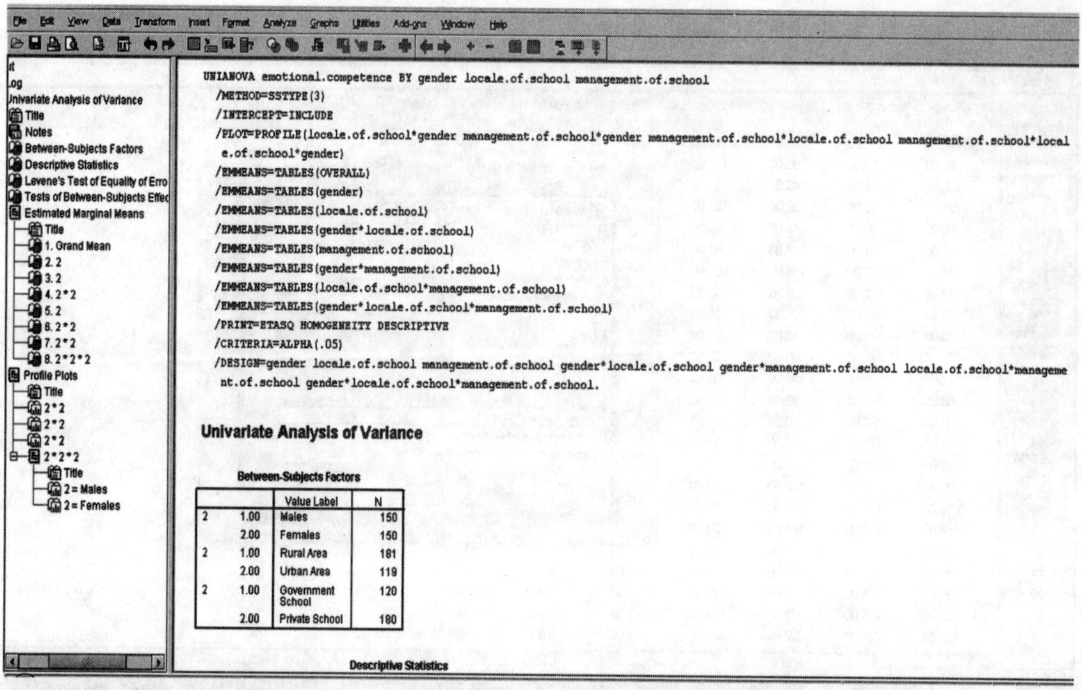

```
UNIANOVA emotional.competence BY gender locale.of.school management.of.school
  /METHOD=SSTYPE(3)
  /INTERCEPT=INCLUDE
  /PLOT=PROFILE(locale.of.school*gender management.of.school*gender management.of.school*locale.of.school management.of.school*local
   e.of.school*gender)
  /EMMEANS=TABLES(OVERALL)
  /EMMEANS=TABLES(gender)
  /EMMEANS=TABLES(locale.of.school)
  /EMMEANS=TABLES(gender*locale.of.school)
  /EMMEANS=TABLES(management.of.school)
  /EMMEANS=TABLES(gender*management.of.school)
  /EMMEANS=TABLES(locale.of.school*management.of.school)
  /EMMEANS=TABLES(gender*locale.of.school*management.of.school)
  /PRINT=ETASQ HOMOGENEITY DESCRIPTIVE
  /CRITERIA=ALPHA(.05)
  /DESIGN=gender locale.of.school management.of.school gender*locale.of.school gender*management.of.school locale.of.school*manageme
   nt.of.school gender*locale.of.school*management.of.school.
```

Univariate Analysis of Variance

Between-Subjects Factors

		Value Label	N
2	1.00	Males	150
	2.00	Females	150
2	1.00	Rural Area	181
	2.00	Urban Area	119
2	1.00	Government School	120
	2.00	Private School	180

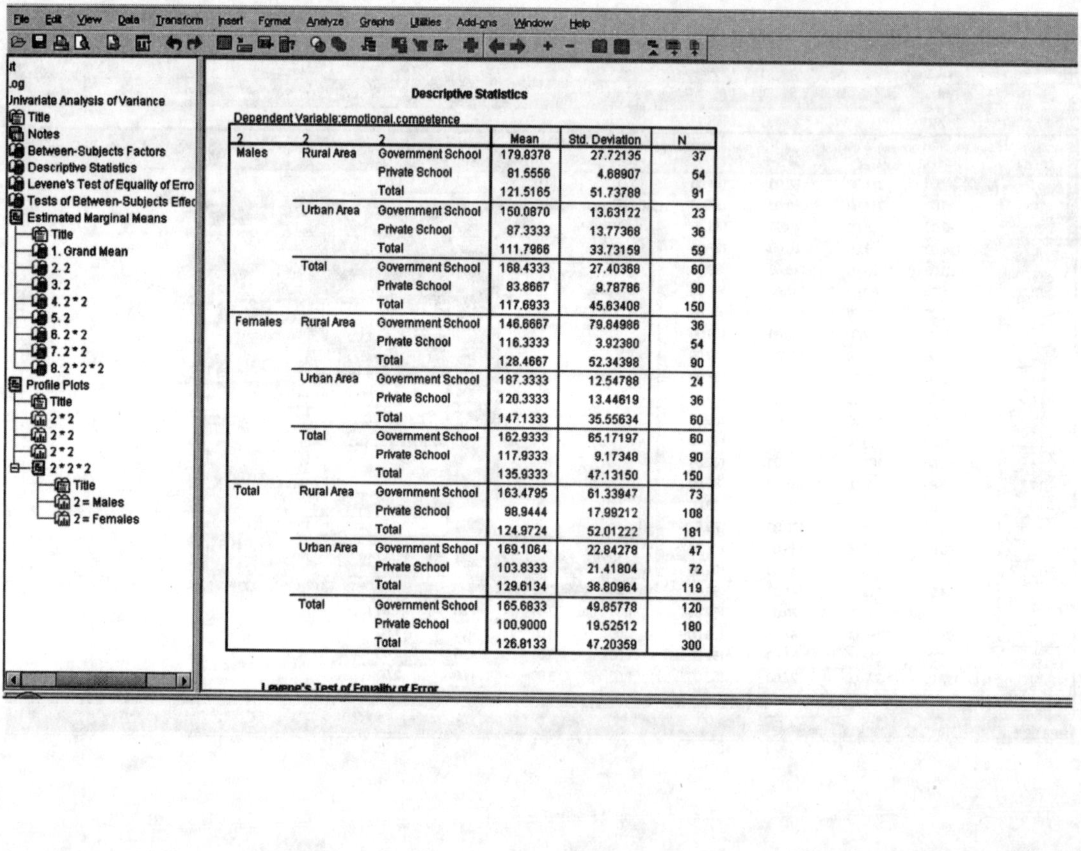

Descriptive Statistics

Dependent Variable:emotional.competence

2	2	2	Mean	Std. Deviation	N
Males	Rural Area	Government School	179.8378	27.72135	37
		Private School	81.5556	4.68907	54
		Total	121.5165	51.73788	91
	Urban Area	Government School	150.0870	13.63122	23
		Private School	87.3333	13.77368	36
		Total	111.7966	33.73159	59
	Total	Government School	168.4333	27.40368	60
		Private School	83.8667	9.78786	90
		Total	117.6933	45.63408	150
Females	Rural Area	Government School	146.6667	79.84986	36
		Private School	116.3333	3.92380	54
		Total	128.4667	52.34398	90
	Urban Area	Government School	187.3333	12.54788	24
		Private School	120.3333	13.44619	36
		Total	147.1333	35.55634	60
	Total	Government School	162.9333	65.17197	60
		Private School	117.9333	9.17348	90
		Total	135.9333	47.13150	150
Total	Rural Area	Government School	163.4795	61.33947	73
		Private School	98.9444	17.99212	108
		Total	124.9724	52.01222	181
	Urban Area	Government School	169.1064	22.84278	47
		Private School	103.8333	21.41804	72
		Total	129.6134	38.80964	119
	Total	Government School	165.6833	49.85778	120
		Private School	100.9000	19.52512	180
		Total	126.8133	47.20359	300

Levene's Test of Equality of Error

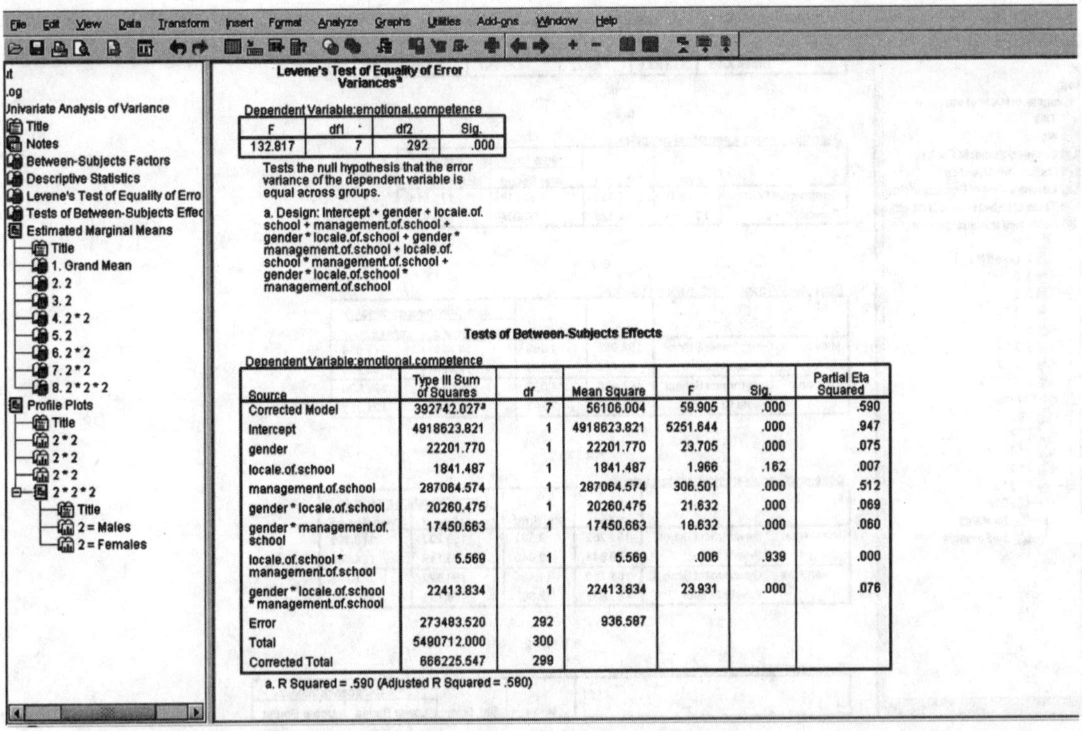

Levene's Test of Equality of Error Variances[a]

Dependent Variable:emotional.competence

F	df1	df2	Sig.
132.817	7	292	.000

Tests the null hypothesis that the error variance of the dependent variable is equal across groups.

a. Design: Intercept + gender + locale.of.school + management.of.school + gender * locale.of.school + gender * management.of.school + locale.of.school * management.of.school + gender * locale.of.school * management.of.school

Tests of Between-Subjects Effects

Dependent Variable:emotional.competence

Source	Type III Sum of Squares	df	Mean Square	F	Sig.	Partial Eta Squared
Corrected Model	392742.027[a]	7	56106.004	59.905	.000	.590
Intercept	4918623.821	1	4918623.821	5251.644	.000	.947
gender	22201.770	1	22201.770	23.705	.000	.075
locale.of.school	1841.487	1	1841.487	1.966	.162	.007
management.of.school	287064.574	1	287064.574	306.501	.000	.512
gender * locale.of.school	20260.475	1	20260.475	21.632	.000	.069
gender * management.of.school	17450.663	1	17450.663	18.632	.000	.060
locale.of.school * management.of.school	5.569	1	5.569	.006	.939	.000
gender * locale.of.school * management.of.school	22413.834	1	22413.834	23.931	.000	.076
Error	273483.520	292	936.587			
Total	5490712.000	300				
Corrected Total	666225.547	299				

a. R Squared = .590 (Adjusted R Squared = .580)

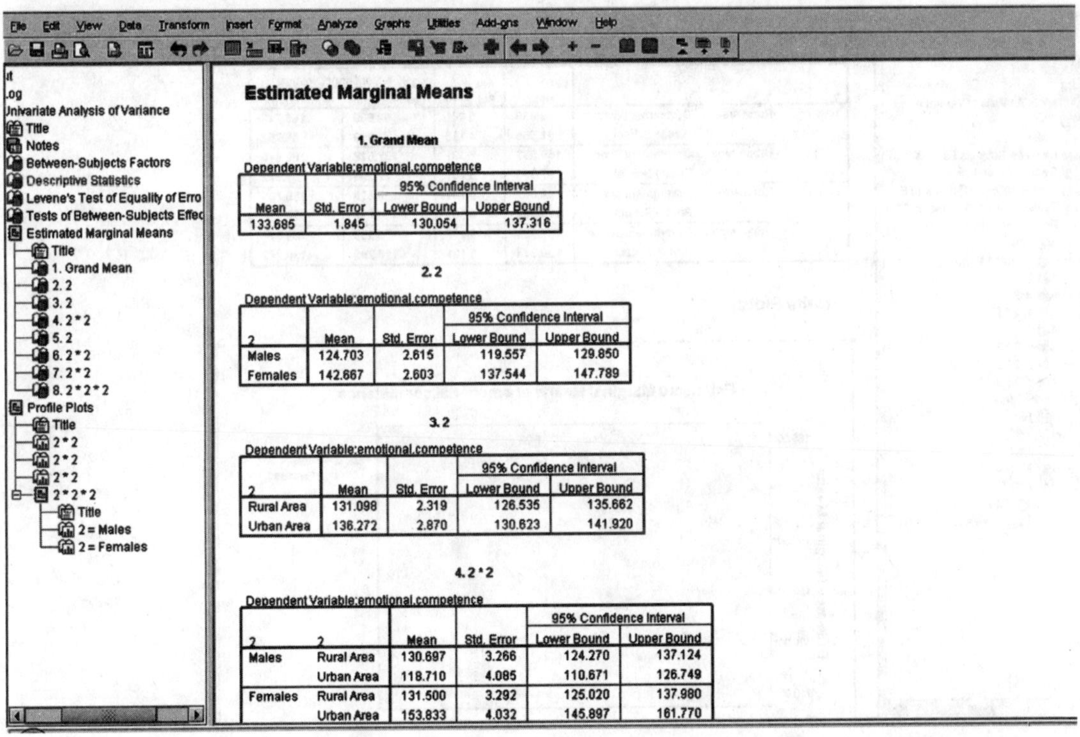

Estimated Marginal Means

1. Grand Mean

Dependent Variable:emotional.competence

Mean	Std. Error	95% Confidence Interval Lower Bound	95% Confidence Interval Upper Bound
133.685	1.845	130.054	137.316

2.2

Dependent Variable:emotional.competence

2	Mean	Std. Error	95% Confidence Interval Lower Bound	95% Confidence Interval Upper Bound
Males	124.703	2.615	119.557	129.850
Females	142.667	2.603	137.544	147.789

3.2

Dependent Variable:emotional.competence

2	Mean	Std. Error	95% Confidence Interval Lower Bound	95% Confidence Interval Upper Bound
Rural Area	131.098	2.319	126.535	135.662
Urban Area	136.272	2.870	130.623	141.920

4.2 * 2

Dependent Variable:emotional.competence

2	2	Mean	Std. Error	95% Confidence Interval Lower Bound	95% Confidence Interval Upper Bound
Males	Rural Area	130.697	3.266	124.270	137.124
	Urban Area	118.710	4.085	110.671	126.749
Females	Rural Area	131.500	3.292	125.020	137.980
	Urban Area	153.833	4.032	145.897	161.770

	Urban Area	153.833	4.032	145.897	161.770

5. 2

Dependent Variable:emotional.competence

2	Mean	Std. Error	95% Confidence Interval Lower Bound	Upper Bound
Government School	165.981	2.862	160.348	171.614
Private School	101.389	2.328	96.807	105.971

6. 2 * 2

Dependent Variable:emotional.competence

2	2	Mean	Std. Error	95% Confidence Interval Lower Bound	Upper Bound
Males	Government School	164.962	4.063	156.966	172.959
	Private School	84.444	3.292	77.965	90.924
Females	Government School	167.000	4.032	159.064	174.936
	Private School	118.333	3.292	111.853	124.813

7. 2 * 2

Dependent Variable:emotional.competence

2	2	Mean	Std. Error	95% Confidence Interval Lower Bound	Upper Bound
Rural Area	Government School	163.252	3.582	156.202	170.303
	Private School	98.944	2.945	93.149	104.740
Urban Area	Government School	168.710	4.465	159.922	177.498
	Private School	103.833	3.607	96.735	110.932

8. 2 * 2 * 2

Dependent Variable:emotional.competence

2	2	2	Mean	Std. Error	95% Confidence Interval Lower Bound	Upper Bound
Males	Rural Area	Government School	179.838	5.031	169.936	189.740
		Private School	81.556	4.165	73.359	89.752
	Urban Area	Government School	150.087	6.381	137.528	162.646
		Private School	87.333	5.101	77.295	97.372
Females	Rural Area	Government School	146.667	5.101	136.628	156.705
		Private School	116.333	4.165	108.137	124.530
	Urban Area	Government School	187.333	6.247	175.039	199.628
		Private School	120.333	5.101	110.295	130.372

Profile Plots

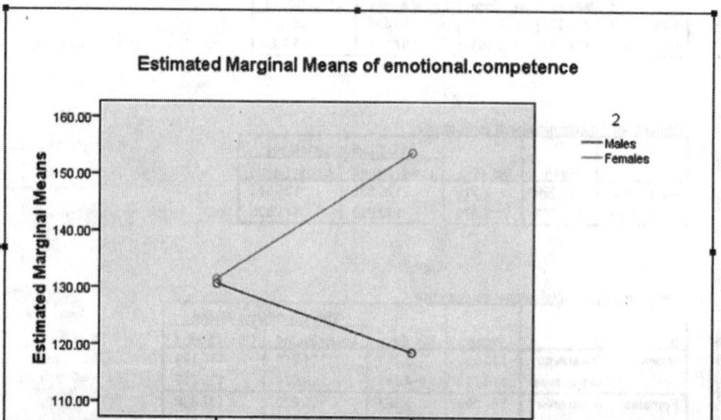

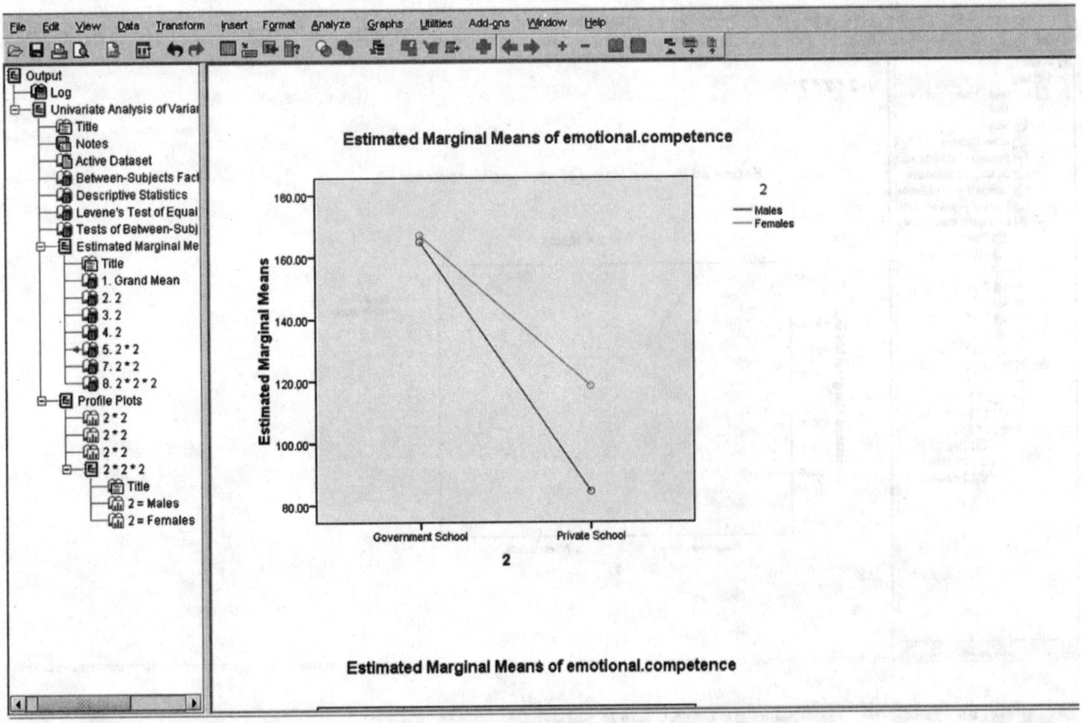
File Edit View Data Transform Insert Format Analyze Graphs Utilities Add-ons Window Help
Output
Log
Univariate Analysis of Variar
Title
Notes
Active Dataset
Between-Subjects Fact
Descriptive Statistics
Levene's Test of Equal
Tests of Between-Subj
Estimated Marginal Me
Title
1. Grand Mean
2. 2
3. 2
4. 2
5. 2 * 2
7. 2 * 2
8. 2 * 2 * 2
Profile Plots
2 * 2
2 * 2
2 * 2
2 * 2 * 2
Title
2 = Males
2 = Females
Estimated Marginal Means of emotional.competence
2
Males
Females
Estimated Marginal Means
180.00
160.00
140.00
120.00
100.00
80.00
Government School
Private School
2
Estimated Marginal Means of emotional.competence

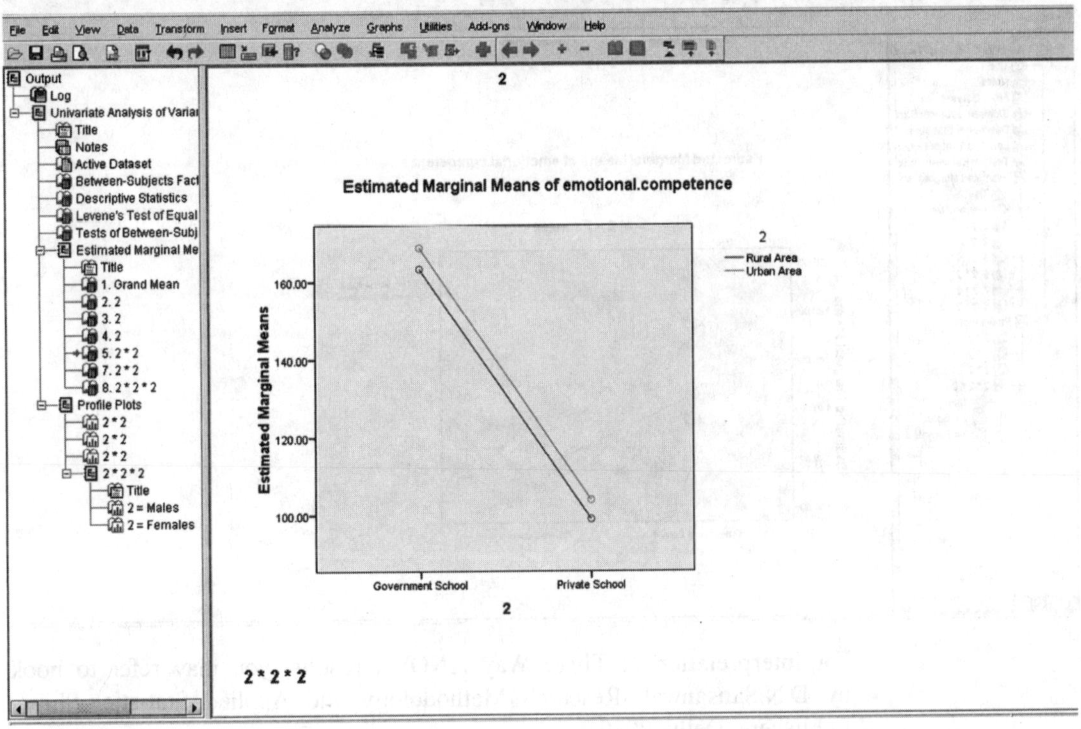
File Edit View Data Transform Insert Format Analyze Graphs Utilities Add-ons Window Help
Output
Log
Univariate Analysis of Variar
Title
Notes
Active Dataset
Between-Subjects Fact
Descriptive Statistics
Levene's Test of Equal
Tests of Between-Subj
Estimated Marginal Me
Title
1. Grand Mean
2. 2
3. 2
4. 2
5. 2 * 2
7. 2 * 2
8. 2 * 2 * 2
Profile Plots
2 * 2
2 * 2
2 * 2
2 * 2 * 2
Title
2 = Males
2 = Females
2
Estimated Marginal Means of emotional.competence
2
Rural Area
Urban Area
Estimated Marginal Means
160.00
140.00
120.00
100.00
Government School
Private School
2
2 * 2 * 2

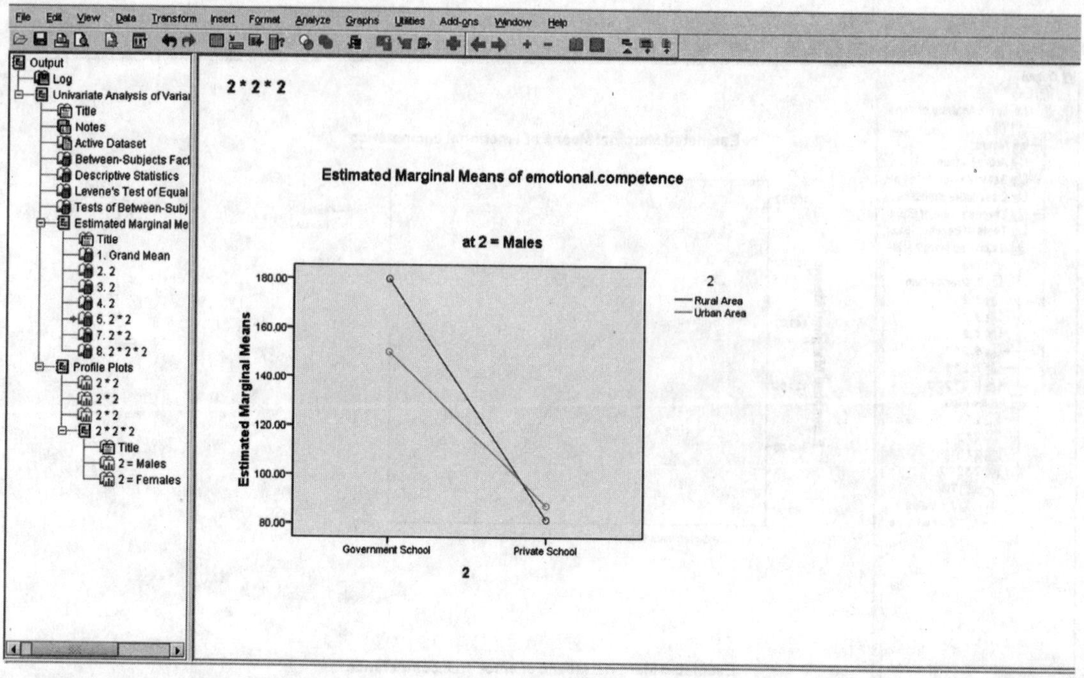

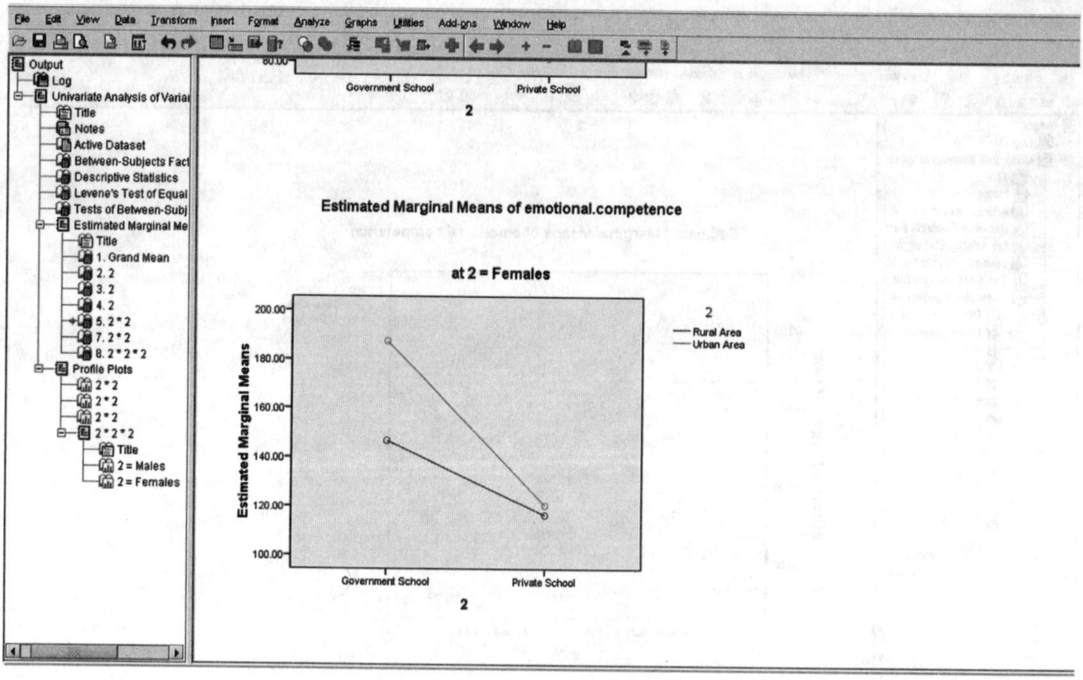

For interpretation of Three Way ANOVA results, you may refer to book by D.N.Sansanwal, Research Methodology and Applied Statistic, Shipra Publishers, Delhi, 2020.

One Way ANCOVA

163. In research there might be intervening variables which need to be controlled. There are many methods of controlling intervening variables. One of the methods is Statistical Control. Only continuous intervening variables can be controlled through the use of Statistical Techniques. Intervening variable that can be controlled through the use of Statistical Technique is called **Covariate.** Analysis of Covariance (ANCOVA) is one of the Statistical Techniques used for controlling intervening variables. In ANCOVA, there must be minimum one covariate or intervening variable which is to be controlled. There may be more than one covariate. **If in a research there is one discontinuous variable having two or more labels, one continuous variable and one or more covariates, it is called One Way ANCOVA**. The wording of objective of research whose data can be analysed with the help of One Way ANCOVA is as follows:

To compare adjusted mean scores of Emotional Competence of Male and Female Teachers by considering their Self-efficacy as covariate.

Click on "**Analyse**", bring curser to "**General Linear Model**" and then to "**Univaraite**" to get the following screen.

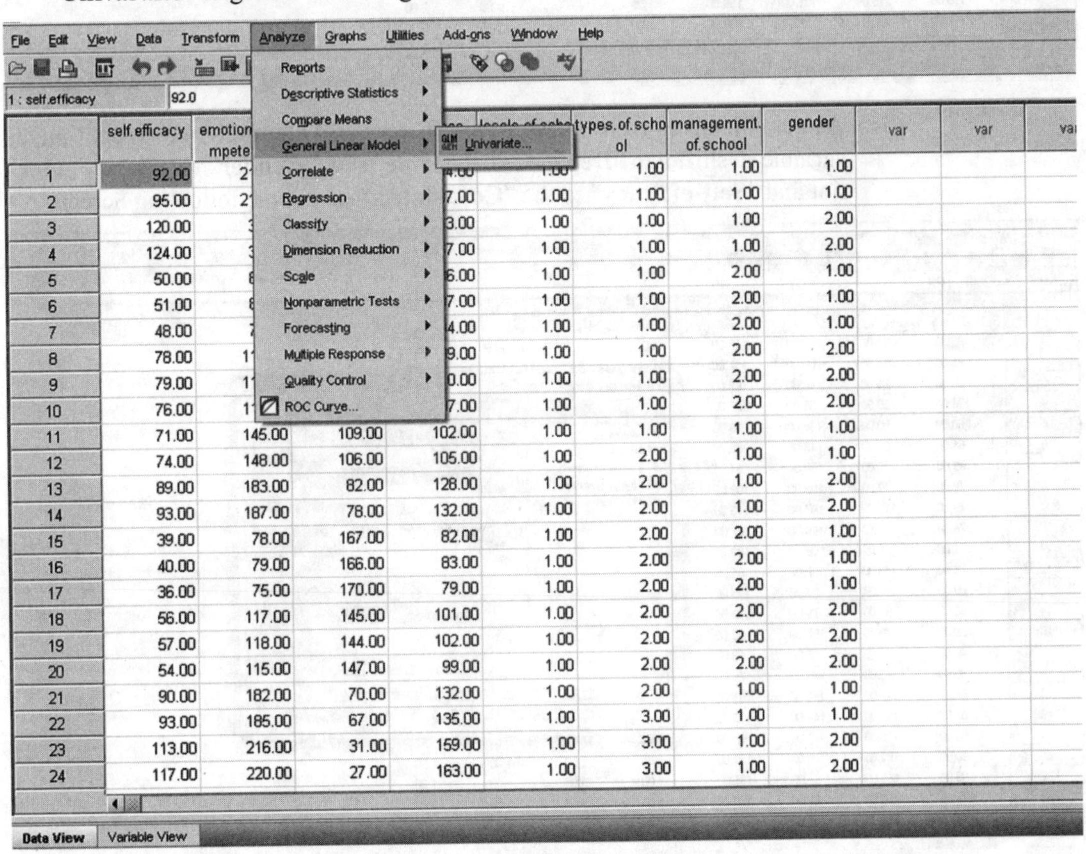

164. Click on "**Univariate**" icon to get the following screen.

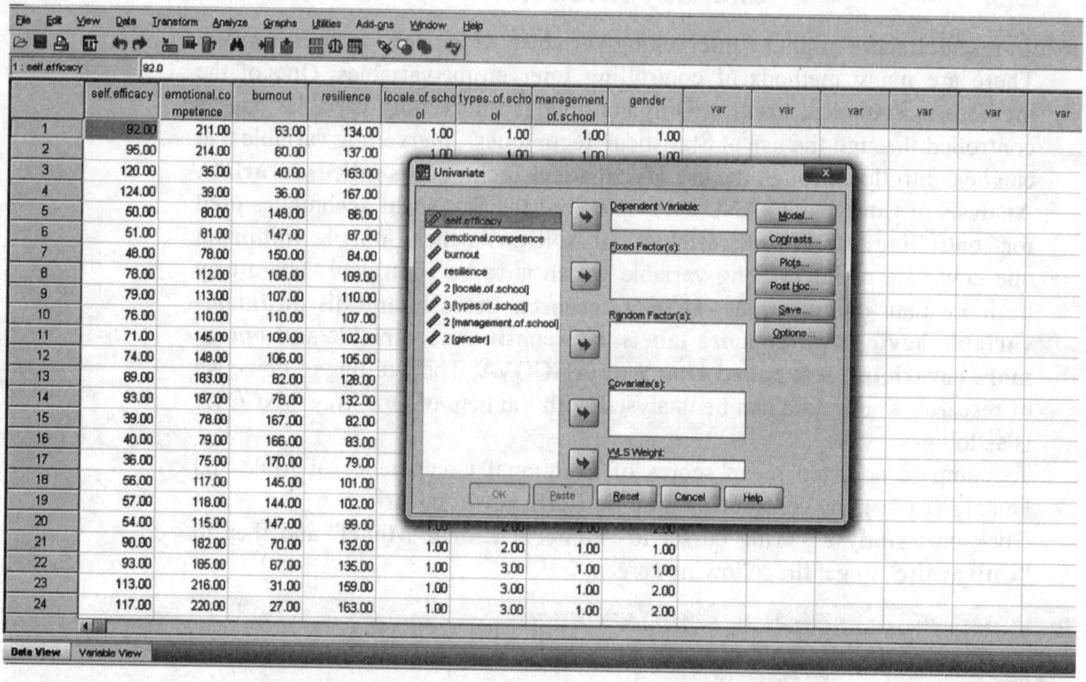

165. As per objective given in frame 163, "**Emotional Competence**" is continuous variable so shift it to "**Dependent Variable**" slot, "**Gender**" to "**Fixed Factor**" slot and "**Self-efficacy**" to the "**Covariate(s)**" to get the following Screen.

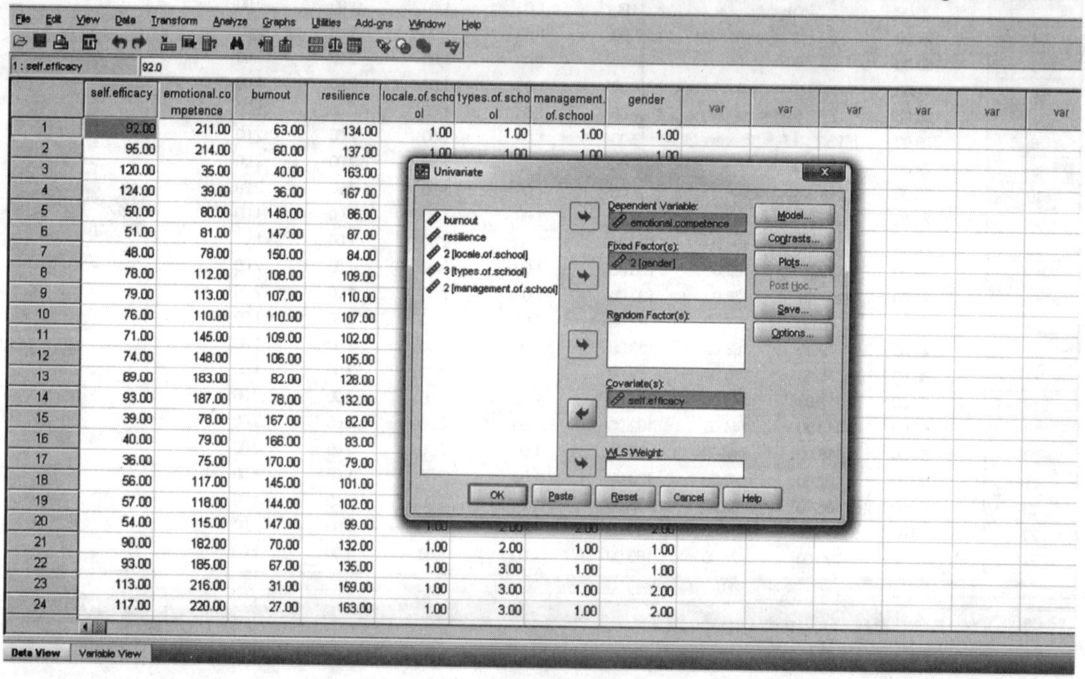

166. Click on "**Options**" to get the following screen.

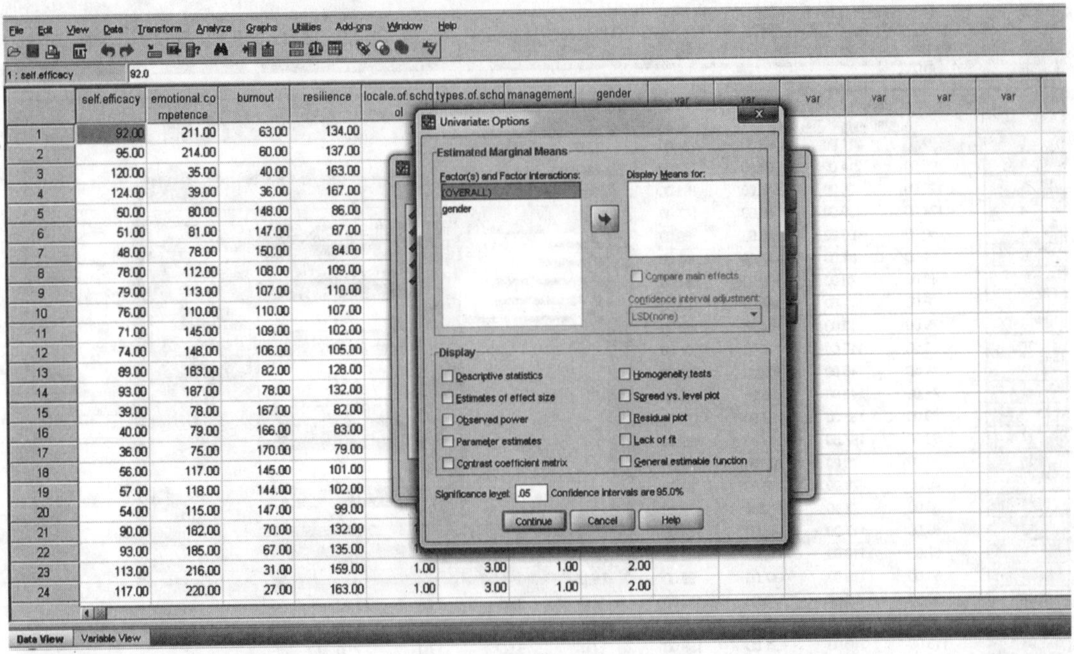

167. Shift all variables from "**Factor(s) and Factor Interactions**" slot to "**Display Means For**" icon. Also highlight "**Descriptive Statistics**" icon, "**Homogeneity Test**" icon and "**Estimates of effect size**" icon as given under "**Display**" to get the following screen.

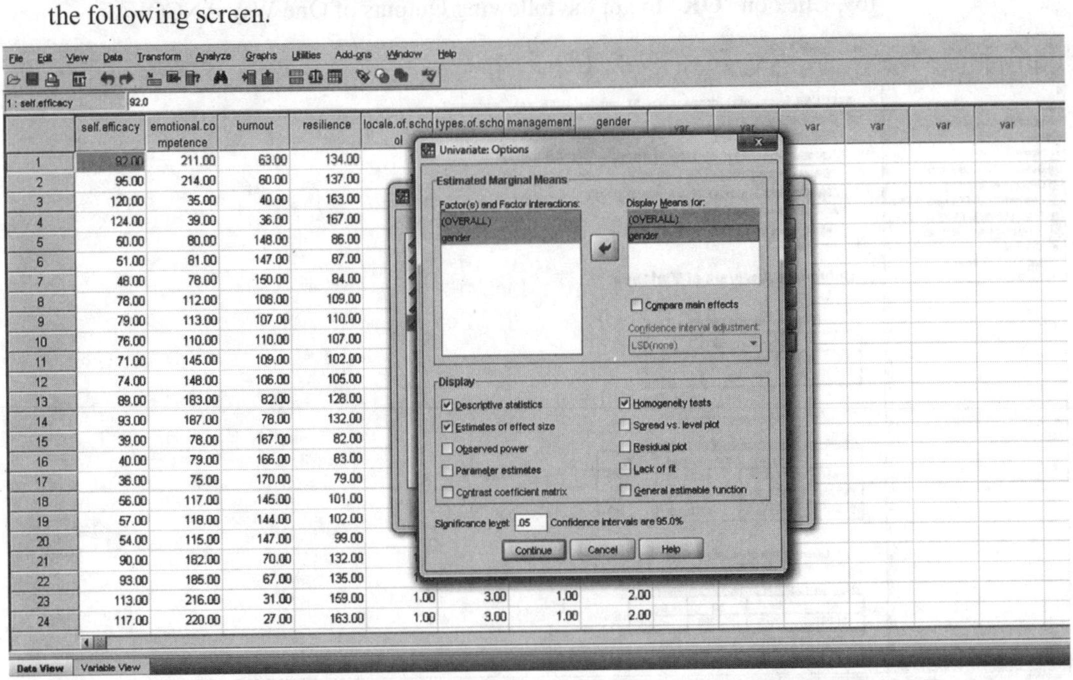

168. Click on "**Continue**" to get the following screen.

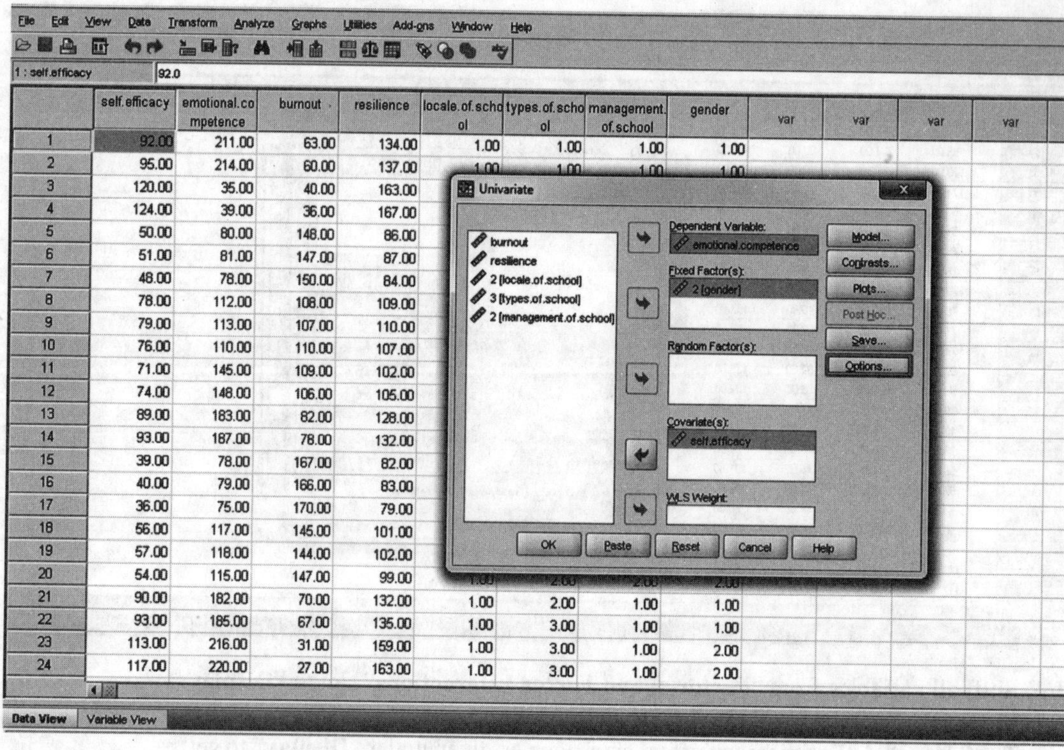

169. Click on "**OK**" to get the following Outputs of One Way ANCOVA.

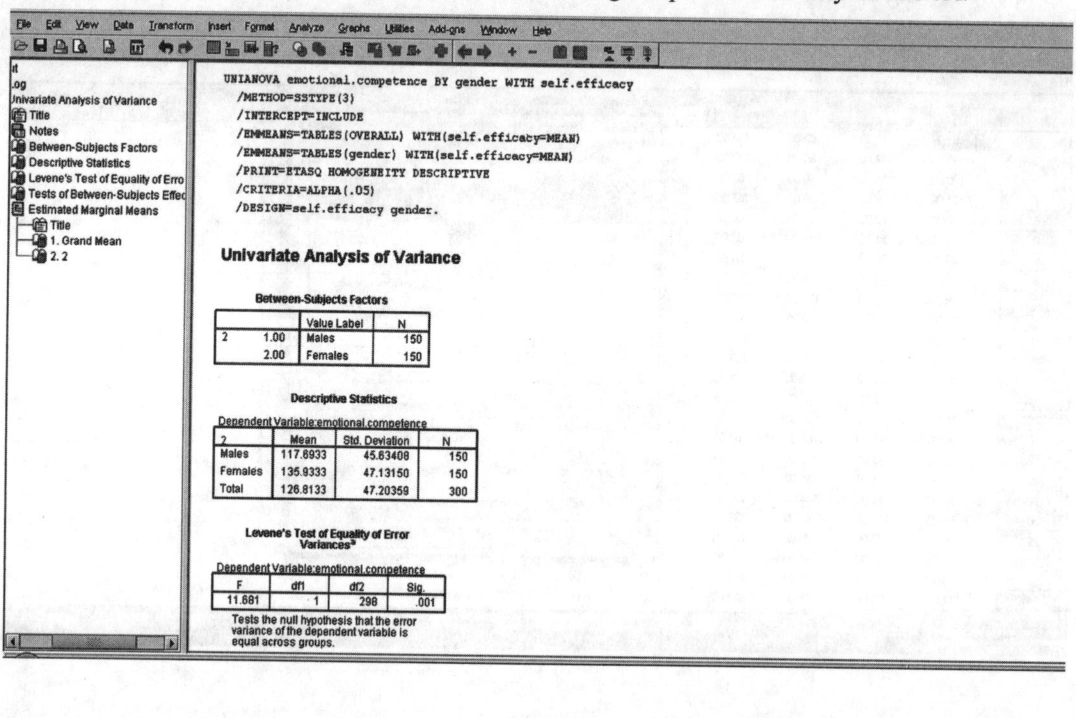

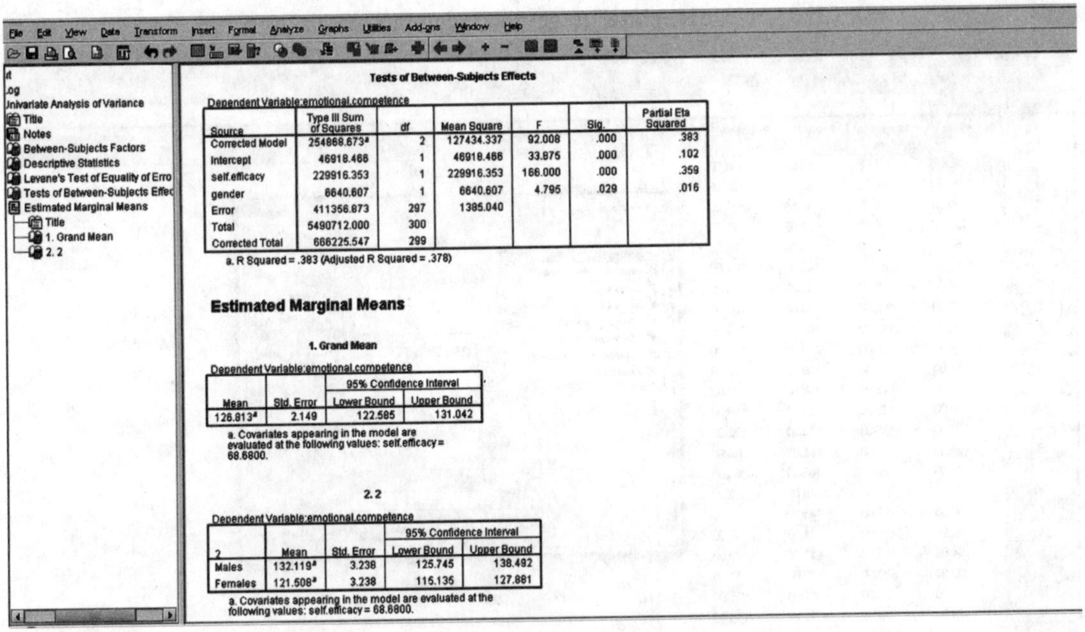

Tests of Between-Subjects Effects

Dependent Variable:emotional.competence

Source	Type III Sum of Squares	df	Mean Square	F	Sig.	Partial Eta Squared
Corrected Model	254868.673[a]	2	127434.337	92.008	.000	.383
Intercept	46918.466	1	46918.466	33.875	.000	.102
self.efficacy	229916.353	1	229916.353	166.000	.000	.359
gender	6640.607	1	6640.607	4.795	.029	.016
Error	411356.873	297	1385.040			
Total	5490712.000	300				
Corrected Total	666225.547	299				

a. R Squared = .383 (Adjusted R Squared = .378)

Estimated Marginal Means

1. Grand Mean

Dependent Variable:emotional.competence

Mean	Std. Error	95% Confidence Interval Lower Bound	95% Confidence Interval Upper Bound
126.813[a]	2.149	122.585	131.042

a. Covariates appearing in the model are evaluated at the following values: self.efficacy = 68.6800.

2.2

Dependent Variable:emotional.competence

2	Mean	Std. Error	95% Confidence Interval Lower Bound	95% Confidence Interval Upper Bound
Males	132.119[a]	3.238	125.745	138.492
Females	121.508[a]	3.238	115.135	127.881

a. Covariates appearing in the model are evaluated at the following values: self.efficacy = 68.6800.

170. Let us take another example of objective with one discontinuous variable, one continuous variable and two covariates. Suppose the objective of research is as given below:
To compare adjusted mean scores of Emotional Competence of Male and Female Teachers by considering their Self-efficacy and Burnout as covariates. Click on "**Analyse**" icon bring curser to "**General Linear Model**" icon and then to "**Univariate**" icon to get the following screen.

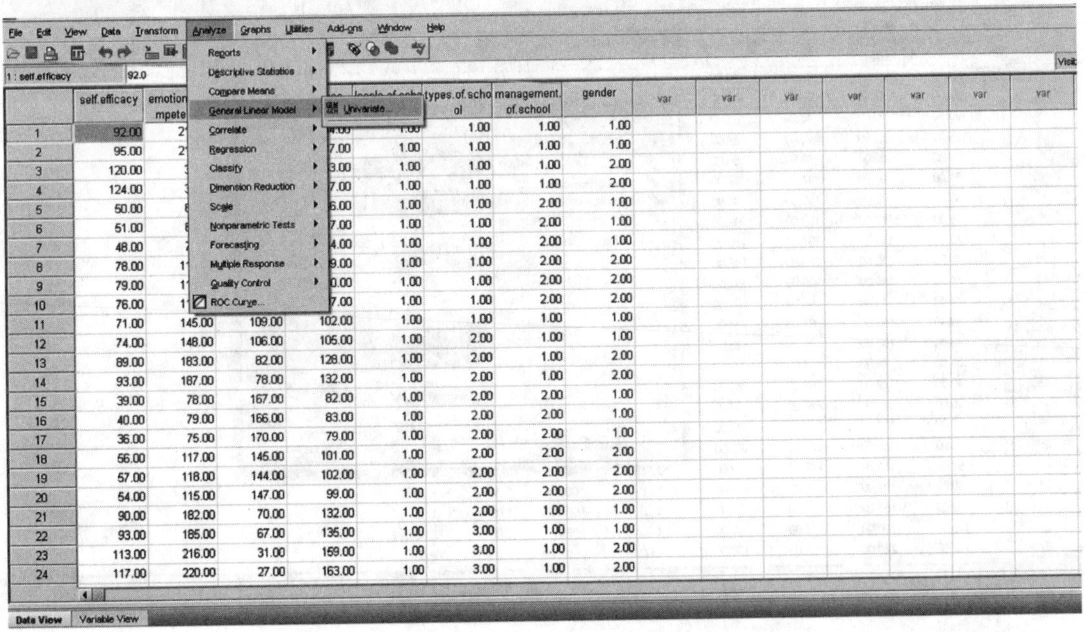

171. Click on "**Univariate**" to get the following screen.

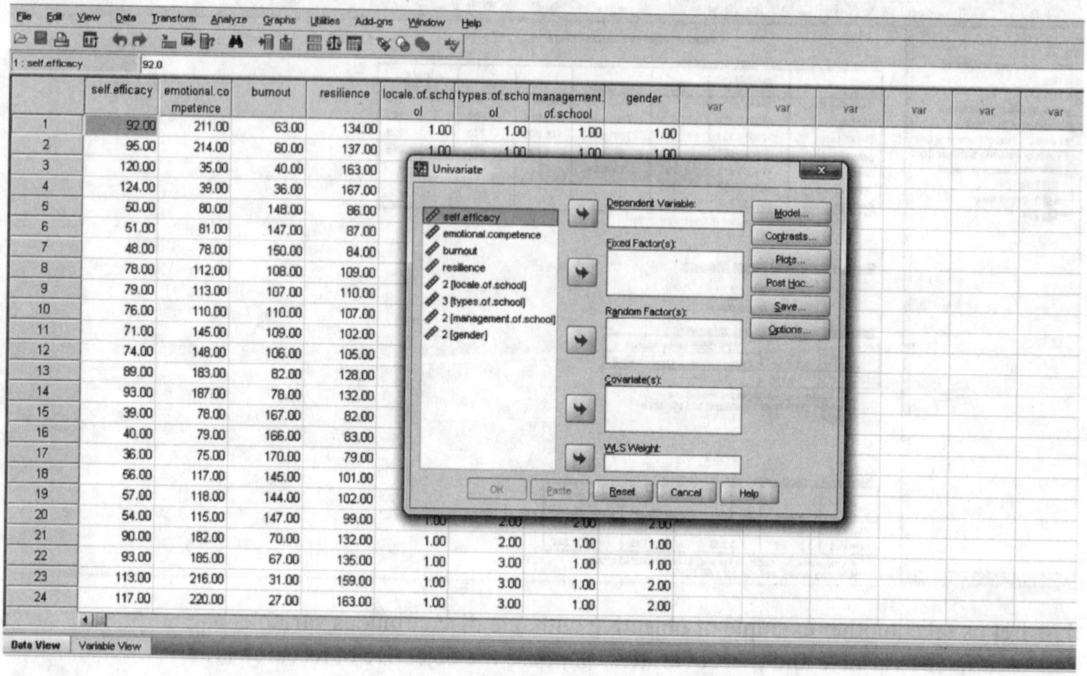

172. According to the objective given in frame 170 shift "**Emotional Competence**" to "**Dependent Variable**" slot, "**Gender**" to "**Fixed Factor**" slot and "**Self-efficacy**" and "**Burnout**" to the "**Covariate(s)**" slot to get the following Screen.

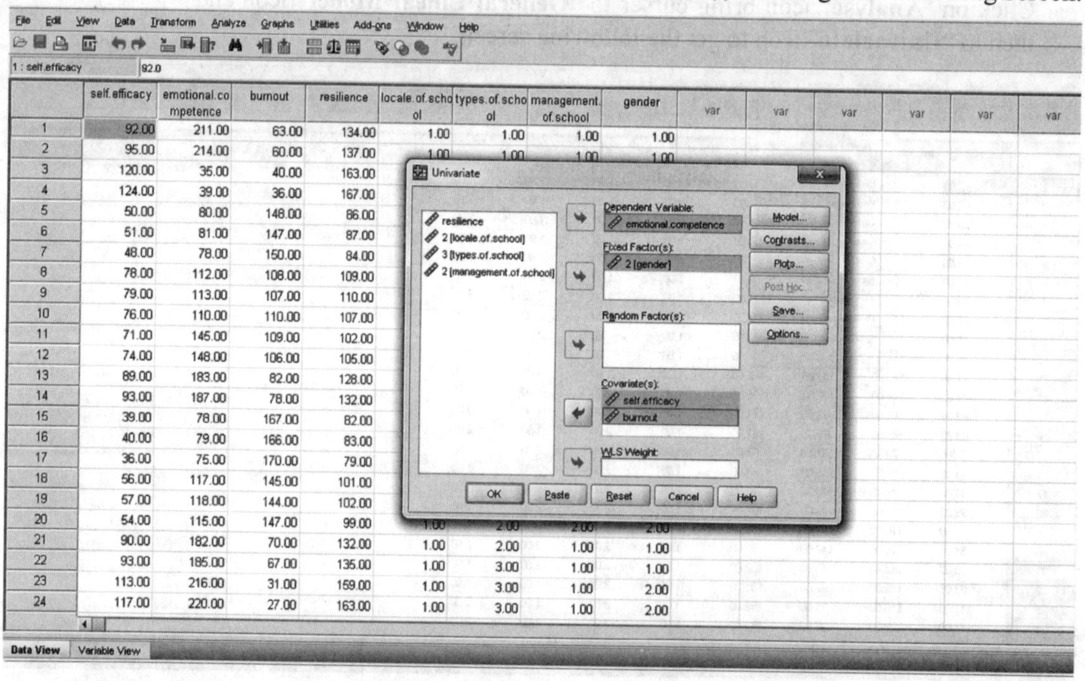

173. Click on "**Options**" and shift variables from "**Factor(s) and Factor Interactions**" to "**Display Means For**" icon. Also highlight "**Descriptive Statistics**" icon, "**Homogeneity Test**" icon "**Estimates of effect size**" icon as given under "**Display**" to get the following screen.

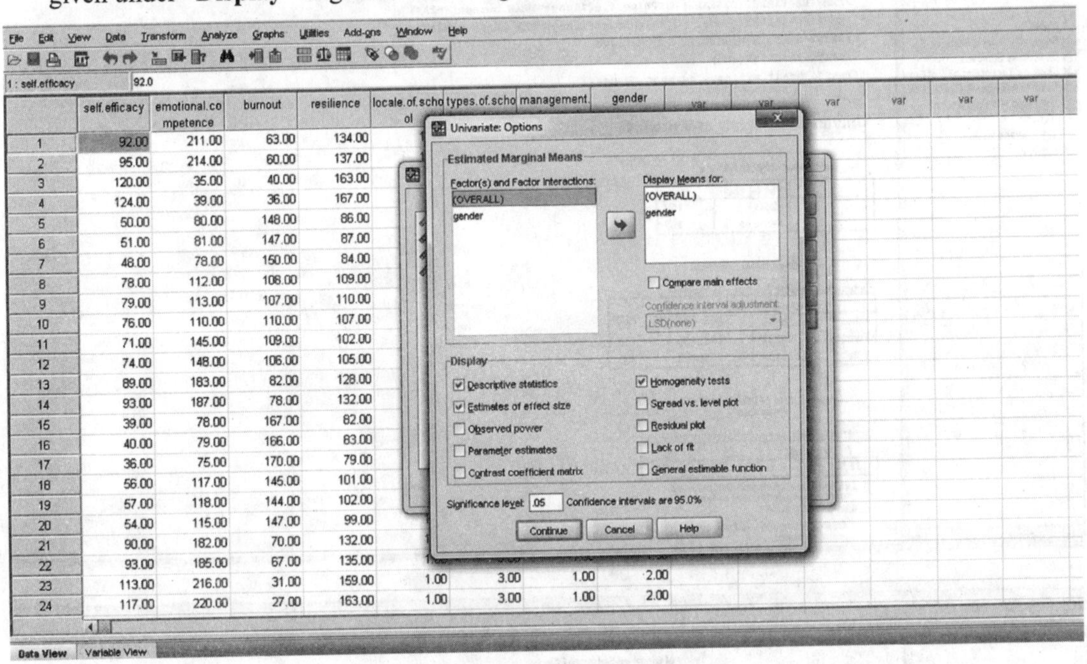

174. Click on "**Continue**" icon to get the following screen.

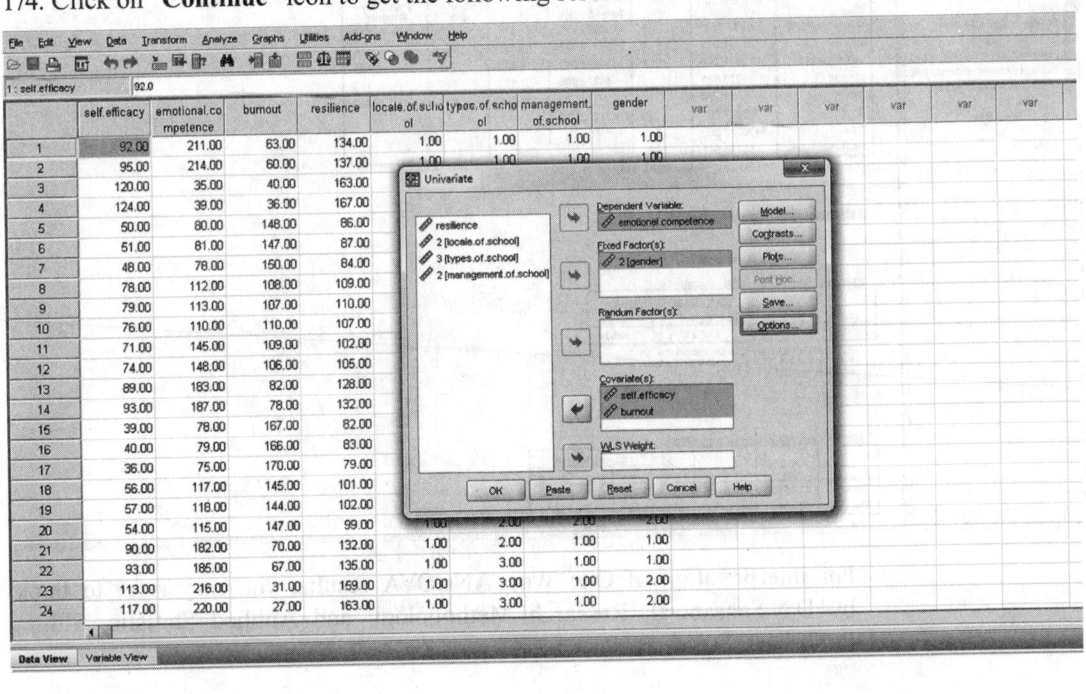

175. Click on "**OK**" to get the following outputs of One Way ANCOVA.

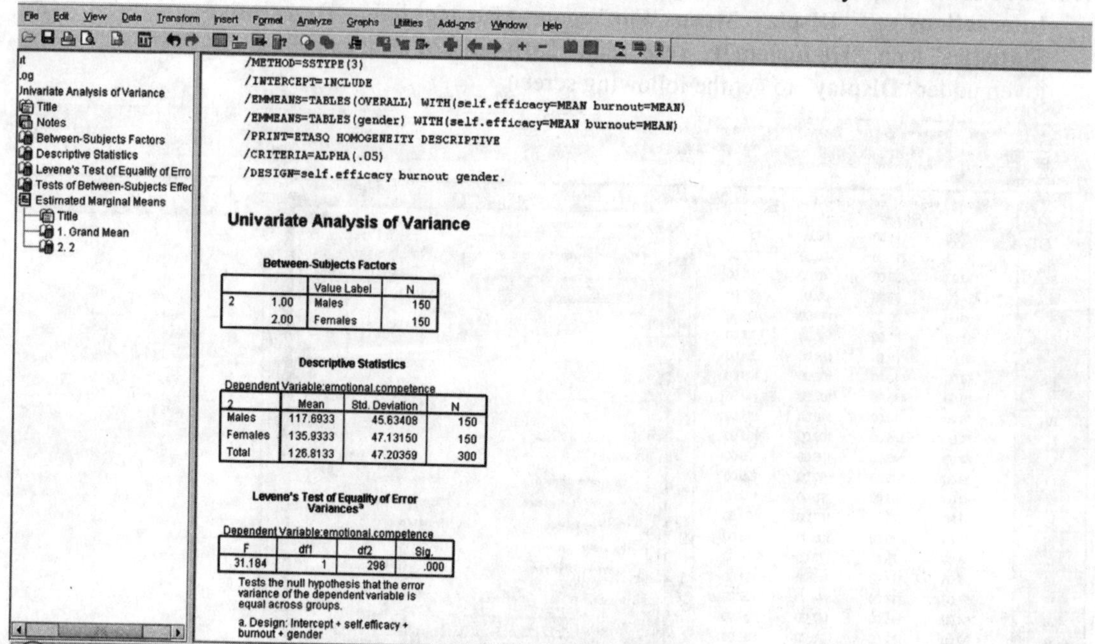

```
/METHOD=SSTYPE(3)
/INTERCEPT=INCLUDE
/EMMEANS=TABLES(OVERALL) WITH(self.efficacy=MEAN burnout=MEAN)
/EMMEANS=TABLES(gender) WITH(self.efficacy=MEAN burnout=MEAN)
/PRINT=ETASQ HOMOGENEITY DESCRIPTIVE
/CRITERIA=ALPHA(.05)
/DESIGN=self.efficacy burnout gender.
```

Univariate Analysis of Variance

Between-Subjects Factors

		Value Label	N
2	1.00	Males	150
	2.00	Females	150

Descriptive Statistics

Dependent Variable:emotional.competence

2	Mean	Std. Deviation	N
Males	117.6933	45.63408	150
Females	135.9333	47.13150	150
Total	126.8133	47.20359	300

Levene's Test of Equality of Error Variances[a]

Dependent Variable:emotional.competence

F	df1	df2	Sig.
31.184	1	298	.000

Tests the null hypothesis that the error variance of the dependent variable is equal across groups.

a. Design: Intercept + self.efficacy + burnout + gender

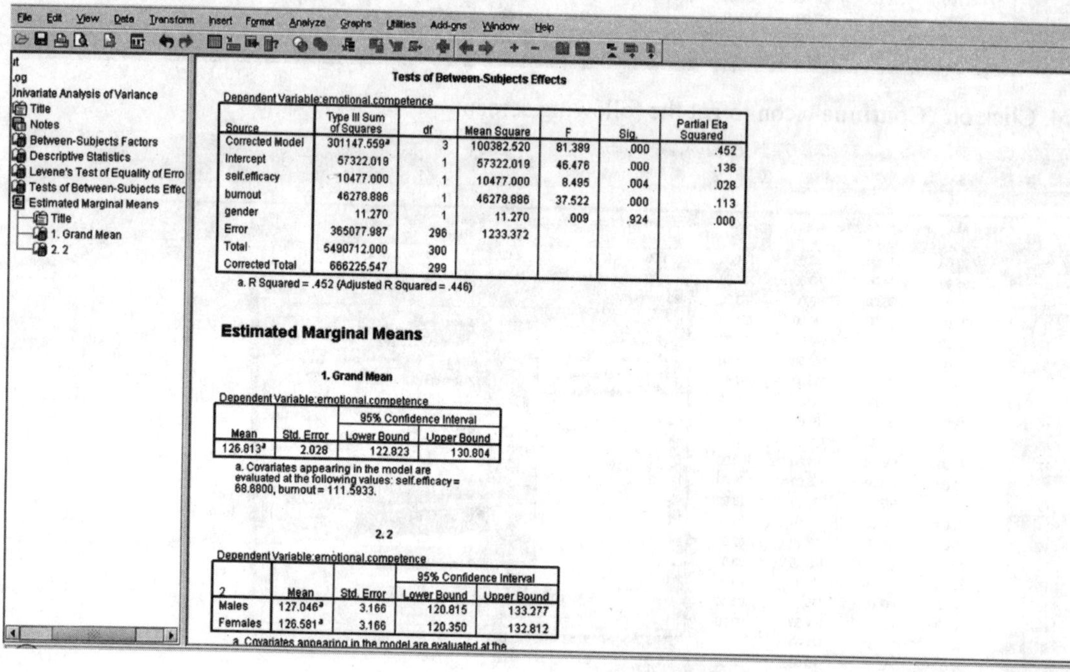

Tests of Between-Subjects Effects

Dependent Variable:emotional.competence

Source	Type III Sum of Squares	df	Mean Square	F	Sig.	Partial Eta Squared
Corrected Model	301147.559[a]	3	100382.520	81.389	.000	.452
Intercept	57322.019	1	57322.019	46.476	.000	.136
self.efficacy	10477.000	1	10477.000	8.495	.004	.028
burnout	46278.886	1	46278.886	37.522	.000	.113
gender	11.270	1	11.270	.009	.924	.000
Error	365077.987	296	1233.372			
Total	5490712.000	300				
Corrected Total	666225.547	299				

a. R Squared = .452 (Adjusted R Squared = .446)

Estimated Marginal Means

1. Grand Mean

Dependent Variable:emotional.competence

Mean	Std. Error	95% Confidence Interval	
		Lower Bound	Upper Bound
126.813[a]	2.028	122.823	130.804

a. Covariates appearing in the model are evaluated at the following values: self.efficacy = 68.6800, burnout = 111.5933.

2. 2

Dependent Variable:emotional.competence

2	Mean	Std. Error	95% Confidence Interval	
			Lower Bound	Upper Bound
Males	127.046[a]	3.166	120.815	133.277
Females	126.581[a]	3.166	120.350	132.812

a. Covariates appearing in the model are evaluated at the

For interpretation of One Way ANCOVA results, you may refer to book by D.N.Sansanwal, Research Methodology and Applied Statistic, Shipra Publishers, Delhi, 2020.

Two Way ANCOVA

176. Hope you can analsye your data with the help of One Way ANCOVA with one or more covariates.

Suppose you have two discontinuous variables, one continuous and at least one continuous covariate, the data can be analysed with the help of Two Way ANCOVA. To understand this, let us consider the following objective of research: To study the effect of Groups (Thinking Strategies), Gender and their interaction on Creativity of students by considering their Pre-Creativity, Intelligence and Achievement Stress as covariates.

After clicking on "**Analyse**" icon bring curser to "**General Linear Model**" icon and then to "**Univariate**" icon to get the following screen.

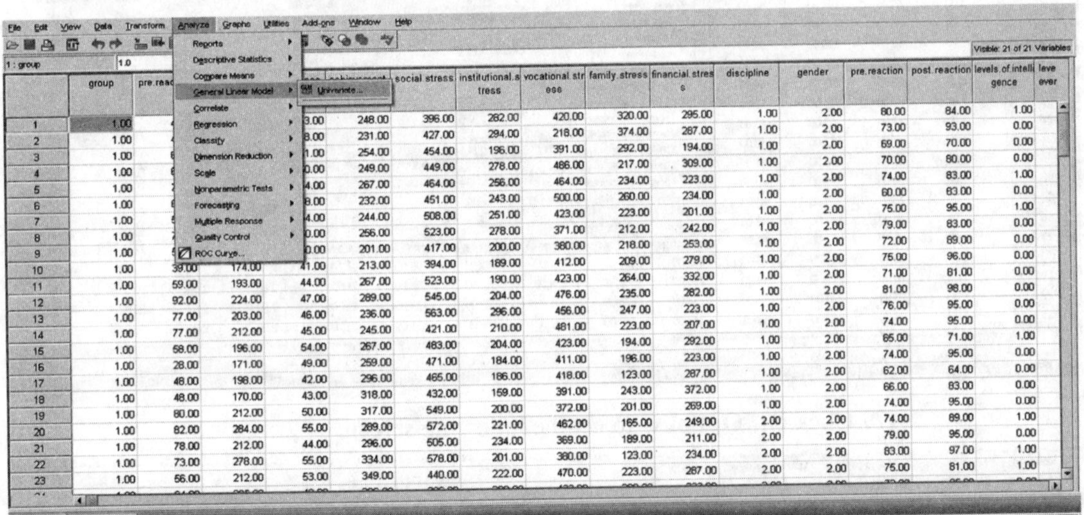

177. Click on "**Univariate**" icon to get the following screen.

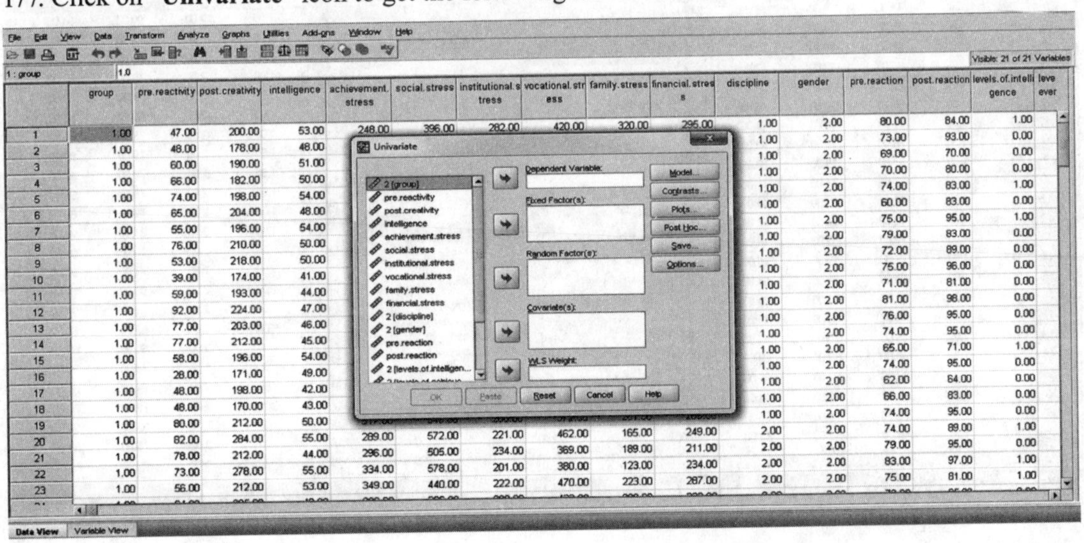

178. Shift "**Post Creativity**" variable to "**Dependent Variable**" slot. Also shift "**Groups**" and "**Gender**" variables to "**Fixed Variable(s)**" slot. Finally shift "**Pre-Creativity**", "**Intelligence**" and "**Achievement Stress**" to "**Covariate(s)**" slot to get the following screen.

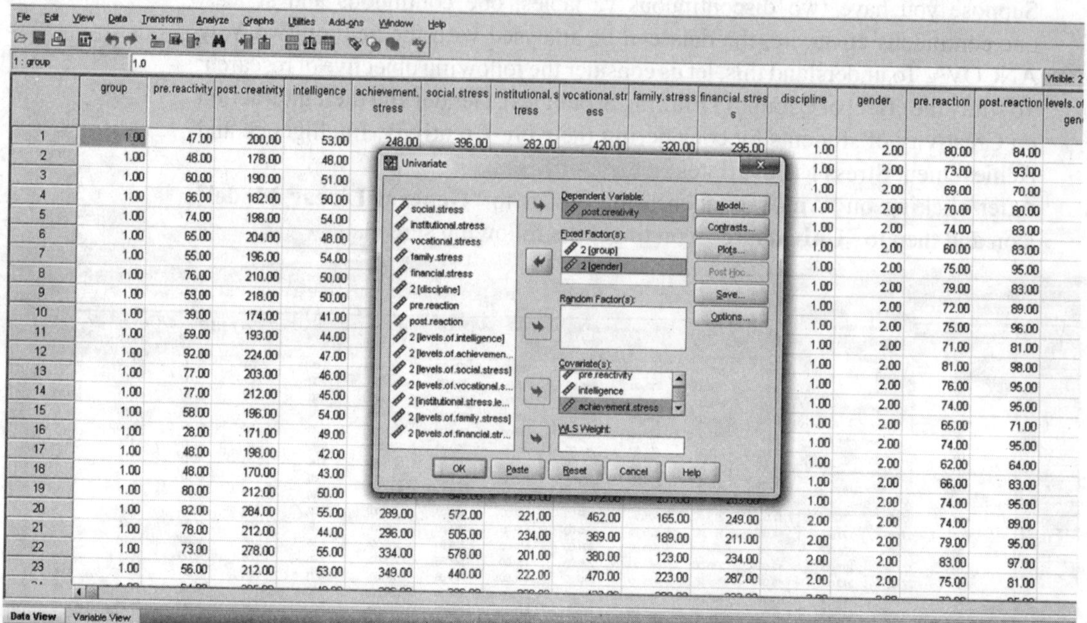

179. Click on "**Options**" to get the following screen.

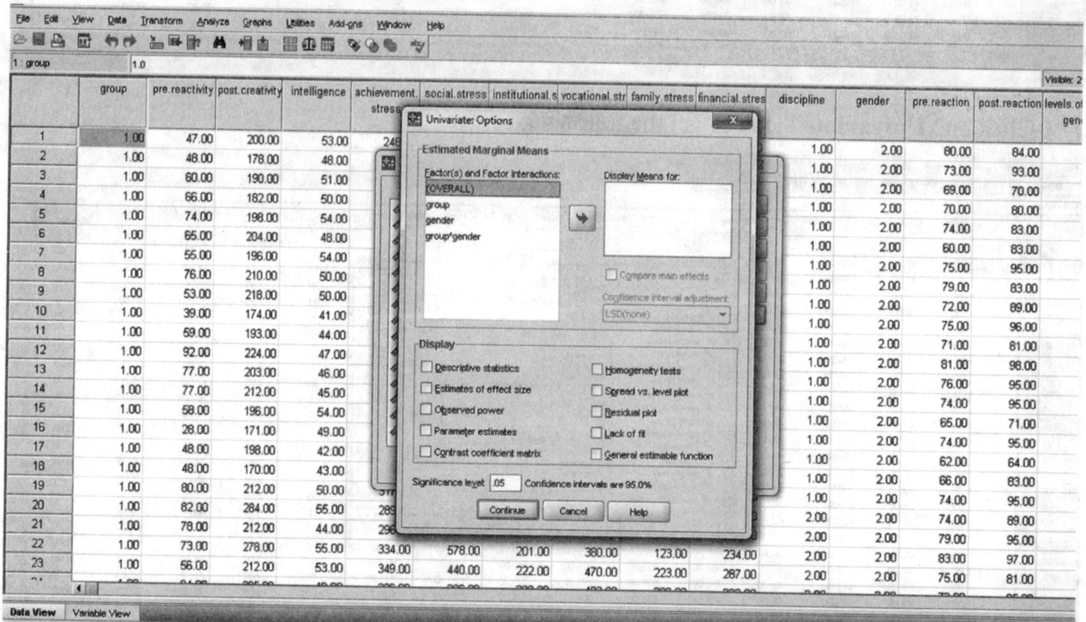

180. Shift all variables from "**Factor(s) and Factor Interactions**" box to "**Display Means for**" box; under "**Display**" icon highlight "**Discriptive Statistics**" icon, "**Homogeneity Tests**" icon and "**Estimates of effect size**" icon to get the following screen.

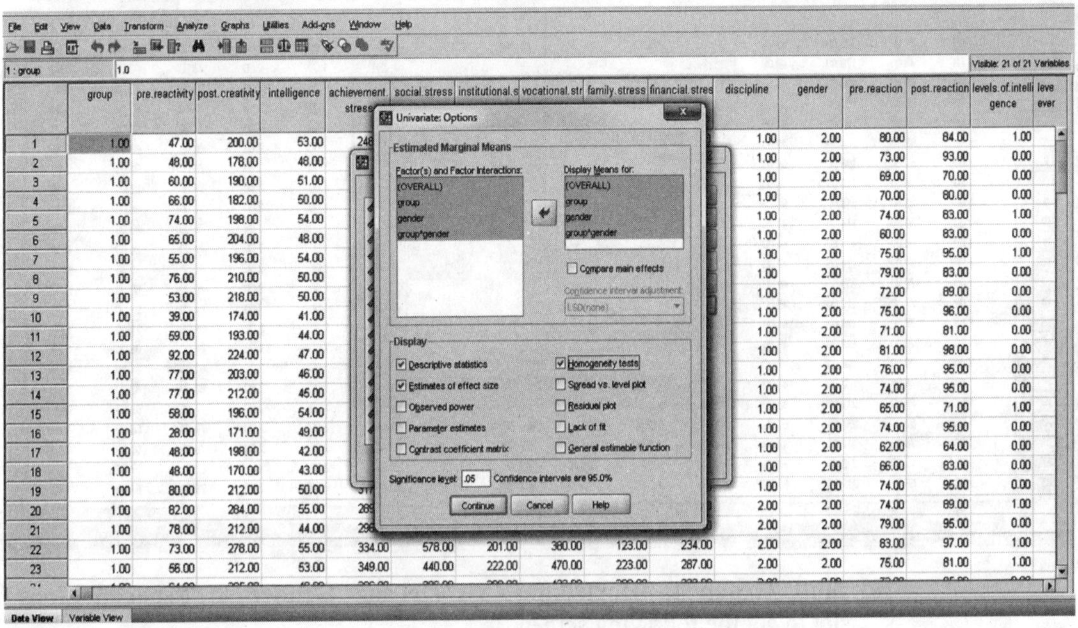

181. Click on "**Continue**" icon to get the following screen.

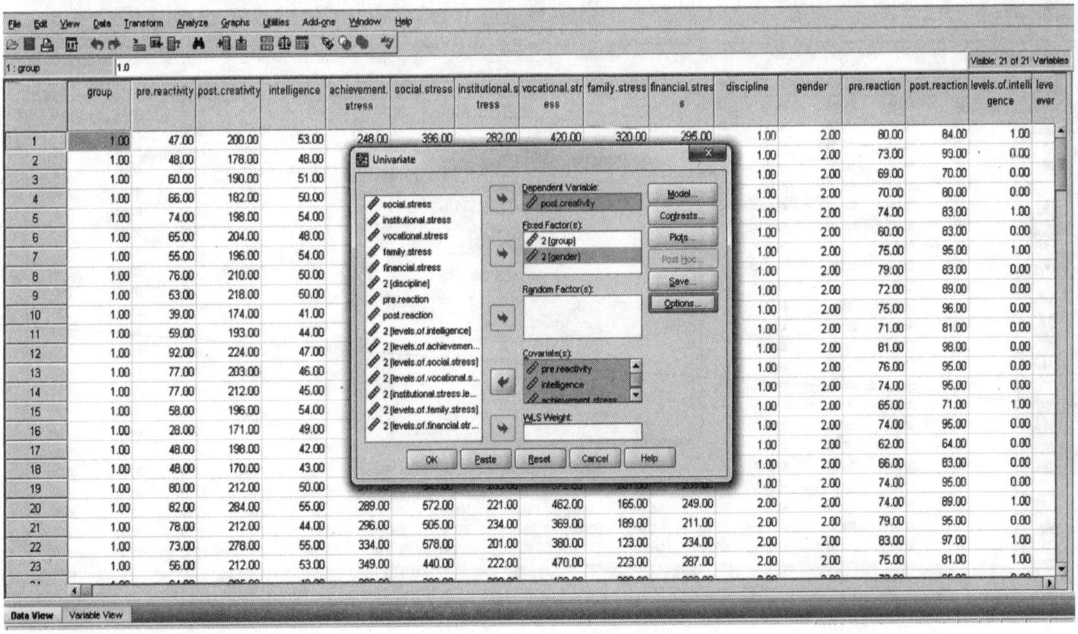

182. Click on "**Plots**" icon to get the following screen.

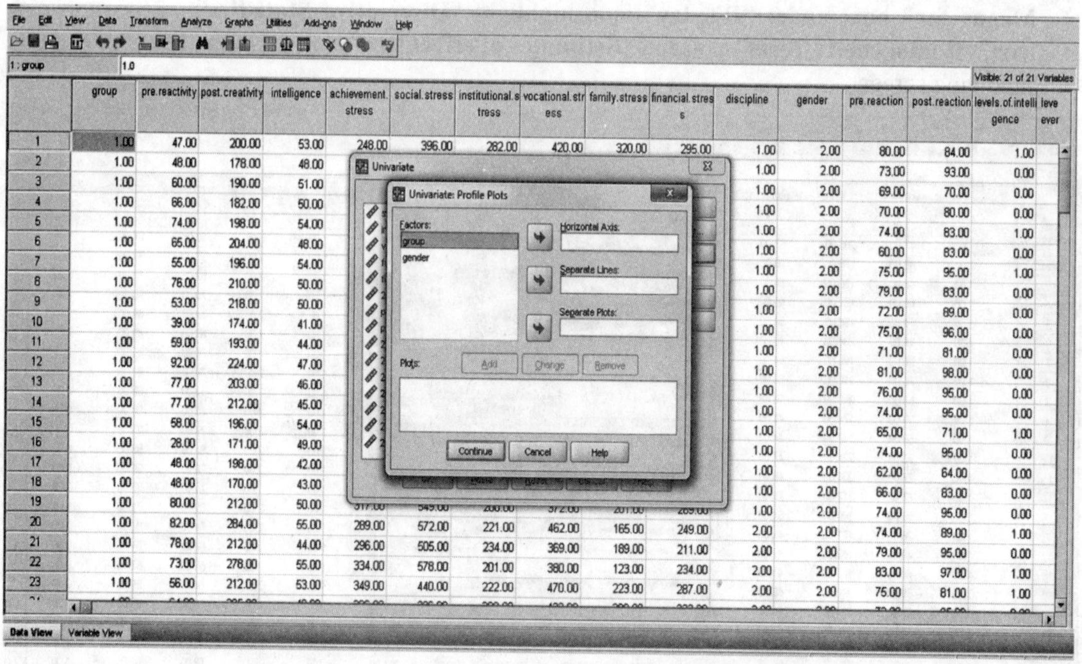

183. Shift "**Group**" to "**Horizontal Axis**" slot and "**Gender**" to "**Separate Lines**" slot to get the following screen.

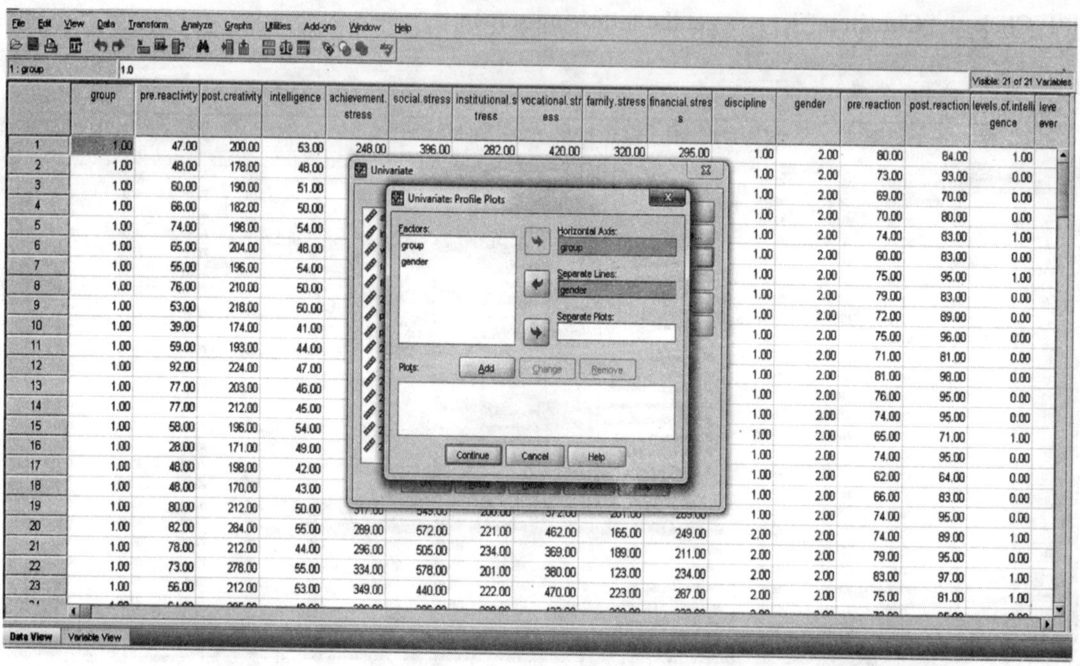

184. Click on "**Add**" to get the following screen.

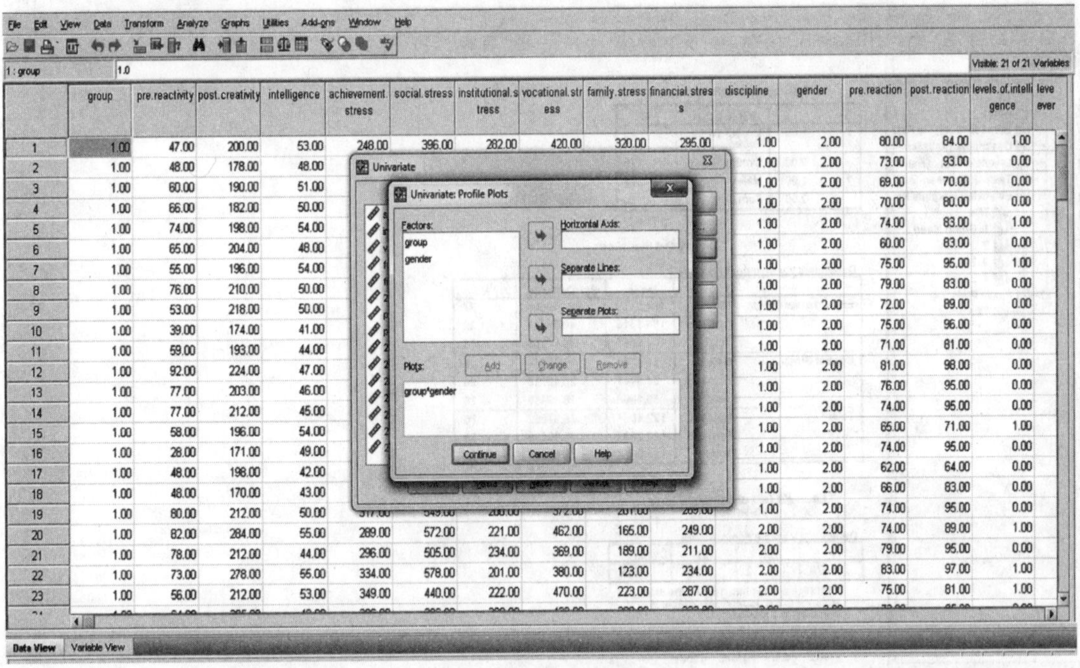

185. Click on "**Continue**" icon to get the following screen.

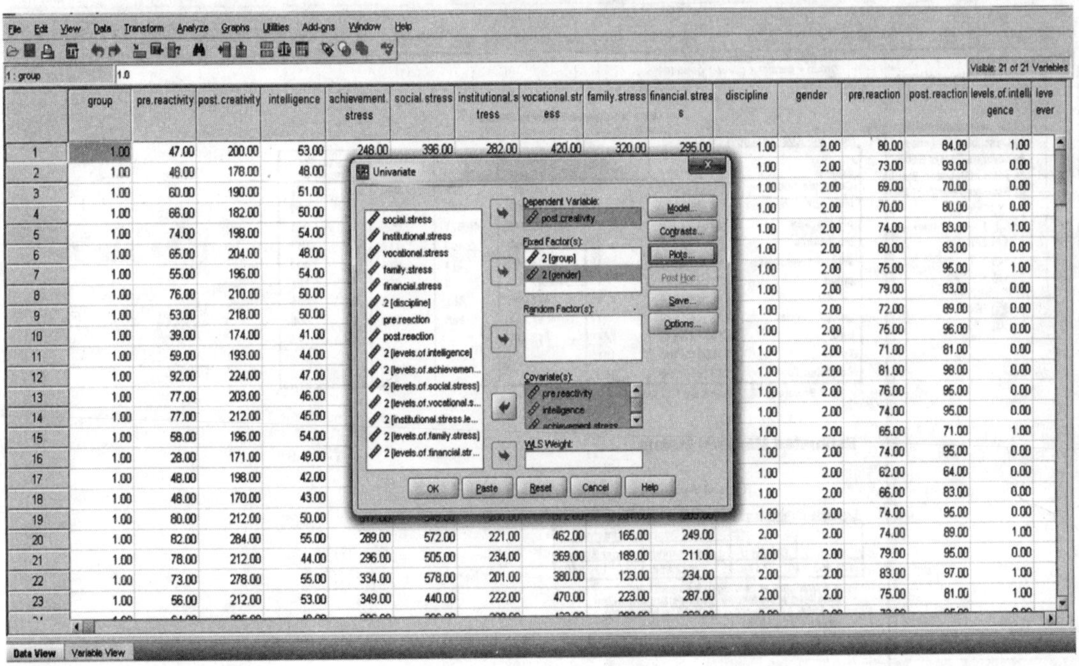

186. Click on "**OK**" icon to get the following outputs of Two Way ANCOVA.

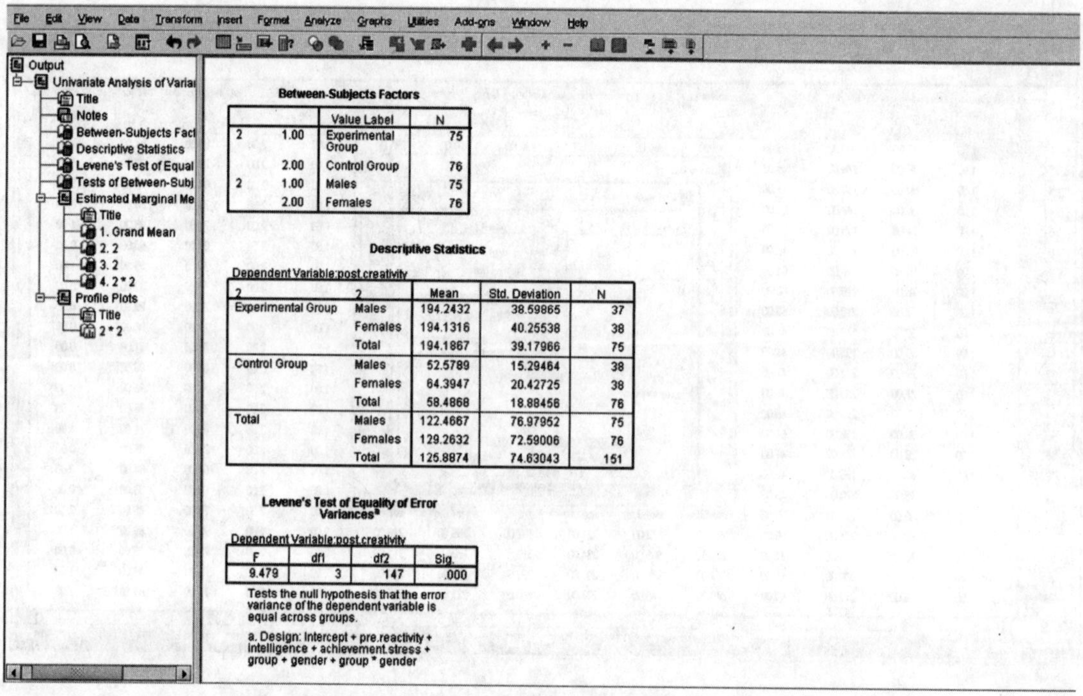

Between-Subjects Factors

		Value Label	N
2	1.00	Experimental Group	75
	2.00	Control Group	76
2	1.00	Males	75
	2.00	Females	76

Descriptive Statistics

Dependent Variable:post.creativity

2	2	Mean	Std. Deviation	N
Experimental Group	Males	194.2432	38.59865	37
	Females	194.1316	40.25538	38
	Total	194.1867	39.17966	75
Control Group	Males	52.5789	15.29464	38
	Females	64.3947	20.42725	38
	Total	58.4868	18.88456	76
Total	Males	122.4667	76.97952	75
	Females	129.2632	72.59006	76
	Total	125.8874	74.63043	151

Levene's Test of Equality of Error Variances[a]

Dependent Variable:post.creativity

F	df1	df2	Sig.
9.479	3	147	.000

Tests the null hypothesis that the error variance of the dependent variable is equal across groups.

a. Design: Intercept + pre.reactivity + intelligence + achievement.stress + group + gender + group * gender

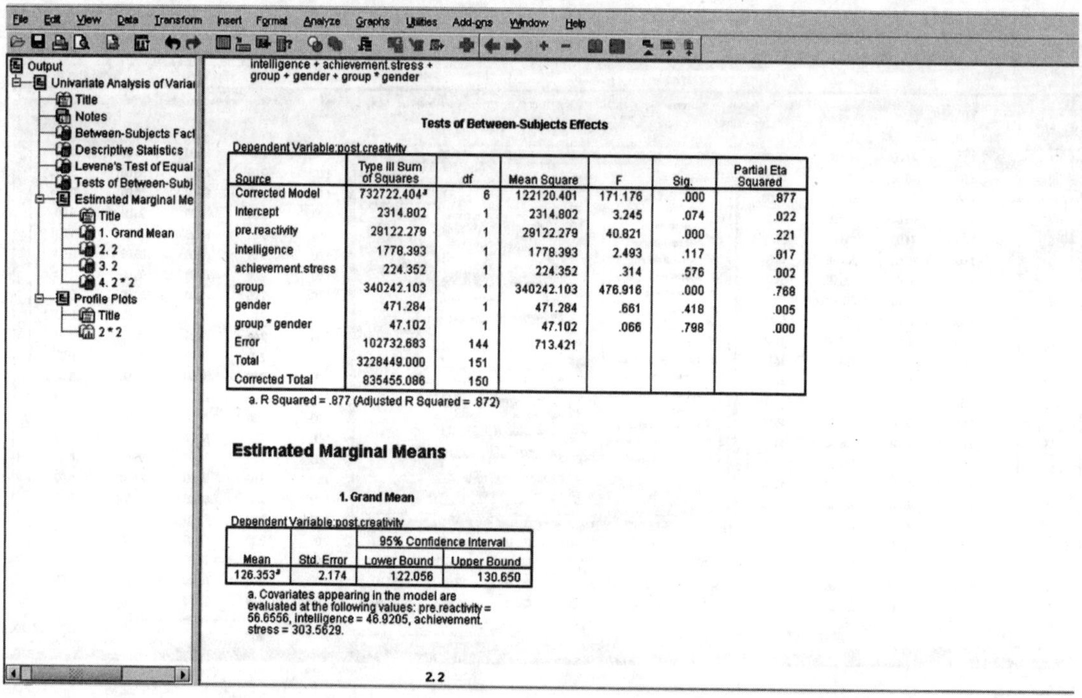

intelligence + achievement.stress + group + gender + group * gender

Tests of Between-Subjects Effects

Dependent Variable:post.creativity

Source	Type III Sum of Squares	df	Mean Square	F	Sig.	Partial Eta Squared
Corrected Model	732722.404[a]	6	122120.401	171.176	.000	.877
Intercept	2314.802	1	2314.802	3.245	.074	.022
pre.reactivity	29122.279	1	29122.279	40.821	.000	.221
intelligence	1778.393	1	1778.393	2.493	.117	.017
achievement.stress	224.352	1	224.352	.314	.576	.002
group	340242.103	1	340242.103	476.916	.000	.768
gender	471.284	1	471.284	.661	.418	.005
group * gender	47.102	1	47.102	.066	.798	.000
Error	102732.683	144	713.421			
Total	3228449.000	151				
Corrected Total	835455.086	150				

a. R Squared = .877 (Adjusted R Squared = .872)

Estimated Marginal Means

1. Grand Mean

Dependent Variable:post.creativity

Mean	Std. Error	95% Confidence Interval Lower Bound	Upper Bound
126.353[a]	2.174	122.056	130.650

a. Covariates appearing in the model are evaluated at the following values: pre.reactivity = 56.6556, intelligence = 46.9205, achievement. stress = 303.5629.

2. 2

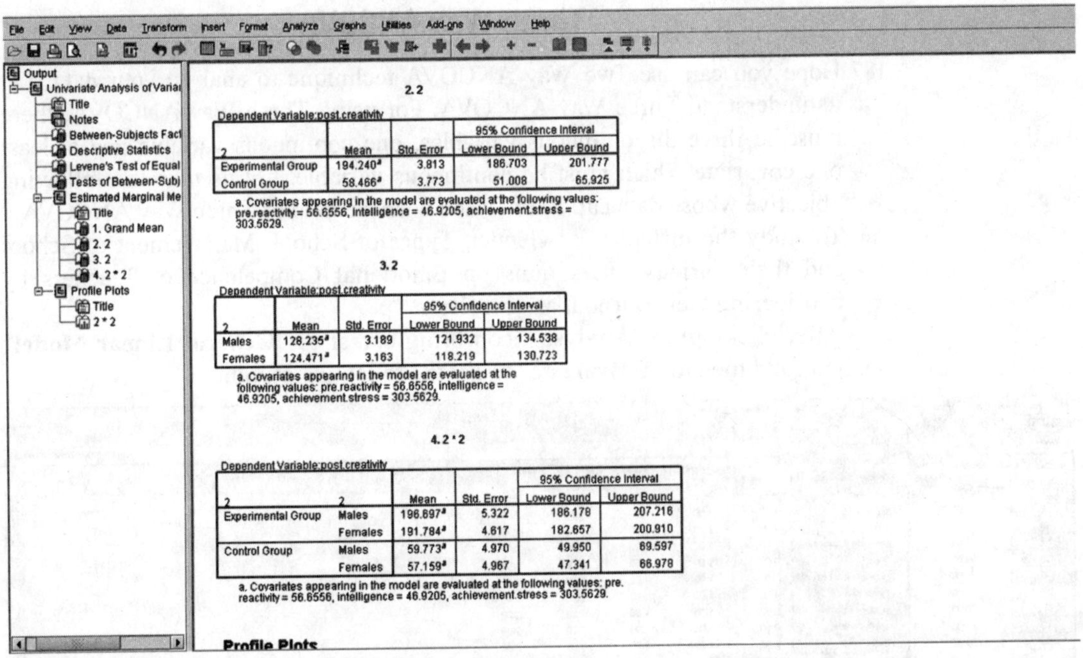

2.2

Dependent Variable:post.creativity

2	Mean	Std. Error	95% Confidence Interval Lower Bound	Upper Bound
Experimental Group	194.240ª	3.813	186.703	201.777
Control Group	58.466ª	3.773	51.008	65.925

a. Covariates appearing in the model are evaluated at the following values: pre.reactivity = 56.6556, intelligence = 46.9205, achievement.stress = 303.5629.

3.2

Dependent Variable:post.creativity

2	Mean	Std. Error	95% Confidence Interval Lower Bound	Upper Bound
Males	128.235ª	3.189	121.932	134.538
Females	124.471ª	3.163	118.219	130.723

a. Covariates appearing in the model are evaluated at the following values: pre.reactivity = 56.6556, intelligence = 46.9205, achievement.stress = 303.5629.

4.2 * 2

Dependent Variable:post.creativity

2	2	Mean	Std. Error	95% Confidence Interval Lower Bound	Upper Bound
Experimental Group	Males	196.697ª	5.322	186.178	207.216
	Females	191.784ª	4.617	182.657	200.910
Control Group	Males	59.773ª	4.970	49.950	69.597
	Females	57.159ª	4.967	47.341	66.978

a. Covariates appearing in the model are evaluated at the following values: pre.reactivity = 56.6556, intelligence = 46.9205, achievement.stress = 303.5629.

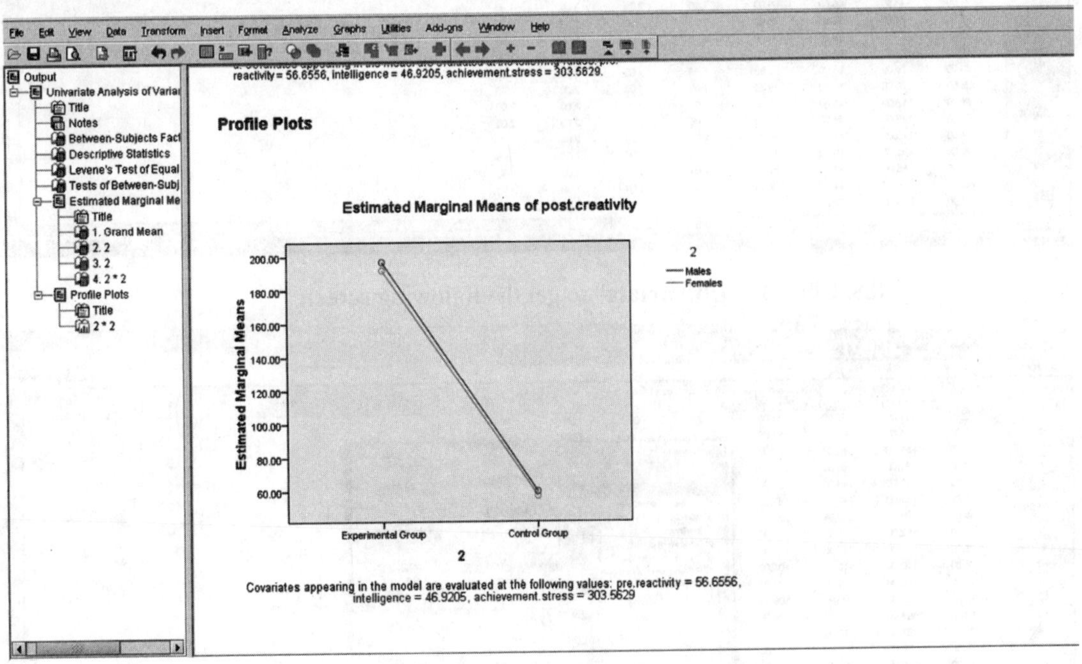

For interpretation of Two Way ANCOVA results, you may refer to book by D.N.Sansanwal, Research Methodology and Applied Statistic, Shipra Publishers, Delhi, 2020.

Three Way ANCOVA

187. Hope you can use Two Way ANCOVA technique to analyse your data. Let us understand Three Way ANCOVA. For using Three Way ANCOVA, there must be three discontinuous variables, one continuous variable and at least one covariate which must be continuous variable. Let us take the following objective whose data can be analysed with the help of Three Way ANCOVA.

To study the influence of Gender, Types of School, Management of School and their various interactions on Emotional Competence of Teachers by considering their Burnout as covariate.

After clicking on "**Analyse**" icon bring curser to "**General Linear Model**" icon and then to "**Univariate**" to get the following screen.

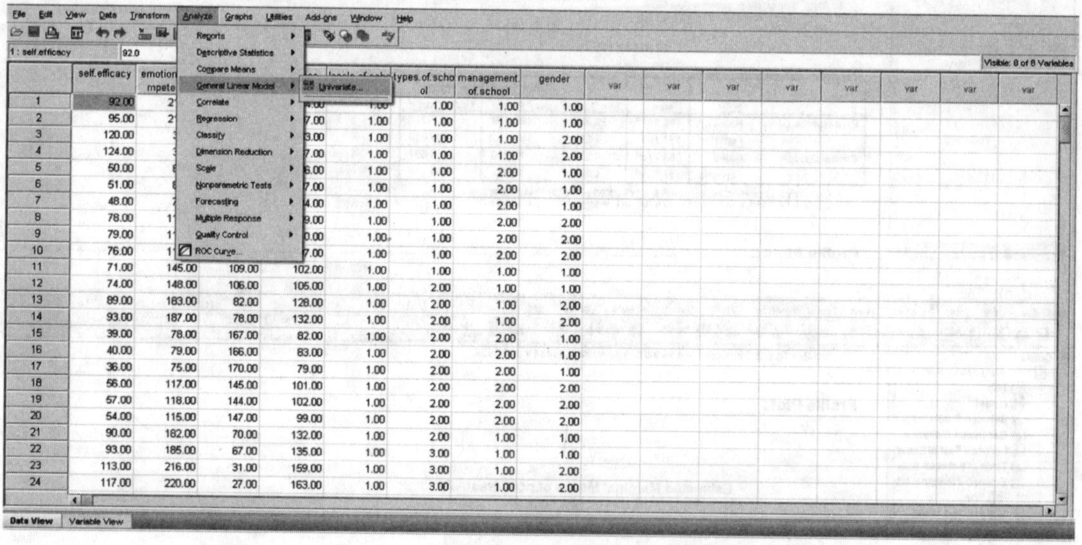

188. Click on "**Univariate**" to get the following screen.

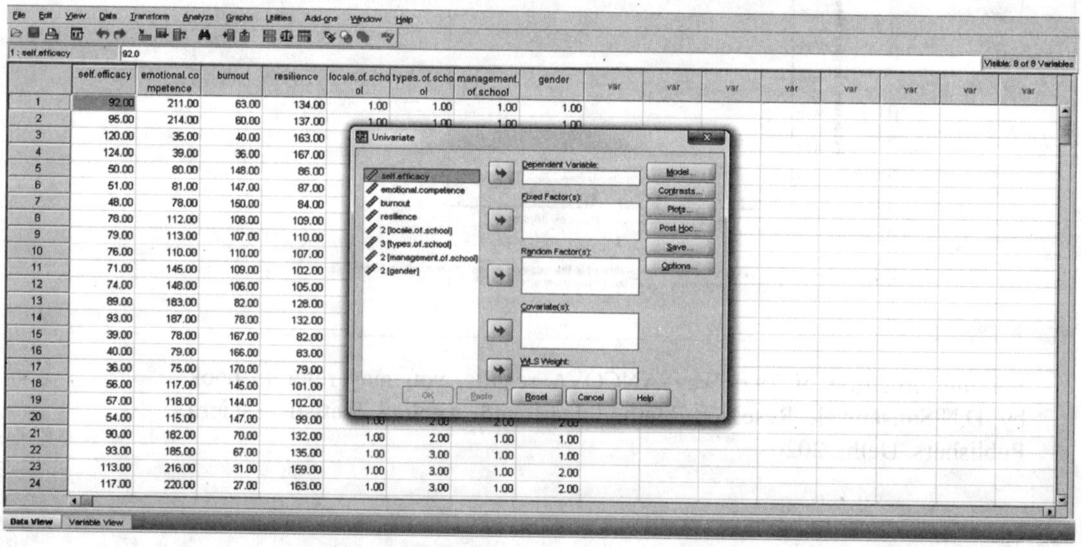

189. As per objective given in frame 187, "**Emotional Competence**" is to be shifted to "**Dependent Variable**" slot to get the following screen.

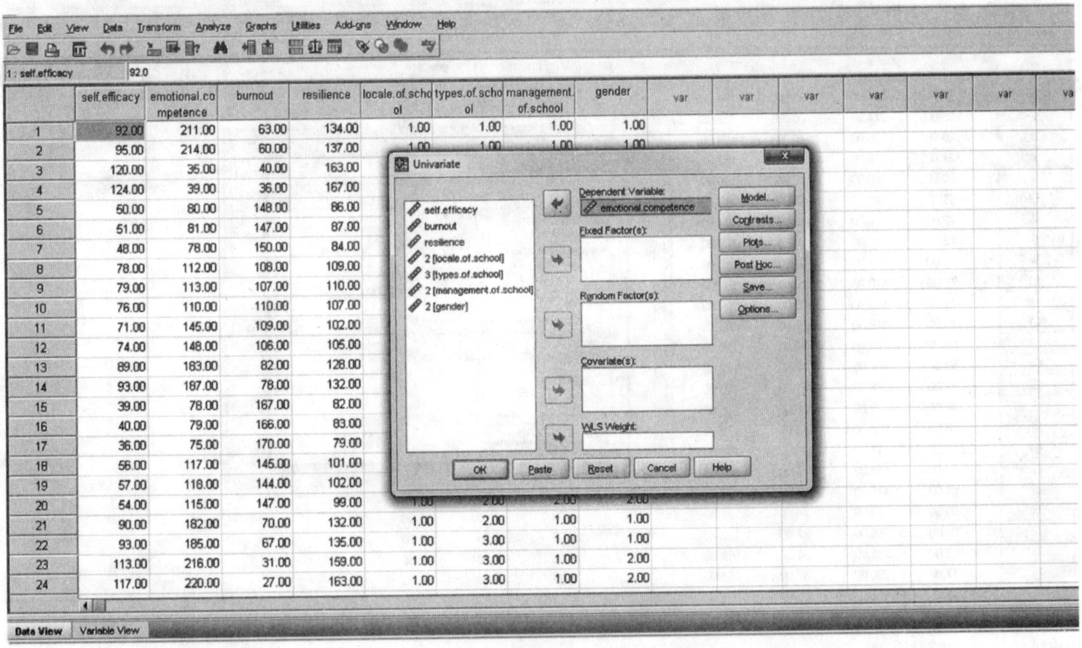

190. "**Gender**", "**Types of School**", "**Management of School**" are the three discontinuous variables and should be shifted to "**Fixed Factor(s)**" box. "**Burnout**" is the covariate and should be shifted to "**Covariate(s)**" box to get the following screen.

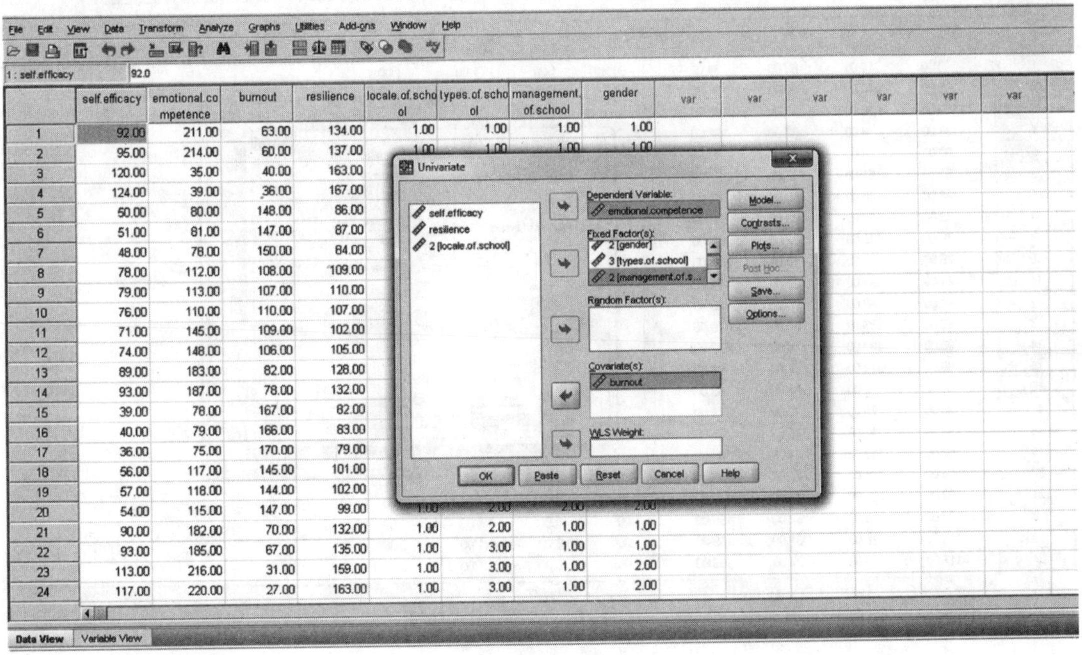

191. Click on "**Plots**" icon to get the following screen.

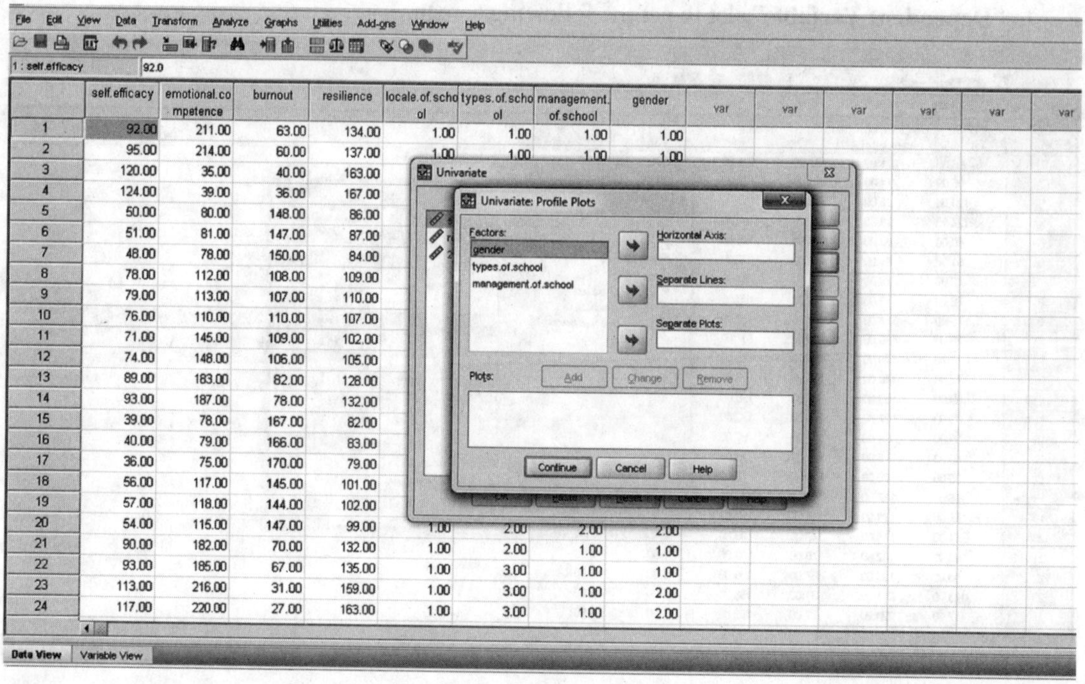

192. Shift "**Types of School**" to "**Horizontal Axis**" slot and "**Gender**" to "**Separate Lines**" slot to get the following screen.

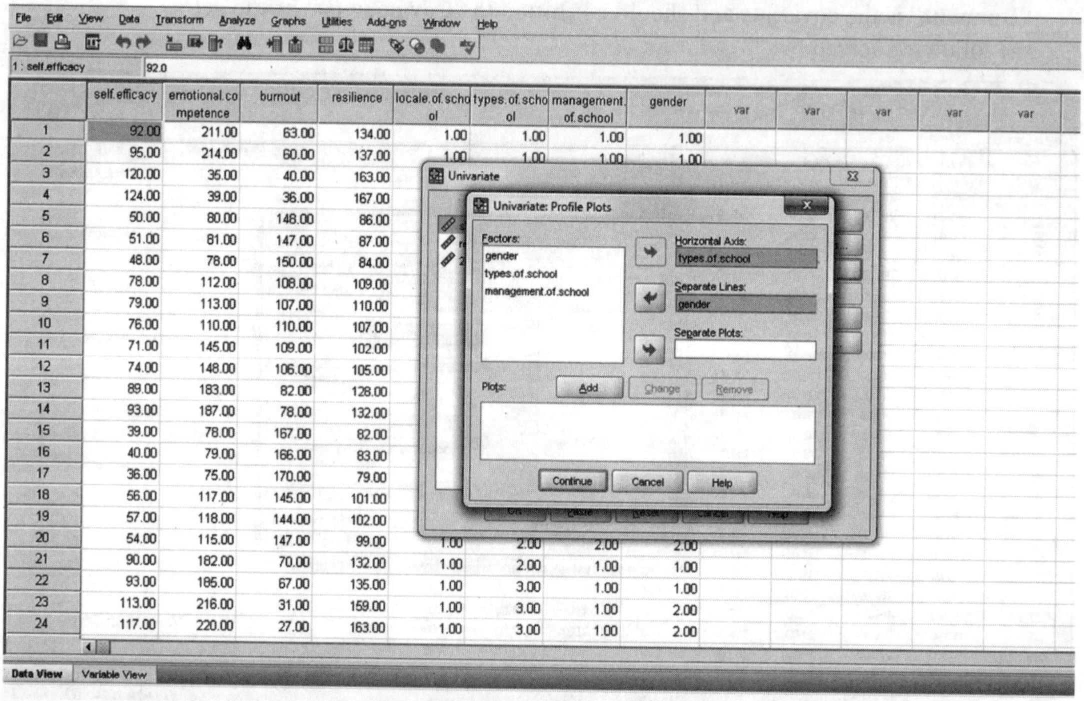

193. Click on "**Add**" icon to get the following screen.

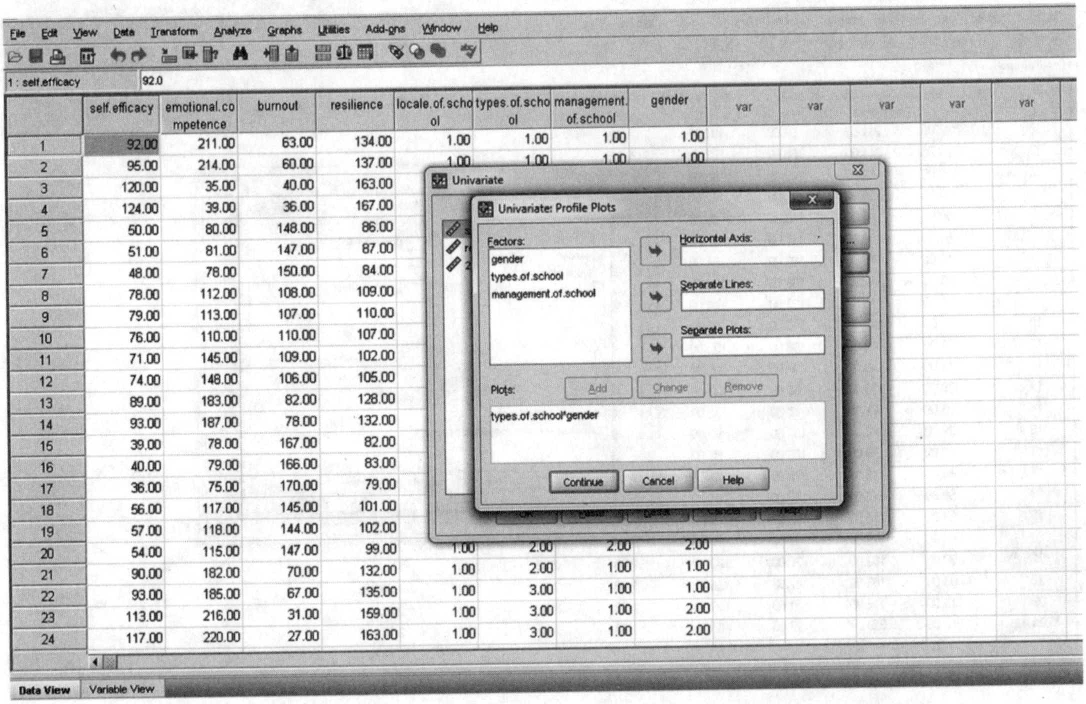

194. Now shift "**Types of School**" to "**Horizontal Axis**" slot and "**Management of School**" to "**Separate Lines**" slot to get the following screen.

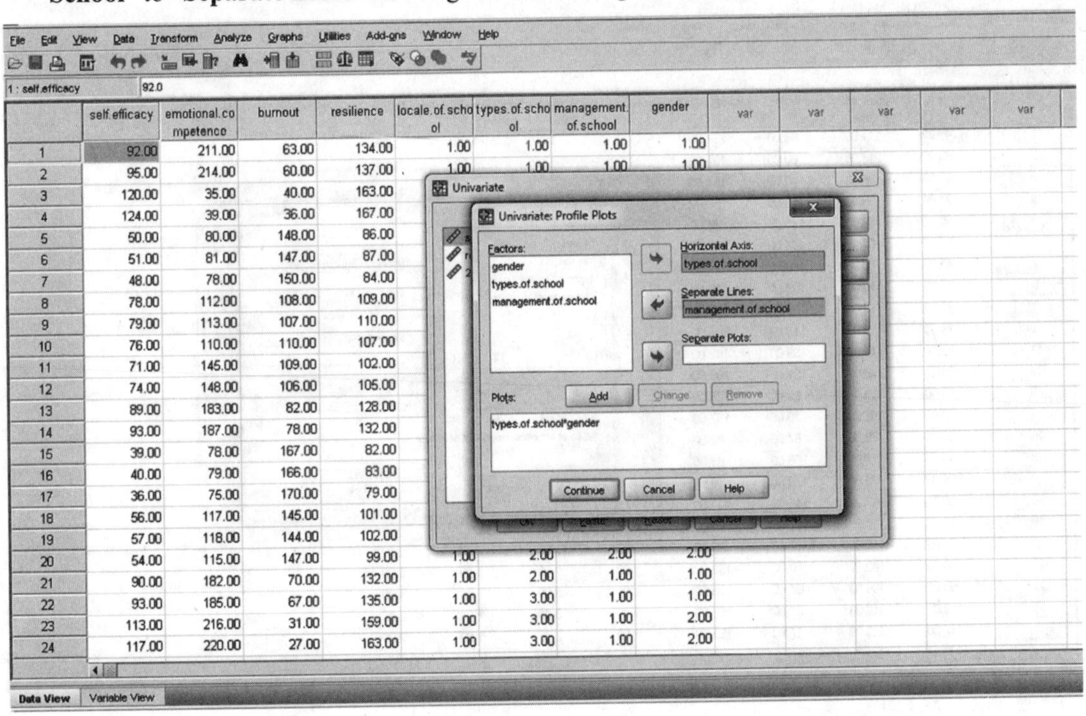

195. Click on "**Add**" to get the following Screen.

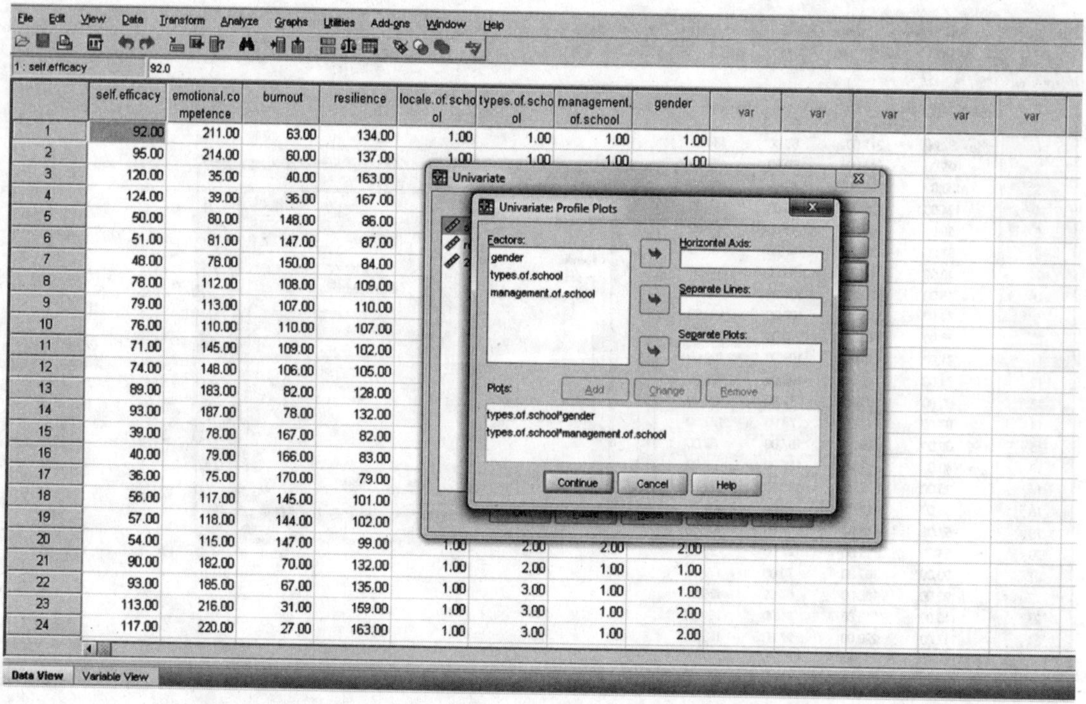

196. Shift "**Management of School**" to "**Horizontal Axis**" slot and "**Gender**" to "**Separate Lines**" slot to get the following screen.

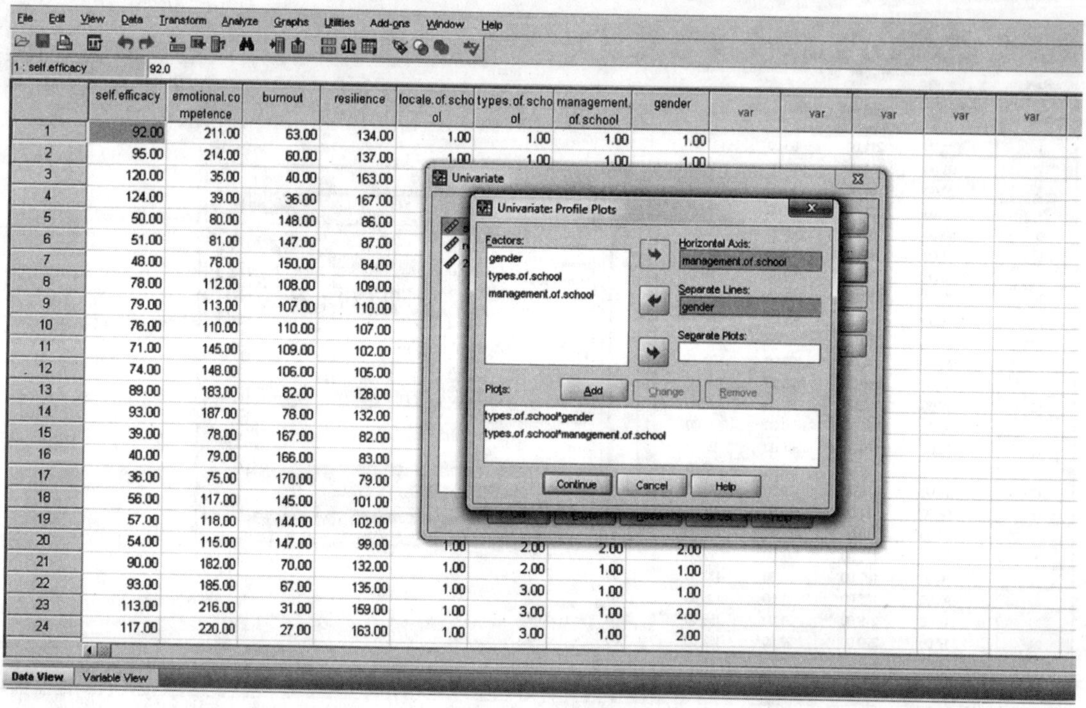

197. Click on "**Add**" to get the following screen.

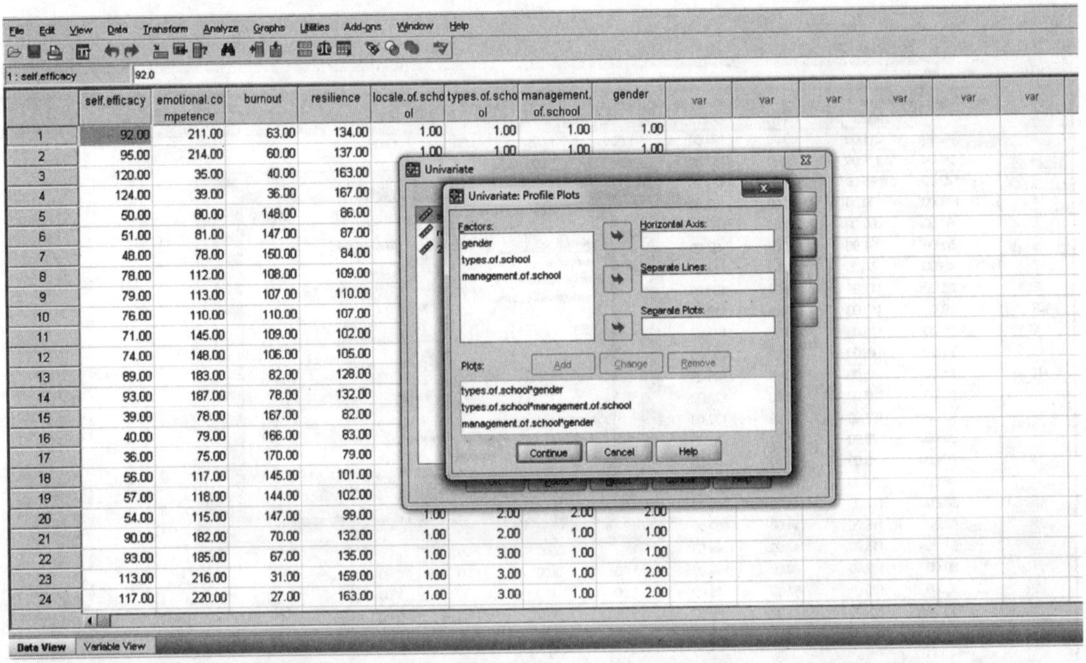

198. Shift "**Types of School**" to "**Horizontal Axis**" slot, "**Management of School**" to "**Separate Lines**" slot and "**Gender**" to "**Separate Plots**" slot to get the following screen.

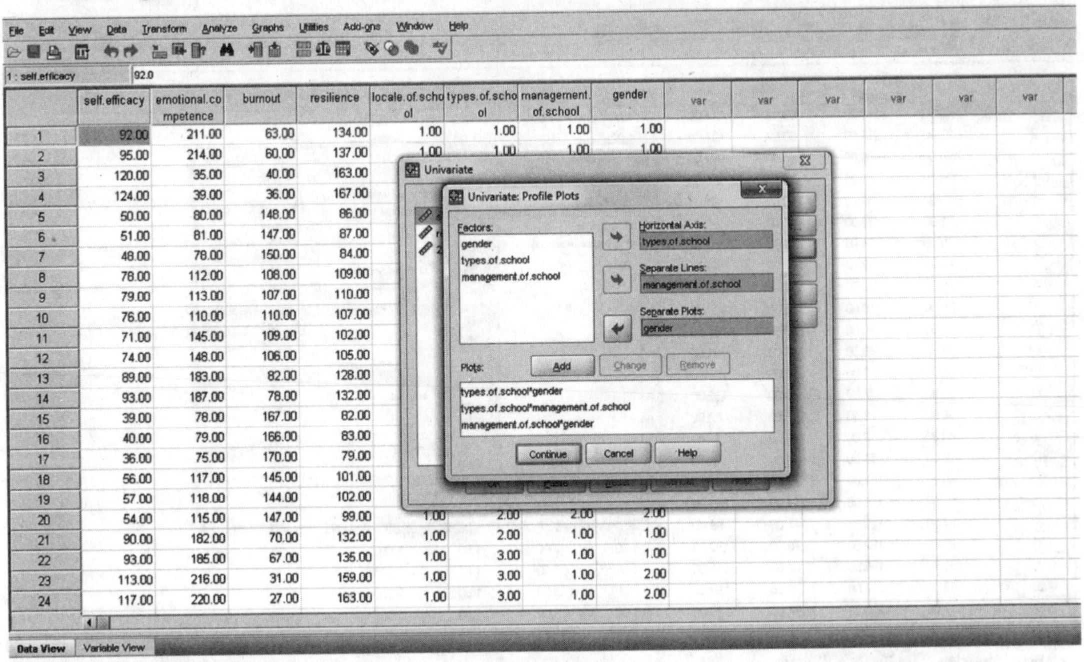

199. Click on "**Add**" to get the following screen.

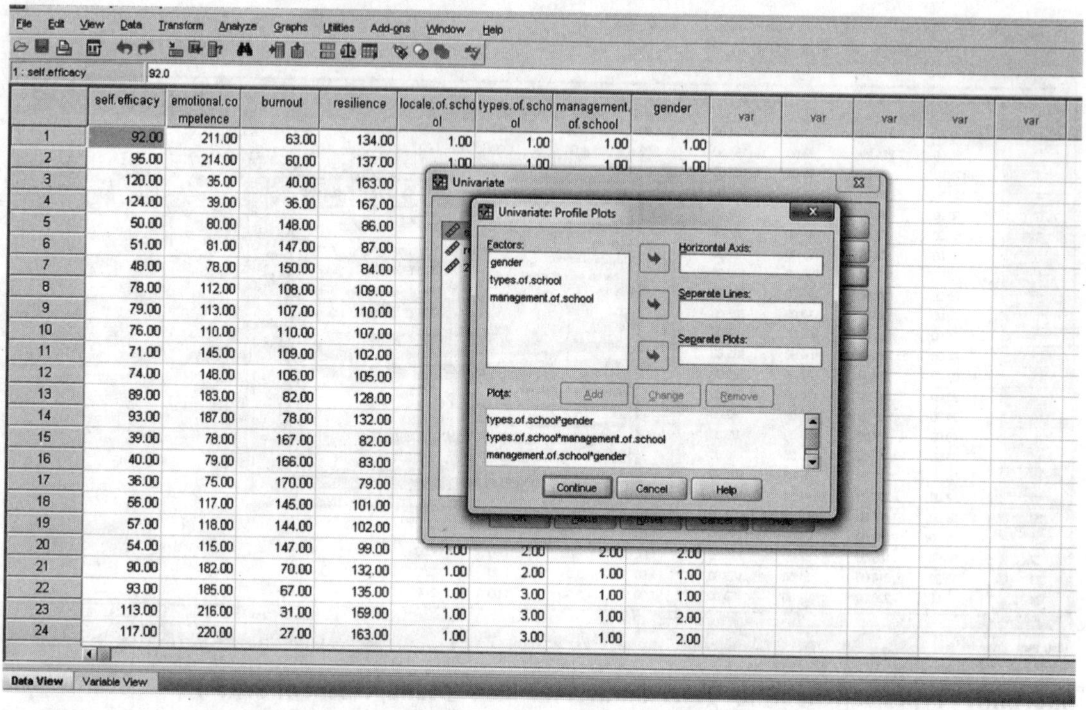

200. Click on "**Continue**" icon to get the following screen.

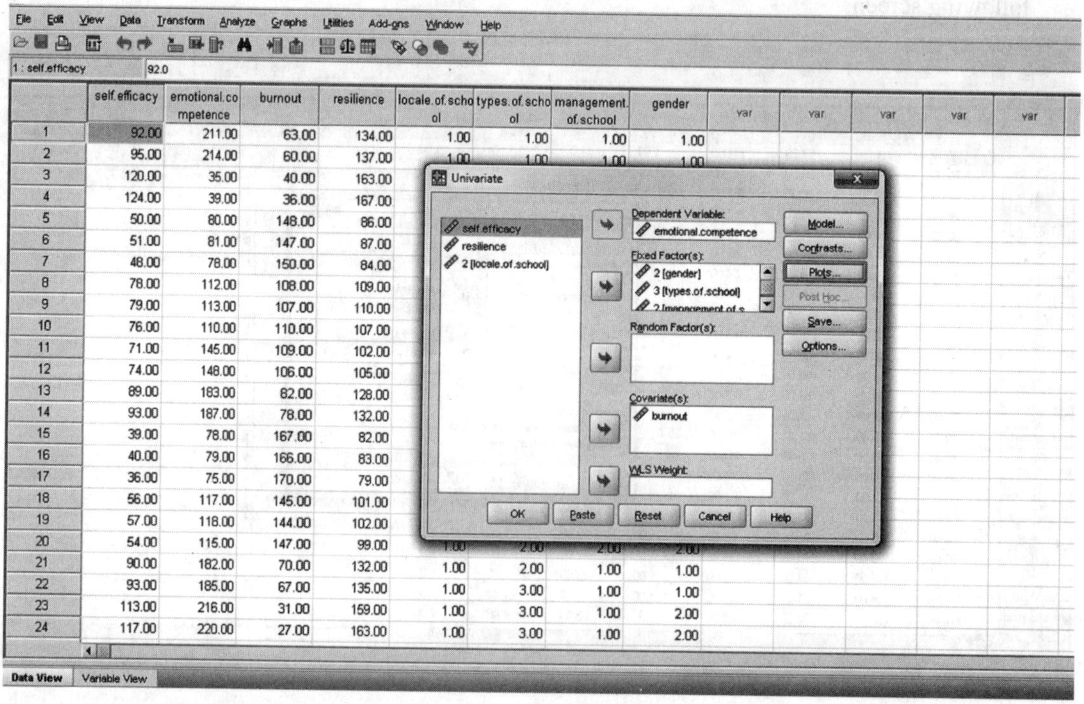

201. Click on "**Options**" icon to get the following screen.

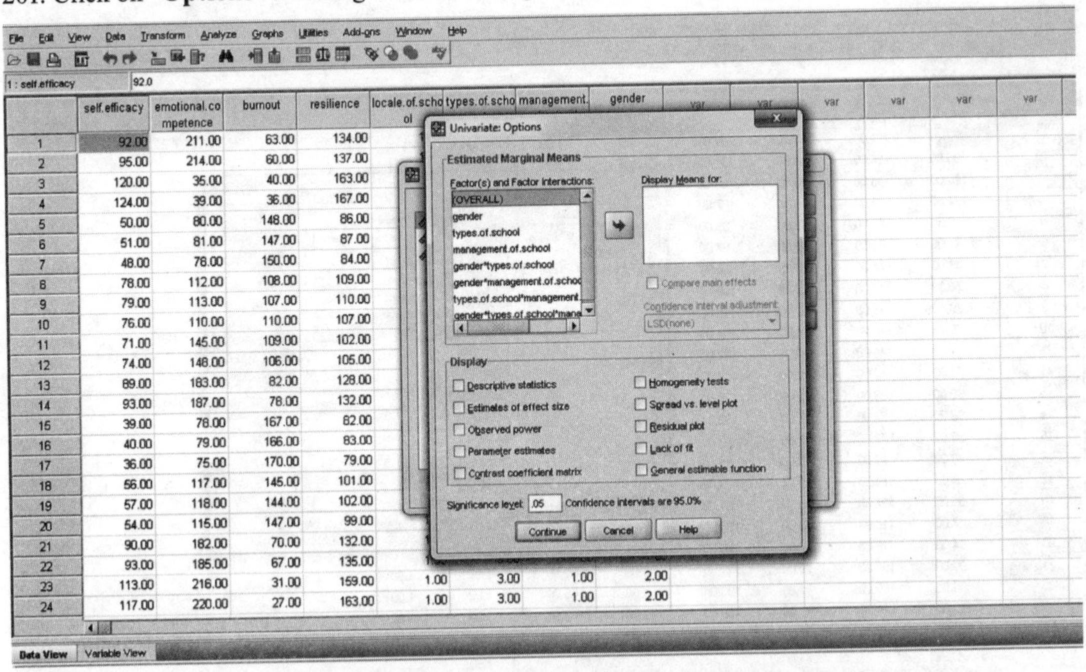

202. Shift all variables from "**Factor(s) and Factor Interactions**" box to "**Display Means For**" box, also highlight under "**Display**" "**Descriptive Statistics**", "**Homogeneity Tests**" and "**Estimates of effect size**" to get the following screen.

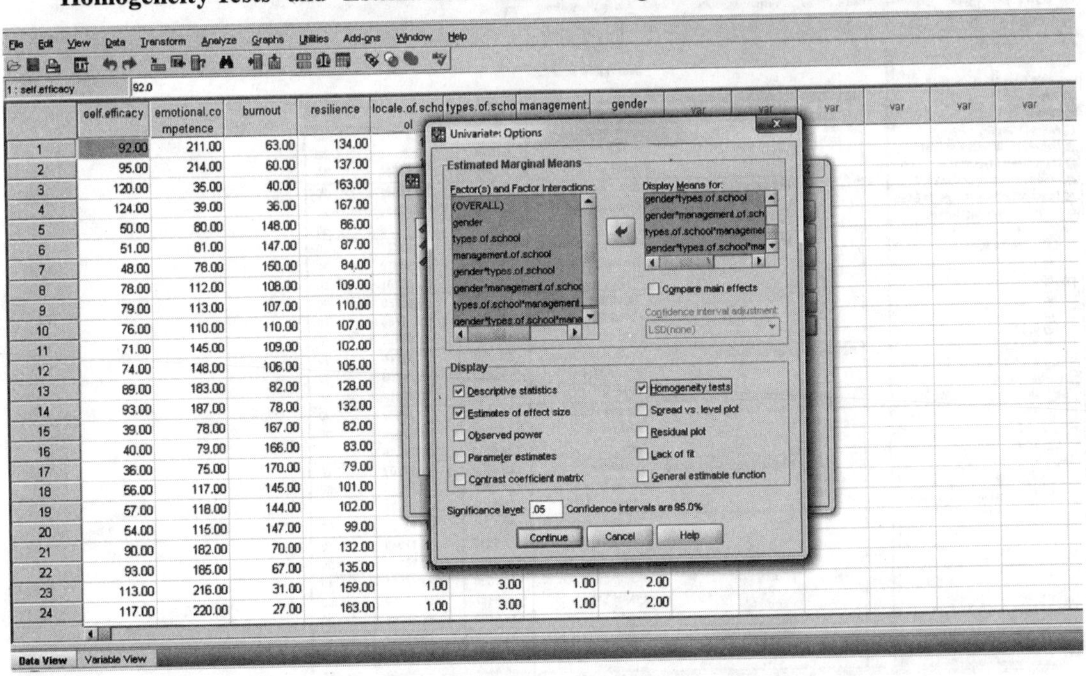

203. Click on "**Continue**" to get the following screen.

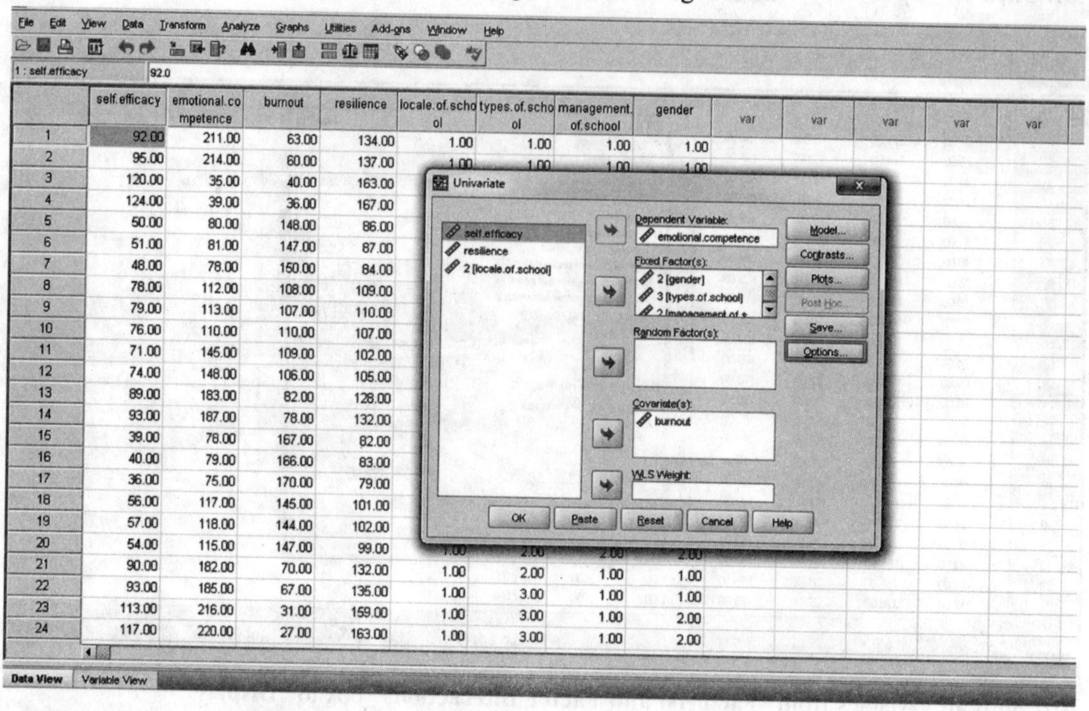

204. Click on "**OK**" to get the following outputs of Three Way ANCOVA.

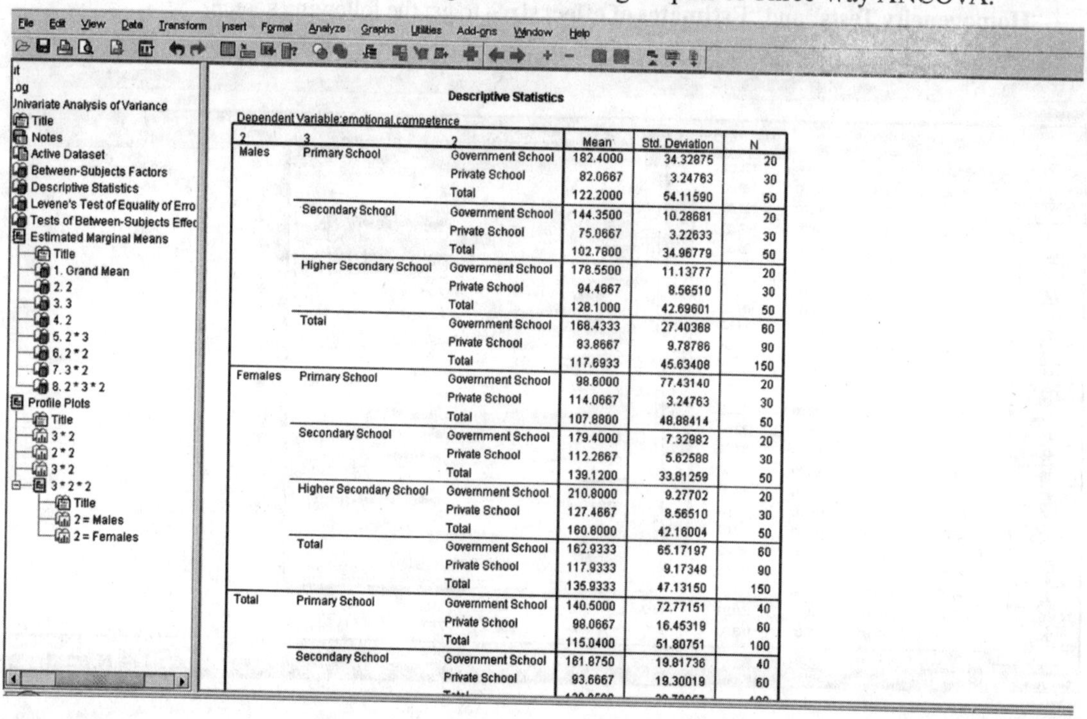

Descriptive Statistics

Dependent Variable:emotional.competence

2	3	2	Mean	Std. Deviation	N
Males	Primary School	Government School	182.4000	34.32875	20
		Private School	82.0667	3.24763	30
		Total	122.2000	54.11590	50
	Secondary School	Government School	144.3500	10.28681	20
		Private School	75.0667	3.22633	30
		Total	102.7800	34.96779	50
	Higher Secondary School	Government School	178.5500	11.13777	20
		Private School	94.4667	8.56510	30
		Total	128.1000	42.69601	50
	Total	Government School	168.4333	27.40368	60
		Private School	83.8667	9.78786	90
		Total	117.6933	45.63408	150
Females	Primary School	Government School	98.6000	77.43140	20
		Private School	114.0667	3.24763	30
		Total	107.8800	48.88414	50
	Secondary School	Government School	179.4000	7.32982	20
		Private School	112.2667	5.62588	30
		Total	139.1200	33.81259	50
	Higher Secondary School	Government School	210.8000	9.27702	20
		Private School	127.4667	8.56510	30
		Total	160.8000	42.16004	50
	Total	Government School	162.9333	65.17197	60
		Private School	117.9333	9.17348	90
		Total	135.9333	47.13150	150
Total	Primary School	Government School	140.5000	72.77151	40
		Private School	98.0667	16.45319	60
		Total	115.0400	51.80751	100
	Secondary School	Government School	161.8750	19.81736	40
		Private School	93.6667	19.30019	60

Levene's Test of Equality of Error Variances[a]

Dependent Variable:emotional.competence

F	df1	df2	Sig.
276.659	11	288	.000

Tests the null hypothesis that the error variance of the dependent variable is equal across groups.

a. Design: Intercept + burnout + gender + types.of.school + management.of.school + gender * types.of.school + gender * management.of.school + types.of.school * management.of.school + gender * types.of.school * management.of.school

Tests of Between-Subjects Effects

Dependent Variable:emotional.competence

Source	Type III Sum of Squares	df	Mean Square	F	Sig.	Partial Eta Squared
Corrected Model	520789.934[a]	12	43399.161	85.643	.000	.782
Intercept	25817.224	1	25817.224	50.947	.000	.151
burnout	3981.887	1	3981.887	7.858	.005	.027
gender	14585.462	1	14585.462	28.783	.000	.091
types.of.school	58173.122	2	29086.561	57.399	.000	.286
management.of.school	51117.414	1	51117.414	100.874	.000	.260
gender * types.of.school	58450.651	2	29225.325	57.673	.000	.287
gender * management.of.school	29241.567	1	29241.567	57.705	.000	.167
types.of.school * management.of.school	16795.578	2	8397.789	16.572	.000	.104
gender * types.of.school * management.of.school	54719.284	2	27359.642	53.991	.000	.273
Error	145435.613	287	506.744			
Total	5490712.000	300				
Corrected Total	666225.547	299				

a. R Squared = .782 (Adjusted R Squared = .773)

Estimated Marginal Means

1. Grand Mean

Dependent Variable:emotional.competence

Mean	Std. Error	95% Confidence Interval	
		Lower Bound	Upper Bound
135.640[a]	1.569	132.552	138.728

a. Covariates appearing in the model are evaluated at the following values: burnout = 111.5933.

2. 2

Dependent Variable:emotional.competence

2	Mean	Std. Error	95% Confidence Interval	
			Lower Bound	Upper Bound
Males	123.110[a]	2.167	118.845	127.375
Females	148.171[a]	3.337	141.602	154.740

a. Covariates appearing in the model are evaluated at the following values: burnout = 111.5933.

3. 3

Dependent Variable:emotional.competence

3	Mean	Std. Error	95% Confidence Interval	
			Lower Bound	Upper Bound
Primary School	123.234[a]	2.695	117.929	128.539
Secondary School	123.523[a]	2.752	118.105	128.940
Higher Secondary School	160.164[a]	3.484	153.306	167.023

a. Covariates appearing in the model are evaluated at the following values: burnout = 111.5933.

4. 2

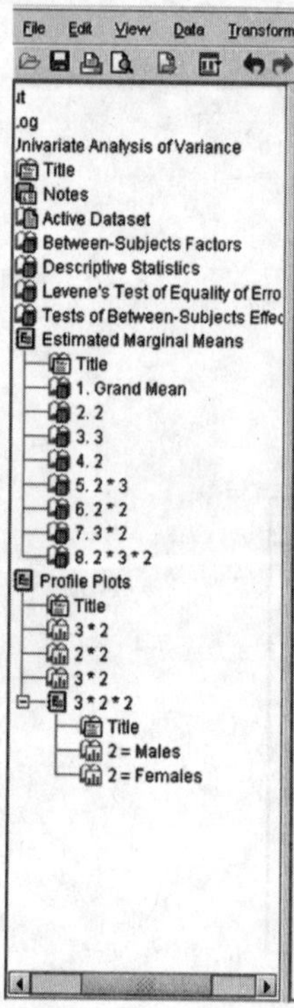

4. 2

Dependent Variable:emotional.competence

2	Mean	Std. Error	95% Confidence Interval Lower Bound	Upper Bound
Government School	179.776ᵃ	5.431	169.086	190.465
Private School	91.505ᵃ	3.748	84.128	98.882

a. Covariates appearing in the model are evaluated at the following values: burnout = 111.5933.

5. 2 * 3

Dependent Variable:emotional.competence

2	3	Mean	Std. Error	95% Confidence Interval Lower Bound	Upper Bound
Males	Primary School	130.852ᵃ	3.286	124.383	137.320
	Secondary School	100.881ᵃ	4.525	91.975	109.787
	Higher Secondary School	137.597ᵃ	3.272	131.156	144.038
Females	Primary School	115.616ᵃ	4.639	106.485	124.748
	Secondary School	146.164ᵃ	3.261	139.764	152.563
	Higher Secondary School	182.732ᵃ	5.839	171.240	194.224

a. Covariates appearing in the model are evaluated at the following values: burnout = 111.5933.

6. 2 * 2

Dependent Variable:emotional.competence

2	2	Mean	Std. Error	95% Confidence Interval Lower Bound	Upper Bound
Males	Government School	177.336ᵃ	4.305	168.863	185.809
	Private School	68.884ᵃ	5.848	57.374	80.394
Females	Government School	182.215ᵃ	7.467	167.518	196.913
	Private School	114.126ᵃ	2.734	108.745	119.508

a. Covariates appearing in the model are evaluated at the following values: burnout = 111.5933.

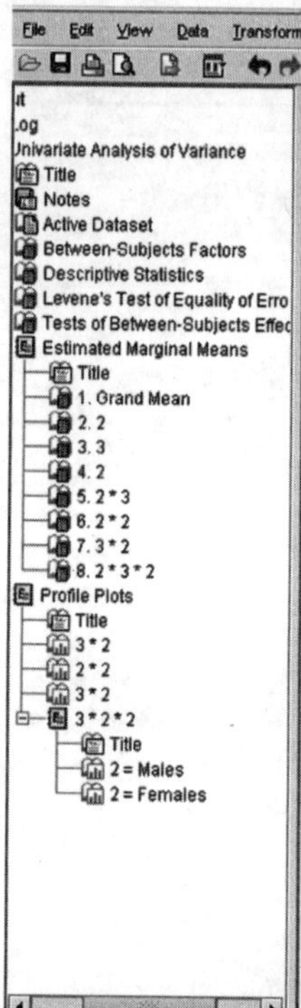

7. 3 * 2

Dependent Variable:emotional.competence

3	2	Mean	Std. Error	95% Confidence Interval Lower Bound	Upper Bound
Primary School	Government School	157.725ᵃ	7.101	143.748	171.702
	Private School	88.743ᵃ	4.417	80.050	97.437
Secondary School	Government School	167.945ᵃ	4.166	159.745	176.145
	Private School	79.100ᵃ	5.954	67.381	90.819
Higher Secondary School	Government School	213.657ᵃ	7.650	198.600	228.714
	Private School	106.672ᵃ	3.285	100.206	113.138

a. Covariates appearing in the model are evaluated at the following values: burnout = 111.5933.

8. 2 * 3 * 2

Dependent Variable:emotional.competence

2	3	2	Mean	Std. Error	95% Confidence Interval Lower Bound	Upper Bound
Males	Primary School	Government School	195.024ᵃ	6.754	181.730	208.318
		Private School	66.680ᵃ	6.857	53.183	80.177
	Secondary School	Government School	145.935ᵃ	5.065	135.965	155.905
		Private School	55.828ᵃ	8.000	40.082	71.573
	Higher Secondary School	Government School	191.049ᵃ	6.725	177.813	204.285
		Private School	84.144ᵃ	5.518	73.283	95.006
Females	Primary School	Government School	120.426ᵃ	9.272	102.177	138.675
		Private School	110.807ᵃ	4.271	102.400	119.214
	Secondary School	Government School	189.955ᵃ	6.286	177.582	202.328
		Private School	102.372ᵃ	5.418	91.709	113.036
	Higher Secondary School	Government School	236.264ᵃ	10.385	215.823	256.706
		Private School	129.200ᵃ	4.156	121.020	137.381

a. Covariates appearing in the model are evaluated at the following values: burnout = 111.5933.

Profile Plots

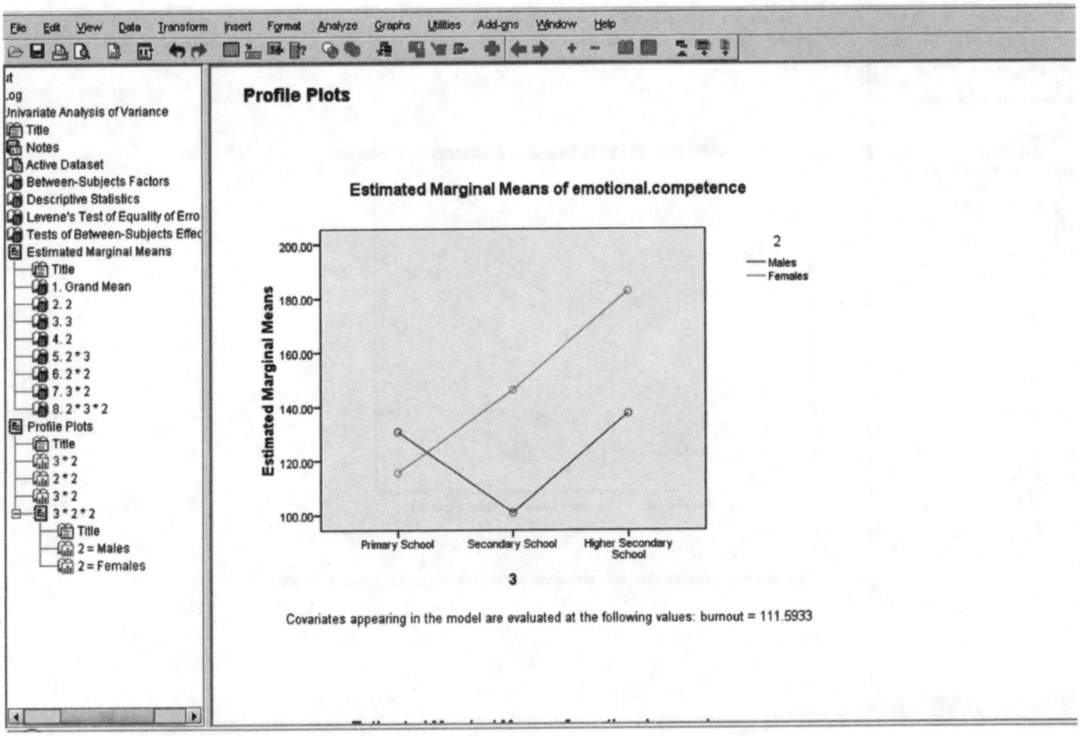
File Edit View Data Transform Insert Format Analyze Graphs Utilities Add-ons Window Help
Profile Plots
Estimated Marginal Means of emotional.competence
Estimated Marginal Means
200.00
180.00
160.00
140.00
120.00
100.00
Primary School
Secondary School
Higher Secondary School
3
2
Males
Females
Covariates appearing in the model are evaluated at the following values: burnout = 111.5933
Univariate Analysis of Variance
Title
Notes
Active Dataset
Between-Subjects Factors
Descriptive Statistics
Levene's Test of Equality of Erro
Tests of Between-Subjects Effec
Estimated Marginal Means
1. Grand Mean
2. 2
3. 3
4. 2
5. 2 * 3
6. 2 * 2
7. 3 * 2
8. 2 * 3 * 2
Profile Plots
3 * 2
2 * 2
3 * 2
3 * 2 * 2
2 = Males
2 = Females

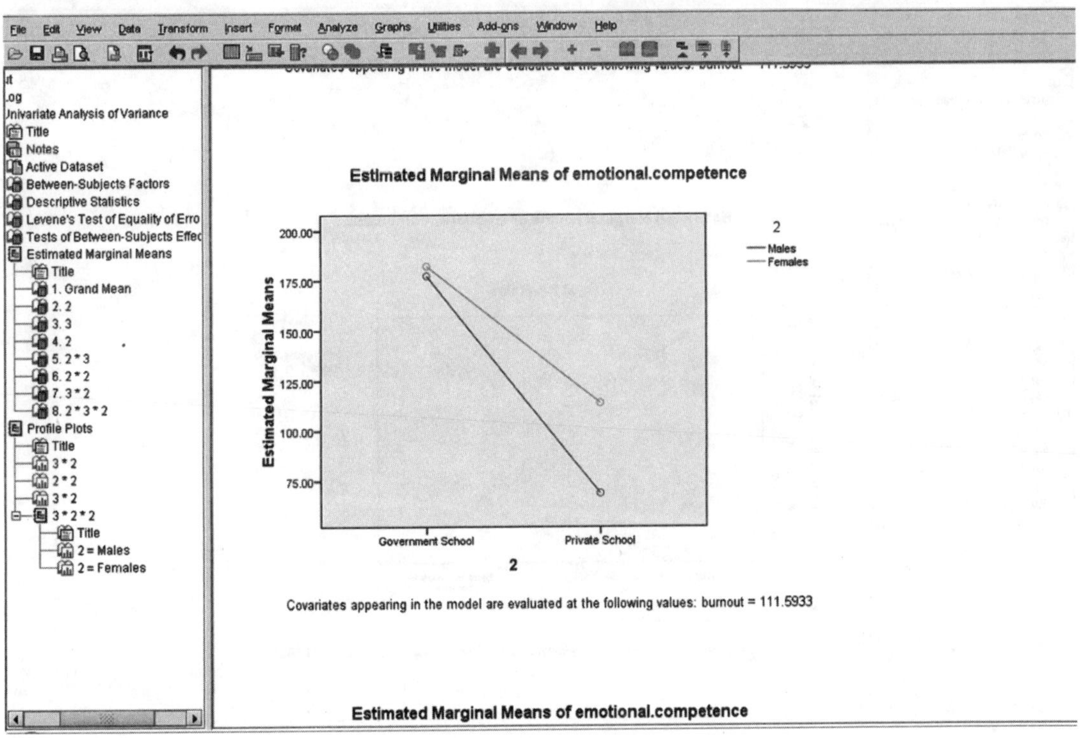
File Edit View Data Transform Insert Format Analyze Graphs Utilities Add-ons Window Help
Estimated Marginal Means of emotional.competence
Estimated Marginal Means
200.00
175.00
150.00
125.00
100.00
75.00
Government School
Private School
2
2
Males
Females
Covariates appearing in the model are evaluated at the following values: burnout = 111.5933
Estimated Marginal Means of emotional.competence
Univariate Analysis of Variance
Title
Notes
Active Dataset
Between-Subjects Factors
Descriptive Statistics
Levene's Test of Equality of Erro
Tests of Between-Subjects Effec
Estimated Marginal Means
1. Grand Mean
2. 2
3. 3
4. 2
5. 2 * 3
6. 2 * 2
7. 3 * 2
8. 2 * 3 * 2
Profile Plots
3 * 2
2 * 2
3 * 2
3 * 2 * 2
2 = Males
2 = Females

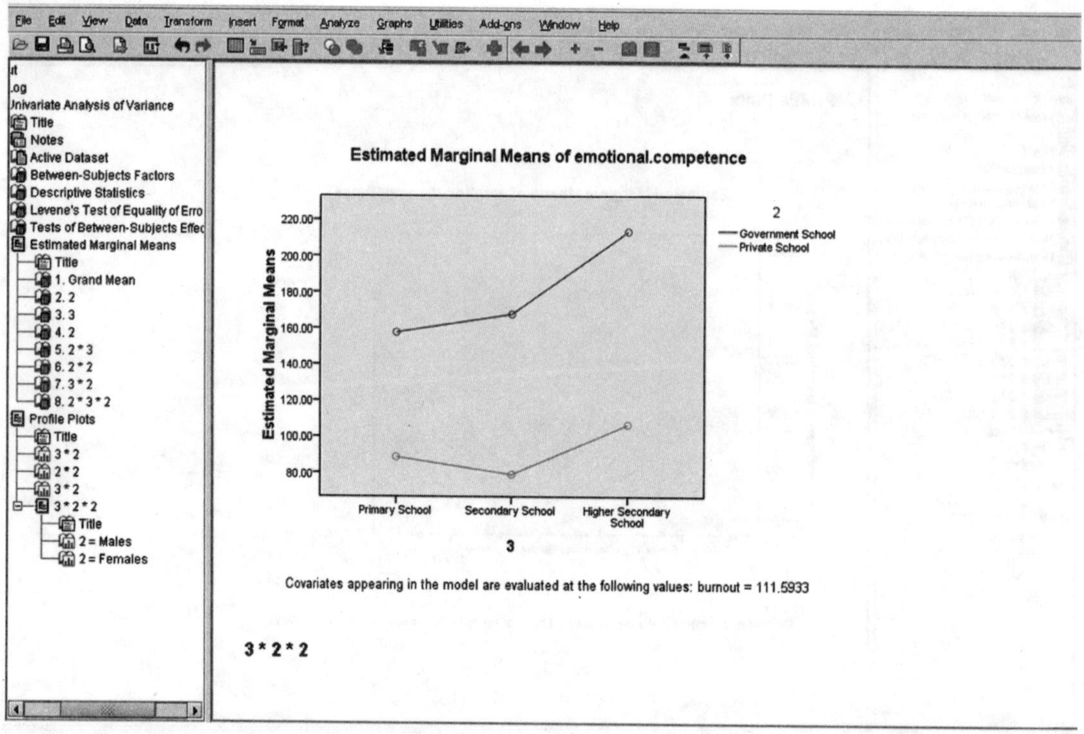
File Edit View Data Transform Insert Format Analyze Graphs Utilities Add-ons Window Help
Univariate Analysis of Variance
Title
Notes
Active Dataset
Between-Subjects Factors
Descriptive Statistics
Levene's Test of Equality of Erro
Tests of Between-Subjects Effec
Estimated Marginal Means
Title
1. Grand Mean
2. 2
3. 3
4. 2
5. 2 * 3
6. 2 * 2
7. 3 * 2
8. 2 * 3 * 2
Profile Plots
Title
3 * 2
2 * 2
3 * 2
3 * 2 * 2
Title
2 = Males
2 = Females
Estimated Marginal Means of emotional.competence
Estimated Marginal Means
220.00
200.00
180.00
160.00
140.00
120.00
100.00
80.00
Primary School
Secondary School
Higher Secondary School
3
2
Government School
Private School
Covariates appearing in the model are evaluated at the following values: burnout = 111.5933
3 * 2 * 2

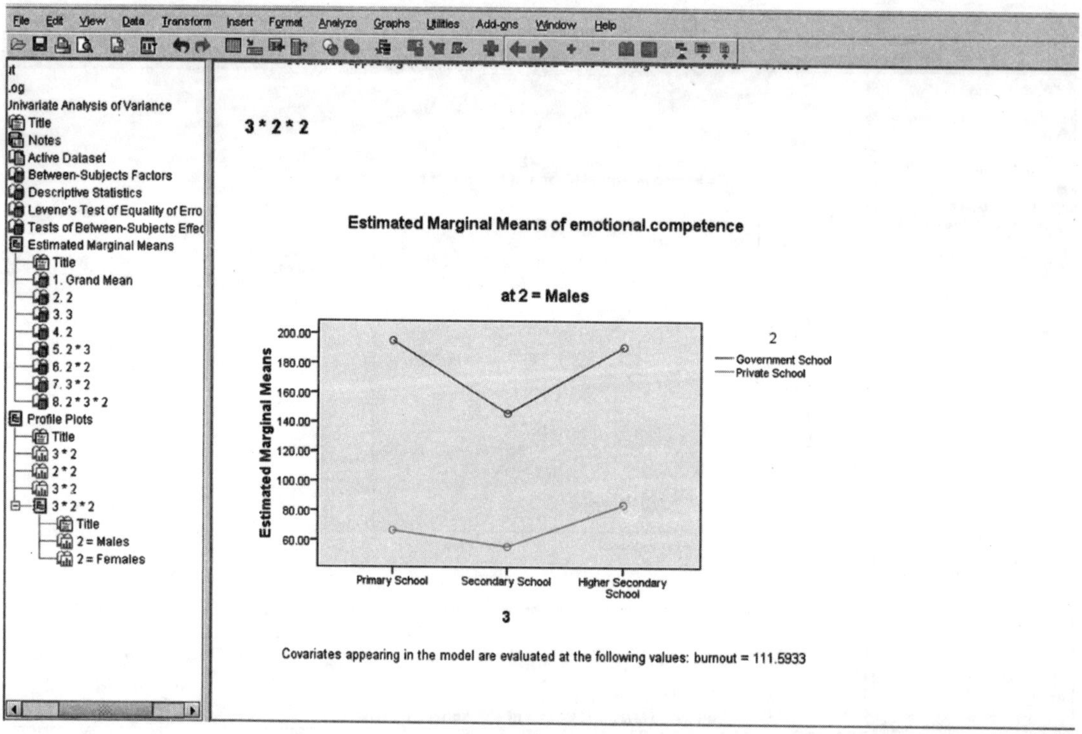
File Edit View Data Transform Insert Format Analyze Graphs Utilities Add-ons Window Help
Univariate Analysis of Variance
Title
Notes
Active Dataset
Between-Subjects Factors
Descriptive Statistics
Levene's Test of Equality of Erro
Tests of Between-Subjects Effec
Estimated Marginal Means
Title
1. Grand Mean
2. 2
3. 3
4. 2
5. 2 * 3
6. 2 * 2
7. 3 * 2
8. 2 * 3 * 2
Profile Plots
Title
3 * 2
2 * 2
3 * 2
3 * 2 * 2
Title
2 = Males
2 = Females
3 * 2 * 2
Estimated Marginal Means of emotional.competence
at 2 = Males
Estimated Marginal Means
200.00
180.00
160.00
140.00
120.00
100.00
80.00
60.00
Primary School
Secondary School
Higher Secondary School
3
2
Government School
Private School
Covariates appearing in the model are evaluated at the following values: burnout = 111.5933

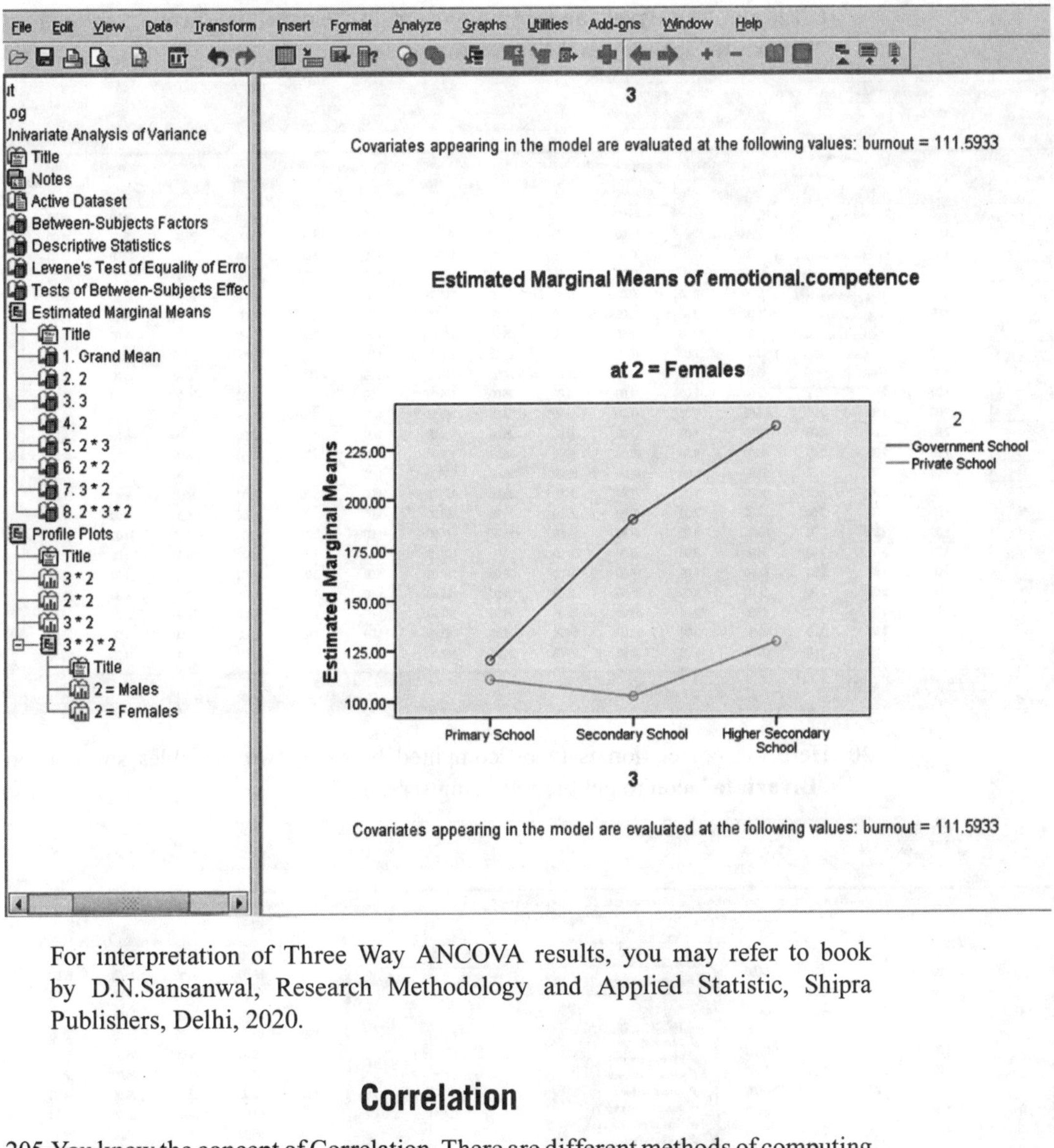

For interpretation of Three Way ANCOVA results, you may refer to book by D.N.Sansanwal, Research Methodology and Applied Statistic, Shipra Publishers, Delhi, 2020.

Correlation

205. You know the concept of Correlation. There are different methods of computing correlation. One of the methods is Pearson Product Moment Correlation which requires two continuous variables having measurement either on Interval Scale or Ratio Scale. Let us understand the use of SPSS for computing correlation with the help of Pearson Product Moment Correlation Method. Let us take the following objective.

To study correlation between Democratic Behaviour and Social Support Behaviour of coaches.

Click on "**Analyse**" and bring curser to "**Correlate**" icon and then to "**Bivariate**" icon to get the following screen.

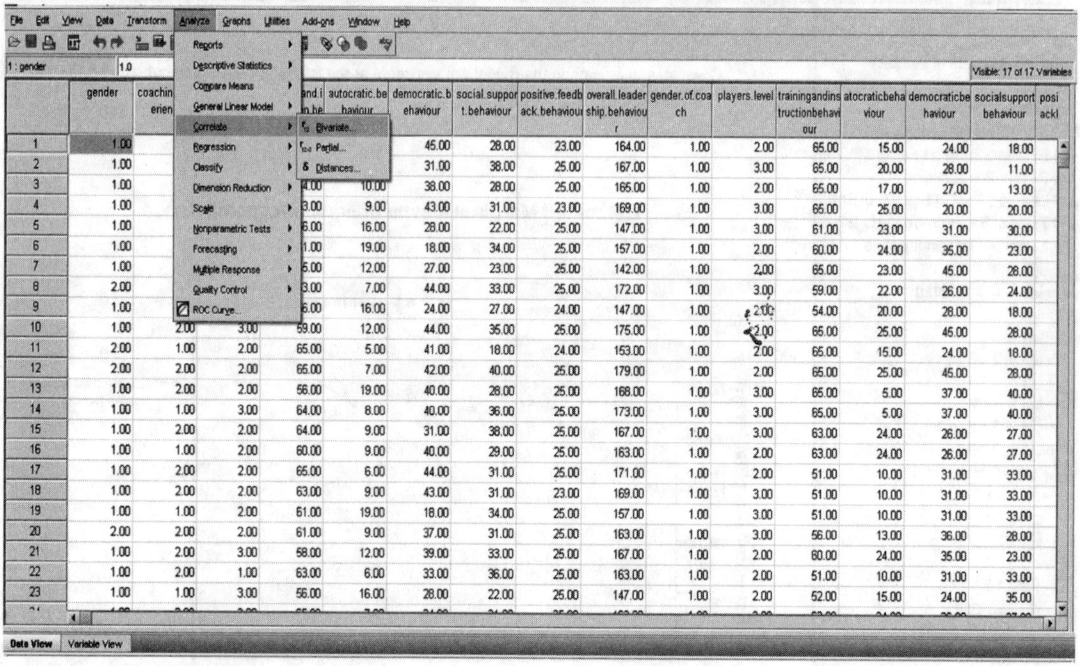

206.Here the correlation is to be computed between two variables so click on "**Bivariate**" icon to get the following screen.

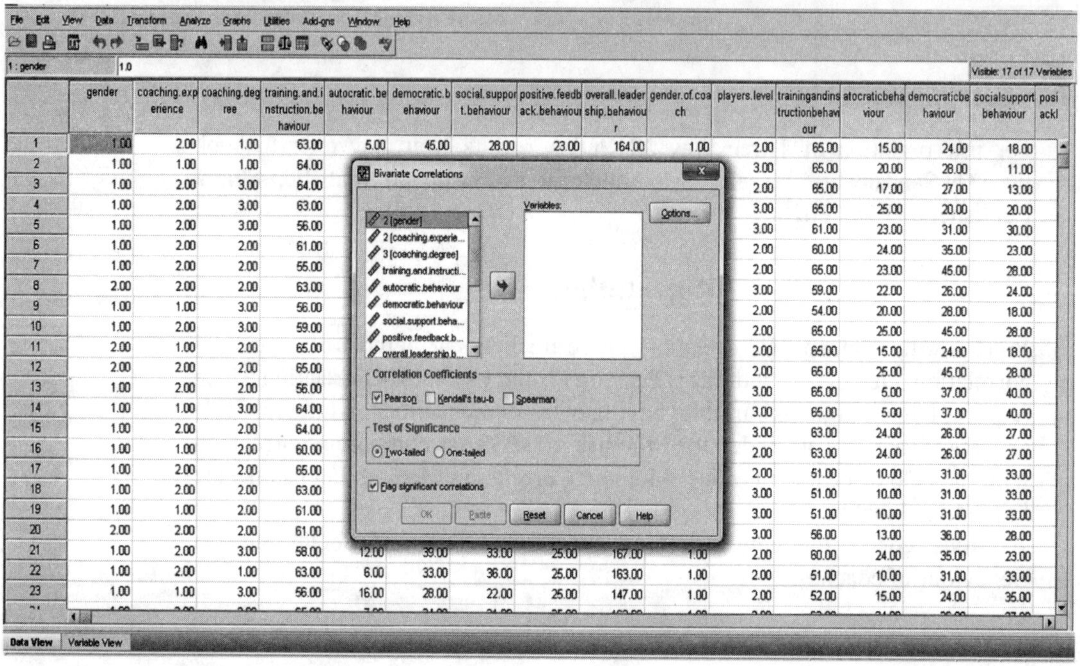

207. The correlation is to be computed between "**Democratic Behaviour** and **Social Support Behaviour**" variables. Shift both these variables under "**Variables**" dialog box to get the following screen.

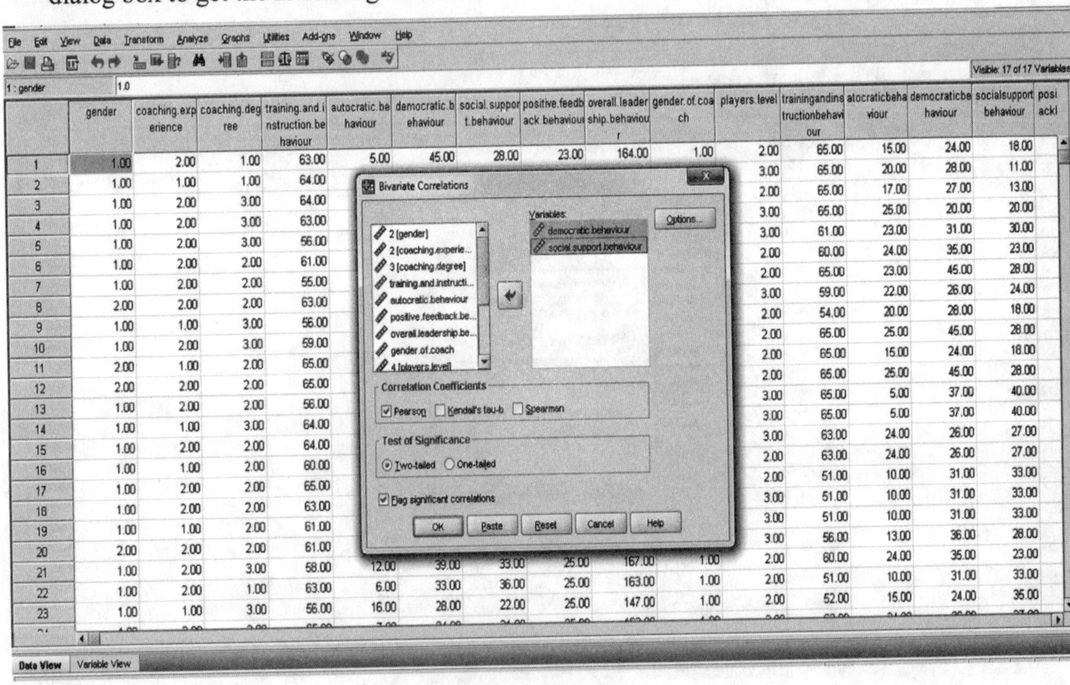

208. Click on "**Options**" to get the following screen.

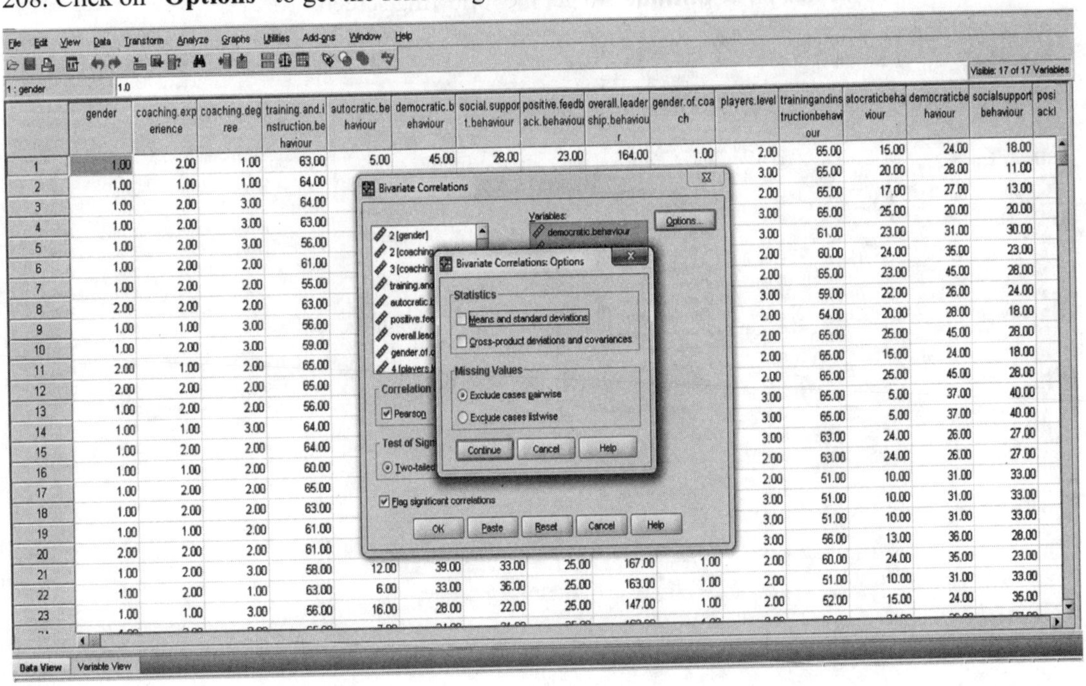

209. In case you want to compute any statistics, you may click on the appropriate "**Statistics**" icon. Suppose you want to calculate "**Means and Standard Deviations**" for both the variables, click on "**Means and Standard Deviations**" slot to get the following screen.

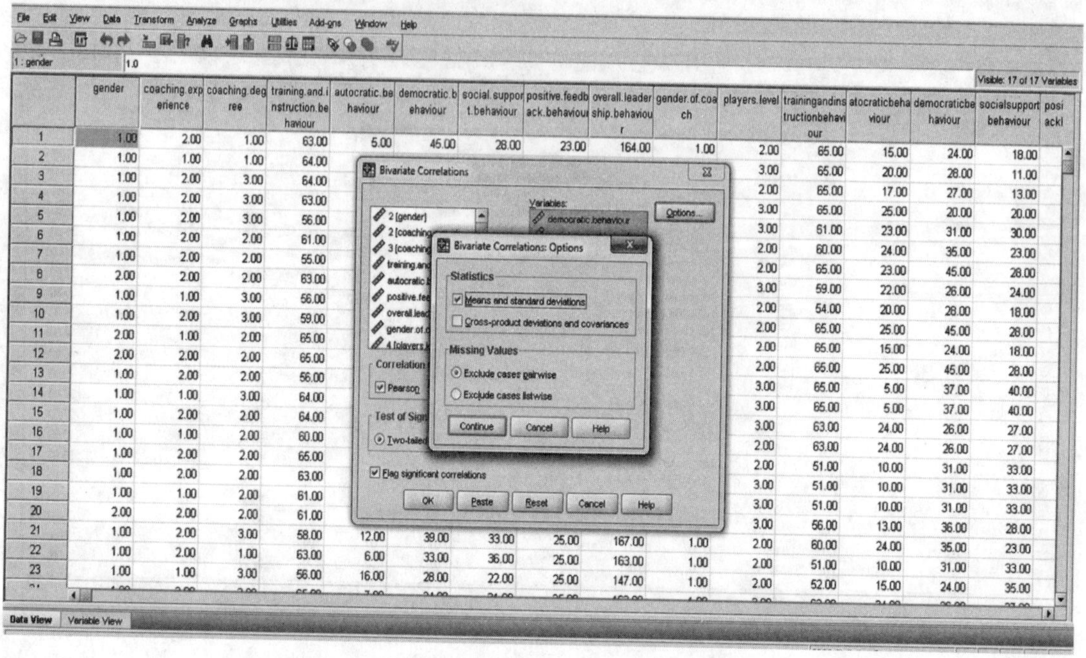

210. Click on "**Continue**" to get the following screen.

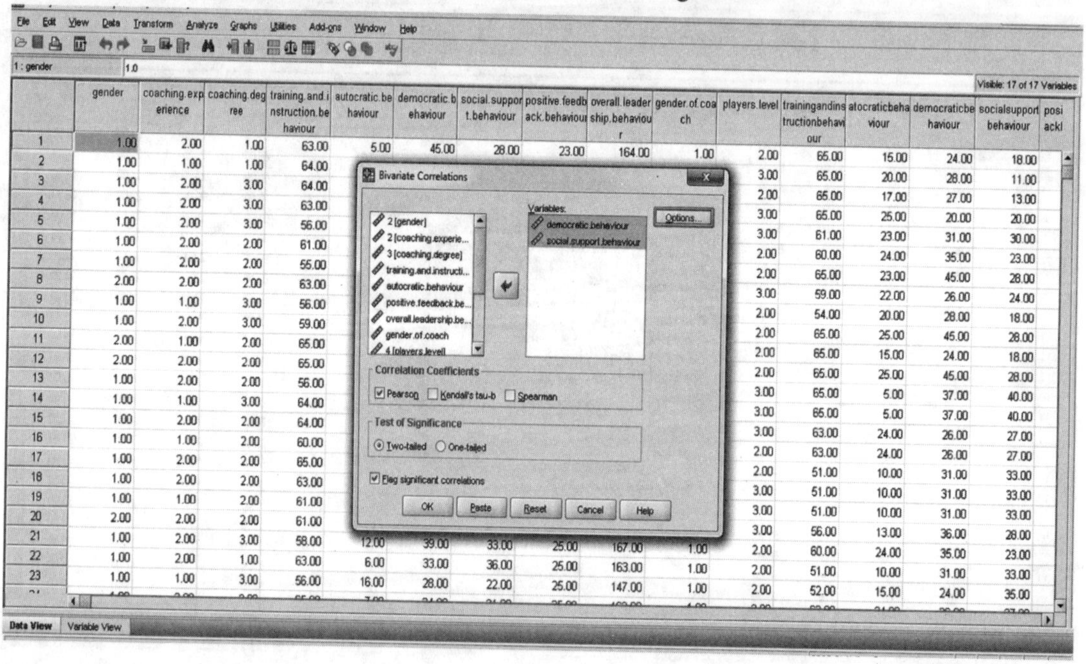

211. In the present case both variables are continuous so Pearson Product Moment Correlation Method is to be used and "**Pearson**" is already highlighted, so click on "**OK**" to get the following outputs of Correlation.

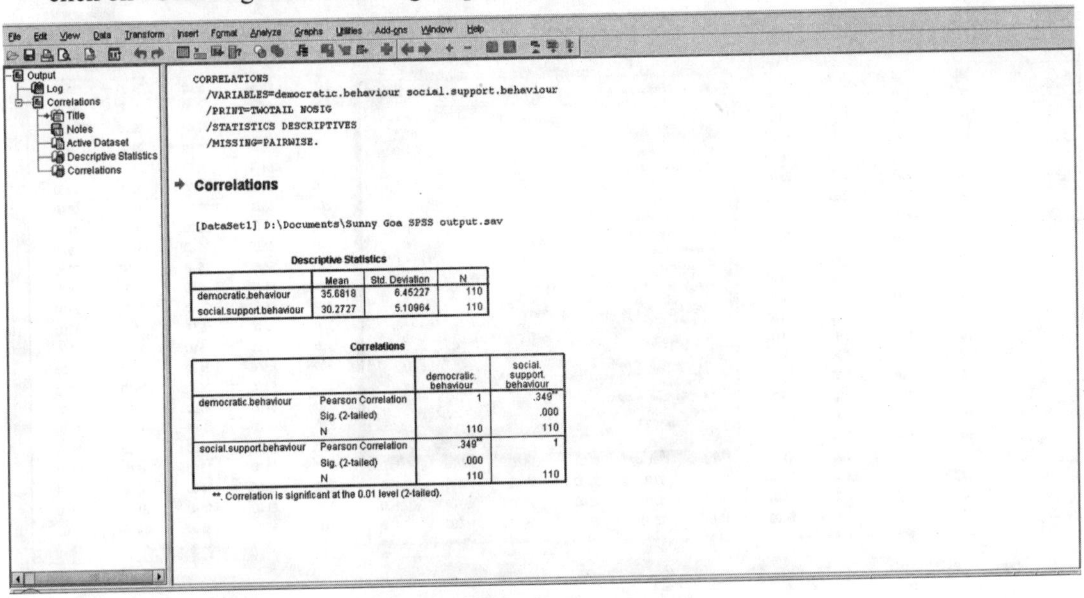

212. Suppose you want to calculate correlation among many continuous variables. Let us take the following objective:
To study correlation among Democratic Behaviour, Social Support Behaviour, Positive Feedback Behaviour and Training & Instruction Behaviour of coaches.
Click on "**Analyse**" bring curser to "**Correlate**" and then to "**Bivariate**" to get the following screen.

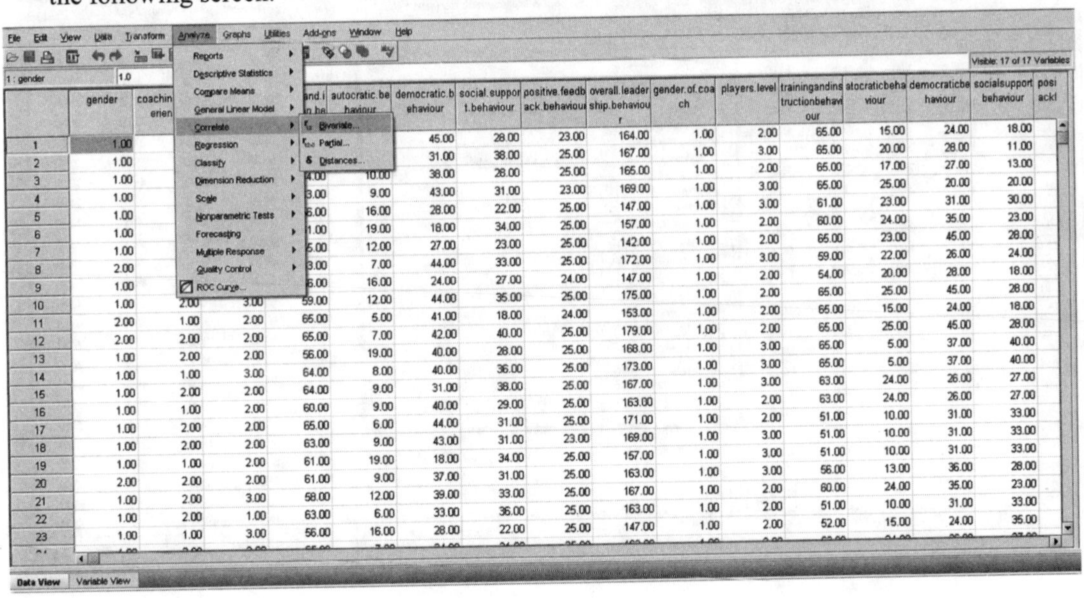

213. Click on "**Bivariate**" to get the following screen.

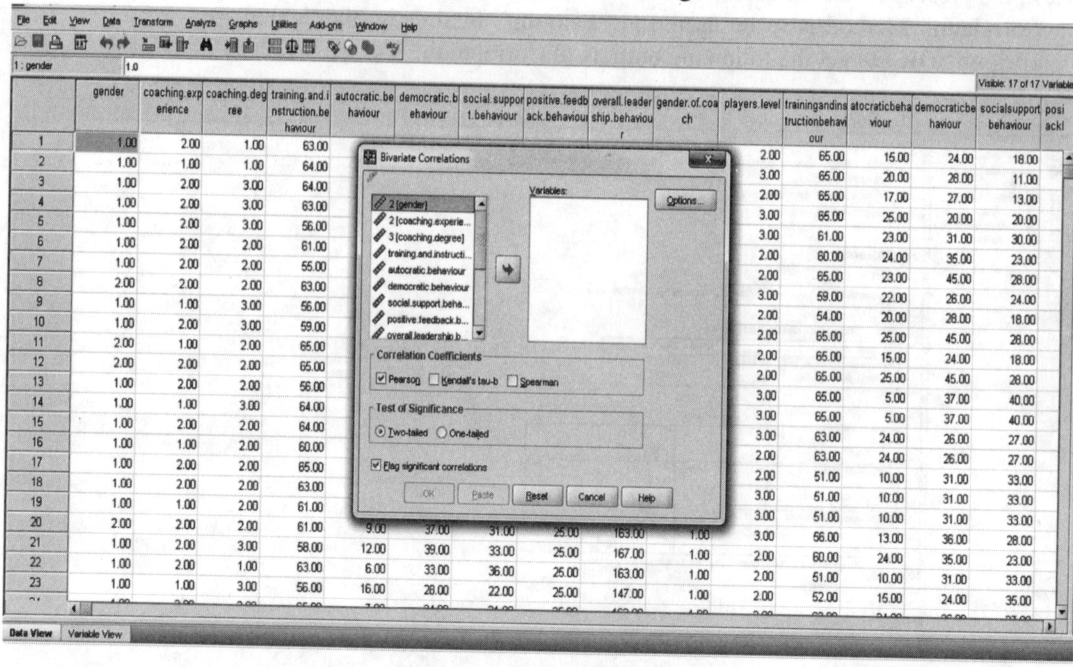

214. Shift "**Democratic Behaviour**", "**Social Support Behaviour**", "**Positive Feedback Behaviour**", and "**Training & Instruction Behaviour**" variables to the "**Variables**" dialogue box to get the following screen.

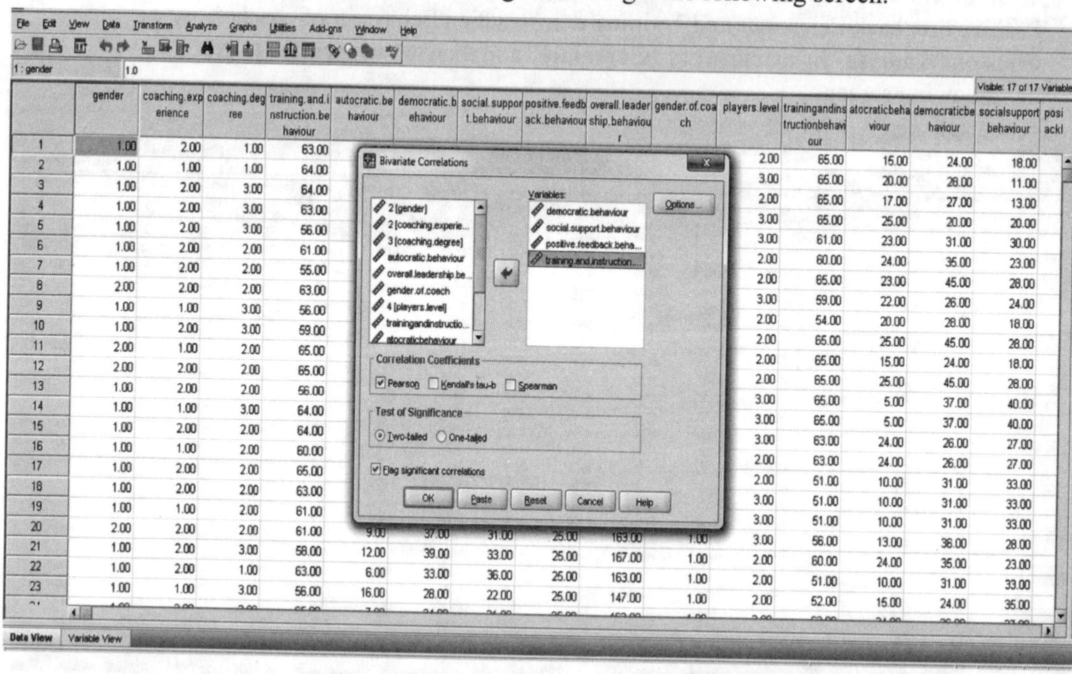

215. In case you do not want to use "**Options**", click on "**OK**" to get the following outputs of Correlation.

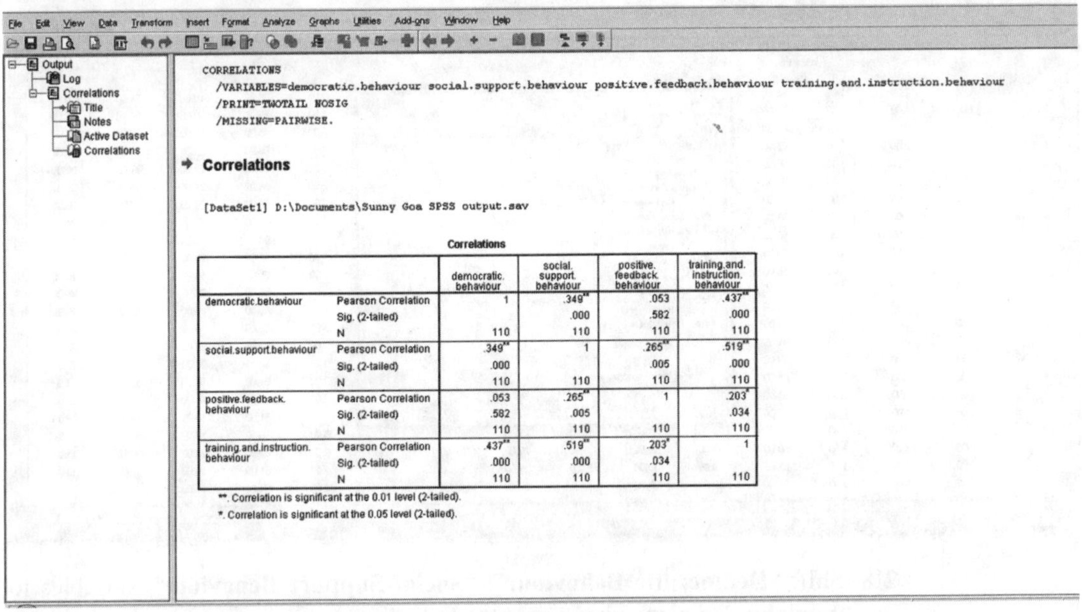

216. Let us consider the following Objective whose data can be analysed with the help of Pearson Product Moment Correlation.

To study correlation between Democratic Behaviour and Social Support Behaviour of Male and Female Coaches separately.

Click on "**Analyse**", bring curser on "**Correlate**" and then to "**Bivariate**" to get the following screen.

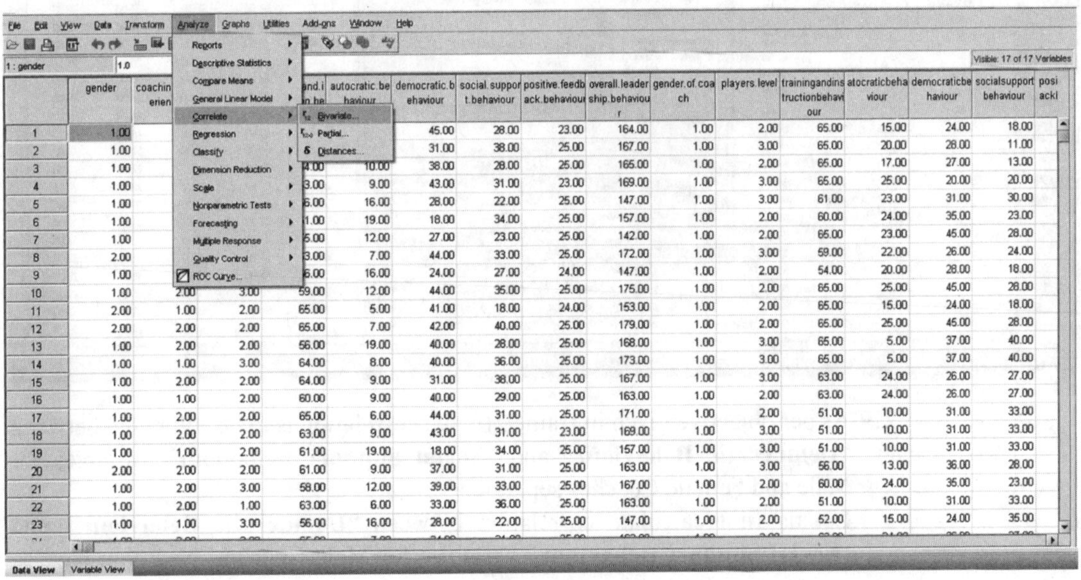

217. Click on "**Bivariate**" to get the following screen.

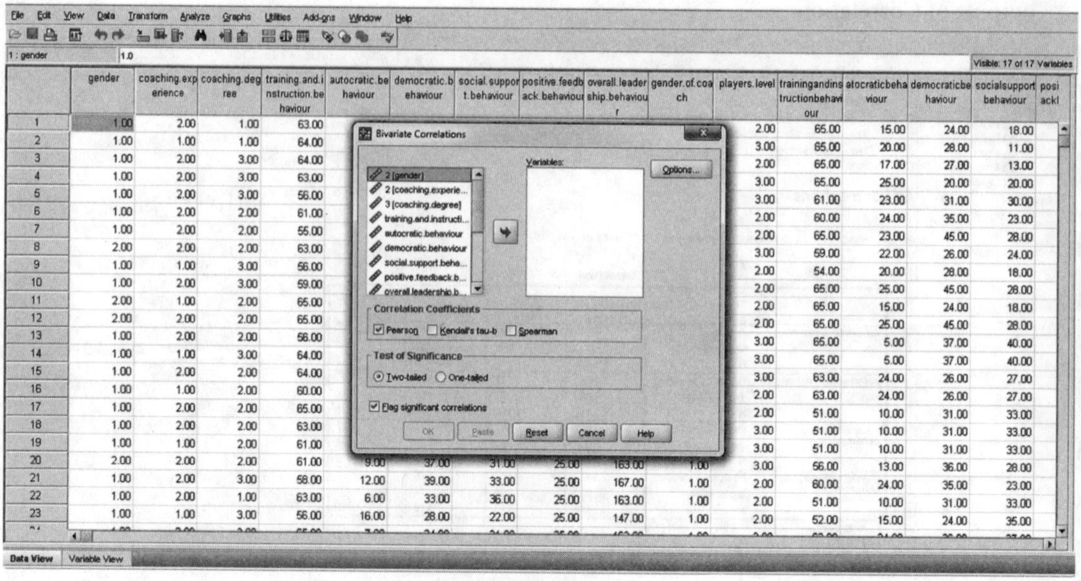

218. Shift "**Democratic Behaviour**", "**Social Support Behaviour**" variables to "**Variables**" dialogue box to get the following screen.

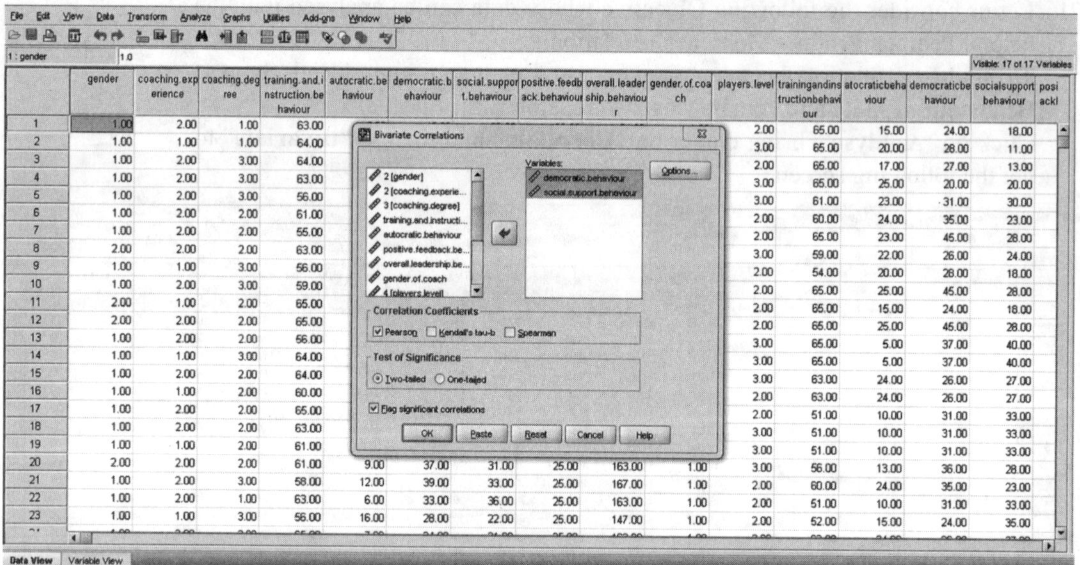

219. As per objective given in frame 216, the correlation is to be computed between "**Democratic Behaviour**" and "**Social Support Behaviour**" variables for Male and Female Coaches separately.

Let us first calculate correlation between "**Democratic Behaviour**", and "**Social Support Behaviour**" variables for Male Coaches. Now you have to take the data only of Male Coaches. So click on "**Data**" icon from the menu bar to get the following screen.

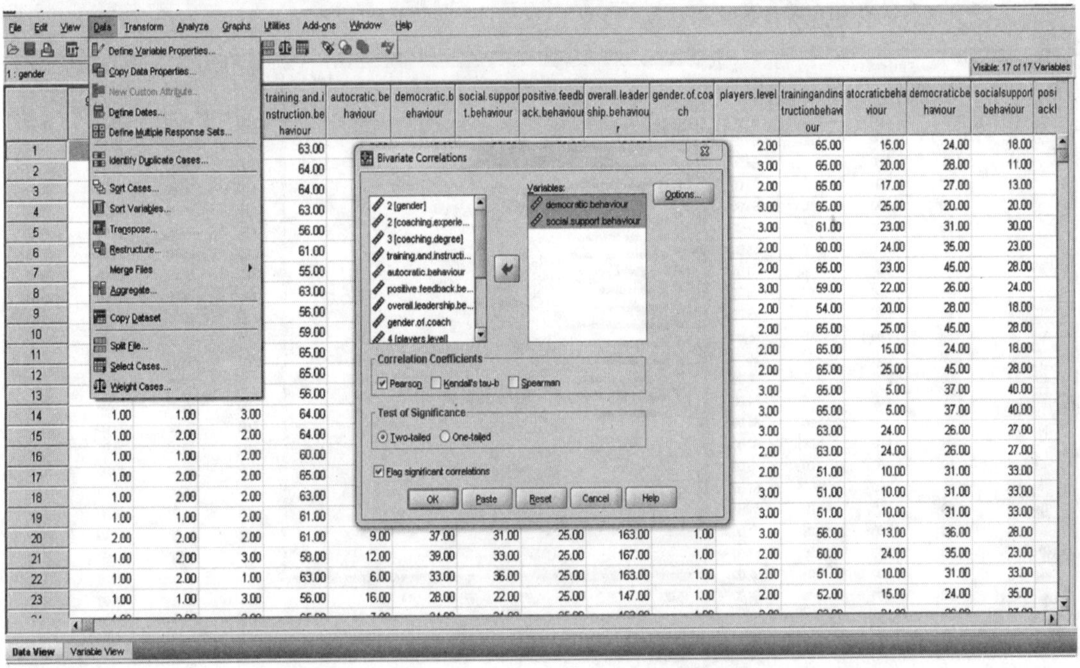

220. Bring curser to '**Split Case**" and click to get the following screen.

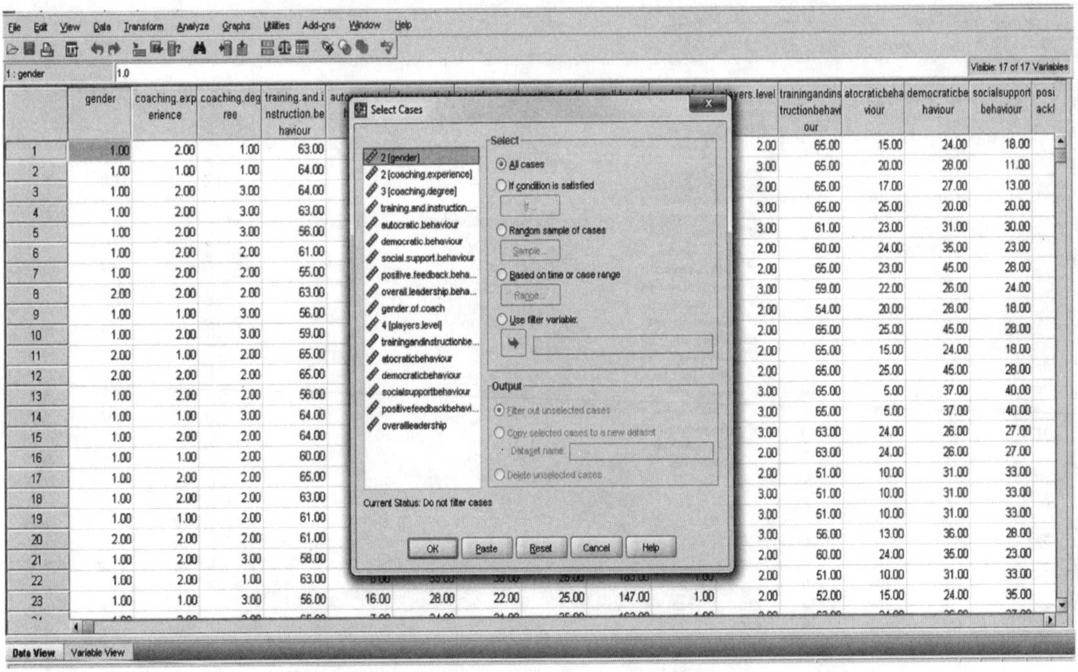

221. Click on "**If condition satisfied**" icon to get the following screen.

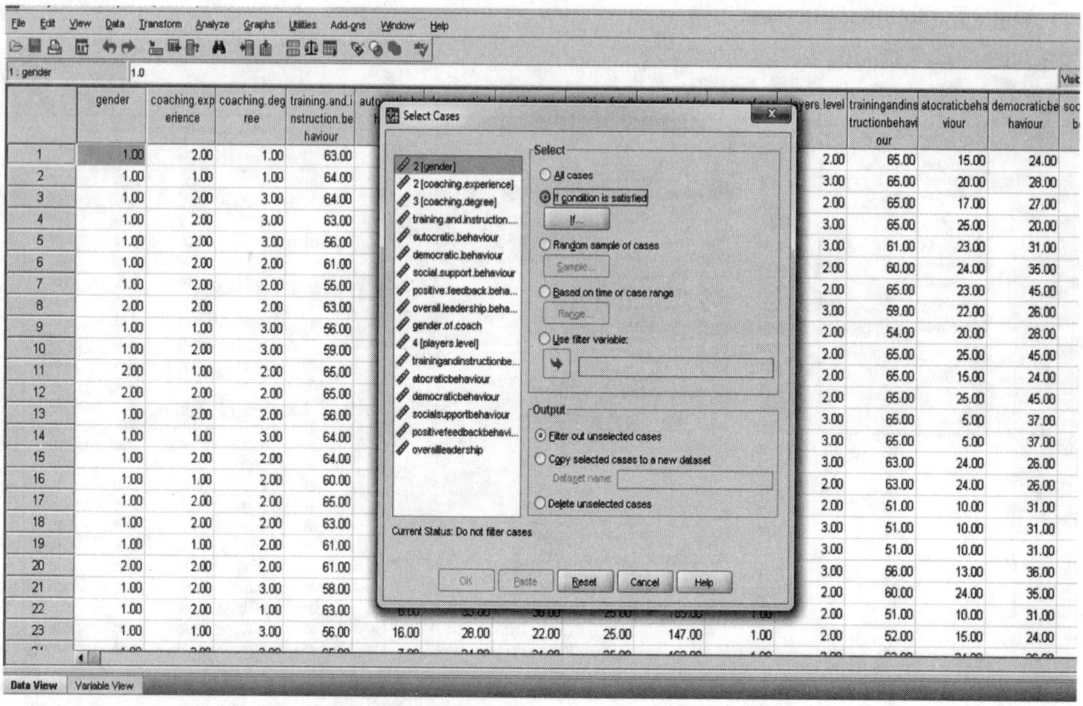

222. Click on "**If...**" icon to get the following screen.

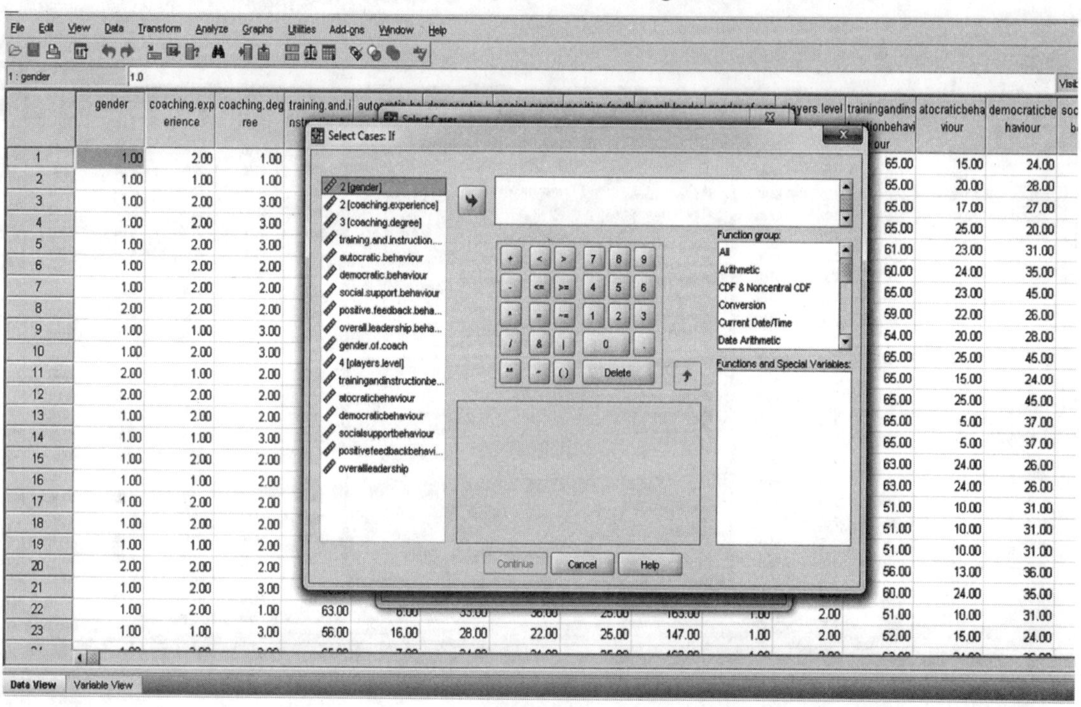

223. You have to split file with respect to "**Gender of Coaches**". Shift "**Gender of Coaches**" to the right hand dialogue box to get the following screen.

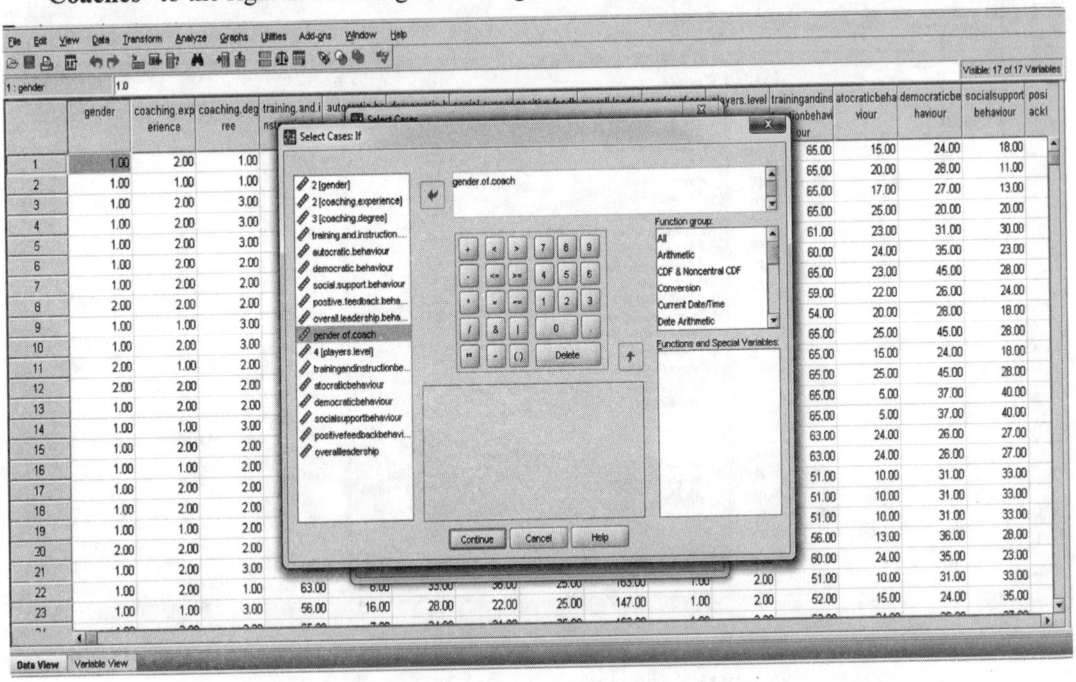

224. You want only "**Male Coaches**" data and Male Coaches is represented by "**1**". Now put "=" sign and type "**1**" to get the following output.

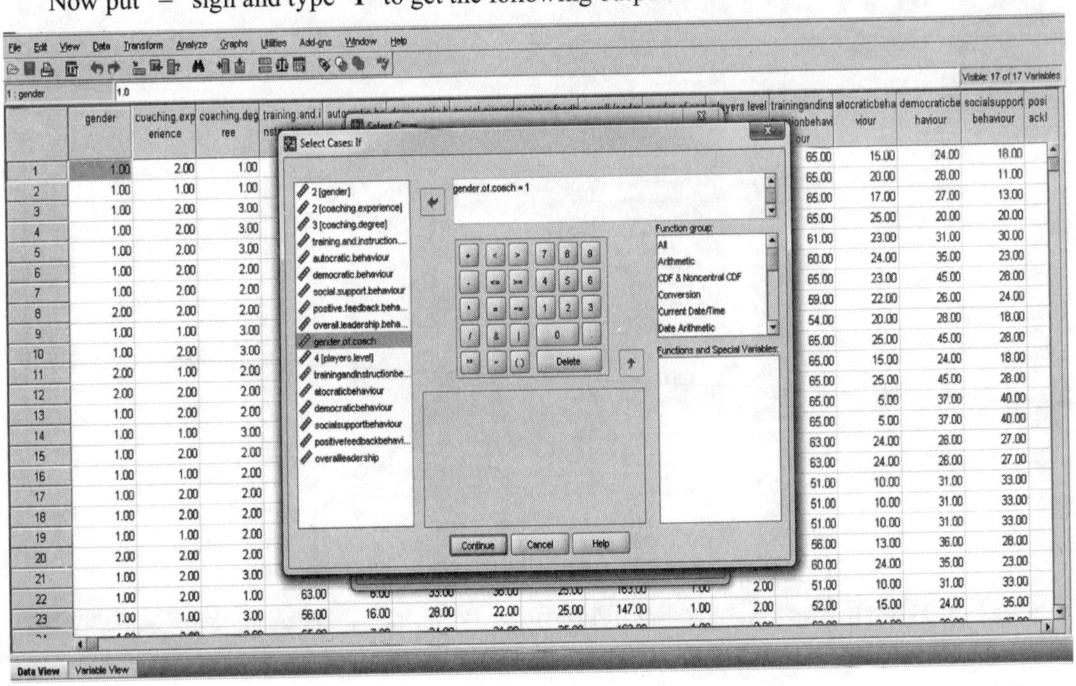

225. Click on "**Continue**" icon to get the following screen.

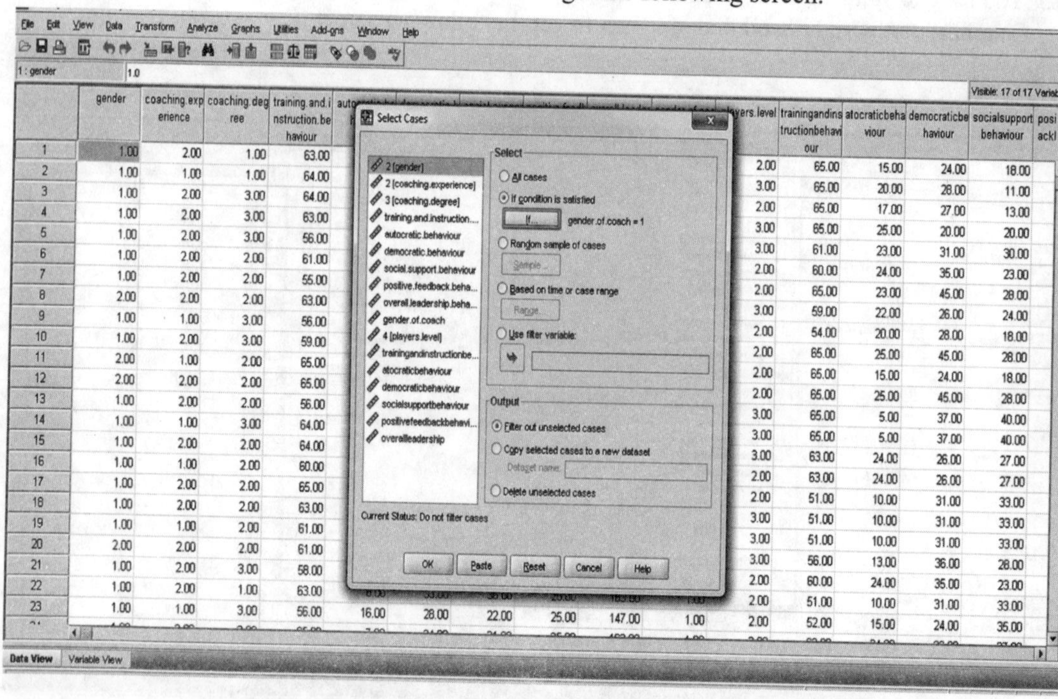

226. Click on "**OK**" to get the following screen.

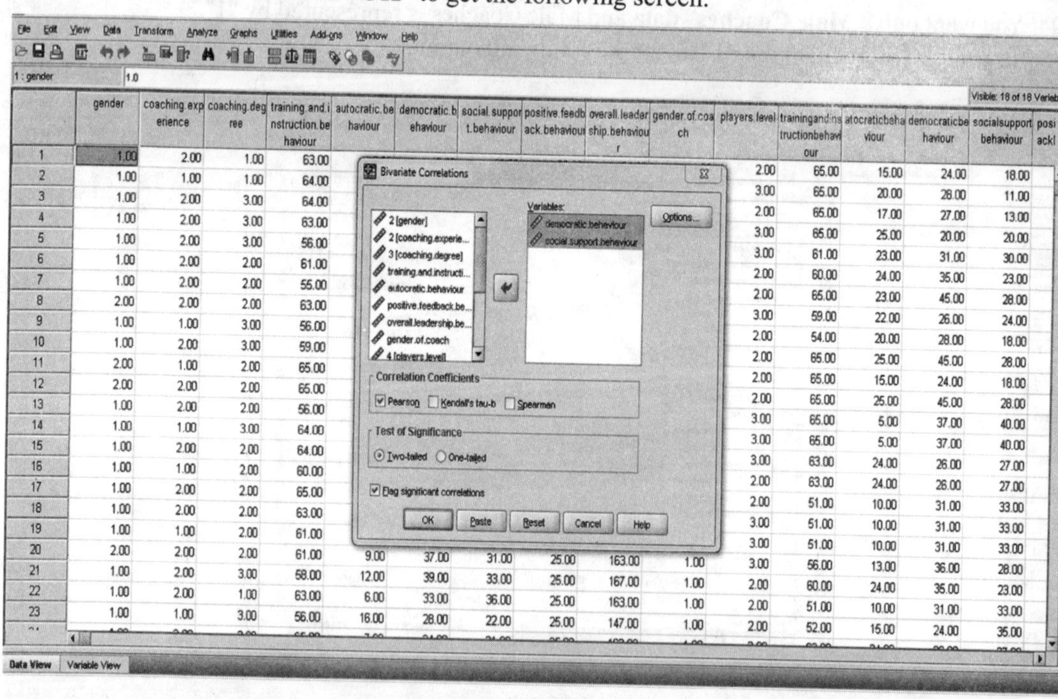

227. Click on "**OK**" to get the following outputs of Correlation coefficient only for "**Male Coaches**".

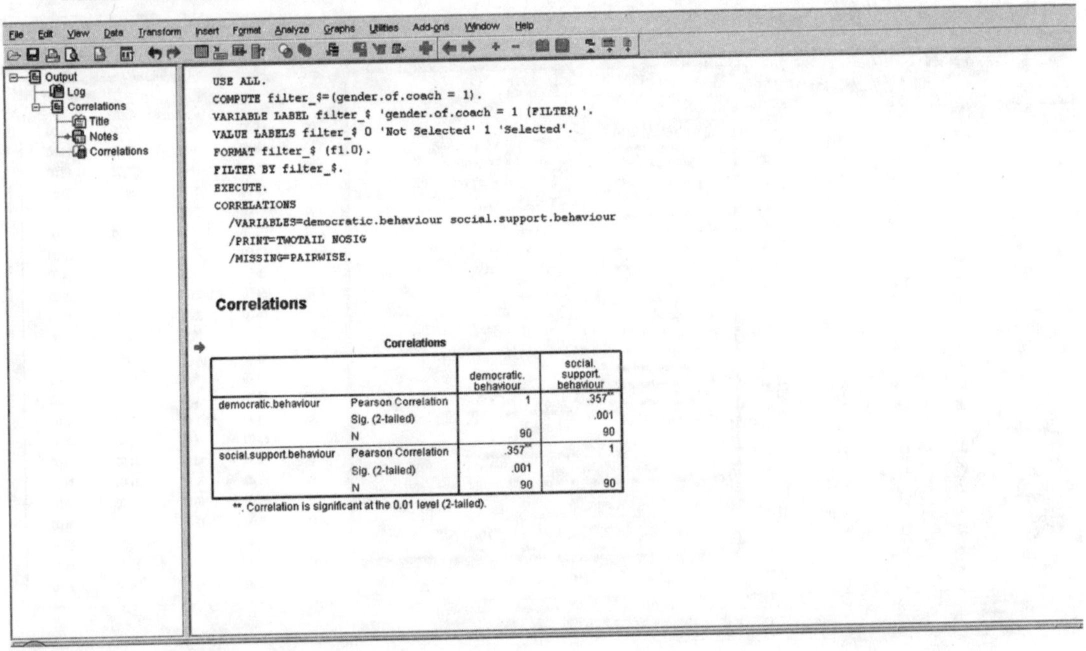

228. To get the output for "**Female Coaches**", click on "**Data**" and bring curser to "**Select Cases**" icon to get the following screen.

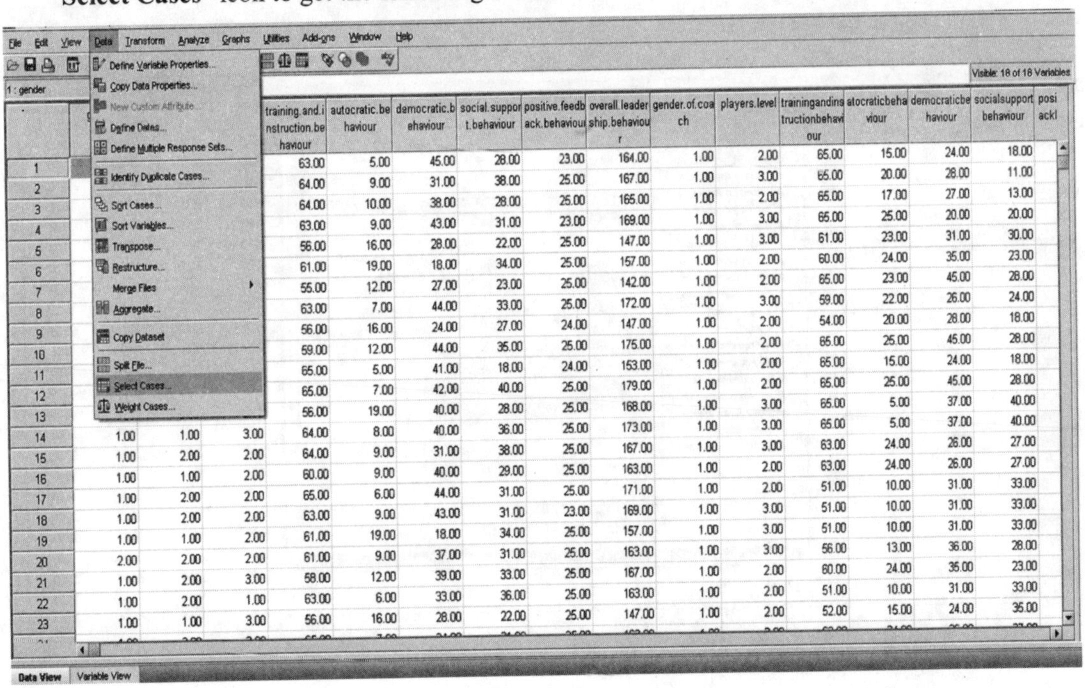

229. Click on "**Select Cases**" icon to get the following screen.

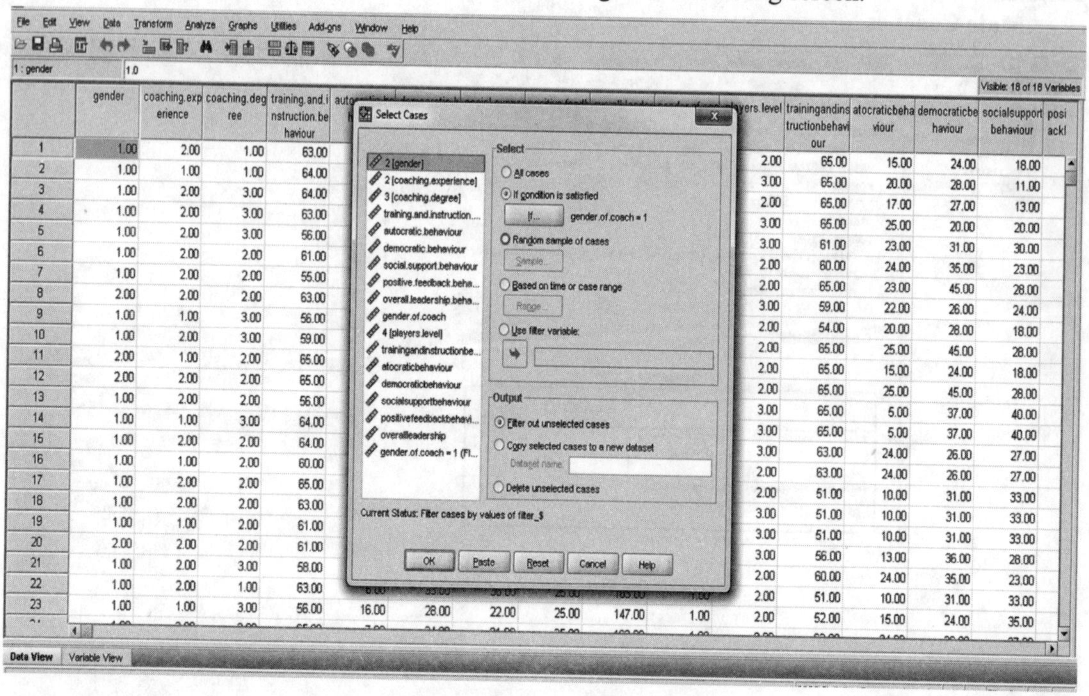

230. Click on "**If...**" icon to get the following screen.

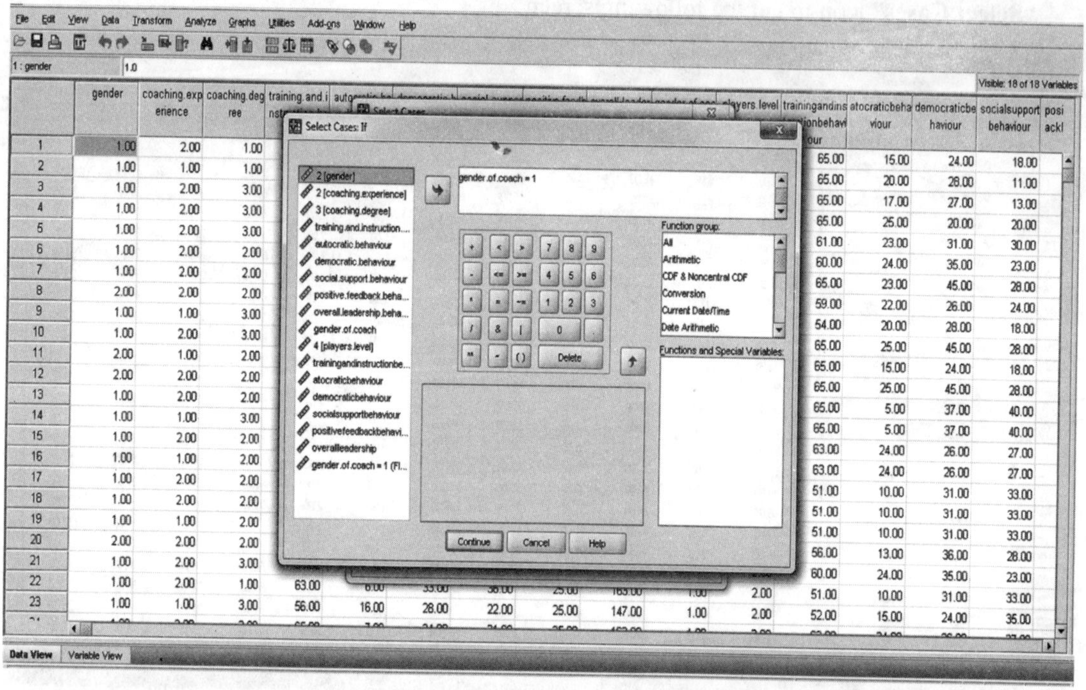

231. In the right hand side slot, type "**2**" in place of "**1**" because "**2**" is the code of "**Female Coaches**" to get the following screen.

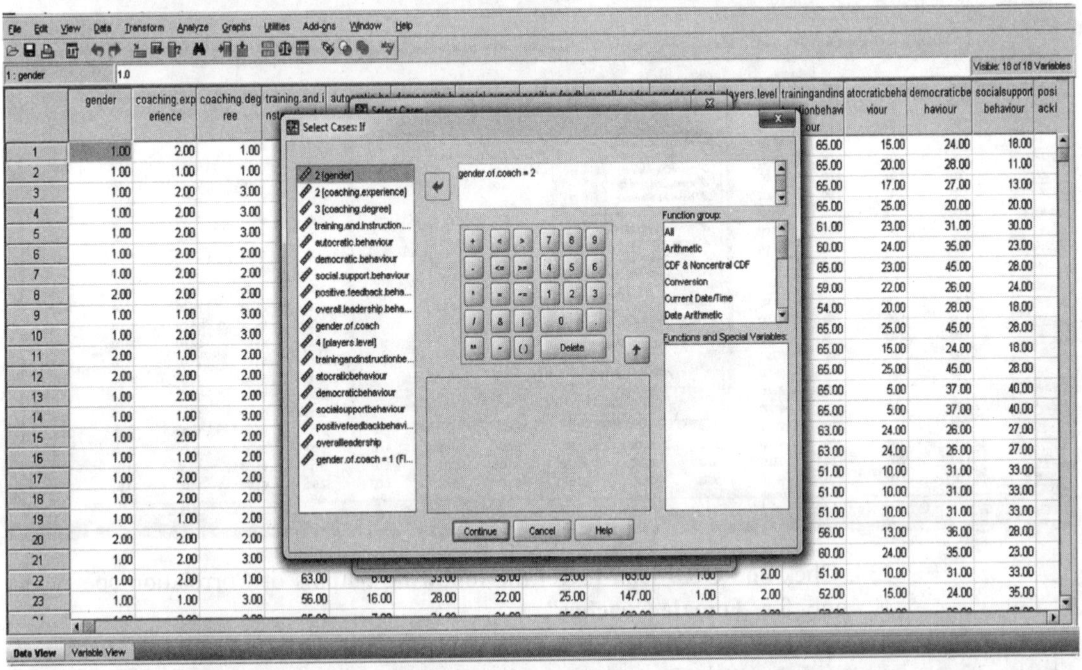

232. Click on "**Continue**" icon to get the following screen.

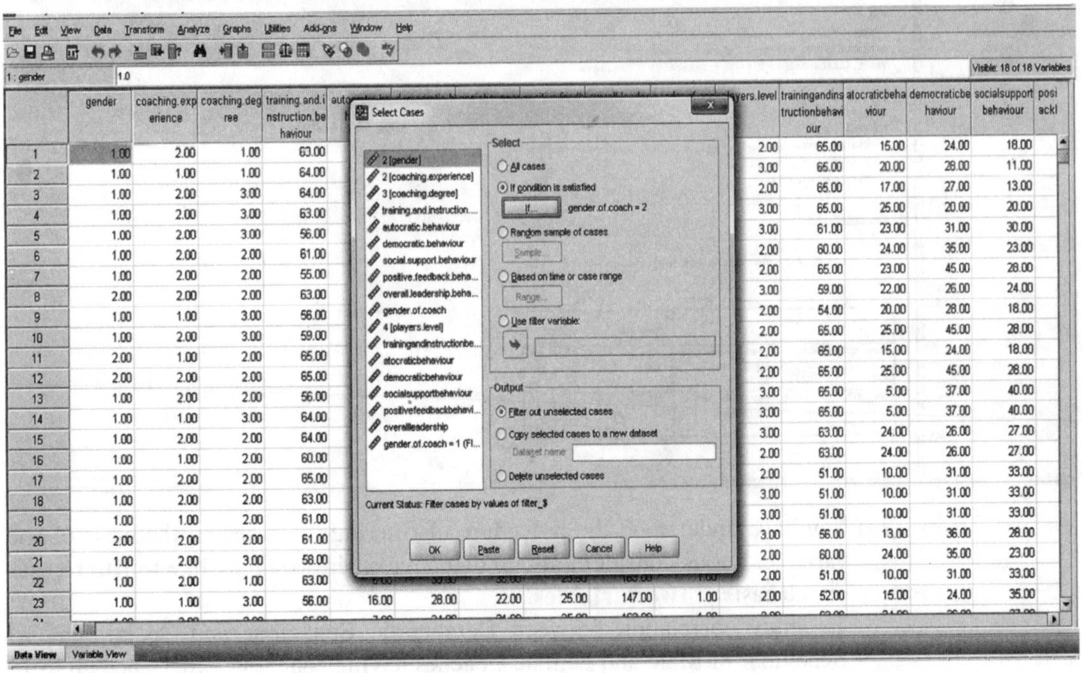

233. Click on "**OK**" to get the following screen.

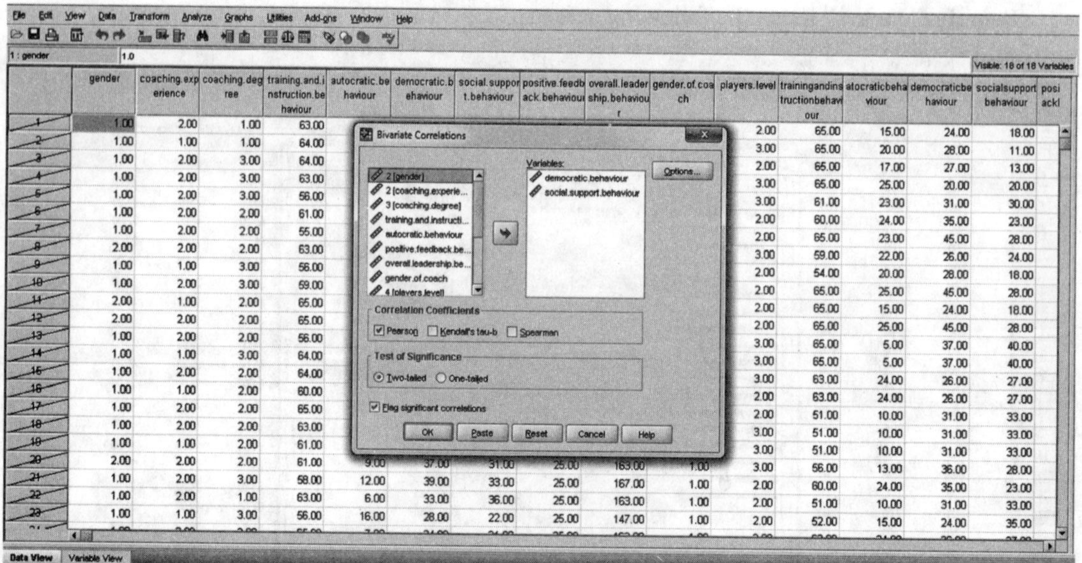

234. Click on "**OK**" icon to get the following outputs of Correlation coefficient only for "**Female Coaches**".

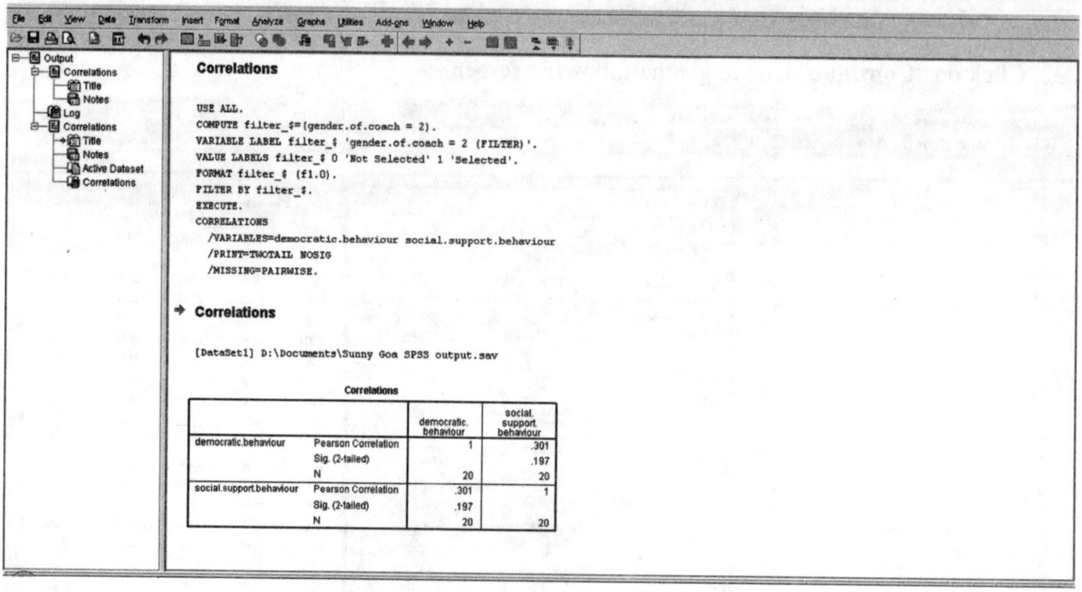

		democratic.behaviour	social.support.behaviour
democratic.behaviour	Pearson Correlation	1	.301
	Sig. (2-tailed)		.197
	N	20	20
social.support.behaviour	Pearson Correlation	.301	1
	Sig. (2-tailed)	.197	
	N	20	20

235. You have understood the procedure of filtering the cases on the basis of one variable. Let us consider another objective where you may like to **filter cases** on the basis of **two variables.**

To study correlation between Democratic Behaviour and Social Support Behaviour of Male and Female Coaches having coaching experience up to 15 years and more than 15 years separately.

Let us first select cases. For selecting cases, click on "**Data**" icon and bring the curser to "**Select Cases**" to get the following screen.

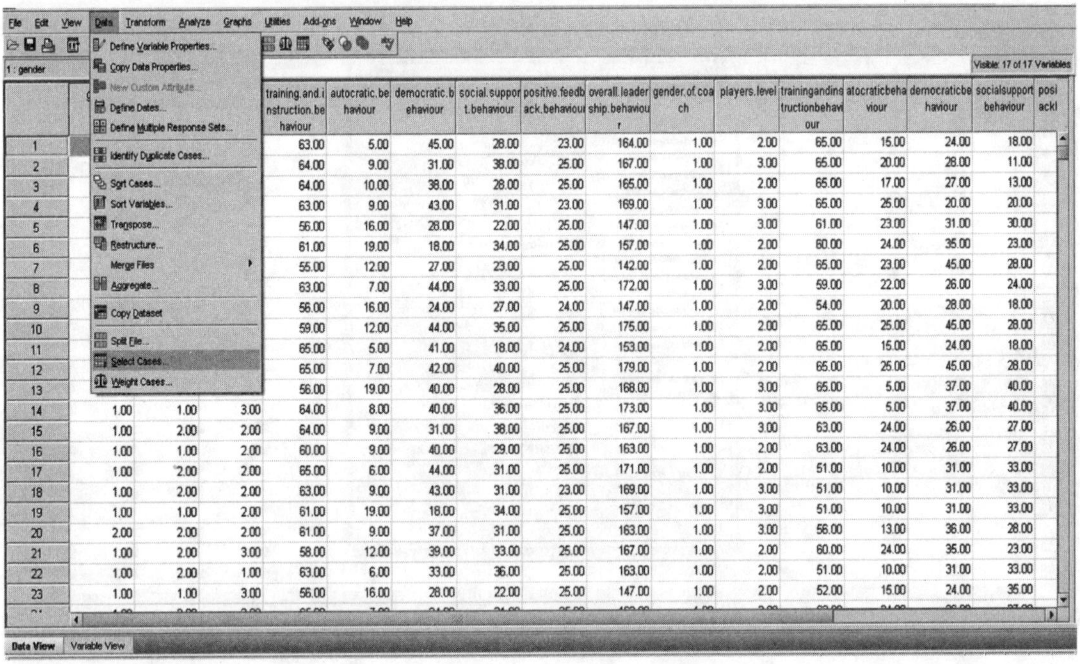

236. Click on "**Select Cases**" icon to get the following screen.

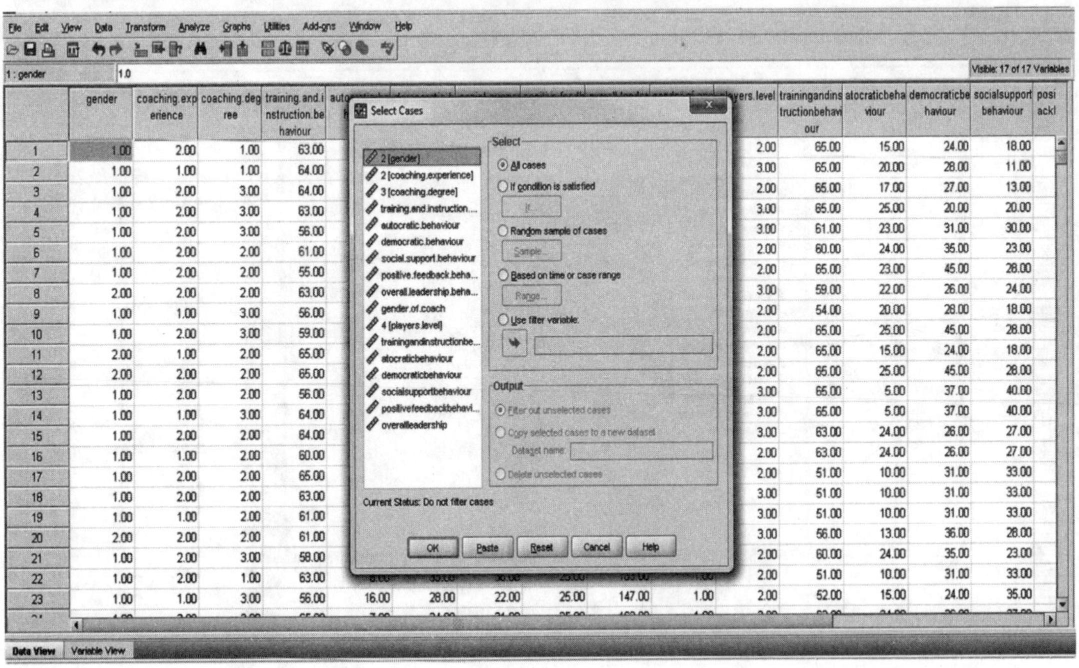

237. Highlight "**If condition is satisfied**" to get the following screen.

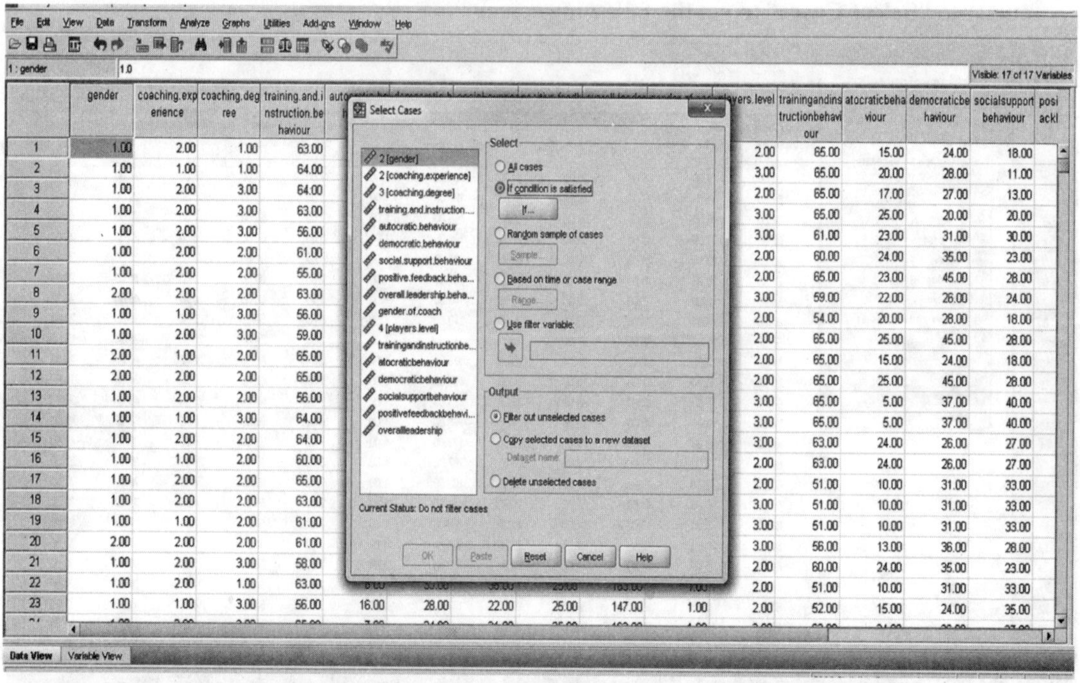

238. Click on "**If....**" icon to get the following screen.

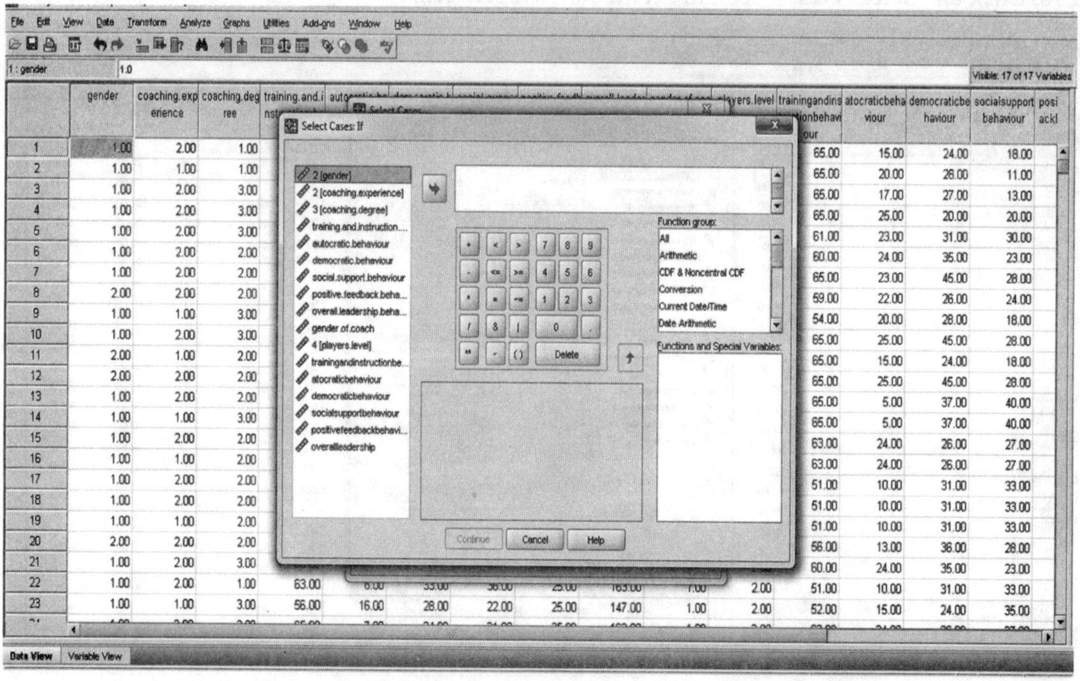

239. Shift "**Gender**" to the right hand side slot and put "**=1**" because "**1**" represents Male Coaches to get the following screen.

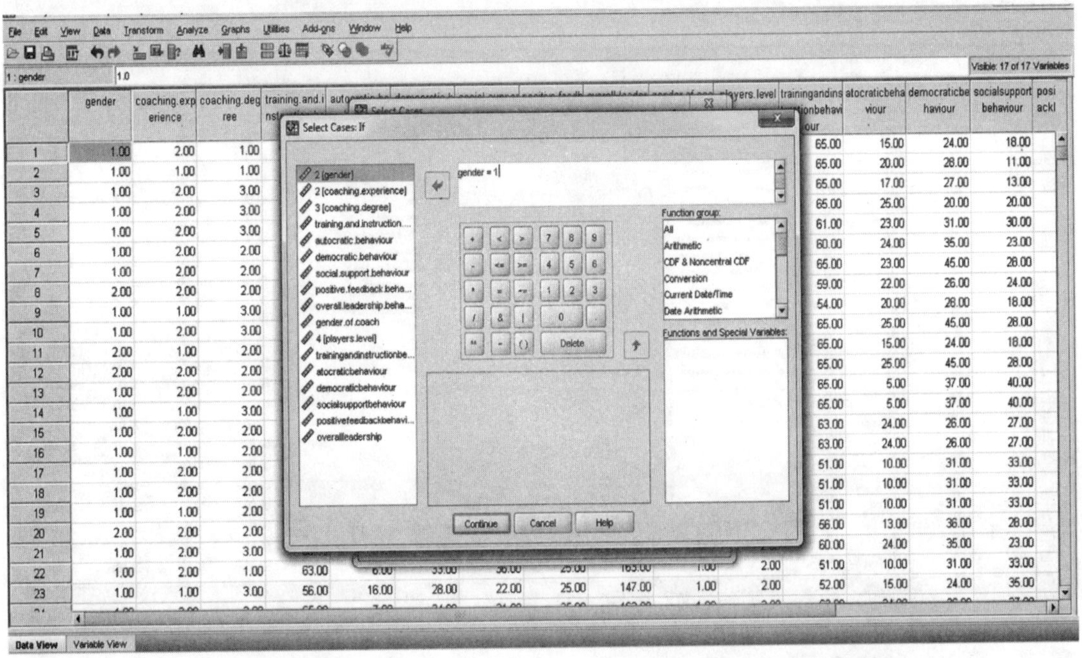

240. As per objective given in frame 235, the "**Data**" are to be filtered on the basis of "**Gender**" and "**Coaching Experience**", so type "**and**" to get the following screen.

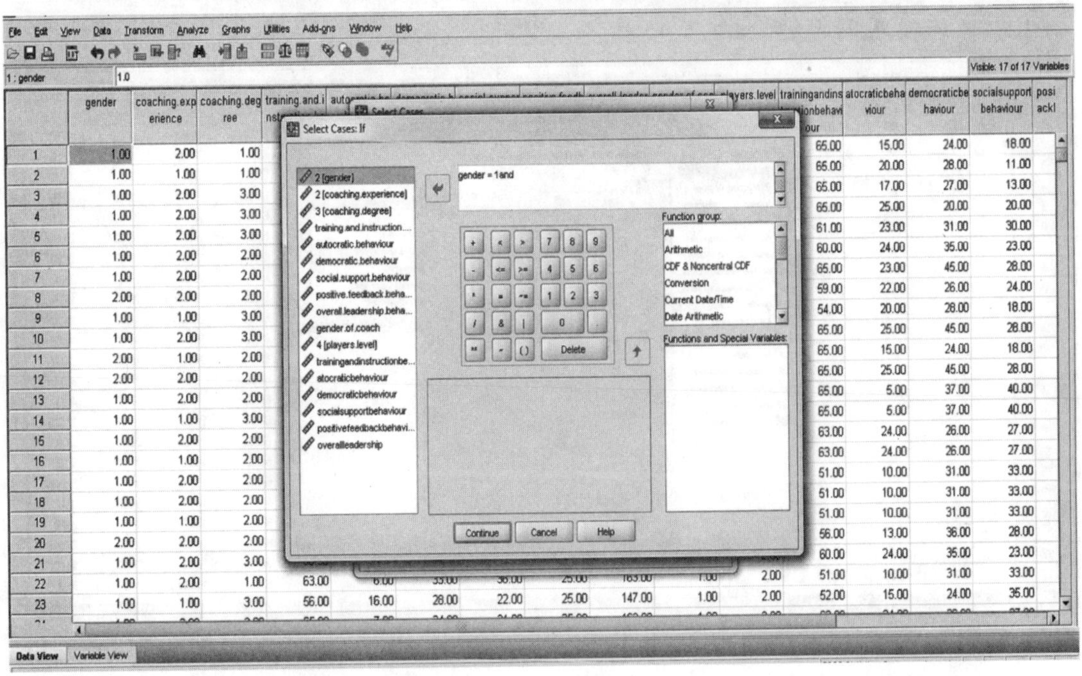

241. Shift "**Coaching Experience**" variable after "**and**" to get the following screen.

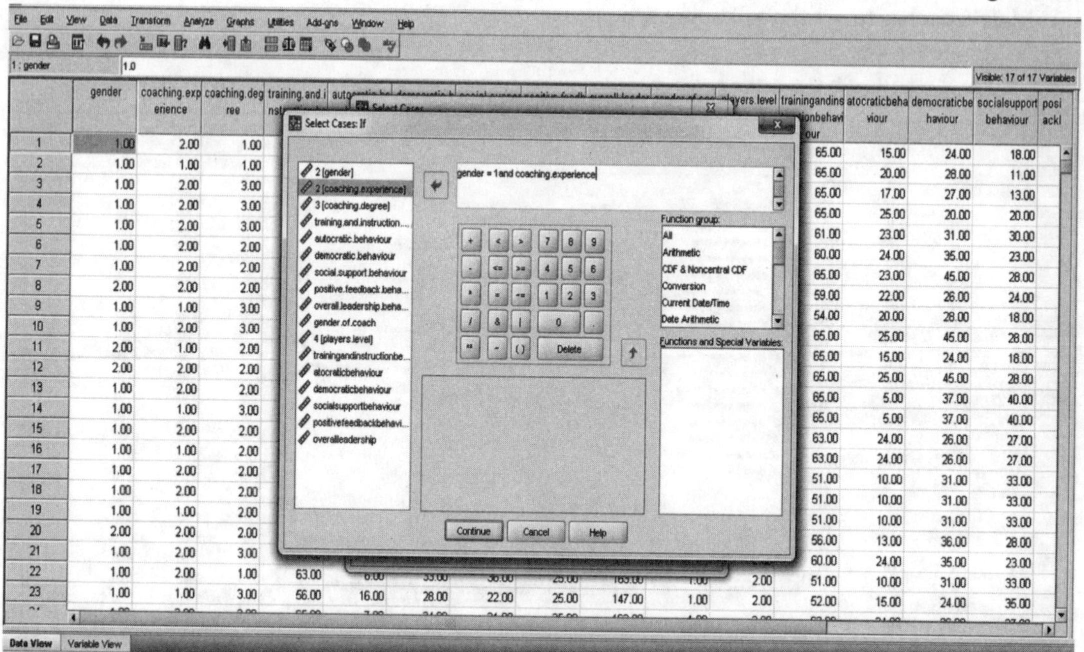

242. Put equal sign "=" and type "**1**" because "**1**" represents Coaching Experience up to 15 Years to get the following screen.

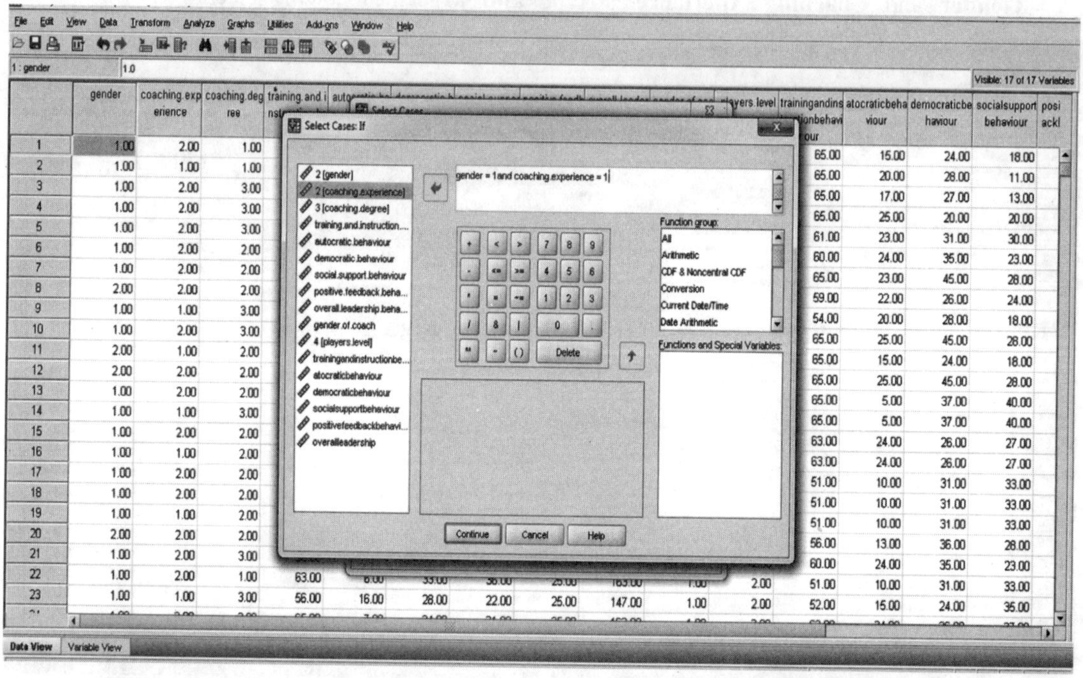

243. Click on "**Continue**" to get the following screen.

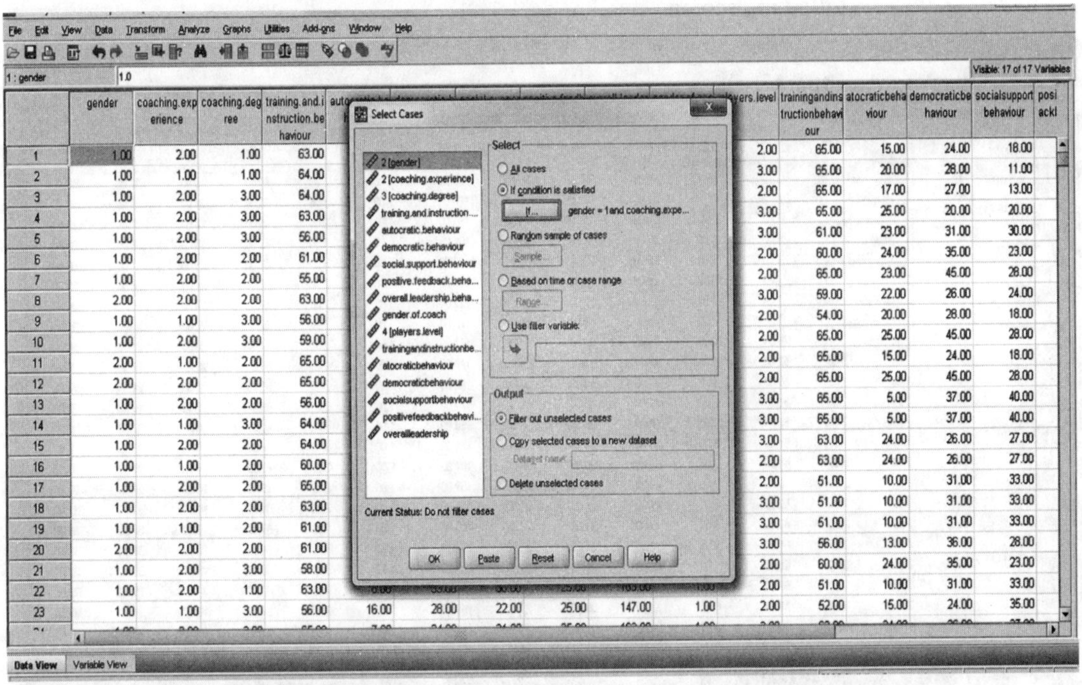

244. Click on "**OK**" to get the following screen.

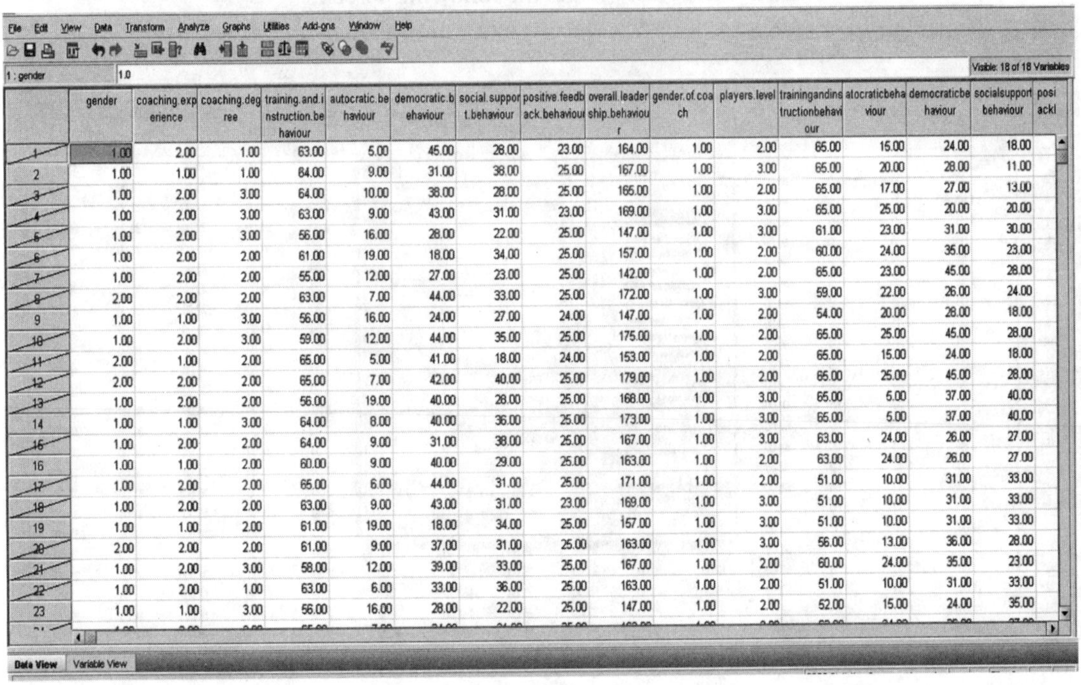

245. Click on "**Analyse**" bring curser on "**Correlate**" then to "**Bivariate**" to get the following screen.

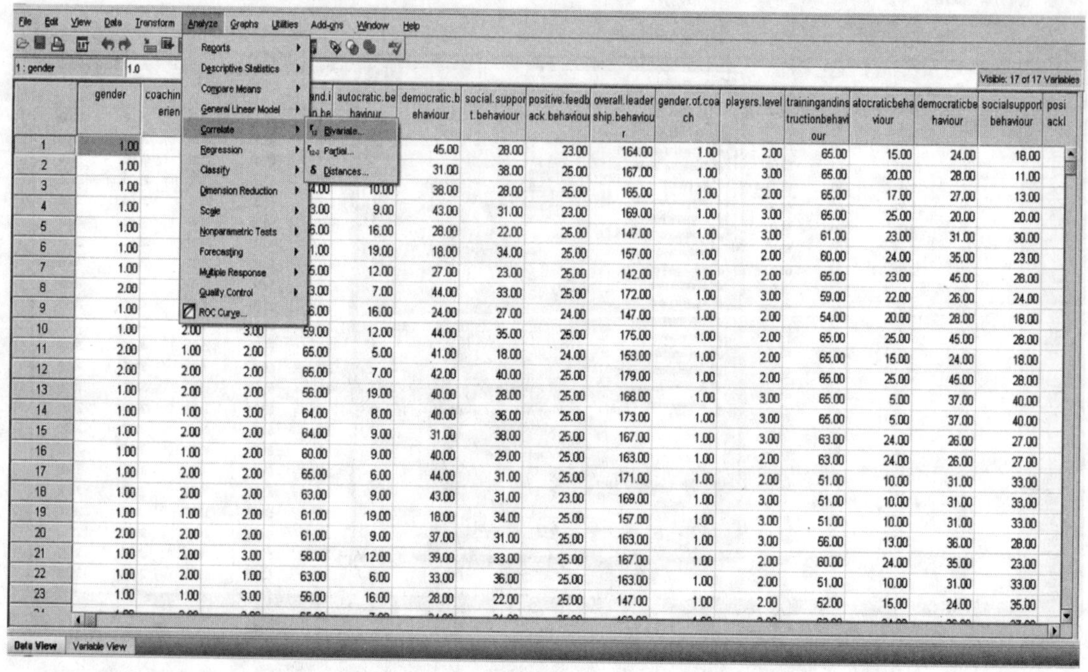

246. Click on "**Bivariate**" to get the following screen.

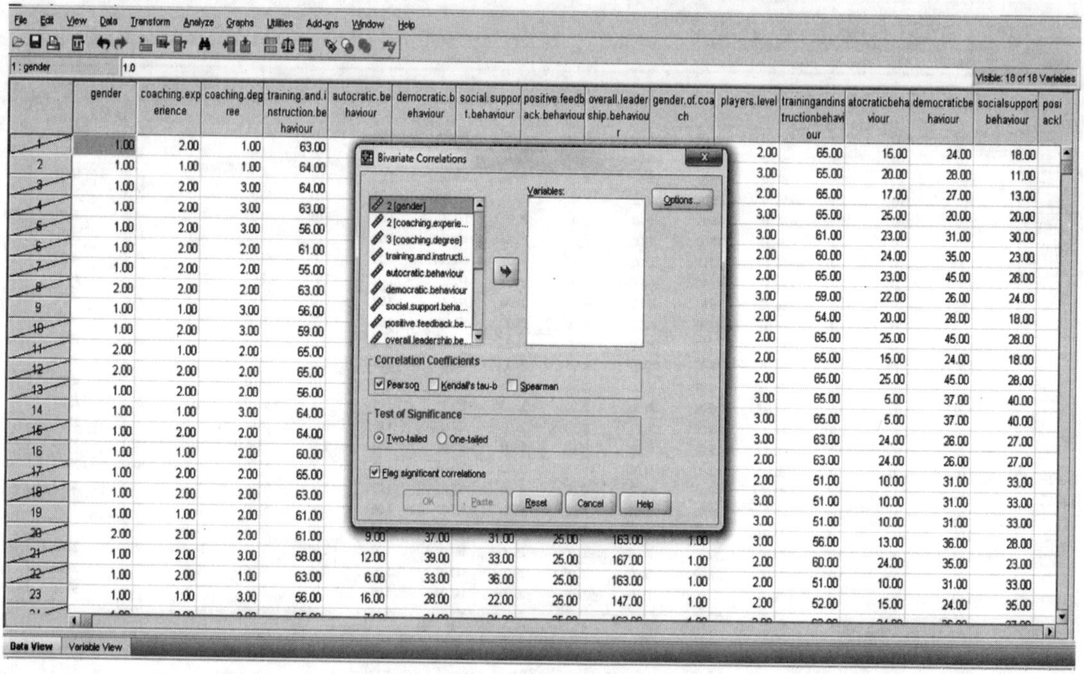

247. Shift "**Democratic Behaviour**" and "**Social Support Behaviour**" to "**Variables**" dialogue box to get the following screen.

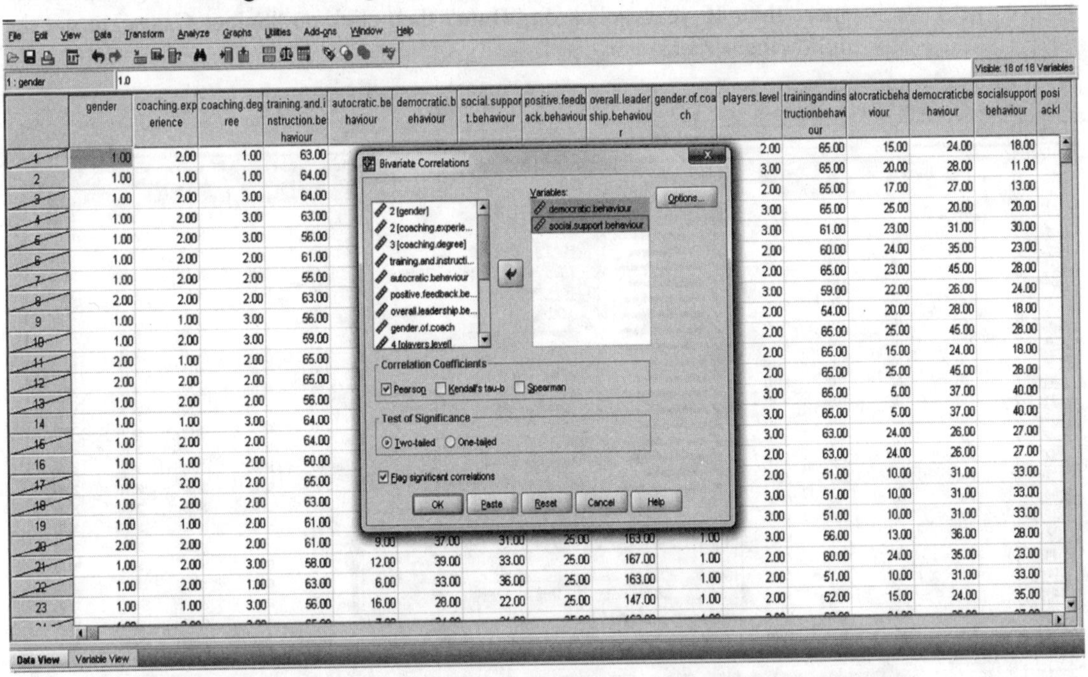

248. Click on "**OK**" to get the following outputs of Correlation between "**Democratic Behaviour**" and "**Social Support Behaviour**" of Male Coaches having Coaching Experience up to 15 years.

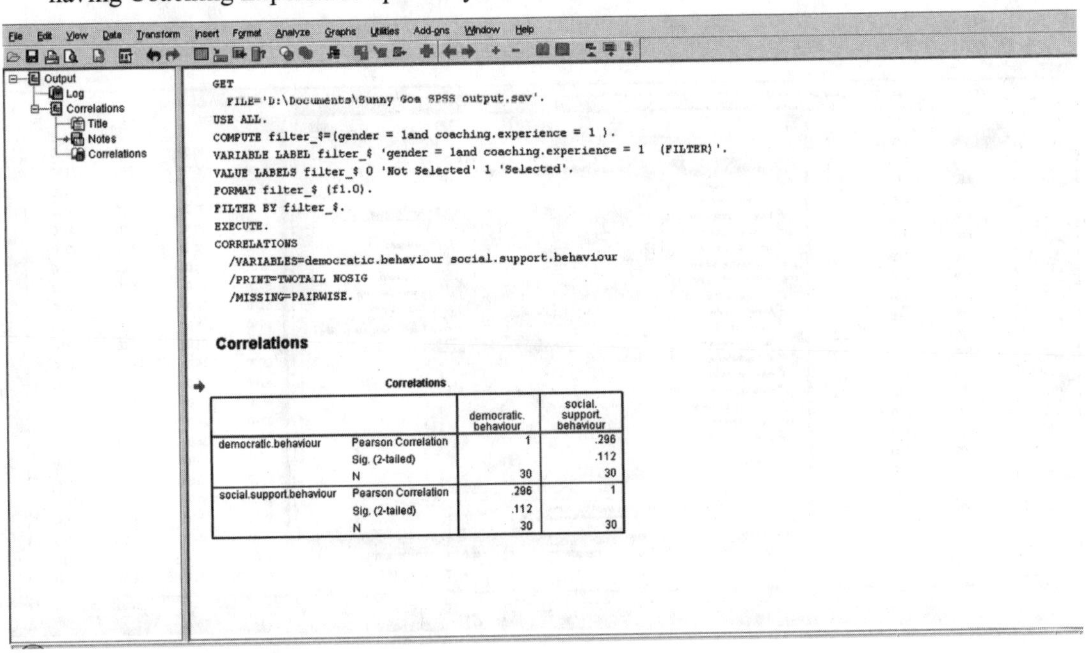

249. In order to calculate correlation between "**Democratic Behaviour**" and "**Social Support Behaviour**" for Male coaches having Coaching Experience more than 15 years, click on "**Data**" then click on "**Select Cases**" to get the following screen.

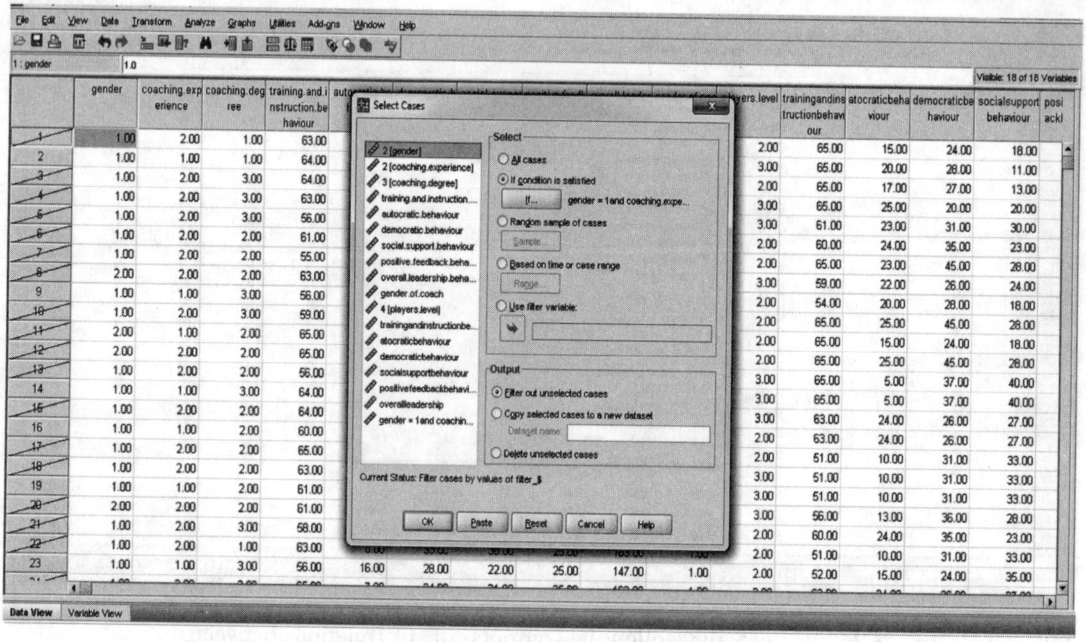

250. Click on "**If...**" icon and under "**Coaching Experience**" type "**2**" in place of"**1**" to get the following screen.

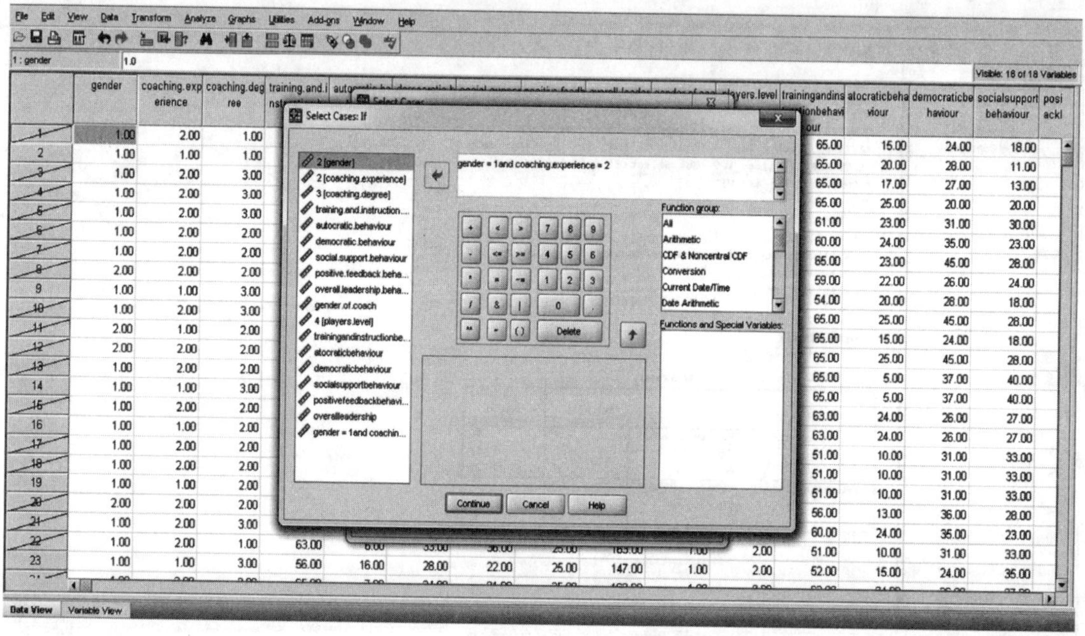

251. Click on "**Continue**" to get the following screen.

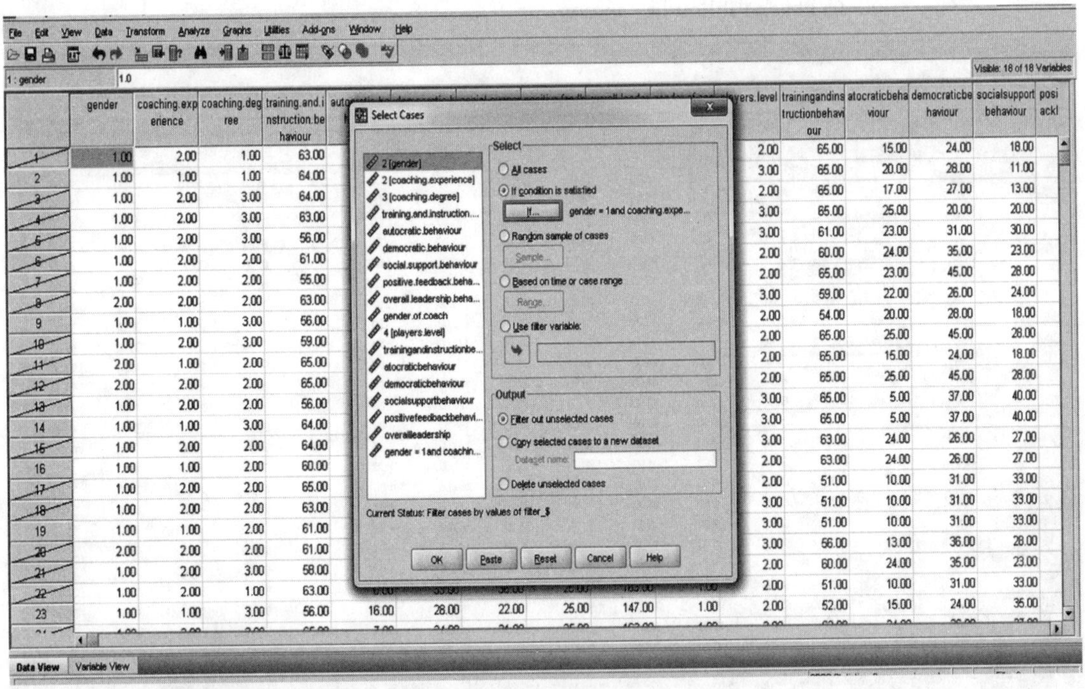

252. Click on "**OK**" icon to get the following screen.

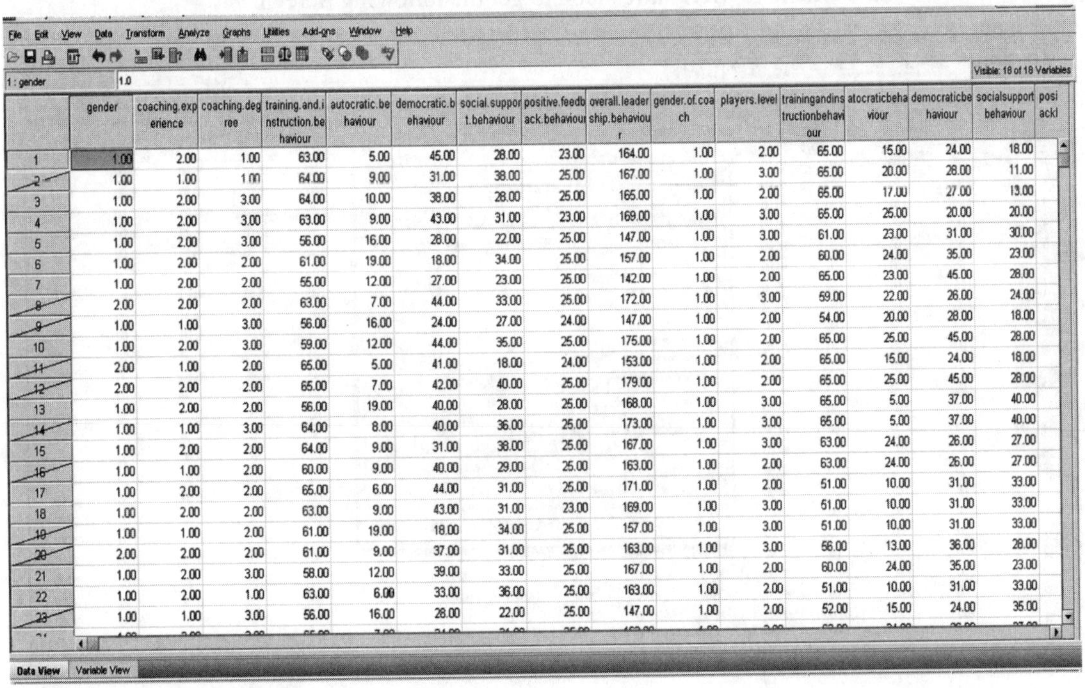

253. Click on "**Analyse**" and bring curser to "**Correlate**" and then to "**Bivariate**" to get the following screen.

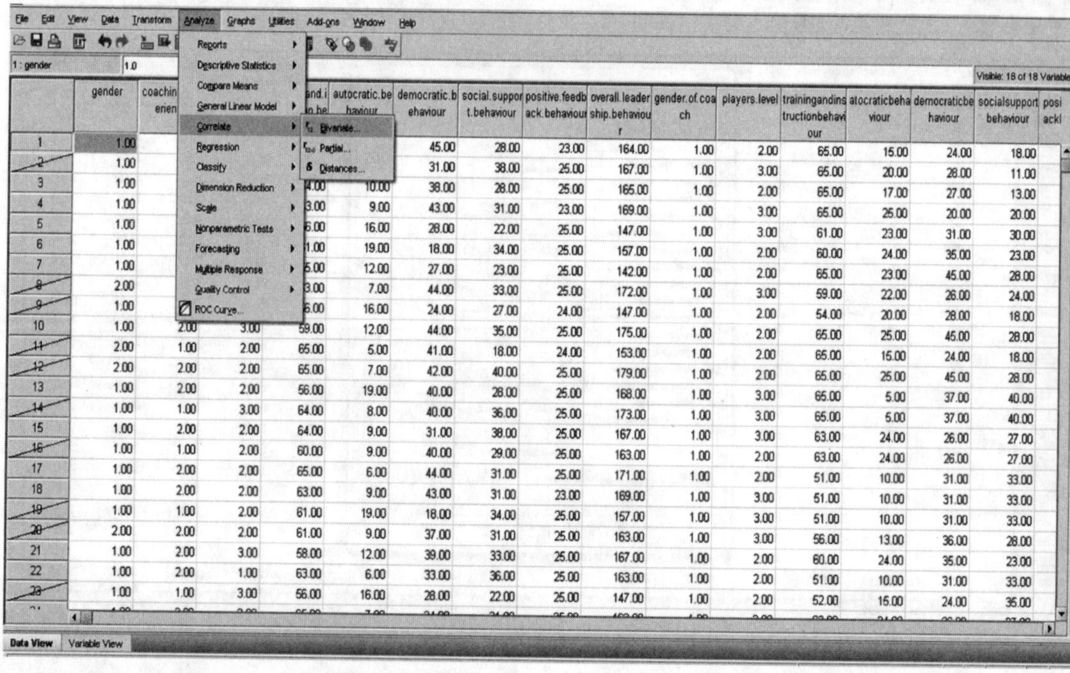

254. Click on "**Bivariate**" icon to get the following Screen.

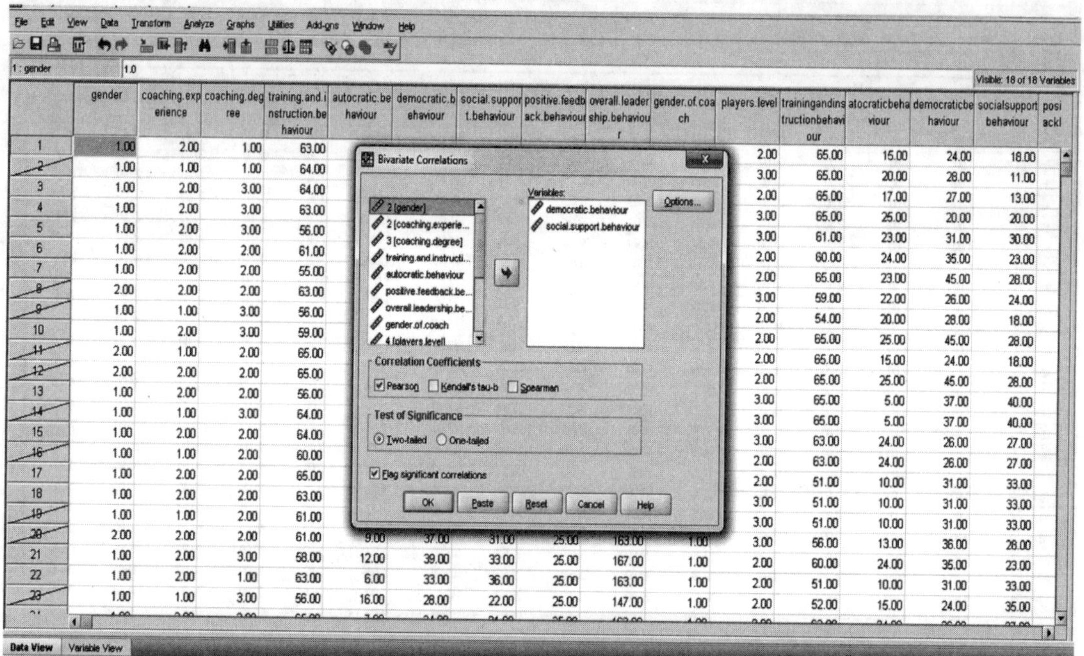

255. Click on "**OK**" to get the following outputs of Correlation between "**Democratic Behaviour**" and "**Social Support Behaviour**" of Male coaches having Coaching Experience more than 15 years.

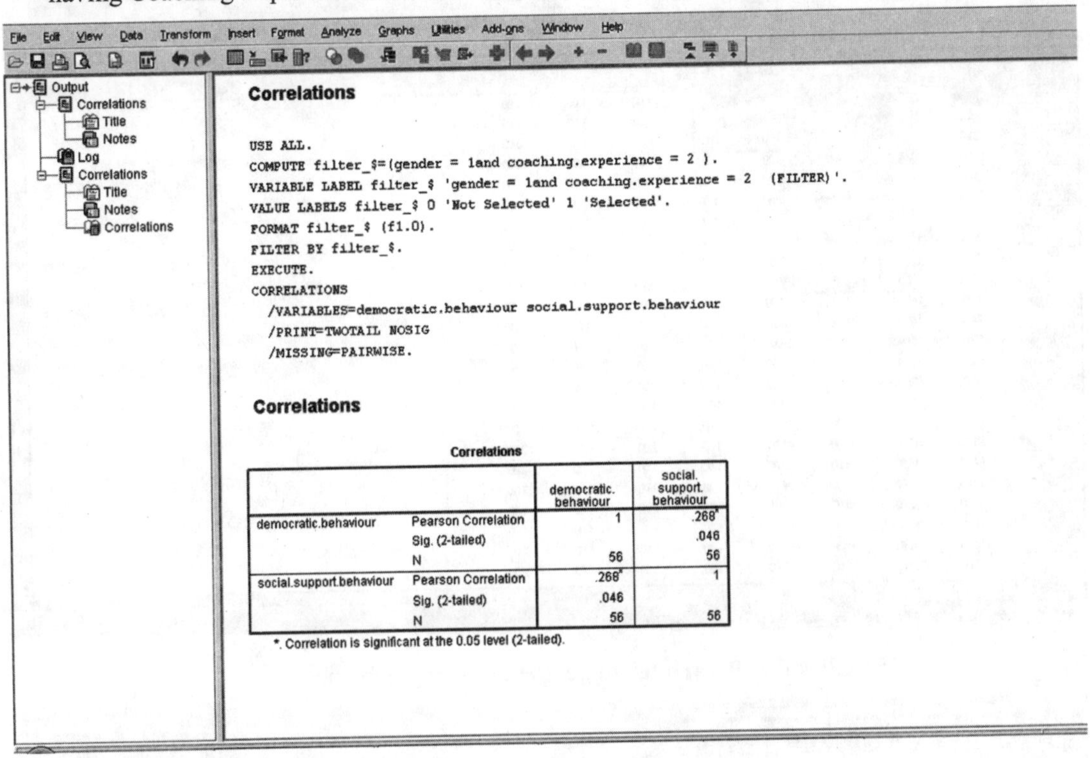

Correlations

```
USE ALL.
COMPUTE filter_$=(gender = 1and coaching.experience = 2 ).
VARIABLE LABEL filter_$ 'gender = 1and coaching.experience = 2  (FILTER)'.
VALUE LABELS filter_$ 0 'Not Selected' 1 'Selected'.
FORMAT filter_$ (f1.0).
FILTER BY filter_$.
EXECUTE.
CORRELATIONS
  /VARIABLES=democratic.behaviour social.support.behaviour
  /PRINT=TWOTAIL NOSIG
  /MISSING=PAIRWISE.
```

Correlations

Correlations

		democratic. behaviour	social. support. behaviour
democratic.behaviour	Pearson Correlation	1	.268*
	Sig. (2-tailed)		.046
	N	56	56
social.support.behaviour	Pearson Correlation	.268*	1
	Sig. (2-tailed)	.046	
	N	56	56

*. Correlation is significant at the 0.05 level (2-tailed).

You may repeat the same steps for "**Female Coaches**" having Coaching Experience up to 15 Years and more than 15 years. So you may use "**Select Cases**" for as many discontinuous variables as you like.

For interpretation of Correlation results, you may refer to the book by D.N.Sansanwal, Research Methodology and Applied Statistic, Shipra Publishers, Delhi, 2020.

Kendall's Tau – b

256. In case two variables do not satisfy the assumptions of Product Moment Correlation, then **Kendall Tau – b Method** can be used for computing correlation between two variables. Kendall Tau – b is a non-parametric statistics. Both the variables must have data on Ordinal Scale. In case you have data on Interval Scale or Ratio Scale but do not satisfy the assumptions of Pearson Product Moment Correlation, then Kendall Tau – b Method can be used for computing correlation.

Let us take the following objective:

To study correlation between Emotional Competence and Resilience of Teachers.

Click on "**Analyse**" bring curse to "**Correlate**" and then to "**Bivariate**" to get the following screen.

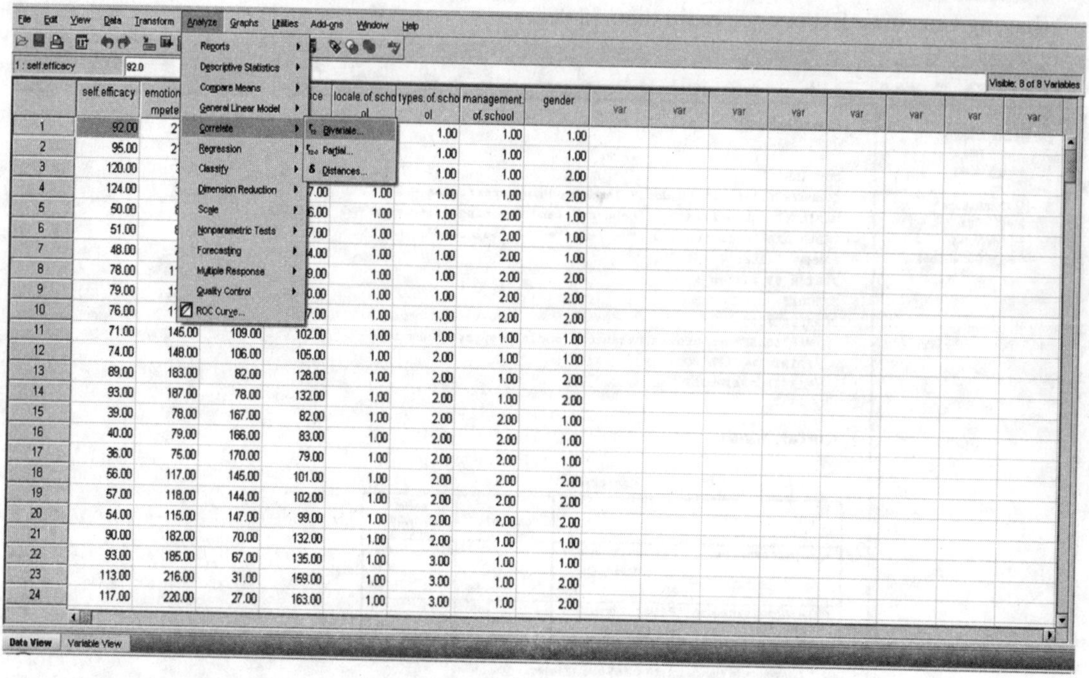

257. Click on "**Bivariate**" to get the following Screen.

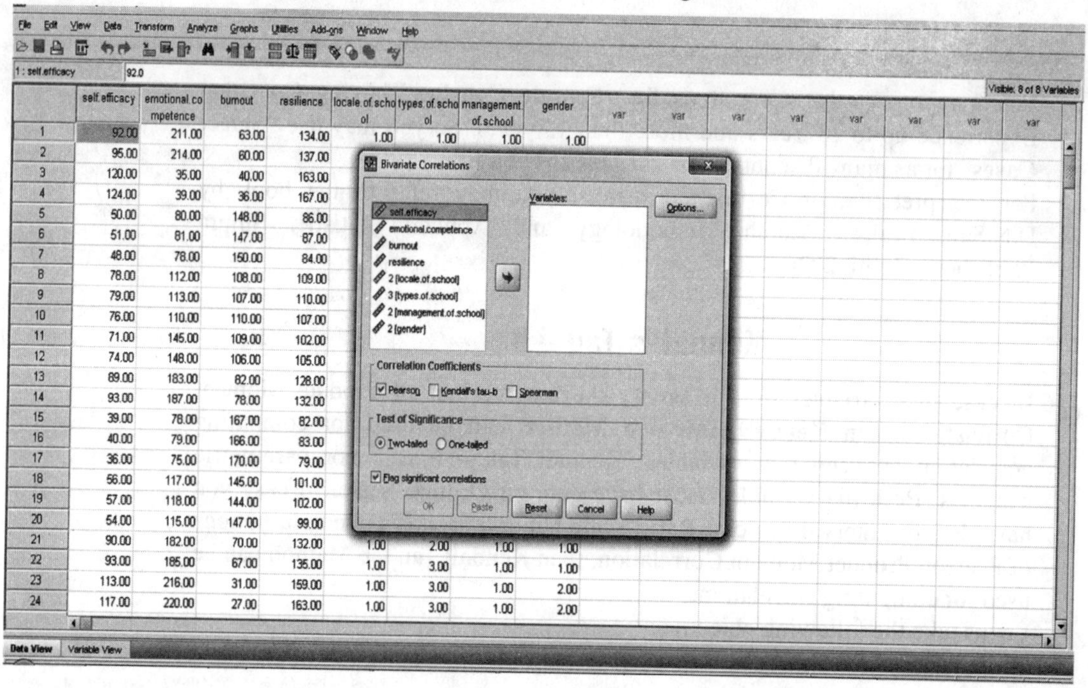

258. Shift "**Emotional Competence**" and "**Resilience**" under "**Variables**" slot to get the following screen.

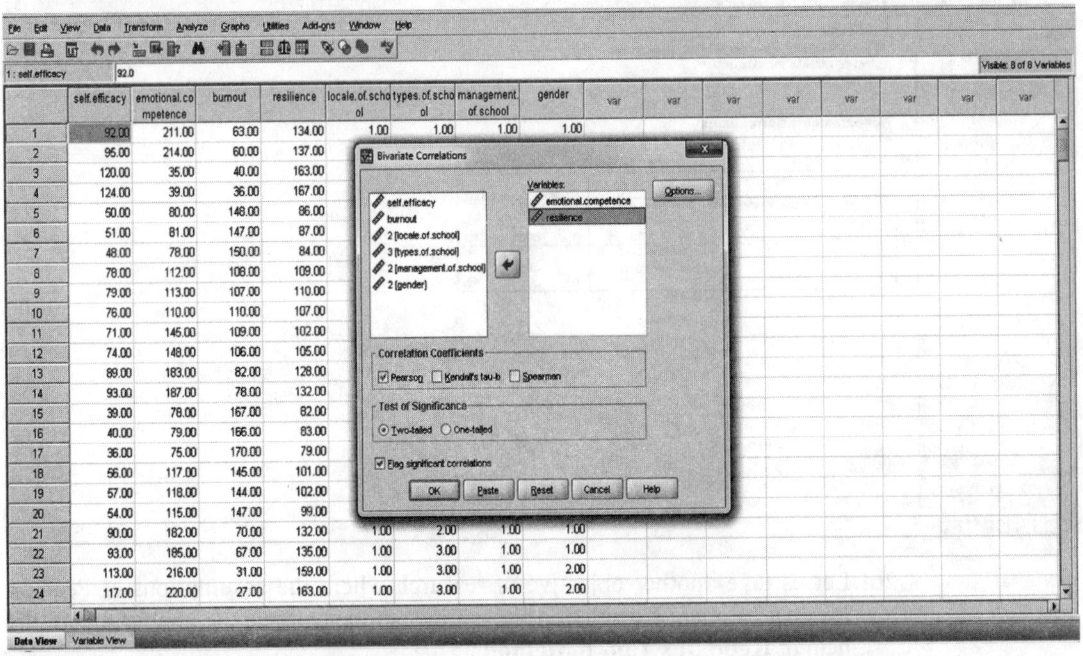

259. "**Pearson**" is by default highlighted. In case you do not want to use "**Pearson**", it can be deactivated and activate "**Kendall's Tau - b**" to get the following screen.

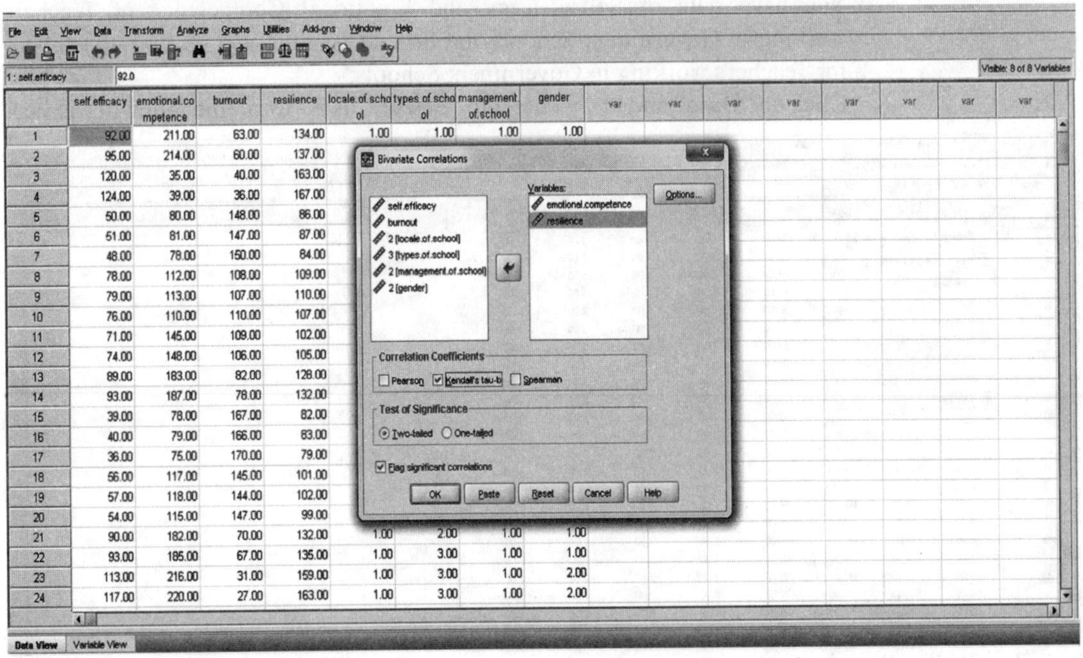

260. Click on "**OK**" to get the following outputs of Kendall's Tau - b.

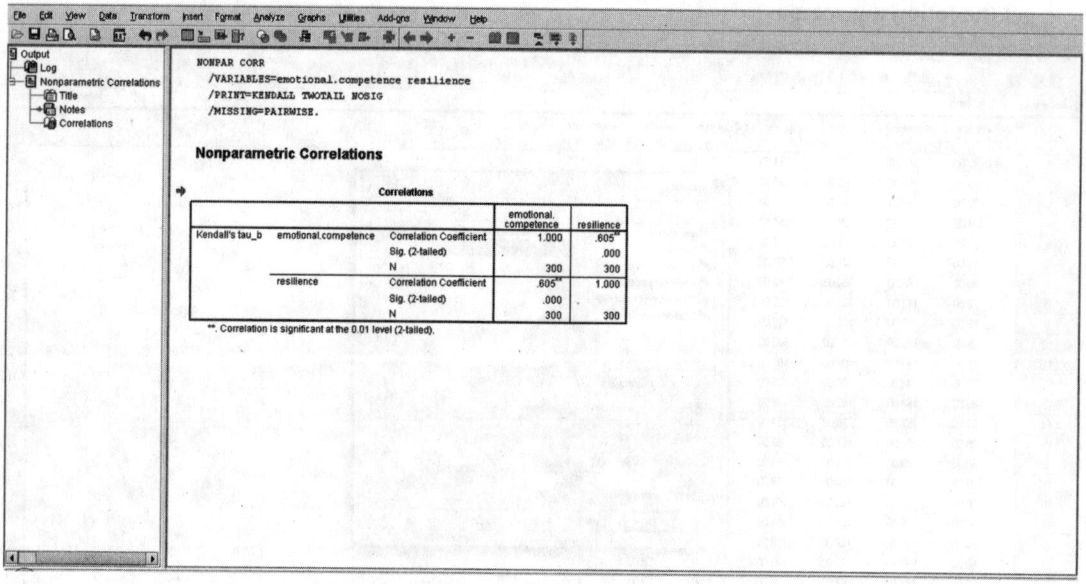

261. Let us take another objective of research where the assumptions of Pearson Product Moment Correlation are not met so the data can be analysed with the help of **Kendall's Tau- b Method**.

To study the correlation between Self-efficacy and Emotional Competence of Teachers working in Government Schools and Private Schools separately.

You have data of Self-efficacy and Emotional Competence of Teachers working in Government Schools and Private Schools. Let us first do analysis for Teachers working in Government Schools.

Click on "**Data**" and bring curser to "**Select Cases**" to get the following screen.

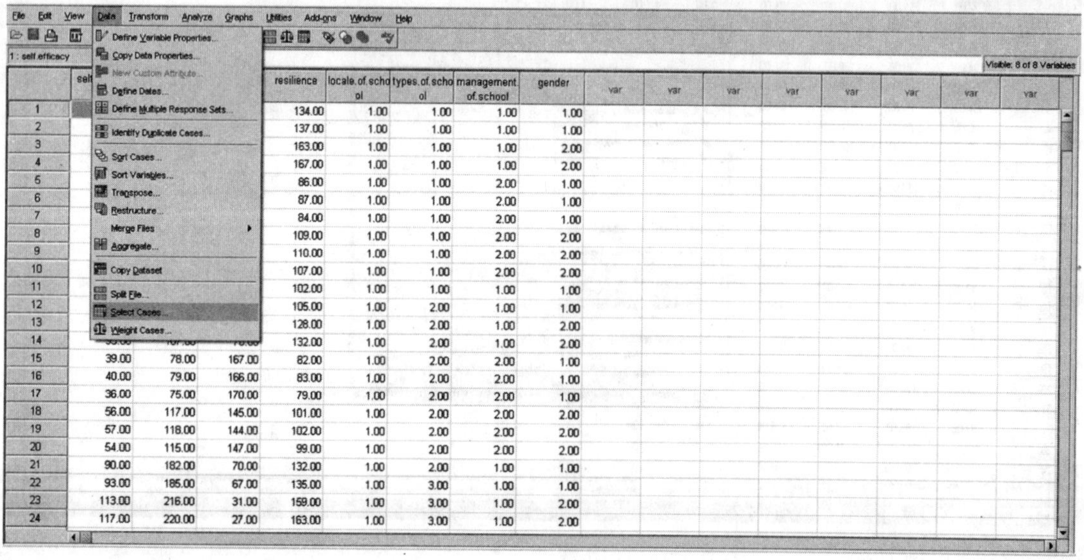

262. Click on "**Select Cases**" to get the following screen.

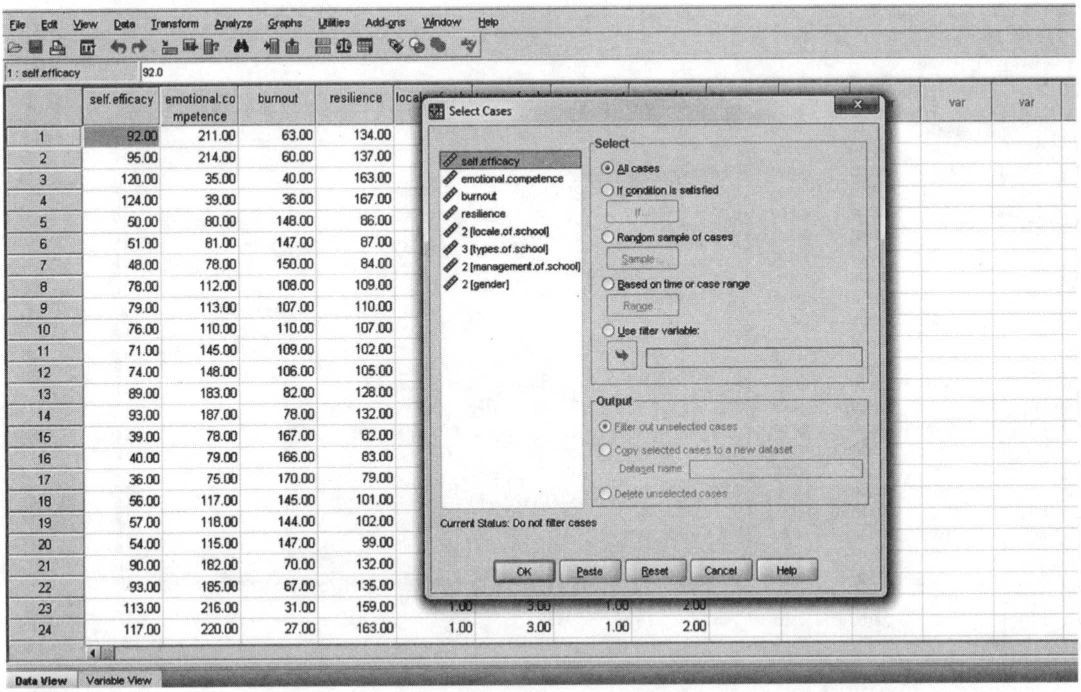

263. Highlight "**If condition is satisfied**" to get the following screen.

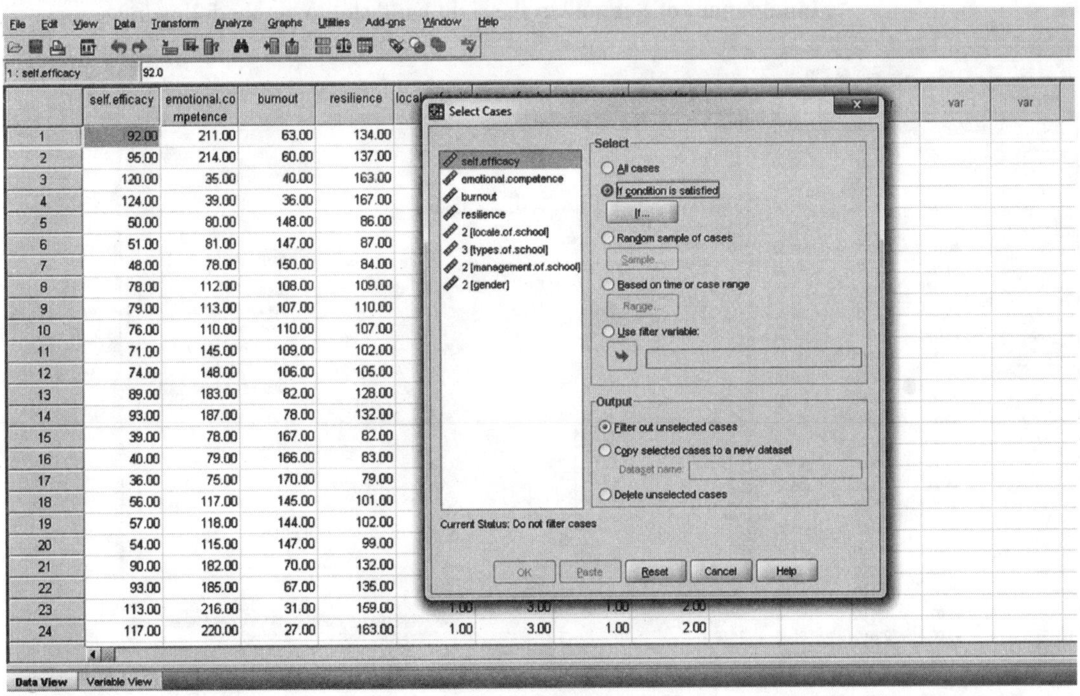

264. Click on "**If...**" to get the following screen.

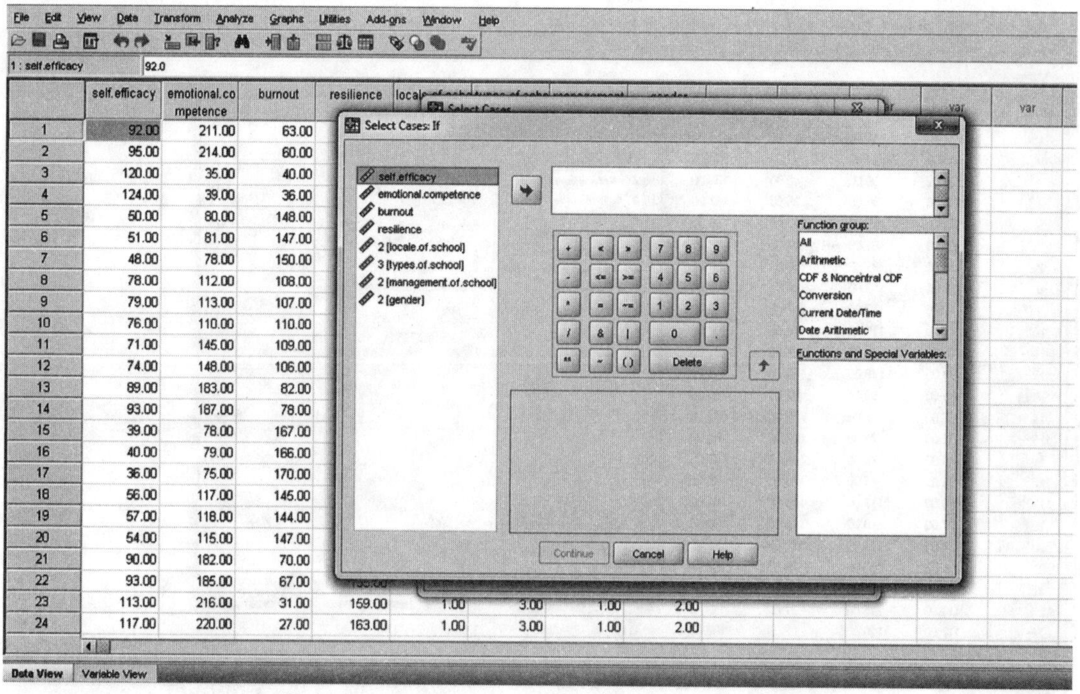

265. Data are to be selected on the basis of "**Management of School**". Shift "**Management of School**" to the right hand slot to get the following screen.

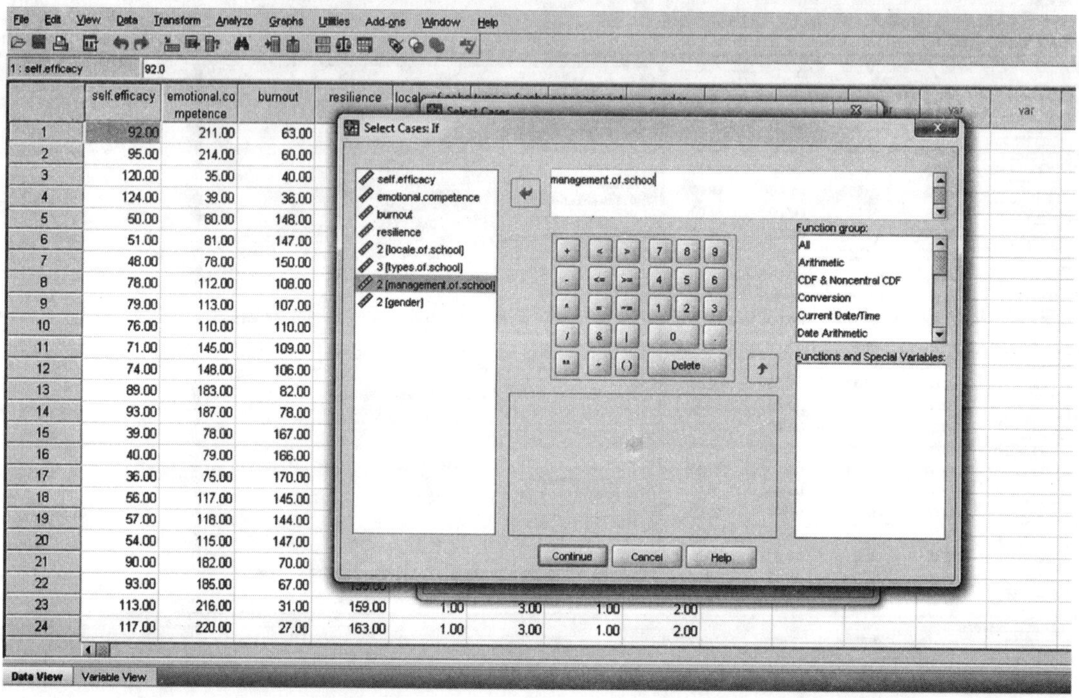

266. Against "**Management of School**" put "=" sign and type "1" because "1" represents Government Schools to get the following screen.

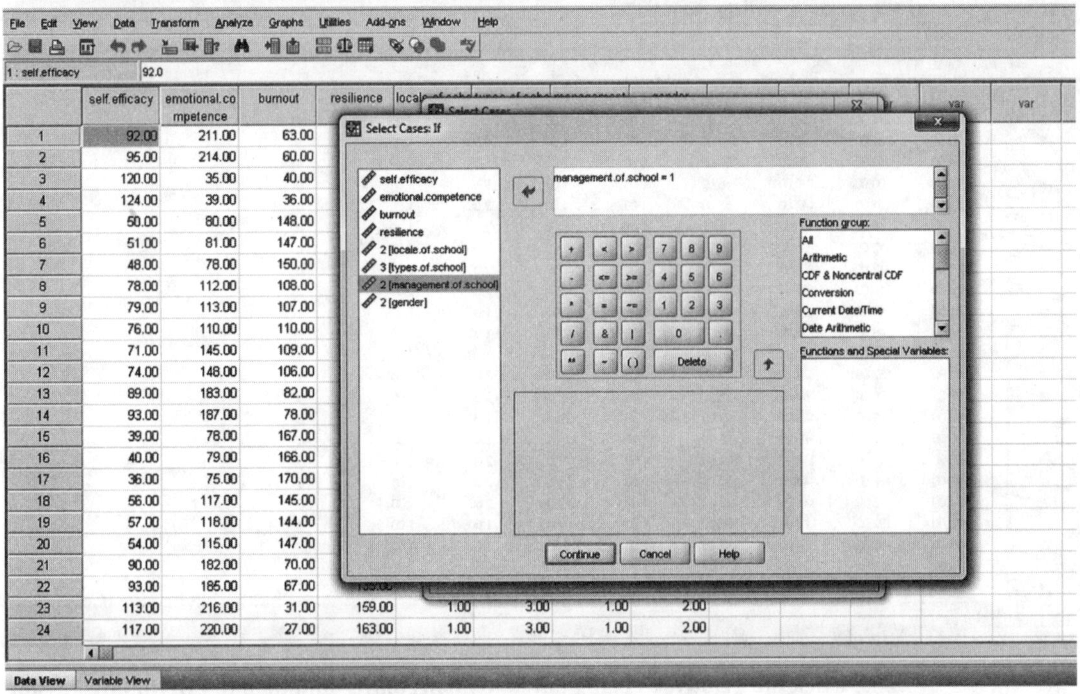

267. Click on "**Continue**" to get the following screen.

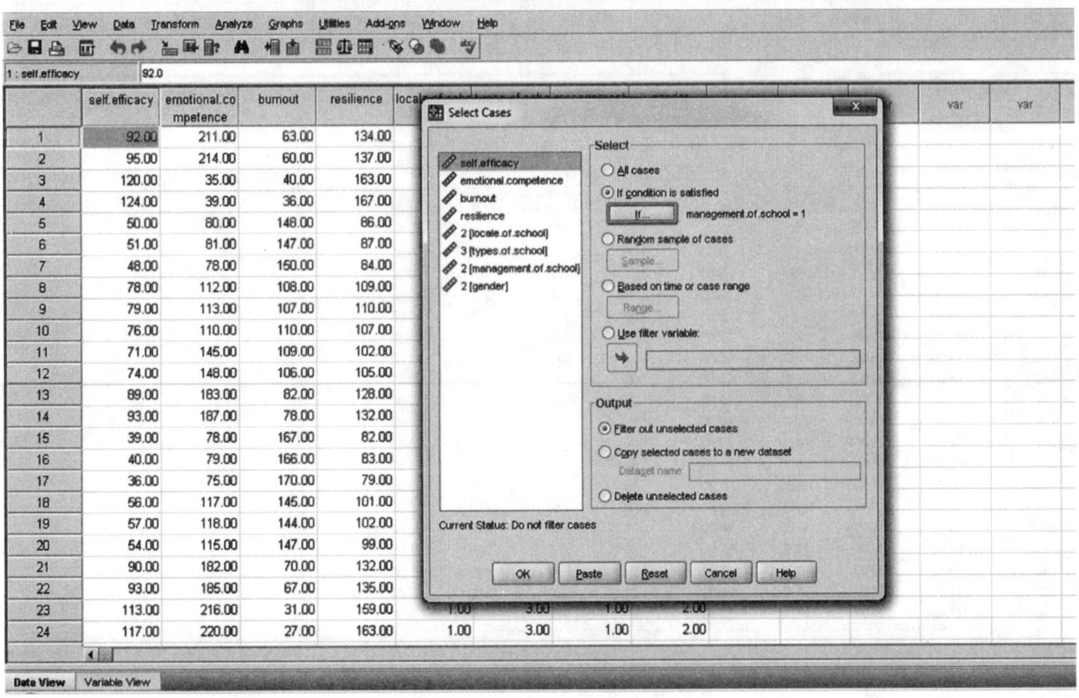

268. Click on "**OK**" to get the following screen.

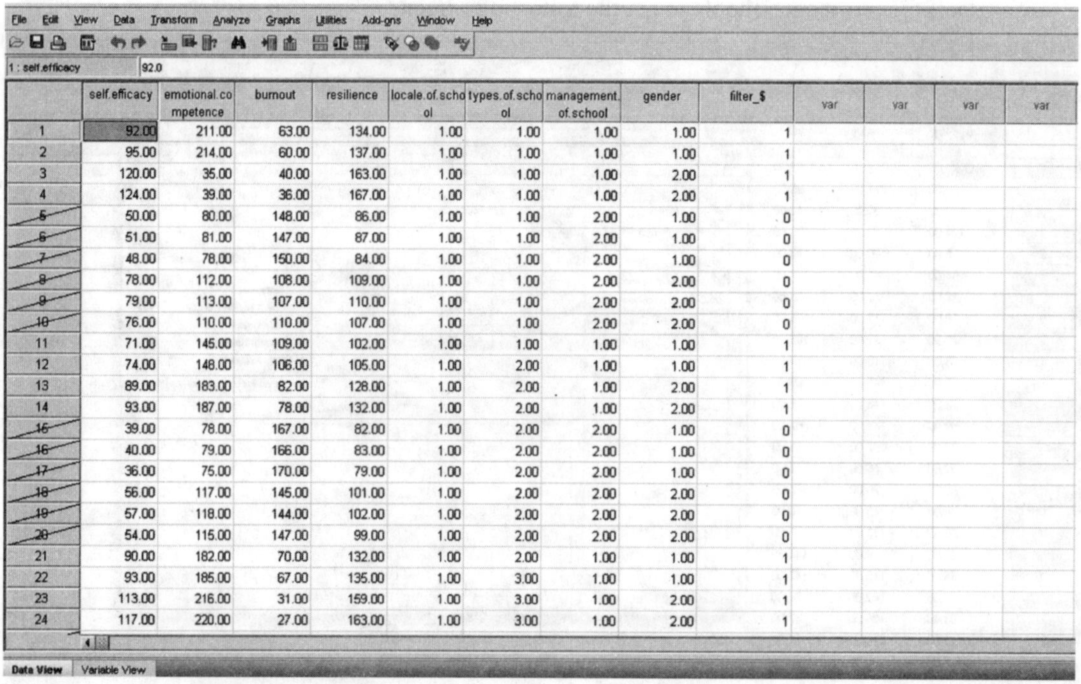

269. Click on "**Analyse**" bring curse to "**Correlate**" and then to "**Bivariate**" to get the following screen.

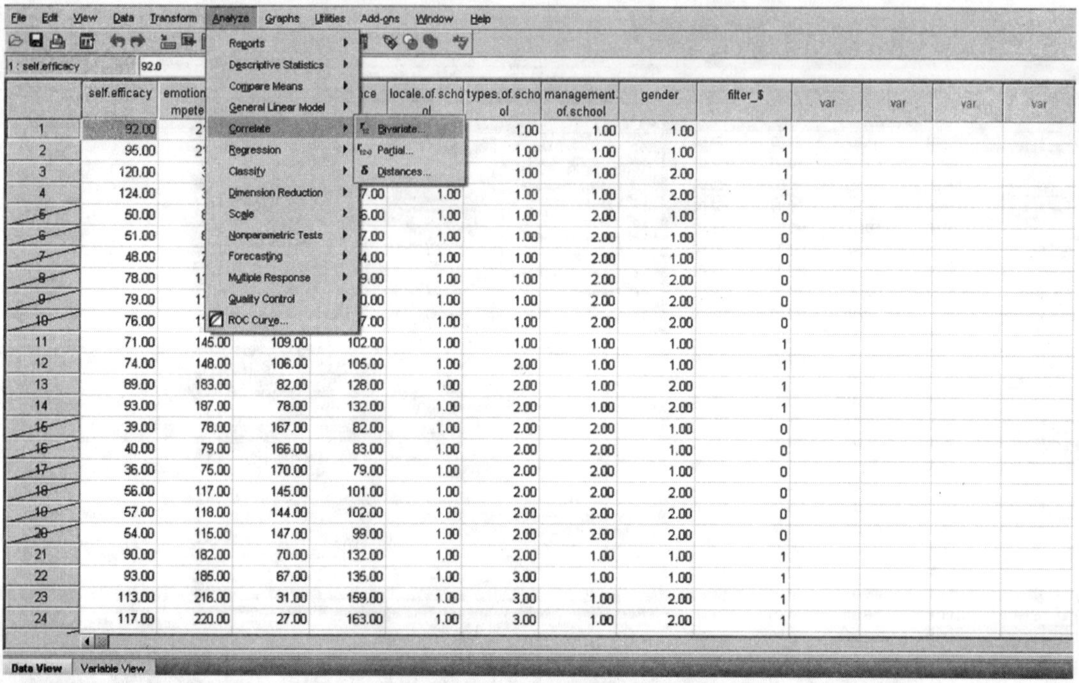

270. Click on "**Bivariate**" to get the following screen.

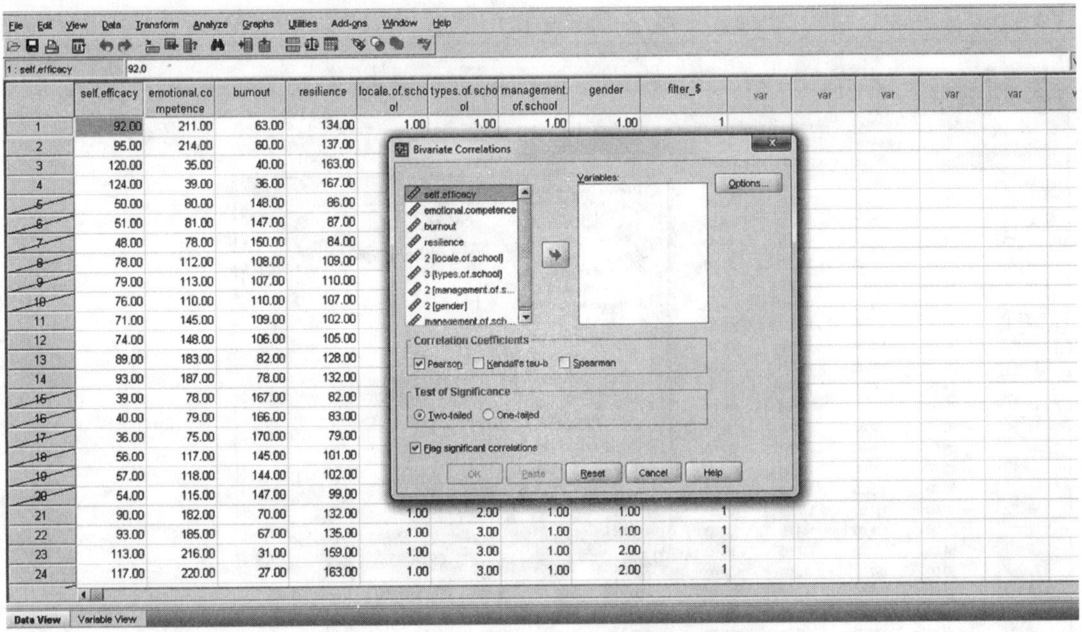

271. As per objective of research given in frame 261, the correlation is to be computed between "**Self-efficacy**" and "**Emotional Competence**", so shift "**Self-efficacy**" and "**Emotional Competence**" to the "**Variables**" dialog box to get the following screen.

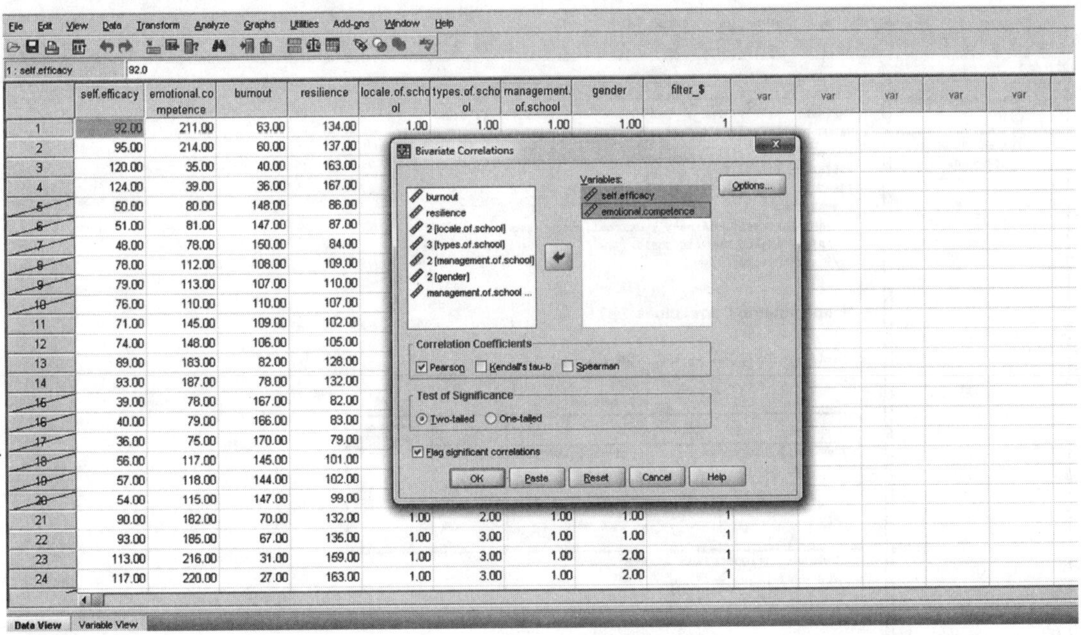

272. Deactivate "**Pearson**" and highlight "**Kendall's Tau-b**" to get the following screen.

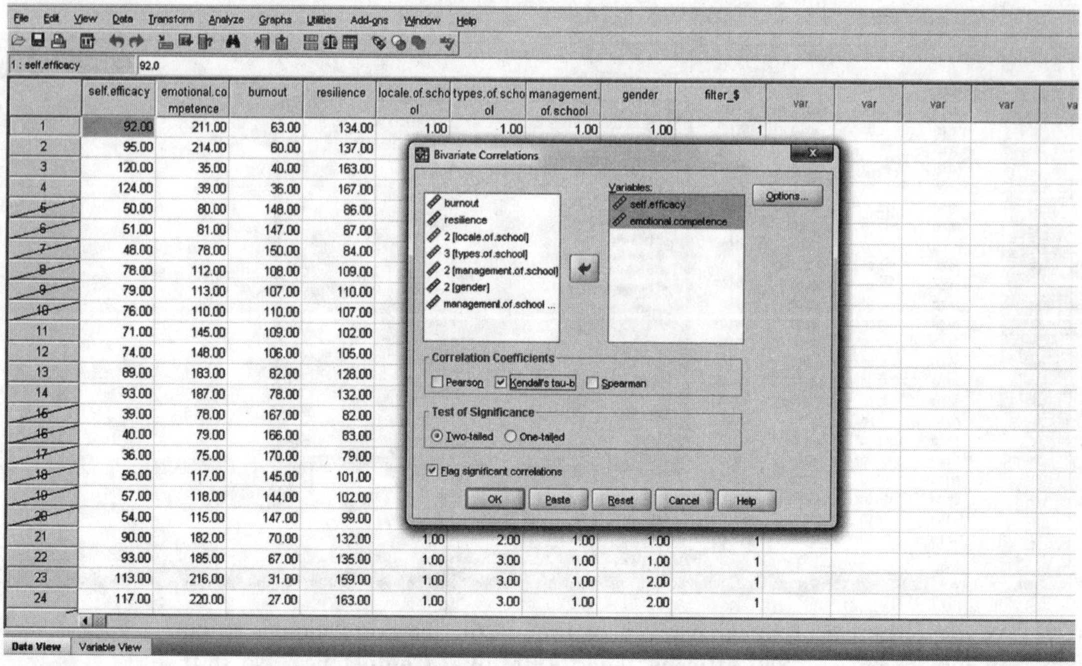

273. Click on "OK" to get the outputs of Kendall's Tau-b for Teachers working in Government Schools.

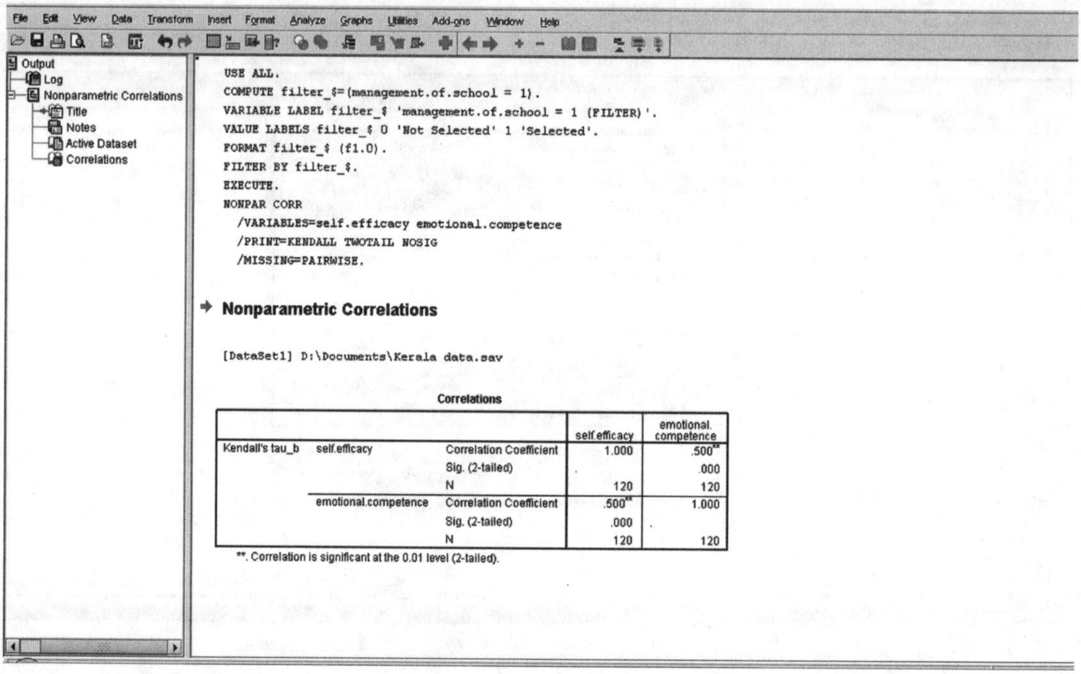

274. For computing correlation between "**Self-efficacy**" and "**Emotional Competence**" for Teachers working in Private Schools, go to "**Data**" and click on "**Select Cases**" to get the following screen.

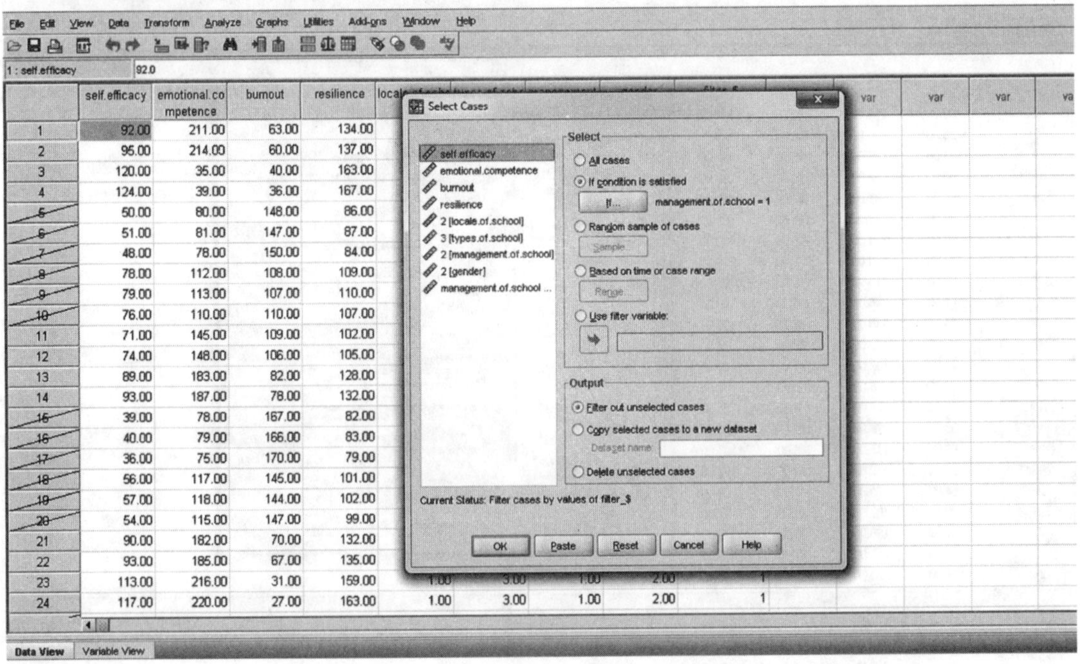

275. Click on "**If...**" icon to get the following screen.

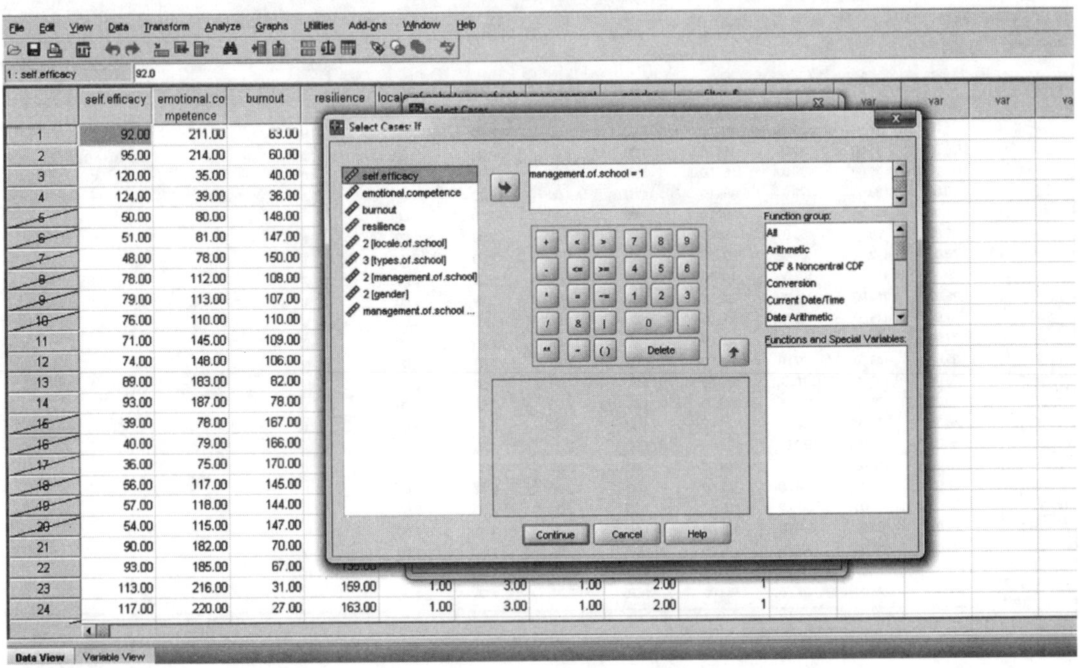

276. Against "**Management of School**" type "**2**" in place of "**1**" because "**2**" is the code of Private School and click on "**Continue**" to get the following screen.

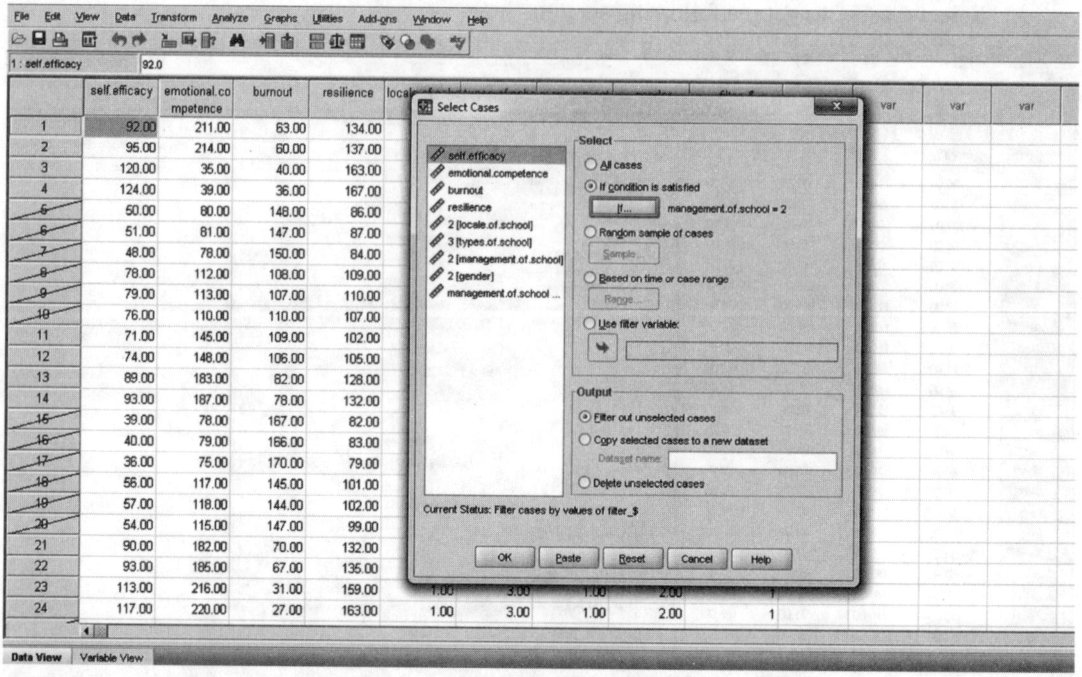

277. Click on "**OK**" to get the following screen.

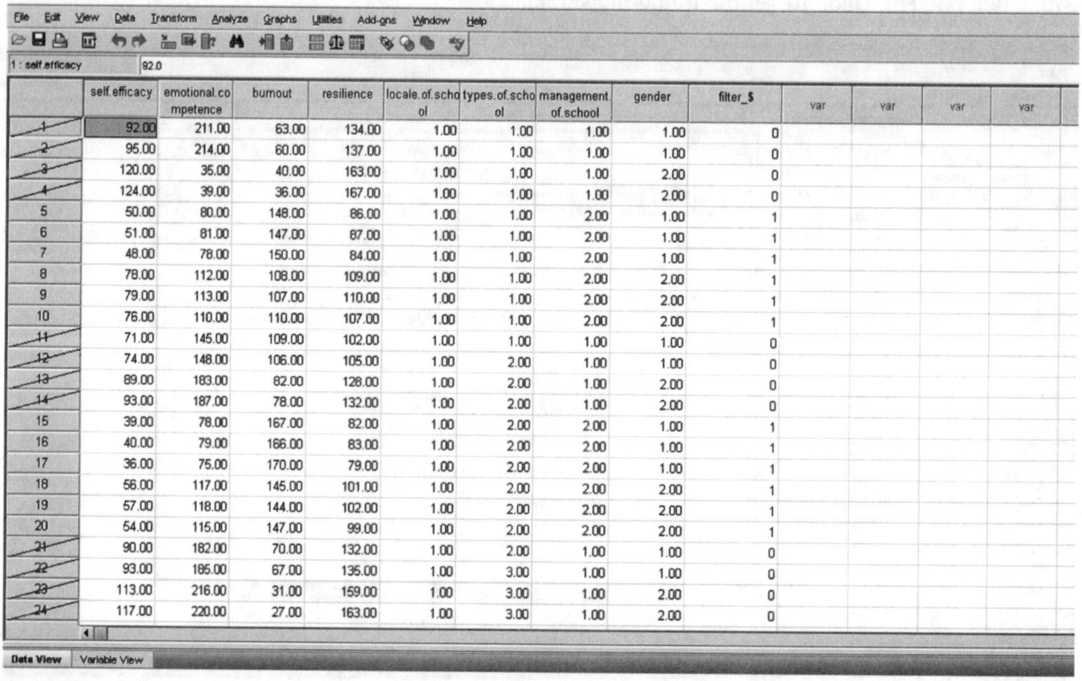

278. Click on "**Analyse**", bring curser to "**Correlate**" and then to "**Bivariate**" to get the following screen.

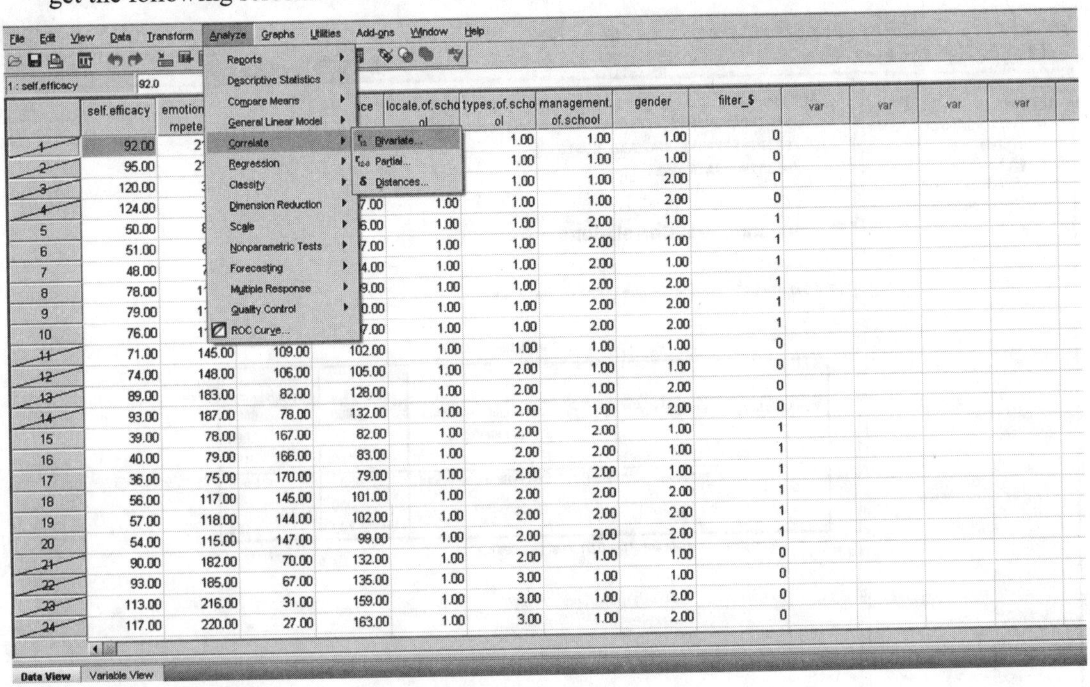

279. Click on "**Bivariate**" to get the following screen.

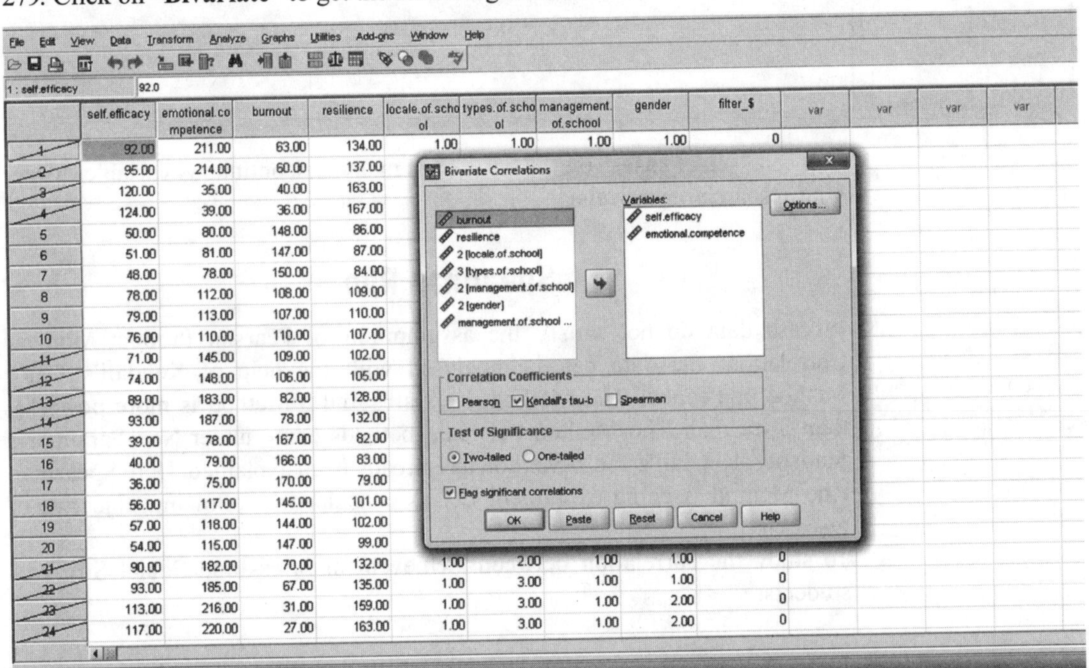

280. Click on "**OK**" to get the following outputs of Kendall's Tau-b coefficient for Teachers working in Private Schools.

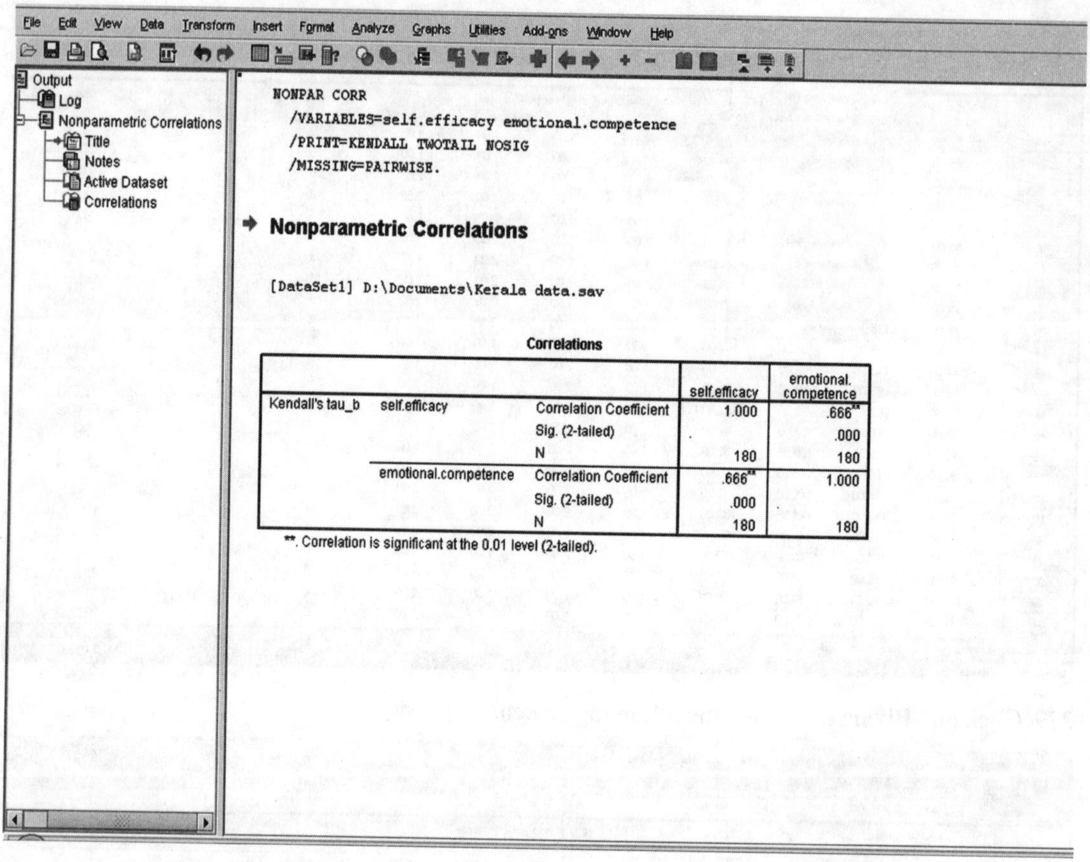


```
NONPAR CORR
  /VARIABLES=self.efficacy emotional.competence
  /PRINT=KENDALL TWOTAIL NOSIG
  /MISSING=PAIRWISE.
```

Nonparametric Correlations

[DataSet1] D:\Documents\Kerala data.sav

Correlations

			self.efficacy	emotional. competence
Kendall's tau_b	self.efficacy	Correlation Coefficient	1.000	.666**
		Sig. (2-tailed)	.	.000
		N	180	180
	emotional.competence	Correlation Coefficient	.666**	1.000
		Sig. (2-tailed)	.000	.
		N	180	180

**. Correlation is significant at the 0.01 level (2-tailed).

You can "**select cases**" on the basis of as many Discontinuous variables as per your research objective(s).

Spearman Rho

281. In case data do not satisfy the assumptions of Pearson Product Moment Correlation, the data can be analysed with the help of Kendall's Tau-b Method or Pearson Rho Method. Kendall's Tau-b Method is more powerful than Spearman Rho Method but both methods come under Non-Parametric Statistics. Kendall's Tau-b Method has already been explained. Here Spearman Rho Method is being explained. Let us consider the following objective of research.

To study the correlation between Achievement Stress and Social Stress of students.

Click on "**Analyse**", bring curser to "**Correlate**" and then to "**Bivariate**" to get the following screen.

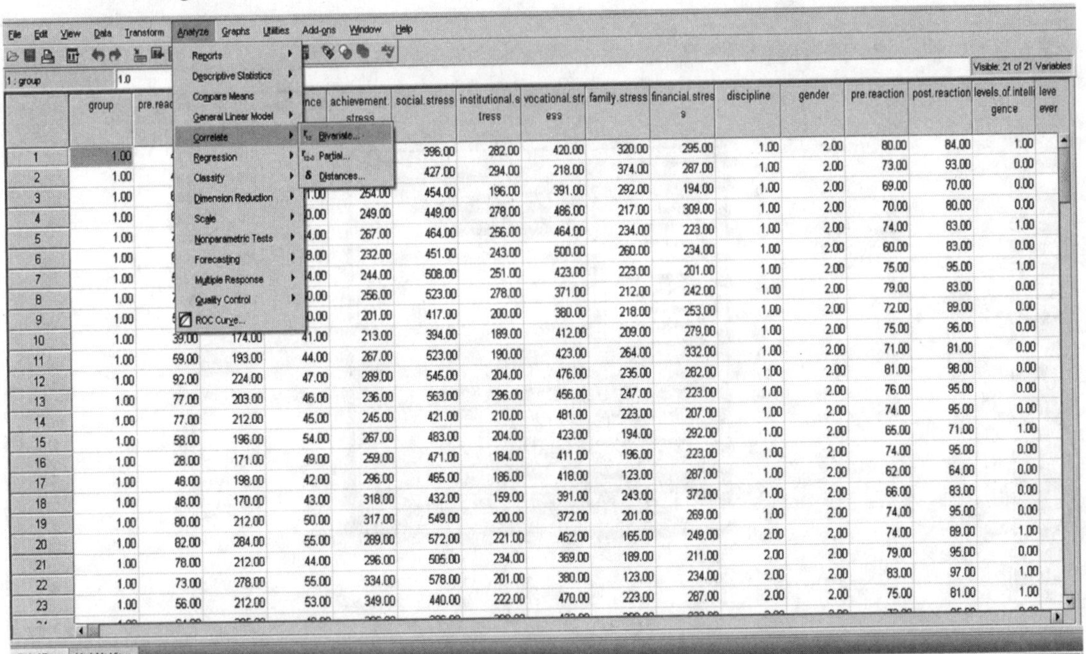

282. Click on "**Bivariate**" to get the following screen.

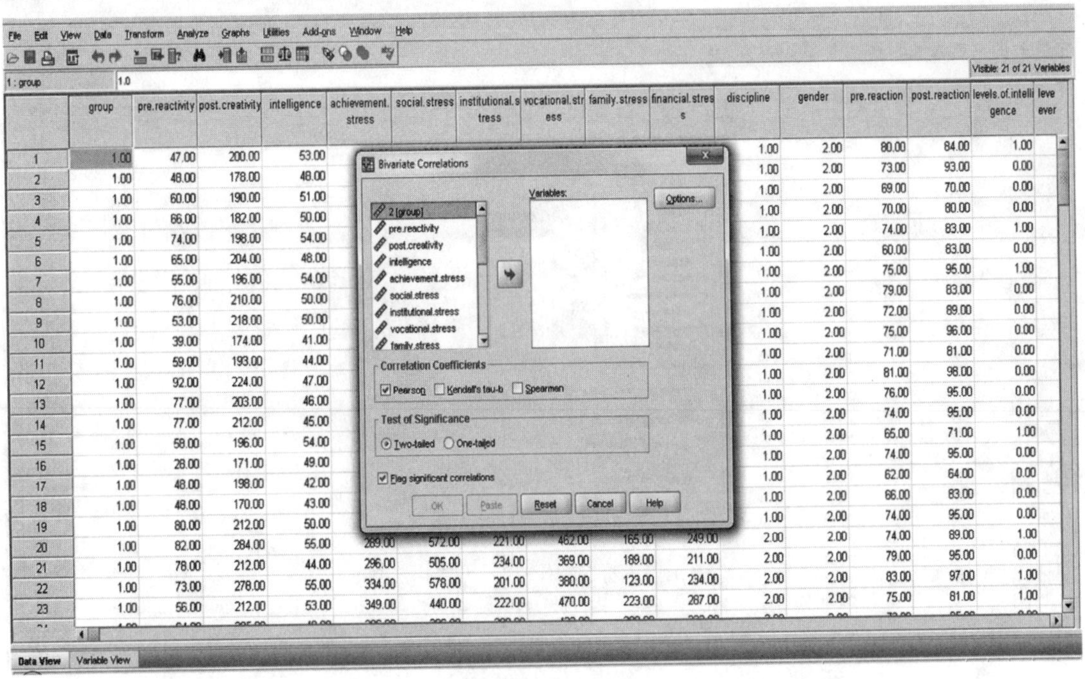

283. Shift "**Achievement Stress**" and "**Social Stress**" under "**Variables**" dialog box to get the following screen.

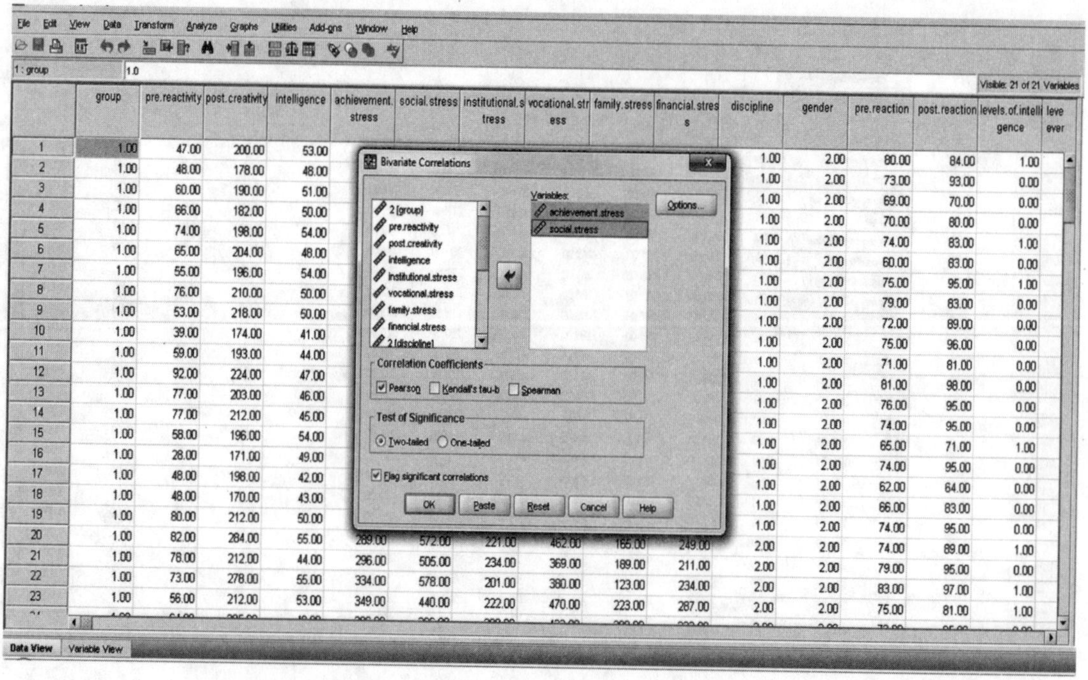

284. Deactivate "**Pearson**" and highlight "**Spearman**" to get the following screen.

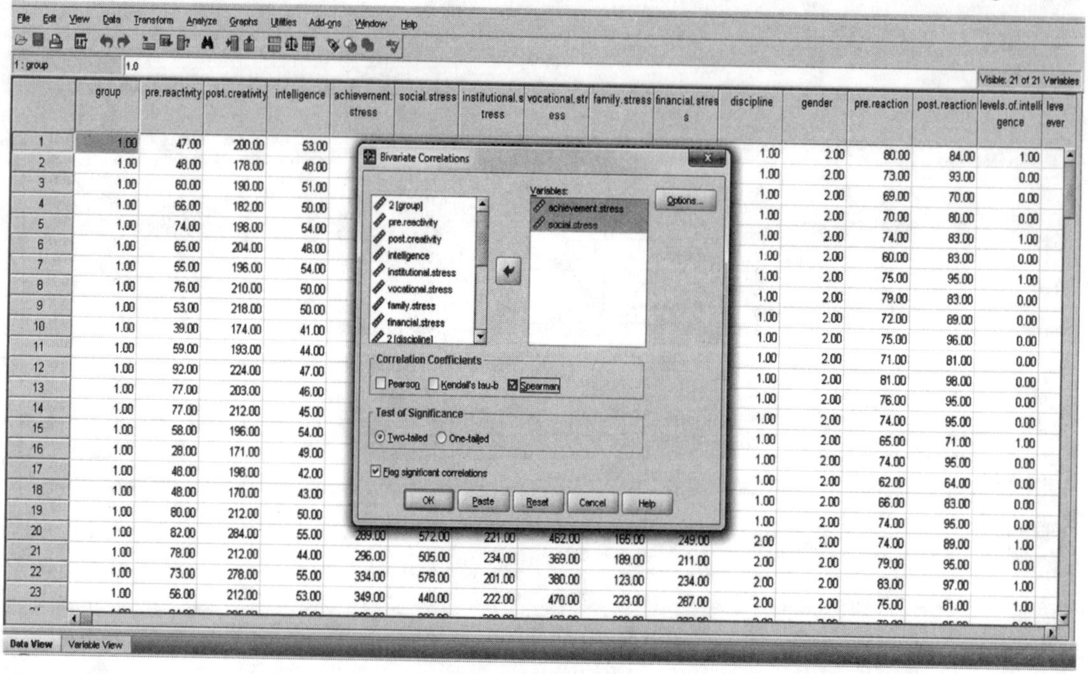

285. Click on "**OK**" to get the following outputs of Spearman Correlation coefficient.

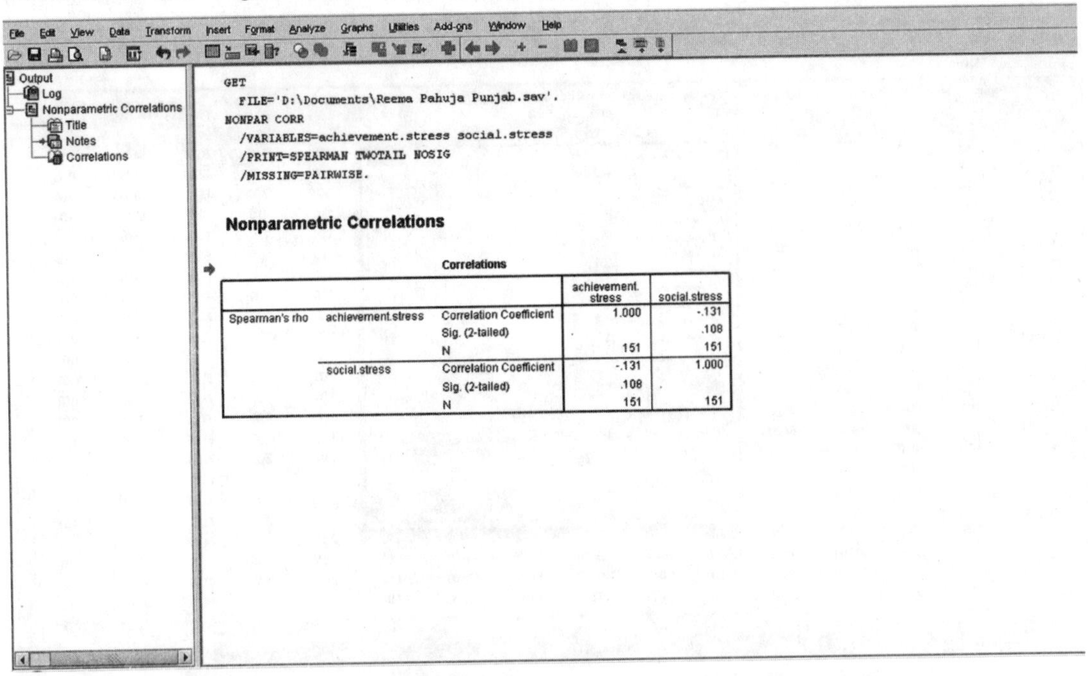

286. Let us consider the following objective of research.

To study the correlation between Family Stress and Financial Stress of Male and Female students belonging to Arts and Science subjects separately.

Click on "**Analyse**", bring curser to "**Correlate**" and then to "**Bivariate**" to get the following screen.

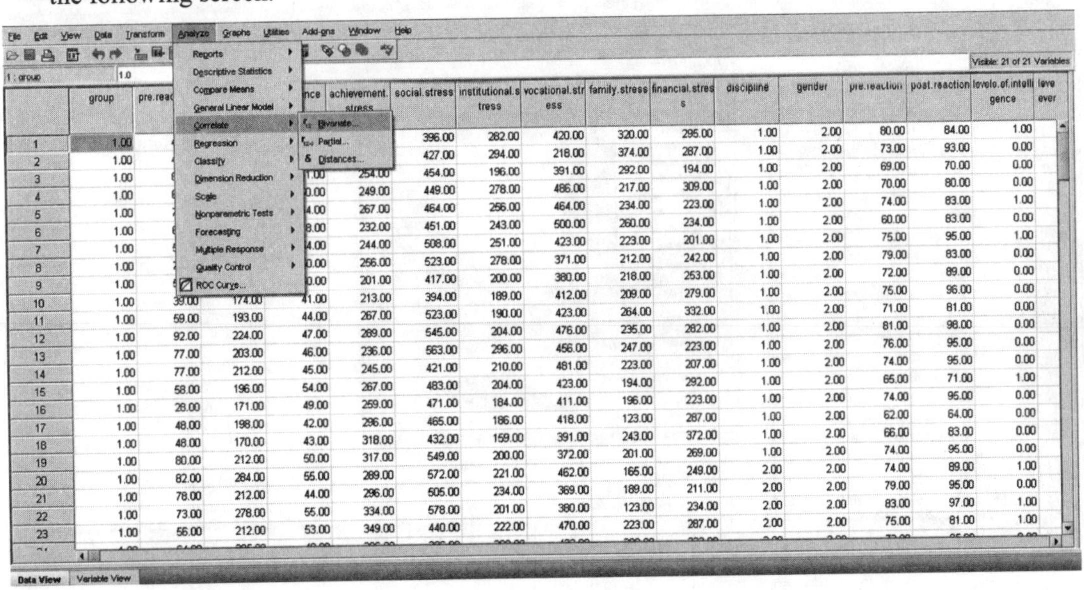

287. Click on "**Bivariate**" to get the following screen.

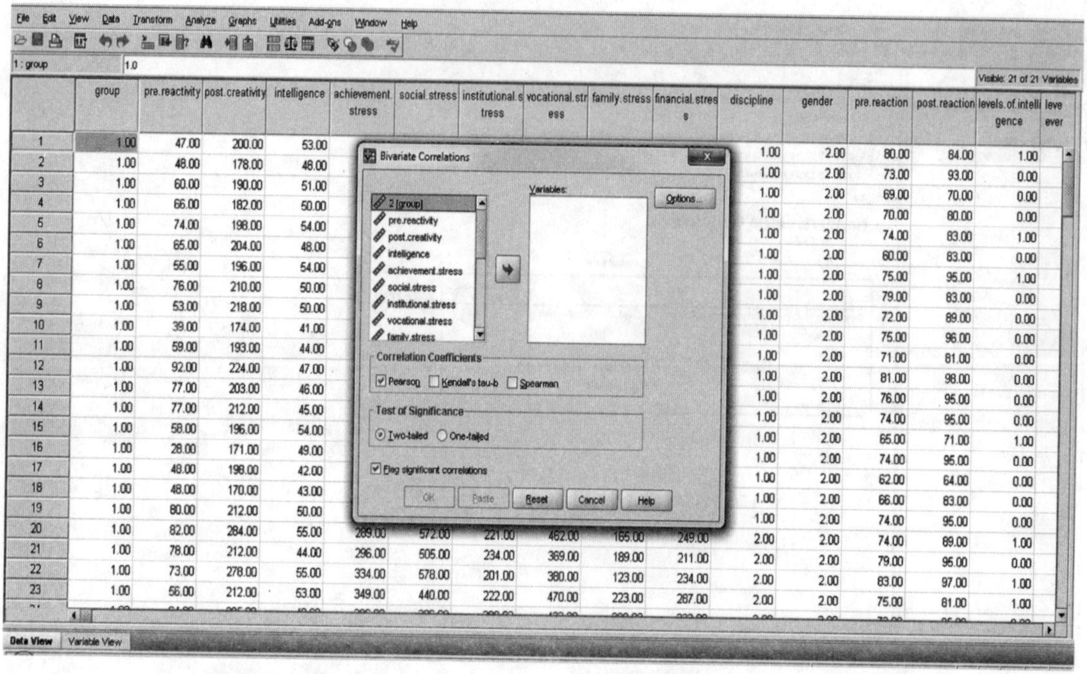

288. Shift "**Family Stress**" and "**Financial Stress**" variables to right hand side dialog box to get the following screen.

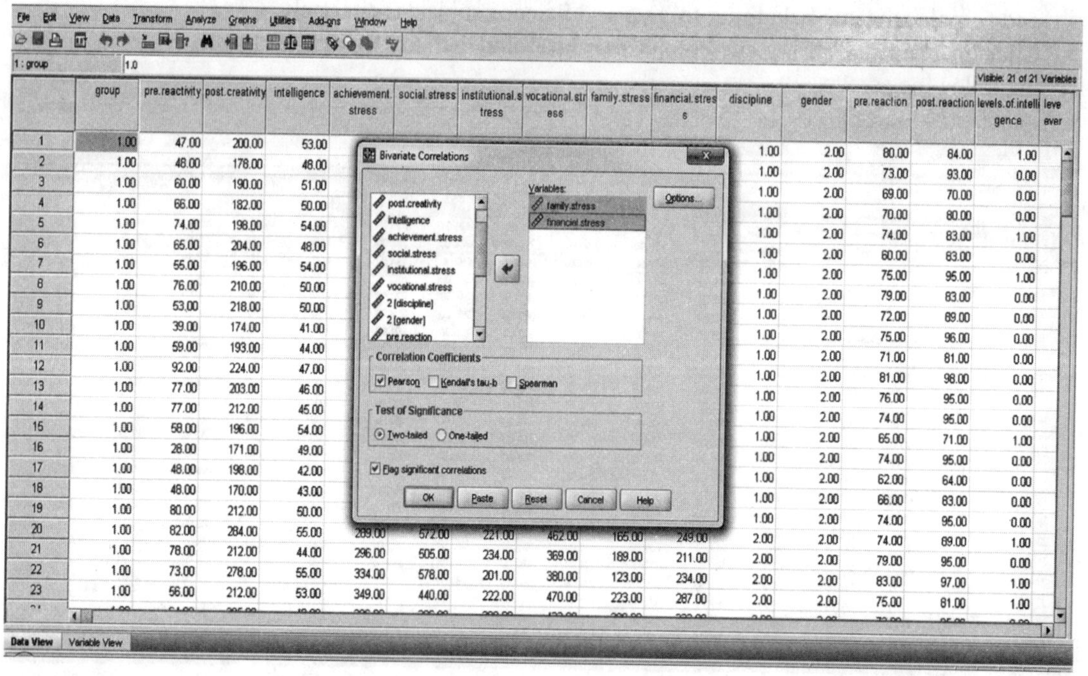

289. Deactivate "**Pearson**" and activate "**Spearman**" to get the following screen.

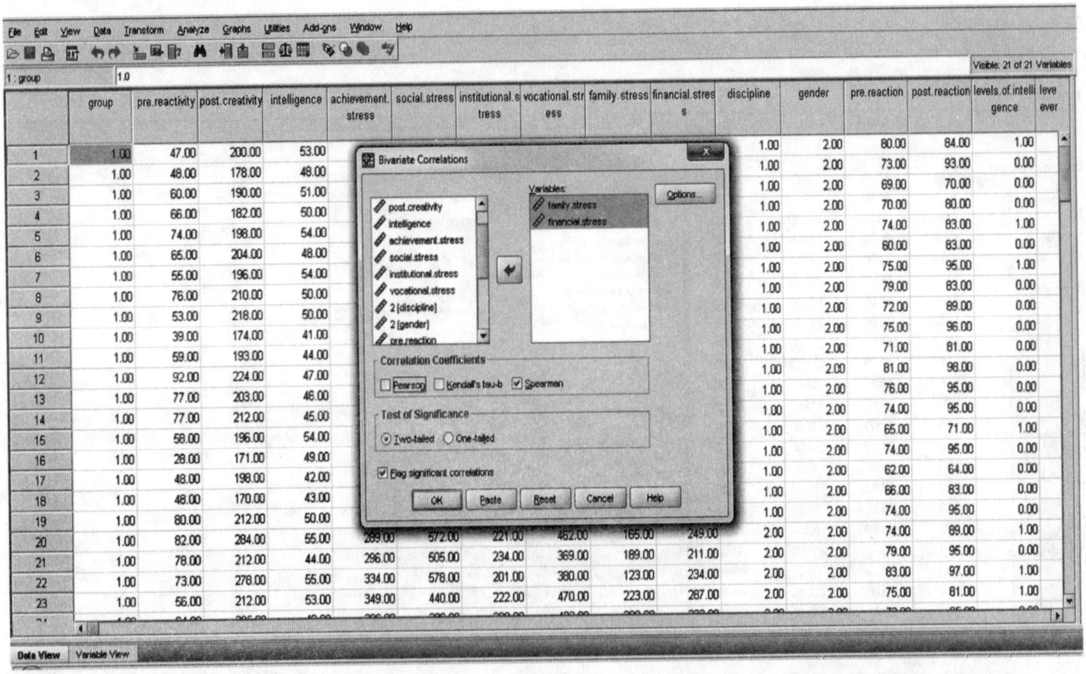

290. You need data of Male students belonging to Arts subjects. For this click on "**Data**" icon and bring curser to "**Select Cases**" to get the following screen.

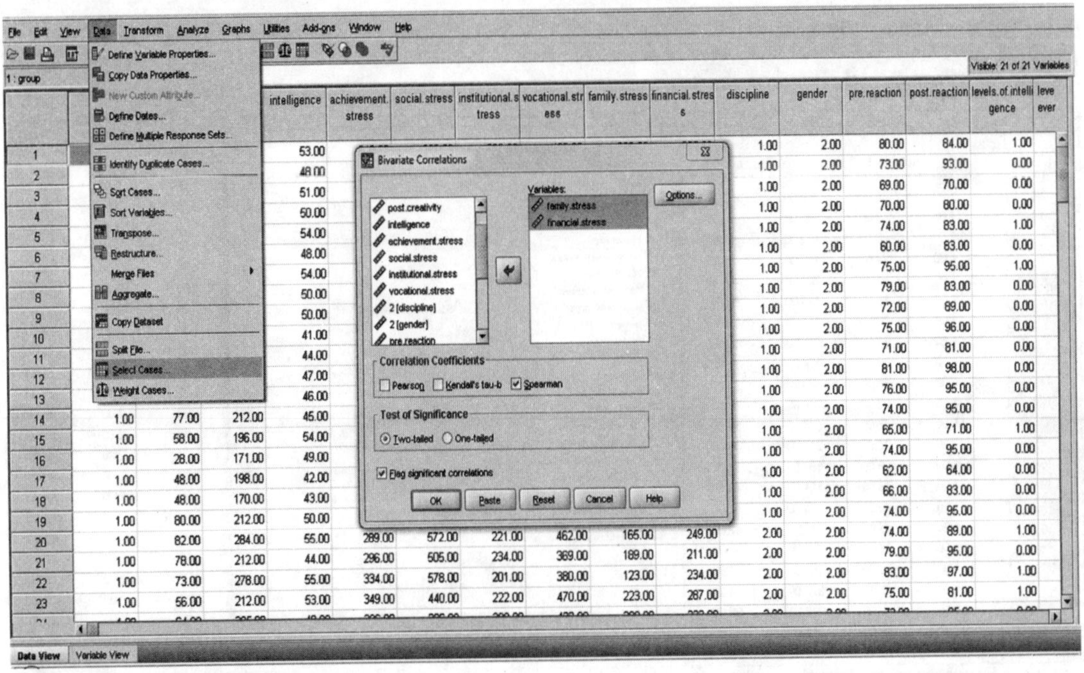

291. Click on "**Select Cases**" to get the following screen.

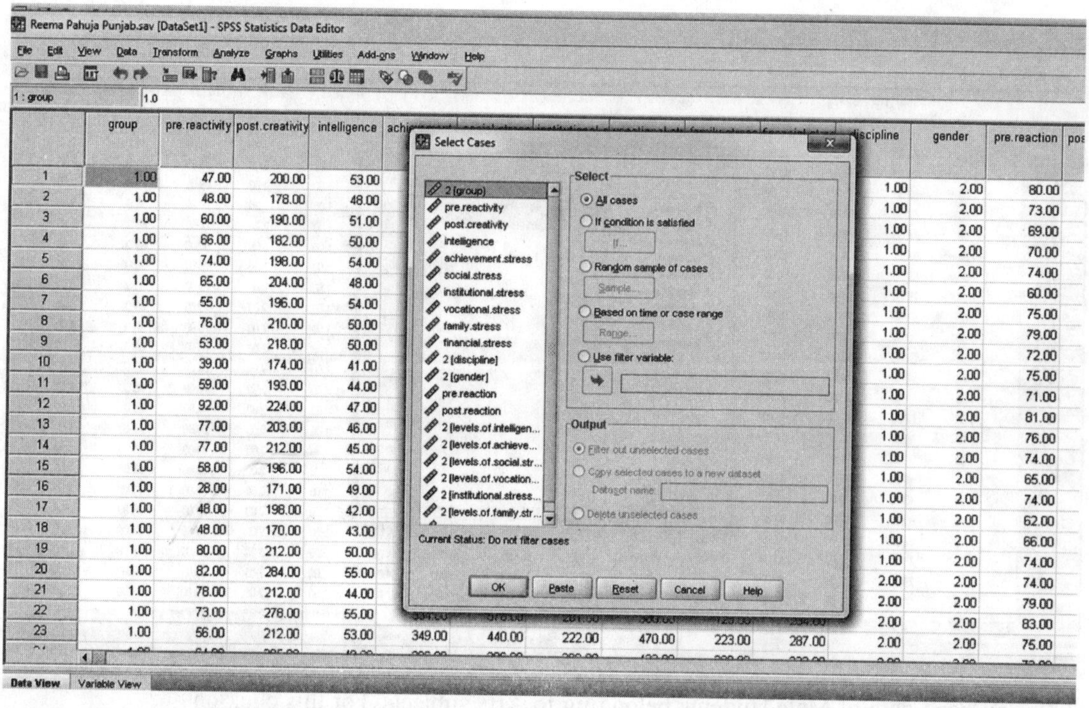

292. Click on "**If condition is satisfied**" to get the following screen.

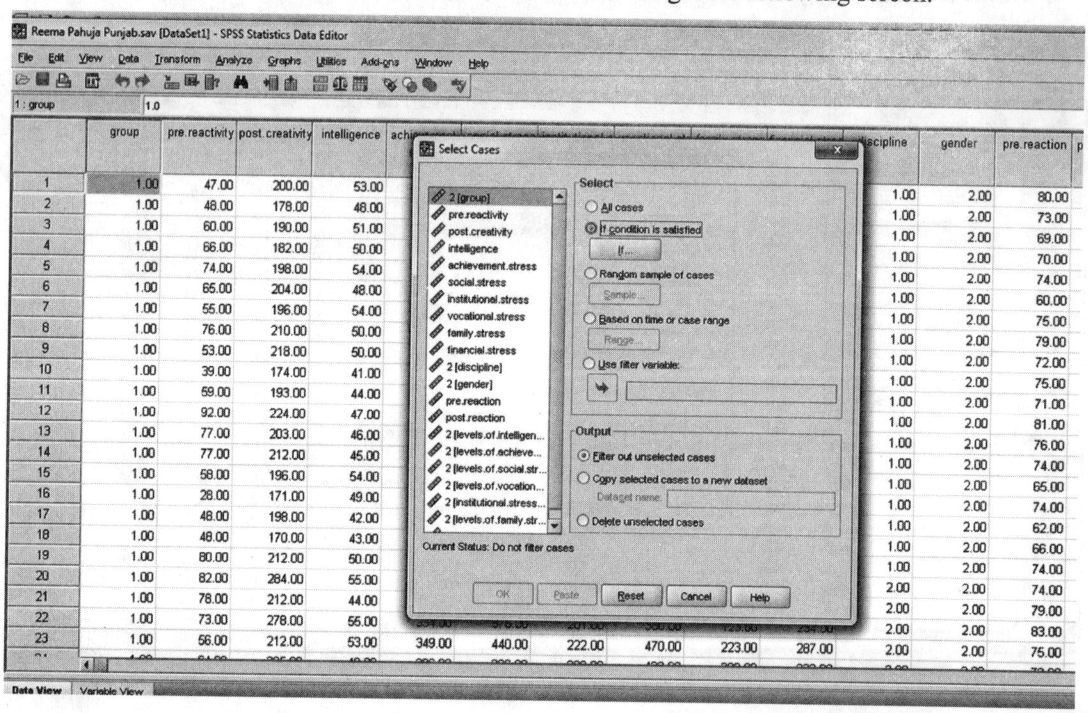

293. Click on "**If.....**" button to get the following screen.

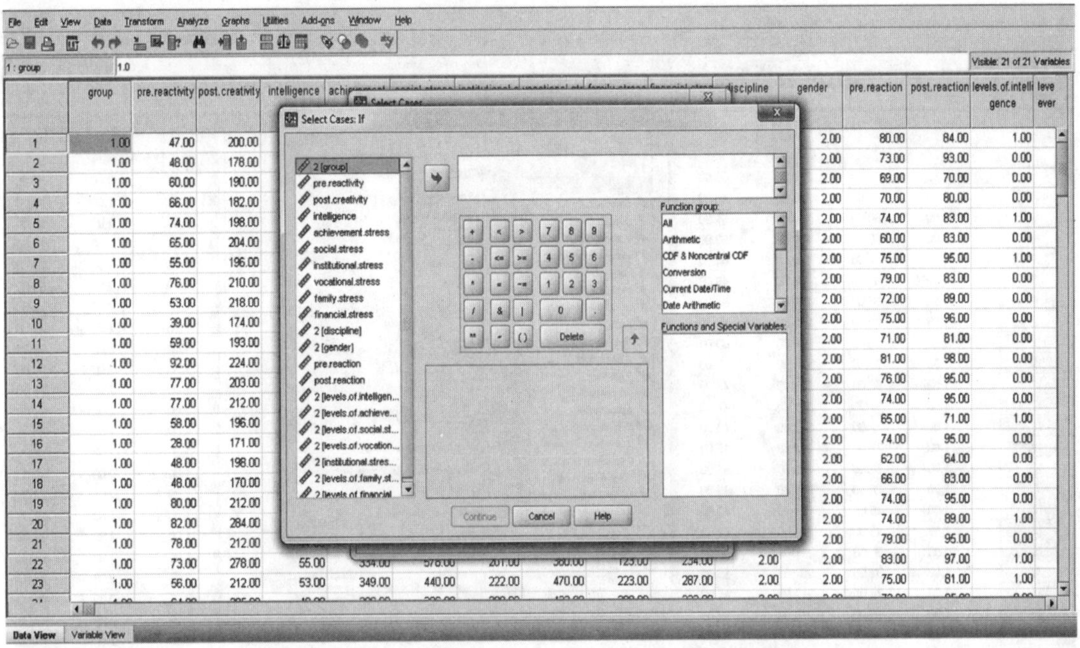

294. To get the data of Male students belonging to Arts subject, shift "**Gender**" to the right hand side slot and put "=" sign and type "**1**". Now typing "**and**" and shift "**Discipline**" to the right hand side slot and put "=" and type "**1**" to get the following screen.

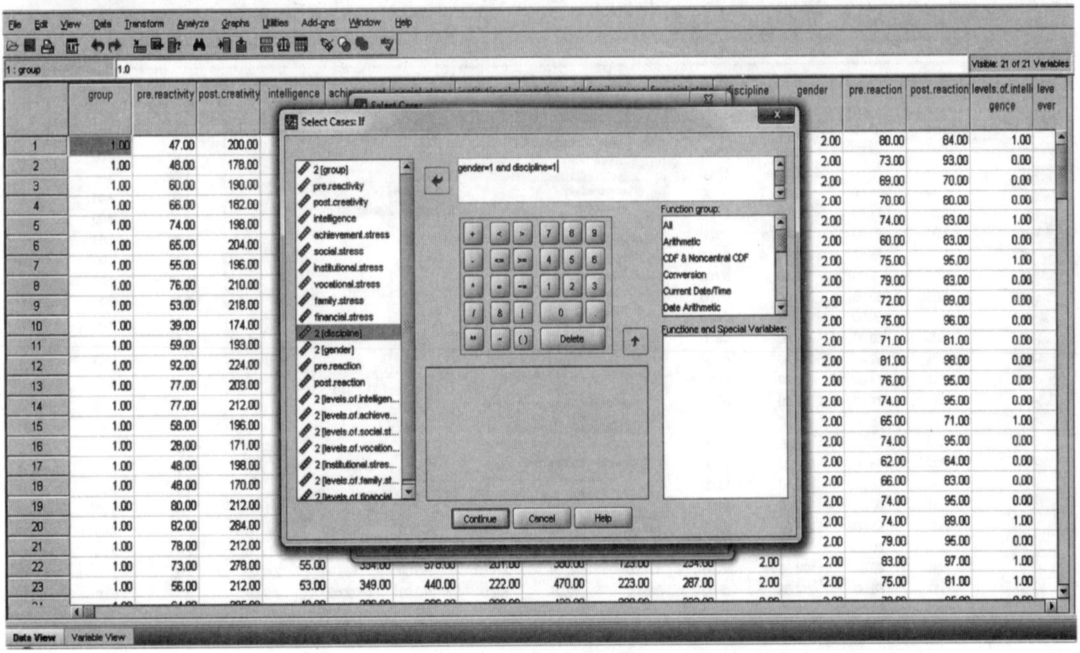

295. Click on "**Continue**" to get the following screen.

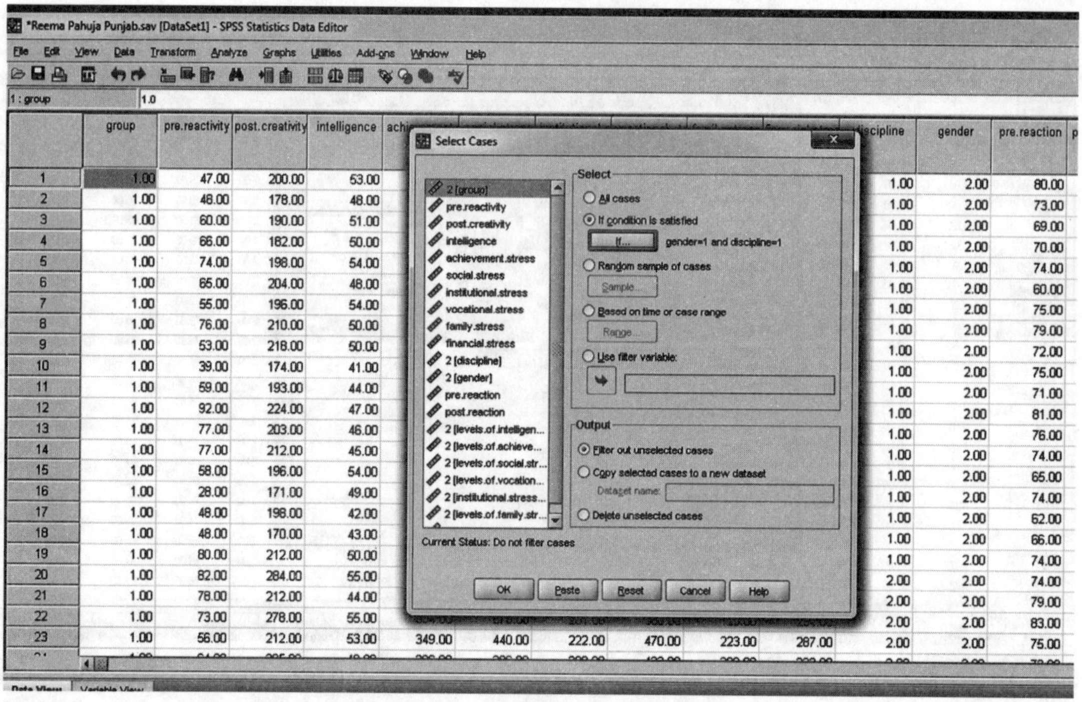

296. Click on "**OK**" to get the following screen.

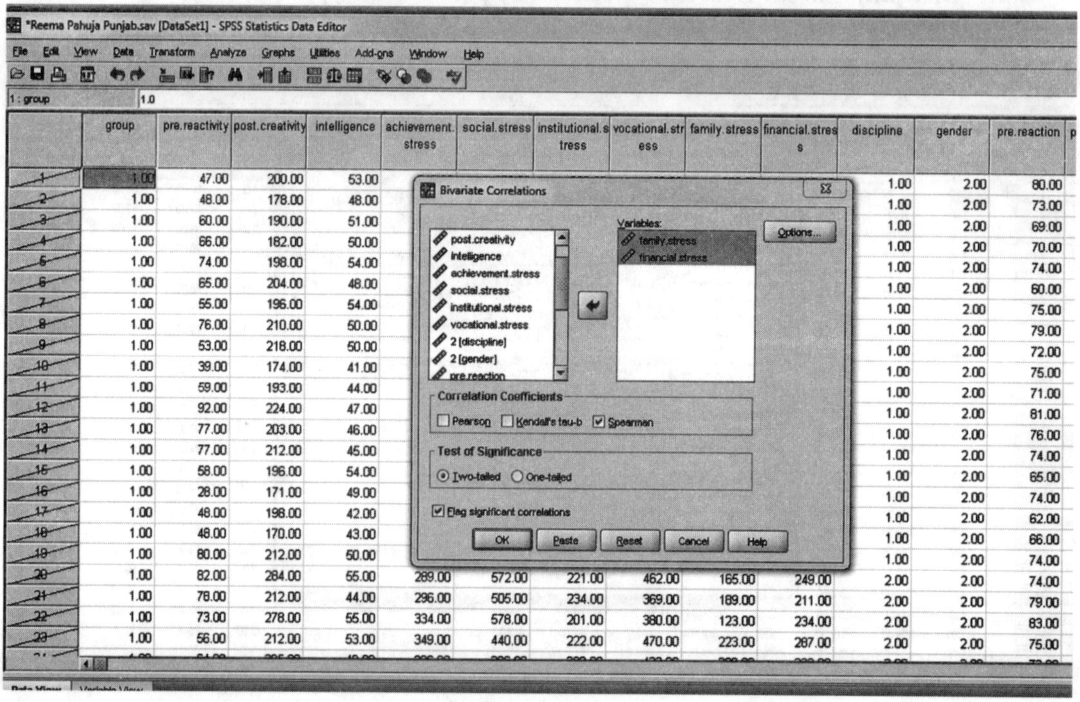

297. Click on "**OK**" to get the following outputs of Spearman correlation between Family Stress and Financial Stress of Male students belonging to Arts subject.

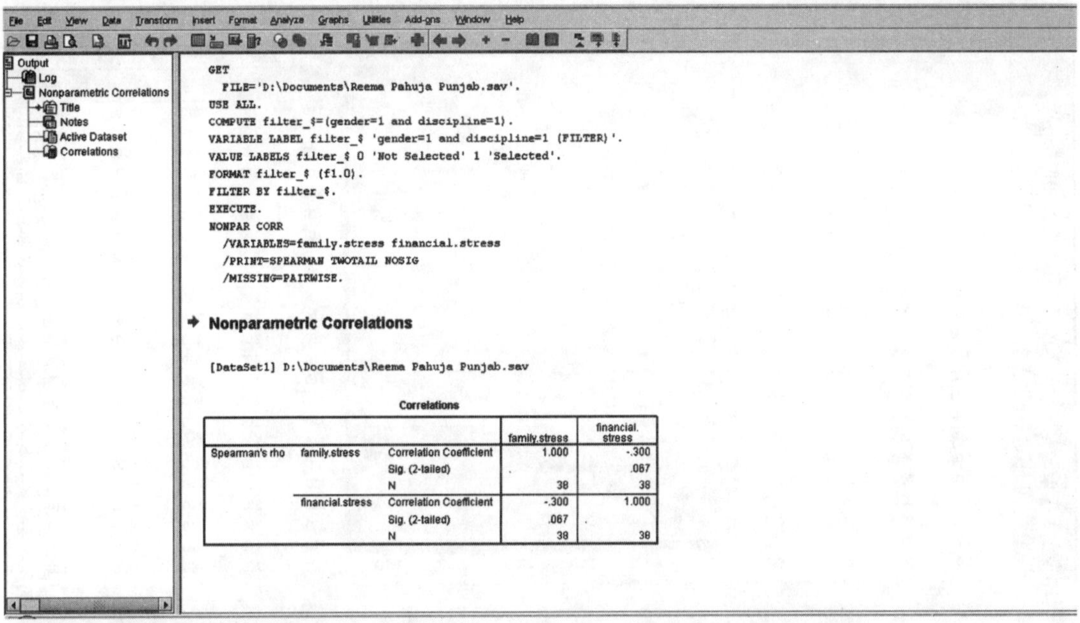

298. To compute correlation between Family Stress and Financial Stress of Male students belonging to Science subject, click on "**Data**" and bring curser to "**Select Cases**" to get the following screen.

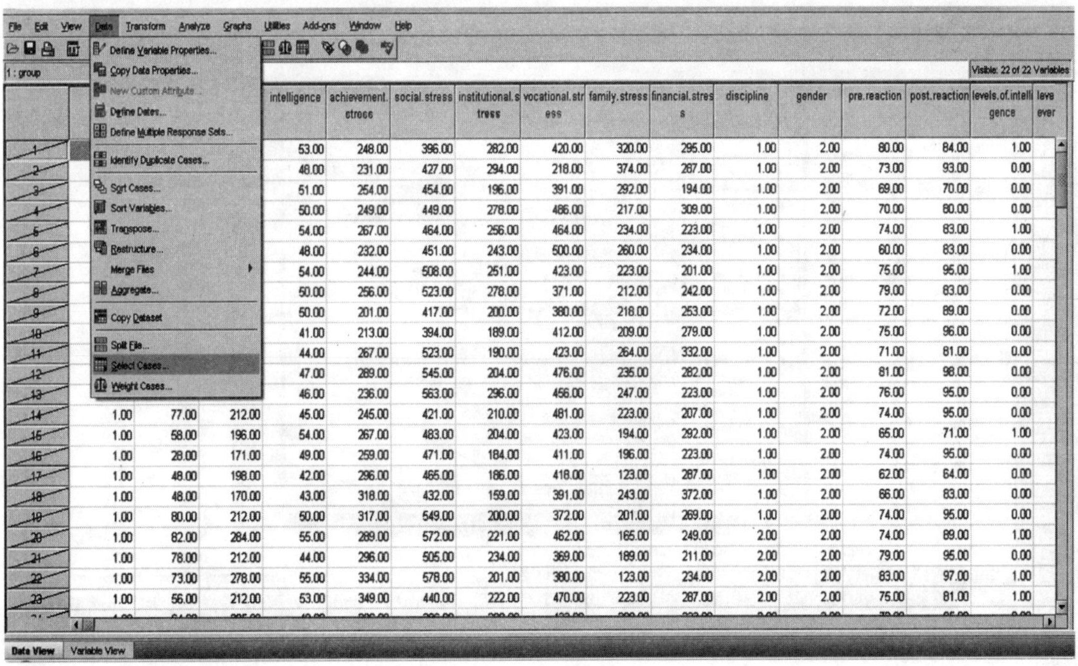

299. Click on "**Select Cases**" to get the following screen.

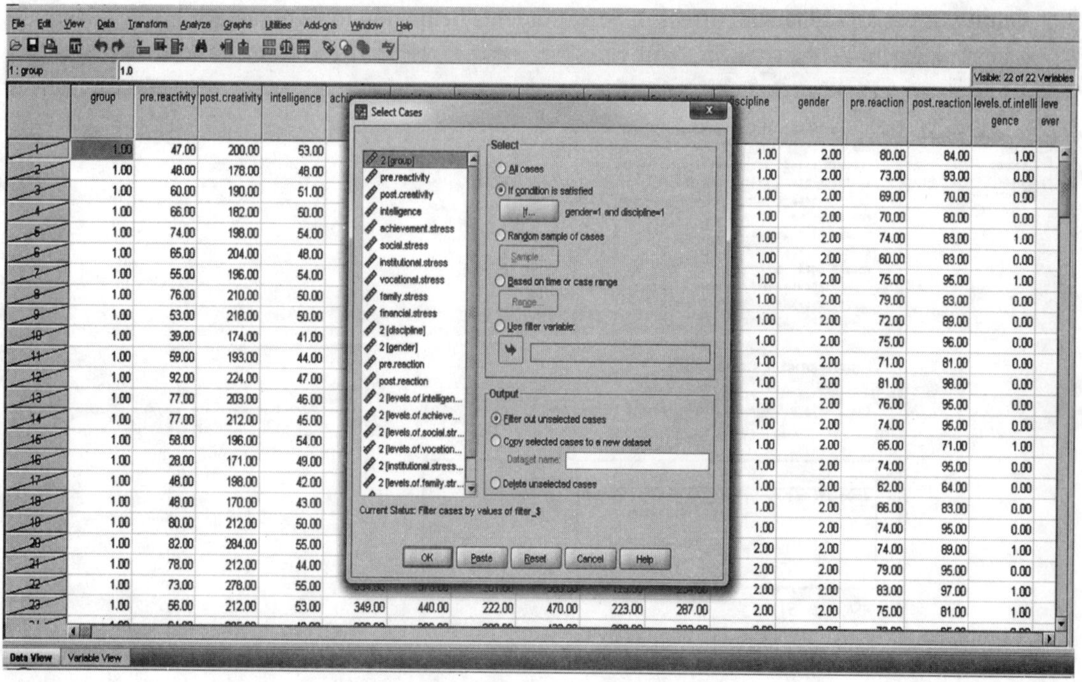

300. Click on "**If....**" button to get the following screen.

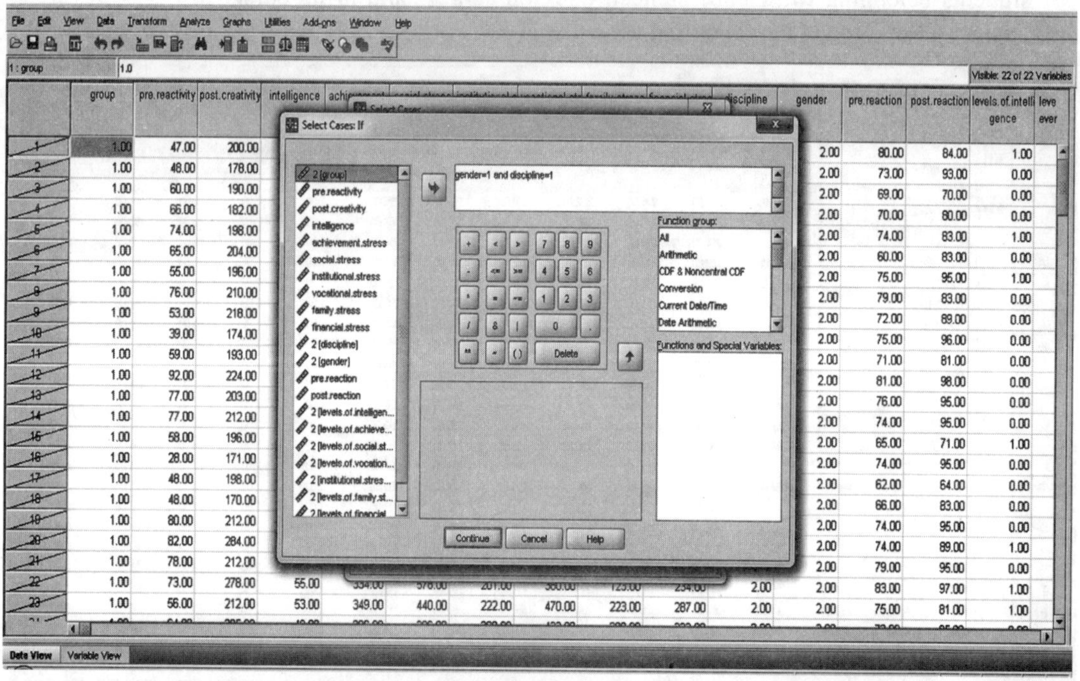

301. To get result for Male students studying Science Subject, against "**Discipline**" replace "**1**" by "**2**" to get the following screen.

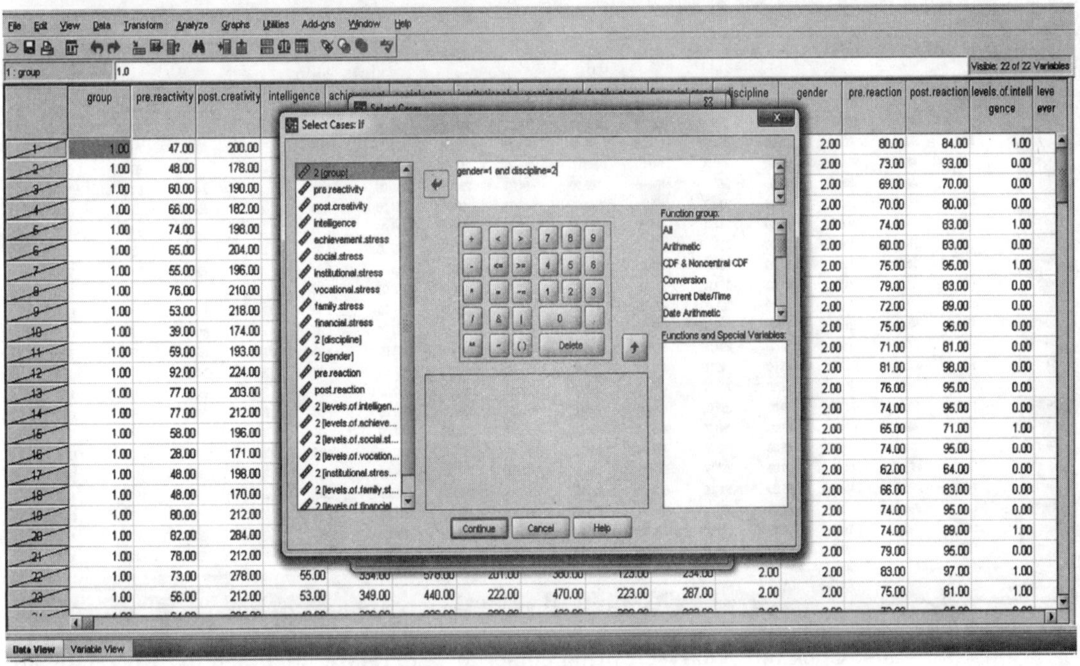

302. Click on "**Continue**" to get the following screen.

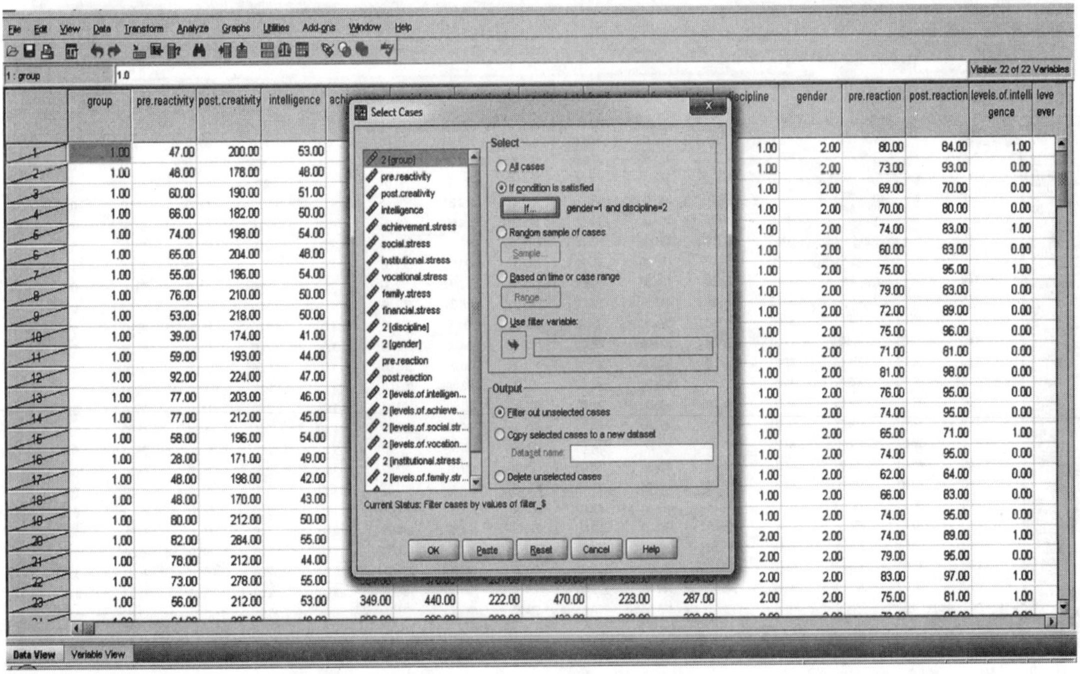

303. Click on "**OK**" to get the following screen.

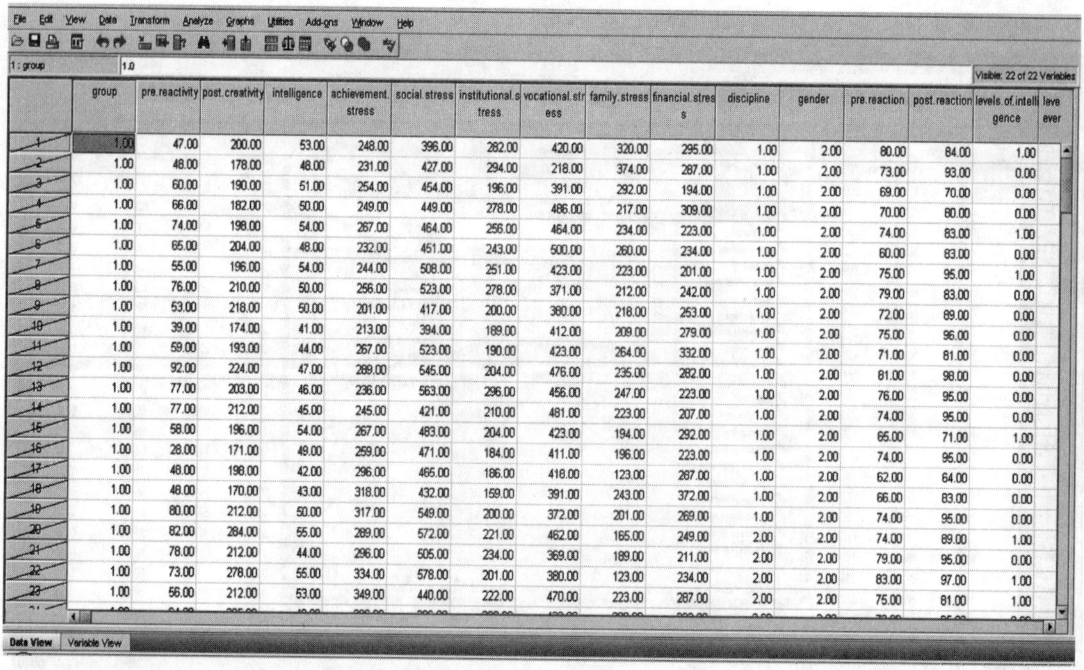

304. Click on "**Analyse**", bring curser to "**Correlate**" and then to "**Bivariate**" to get the following screen.

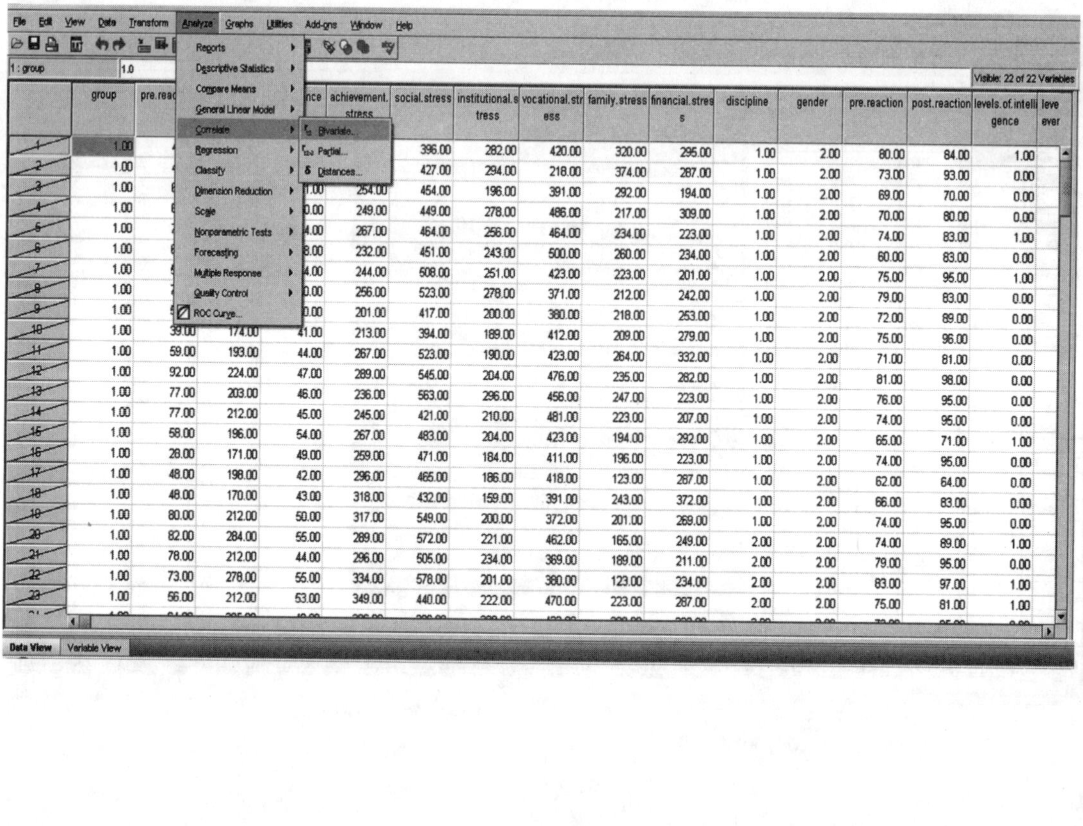

305. Click on "**Bivariate**" to get the following screen.

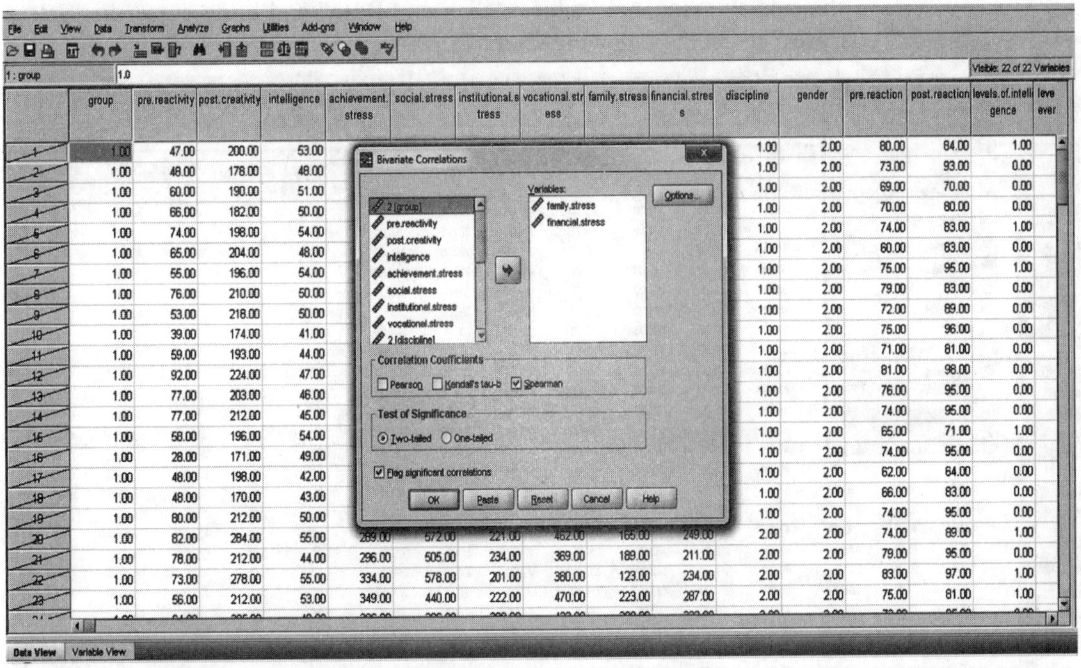

306. Click on "**OK**" to get the following outputs of Correlation between Family Stress and Financial Stress of Male students belonging to Science subject.

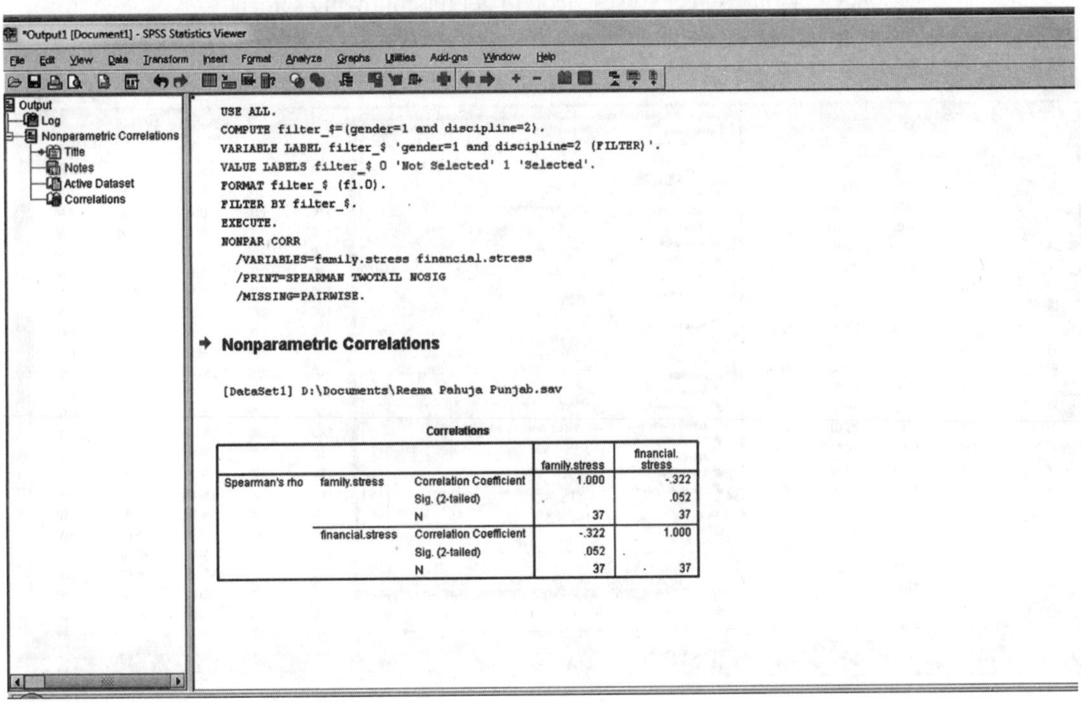

			family.stress	financial. stress
Spearman's rho	family.stress	Correlation Coefficient	1.000	-.322
		Sig. (2-tailed)	.	.052
		N	37	37
	financial.stress	Correlation Coefficient	-.322	1.000
		Sig. (2-tailed)	.052	.
		N	37	37

307. To get Correlation between Family Stress and Financial Stress of Female students studying Arts subject, click on "**Data**" and bring curser to "**Select Cases**" to get the following screen.

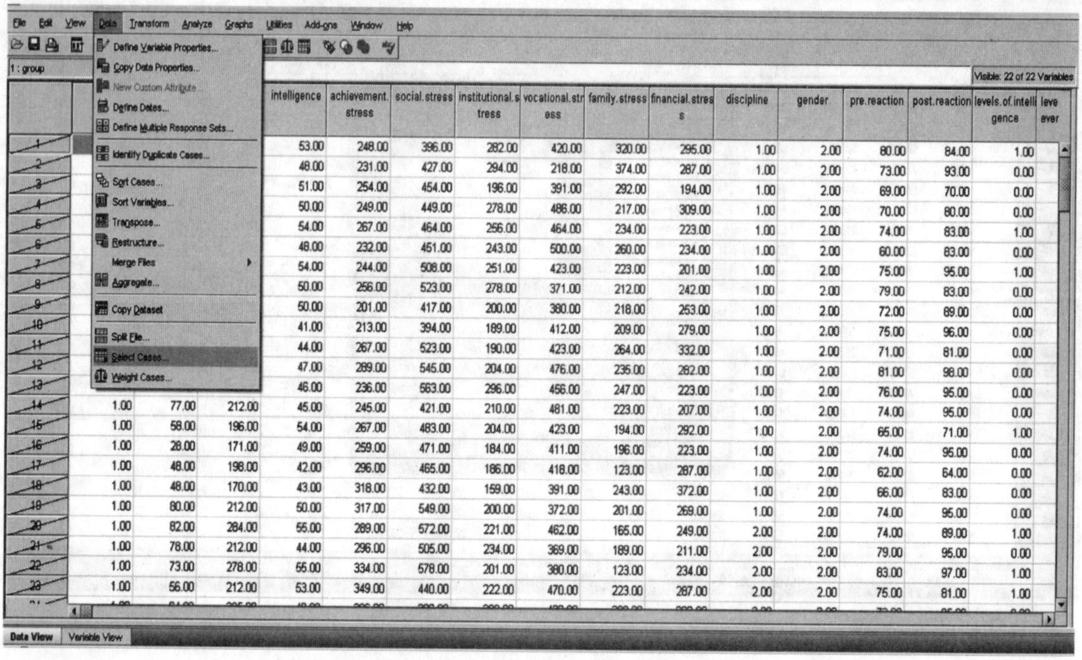

308. Click on "**Select Cases**" icon to get the following screen.

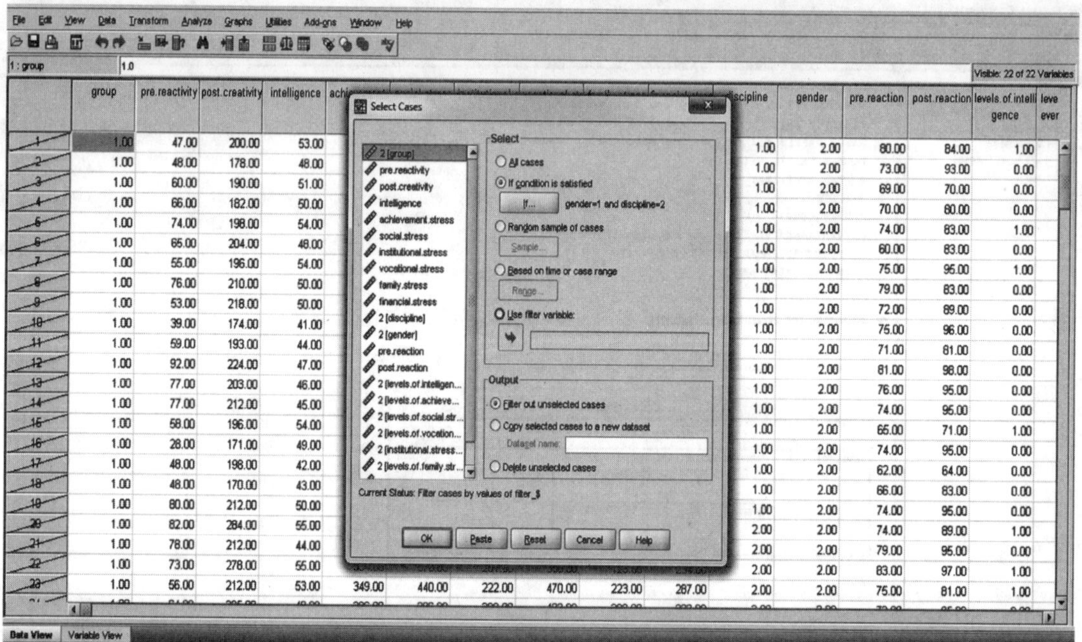

309. Click on "**If...**" and against "**Gender**" replace "**1**" by "**2**" and against "**Discipline**" replace "**2**" by "**1**" to get the following screen.

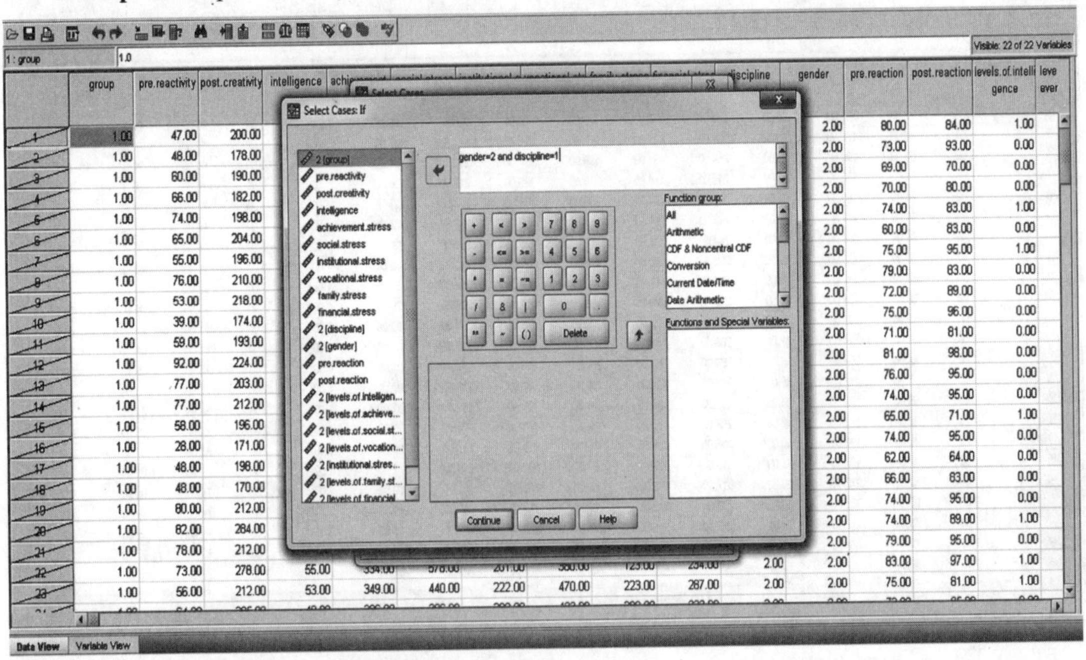

310. Click on "**Continue**" to get the following screen.

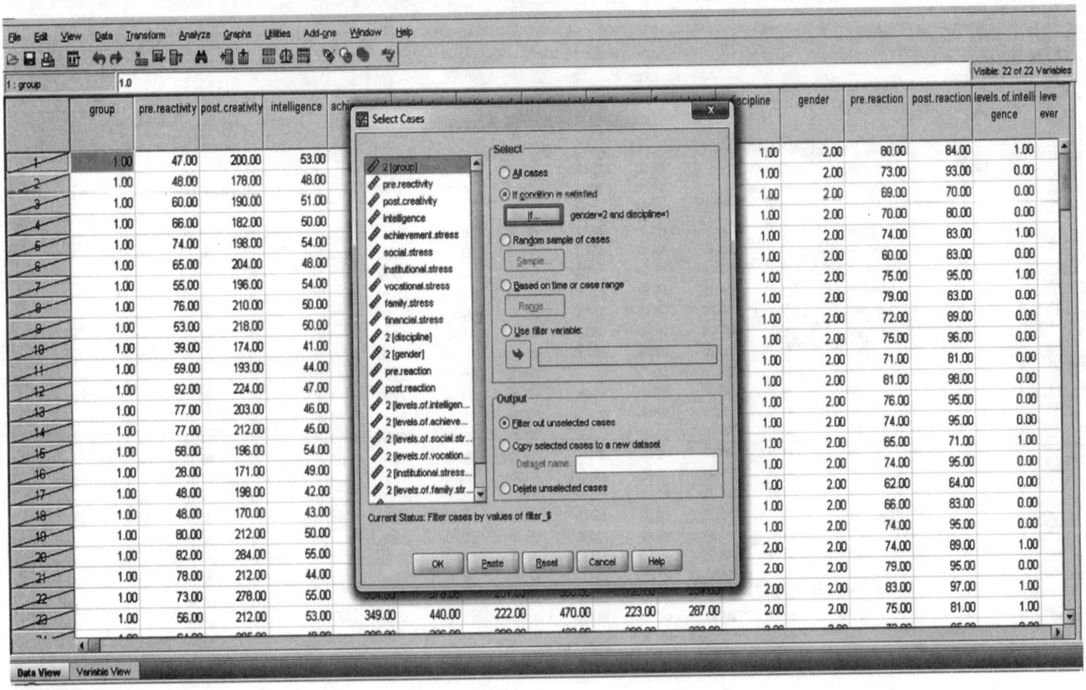

311. Click on "**OK**" to get the following screen.

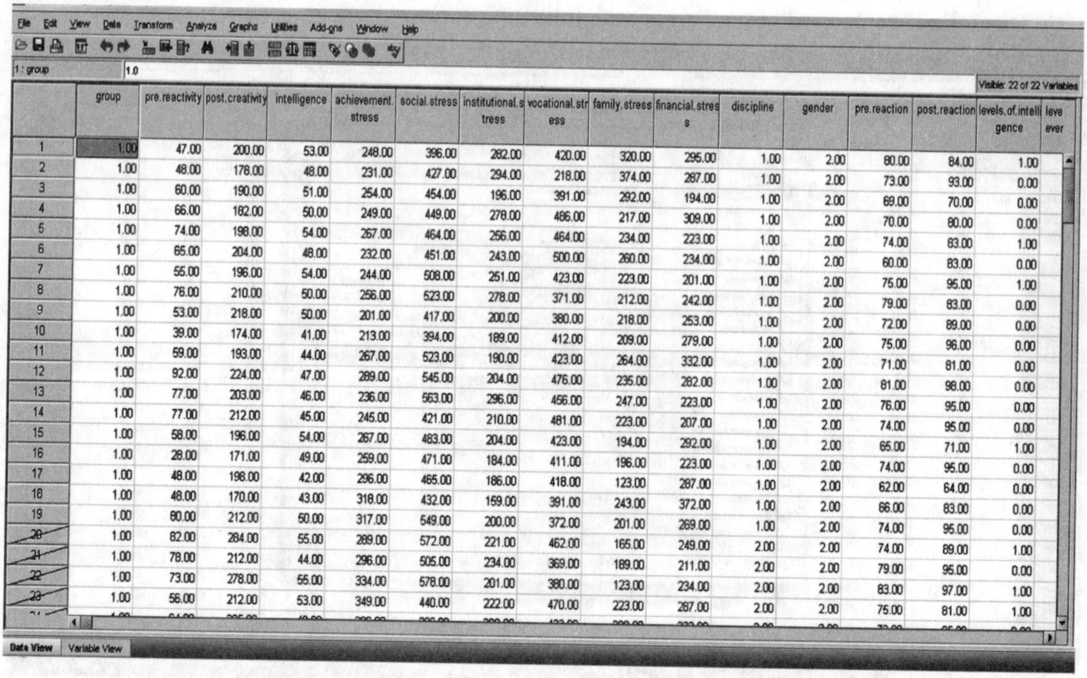

312. Click on "**Analyse**", bring curser to "**Correlate**" and then to "**Bivariate**" to get the following screen.

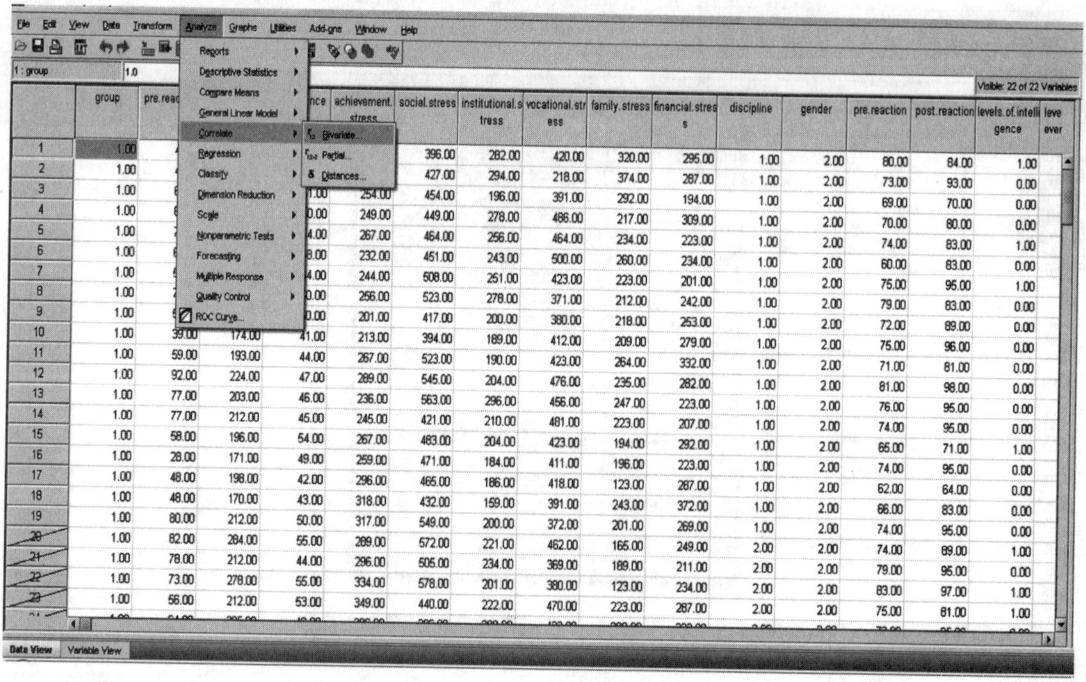

313. Click on "**Bivariate**" to get the following screen.

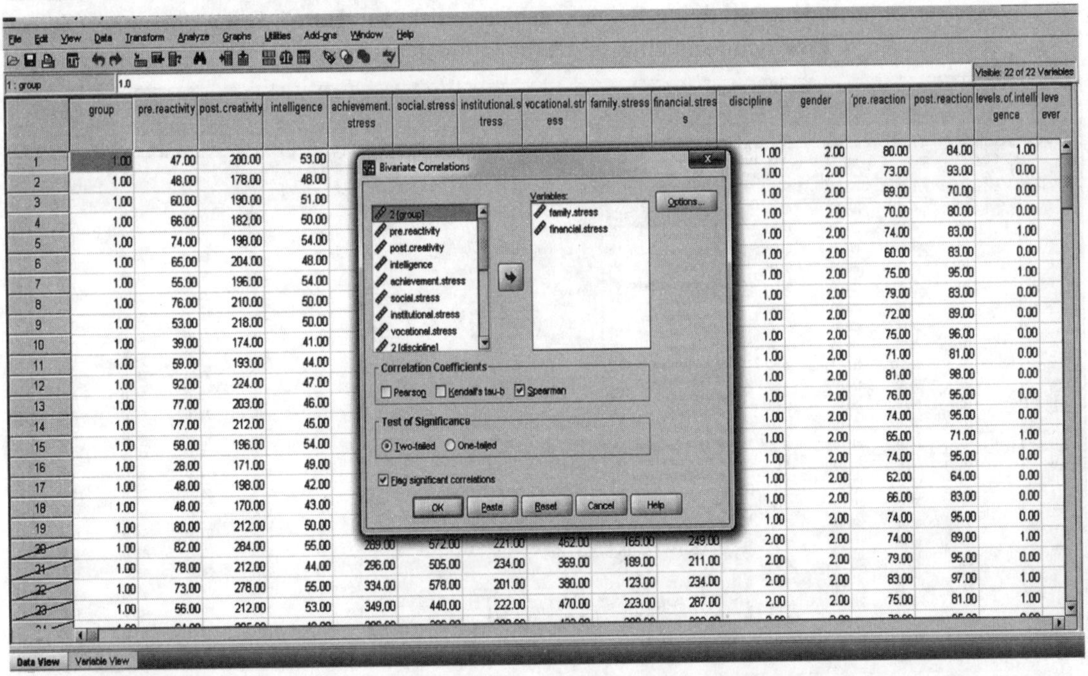

314. Click on "**OK**" to get the following Outputs of Correlation between Family Stress and Financial Stress of Female Students belonging to Arts subject.

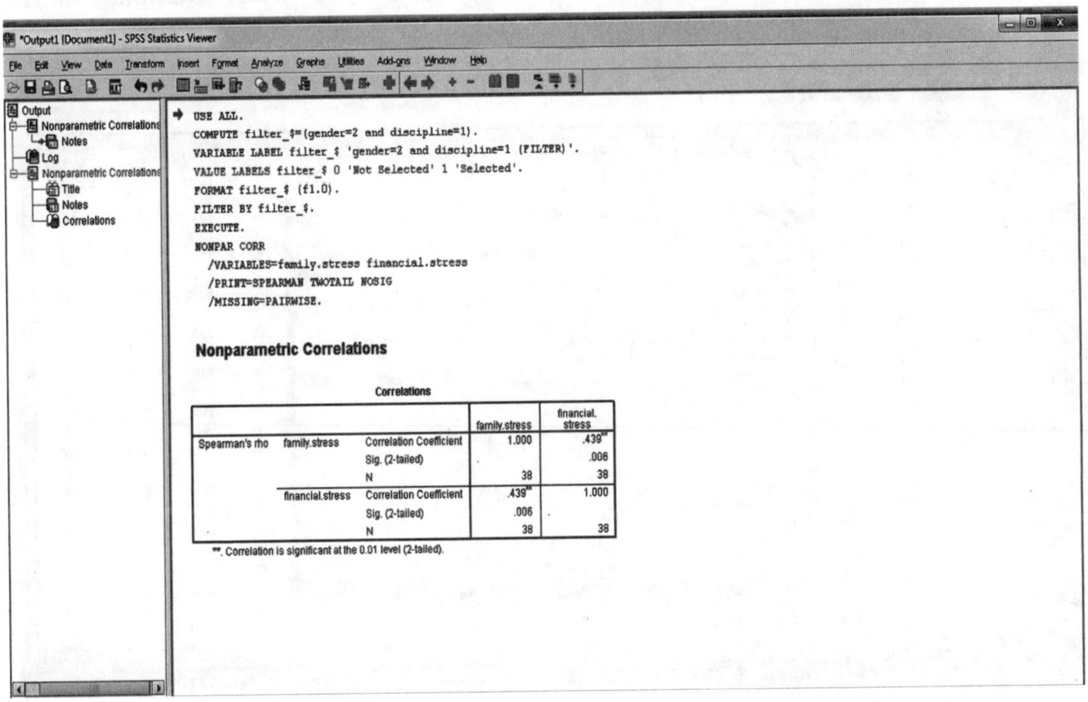

315. To calculate correlation between Family Stress and Financial Stress of Female students studying Science subject, click on "**Data**", bring curser to "**Select Cases**" icon and click to get the following screen.

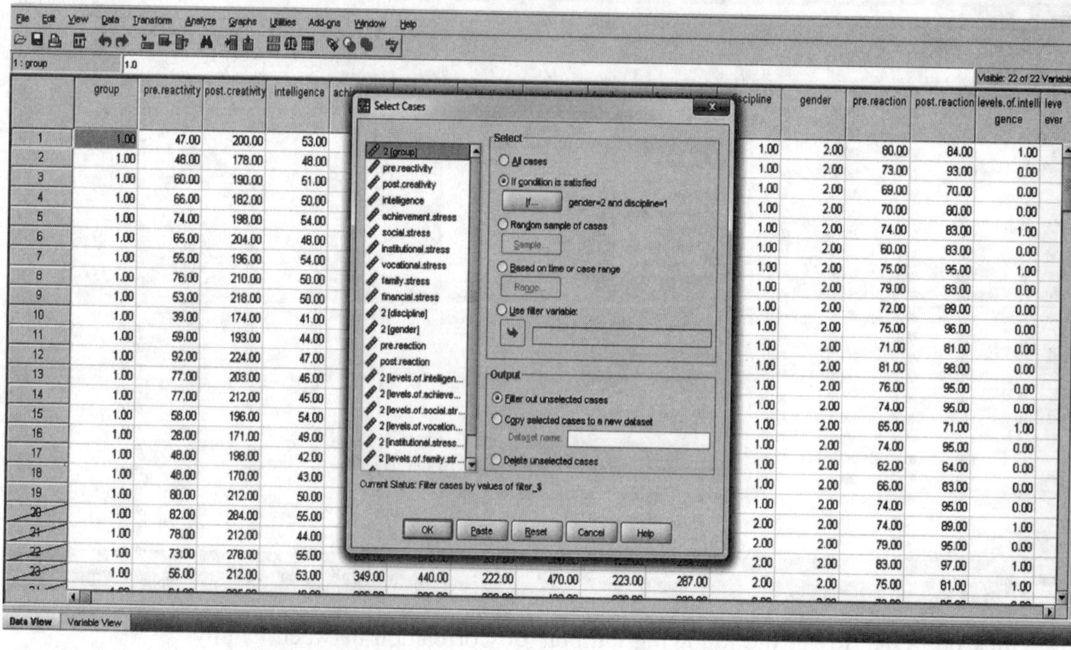

316. After clicking on "**If...**" button replace "**1**" by "**2**" under "**Discipline**" to get the following screen.

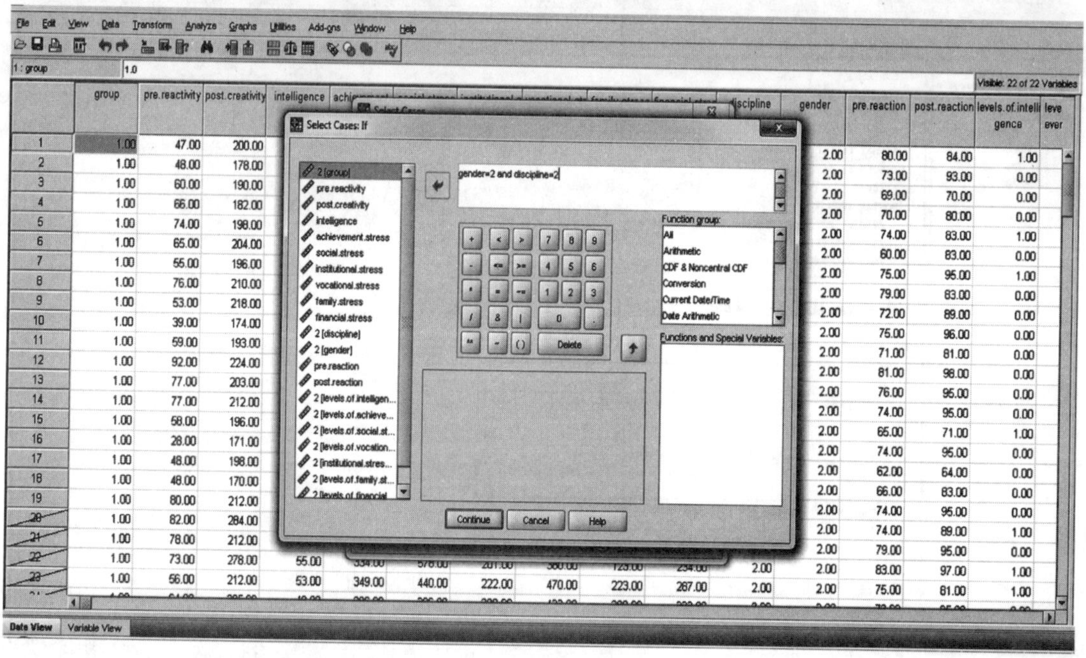

317. Click on "**Continue**" to get the following screen.

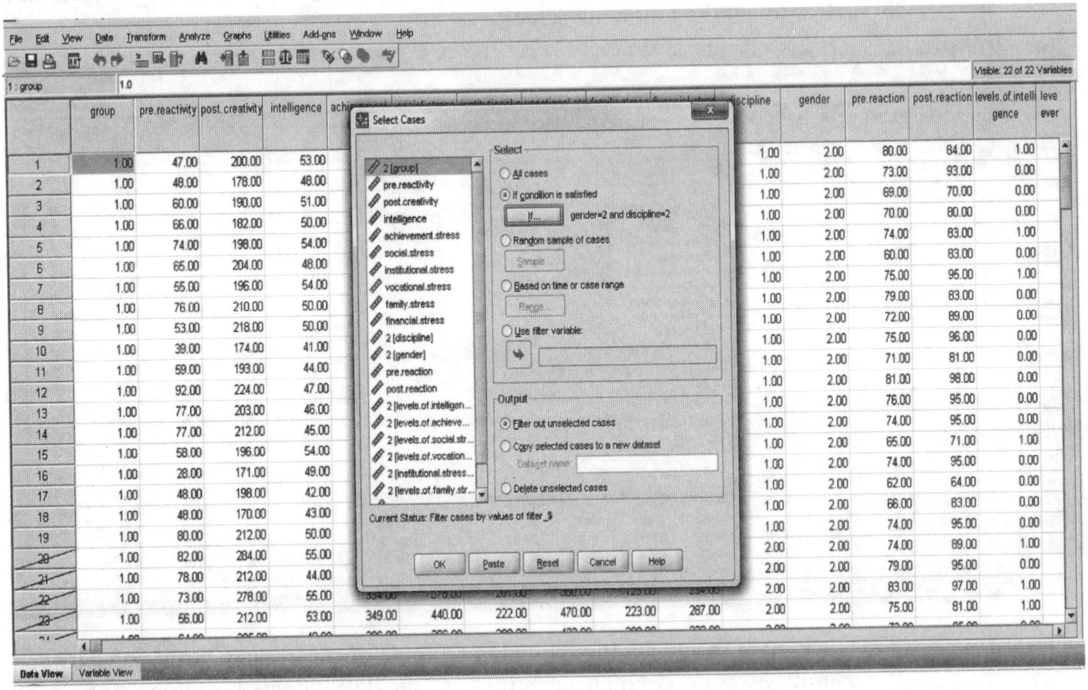

318. Click on "**OK**" to get the following screen.

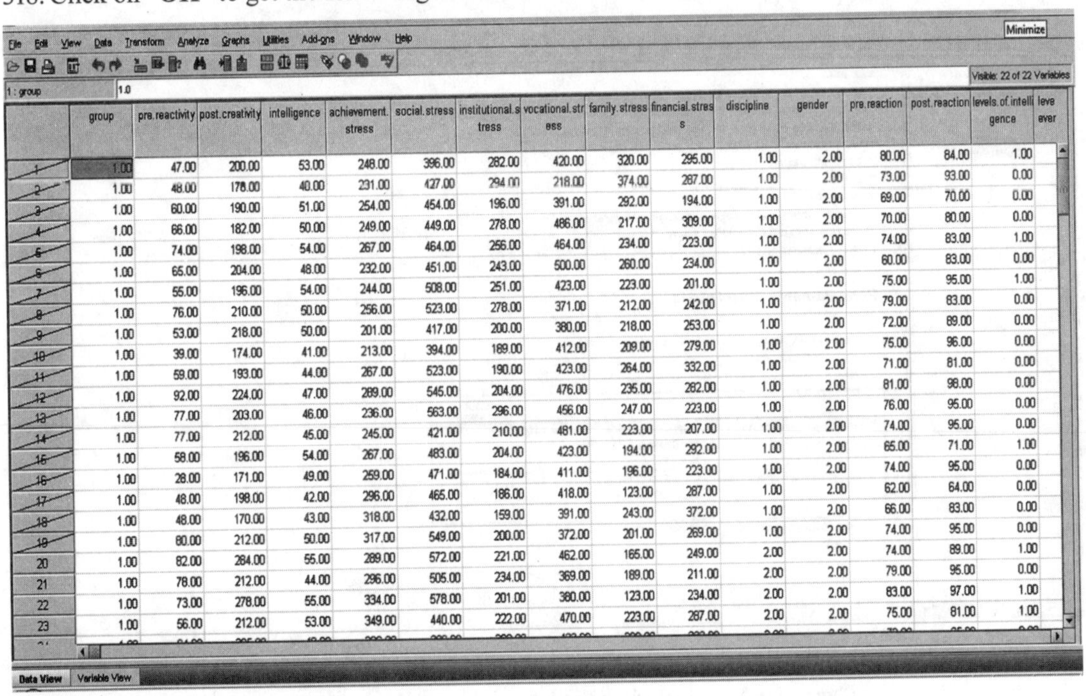

319. Click on "**Analyse**", bring curser to "**Correlate**" and then to "**Bivariate**" and click to get the following screen.

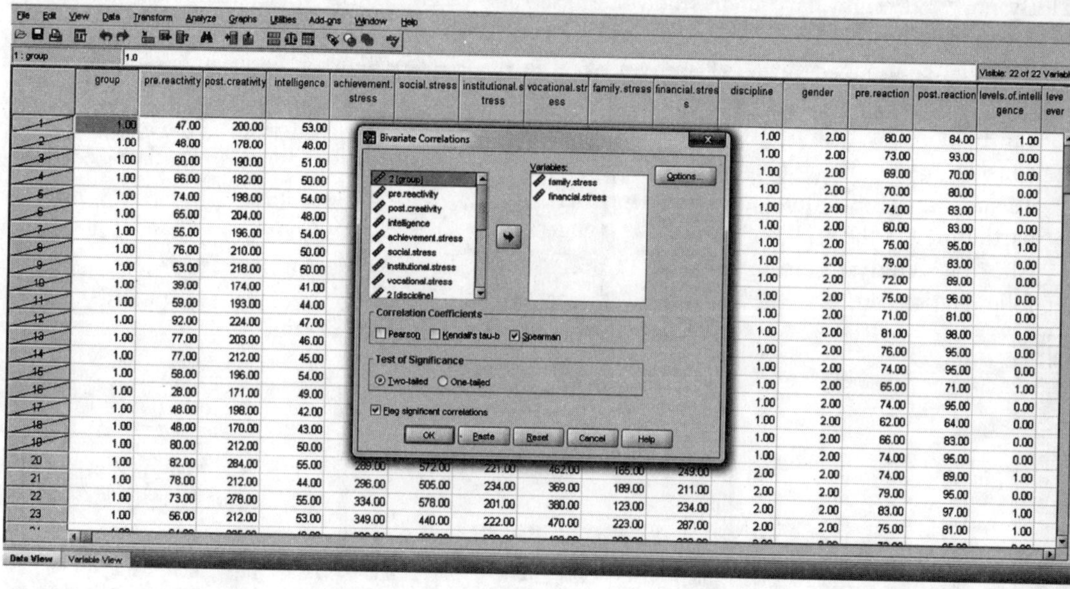

320. Click on "**OK**" to get the following Outputs of spearman Correlation between Family Stress and Financial Stress of Female Students belonging to Science subject.

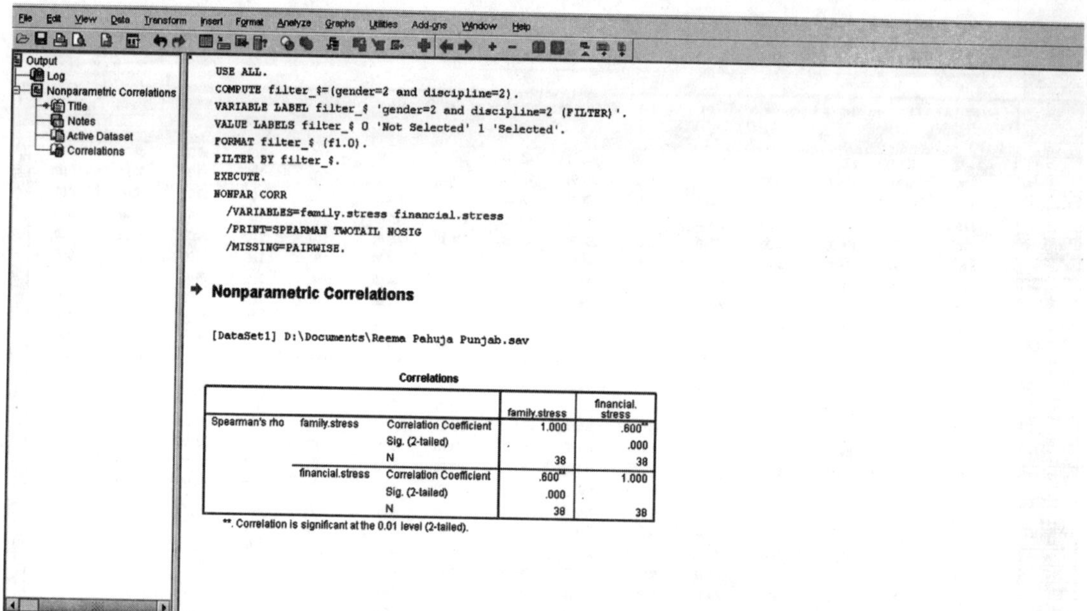

By now you must have understood the process of using "**Select Cases**" option. Cases can be selected on the basis of more than two discontinuous variables also.

Partial Correlation

321. By now you might have understood the procedure of computing correlation between two continuous variables with the help of SPSS. In case there are more than two continuous variables and you want to compute correlation between two continuous variables by keeping other continuous variables constant, this can be done by using Partial Correlation technique. To understand it let us consider the following objective.

To study the correlation between Self-efficacy and Emotional Competence by partialling out the effect of Burnout of Teachers.

Click on "**Analyse**", bring curser to "**Correlate**" then to "**Partial**" to get the following screen.

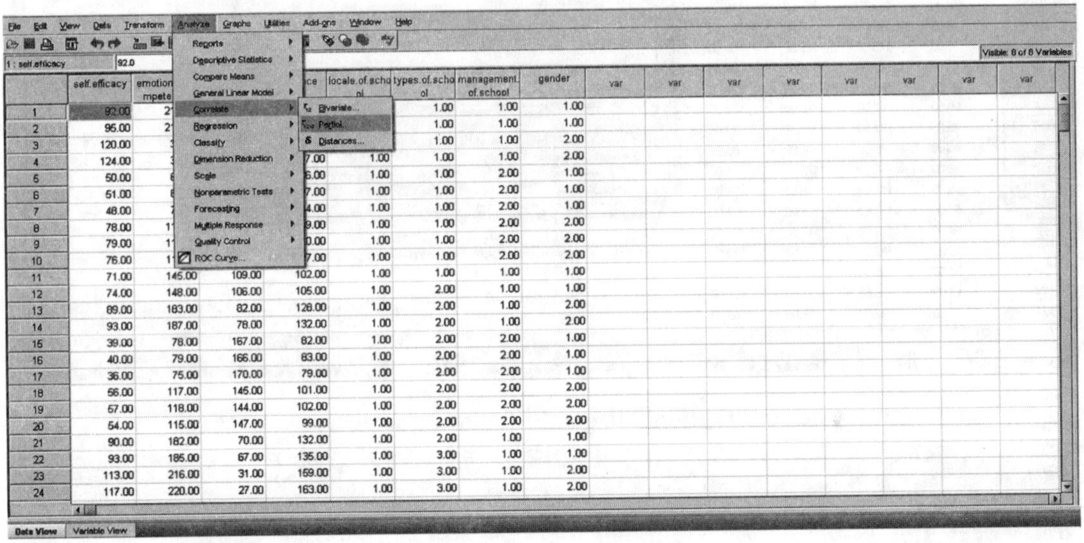

322. Click on "**Partial**" to get the following screen.

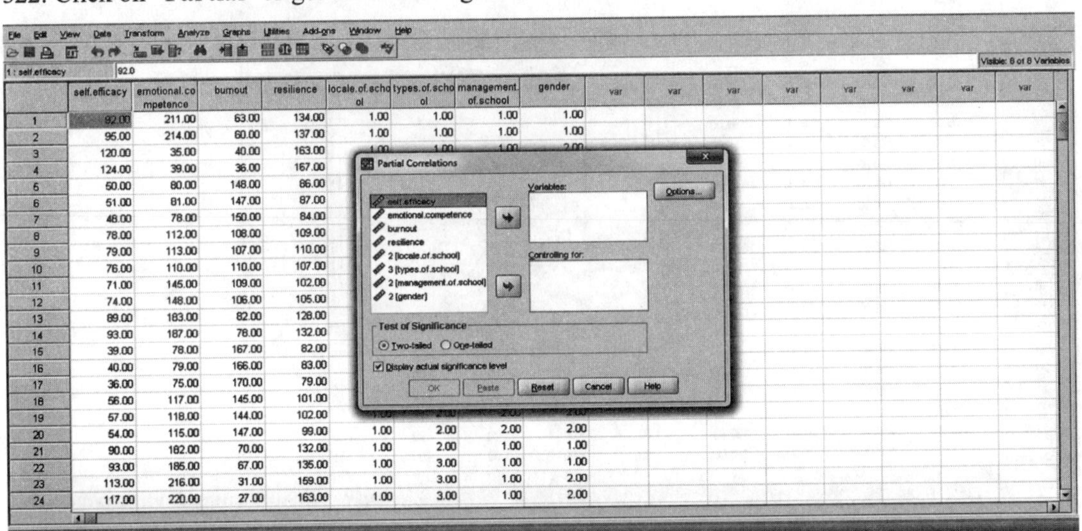

323. Shift "**Self-efficacy** and **Emotional Competence**" to the "**Variable**" dialog box and "**Burnout**" to "**Controlling for**" dialog box to get the following Screen.

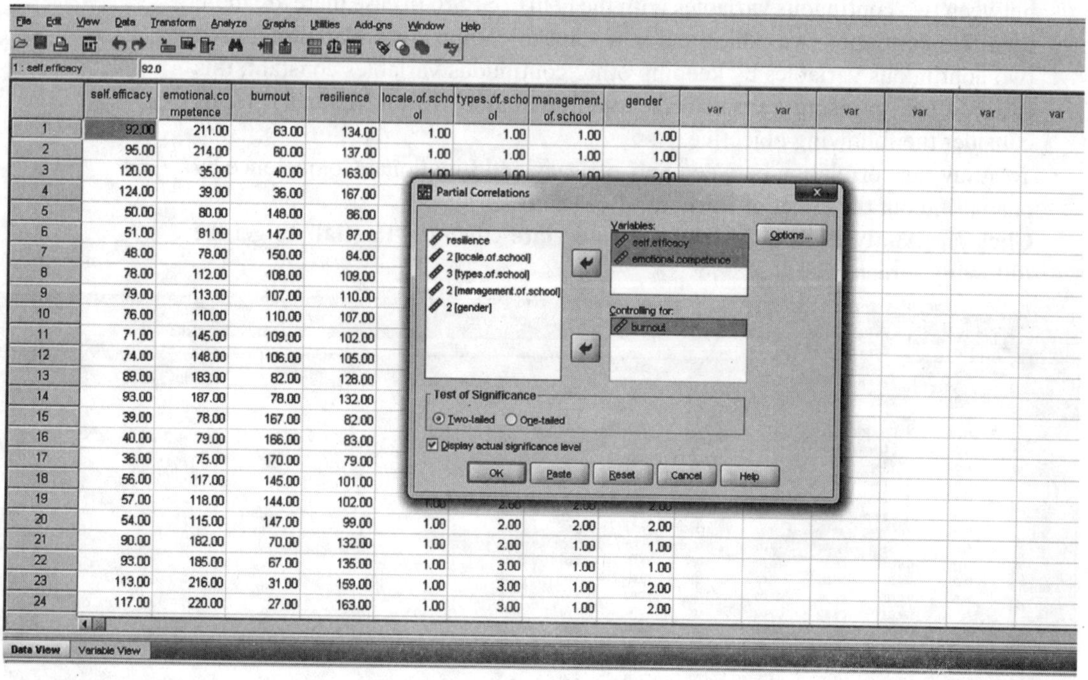

324. Click on "**Options**" to get the following screen.

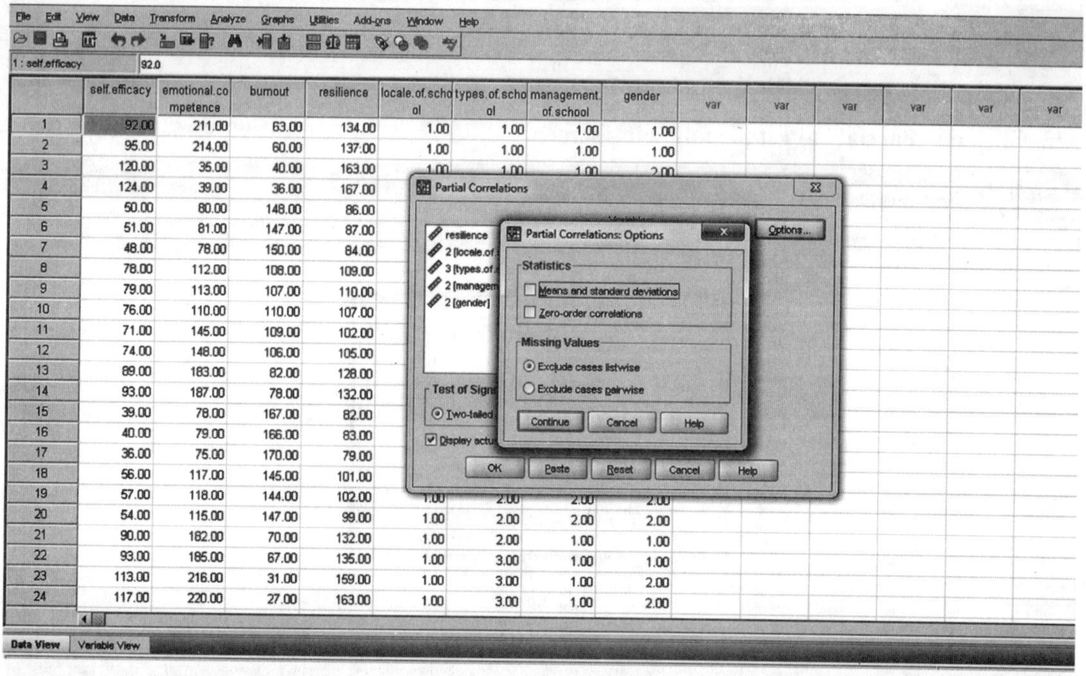

325. In case you want to calculate any "**Statistics**" then you may highlight the appropriate option(s) under it. Suppose you want to calculate "**Means and Standard Deviations**" than highlight by clicking on "**Means and Standard Deviations**" to get the following screen.

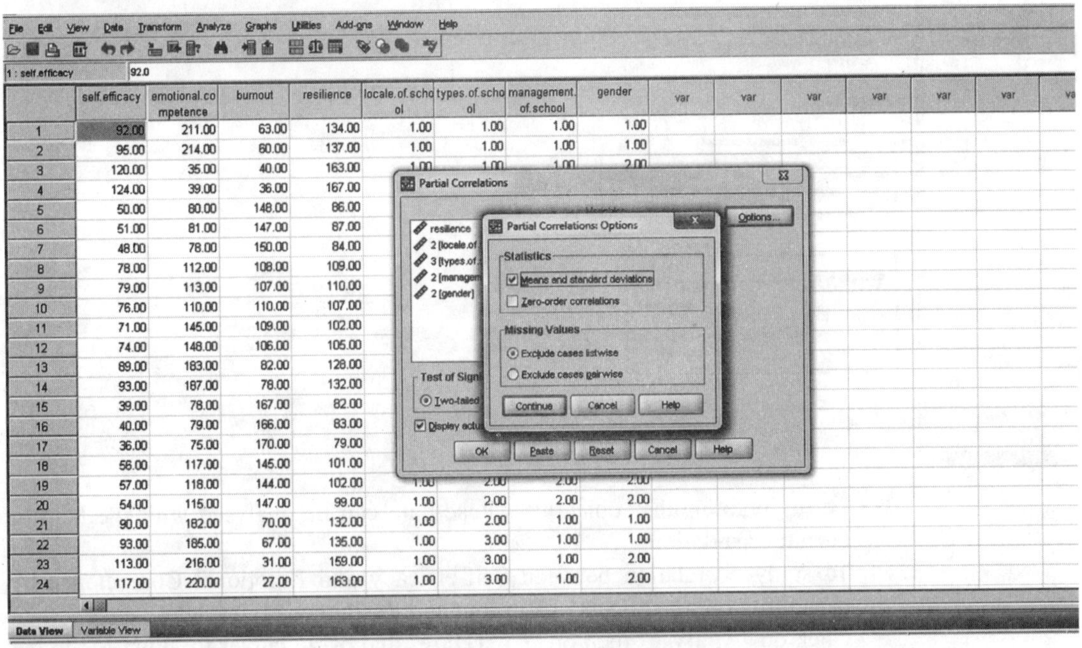

326. Click on "**Continue**" to get the following the following screen.

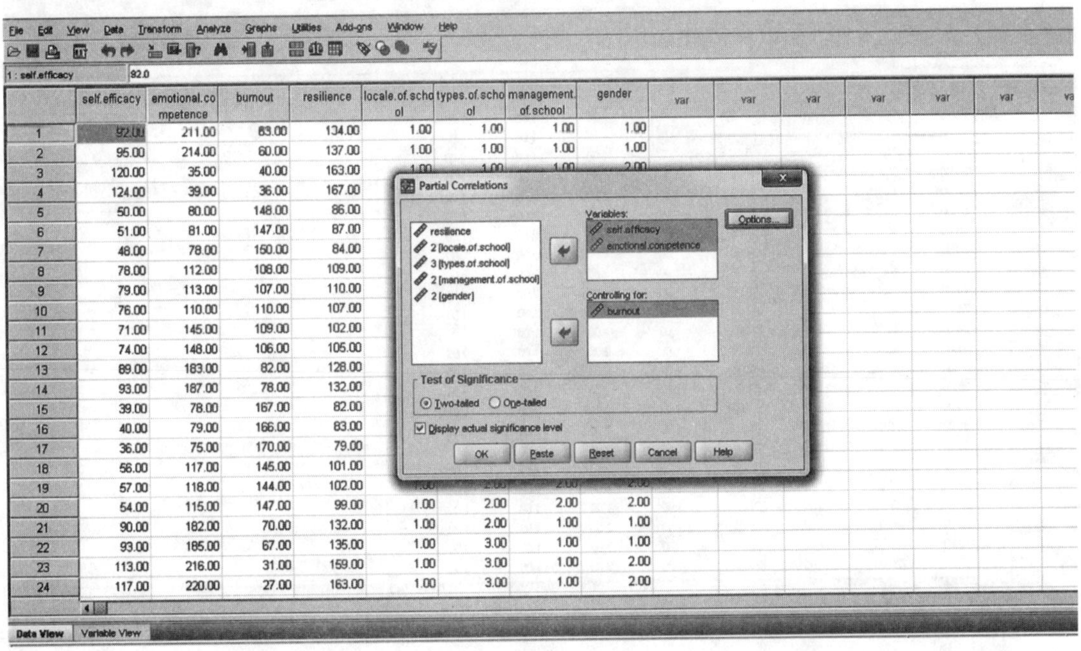

327. Click on "**OK**" to get the following outputs of Partial Correlation.

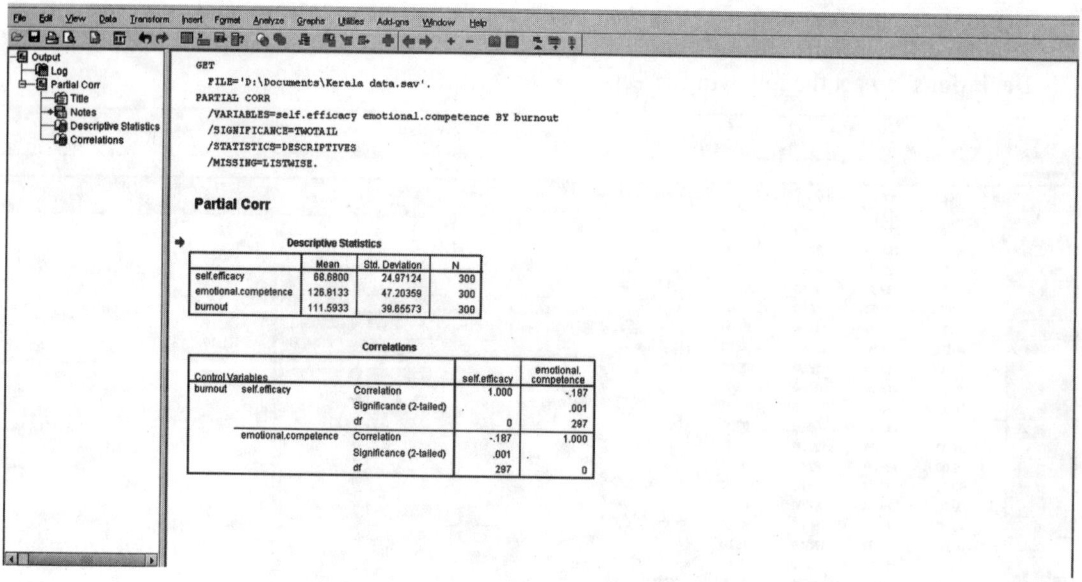

328. Let us take another objective whose data can be analysed with the help of Partial Correlation.
To study correlation between Self-efficacy and Emotional Competence by partialling out the effects of Burnout and Resilience of Teachers.
Click on "**Analyse**" then on "**Correlate**" and bring curser to "**Partial**" to get the following screen.

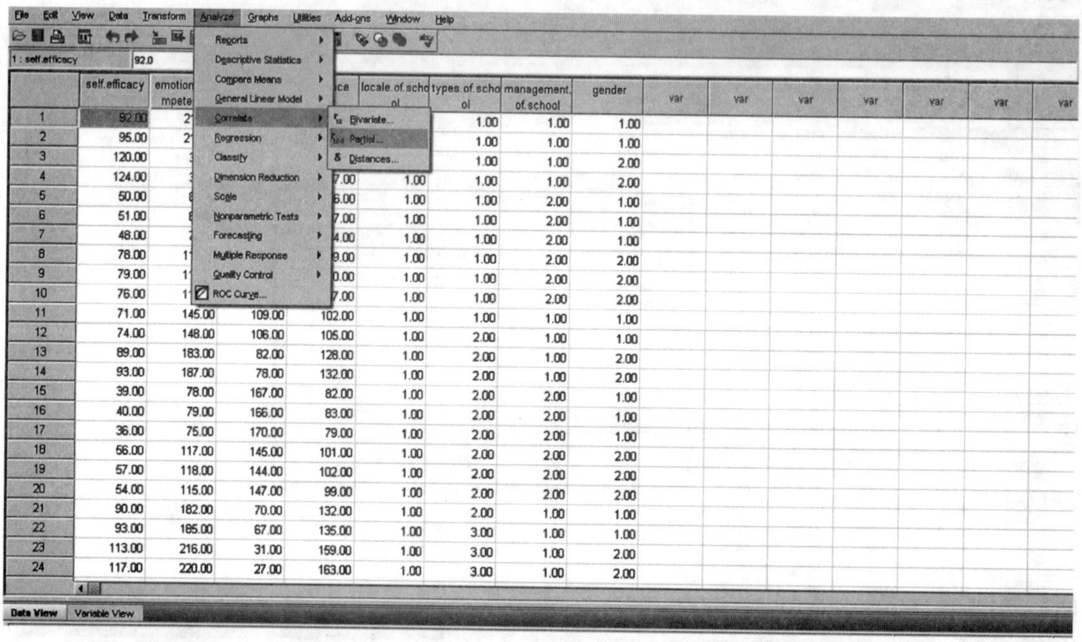

329. Click on "**Partial**" icon to get the following screen.

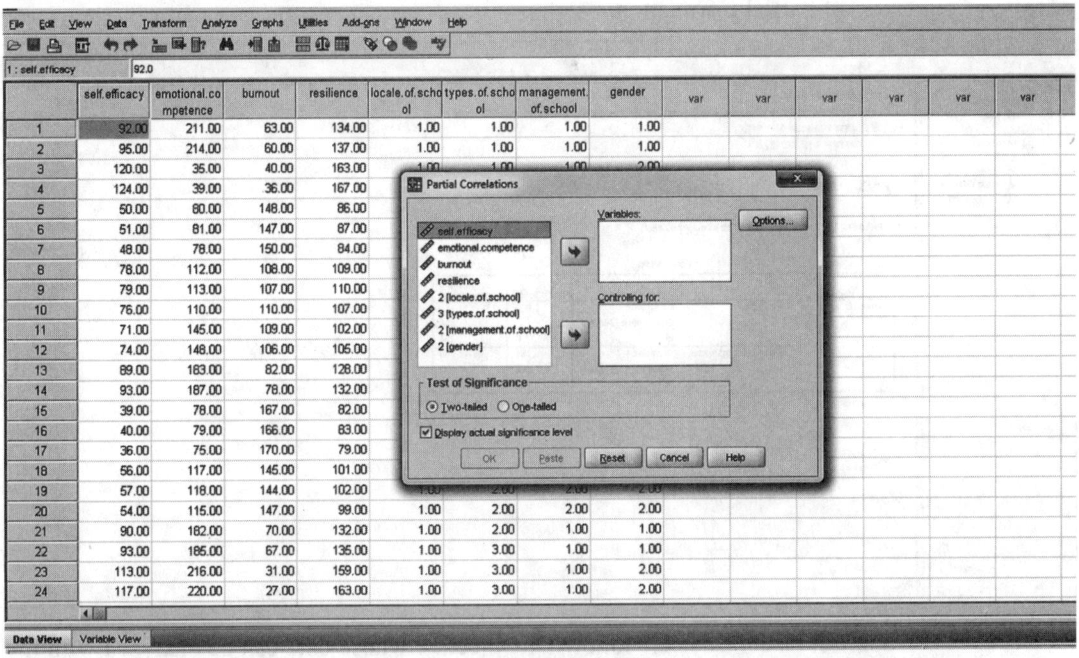

330. Shift "**Self-efficacy** and **Emotional Competence**" under "**Variables**" dialog box and "**Burnout** and **Resilience**" to "**Controlling For**" dialog box to get the following screen.

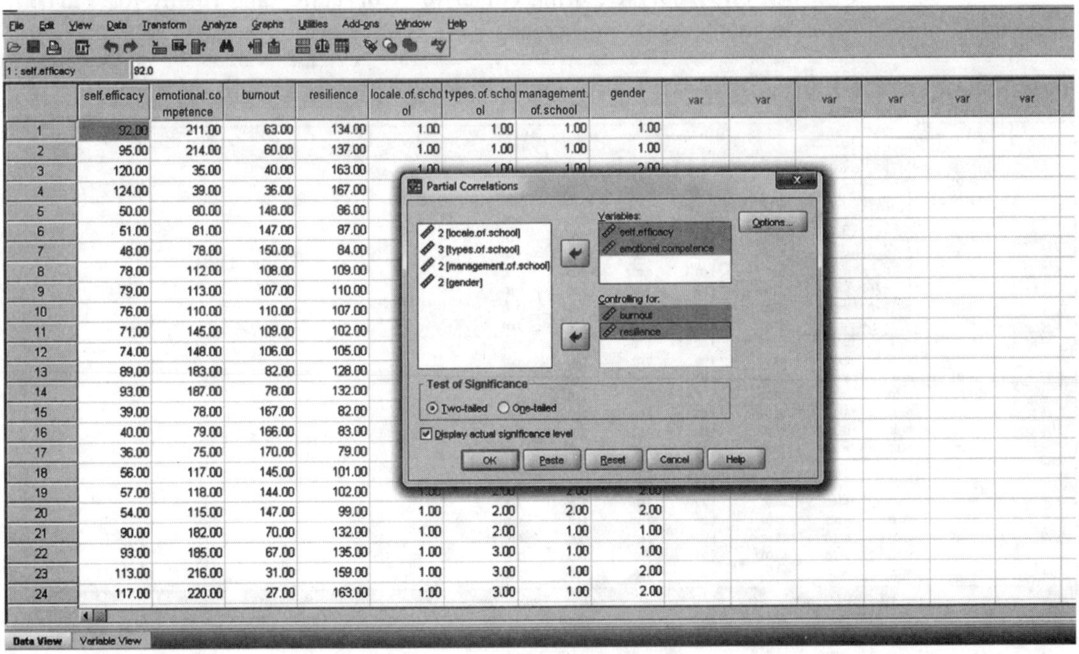

331. If you do not want to use "**Options**" click on "**OK**" to get the following Outputs of Partial Correlation.

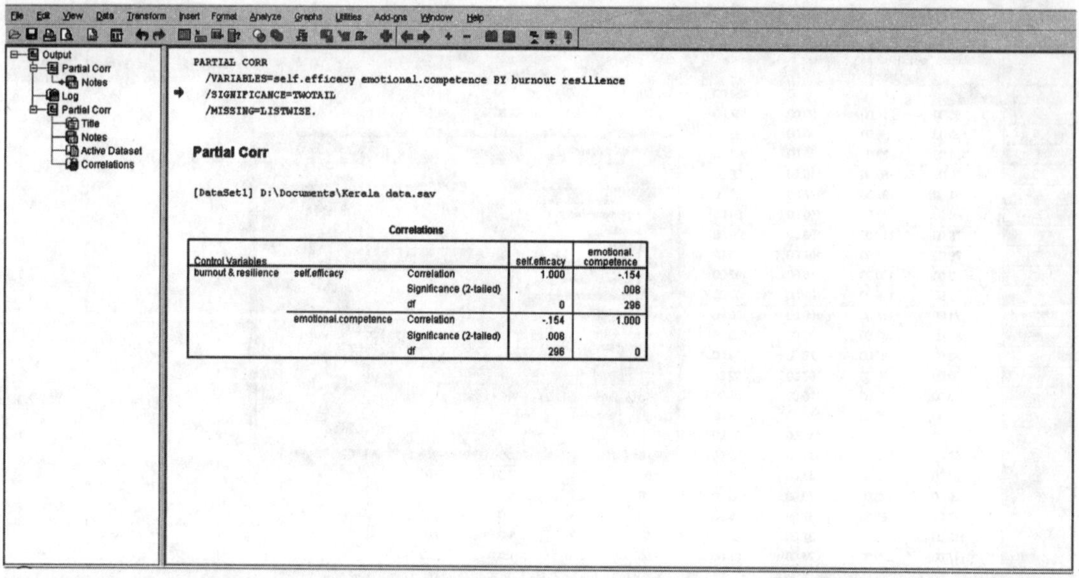

332. Let us consider the following Objective whose data can be analyzed with the help of Partial Correlation.

To study the correlation between Emotional Intelligence and Burnout by considering Self-efficacy and Resilience of Male and Female Teachers separately.

Click on "**Analyse**", bring curser to "**Correlate**" and finally to "**Partial**" icon to get the following screen.

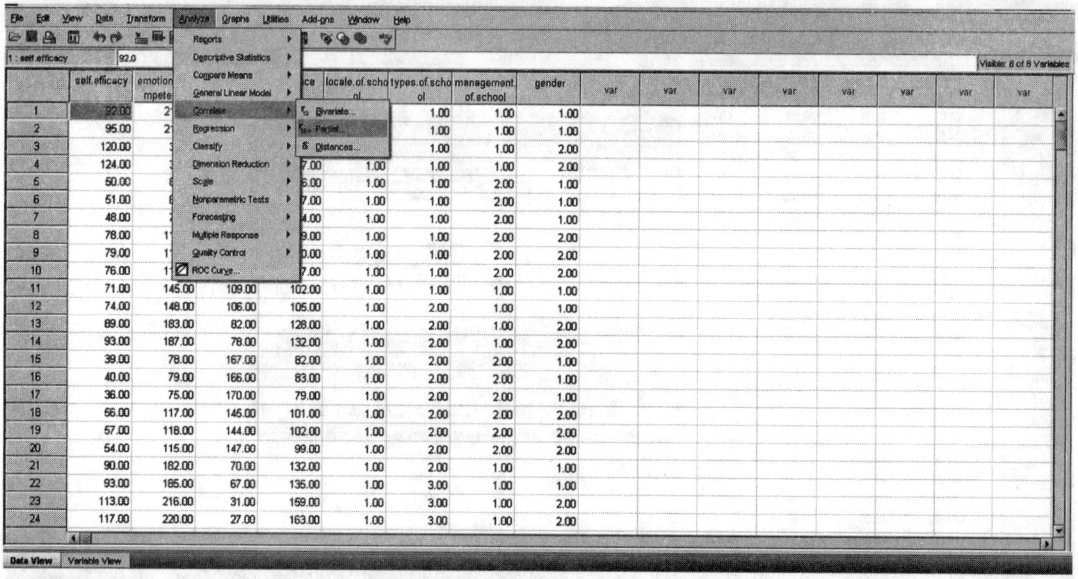

333. Click on "**Partial**" icon to get the following screen.

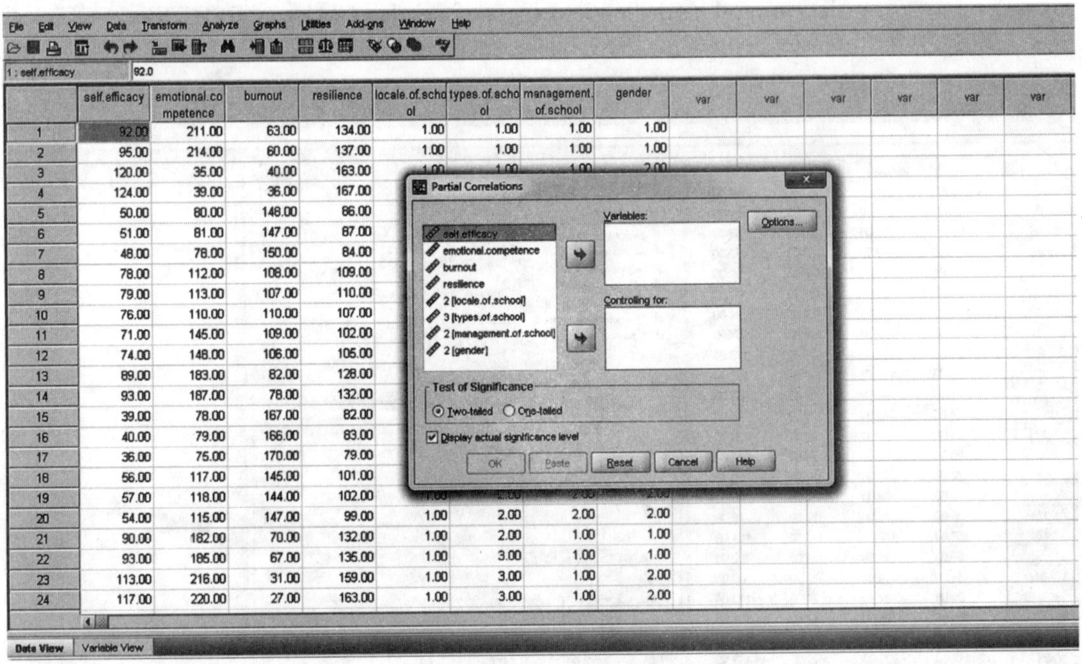

334. Shift "**Emotional Intelligence** and **Burnout**" to the "**Variables**" dialog box and "**Self-efficacy** and **Resilience**" to "**Controlling For**" dialog box to get the following screen.

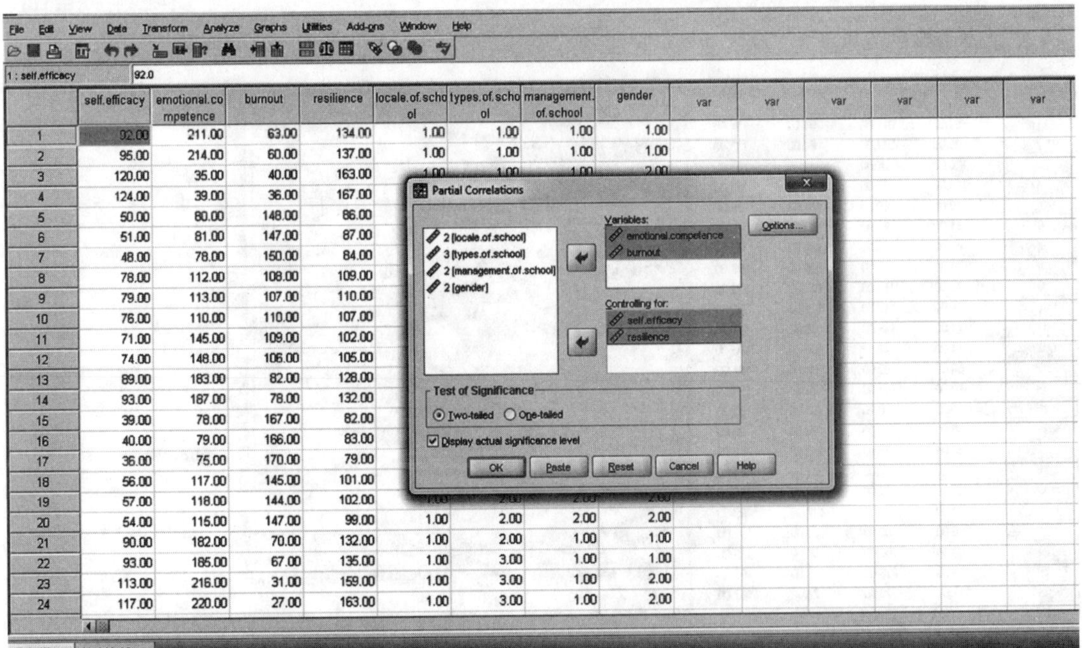

335. Since correlation is to be computed for Male and Female Teachers separately, data are to be selected in respect of Gender. Click on "**Data**" then on "**Select Cases**" icon to get the following screen.

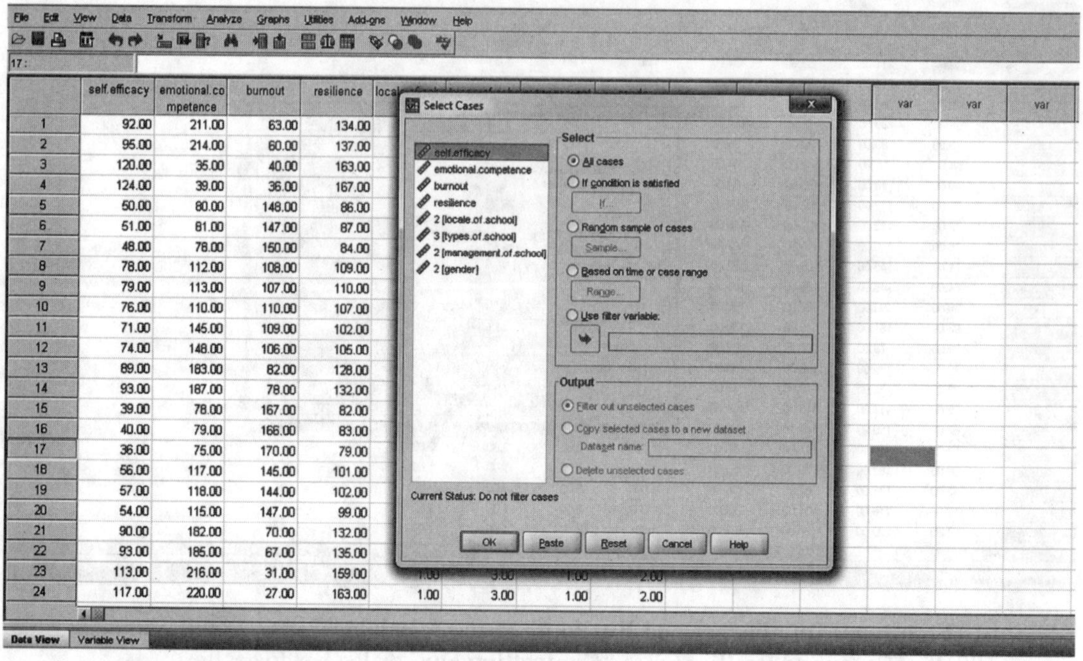

336. Highlight "**If condition is satisfied**" to get the following screen.

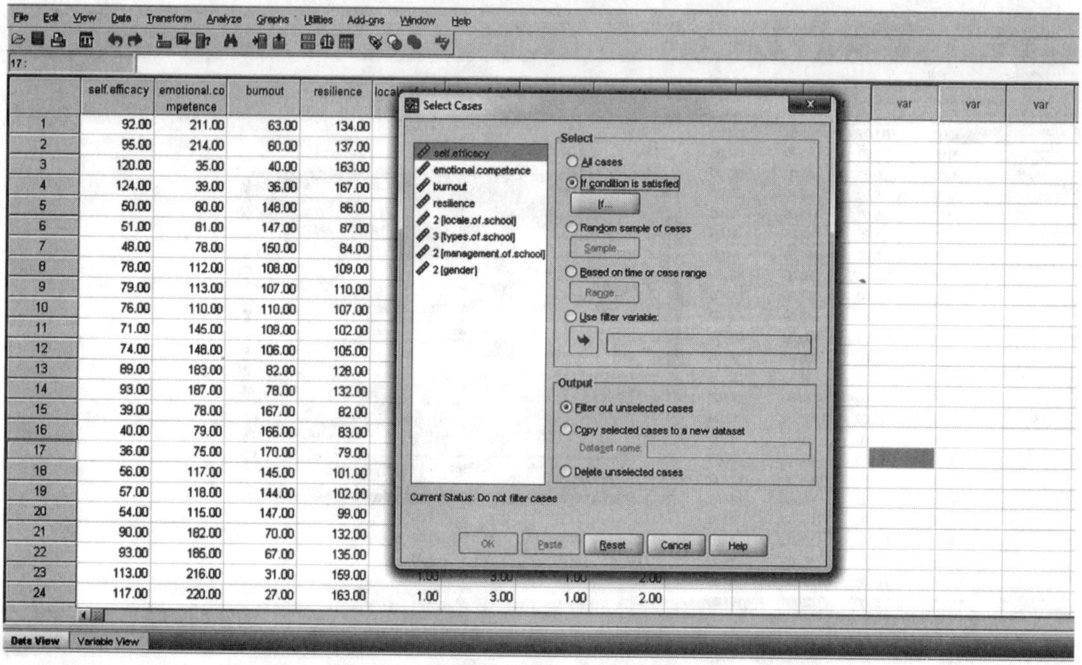

337. Click on "**If.....**" button to get the following screen.

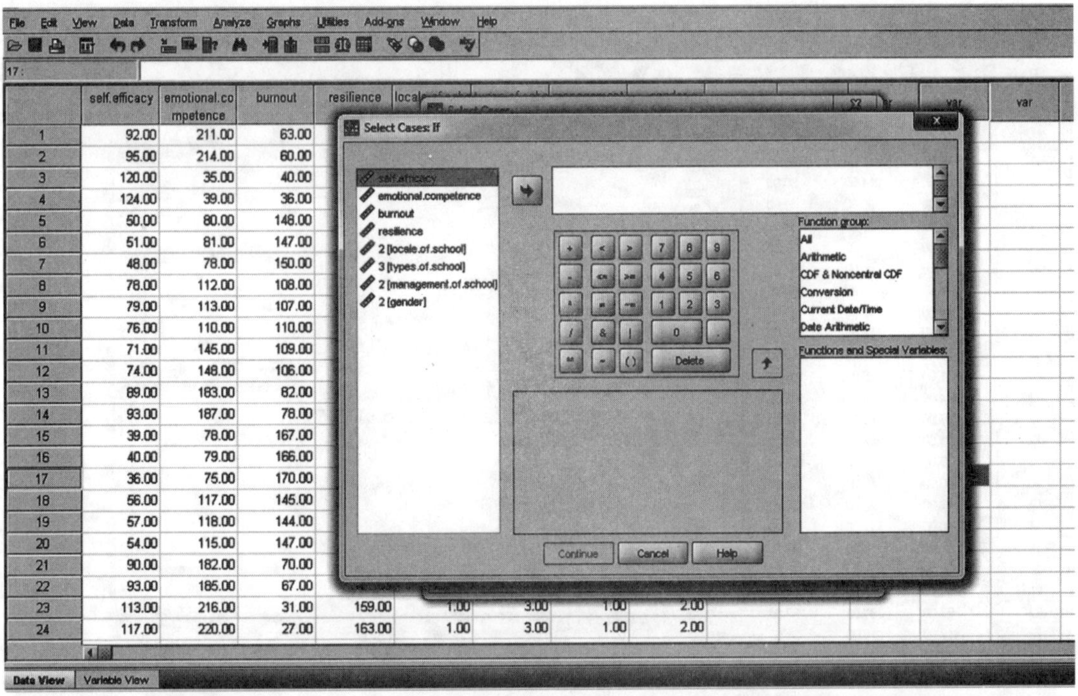

338. Data are to be selected on the basis of "**Gender**". Shift "**Gender**" to the right hand side slot to get the following screen.

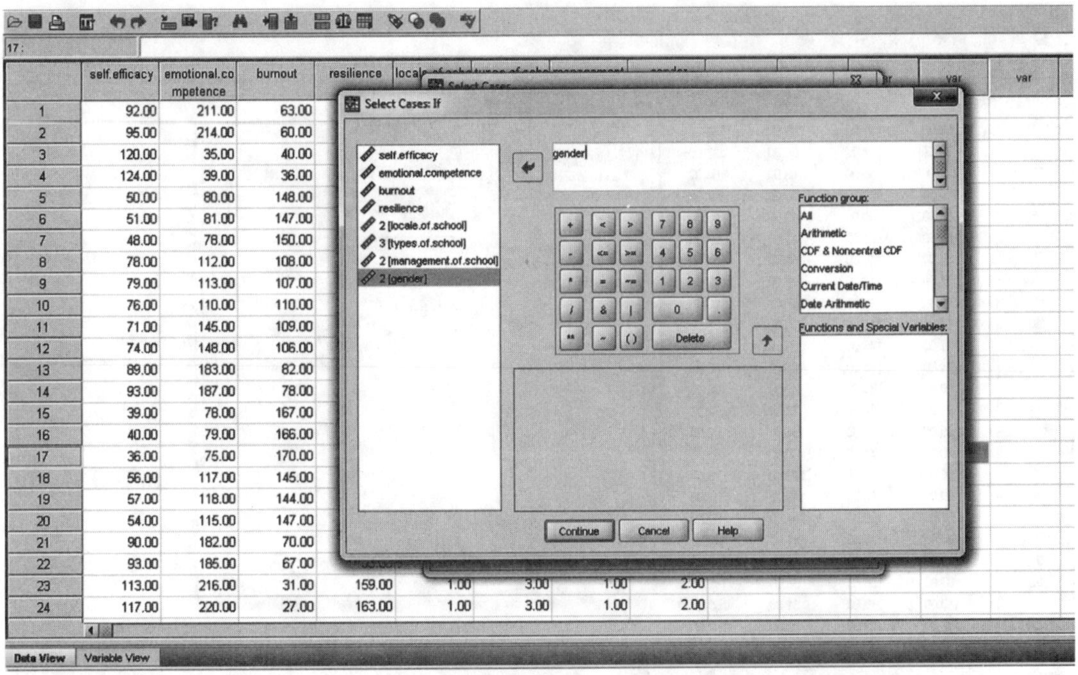

339. The code for "**Male**" is "**1**". Put "=" sign and then type "**1**" to get the following screen.

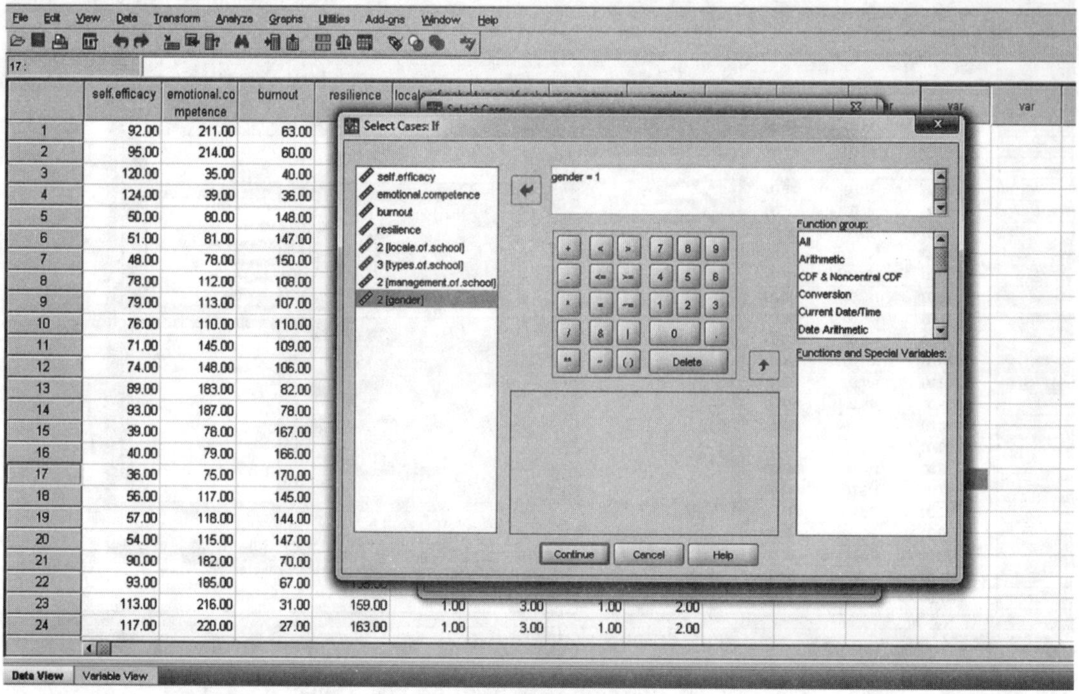

340. Click on "**Continue**" to get the following screen.

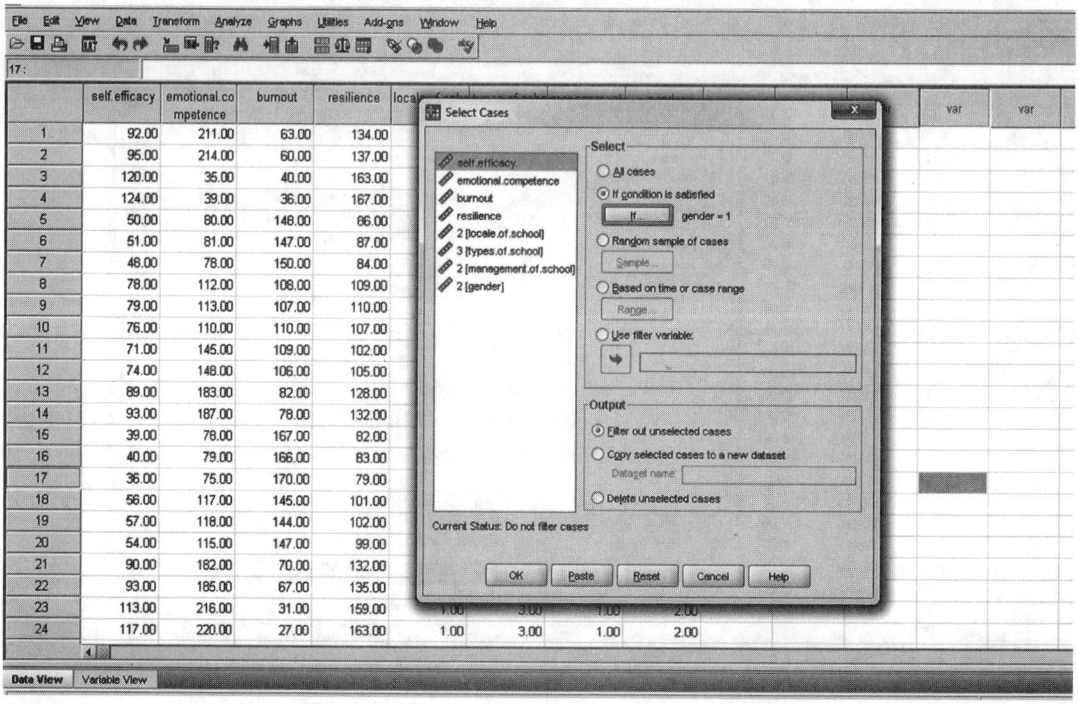

341. Click on "**OK**" to get the following screen.

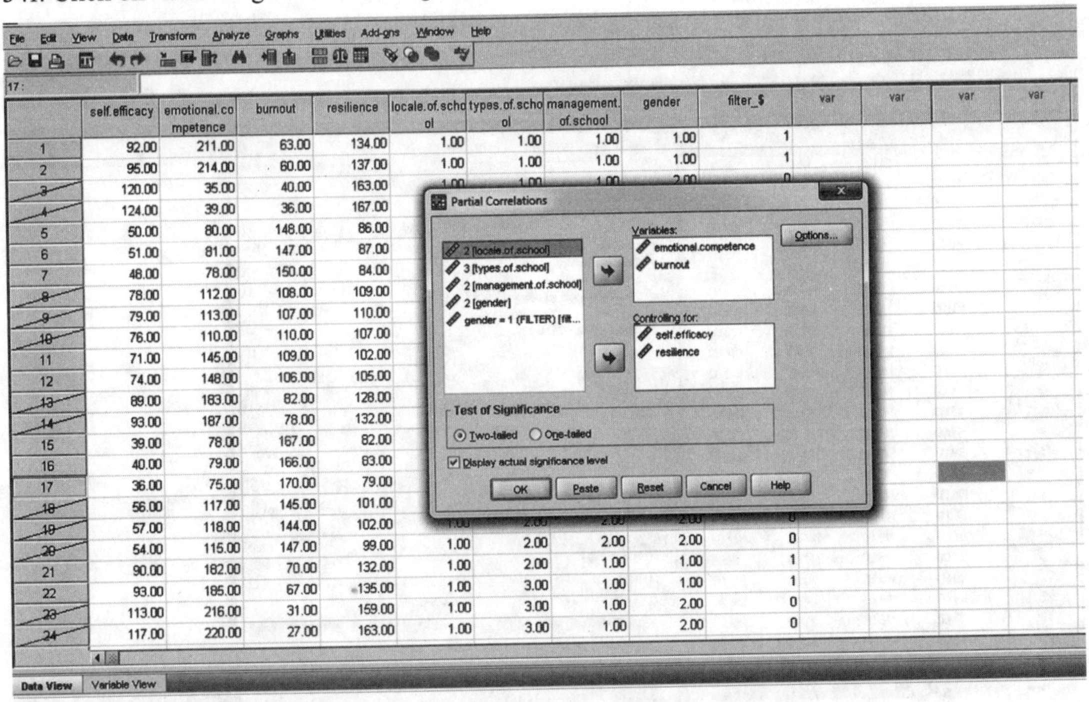

342. Click on "**OK**" to get the outputs of Partial Correlation for Male Teachers.

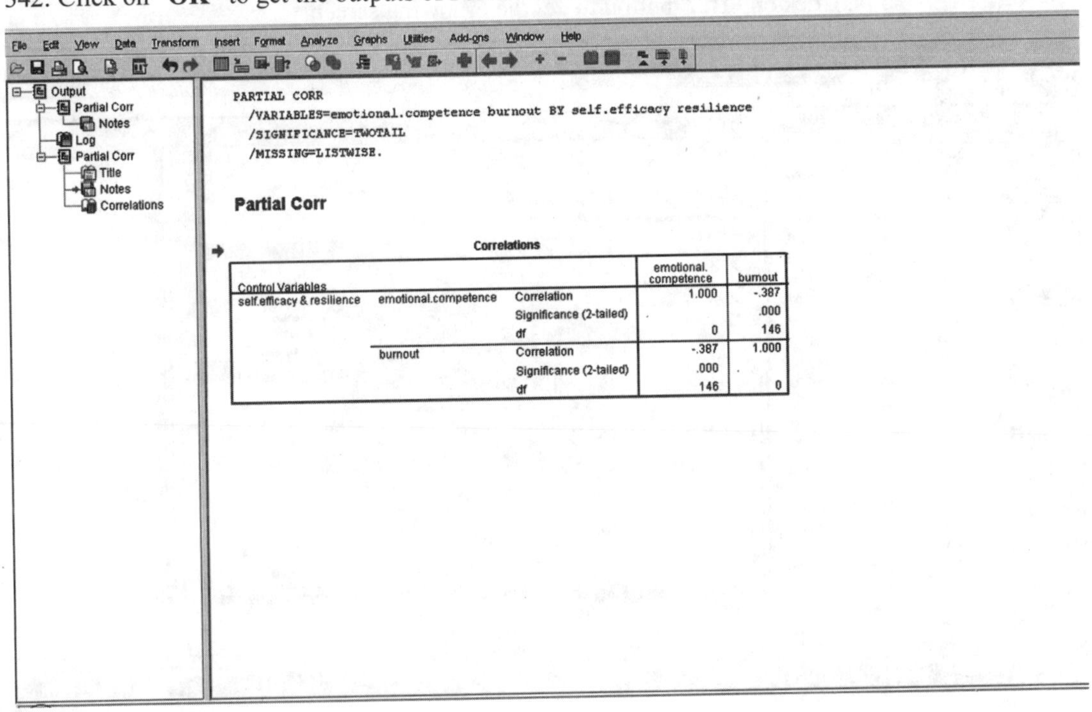

343. To do calculation for Female Teachers, click on "**Data**" icon then on "**Select Cases**" icon to get the following screen.

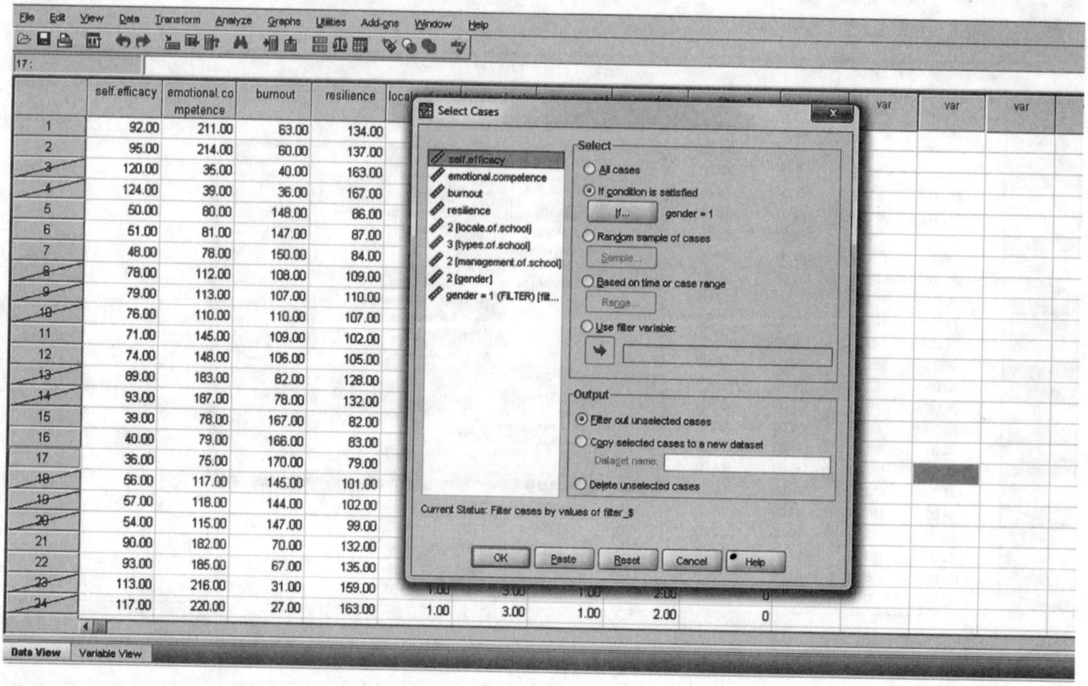

344. Click on "**If...**" button to get the following screen.

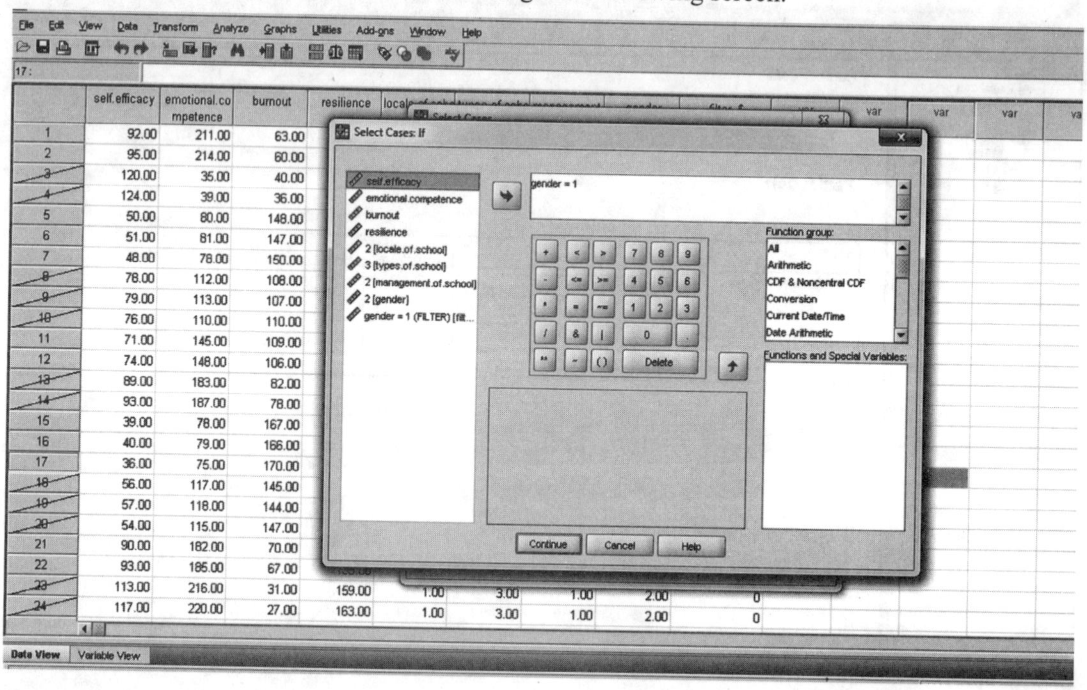

345. Against "**Gender**" replace "1" by "2" because the code for Female is "2" to get the following screen.

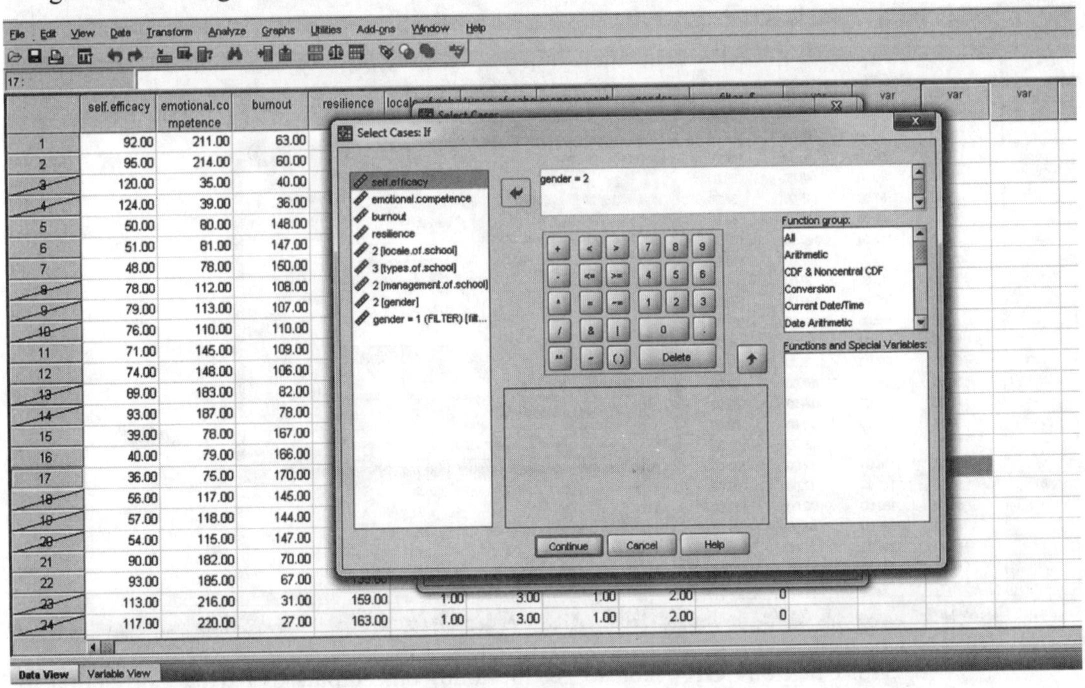

346. Click on "**Continue**" button to get the following screen.

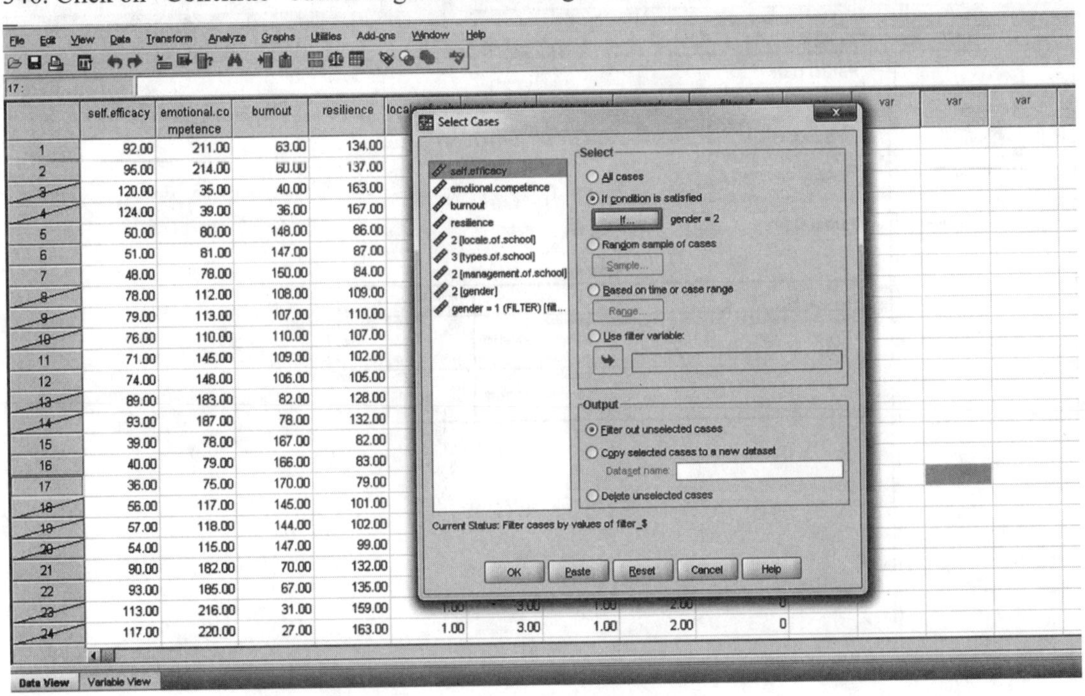

347. Click on "**OK**" to get the following screen.

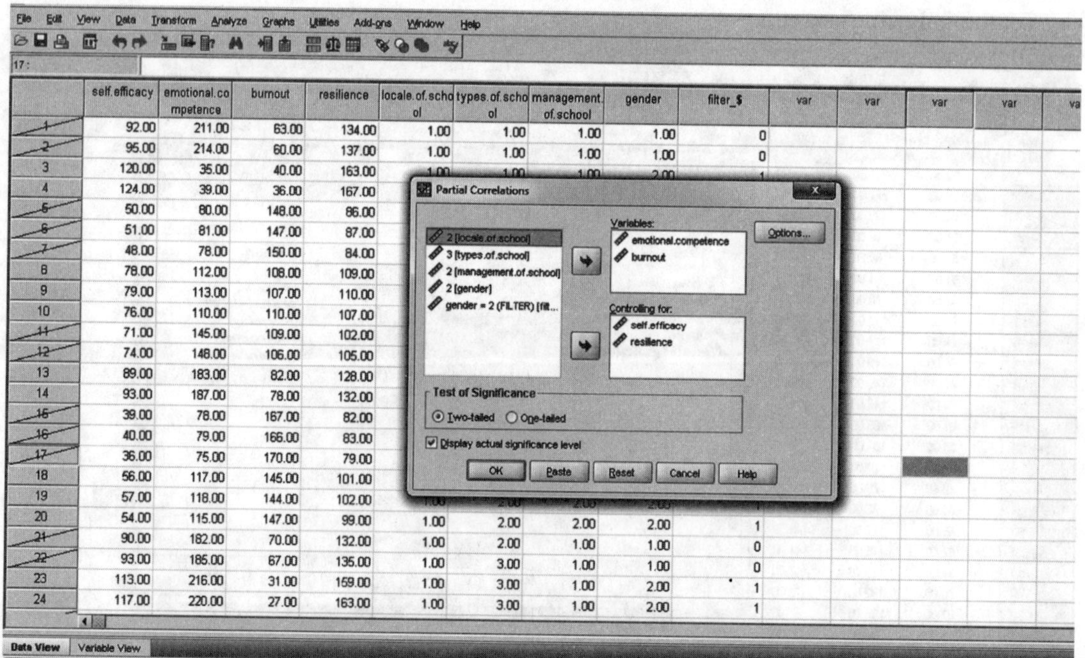

348. Click on "**OK**" icon to get the following outputs of Partial Correlation for Female Teachers.

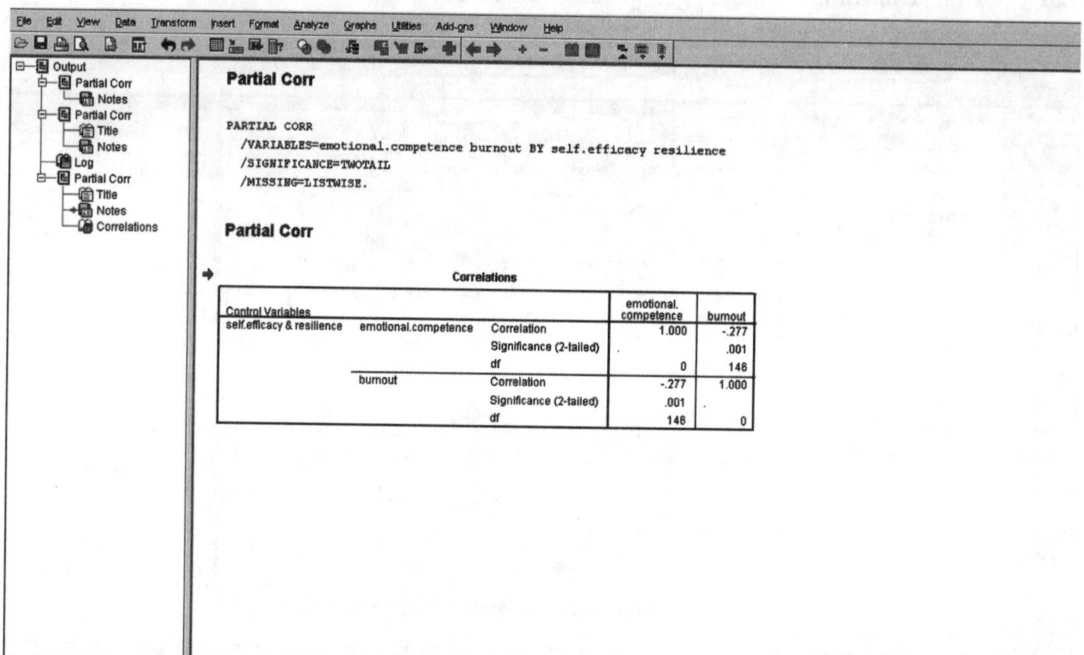

349. Let us take the following objective.
To study correlation between Emotional Intelligence and Burnout by considering Self-efficacy and Resilience of Male and Female Teachers working in Urban and Rural Schools separately.
Click on "**Analyse**" then on "**Correlation**" and finally on "**Partial**" to get the following screen.

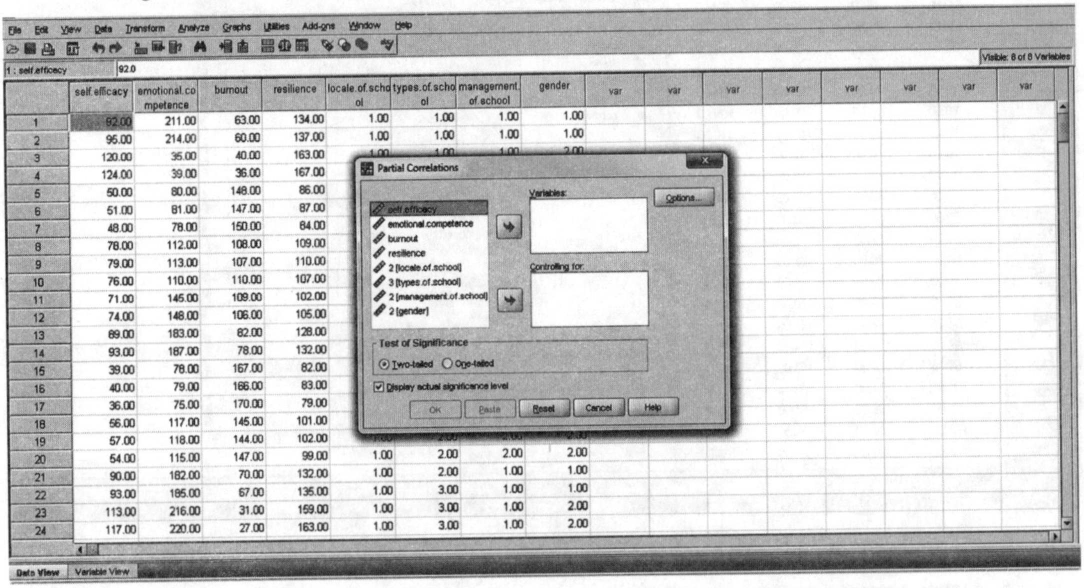

350. Shift "**Emotional Intelligence** and **Burnout**" to the "**Variables**" dialog box and "**Self-efficacy** and **Resilience**" to the "**Controlling For**" dialog box to get the following screen.

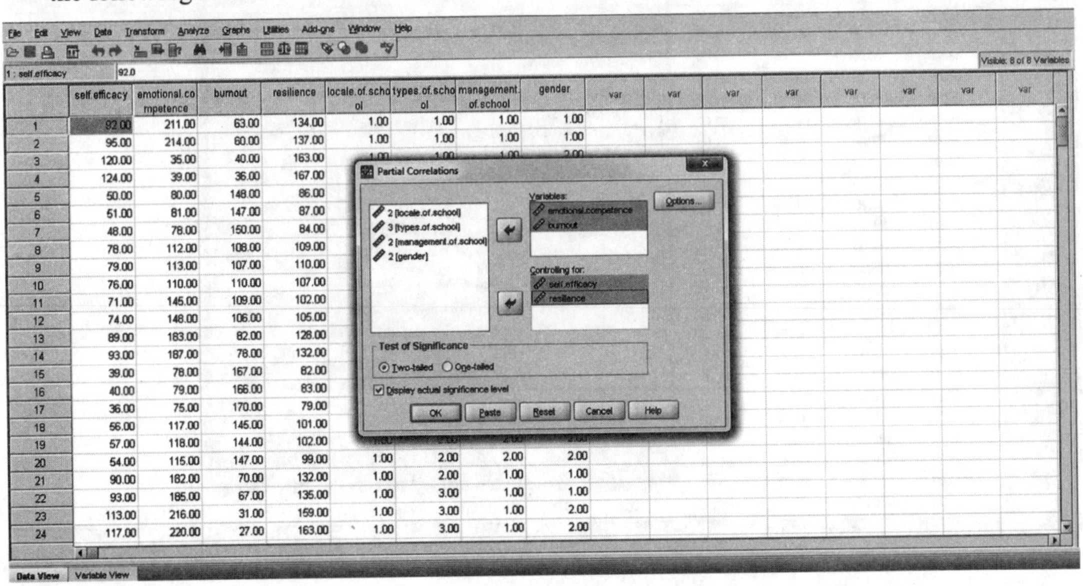

351. Click on "**Data**" then on "**Select Cases**" to get the following screen.

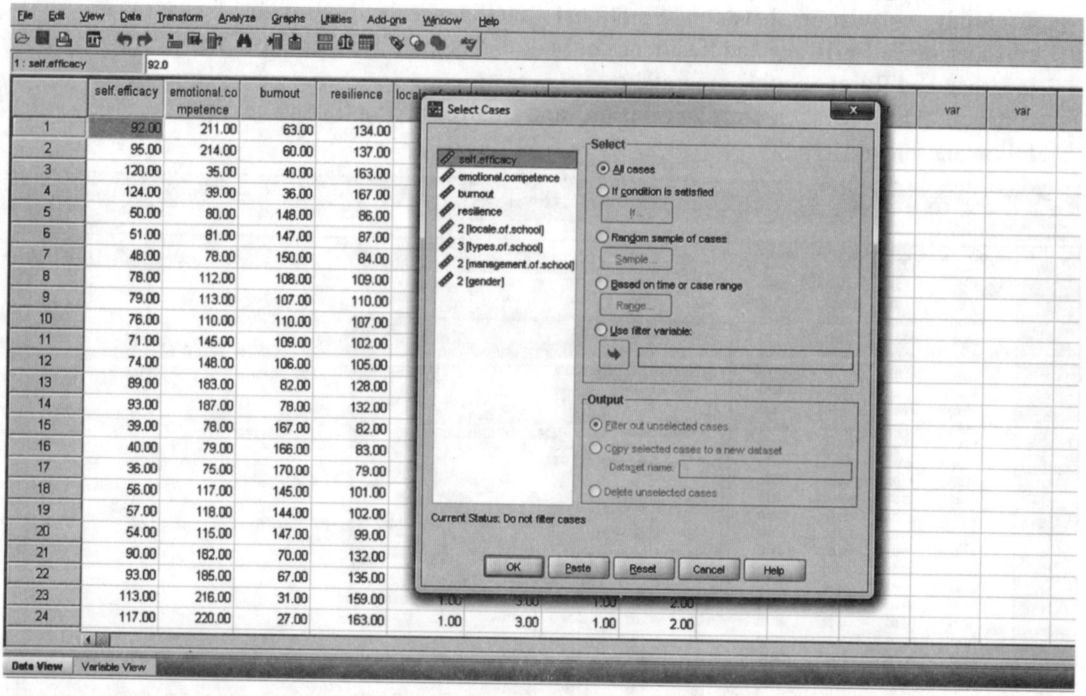

352. Click on "**If condition is satisfied**" to get the following screen.

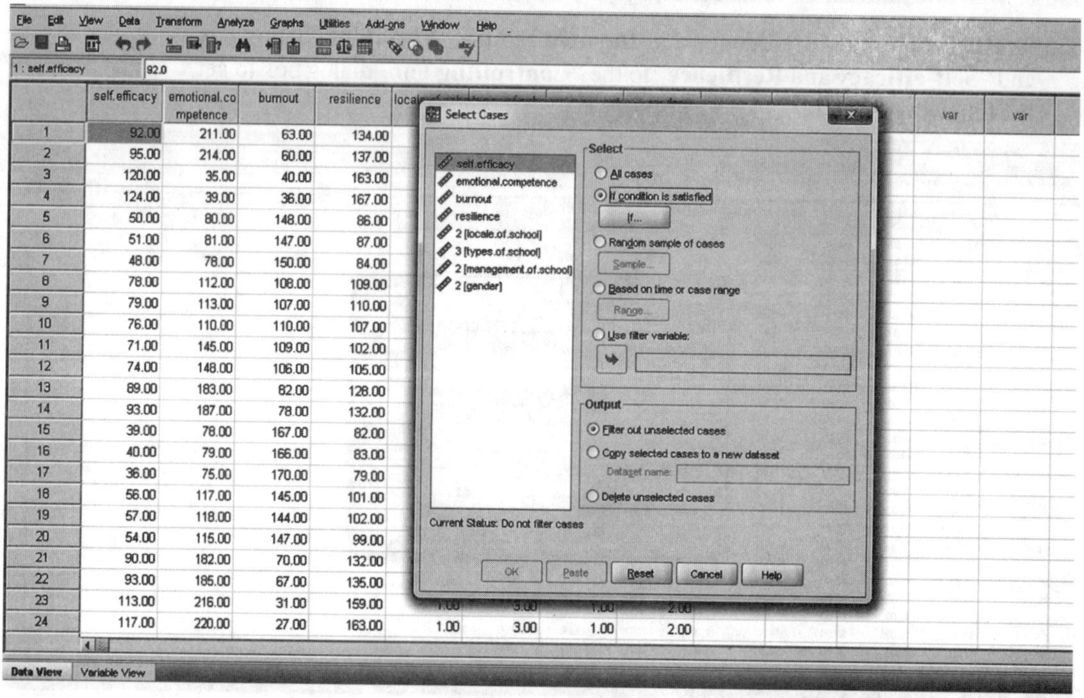

353. Click on "**If...**" to get the following screen.

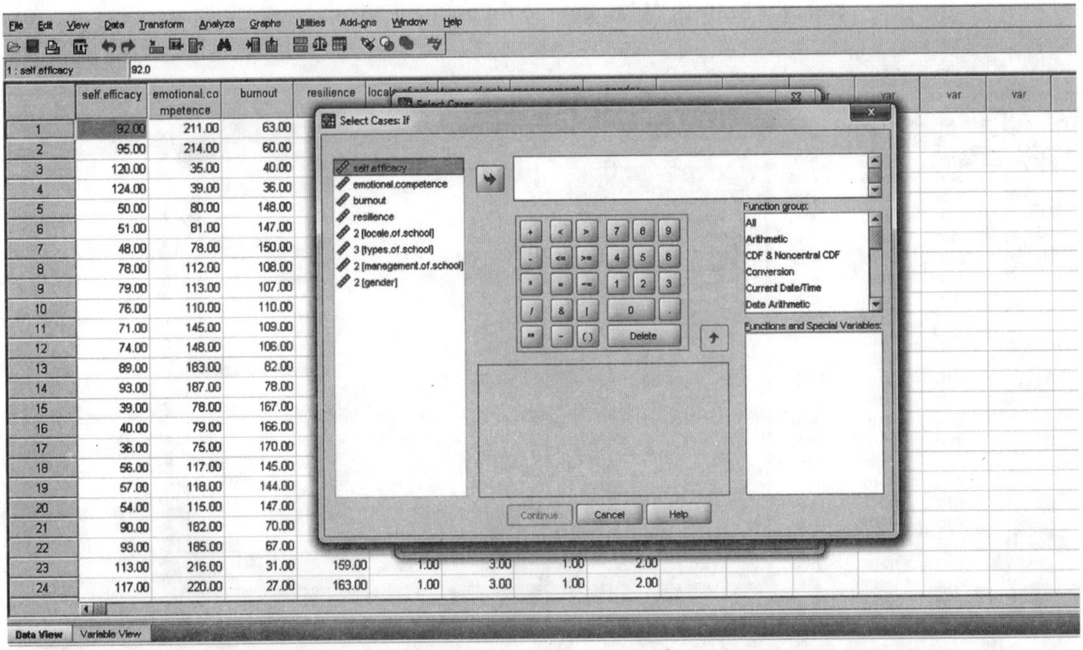

354. According to objective given in Frame 349, Cases are to be selected on the basis of "**Gender**" and "**Locale of School**". You may shift any of these variables on the right hand side dialog box. Suppose you shift "**Gender**" in the right hand side dialog box to get the following screen.

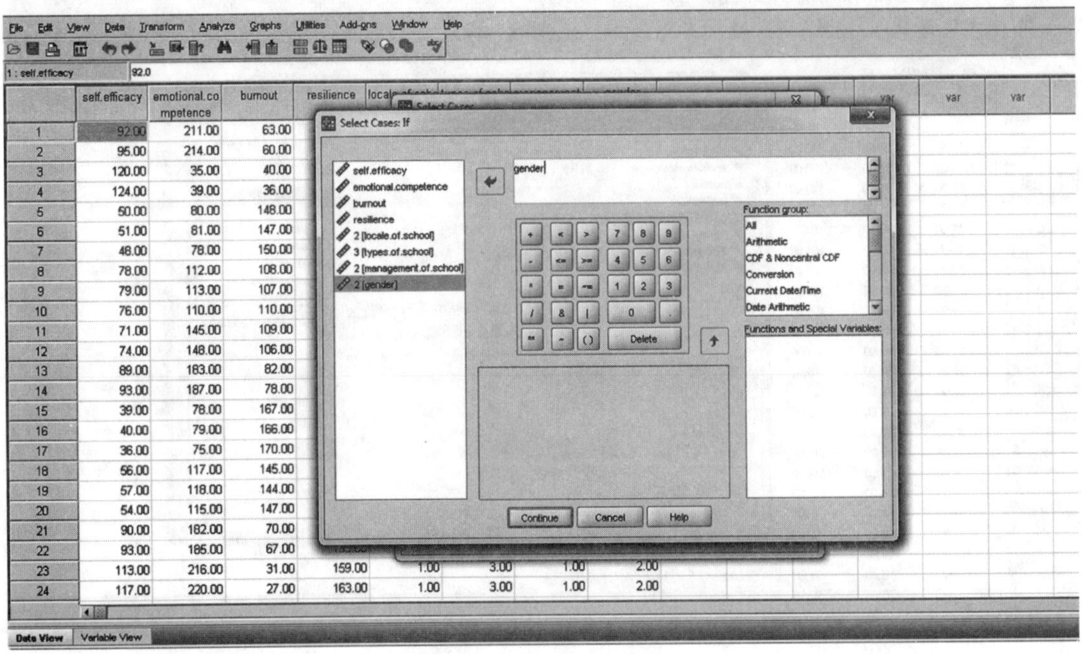

355. In case you want Male Teachers data put "=" sign and type "1" because the code for Male is "1" to get the following screen.

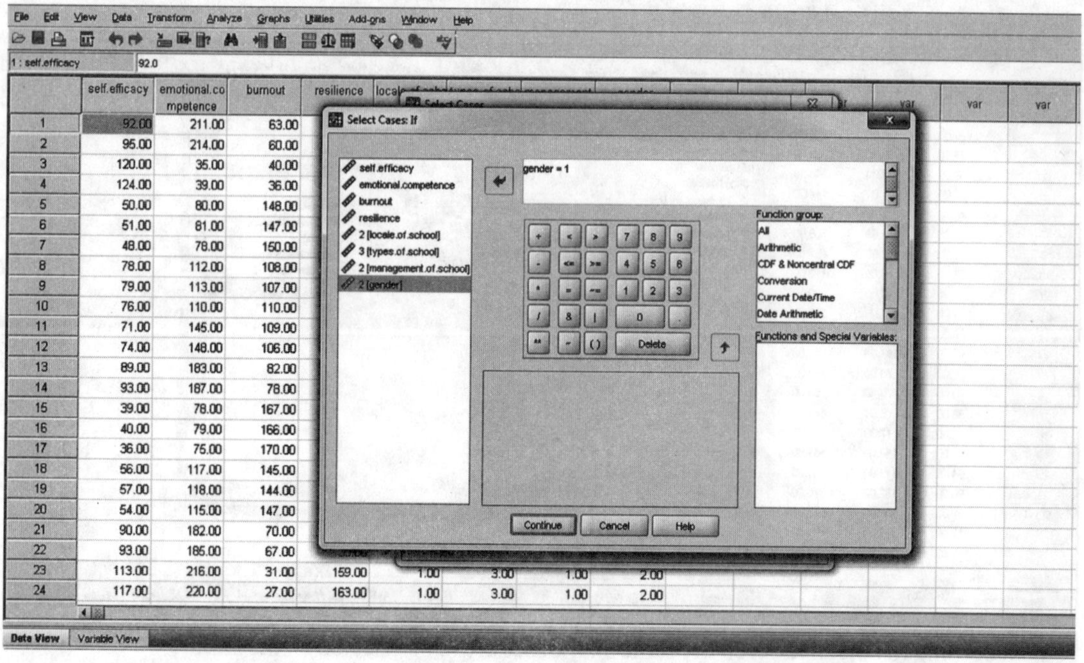

356. Type "**and**" and shift "**Local of School**" to the right hand side dialog box to get the following screen.

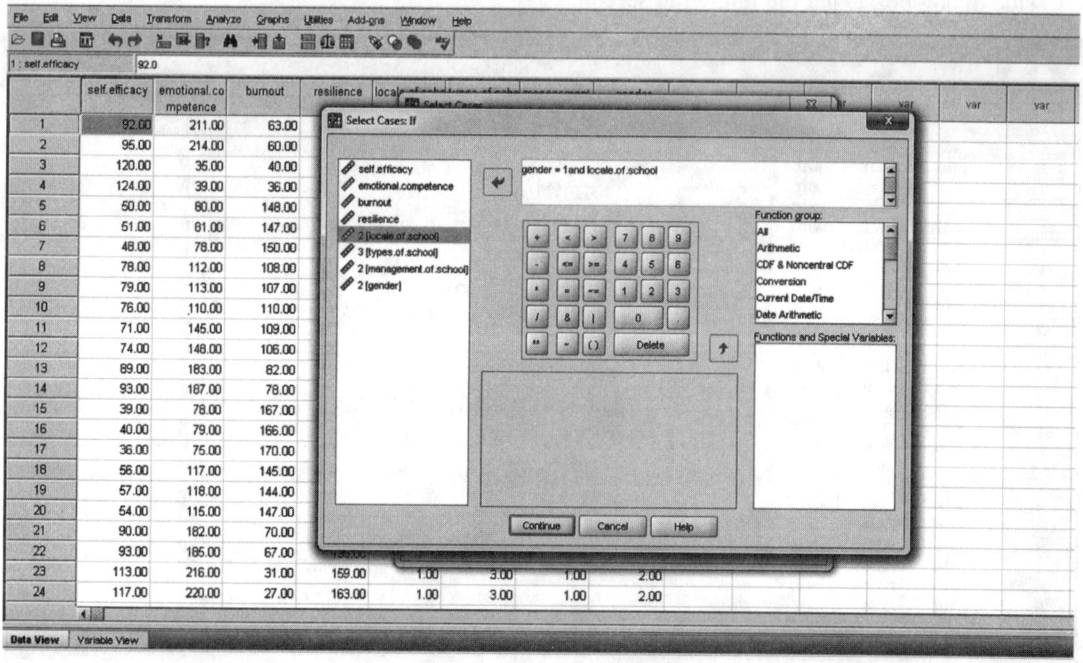

357. Against "**Local of School**" put "**=**" sign and type "**1**" **because "1"** is the code for Urban School to get the following screen.

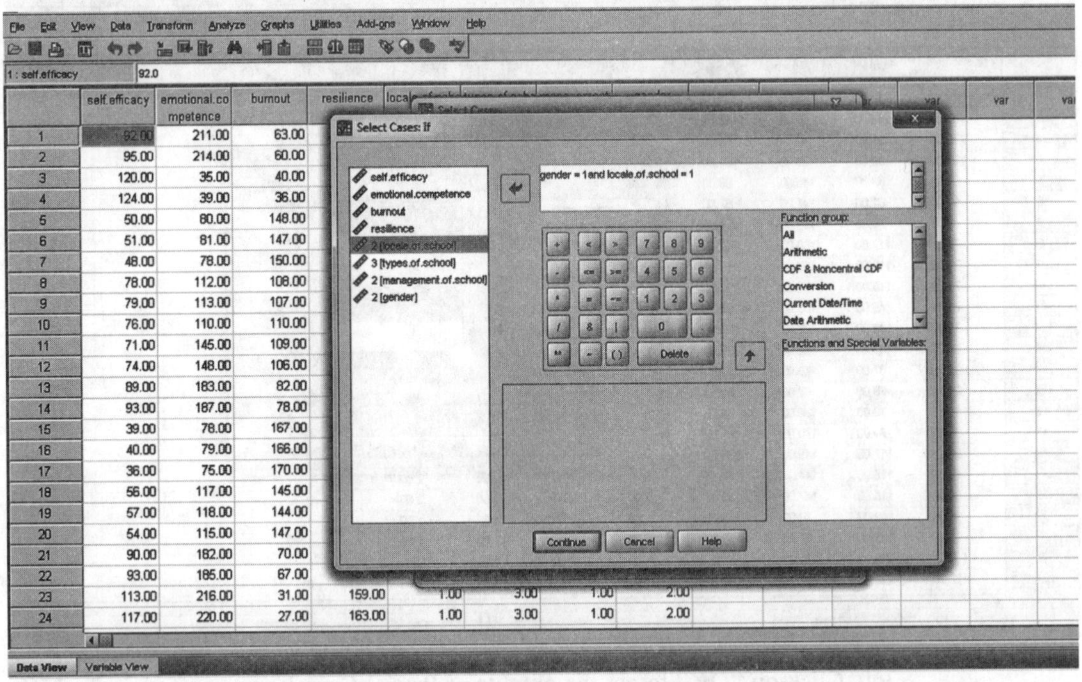

358. Click on "**Continue**" to get the following Screen.

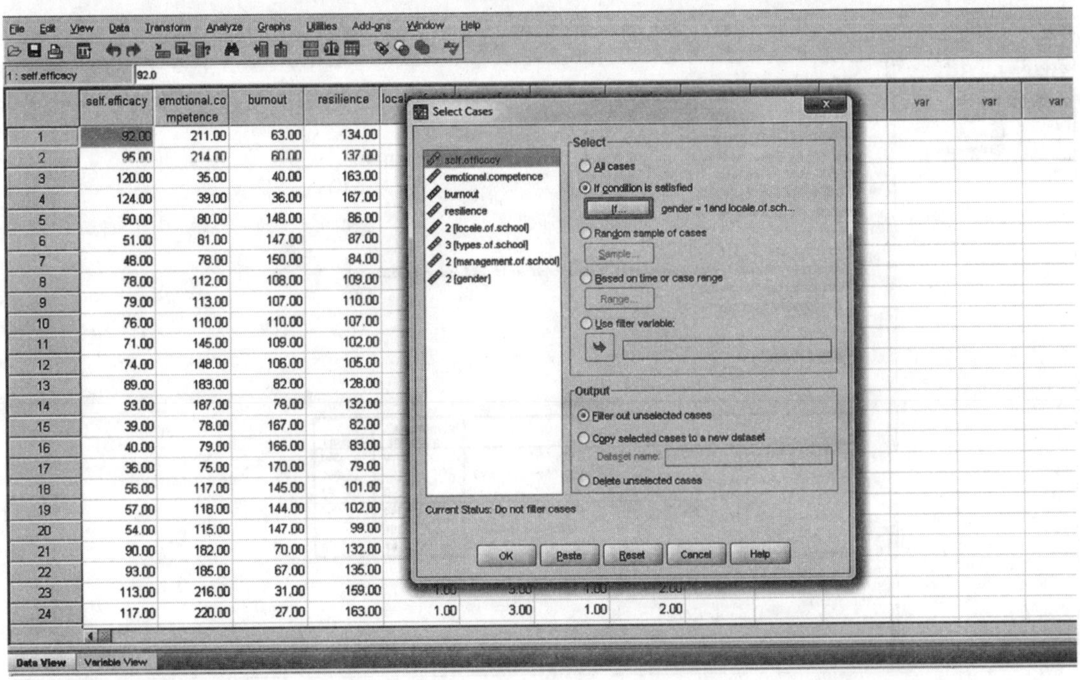

359. Click on "**OK**" to get the following screen.

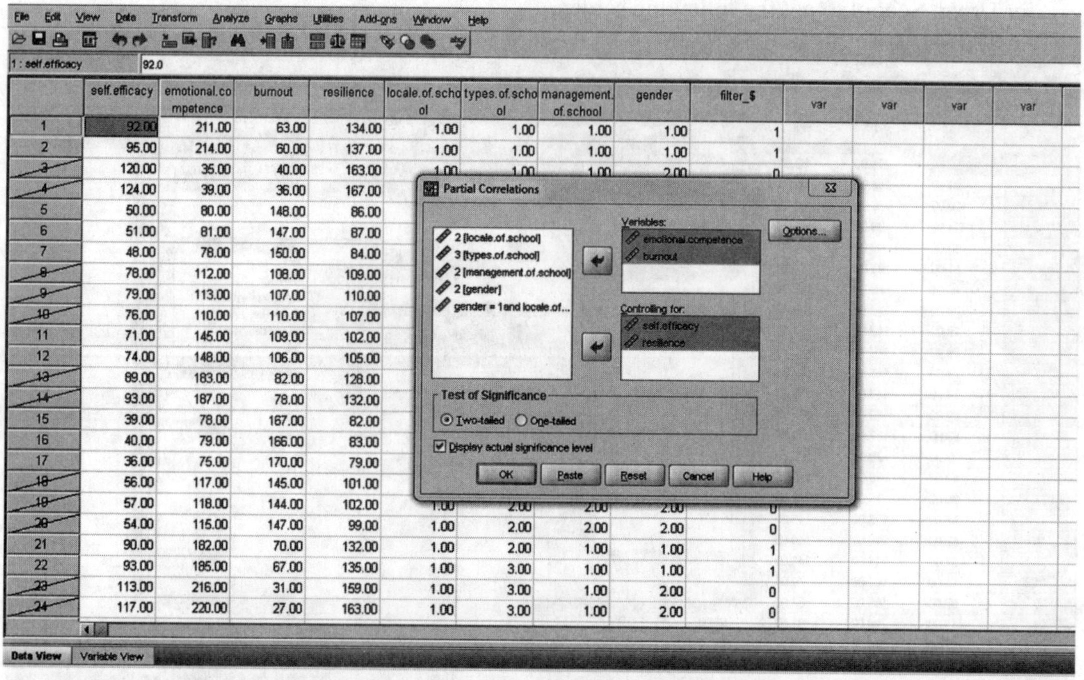

360. Click on "**OK**" to get the outputs of Partial Correlation coefficient for Male Teachers working in Urban Schools.

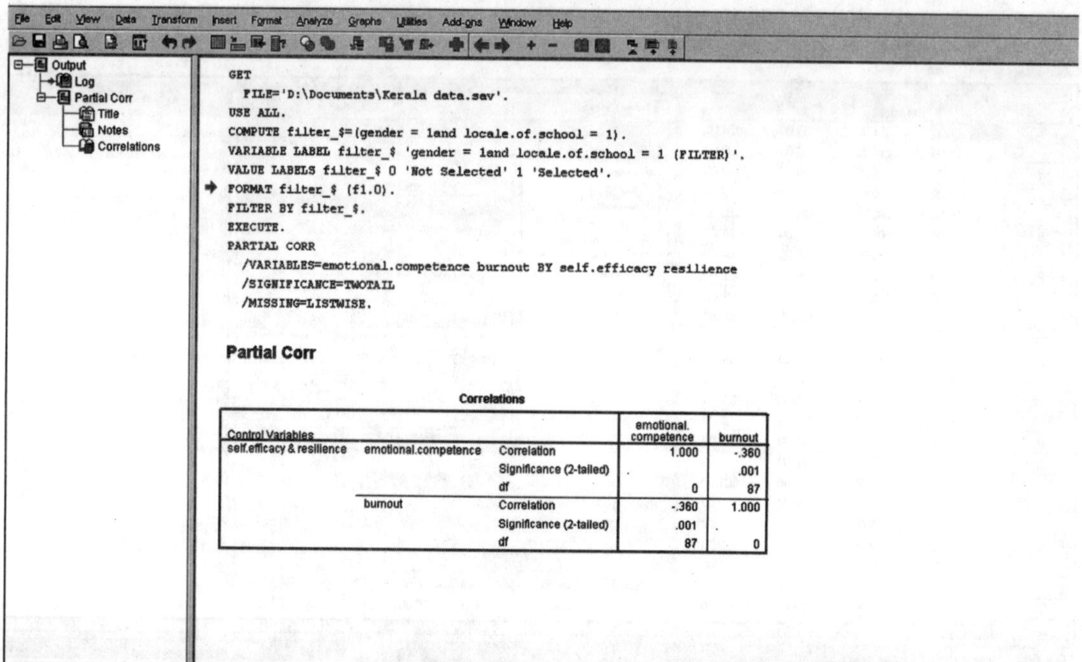

Control Variables			emotional.competence	burnout
self.efficacy & resilience	emotional.competence	Correlation	1.000	-.360
		Significance (2-tailed)	.	.001
		df	0	87
	burnout	Correlation	-.360	1.000
		Significance (2-tailed)	.001	.
		df	87	0

361. To get the Partial Correlation coefficient for Male Teachers working in Rural Schools. Click on "**Data**" then on "**Select Cases**" to get the following screen.

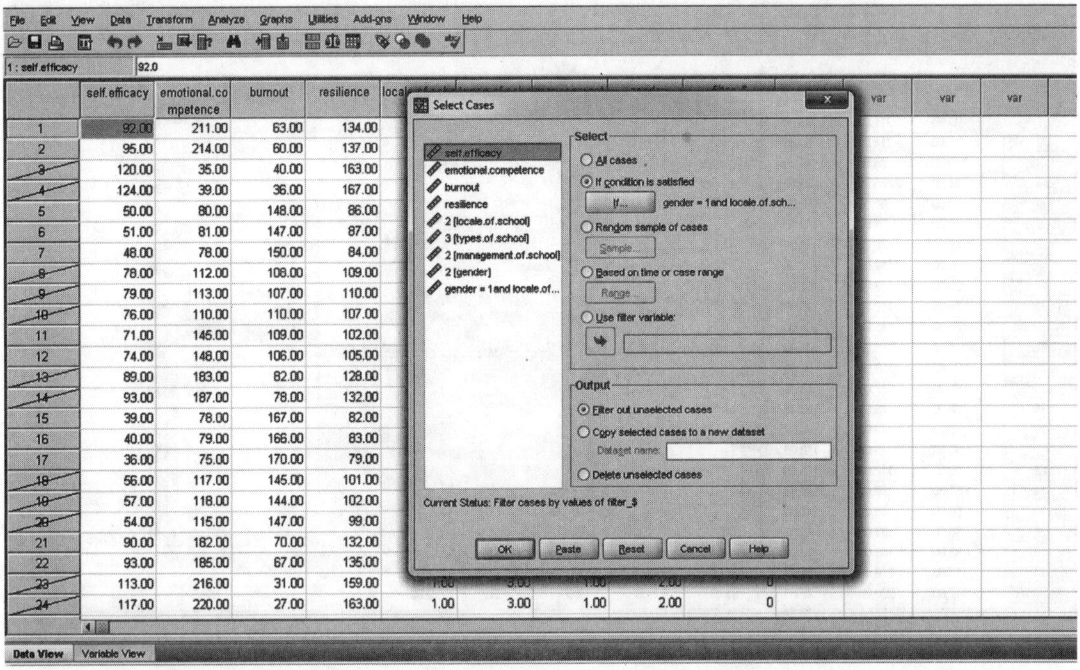

362. Click on "**If...**" button to get the following screen.

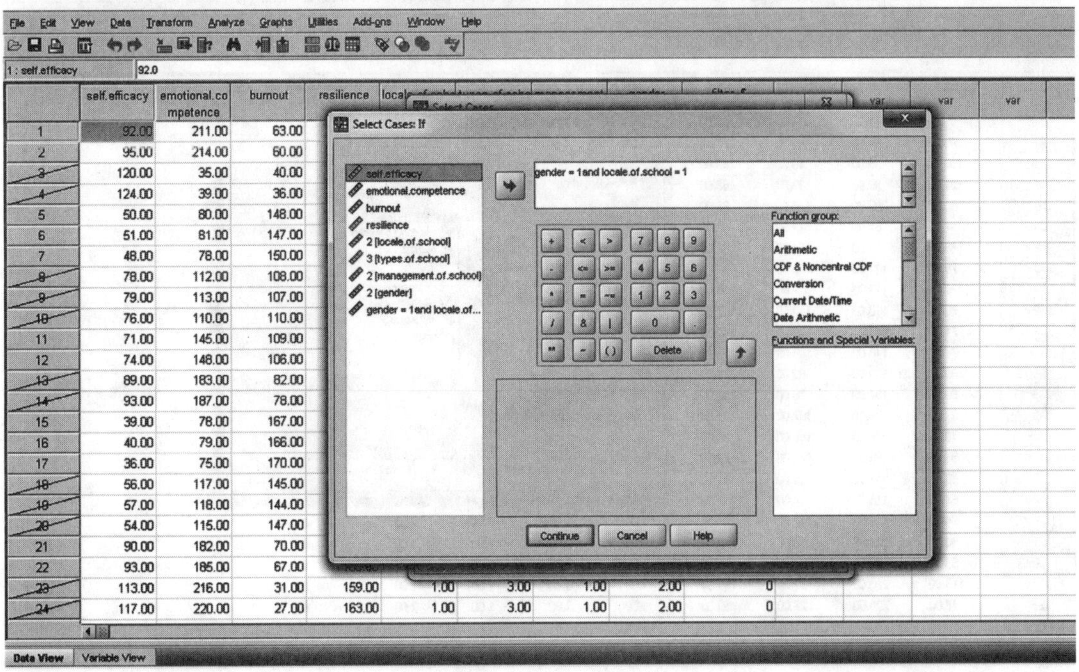

363. Rural Schools are represented by "**2**", so type "**2**" against "**Local of School**" to get the following screen.

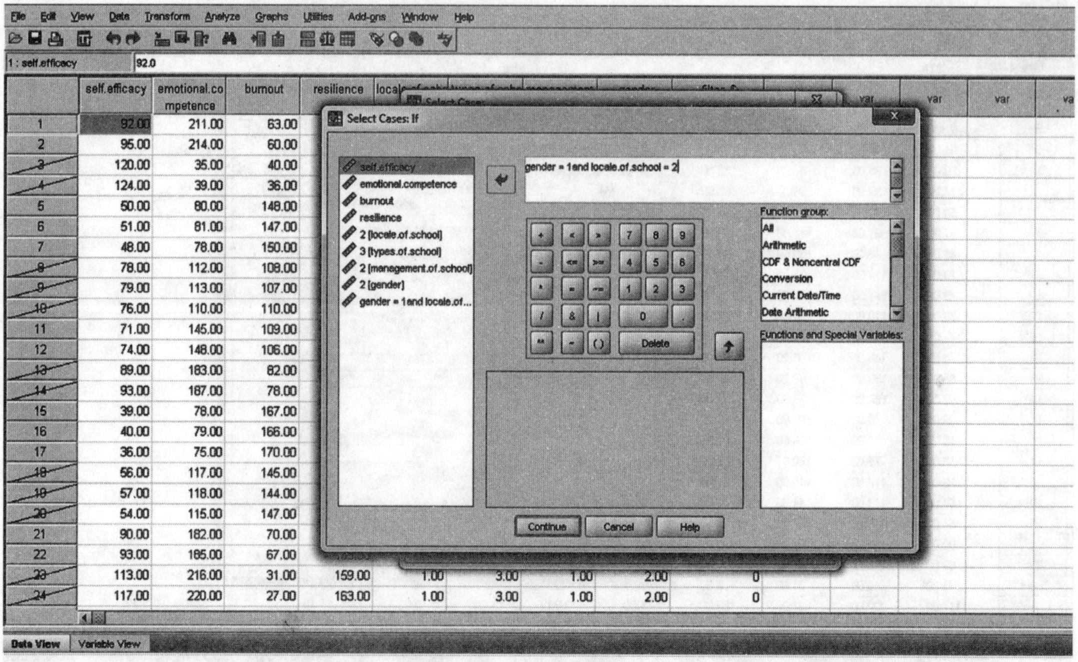

364. Click on "**Continue**" to get the following screen.

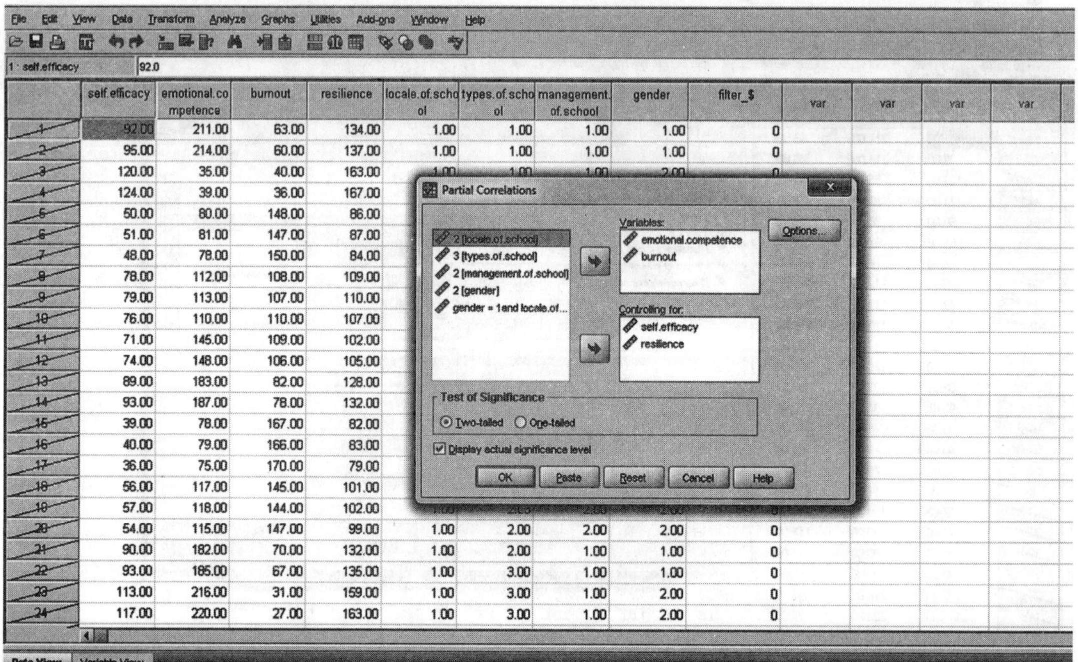

365. Click on "**OK**" to get the outputs of Partial Correlation coefficient of Male Teachers working in Rural School.

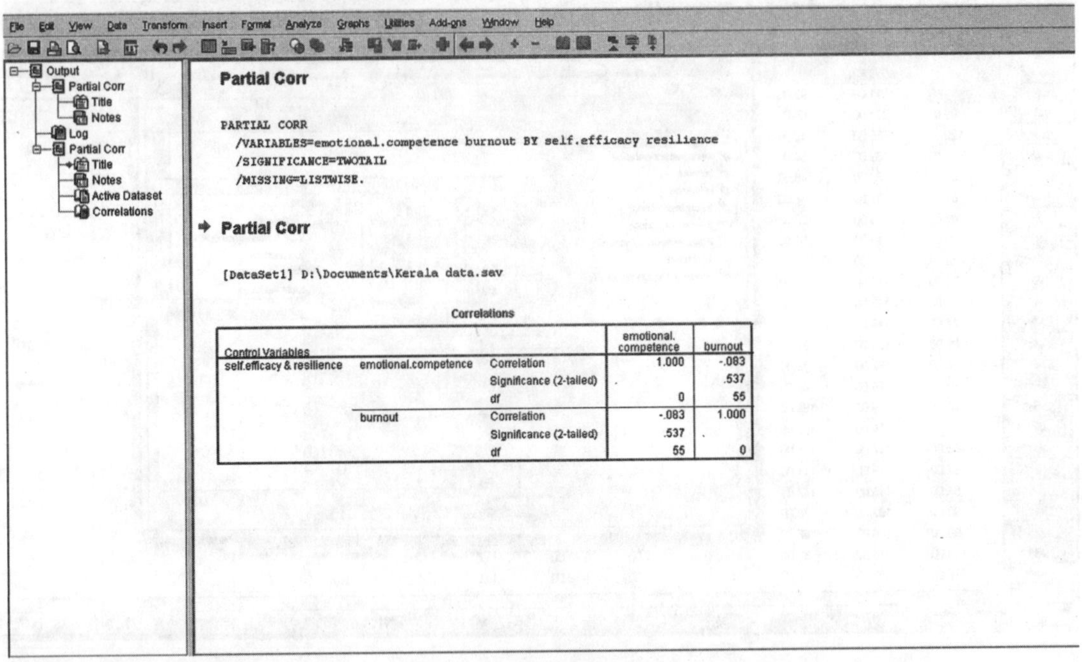

366. For Female Teachers working in Urban Schools, click on "**Data**" than on "**Select Cases**" to get the following screen.

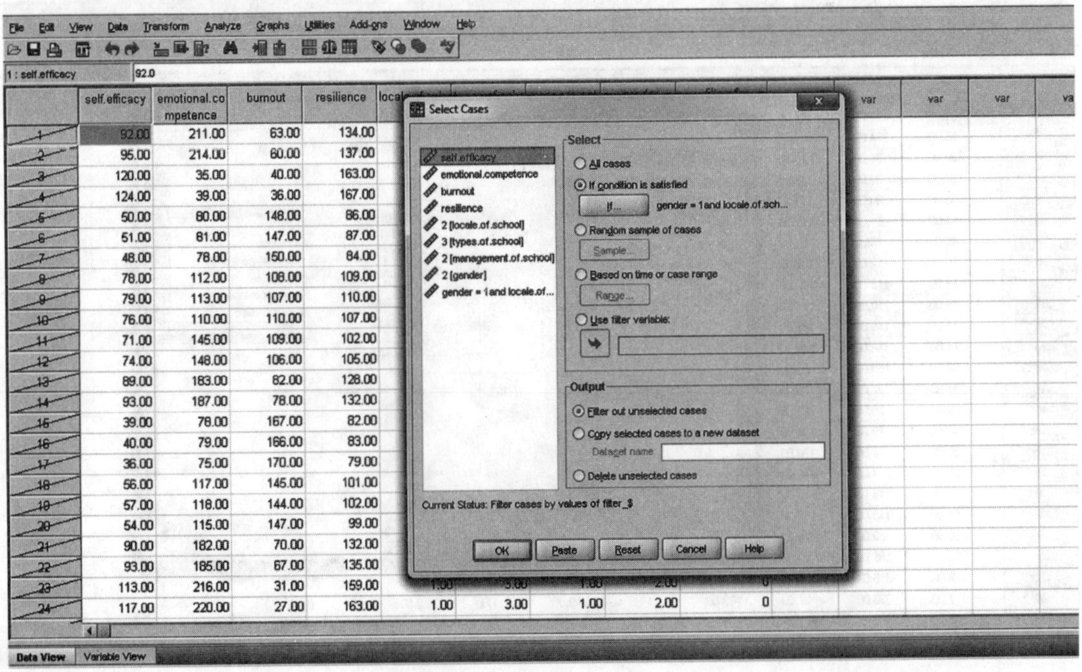

367. Click on "**If...**" button to get the following screen.

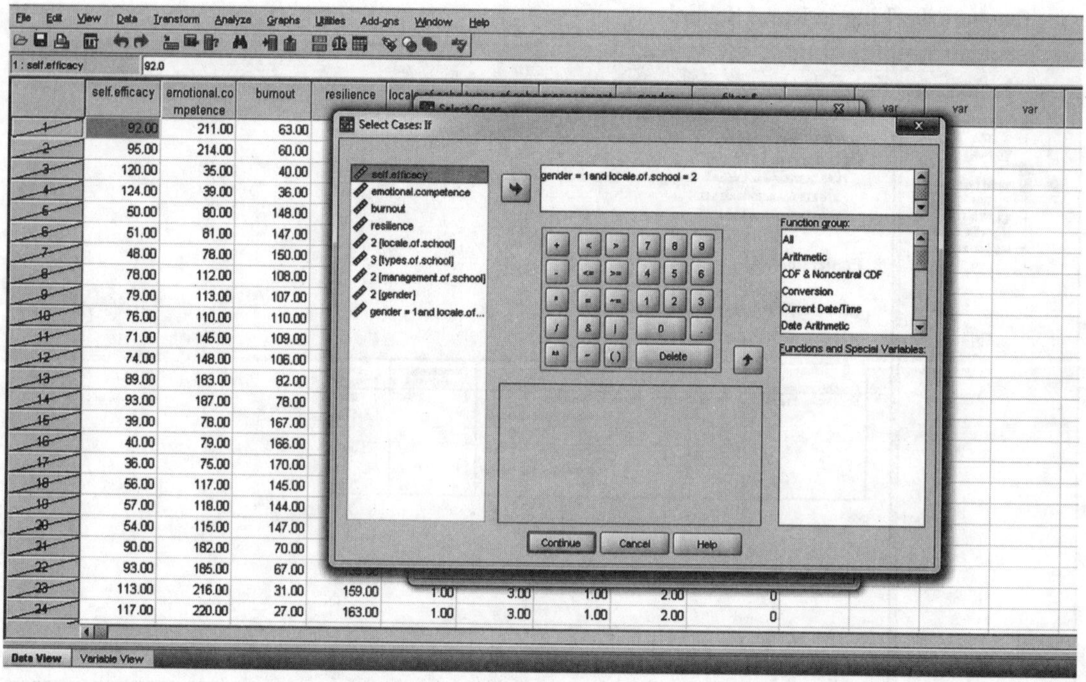

368. Against "**Gender**" type "**2**" and type "**1**" against "**Locale of School**" to get the following screen.

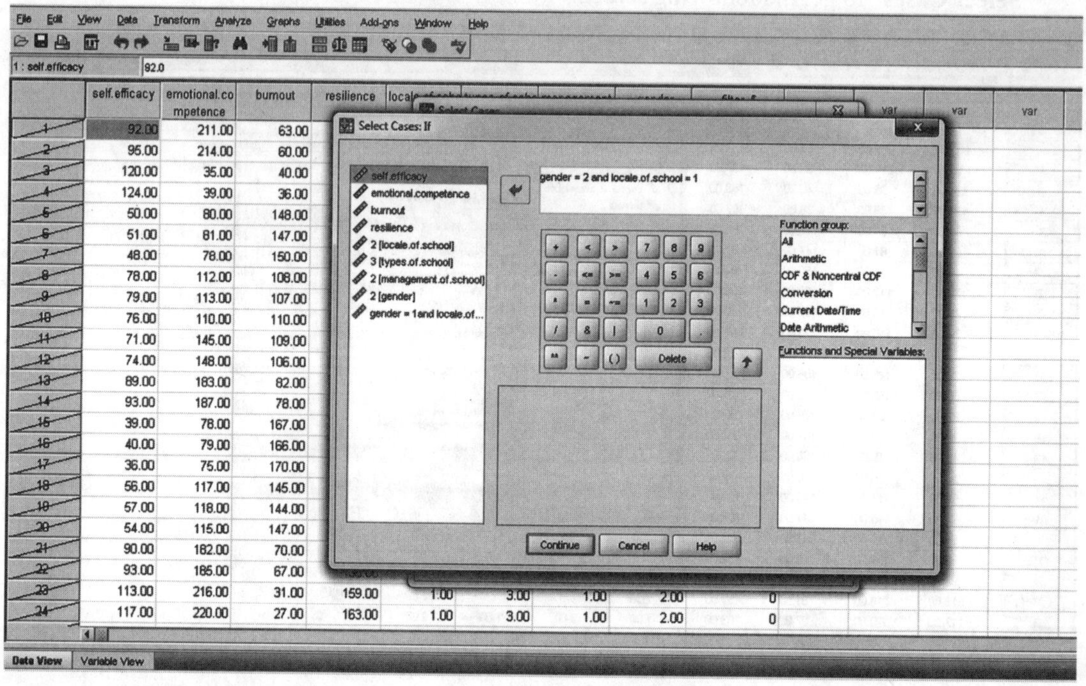

369. Click on "**Continue**" button to get the following screen.

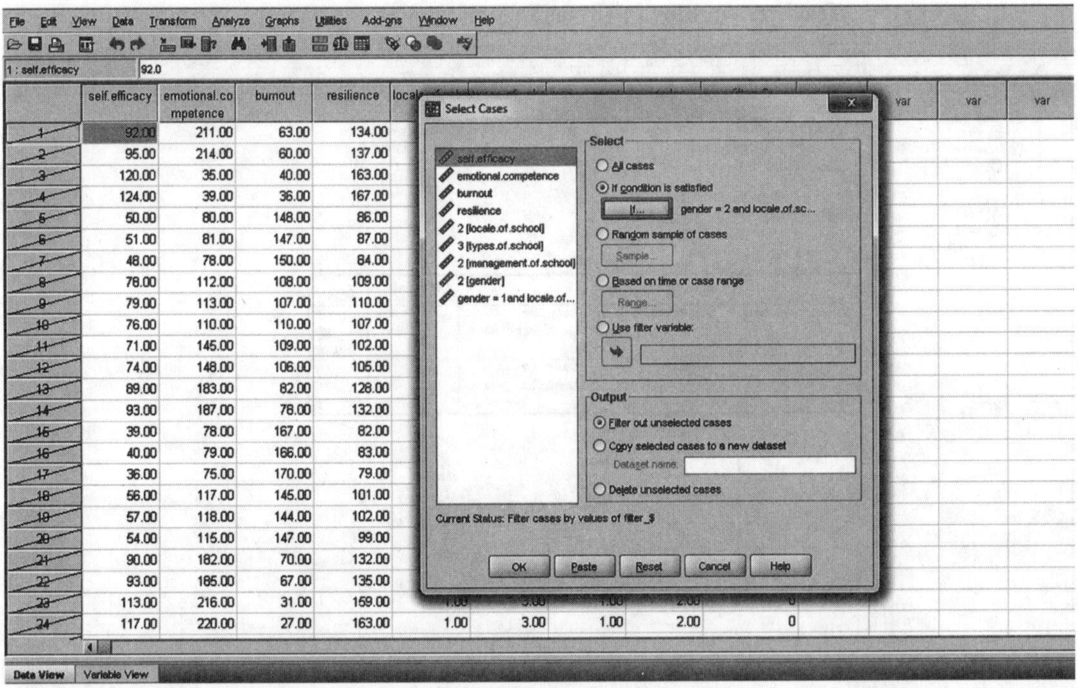

370. Click on "**OK**" to get the following screen.

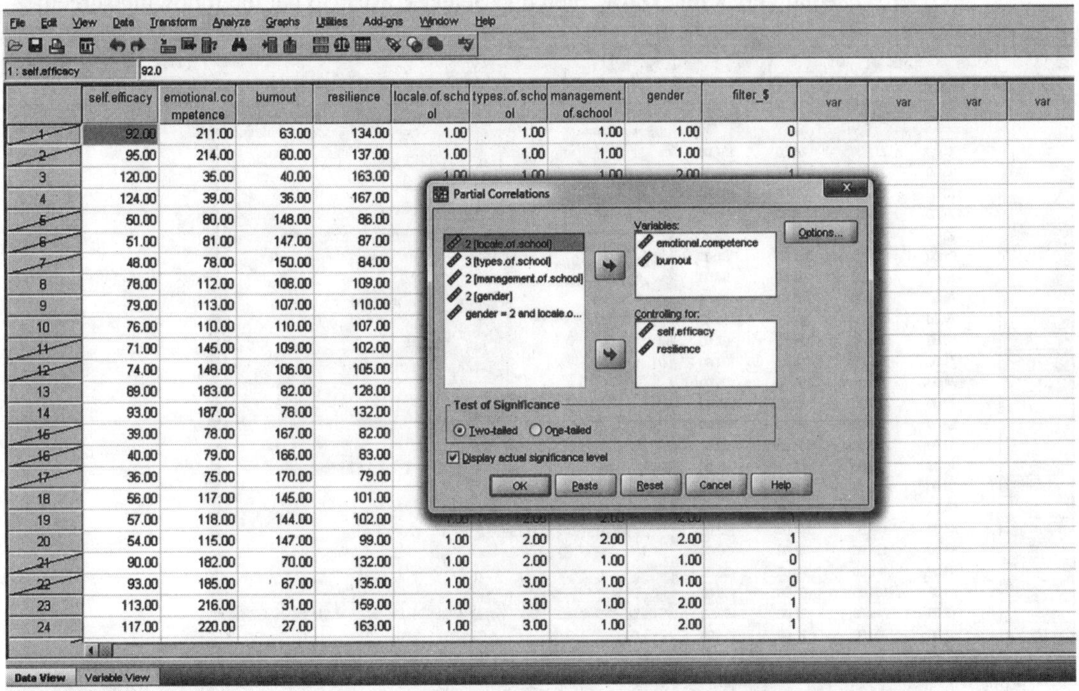

371. Click on "**OK**" to get the outputs of Partial Correlation coefficient for Female Teachers working in Urban Schools.

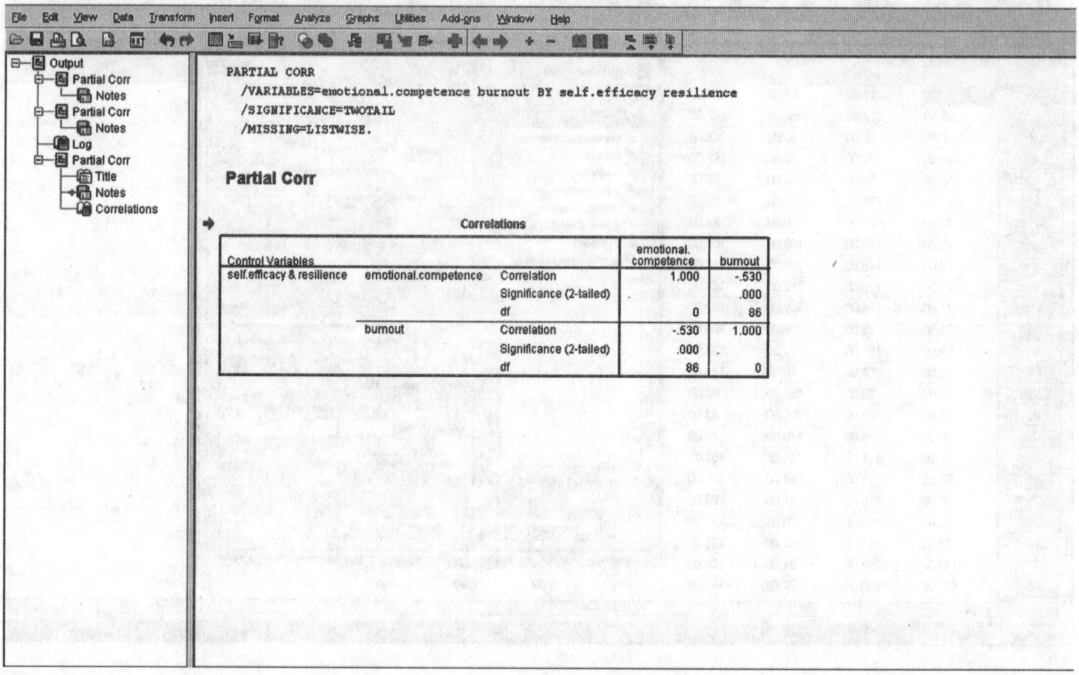

372. Again click on "**Data**" then on "**Select Cases**" to get the following screen.

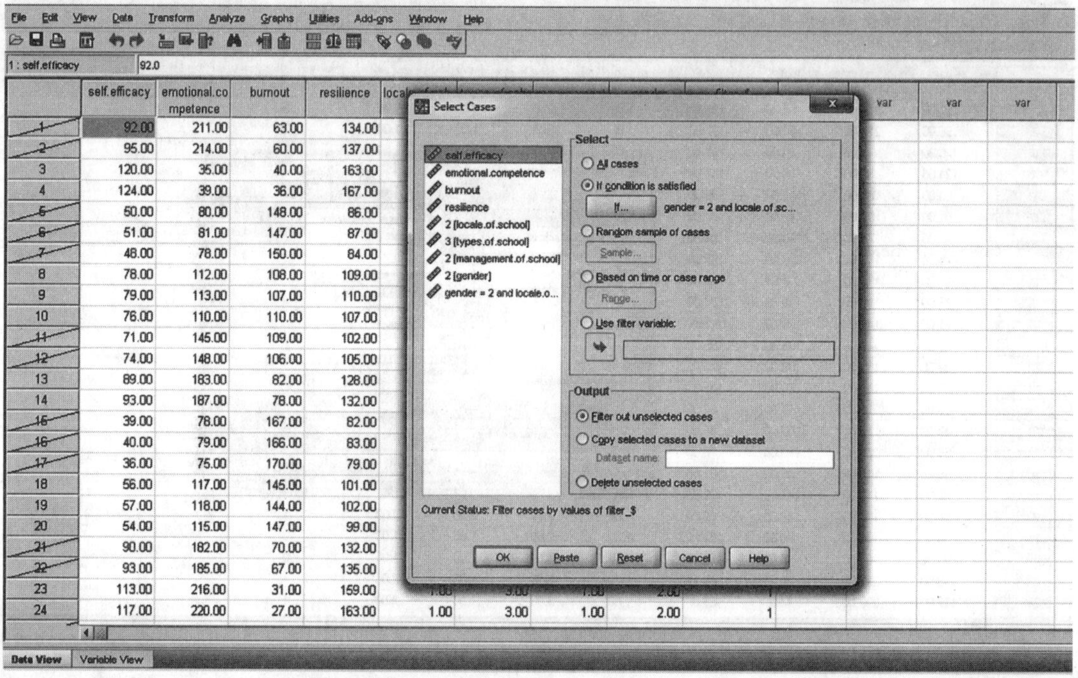

373. Click on "**If...**" button to get the following screen.

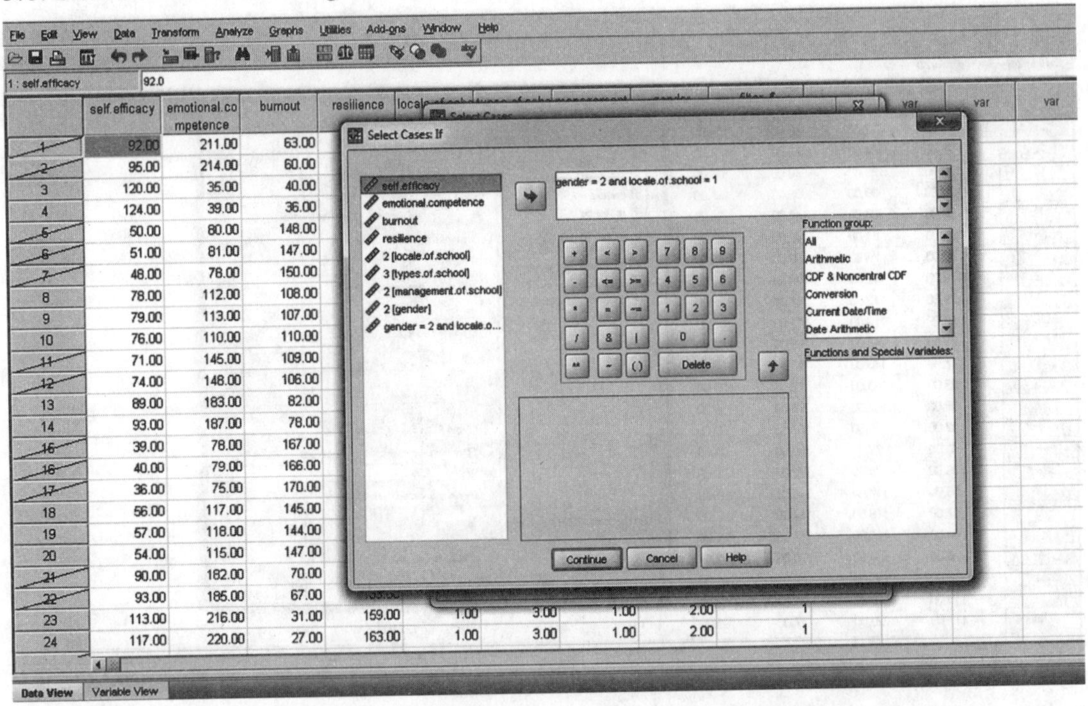

374. Against "**Locale of School**" type "**2**" to get the following screen.

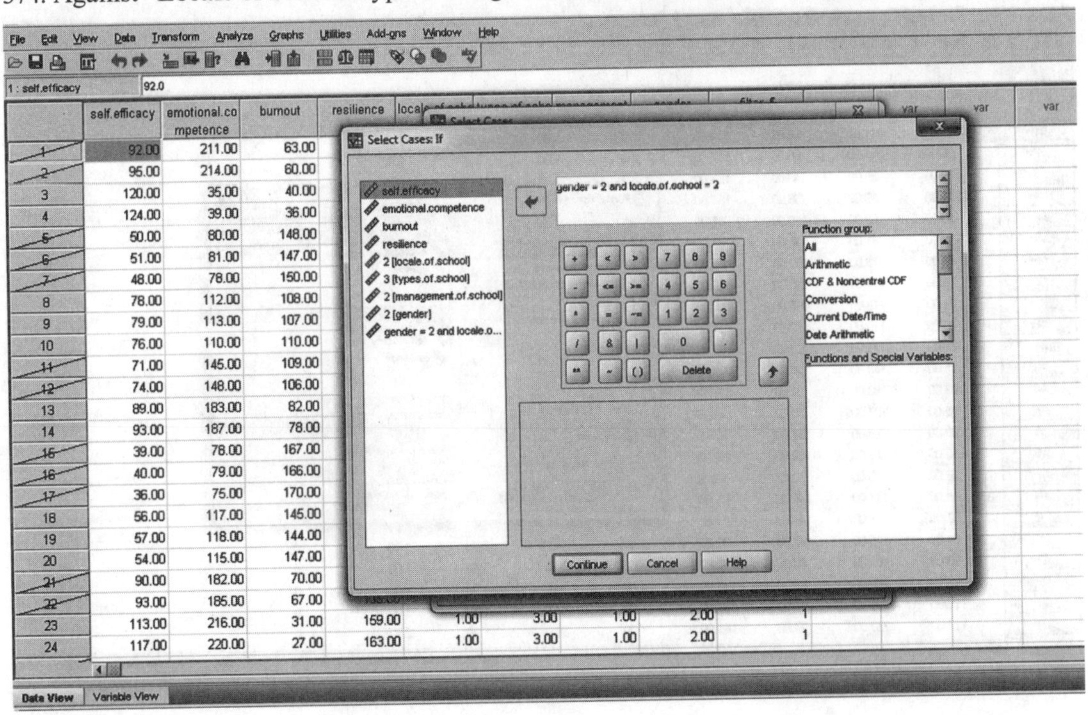

375. Click on "**Continue**" to get the following screen.

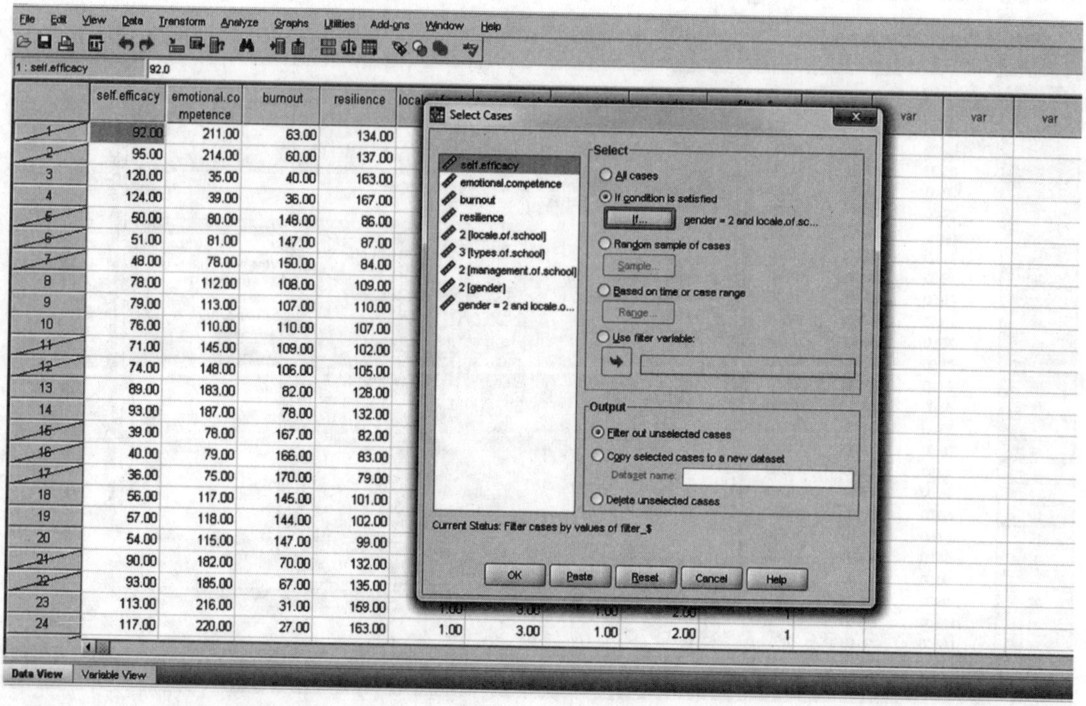

376. Click on "**OK**" to get the following screen.

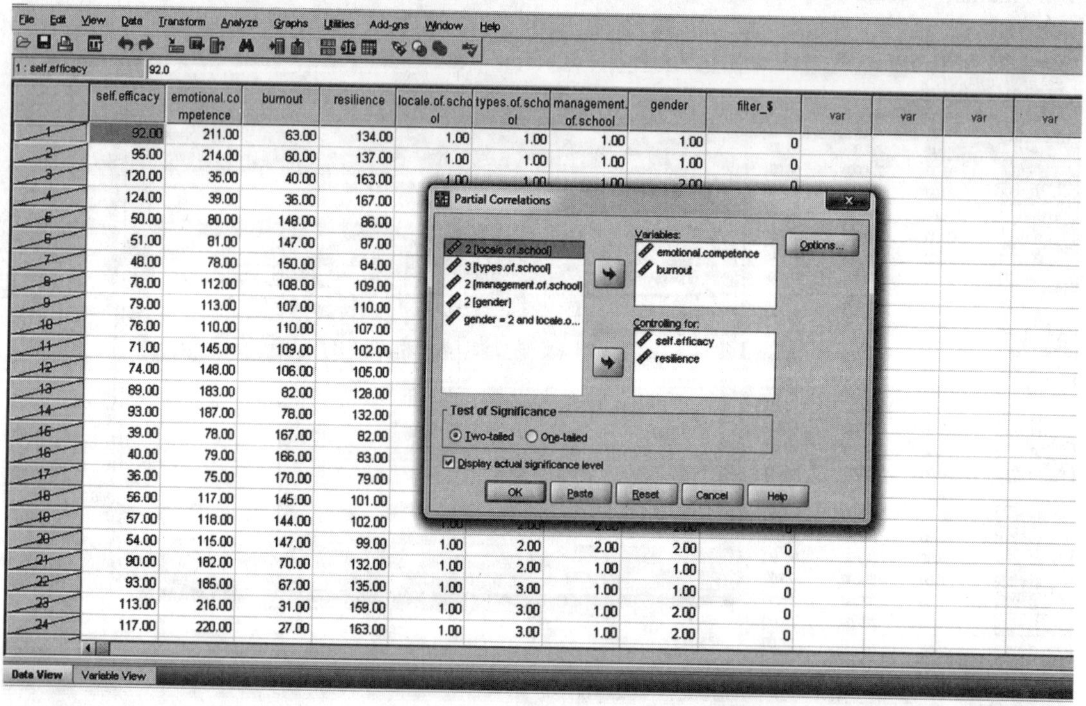

377. Click on "**OK**" to get the outputs of Partial Correlation coefficient for Female Teachers working in Rural Schools.

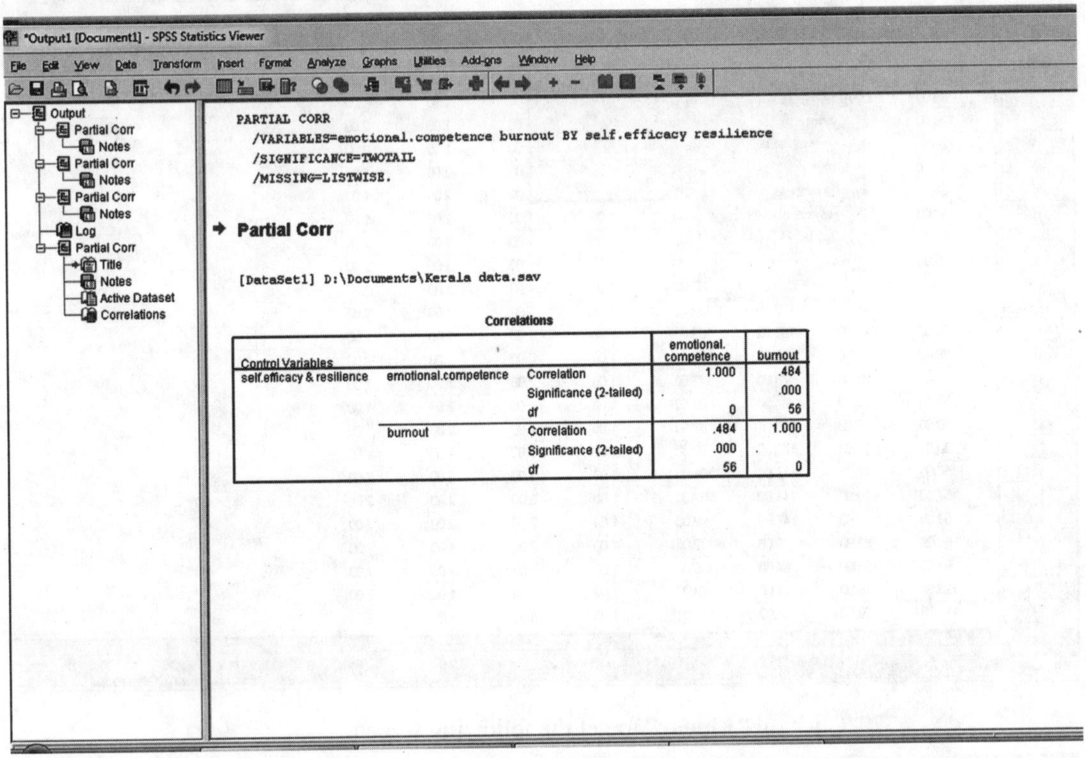

Control Variables			emotional. competence	burnout
self.efficacy & resilience	emotional.competence	Correlation	1.000	.484
		Significance (2-tailed)	.	.000
		df	0	56
	burnout	Correlation	.484	1.000
		Significance (2-tailed)	.000	.
		df	56	0

The same procedure is to be used to "**Select Cases**" for more than two discontinuous variables.

For interpretation of Partial Correlation results, you may refer to the book by D.N.Sansanwal, Research Methodology and Applied Statistic, Shipra Publishers, Delhi, 2020.

Multiple Correlation

378. Multiple Correlation technique is used for studying joint contribution of two or more continuous variables in predicting a continuous variable. All variables must be correlated among themselves. There must be minimum three continuous variables out of which two variables must be predictors and one variable is to be predicted. Multiple Correlation is denoted by **R**. Let us take the following objective.

To study joint contribution of Self-efficacy and Burnout in predicting Emotional Competence of Teachers.

Click on "**Analyse**" bring curser to "**Regression**" icon and finally to "**Linear**" icon to get the following screen.

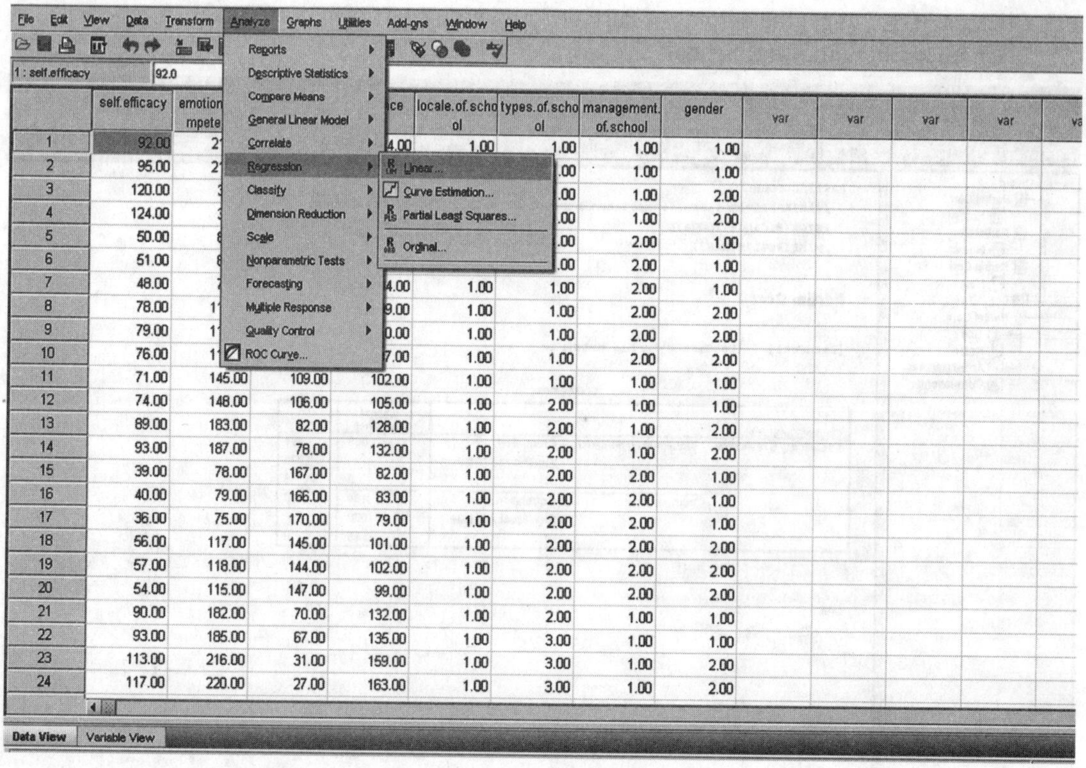

379. Click on "**Linear**" to get the following screen.

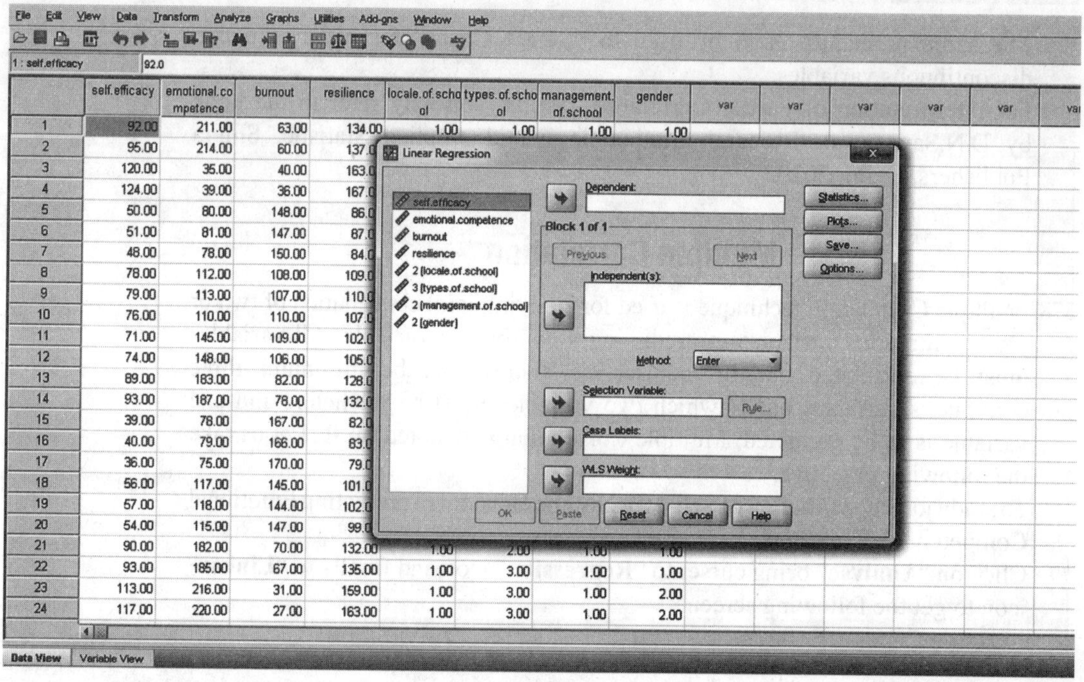

380. Shift "**Emotional Competence**" to the "**Dependent**" slot and "**Self-efficacy** and **Burnout**" variables to the "**Independent(s)**" slot to get the following screen.

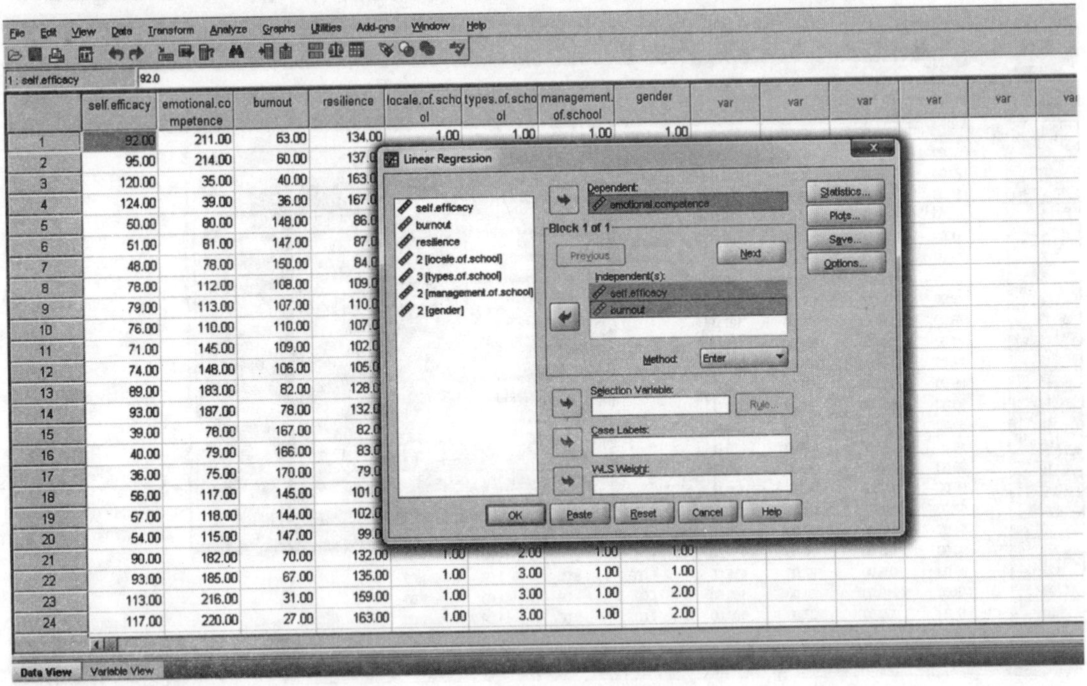

381. Click on "**Statistics**" icon to get the following screen.

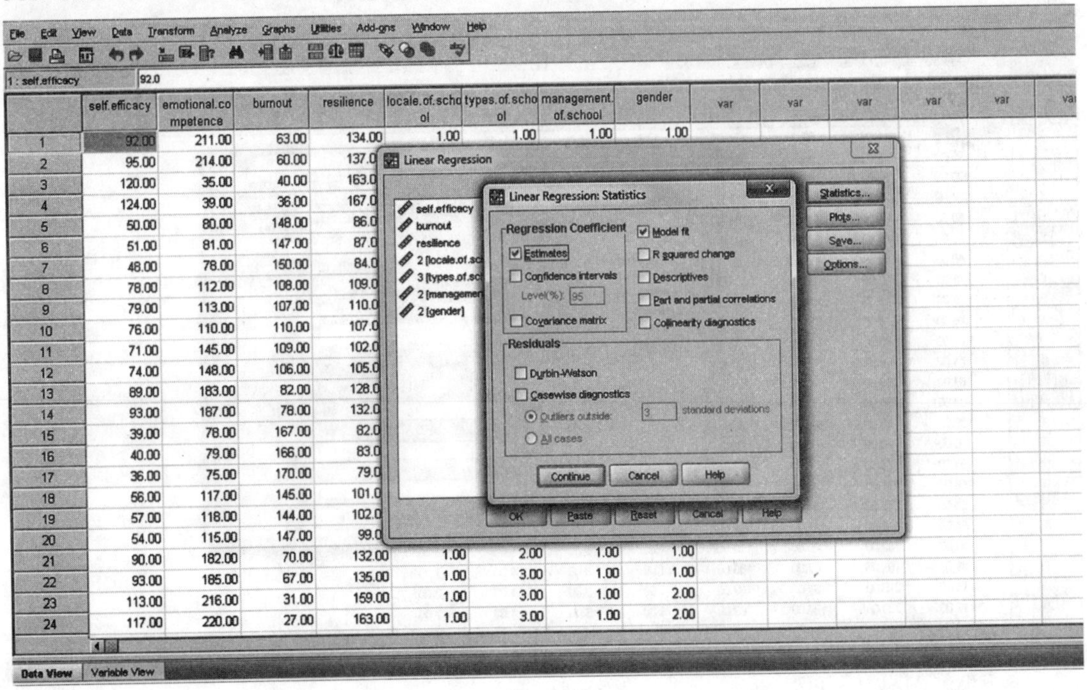

382. "Under "**Regression Coefficient**", "**Estimates**" and "**Model Fit**" are already highlighted. Now highlight "**R squared Change**" to get the following screen.

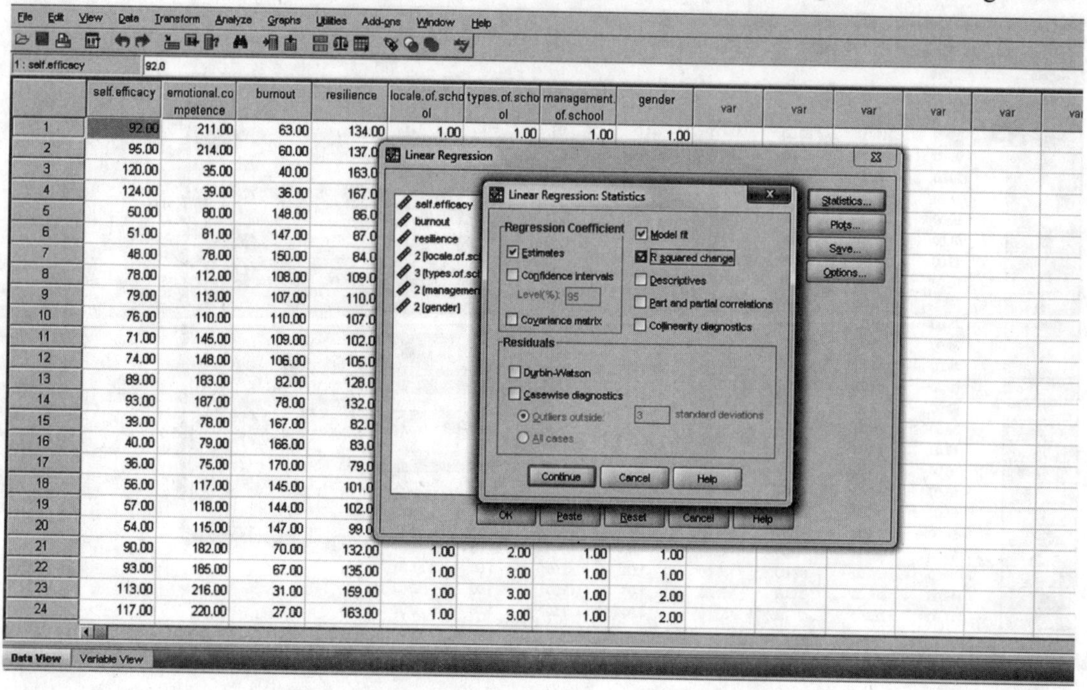

383. Click on "**Continue**" to get the following screen.

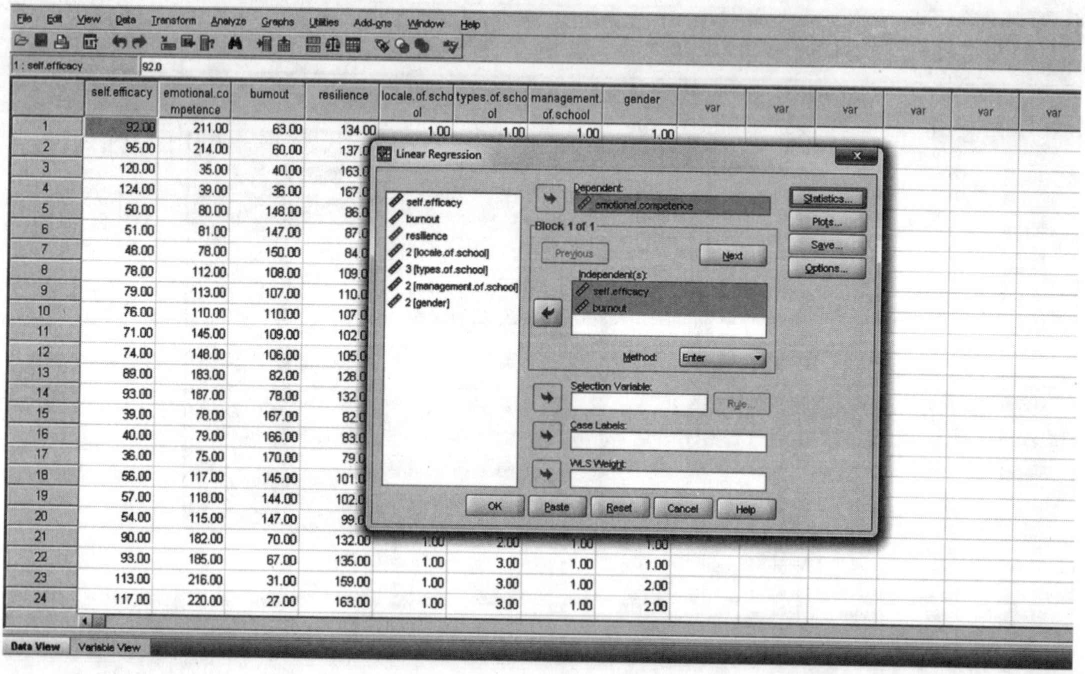

384. Click on "**OK**" to get the following Outputs of Multiple Correlation which is part of Regression Analysis in SPSS Software.

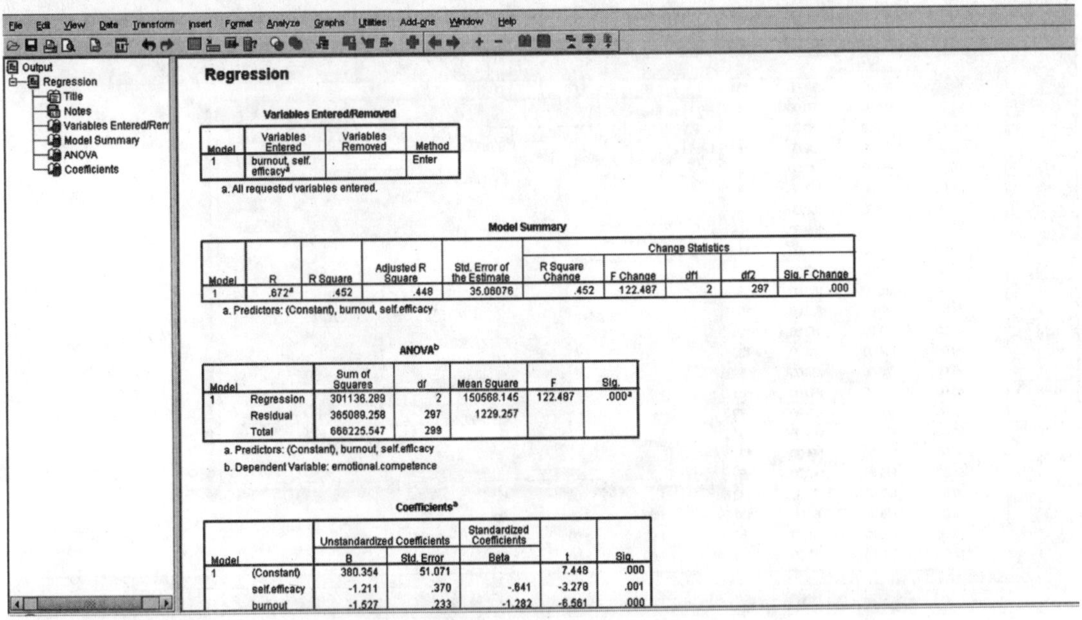

Regression

Variables Entered/Removed

Model	Variables Entered	Variables Removed	Method
1	burnout, self. efficacy[a]	.	Enter

a. All requested variables entered.

Model Summary

Model	R	R Square	Adjusted R Square	Std. Error of the Estimate	Change Statistics				
					R Square Change	F Change	df1	df2	Sig. F Change
1	.672[a]	.452	.448	35.08076	.452	122.487	2	297	.000

a. Predictors: (Constant), burnout, self.efficacy

ANOVA[b]

Model		Sum of Squares	df	Mean Square	F	Sig.
1	Regression	301136.289	2	150568.145	122.487	.000[a]
	Residual	365089.258	297	1229.257		
	Total	666225.547	299			

a. Predictors: (Constant), burnout, self.efficacy

b. Dependent Variable: emotional.competence

Coefficients[a]

Model		Unstandardized Coefficients		Standardized Coefficients	t	Sig.
		B	Std. Error	Beta		
1	(Constant)	380.354	51.071		7.448	.000
	self.efficacy	-1.211	.370	-.641	-3.278	.001
	burnout	-1.527	.233	-1.282	-6.561	.000

385. Let us take the following objective.

To study joint contribution of Self-efficacy and Burnout in predicting Emotional Competence of Male and Female Teachers separately.

Click on "**Analyse**" bring curser to "**Regression**" icon and finally to "**Linear**" icon to get the following screen.

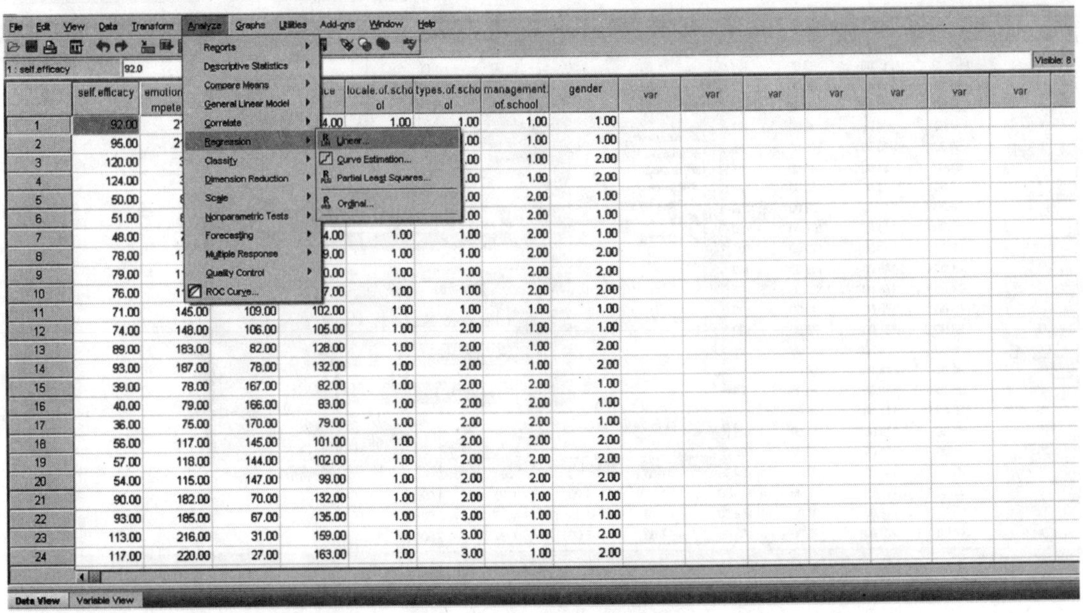

	self.efficacy	emotional.competence		burnout	locale.of.school	types.of.school	management.of.school	gender	var	var	var	var	var	var	var
1	92.00	2		4.00	1.00	1.00	1.00	1.00							
2	95.00	2				.00	1.00	1.00							
3	120.00	3				.00	1.00	2.00							
4	124.00	3				.00	1.00	2.00							
5	50.00	8				.00	2.00	1.00							
6	51.00	8				.00	2.00	1.00							
7	48.00	7		4.00	1.00	1.00	2.00	1.00							
8	78.00	1		9.00	1.00	1.00	2.00	2.00							
9	79.00	1		0.00	1.00	1.00	2.00	2.00							
10	76.00	1		7.00	1.00	1.00	2.00	2.00							
11	71.00	145.00	109.00	102.00	1.00	1.00	1.00	1.00							
12	74.00	148.00	106.00	105.00	1.00	2.00	1.00	1.00							
13	89.00	183.00	82.00	128.00	1.00	2.00	1.00	2.00							
14	93.00	187.00	78.00	132.00	1.00	2.00	1.00	2.00							
15	39.00	78.00	167.00	82.00	1.00	2.00	2.00	1.00							
16	40.00	79.00	166.00	83.00	1.00	2.00	2.00	1.00							
17	36.00	75.00	170.00	79.00	1.00	2.00	2.00	1.00							
18	56.00	117.00	145.00	101.00	1.00	2.00	2.00	2.00							
19	57.00	118.00	144.00	102.00	1.00	2.00	2.00	2.00							
20	54.00	115.00	147.00	99.00	1.00	2.00	2.00	2.00							
21	90.00	182.00	70.00	132.00	1.00	2.00	1.00	1.00							
22	93.00	185.00	67.00	135.00	1.00	3.00	1.00	1.00							
23	113.00	216.00	31.00	159.00	1.00	3.00	1.00	2.00							
24	117.00	220.00	27.00	163.00	1.00	3.00	1.00	2.00							

386. Click on "**Linear**" to get the following screen.

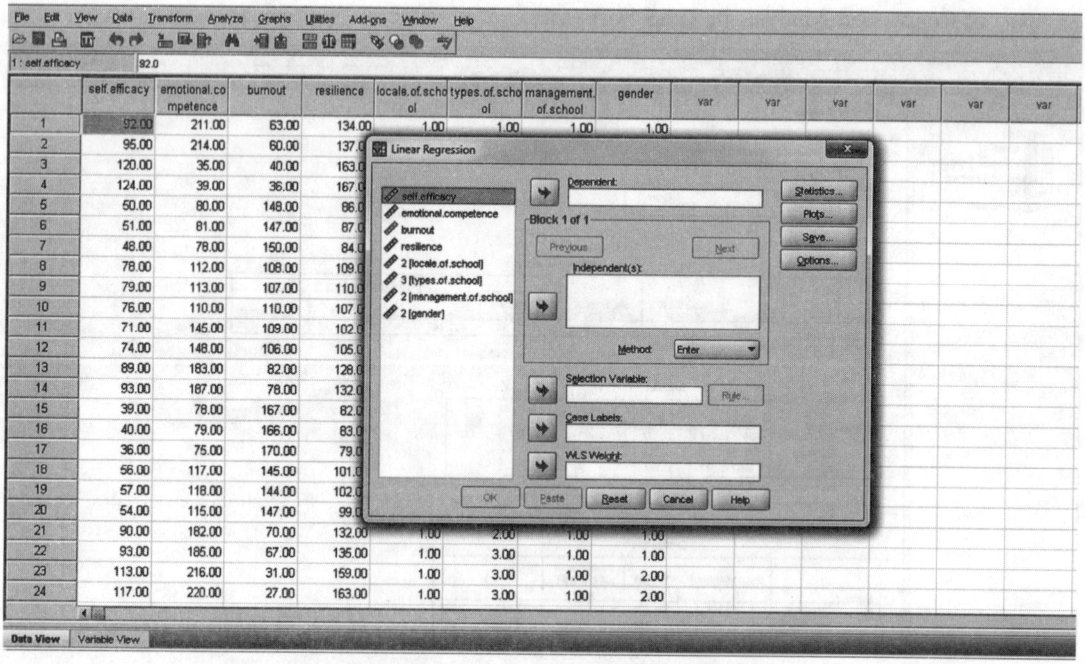

387. Shift "**Emotional Competence**" variable to "**Dependent**" slot and "**Self-efficacy** and **Burnout**" variables to "**Independent(s)**" dialogue box to get the following screen.

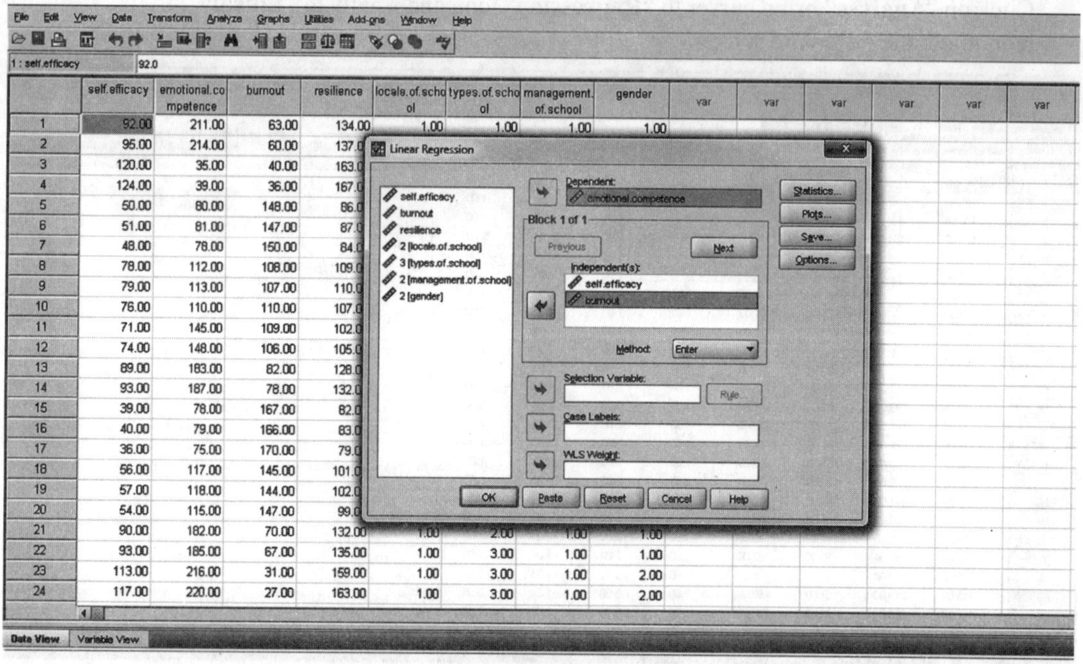

388. Click on "**Statistics**" icon to get the following screen where "**Estimates**" and "**Model Fit**" are pre-highlighted.

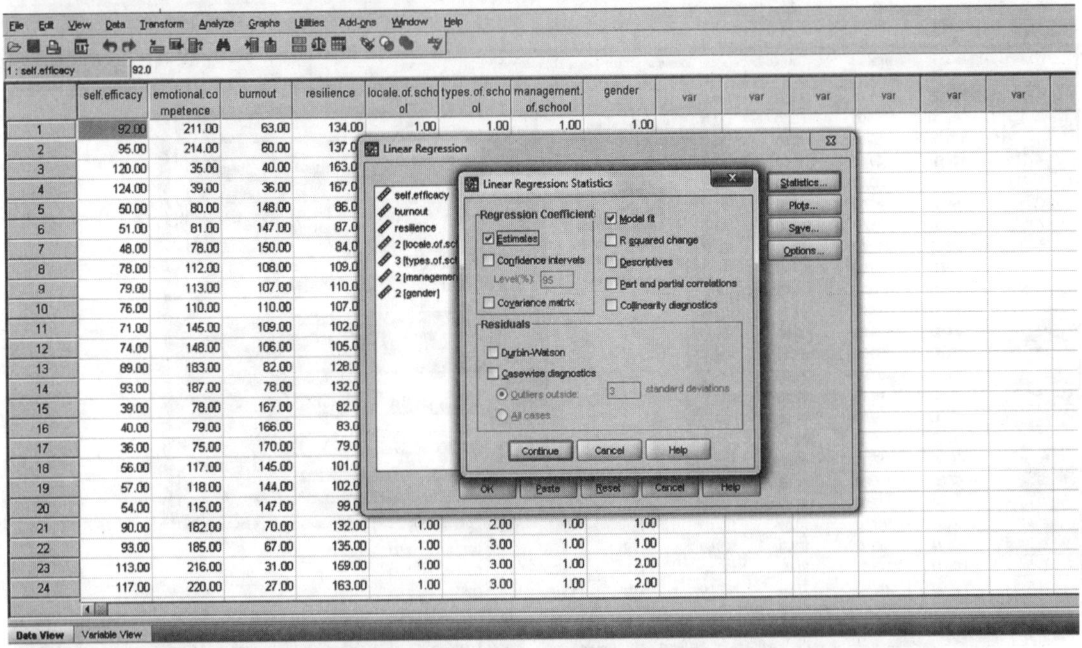

389. Highlight "**R Squared Change**" to get the following screen.

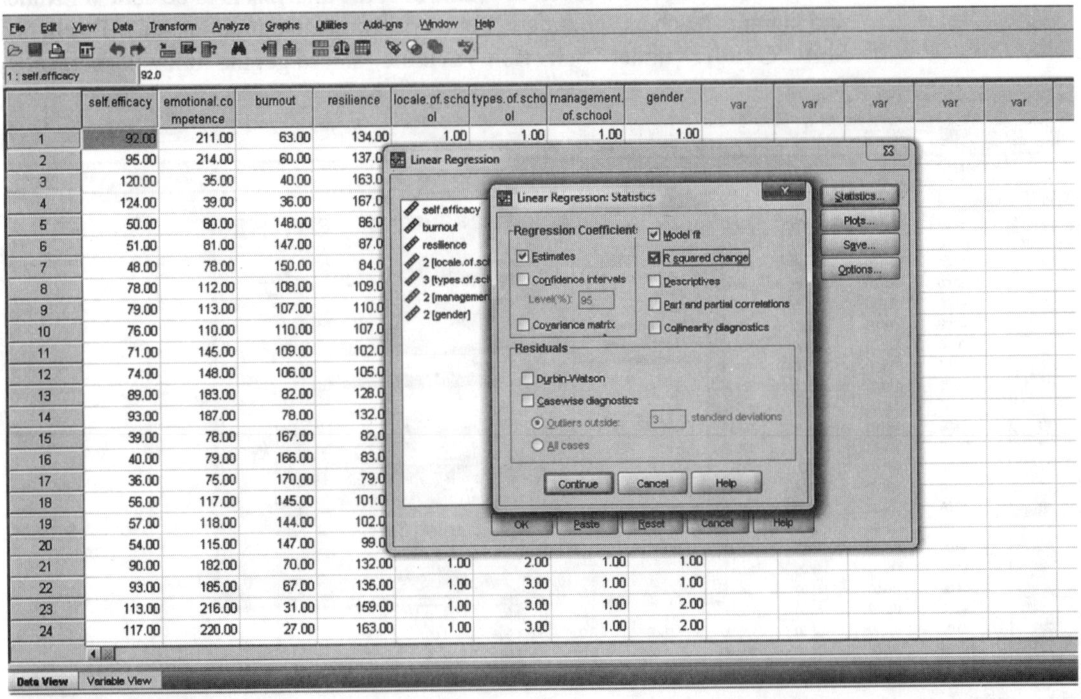

390. Click on "**Continue**" to get the following screen.

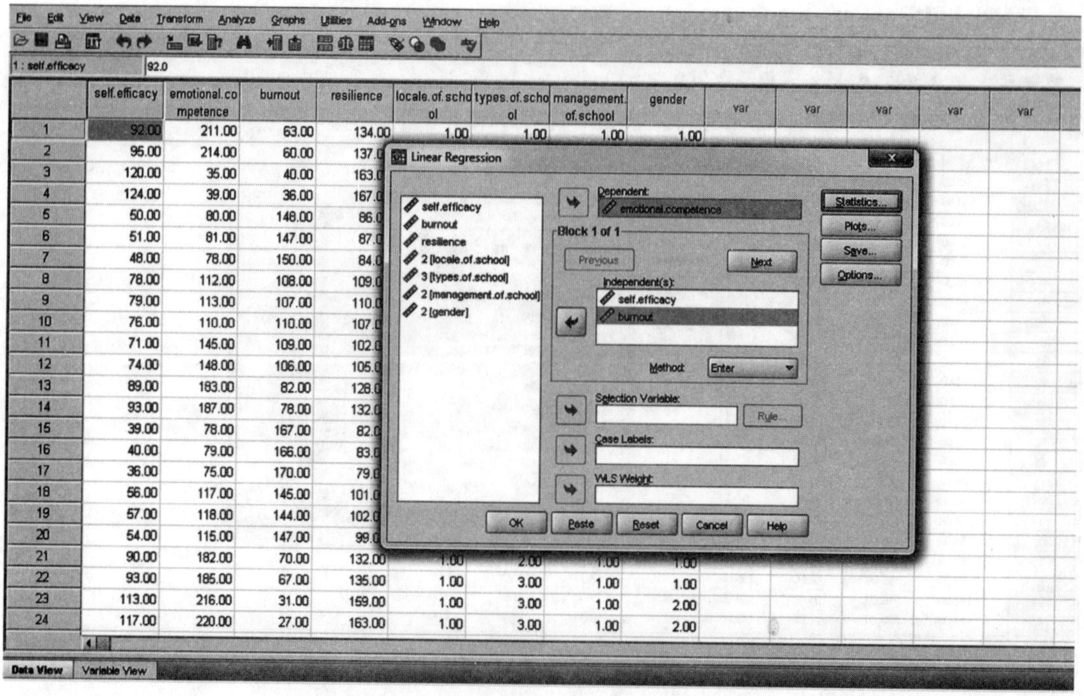

391. According to objective given in Frame 385, the analysis is to be done for Male and Female Teachers separately. Let us first do calculation for Male Teachers. Shift "**Gender**" under "**Selection Variable**" slot to get the following screen.

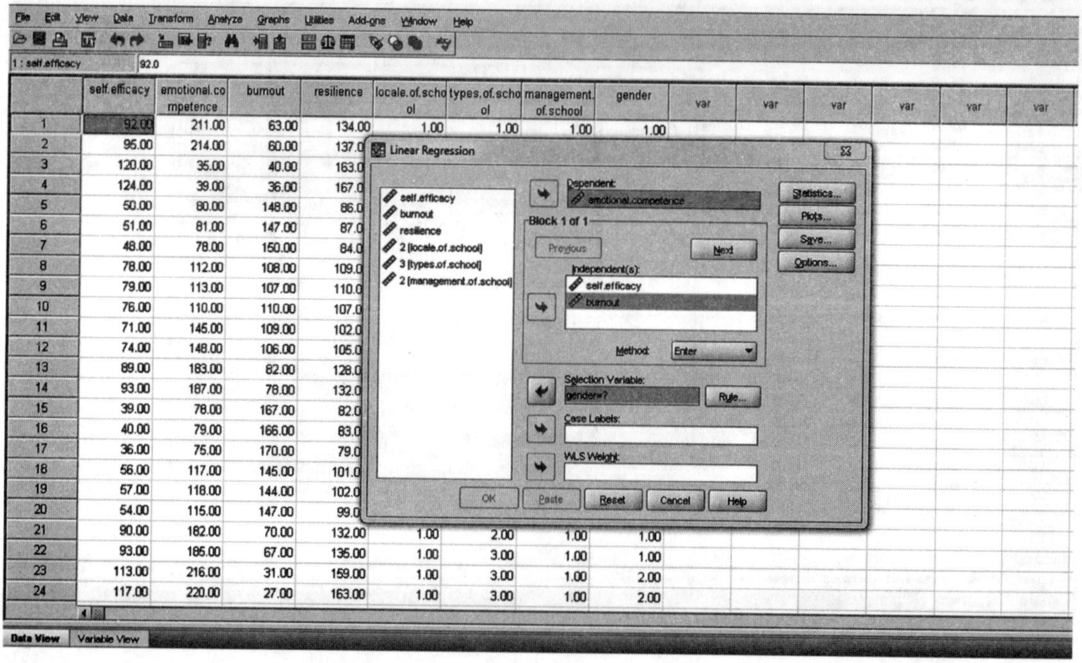

392. Click on "**Rule**" to get the following screen.

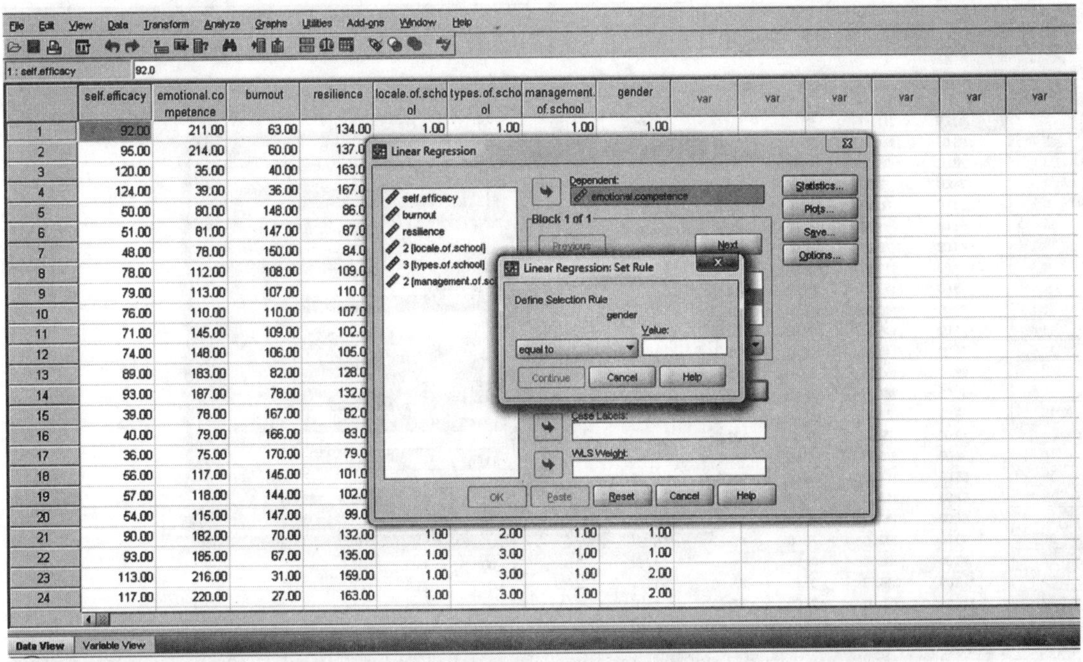

393. Male Teachers are represented by "**1**". Under "**Value**" slot type "**1**" to get the following screen.

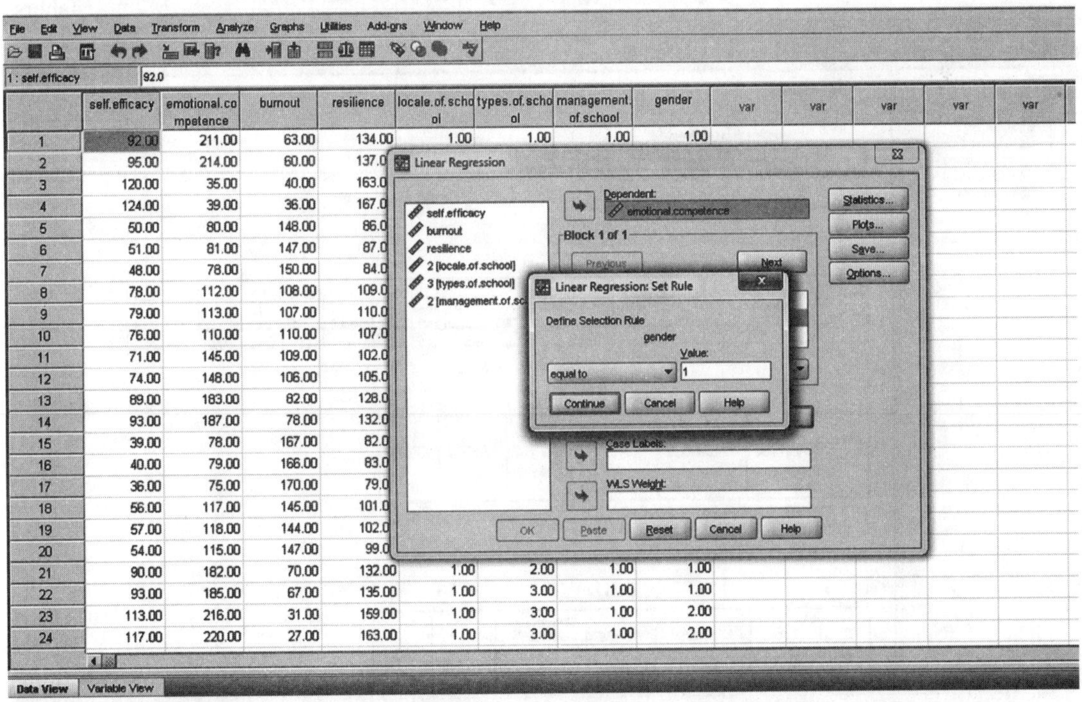

394. Click on "**Continue**" to get the following screen.

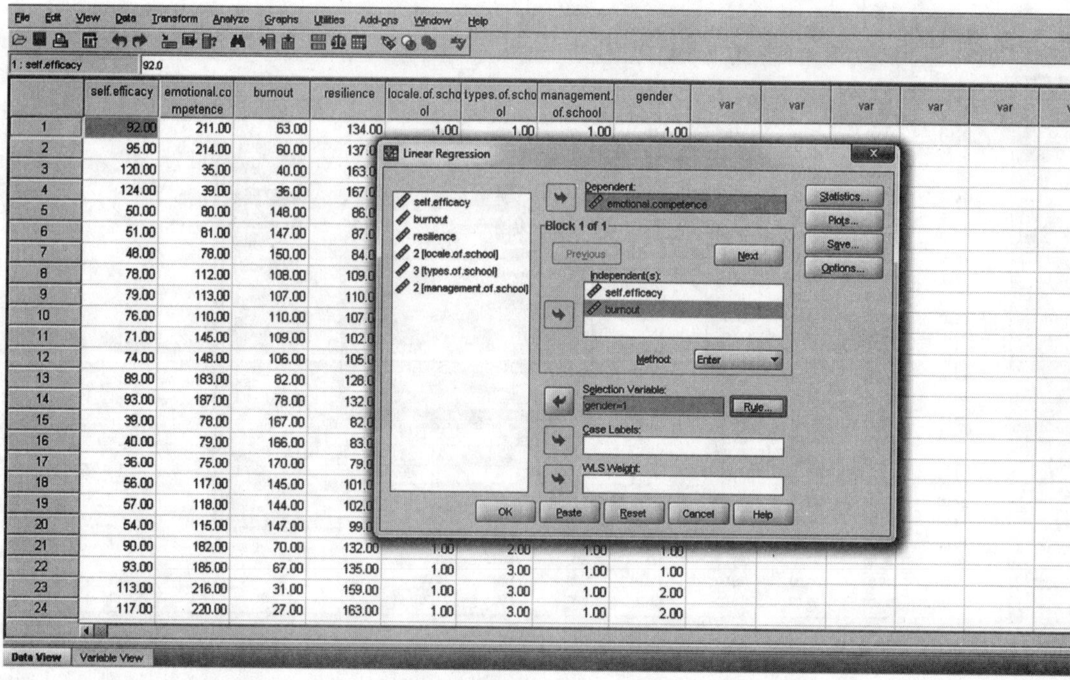

395. Click on "**OK**" to get the outputs of Multiple Correlation for Male Teachers which is part of Regression Analysis in SPSS Software.

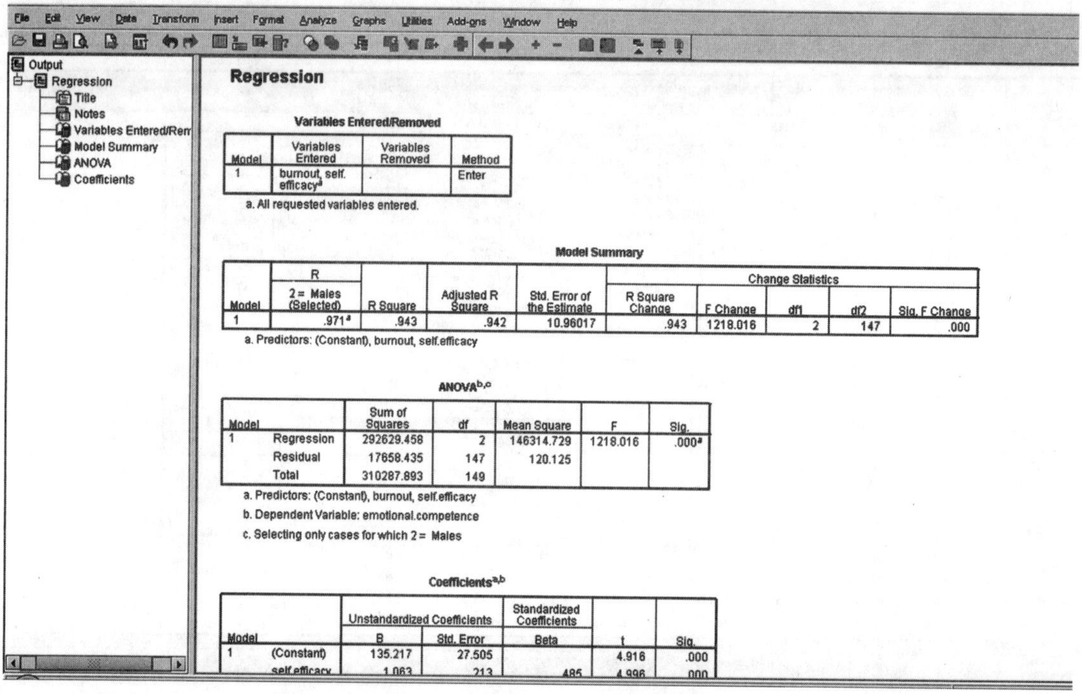

Regression

Variables Entered/Removed

Model	Variables Entered	Variables Removed	Method
1	burnout, self. efficacy[a]	.	Enter

a. All requested variables entered.

Model Summary

Model	R	R Square	Adjusted R Square	Std. Error of the Estimate	Change Statistics				
	2 = Males (Selected)				R Square Change	F Change	df1	df2	Sig. F Change
1	.971[a]	.943	.942	10.96017	.943	1218.016	2	147	.000

a. Predictors: (Constant), burnout, self.efficacy

ANOVA[b,c]

Model		Sum of Squares	df	Mean Square	F	Sig.
1	Regression	292629.458	2	146314.729	1218.016	.000[a]
	Residual	17658.435	147	120.125		
	Total	310287.893	149			

a. Predictors: (Constant), burnout, self.efficacy

b. Dependent Variable: emotional.competence

c. Selecting only cases for which 2 = Males

Coefficients[a,b]

Model		Unstandardized Coefficients B	Std. Error	Standardized Coefficients Beta	t	Sig.
1	(Constant)	135.217	27.505		4.916	.000
	self.efficacy	1.063	.213	.485	4.996	.000

396. To get the output for Female Teachers.
Click on "**Analyse**" then on "**Regression**" and finally on "**Linear**" to get the following screen.

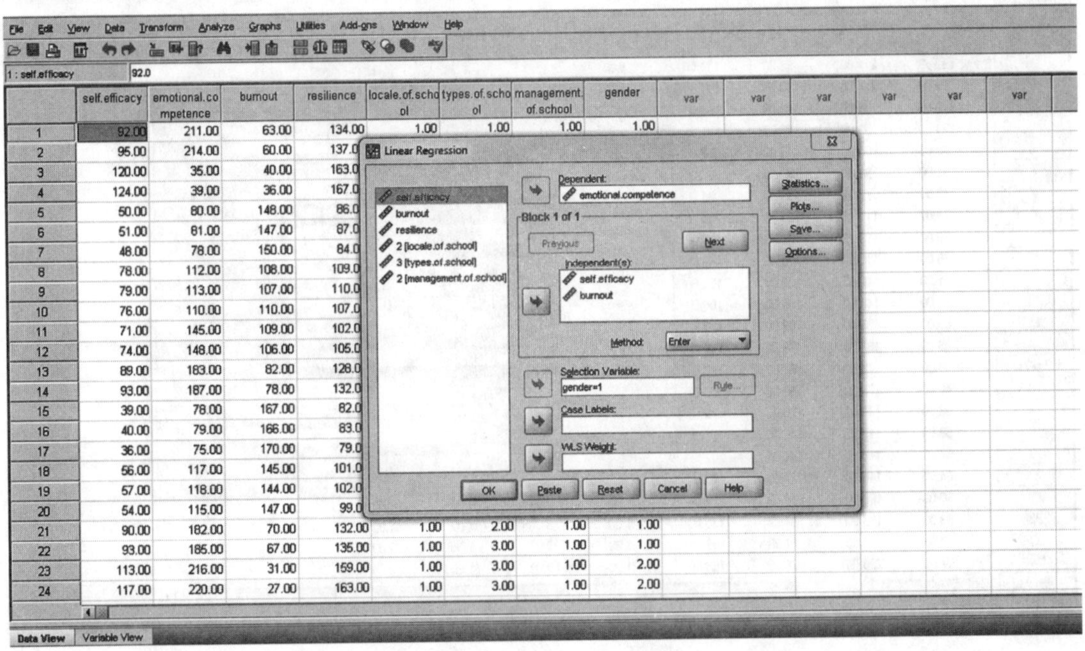

397. Female Teachers are represented by "**2**". Click on "**Select Variable**" to get the following screen.

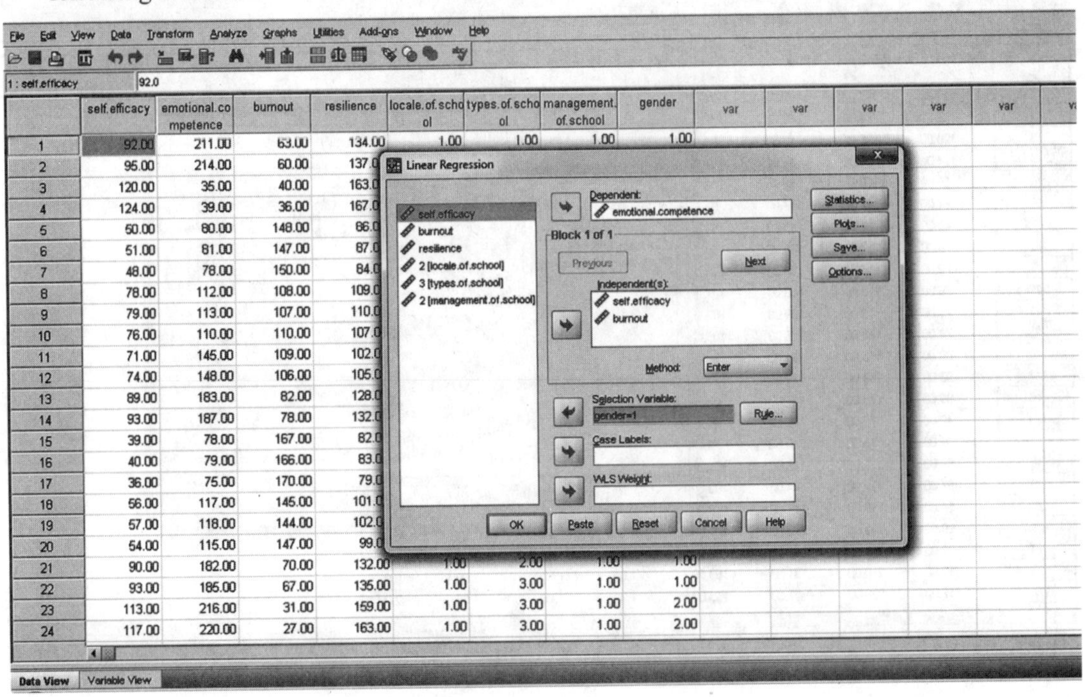

398. Click on "**Rule**" and type "2" under "**Value**" slot to get the following screen.

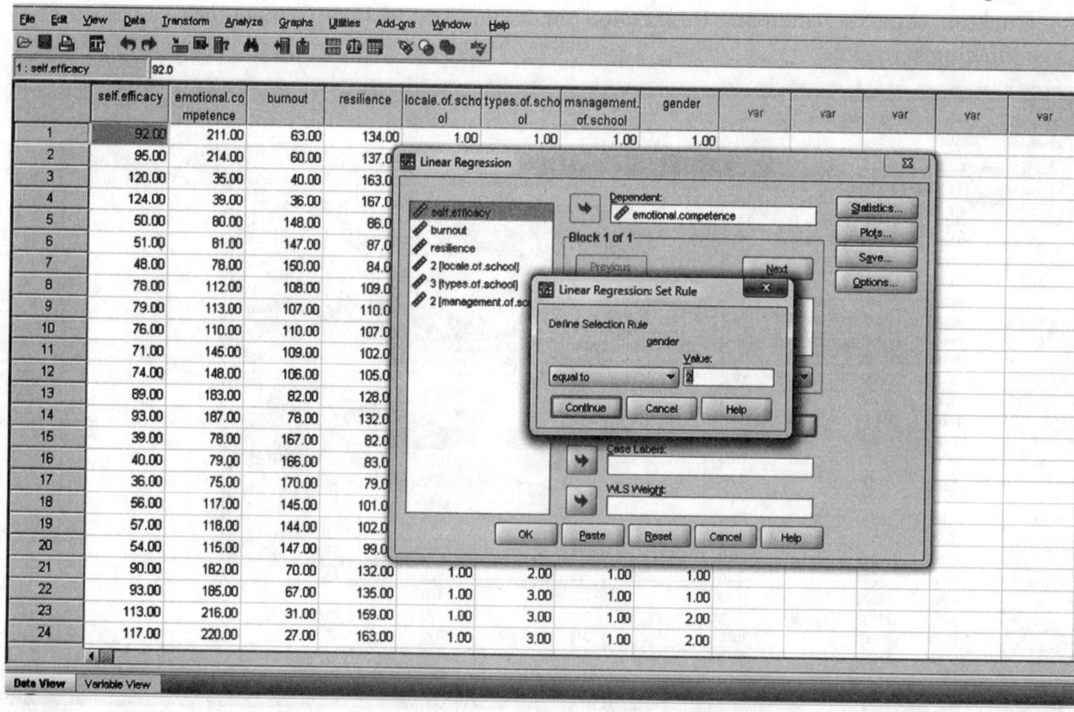

399. Click on "**Continue**" to get the following screen.

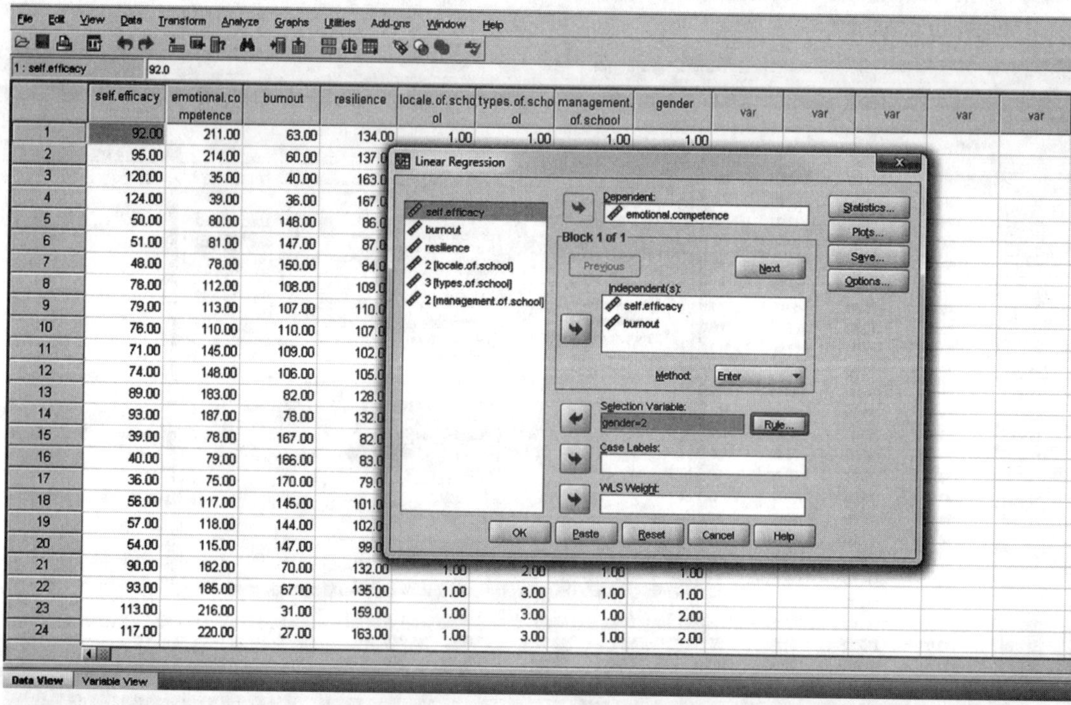

401. Click on "**OK**" to get the following outputs of Multiple Correlation for Female Teachers which is part of Regression Analysis in SPSS Software.

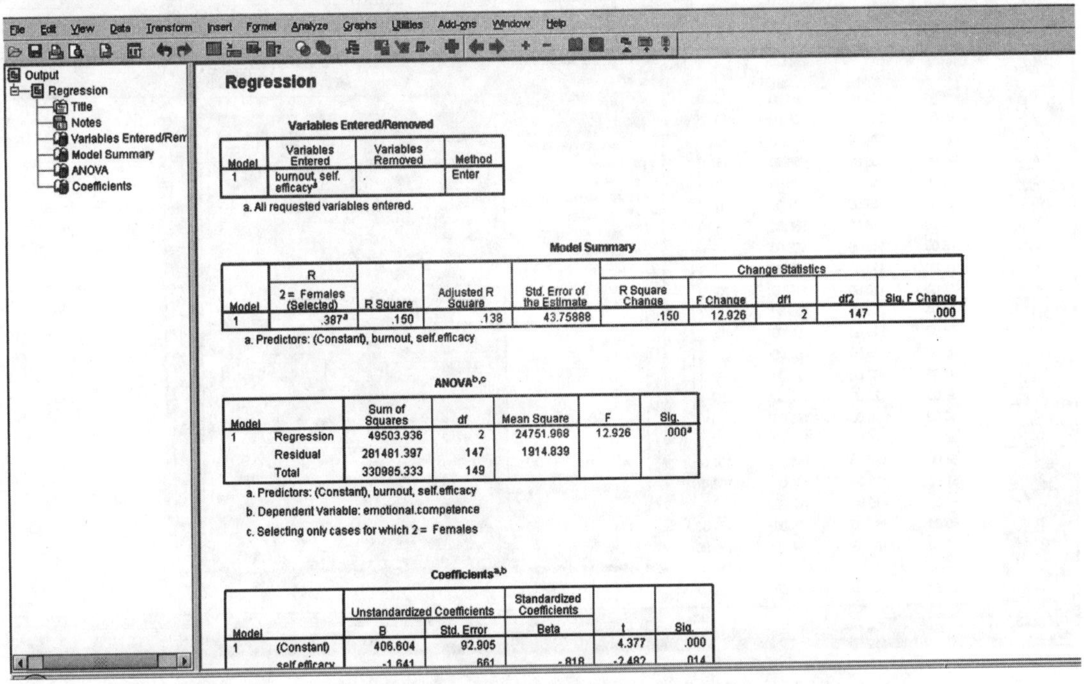

402. Another way to select cases is by clicking on "**Data**" icon and brings curser to "**Select Cases**" and click to get the following screen.

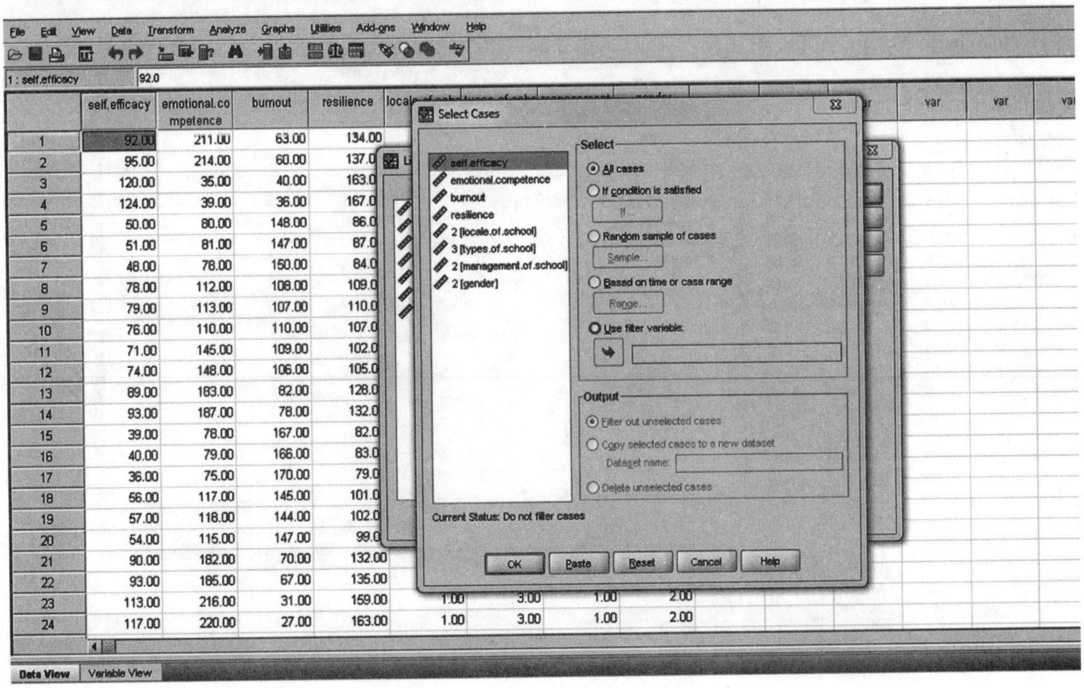

403. Highlight "**If condition is satisfied**" to get the following screen.

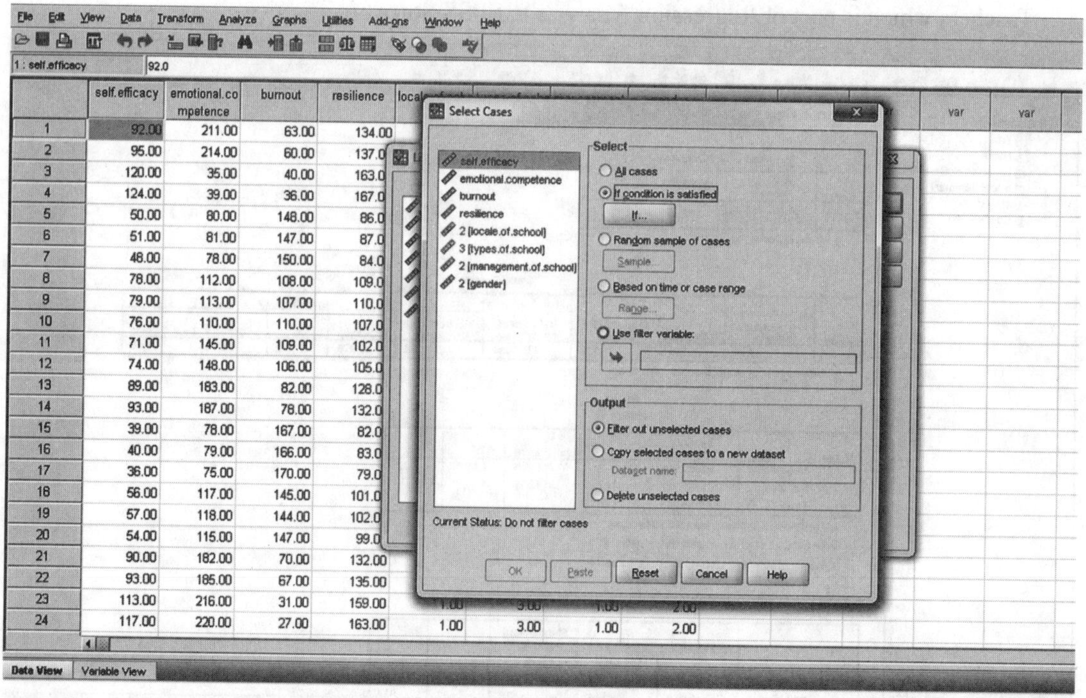

404. Click on "**If...**" to get the following screen.

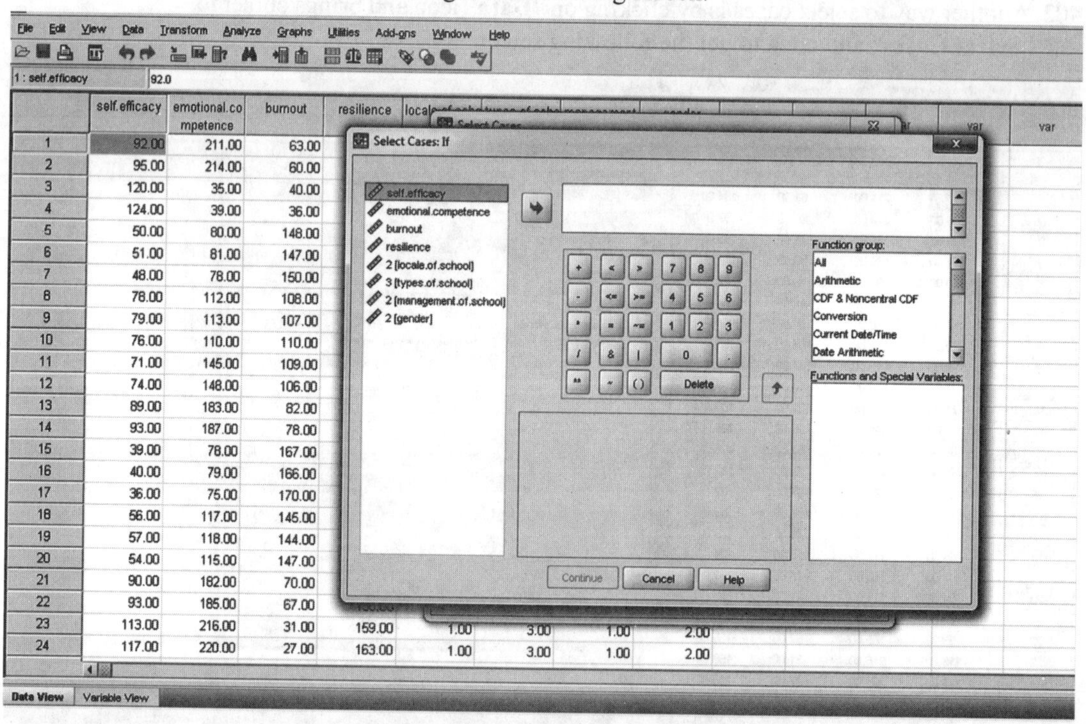

405. Shift "**Gender**" to the right hand slot and put "**=**" sign and type "**1**" to get the following screen.

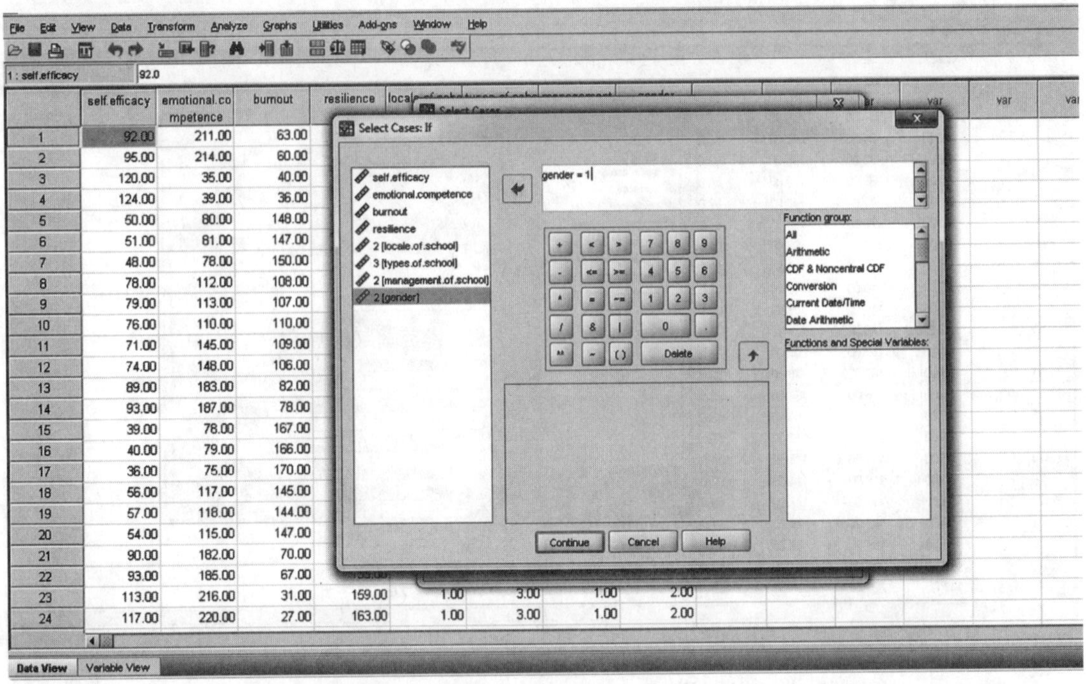

406. Click on "**Continue**" to get the following screen.

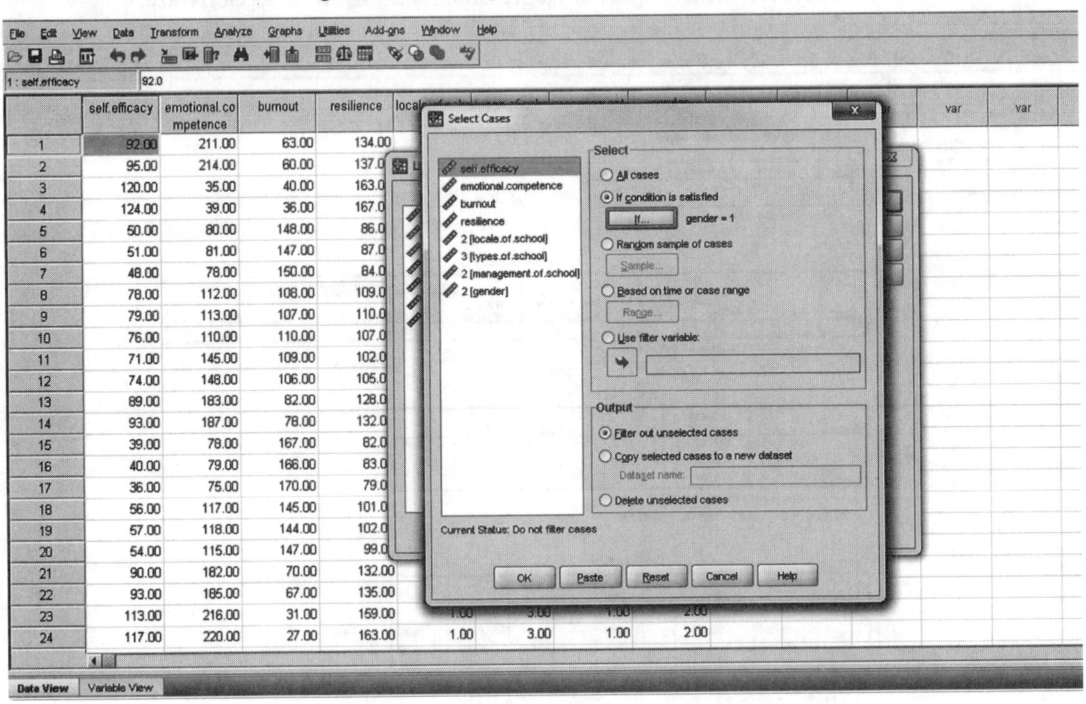

407. Click "**OK**" to get the following screen.

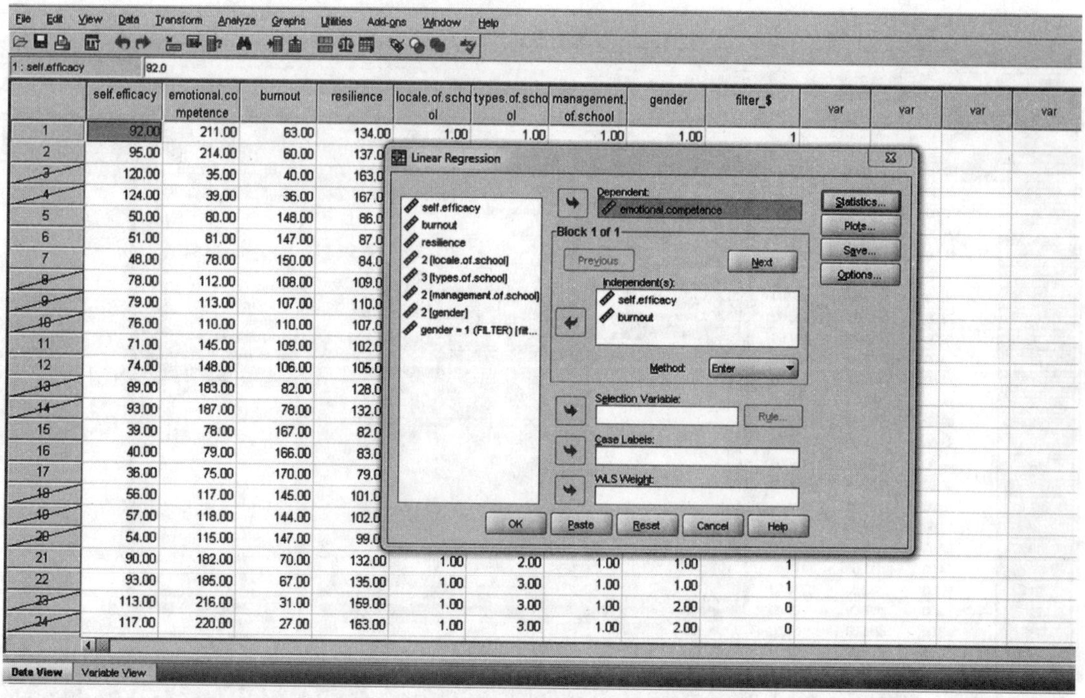

408. Click on "**OK**" to get the following Outputs of Multiple Correlation for Male Teachers which is part of Regression Analysis in SPSS Software.

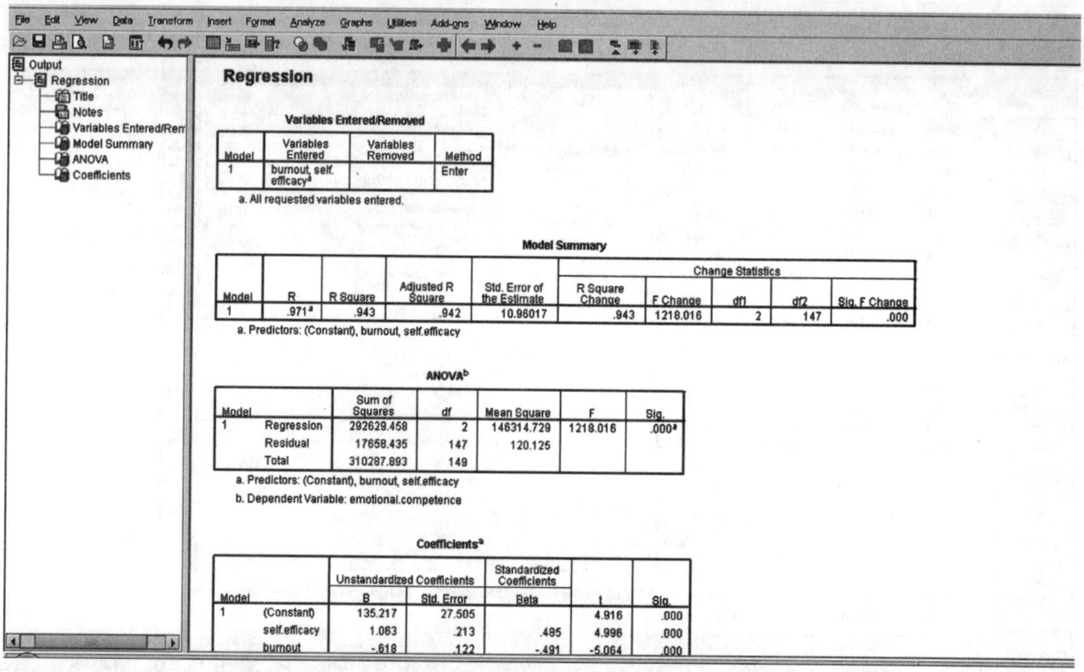

Regression

Variables Entered/Removed

Model	Variables Entered	Variables Removed	Method
1	burnout, self. efficacy[a]	.	Enter

a. All requested variables entered.

Model Summary

Model	R	R Square	Adjusted R Square	Std. Error of the Estimate	Change Statistics: R Square Change	F Change	df1	df2	Sig. F Change
1	.971[a]	.943	.942	10.96017	.943	1218.016	2	147	.000

a. Predictors: (Constant), burnout, self.efficacy

ANOVA[b]

Model		Sum of Squares	df	Mean Square	F	Sig.
1	Regression	292629.458	2	146314.729	1218.016	.000[a]
	Residual	17658.435	147	120.125		
	Total	310287.893	149			

a. Predictors: (Constant), burnout, self.efficacy

b. Dependent Variable: emotional.competence

Coefficients[a]

Model		Unstandardized Coefficients B	Std. Error	Standardized Coefficients Beta	t	Sig.
1	(Constant)	135.217	27.505		4.916	.000
	self.efficacy	1.063	.213	.485	4.996	.000
	burnout	-.618	.122	-.491	-5.064	.000

409. For analysing Female Teachers data, click on "**Data**" icon then on "**Select Cases**" to get the following screen.

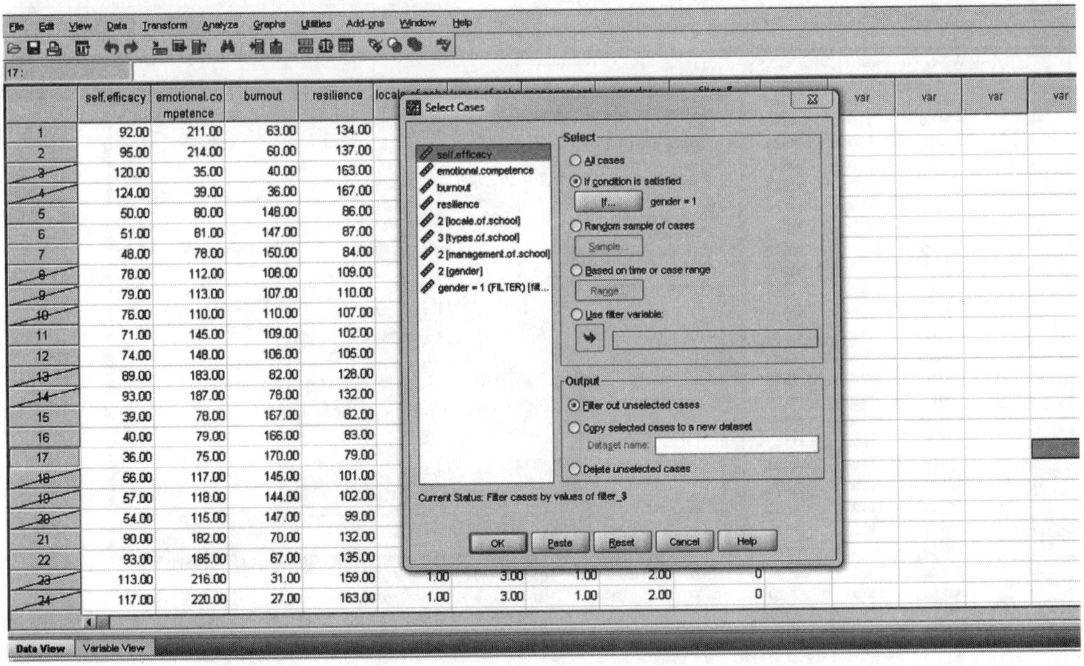

410. Click on "**If...**" to get the following screen.

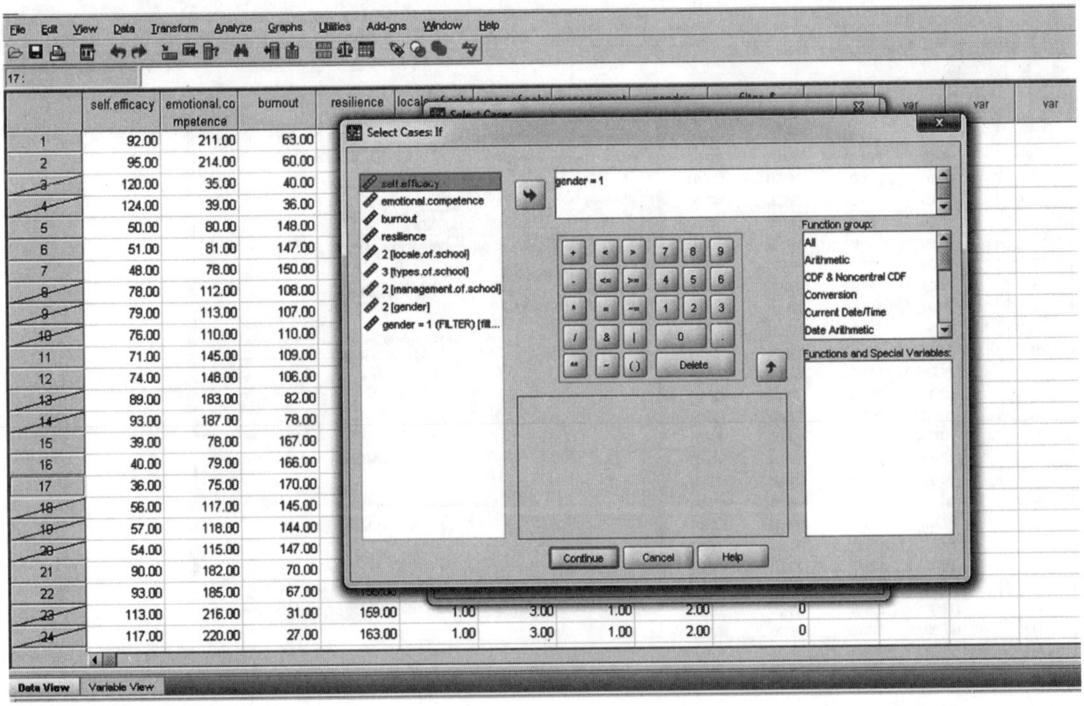

411. Female is coded as **2**, so replace "**1**" by "**2**" to get the following screen.

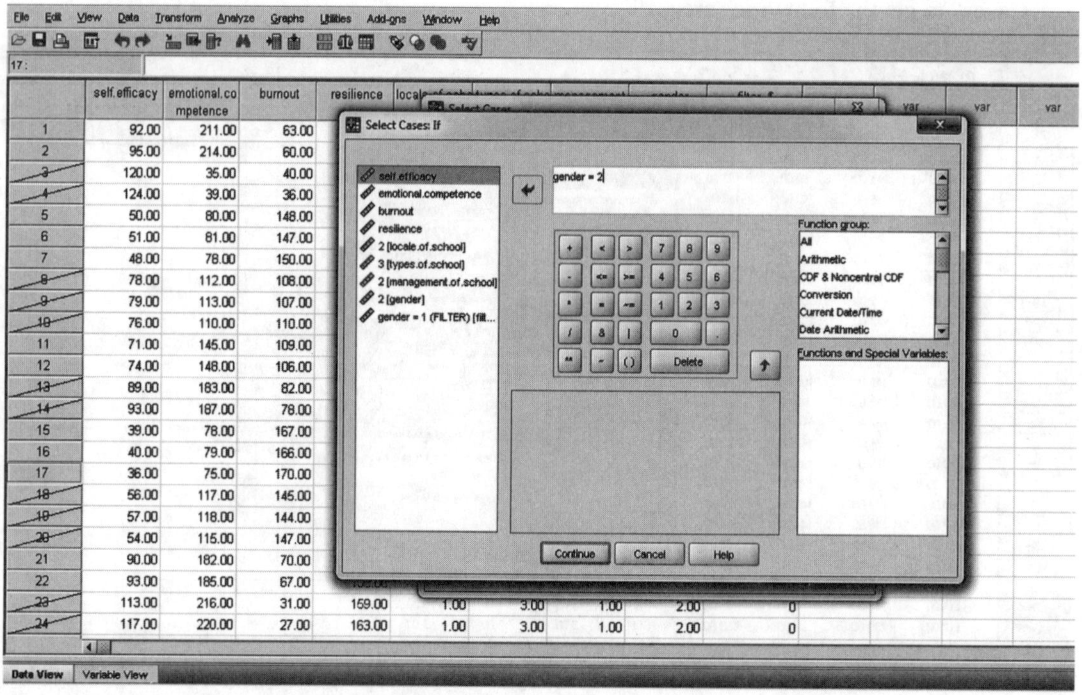

412. Click on "**Continue**" to get the following screen.

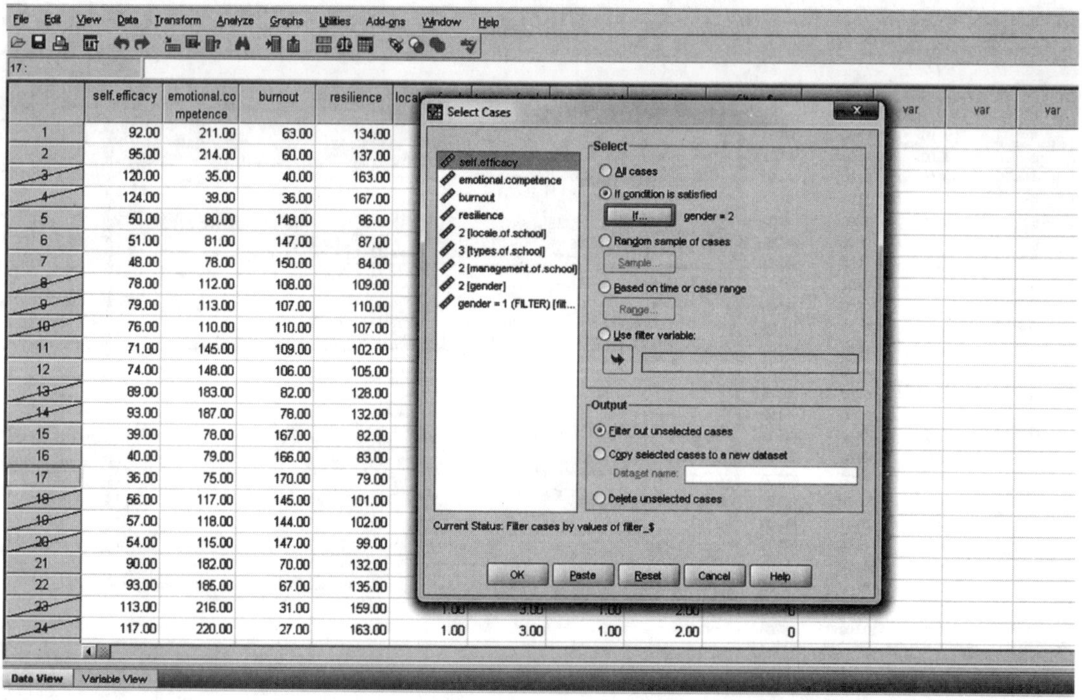

413. Click on "**OK**" to get the following screen.

414. Click on "**Analyse**" then on "**Regression**" and finally on "**Linear**" to get the following screen.

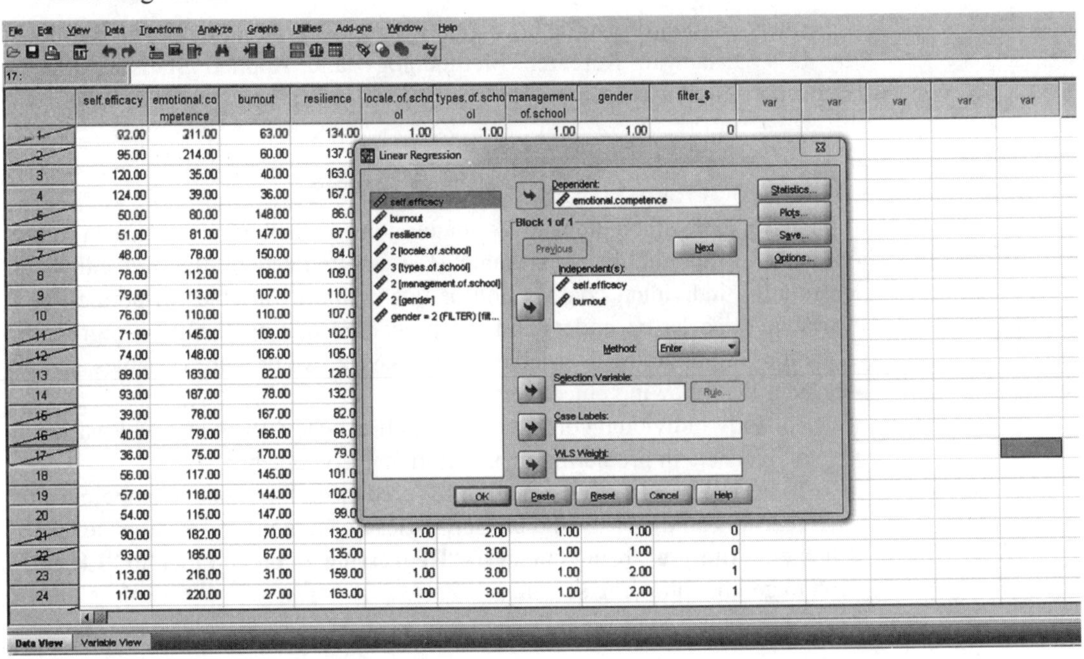

415. Click on "**OK**" to get the following Outputs of Multiple Correlation for Female Teachers which is part of Regression Analysis in SPSS Software.

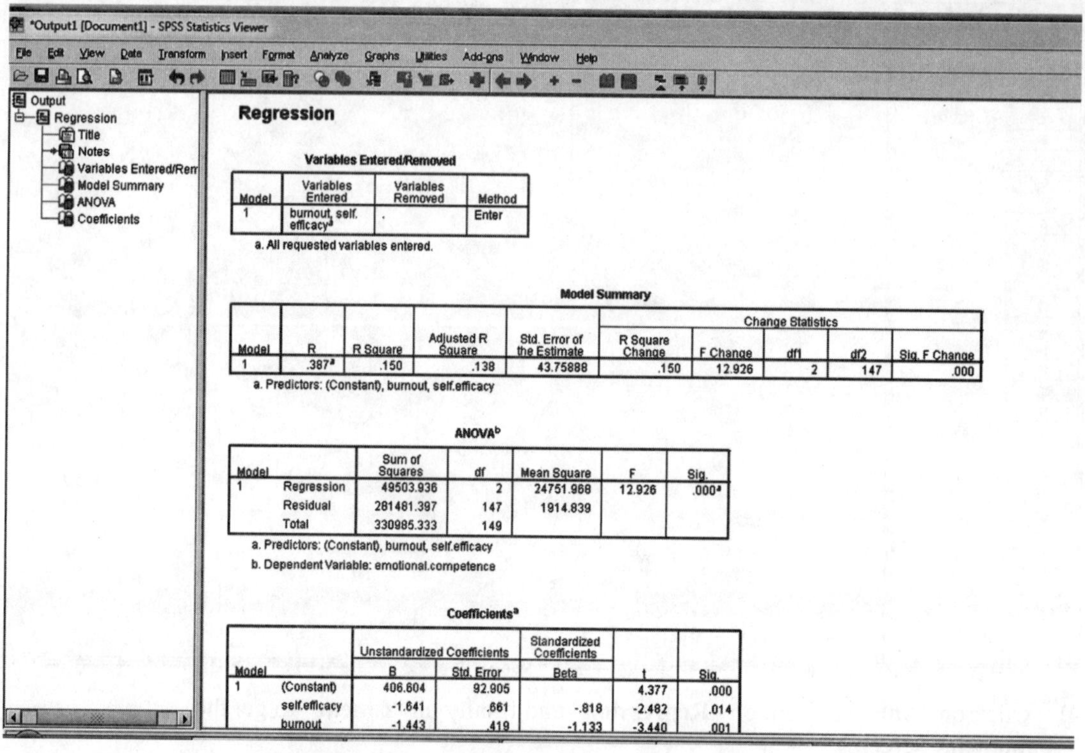

Regression

Variables Entered/Removed

Model	Variables Entered	Variables Removed	Method
1	burnout, self. efficacy[a]	.	Enter

a. All requested variables entered.

Model Summary

Model	R	R Square	Adjusted R Square	Std. Error of the Estimate	Change Statistics				
					R Square Change	F Change	df1	df2	Sig. F Change
1	.387[a]	.150	.138	43.75888	.150	12.926	2	147	.000

a. Predictors: (Constant), burnout, self.efficacy

ANOVA[b]

Model		Sum of Squares	df	Mean Square	F	Sig.
1	Regression	49503.936	2	24751.968	12.926	.000[a]
	Residual	281481.397	147	1914.839		
	Total	330985.333	149			

a. Predictors: (Constant), burnout, self.efficacy

b. Dependent Variable: emotional.competence

Coefficients[a]

Model		Unstandardized Coefficients		Standardized Coefficients	t	Sig.
		B	Std. Error	Beta		
1	(Constant)	406.604	92.905		4.377	.000
	self.efficacy	-1.641	.661	-.818	-2.482	.014
	burnout	-1.443	.419	-1.133	-3.440	.001

For interpretation of Multiple Correlation results, you may refer to the book by D.N.Sansanwal, Research Methodology and Applied Statistic, Shipra Publishers, Delhi, 2020.

Regression Analysis

416. You have understood how to computer joint contribution of two or more variables in predicting a variable. Let us understand the procedure of calculating individual contribution of two or more variables in predicting a variable. Also let us understand the procedure of establishing a regression equation for predicting a variable on the basis of two or more variables. Let us consider the following objectives:

A. To study individual contribution of Self-efficacy, Burnout and Resilience of Teachers in predicting their Emotional Competence.

B. To establish regression equation for predicting Emotional Competence of Teachers on the basis of their Self-efficacy, Burnout and Resilience.

Click on "**Analyse**", bring curser to "**Regression**" icon and then to "**Linear**" icon to get the following screen.

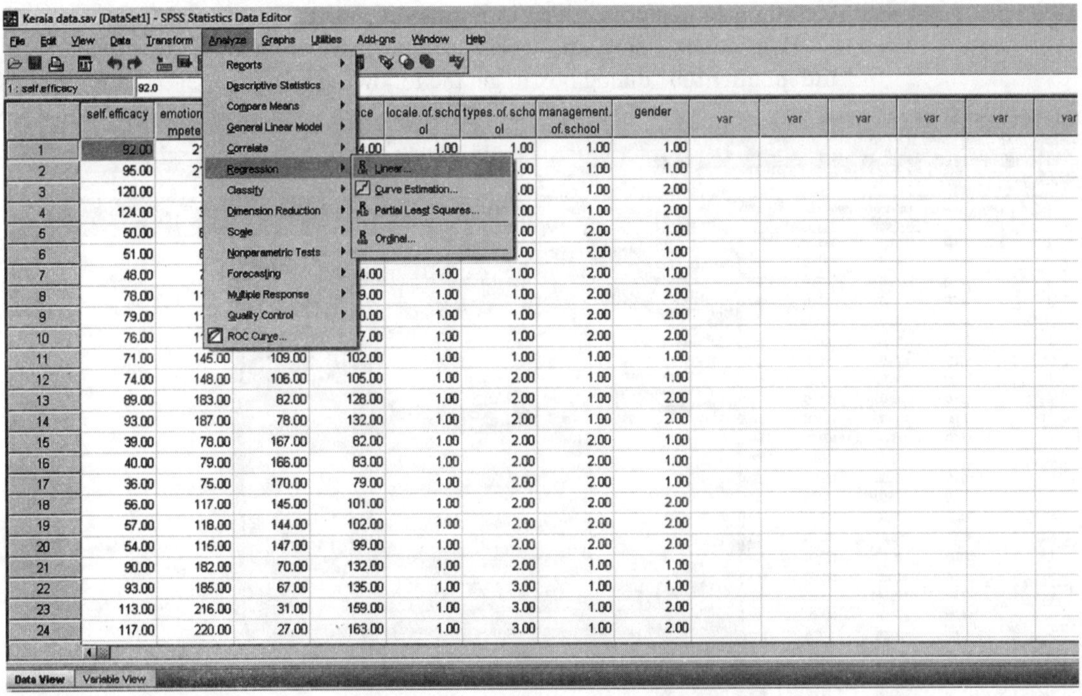

417. Click on "**Linear**" to get the following screen.

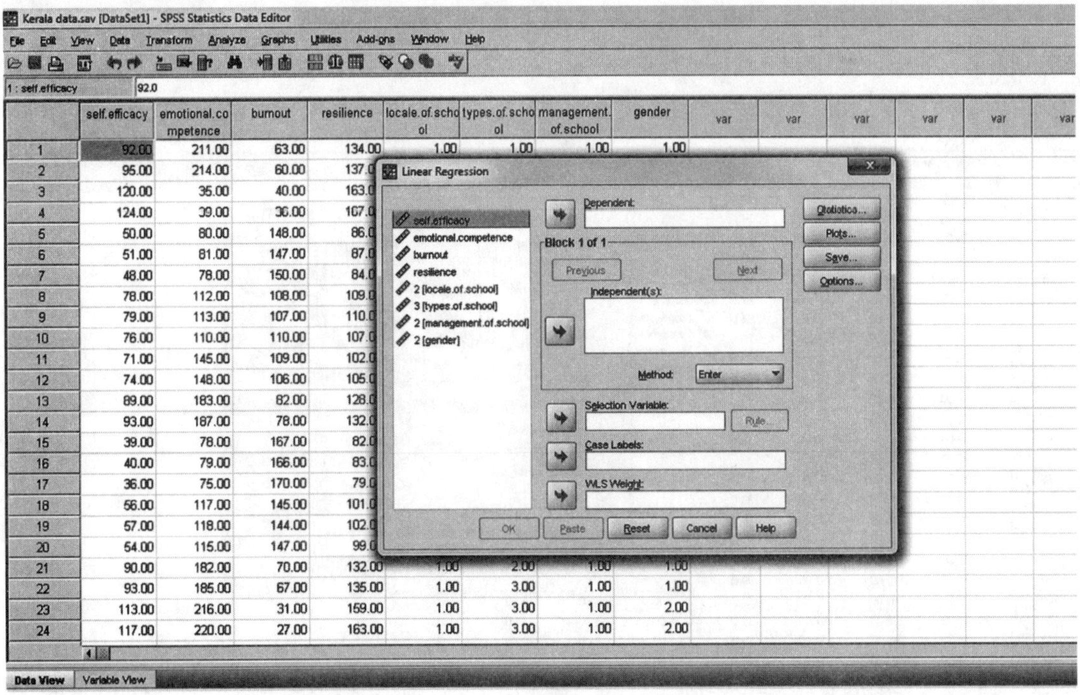

418. According to objective given in Frame 416, shift "**Emotional Competence**" to "**Dependent**" slot and "**Self-efficacy, Burnout** and **Resilience**" to "**Independent(s)**" dialog box to get the following screen.

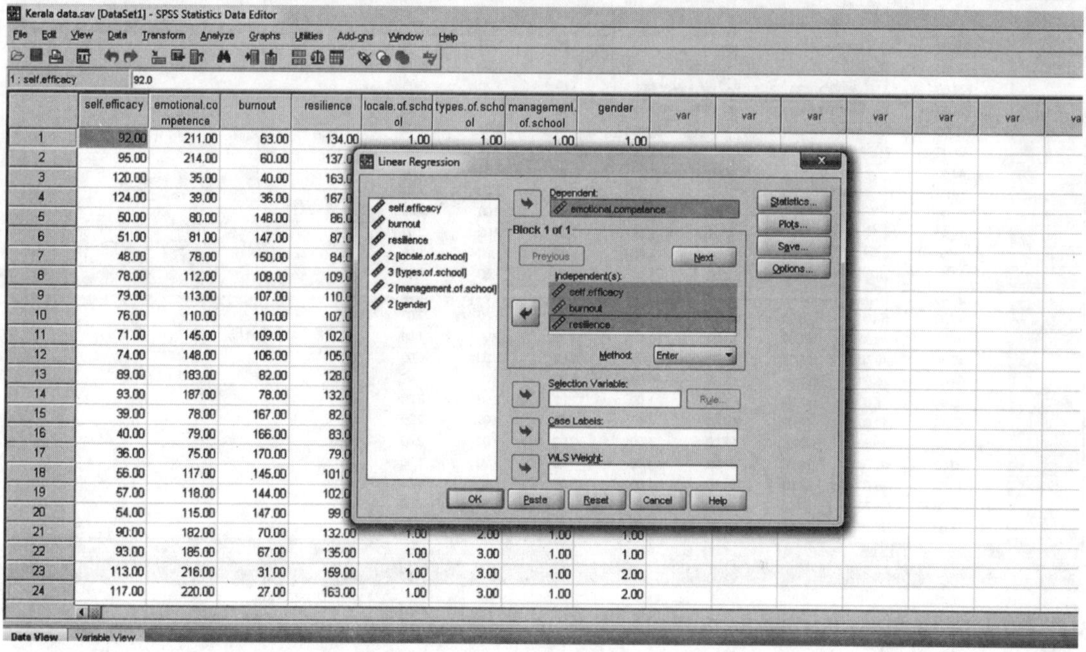

419. Click on "**Statistics**" button to get the following screen.

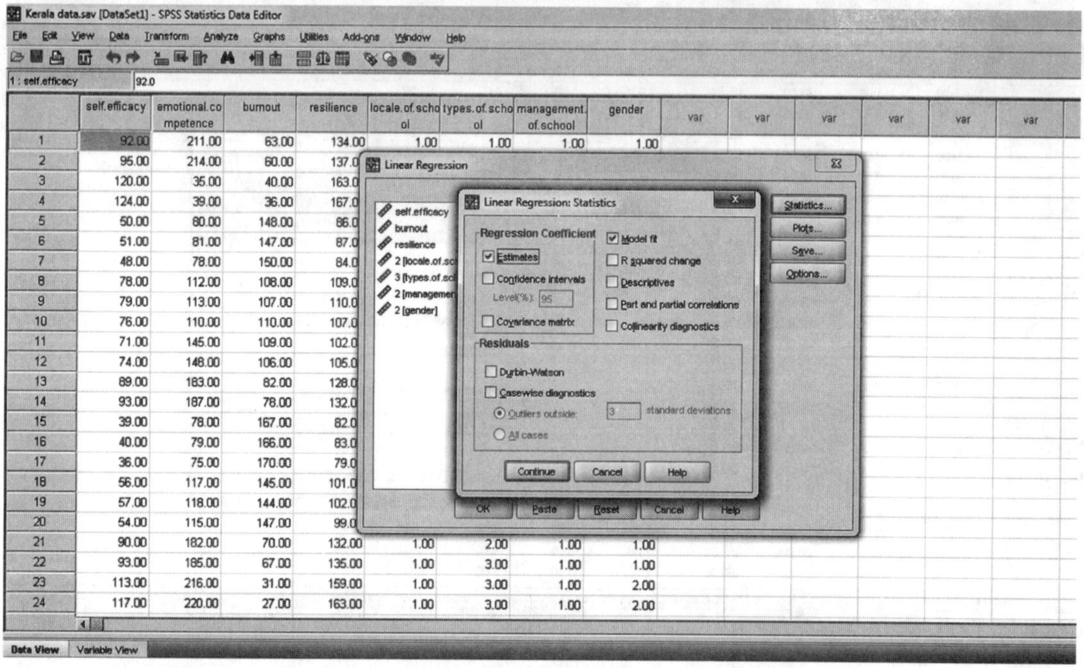

420. "**Estimates** and **Model Fit**" are pre-highlighted. Now highlight "**R Squared Change**", and "**Part and Partial Correlation**" to get the following screen.

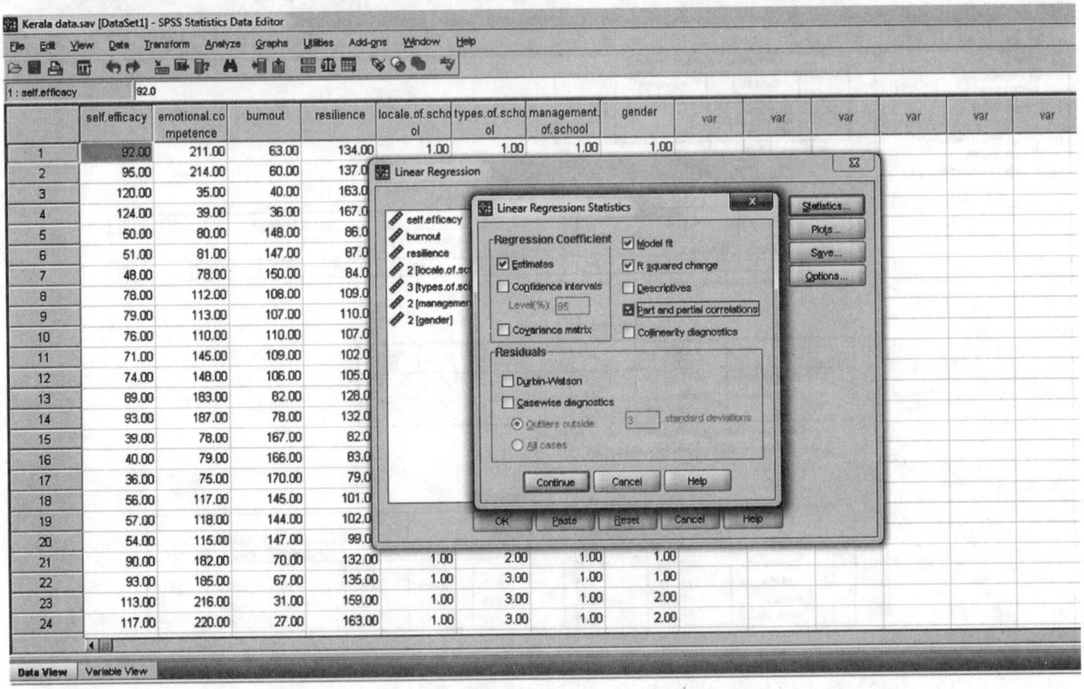

421. Click on "**Continue**" icon to get the following screen.

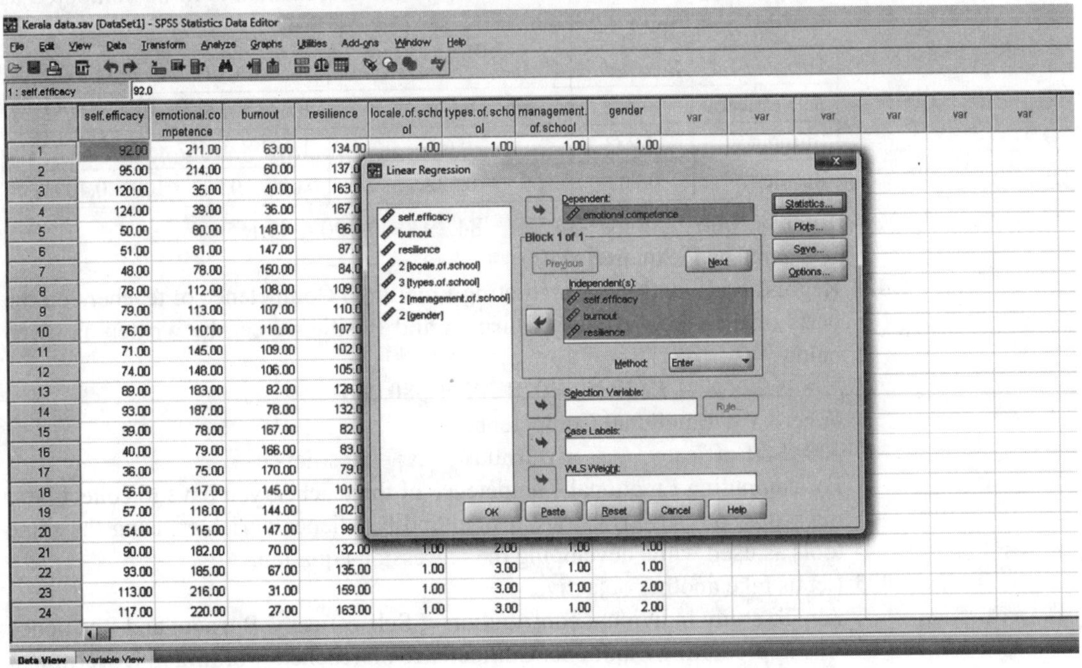

422. Click on "**OK**" to get the following outputs of Regression Analysis.

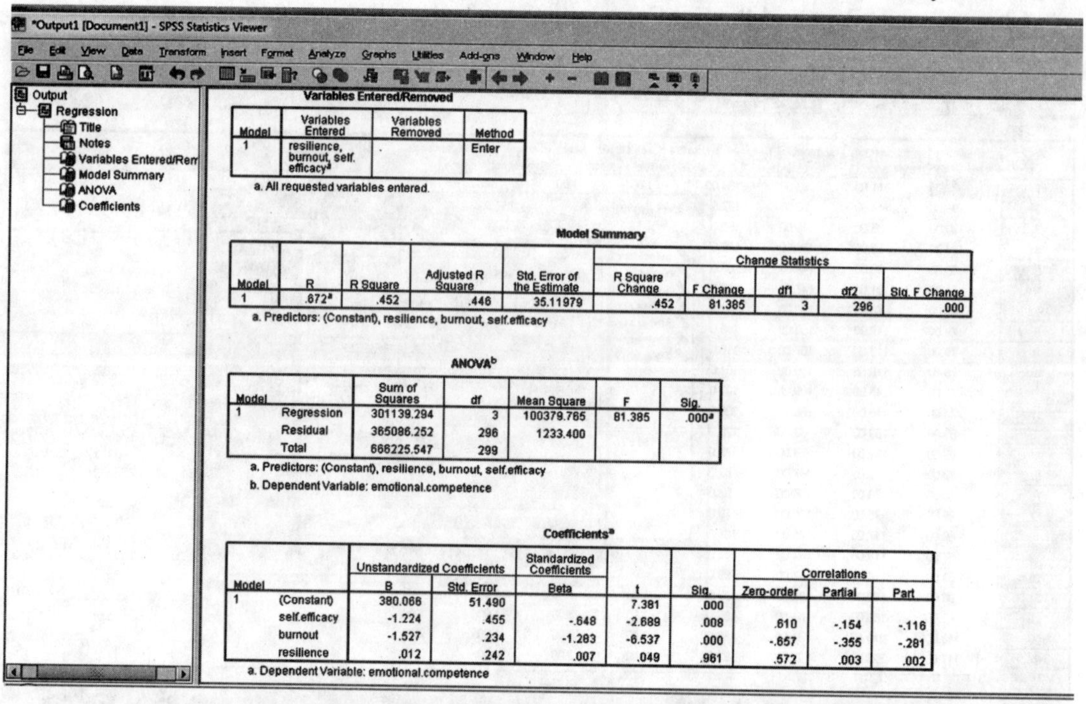

Variables Entered/Removed

Model	Variables Entered	Variables Removed	Method
1	resilience, burnout, self.efficacy[a]	.	Enter

a. All requested variables entered.

Model Summary

Model	R	R Square	Adjusted R Square	Std. Error of the Estimate	Change Statistics: R Square Change	F Change	df1	df2	Sig. F Change
1	.672[a]	.452	.446	35.11979	.452	81.385	3	296	.000

a. Predictors: (Constant), resilience, burnout, self.efficacy

ANOVA[b]

Model		Sum of Squares	df	Mean Square	F	Sig.
1	Regression	301139.294	3	100379.765	81.385	.000[a]
	Residual	365086.252	296	1233.400		
	Total	666225.547	299			

a. Predictors: (Constant), resilience, burnout, self.efficacy
b. Dependent Variable: emotional.competence

Coefficients[a]

Model		Unstandardized Coefficients B	Std. Error	Standardized Coefficients Beta	t	Sig.	Correlations Zero-order	Partial	Part
1	(Constant)	380.066	51.490		7.381	.000			
	self.efficacy	-1.224	.455	-.648	-2.689	.008	.610	-.154	-.116
	burnout	-1.527	.234	-1.283	-6.537	.000	-.657	-.355	-.281
	resilience	.012	.242	.007	.049	.961	.572	.003	.002

a. Dependent Variable: emotional.competence

423. Individual contribution of Self-efficacy, Burnout and Resilience of Teachers in predicting their Emotional Competence of Teachers is to be computed as shown in the following table.

Variable	*Beta value*	*Zero-order correlation*	*% of Contribution*
Self-efficacy	-0.648	0.610	-0.648 × 0.610 × 100 = -39.528%
Burnout	-1.283	-0.657	-1.283 × -0.657 × 100 = 84.293%
Resilience	0.007	0.572	0.007 × 0.572 × 100 = 0.400%

Total % contribution = -39.528 + 84.293 + 0.400 = 45.165
It is same as R Squared × 100

424. Regression Equation for predicting Emotional Competence of teachers on the basis of their Self-efficacy, Burnout and Resilience can be written as given below:

$Y = -1.224\ X_1 - 1.527\ X_2 + 0.012\ X_3 + 380.066$

Where Y = Emotional Competence

X_1 = Self-efficacy X_2 = Burnout X_3 = Resilience

For computing Emotional Competence of the teacher, you have to collect her / his scores on Self-efficacy, Burnout and Resilience variables using the same tools as used while developing the regression equation.

425. Let us take another objective:

A. To study individual contribution of Self-efficacy, Burnout and Resilience in predicting Emotional Competence of Teachers working in Government Schools and Private Schools separately.

B. To establish regression equation for predicting Emotional Competence on the basis of Self-efficacy, Burnout and Resilience of Teachers working in Government Schools and Private Schools separately.

You want to do analysis for Teachers working in Government Schools and Private Schools separately. Let us do analysis for Teachers working in Government Schools.

Shift "**Management of School**" to "**Selection Variable**" slot to get the following screen.

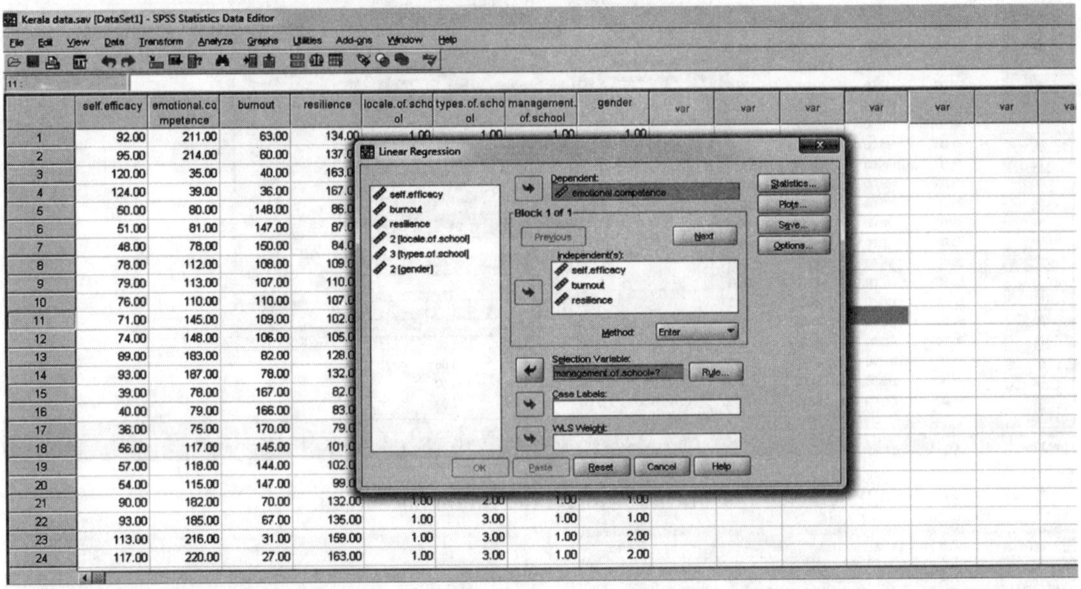

426. Click on "**Rule**" to get the following screen.

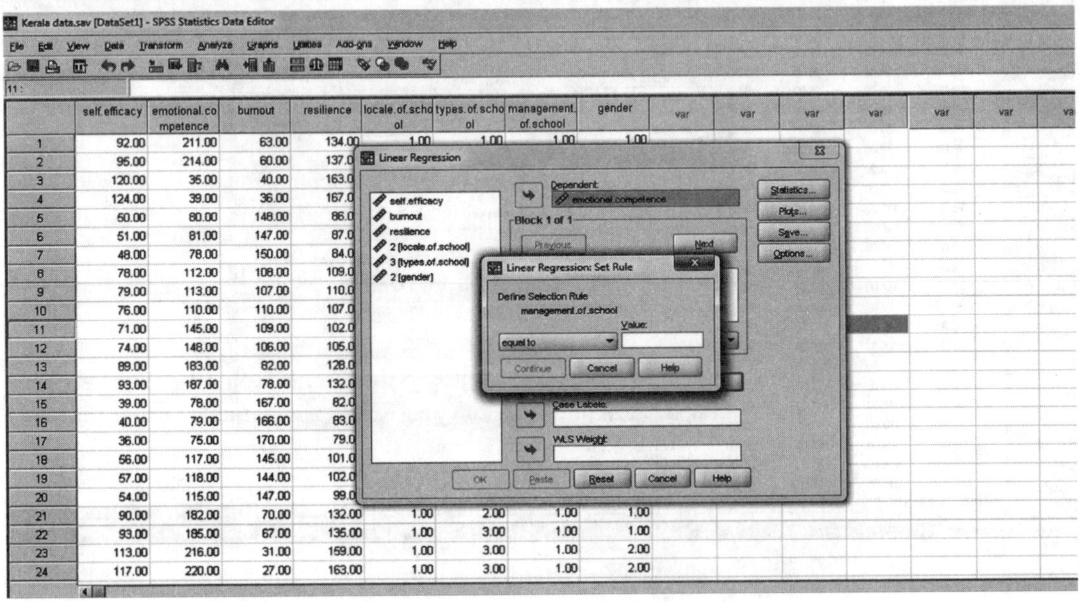

427. The code for Government schools is "1" so type "1" under "**Value**" slot to get the following screen.

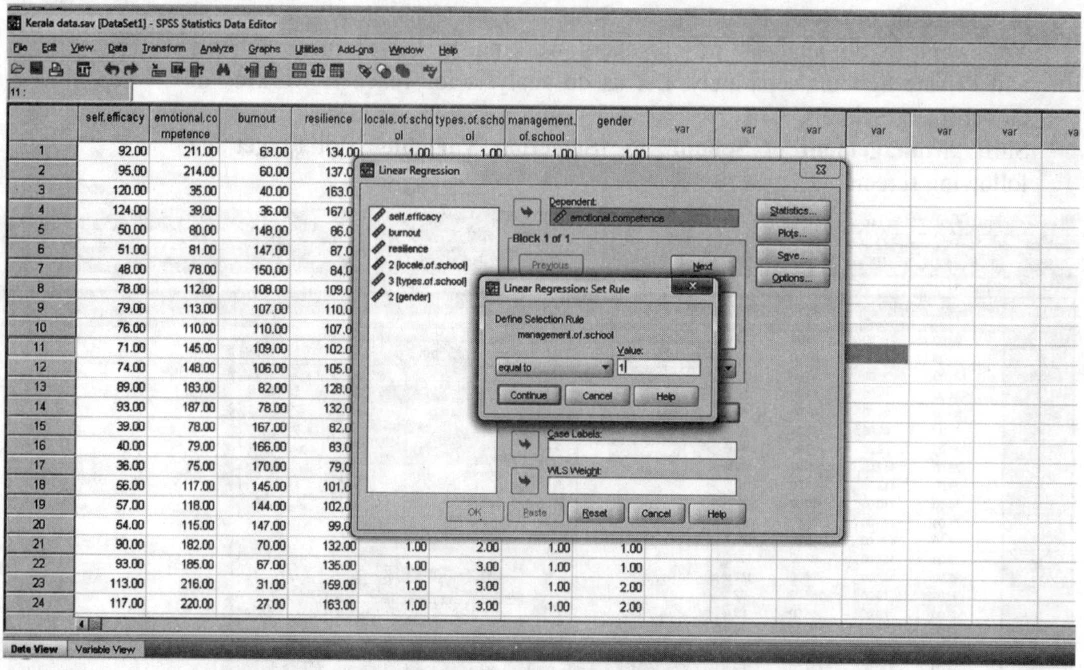

428. Click on "**Continue**" to get the following screen.

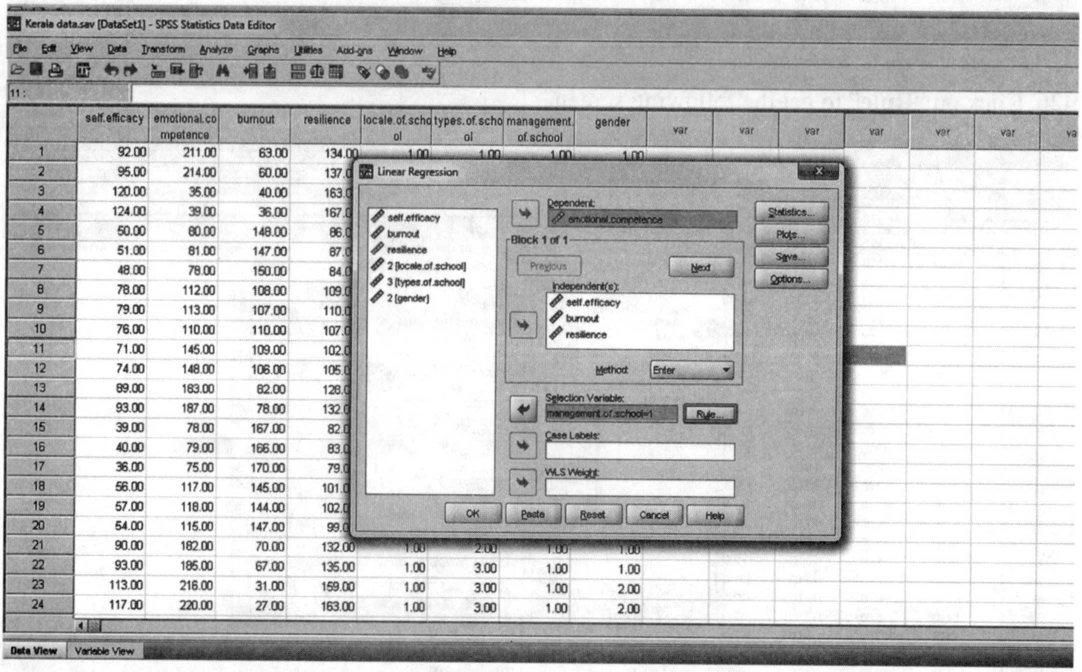

429. Click on "**Statistics**" and highlight "**R Squared Change**", and "**Part and Partial Correlations**" to get the following screen.

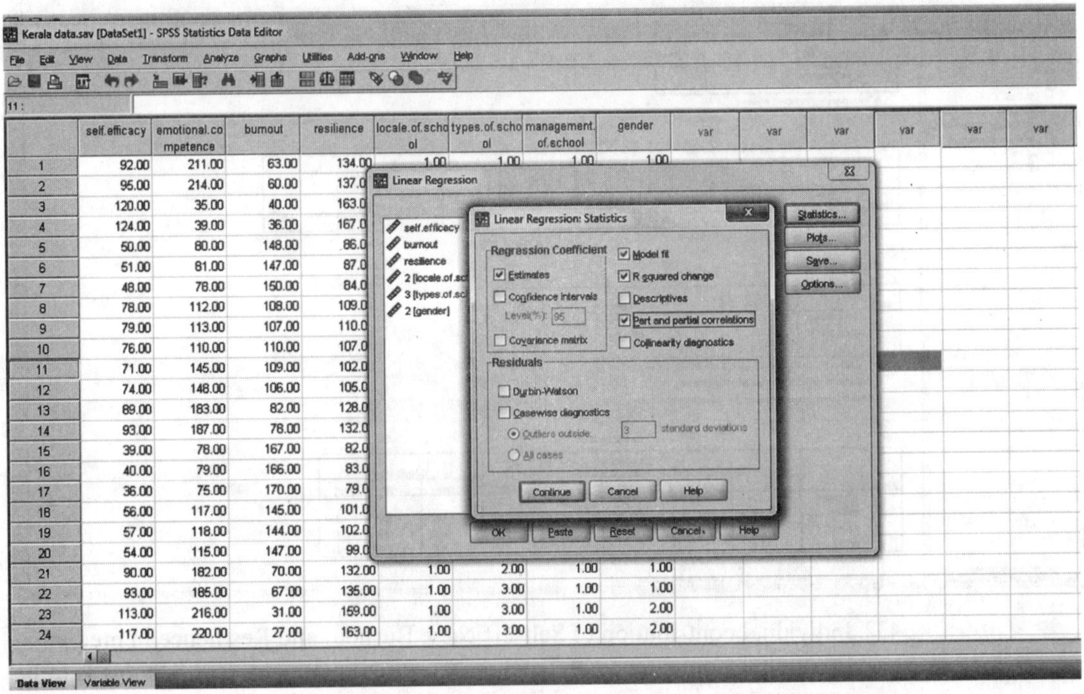

430. Click on "**Continue**" to get the following screen.

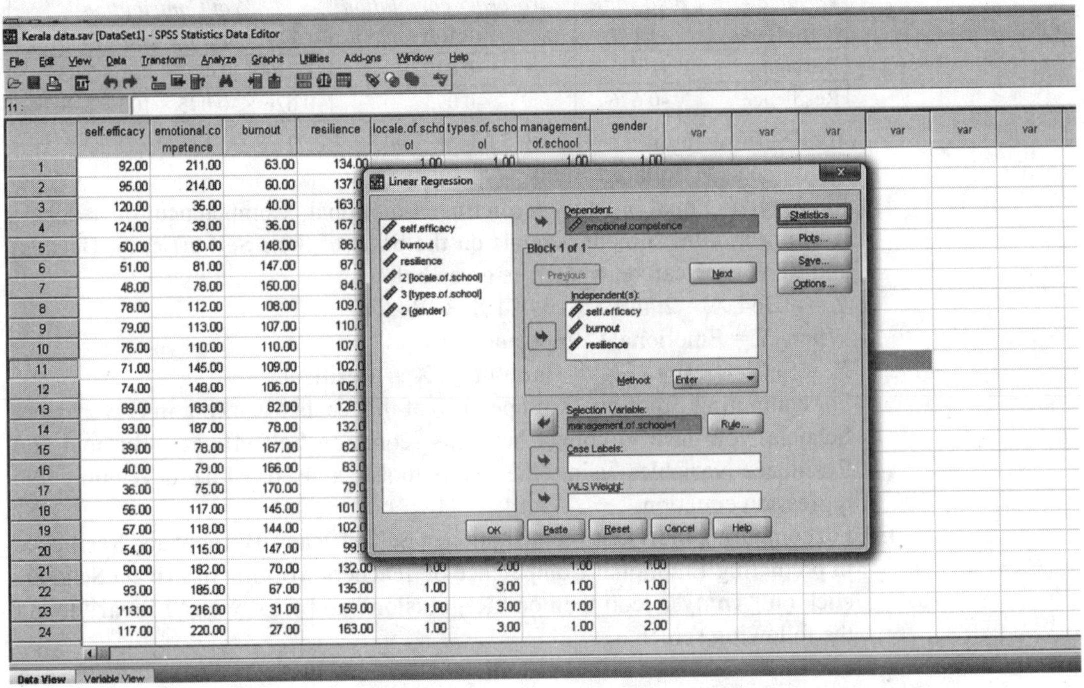

431. Click on "**OK**" to get the following outputs of Regression Analysis for Teachers working in Government Schools.

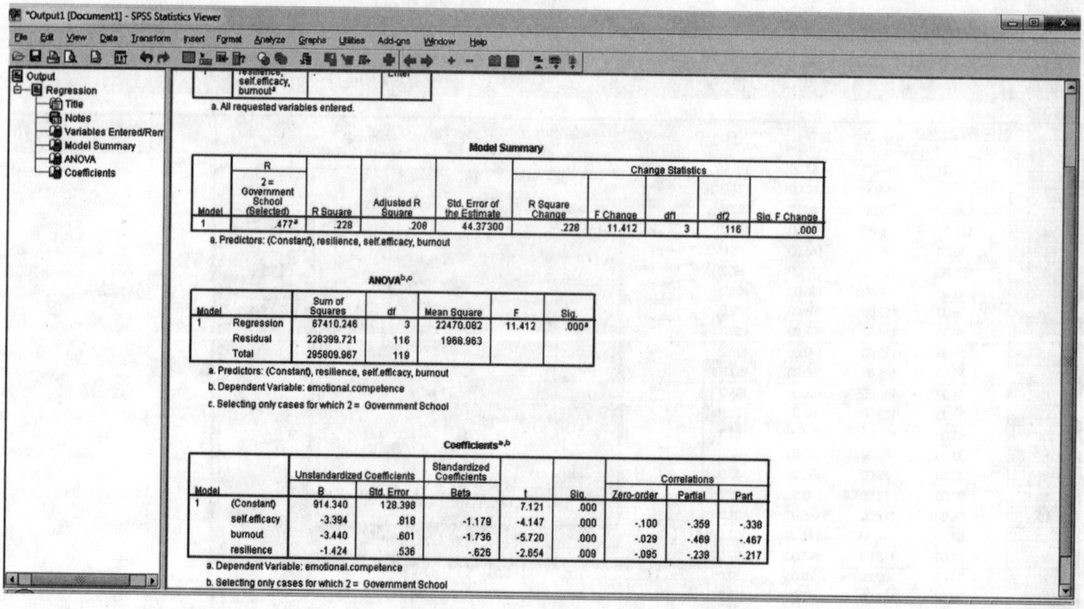

*Output1 [Document1] - SPSS Statistics Viewer

a. All requested variables entered.

Model Summary

Model	R 2 = Government School (Selected)	R Square	Adjusted R Square	Std. Error of the Estimate	Change Statistics: R Square Change	F Change	df1	df2	Sig. F Change
1	.477[a]	.228	.208	44.37300	.228	11.412	3	116	.000

a. Predictors: (Constant), resilience, self.efficacy, burnout

ANOVA[b,c]

Model		Sum of Squares	df	Mean Square	F	Sig.
1	Regression	67410.246	3	22470.082	11.412	.000[a]
	Residual	228399.721	116	1968.963		
	Total	295809.967	119			

a. Predictors: (Constant), resilience, self.efficacy, burnout
b. Dependent Variable: emotional.competence
c. Selecting only cases for which 2 = Government School

Coefficients[a,b]

Model		Unstandardized Coefficients B	Std. Error	Standardized Coefficients Beta	t	Sig.	Correlations Zero-order	Partial	Part
1	(Constant)	914.340	128.398		7.121	.000			
	self.efficacy	-3.394	.818	-1.179	-4.147	.000	-.100	-.359	-.338
	burnout	-3.440	.601	-1.736	-5.720	.000	-.029	-.469	-.467
	resilience	-1.424	.536	-.626	-2.654	.009	-.095	-.239	-.217

a. Dependent Variable: emotional.competence
b. Selecting only cases for which 2 = Government School

432. Individual contribution of Self-efficacy, Burnout and Resilience in predicting Emotional Competence of Teachers working in Government Schools is to be computed as shown in the following table.

Variable	*Beta value*	*Zero-order correlation*	*% of Contribution*
Self-efficacy	-1.179	-0.100	-1.179 × -0.100 × 100 = 11.79%
Burnout	-1.736	-0.029	-1.736 × -0.029 × 100 = 5.034%
Resilience	-0.626	-0.095	-0.626 × -0.095 × 100 = 5.947%

Total % contribution = 11.79 + 5.034 + 5.947 = 22.71
It is same as R Squared × 100

433. Regression Equation for predicting Emotional Competence of teachers working in Government Schools on the basis of their Self-efficacy, Burnout and Resilience can be written as given below:

$Y = -3.364\ X_1 - 2.440\ X_2 - 1.424\ X_3 + 914.240$

Where Y = Emotional Competence

X_1 = Self-efficacy X_2 = Burnout X_3 = Resilience

For computing Emotional Competence of the teacher working in Government Schools, you have to collect her / his scores on Self-efficacy, Burnout and Resilience variables using the same tools as used while developing the regression equation.

434. For computing individual contribution of Self-efficacy, Burnout and Resilience in predicting Emotional Competence of Teachers working in Private Schools, click on "**Analyse** icon then on "**Regression"** and finally on "**Linear**" to get the following screen.

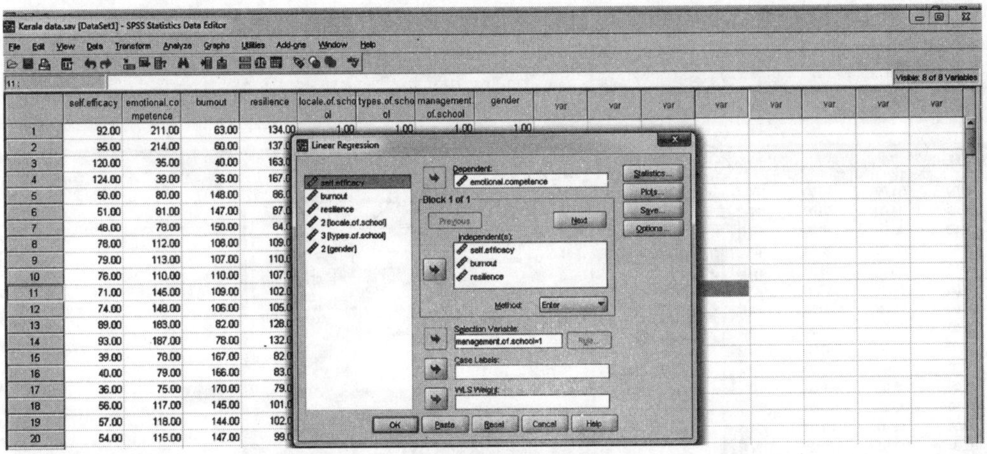

435. Click on "**Selection Variable**" slot to get the following screen

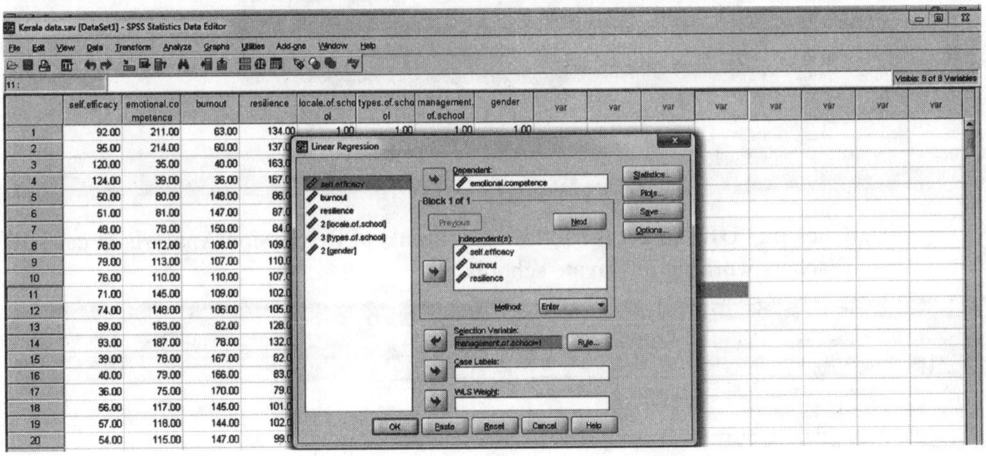

436. Click on "**Rule**" and type "**2**" in place of "**1**" in the "**Value**" slot to get the following screen.

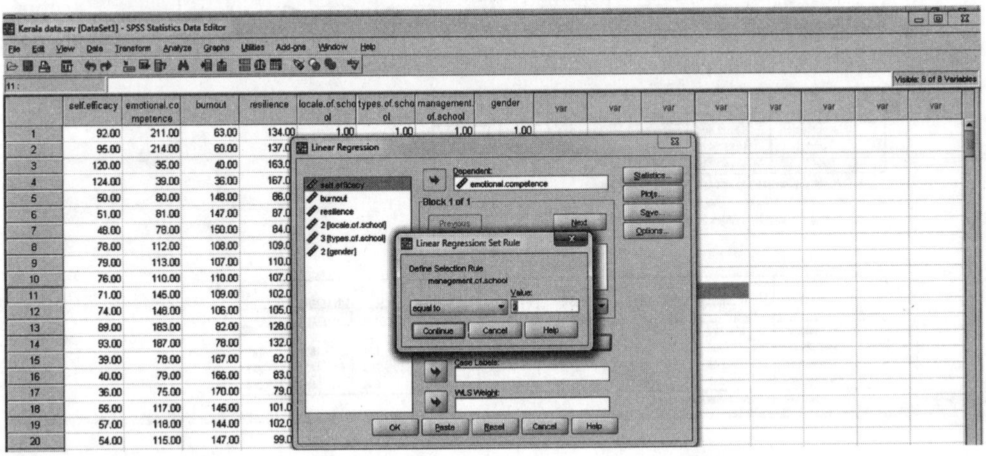

437. Click on "**Continue**" to get the following screen.

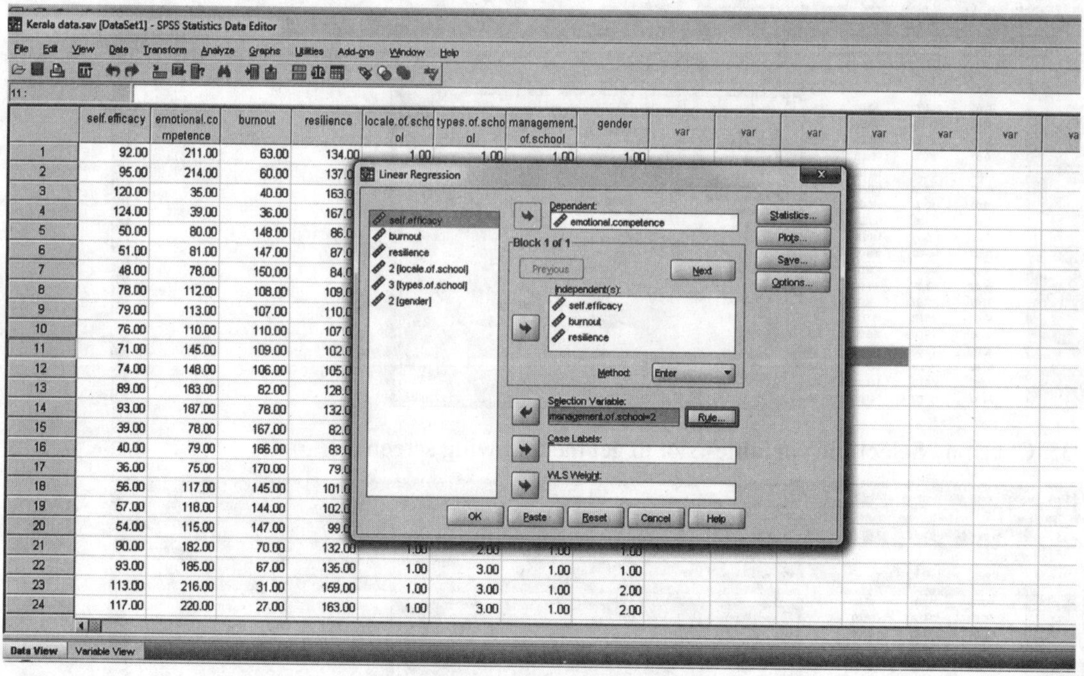

438. Click on "**OK**" to get the following outputs of Regression Analysis in case of Teachers working in Private schools.

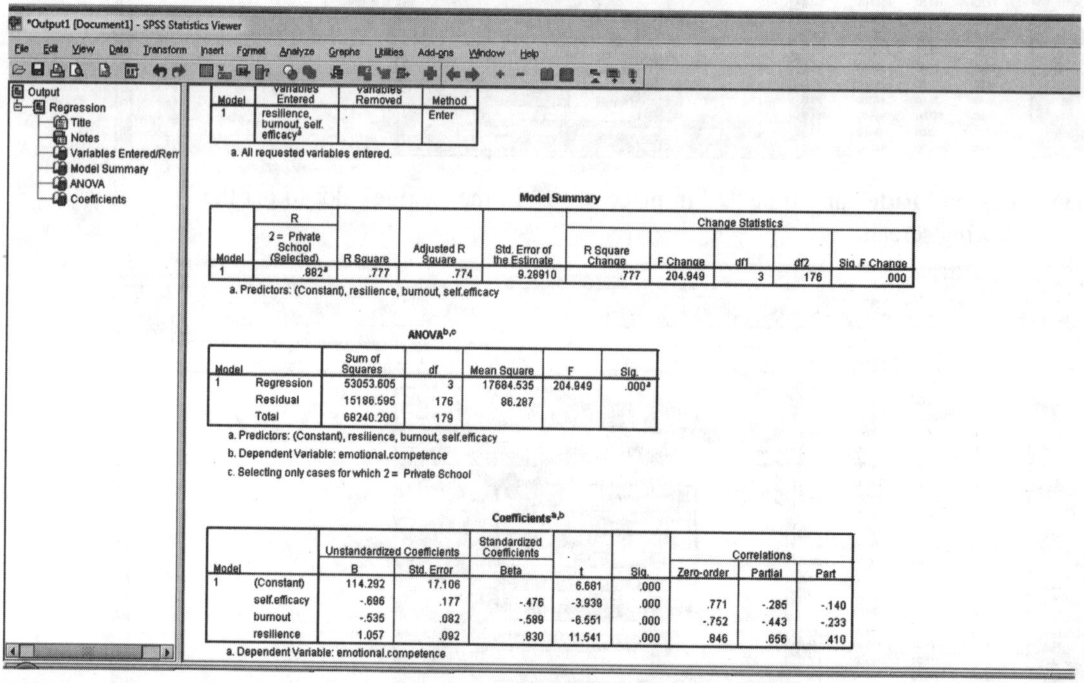

Model	Variables Entered	Variables Removed	Method
1	resilience, burnout, self.efficacy[a]	.	Enter

a. All requested variables entered.

Model Summary

Model	R: 2 = Private School (Selected)	R Square	Adjusted R Square	Std. Error of the Estimate	Change Statistics: R Square Change	F Change	df1	df2	Sig. F Change
1	.882[a]	.777	.774	9.28910	.777	204.949	3	176	.000

a. Predictors: (Constant), resilience, burnout, self.efficacy

ANOVA[b,c]

Model		Sum of Squares	df	Mean Square	F	Sig.
1	Regression	53053.605	3	17684.535	204.949	.000[a]
	Residual	15186.595	176	86.287		
	Total	68240.200	179			

a. Predictors: (Constant), resilience, burnout, self.efficacy

b. Dependent Variable: emotional.competence

c. Selecting only cases for which 2 = Private School

Coefficients[a,b]

Model		Unstandardized Coefficients B	Std. Error	Standardized Coefficients Beta	t	Sig.	Correlations Zero-order	Partial	Part
1	(Constant)	114.292	17.106		6.681	.000			
	self.efficacy	-.696	.177	-.476	-3.939	.000	.771	-.285	-.140
	burnout	-.535	.082	-.589	-6.551	.000	-.752	-.443	-.233
	resilience	1.057	.092	.830	11.541	.000	.846	.656	.410

a. Dependent Variable: emotional.competence

439. Individual contribution of Self-efficacy, Burnout and Resilience in predicting Emotional Competence of Teachers working in Private Schools is to be computed as shown in the following table.

Variable	*Beta value*	*Zero-order correlation*	*% of Contribution*
Self-efficacy	-0.478	0.771	$-0.478 \times 0.771 \times 100 = -36.854\%$
Burnout	-0.589	-0.752	$-0.589 \times -0.752 \times 100 = 44.293\%$
Resilience	0.830	0.846	$0.830 \times 0.846 \times 100 = 70.218\%$

Total % contribution = - 36.854 + 44.293 + 70.218 = 77.657

It is same as R Squared X 100

440. Regression Equation for predicting Emotional Competence of teachers working in Private Schools on the basis of their Self-efficacy, Burnout and Resilience can be written as given below:

$Y = -0.696\, X_1 - 0.535\, X_2 + 1.057\, X_3 + 114.292$

Where Y = Emotional Competence

X_1 = Self-efficacy X_2 = Burnout X_3 = Resilience

For computing Emotional Competence of the teacher working in Private Schools, you have to collect her / his scores on Self-efficacy, Burnout and Resilience variables using the same tools as used while developing the regression equation.

441. Let us take another objective of research.

1. To study the individual contribution of Study Habits and Personality in predicting Academic Performance of Male and Female students belonging to 18 to 20 years age group and 21 to 22 years age group separately.
2. To establish the regression equation for predicting Academic Performance on the basis of Study Habits and Personality of Male and Female students belonging to 18 to 20 years age group and 21 to 22 years age group separately.

Click on "**Analyse**" icon, bring curser to "**Regression**" icon and finally to "**Linear**" icon to get the following screen.

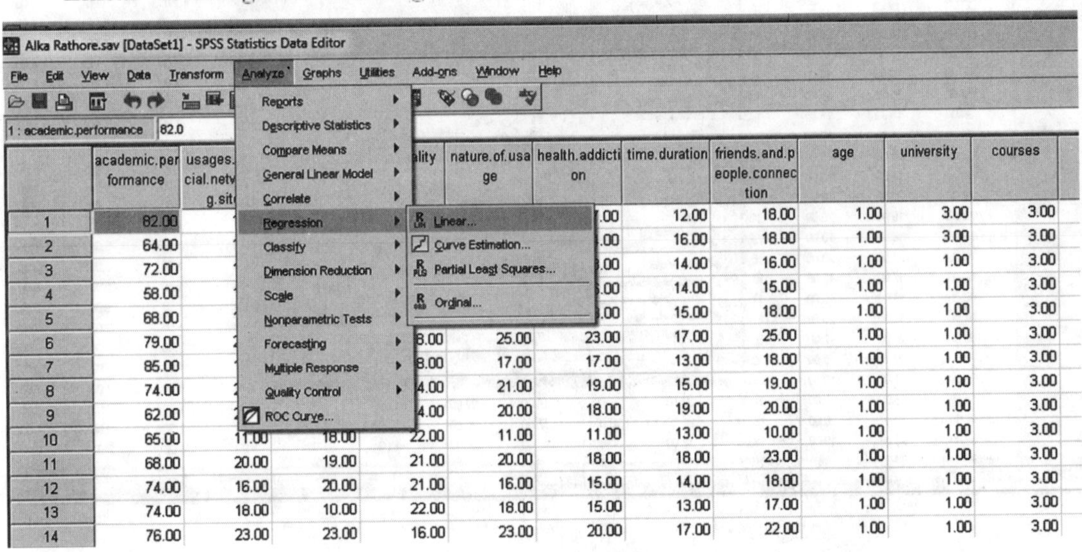

442. Click on "**Linear**" to get the following screen.

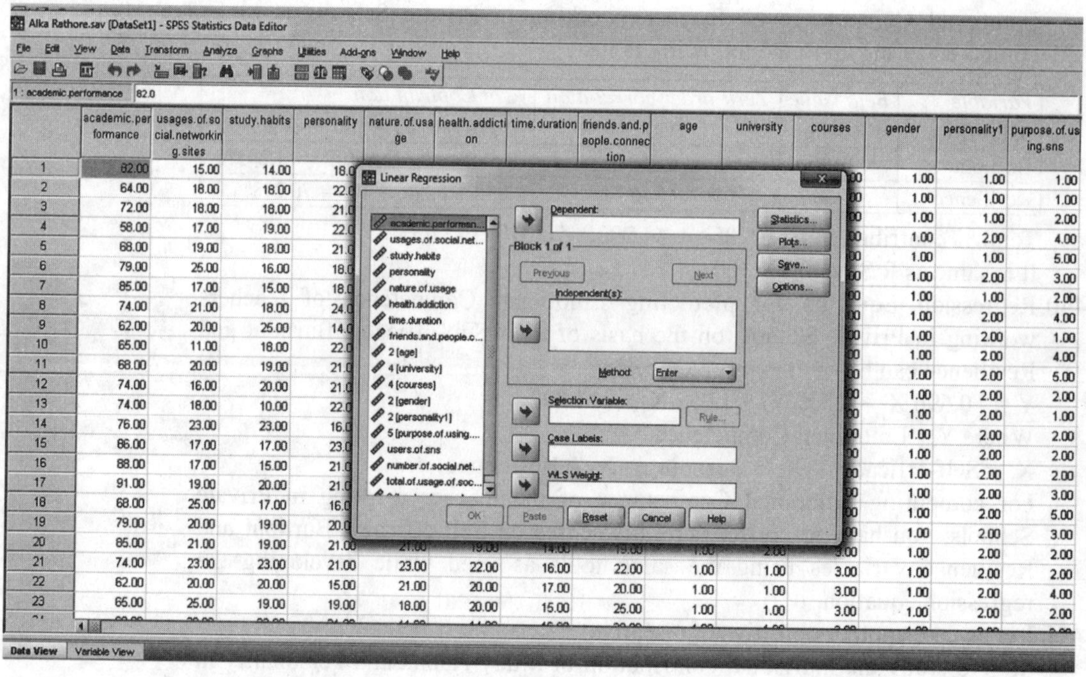

443. Shift "**Academic Performance**" to "**Dependent**" slot and "**Study Habits and Personality**" to "**Independent(s)**" dialog box to get the following screen.

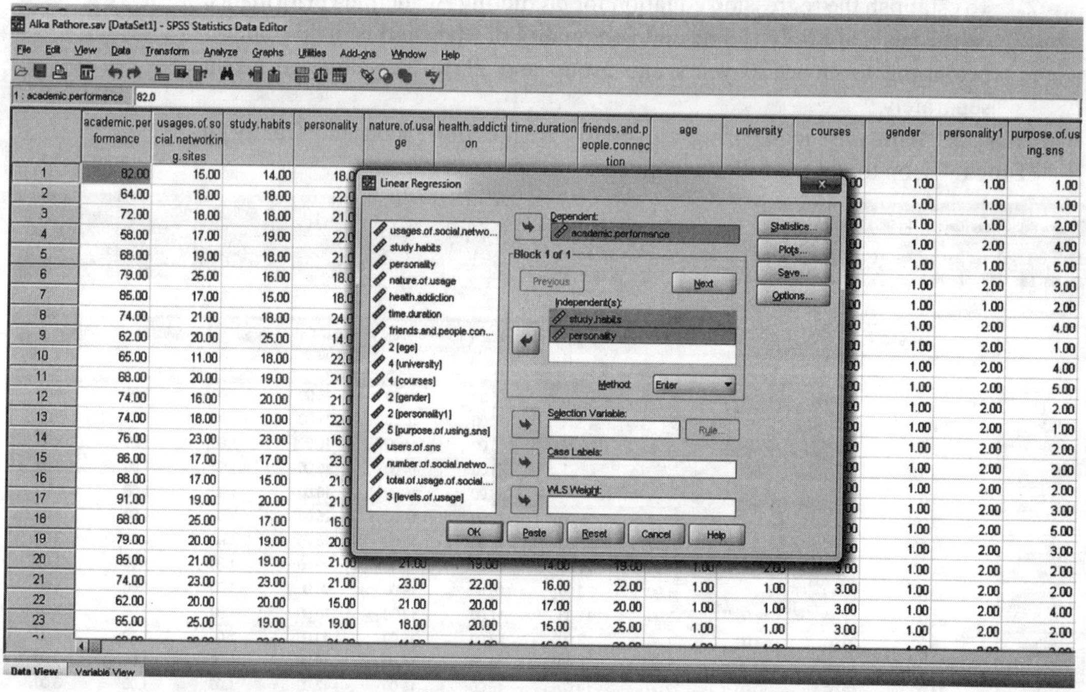

444. Click on "**Statistics**" button to get the following screen.

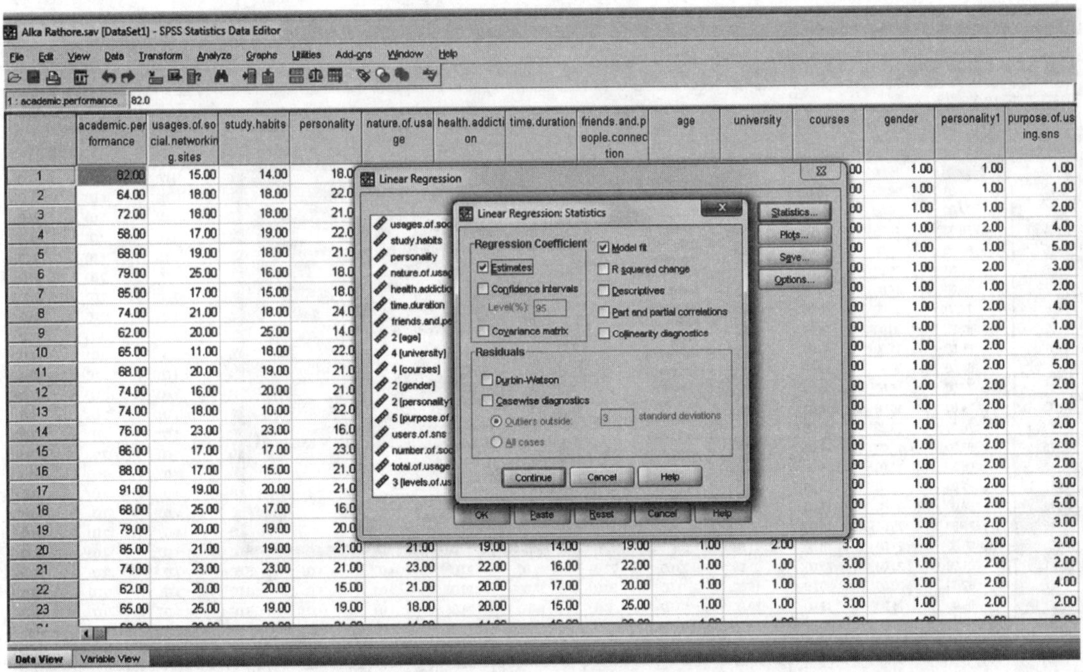

445. "**Estimates**" and "**Model Fit**" are highlighted by default. Now highlight "**R Squared Change**" and "**Part and Partial Correlations**" to get the following screen.

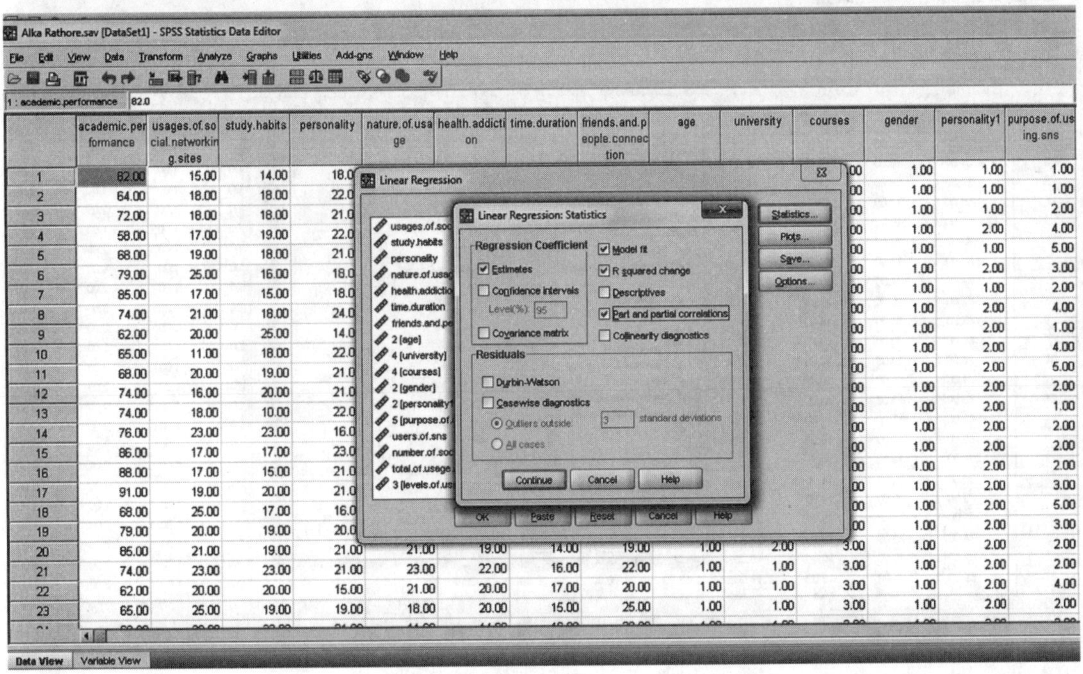

446. Click on "**Continue**" to get the following screen.

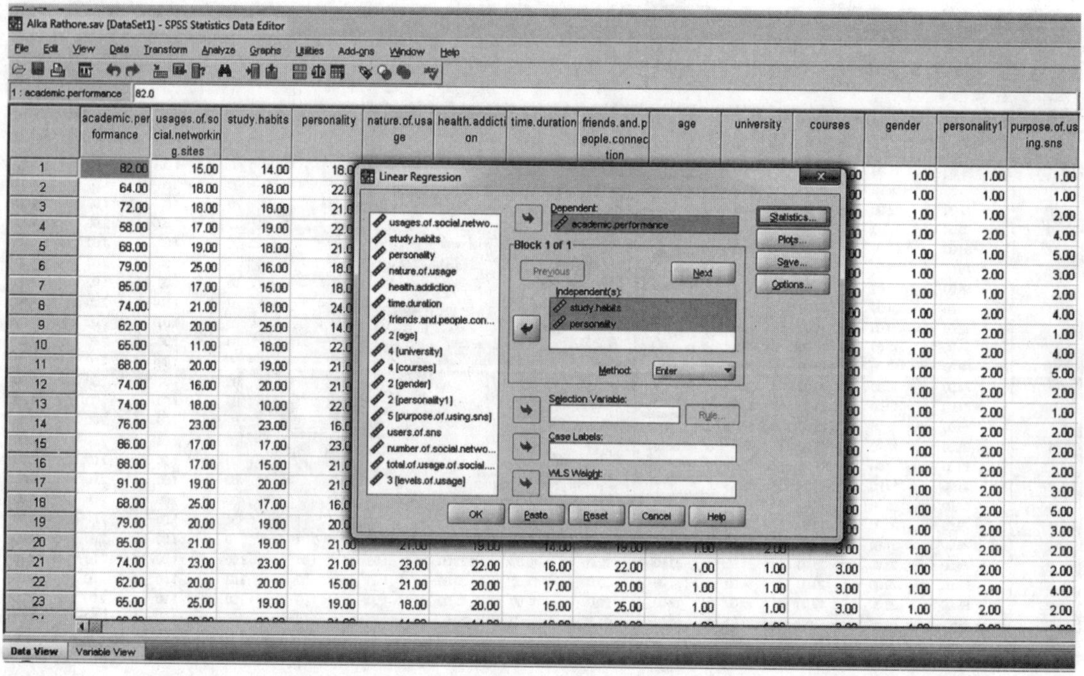

447. In order to select cases. First click on "**Data**" then click on "**Select Cases**" to get the following screen.

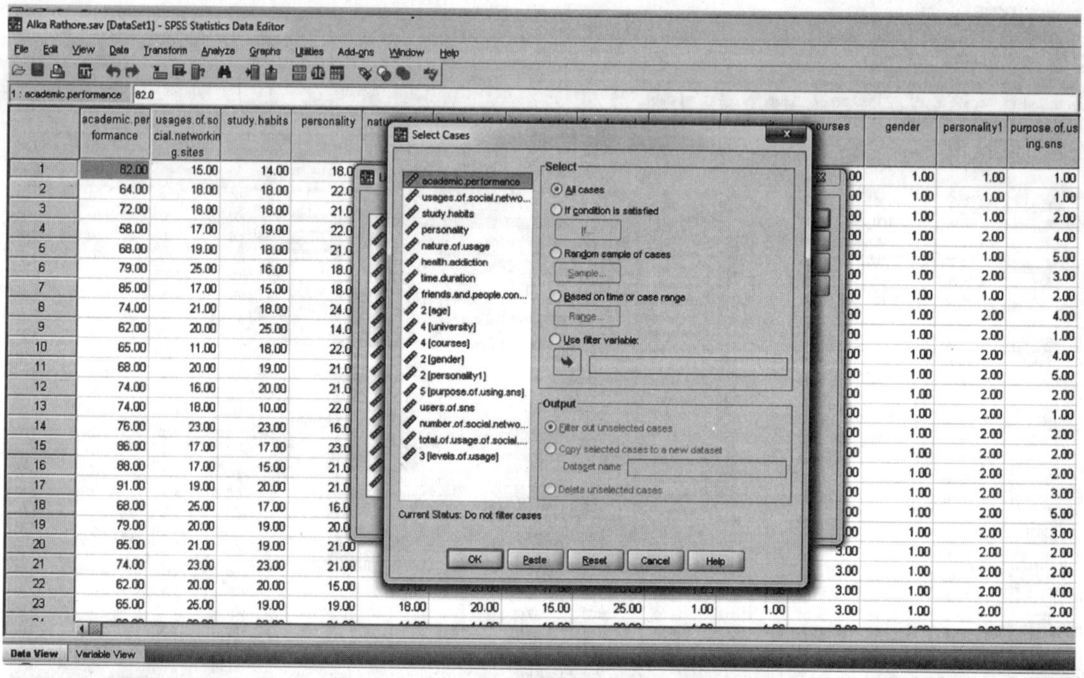

448. Click on "**If condition is satisfy**" to get the following screen.

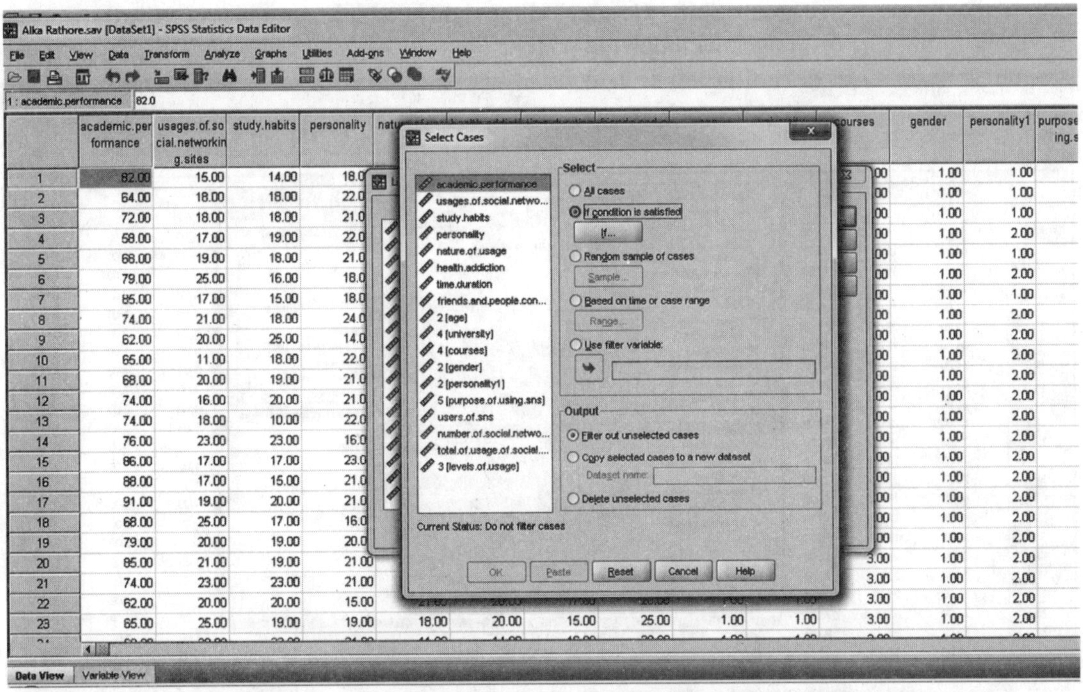

449. Click on "**If...**" to get the following screen.

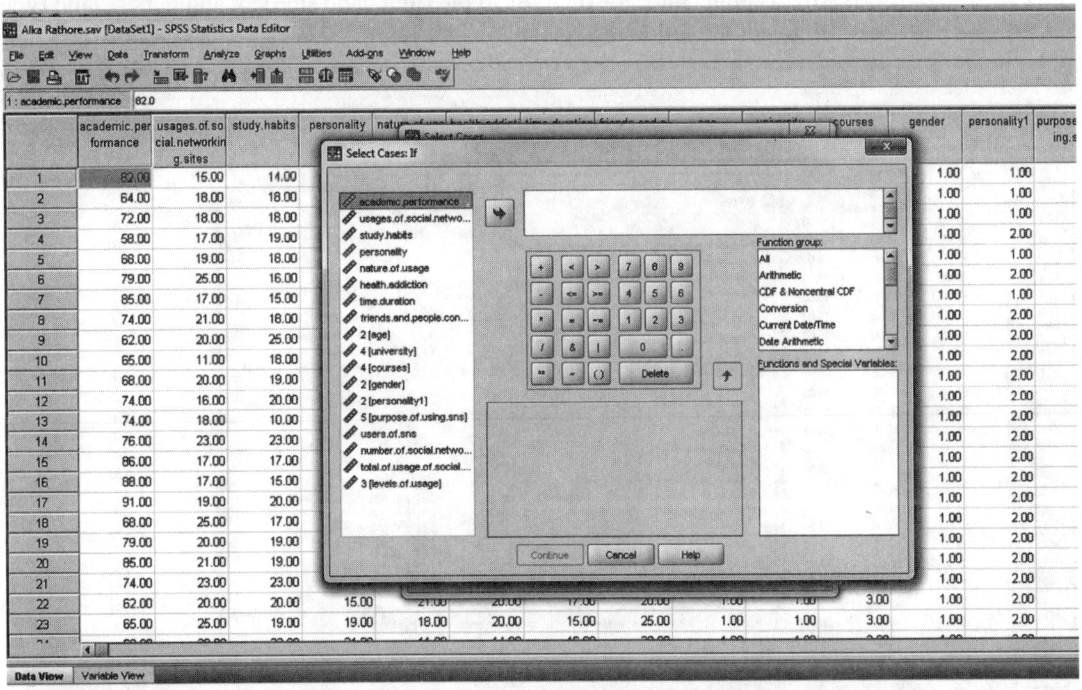

450. Suppose you want to do calculations for Male students belonging to 18 to 20 age group. Shift "**Gender**" to the right hand side slot and type "**1**" after putting "=" to get the following screen.

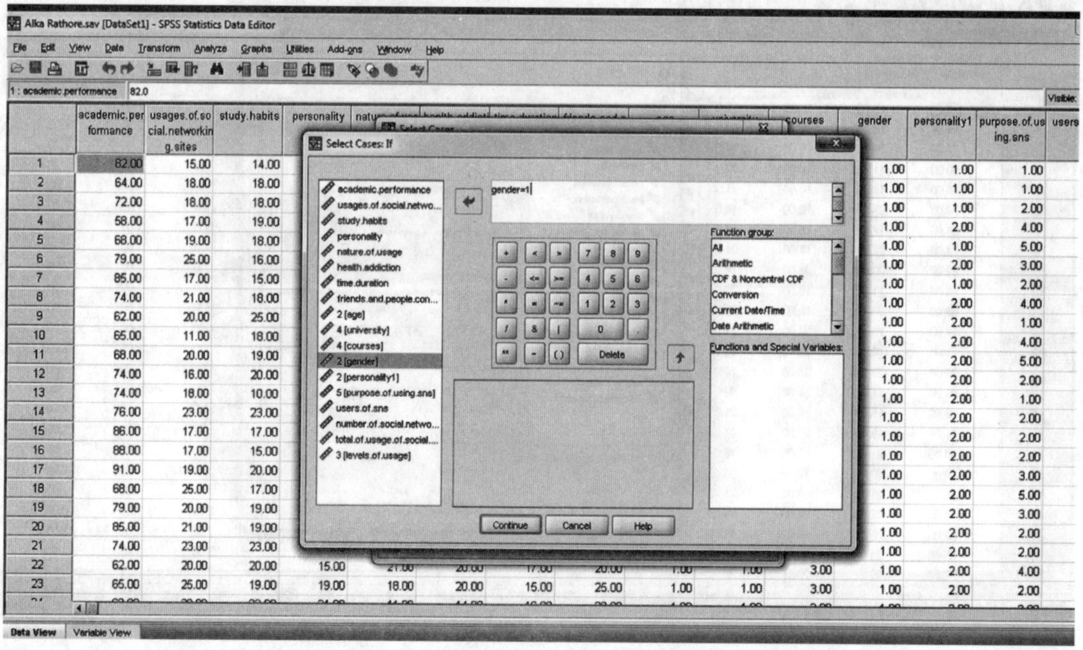

451. After typing "**and**" shift "**Age**" to the right hand side slot and put "=" and type "**1**" to get the following screen.

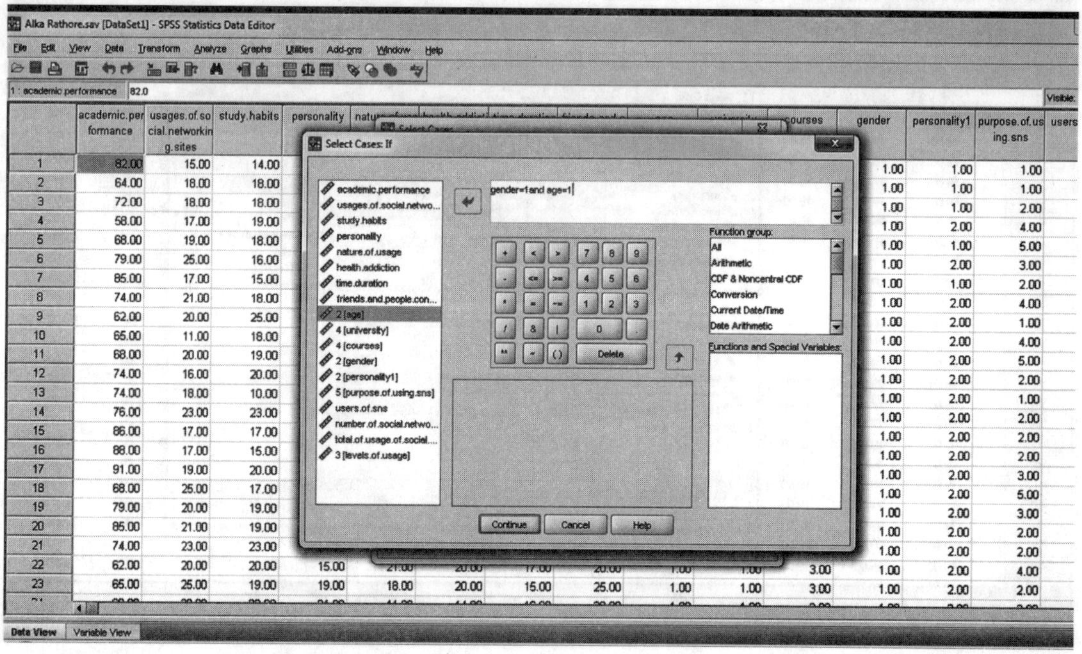

452. Click on "**Continue**" to get the following screen.

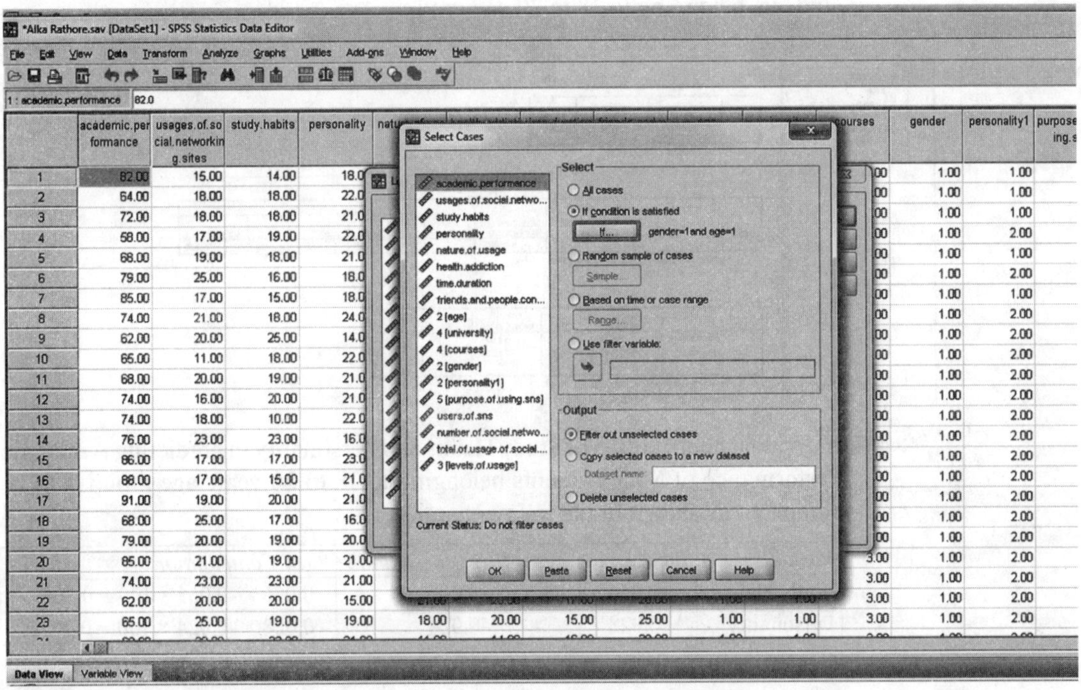

453. Click on "**OK**" to get the following screen.

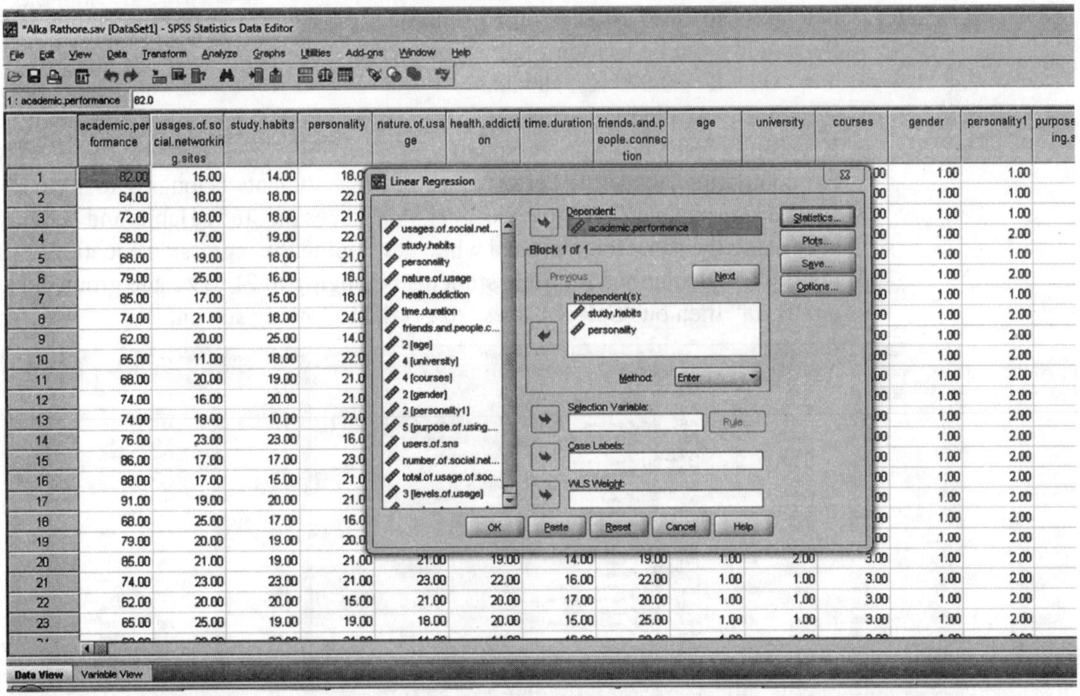

454. Click on "**OK**" to get the following outputs of Regression Analysis for Male students belonging to 18 to 20 age group.

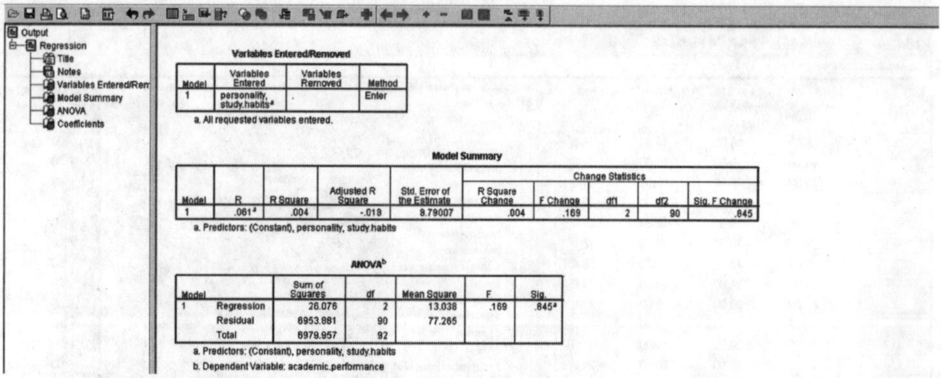

455. Individual contribution of Study Habits and Personality in predicting Academic Performance of Male students belonging to 18 to 20 years age group is to be computed as shown in the following table.

Variable	*Beta value*	*Zero-order correlation*	*% of Contribution*
Study Habits	-0.056	-0.055	$-0.056 \times -0.055 \times 100 = 0.308\%$
Personality	-0.028	-0.024	$-0.028 \times -0.024 \times 100 = 0.0672\%$

Total % contribution= 0.308 +0.067=0.3752

It is same as R Squared X 100

456. Regression Equation for predicting Academic Performance of Male students belonging to 18 to 20 years age group on the basis of their Study Habits and Personality can be written as given below:

$Y = -0.11\ X_1 - 0.079\ X_2 + 80.343$

Where Y = Academic Performance

X_1 = Study Habits X_2 = Personality

For computing Academic Performance of Male students belonging to 18 to 20 years age group, you have to collect her / his scores on Study Habits and Personality using the same tools as used while developing the regression equation.

457. For doing calculations for Male students belonging to 21 to 22 age group click on "**Data**" then on "**Select Cases**" to get the following screen.

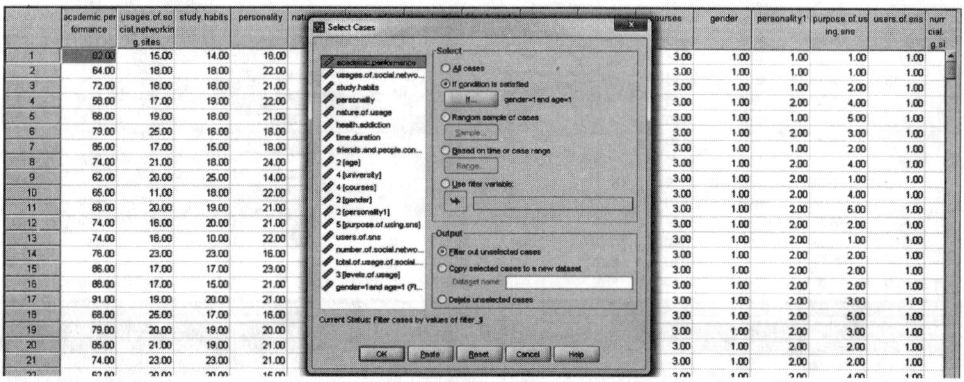

458. Click on "**If...**" icon to get the following screen.

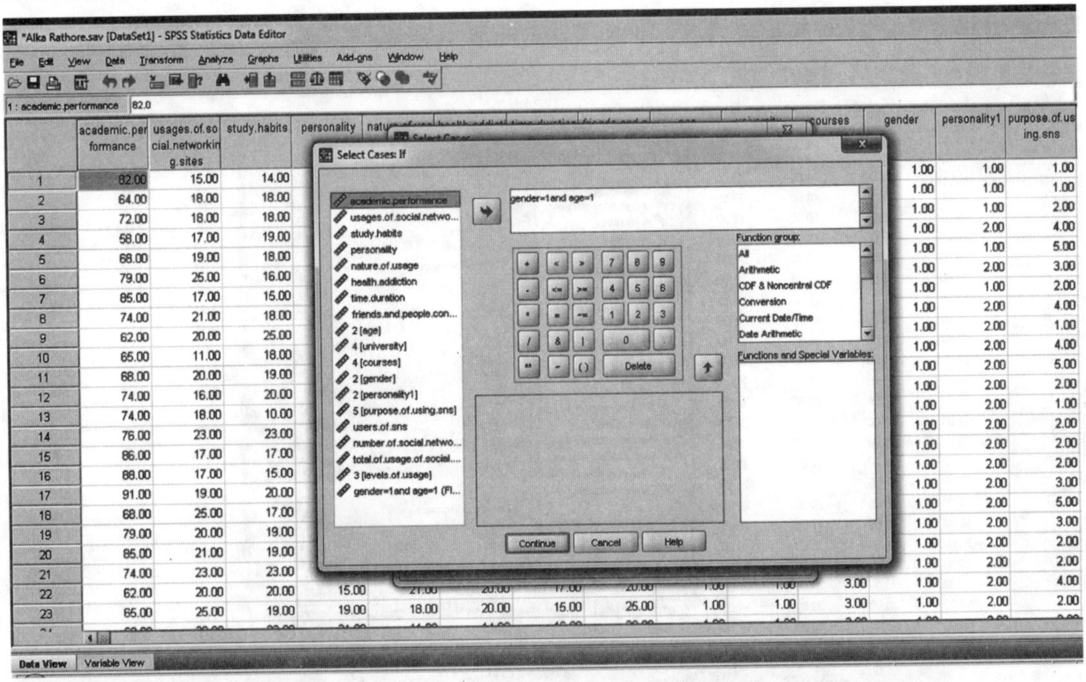

459. Age group 21 to 22 is coded as "**2**" so replace "**1**" by "**2**" against "**Age**" to get the following screen.

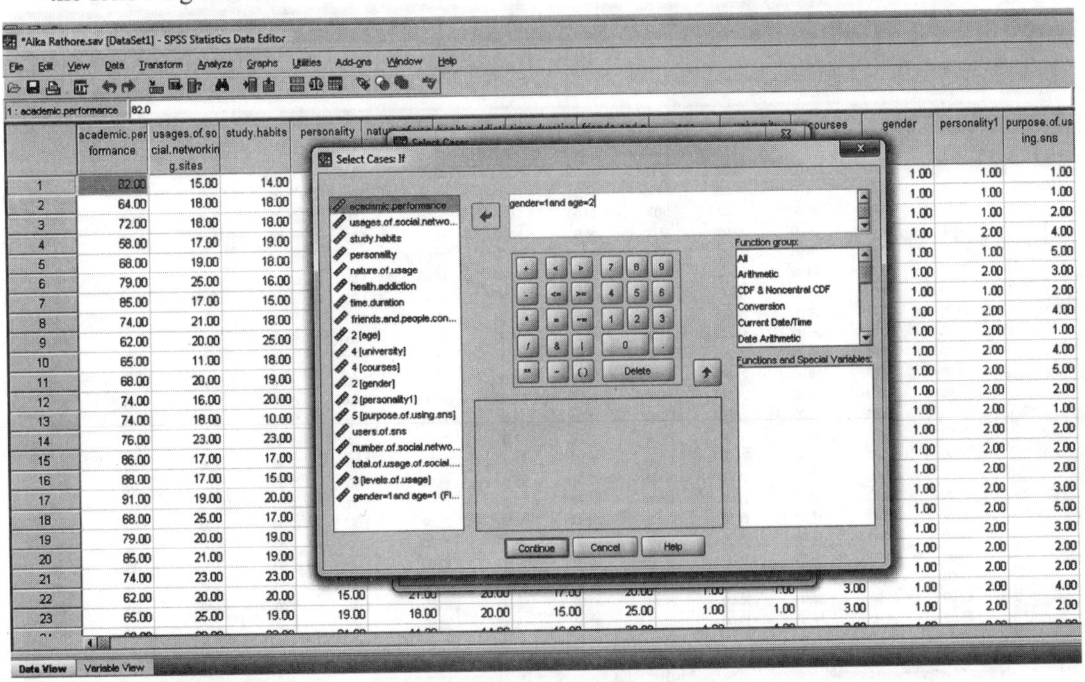

460. Click on "**Continue**" icon to get the following screen.

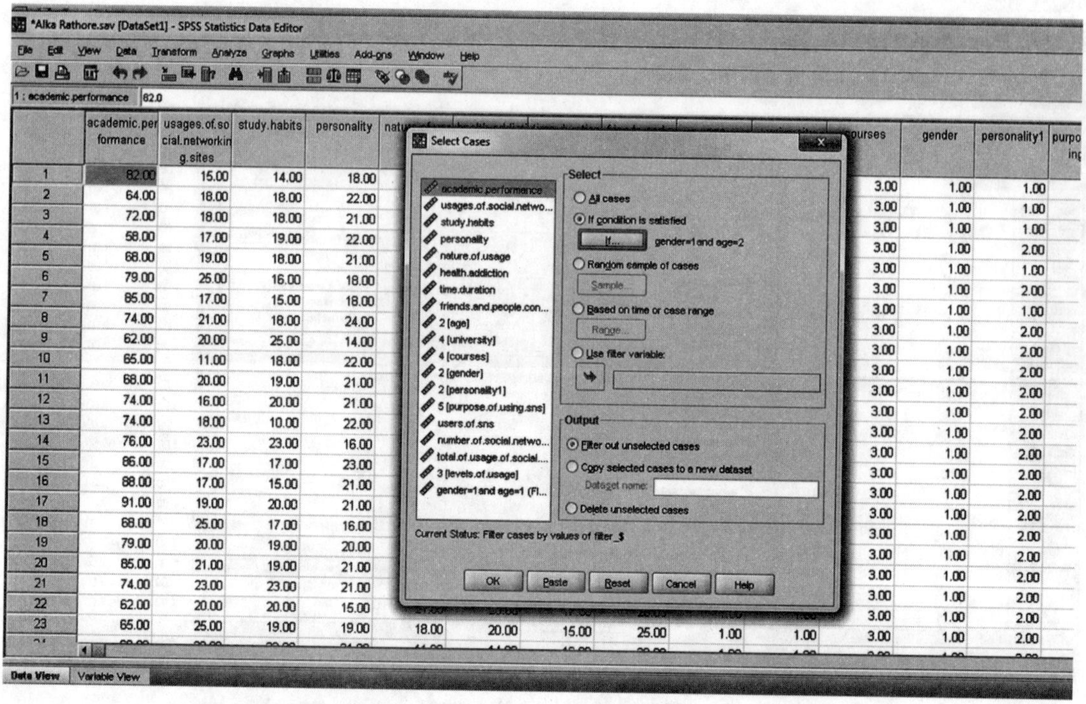

461. Click on "**OK**" to get the following screen.

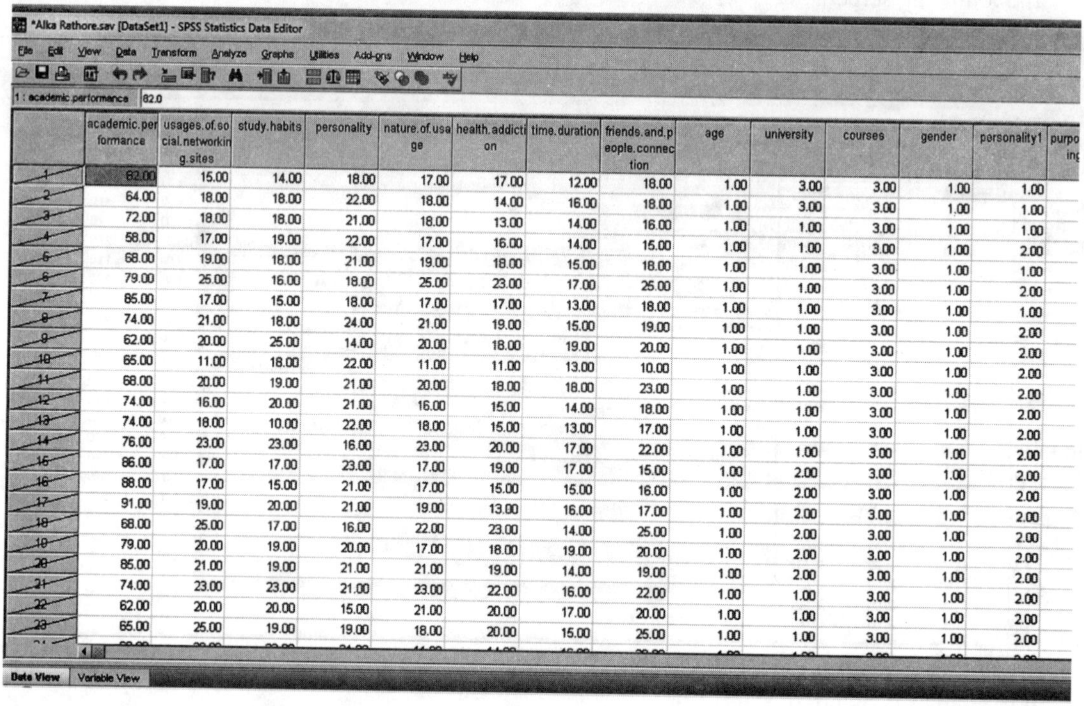

462. Click on "**Analyse**" then on "**Regression**" and finally on "**Linear**" to get the following screen.

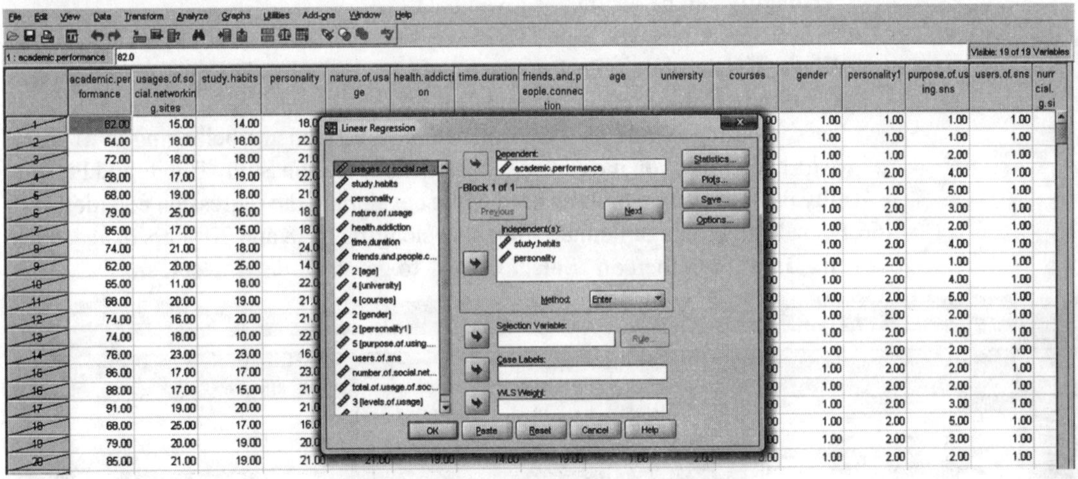

463. Click on "**OK**" to get the following outputs of Regression Analysis for Male students belonging to 21 to 22 year age group.

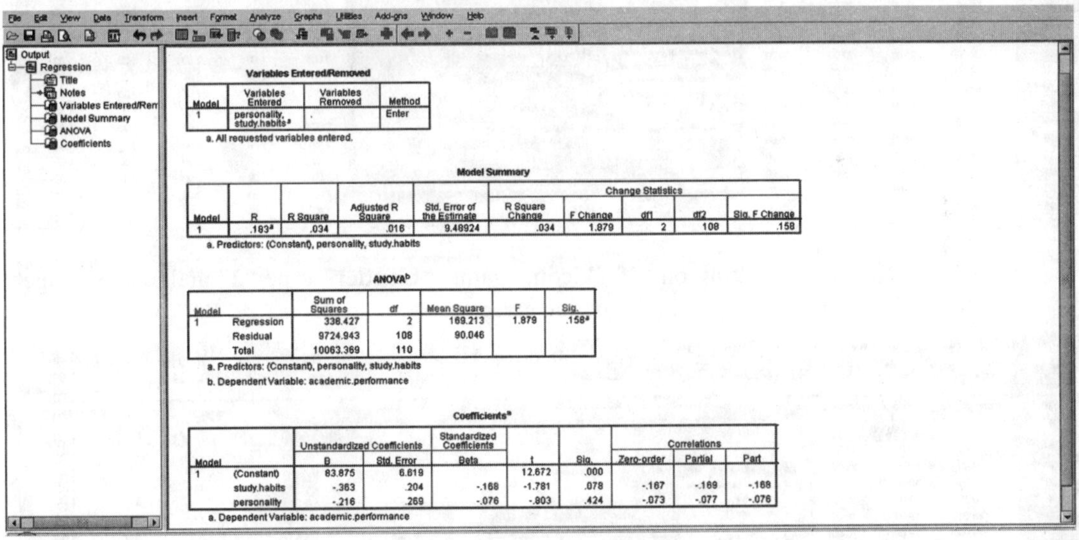

464. Individual contribution of Study Habits and Personality in predicting Academic Performance of Male students belonging to 21 to 22 years age group is to be computed as shown in the following table.

Variable	*Beta value*	*Zero-order correlation*	*% of Contribution*
Study Habits	-0.168	-0.167	-0.168 × -0.167 × 100 = 2.8056%
Personality	-0.076	-0.073	-0.076 × -0.073 × 100 = 0.5548%

Total % contribution= 2.8056 +0.5548= 3.3604

It is same as R Squared X 100

465. Regression Equation for predicting Academic Performance of Male students belonging to 21 to 22 years age group on the basis of their Study Habits and Personality can be written as given below:

$Y = - 0.363\ X_1 - 0.079\ X_2 + 83.876$

Where Y = Academic Performance

X_1 = Study Habits X_2 = Personality

For computing Academic Performance of Male students belonging to 21 to 22 years age group, you have to collect her / his scores on Study Habits and Personality using the same tools as used while developing the regression equation.

466. For selecting data of Female students belonging to 18 and 20 years of age, click on "**Data**" icon then on "**Select Cases**" to get the following screen.

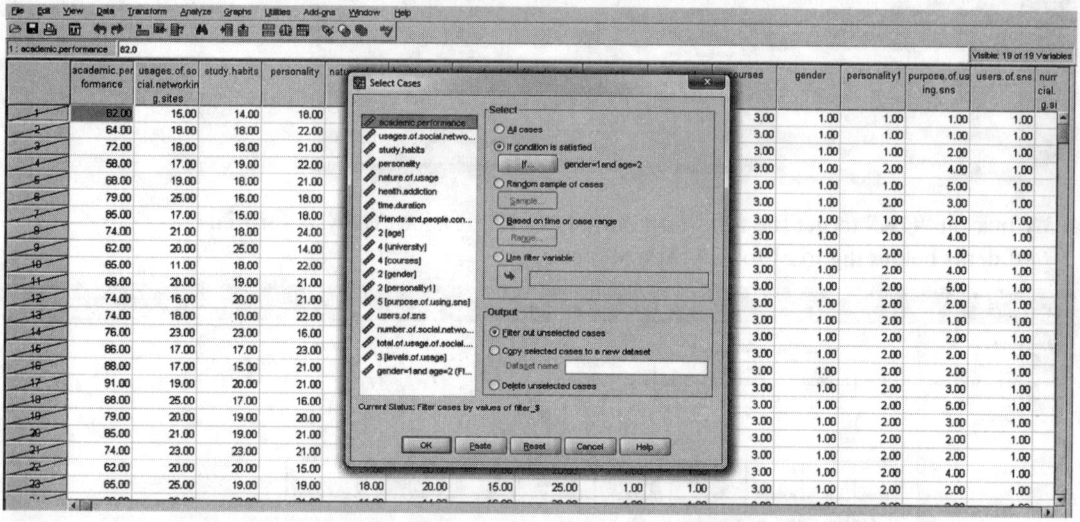

467. After clicking on "**If...**" icon, against "**Gender**" type "**2**" and against "Age" type "**1**" to get the following screen.

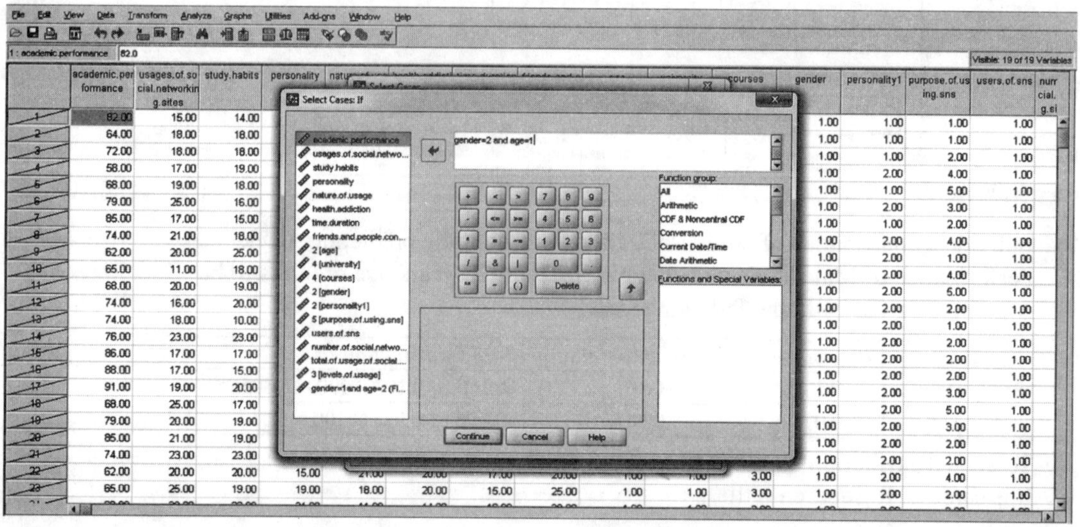

468. Click on "**Continue**" to get the following screen.

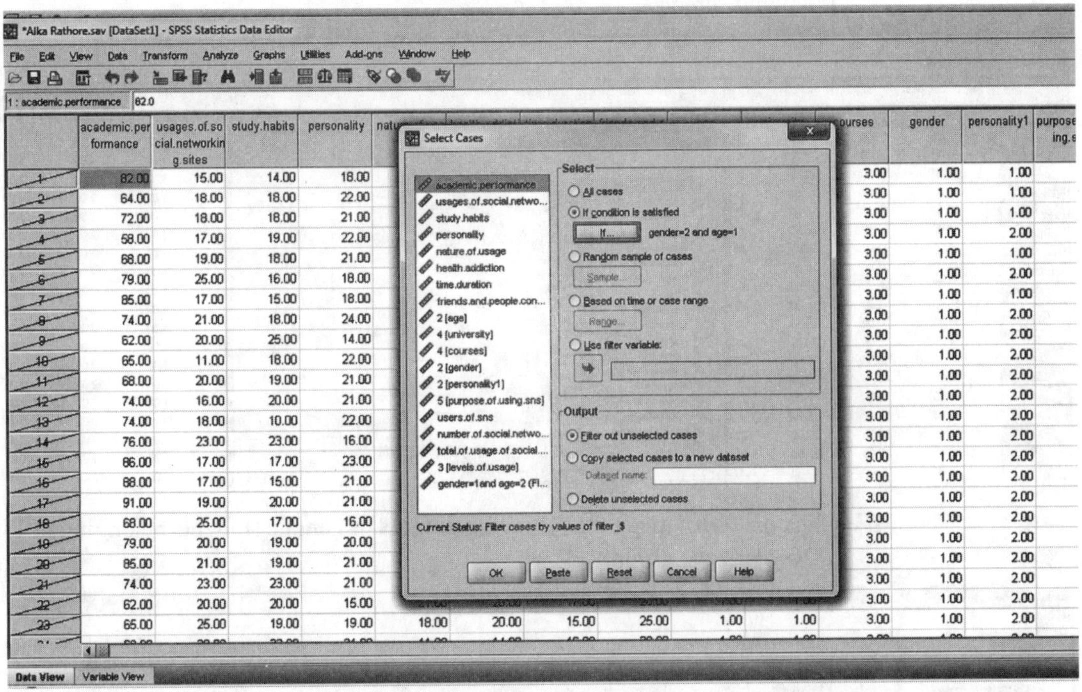

469. Click on "**OK**" to get the following screen.

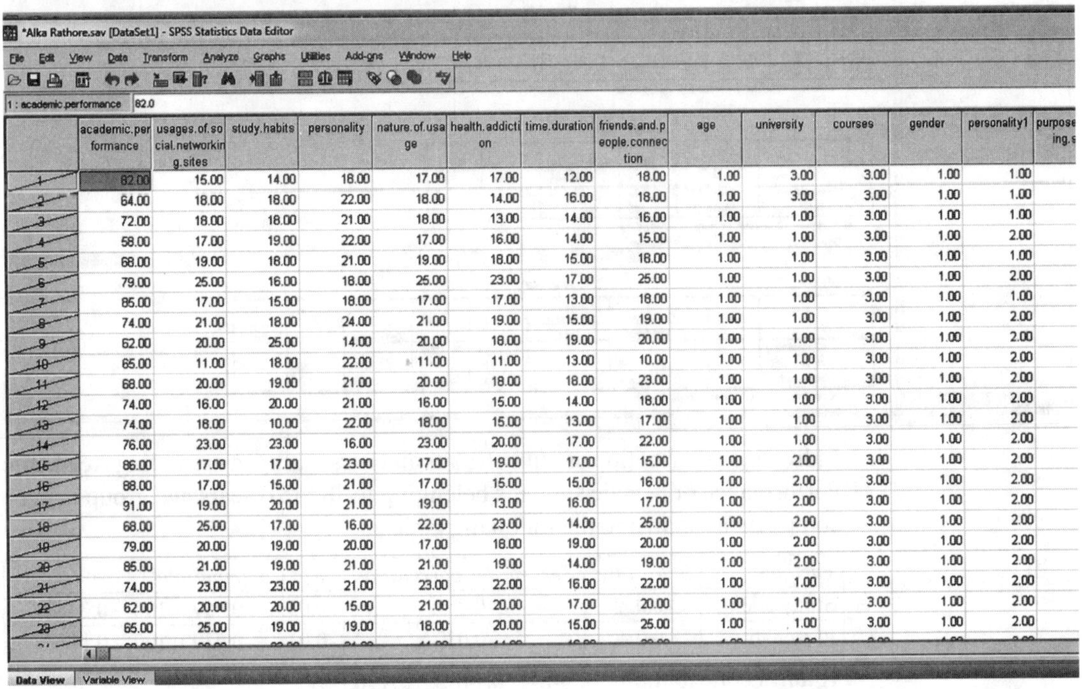

470. Click on "**Analyse**" icon then "**Regression**" and finally on "**Linear**" to get the following screen.

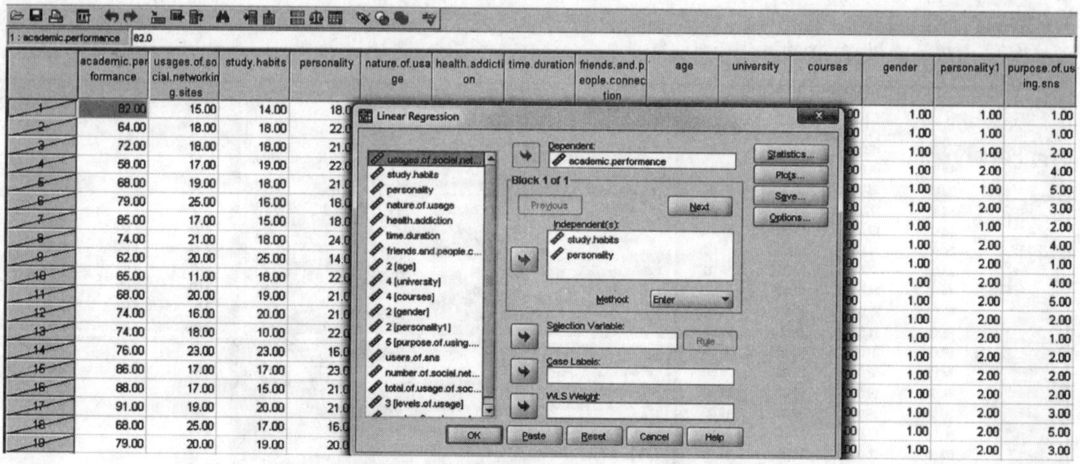

471. Click on "**OK**" to get the following outputs of Female students belonging to 18 to 20 years age group.

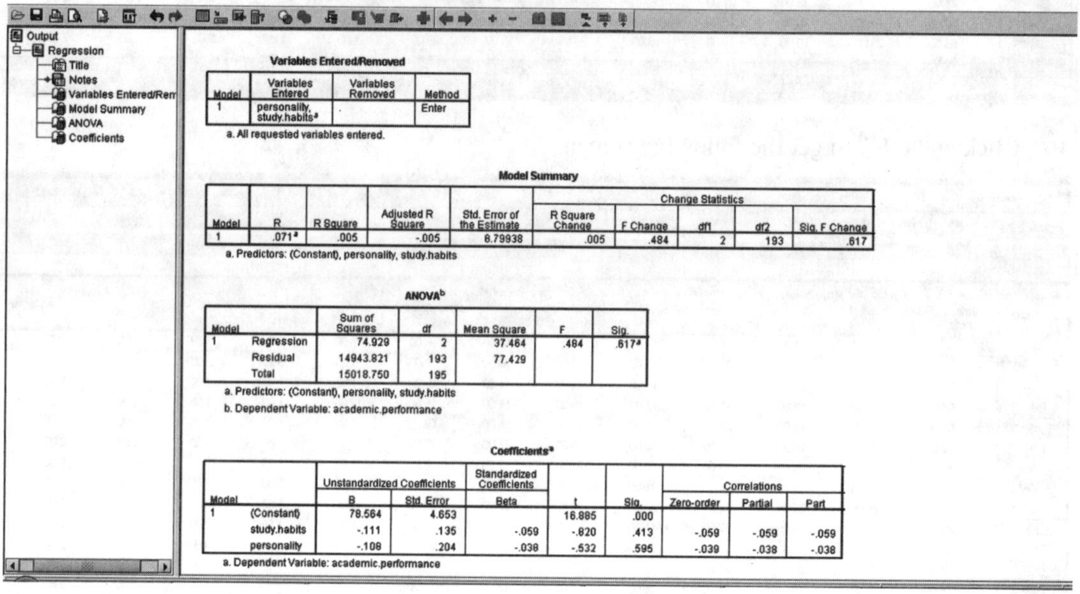

472. Individual contribution of Study Habits and Personality in predicting Academic Performance of Female students belonging to 18 to 20 years age group is to be computed as shown in the following table.

Variable	*Beta value*	*Zero-order correlation*	*% of Contribution*
Study Habits	-0.059	-0.059	-0.059 × -0.059 × 100 = 0.3481%
Personality	-0.038	-0.039	-0.038 × -0.039 × 100 = 0.1482%

Total % contribution= 0.3481 +0.1482= 0.4963

It is same as R Squared X 100

473. Regression Equation for predicting Academic Performance of Female students belonging to 18 to 20 years age group on the basis of their Study Habits and Personality can be written as given below:

$Y = -0.11 X_1 - 0.108 X_2 + 88.564$

Where Y = Academic Performance

X_1 = Study Habits X_2 = Personality

For computing Academic Performance of Female students belonging to 18 to 20 years age group, you have to collect her / his scores on Study Habits and Personality using the same tools as used while developing the regression equation.

474. For selecting data for Female students belonging to 21 and 22 years of age, click on "**Data**" icon then on "**Select Cases**" to get the following screen.

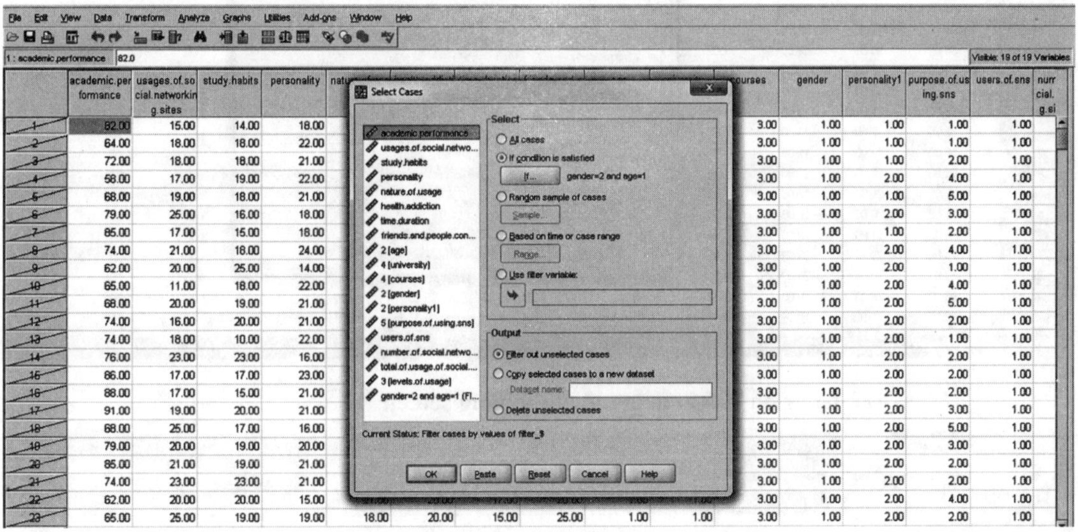

475. Click on "**If....**" icon and replace against "**Age**" "1" by "2" to get the following screen.

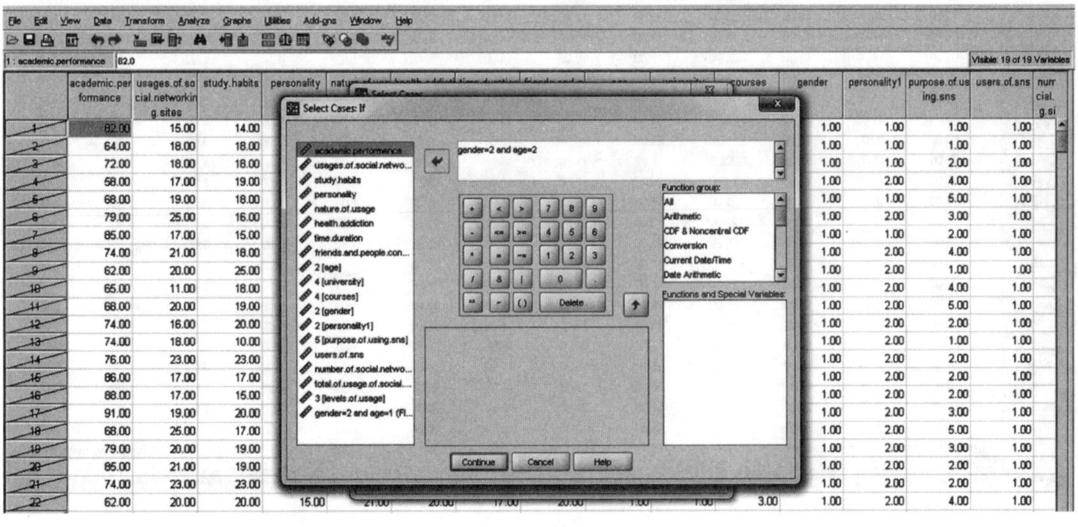

476. Click on "**Continue**" to get the following screen.

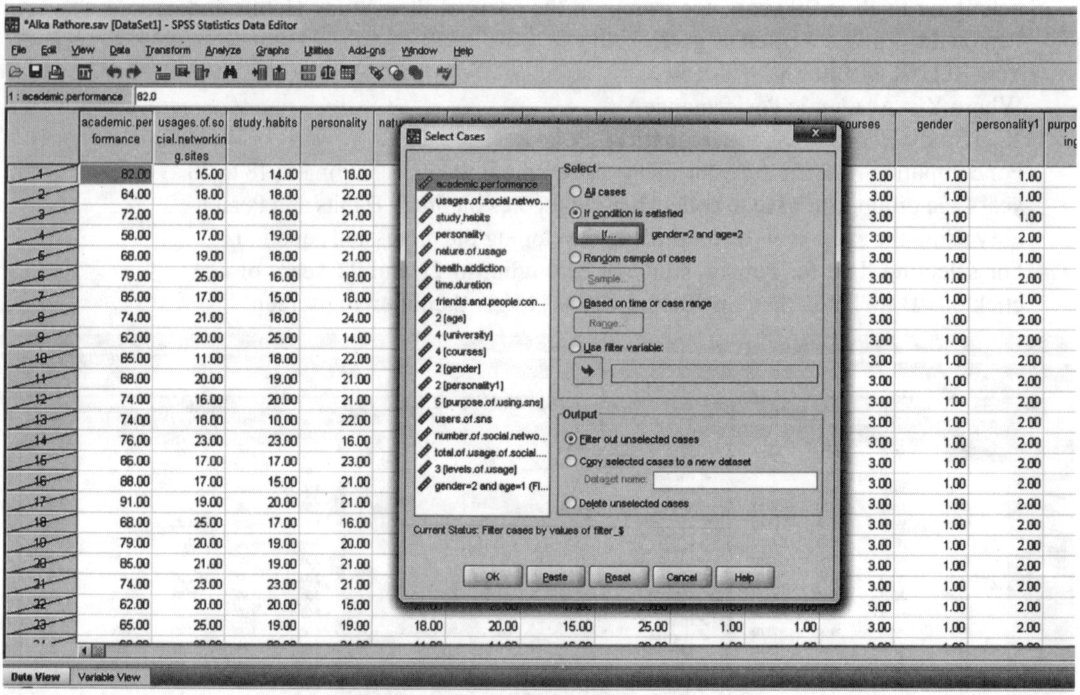

477. Click on "**OK**" to get the following screen.

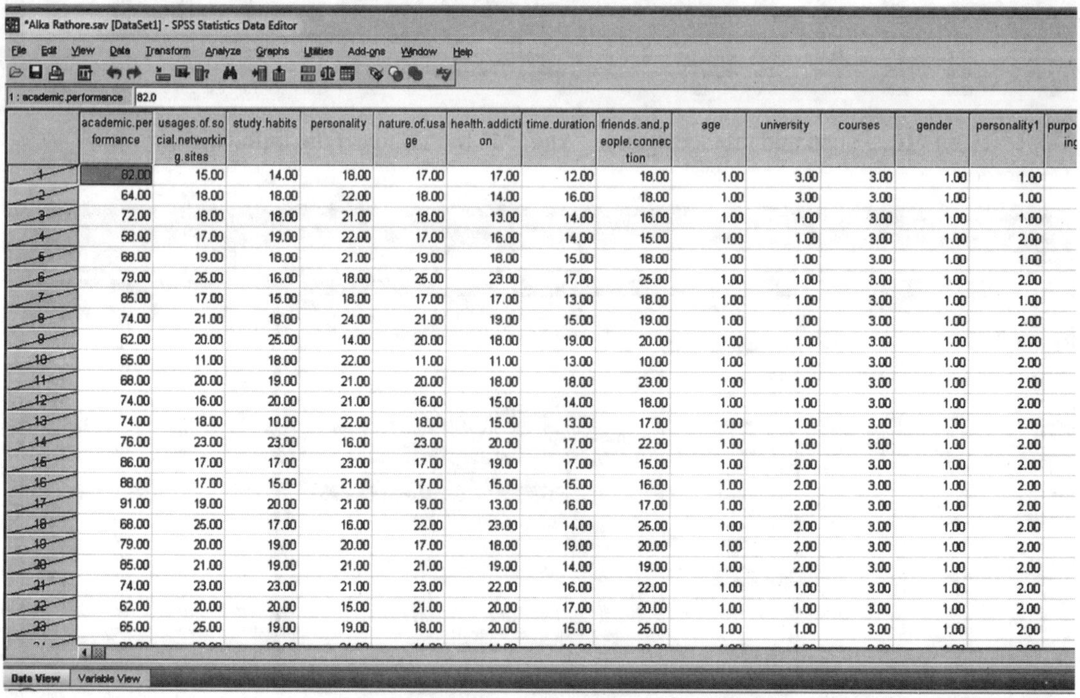

478. Click on "**Analyse**" then on "**Regression**" and finally on "**Linear**" to get the following screen.

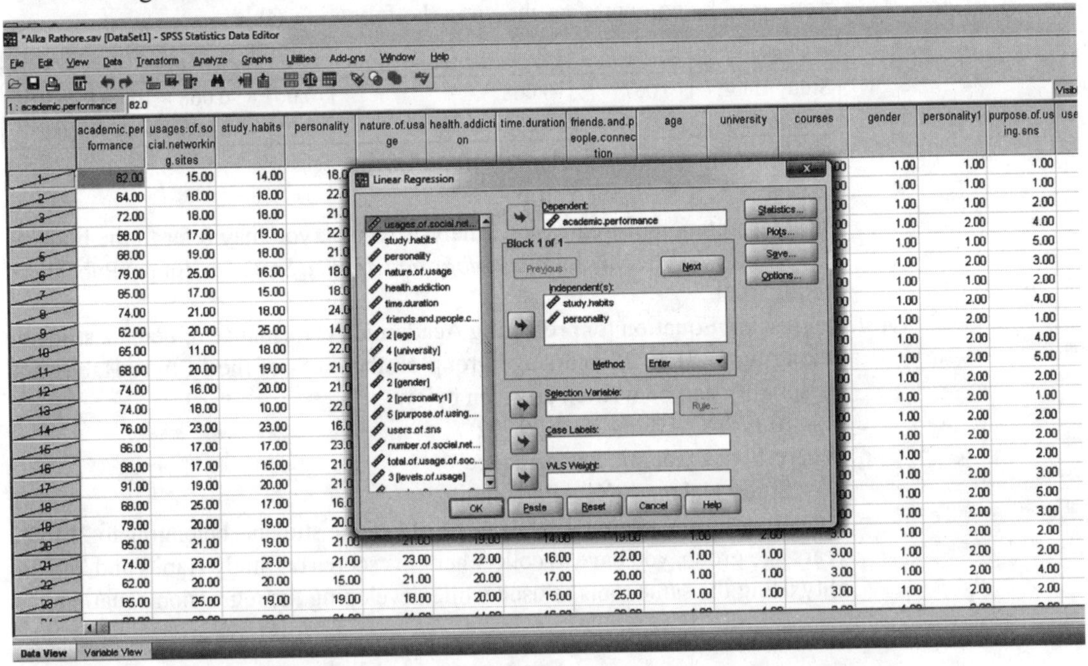

479. Click on "**OK**" to the following outputs of Regression Analysis of Female students belonging to 21 to 22 Years of age.

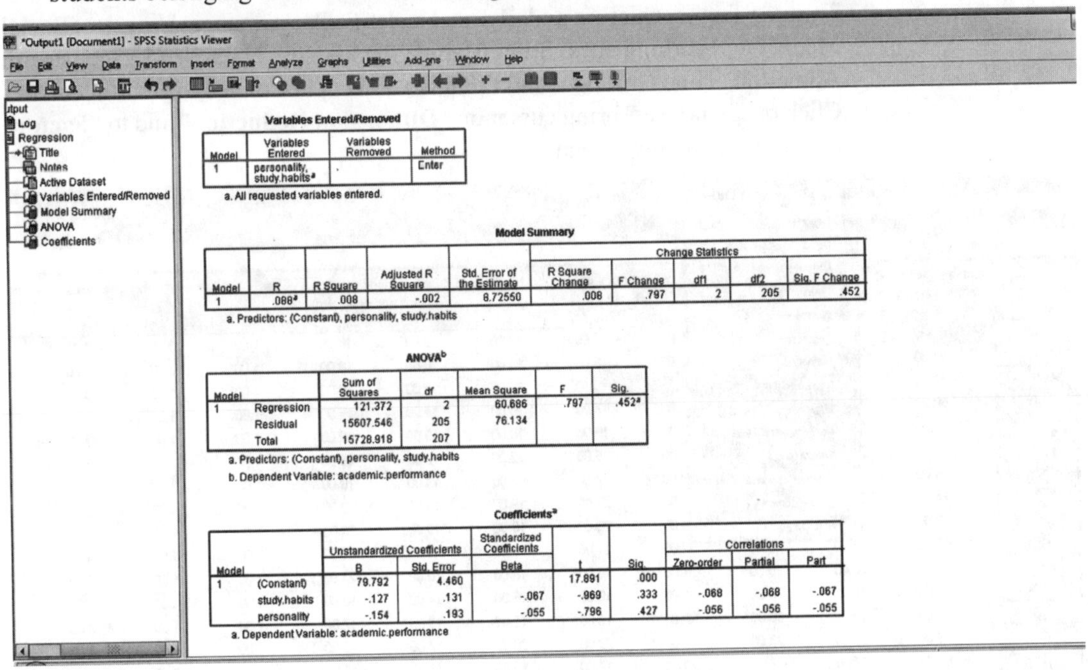

Variables Entered/Removed

Model	Variables Entered	Variables Removed	Method
1	personality, study.habits[a]	.	Enter

a. All requested variables entered.

Model Summary

Model	R	R Square	Adjusted R Square	Std. Error of the Estimate	R Square Change	F Change	df1	df2	Sig. F Change
					Change Statistics				
1	.088[a]	.008	-.002	8.72550	.008	.797	2	205	.452

a. Predictors: (Constant), personality, study.habits

ANOVA[b]

Model		Sum of Squares	df	Mean Square	F	Sig.
1	Regression	121.372	2	60.686	.797	.452[a]
	Residual	15607.546	205	76.134		
	Total	15728.918	207			

a. Predictors: (Constant), personality, study.habits

b. Dependent Variable: academic.performance

Coefficients[a]

Model		Unstandardized Coefficients B	Std. Error	Standardized Coefficients Beta	t	Sig.	Correlations Zero-order	Partial	Part
1	(Constant)	79.792	4.460		17.891	.000			
	study.habits	-.127	.131	-.067	-.969	.333	-.068	-.068	-.067
	personality	-.154	.193	-.055	-.796	.427	-.056	-.056	-.055

a. Dependent Variable: academic.performance

480. Individual contribution of Study Habits and Personality for predicting Academic Performance of Female students belonging to 21 to 22 years age group is to be computed as shown in the following table.

Variable	*Beta value*	*Zero-order correlation*	*% of Contribution*
Study Habits	-0.067	-0.068	-0.067 × -0.068 × 100 = 0.4556%
Personality	-0.055	-0.056	-0.055 × -0.056 × 100 = 0.308%

Total % contribution= 0.4556 +0.308= 0.7636
It is same as R Squared X 100
For interpretation of Regression Analysis results, you may refer to the book by D.N.Sansanwal, *Research Methodology and Applied Statistics*, Shipra Publishers, Delhi, 2020.

481. Regression Equation for predicting Academic Performance of Female students belonging to 21 to 22 years age group on the basis of their Study Habits and Personality can be written as given below:
$Y = - 0.127\ X_1 - 0.154\ X_2 + 79.792$
Where Y = Academic Performance
X_1 = Study Habits X_2 = Personality
For computing Academic Performance of Female students belonging to 21 to 22 years age group, you have to collect her / his scores on Study Habits and Personality using the same tools as used while developing the regression equation.

Factor Analysis

482. Let us consider the following objective of research.
To study factor structure underlying Academic Performance, Usages of Social Media Net Working sites, Study Habits, Personality, Nature of Usage, Health Addiction, Time Duration, and Friends and People Connection of students.
Click on "**Analysis**" bring curser on "**Dimension Reduction**" and to "**Factor**" to get the following screen.

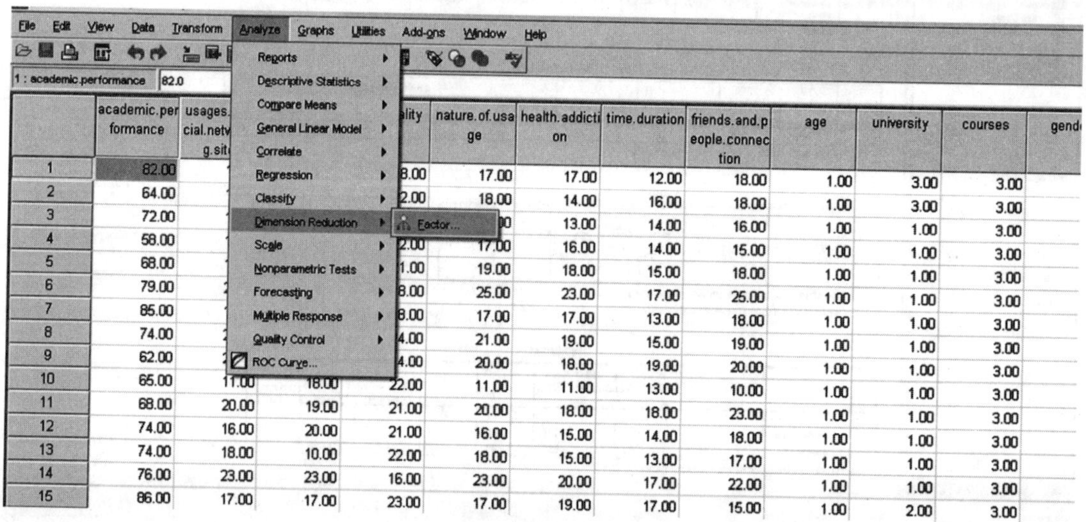

483. Click on "**Factor**" to get the following screen.

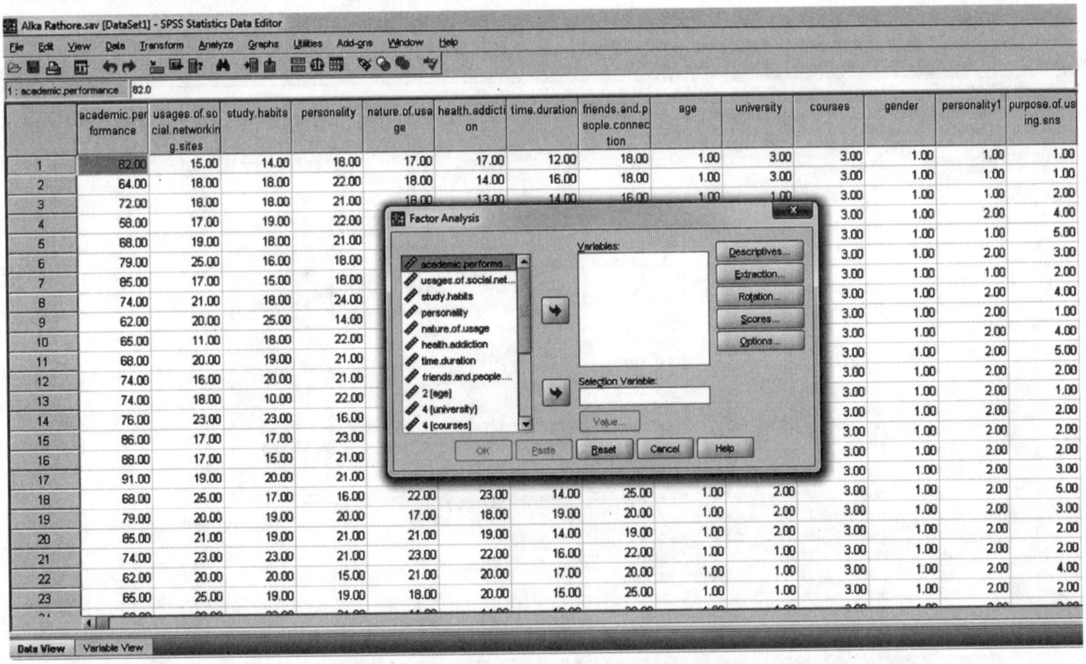

484. Shift "**Academic Performance, Usages of Social Media Net Working sites, Study Habits, Personality, Nature of Usage, Health Addiction, Time Duration, and Friends and People Connection**" under "**Variables**" dialog box to get the following screen.

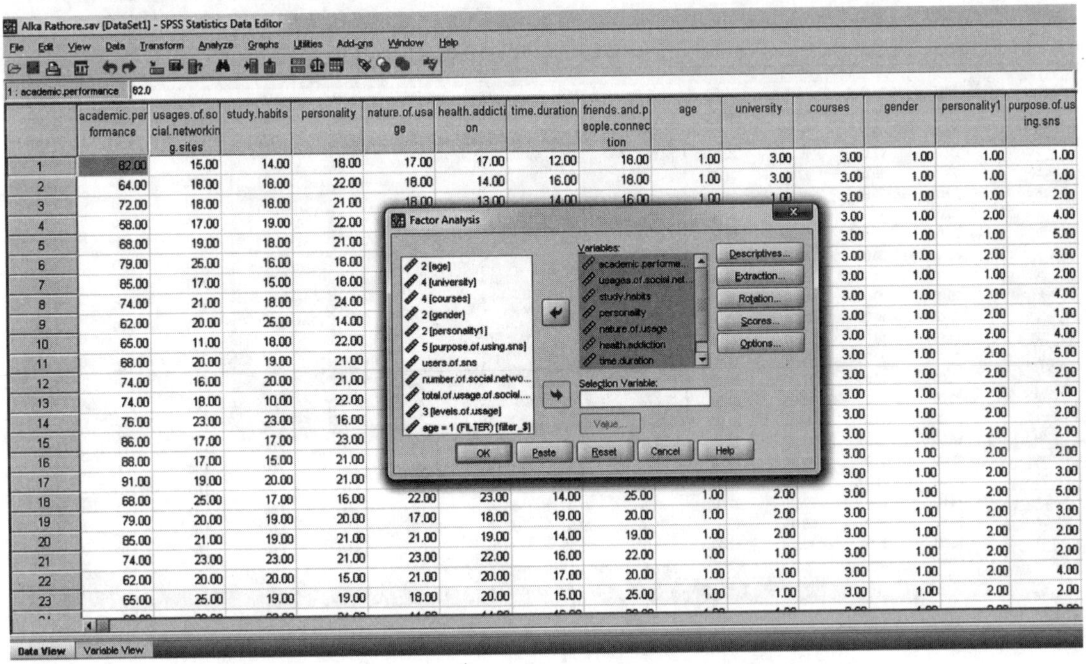

485. Click on "**Rotation**" icon to get the following screen.

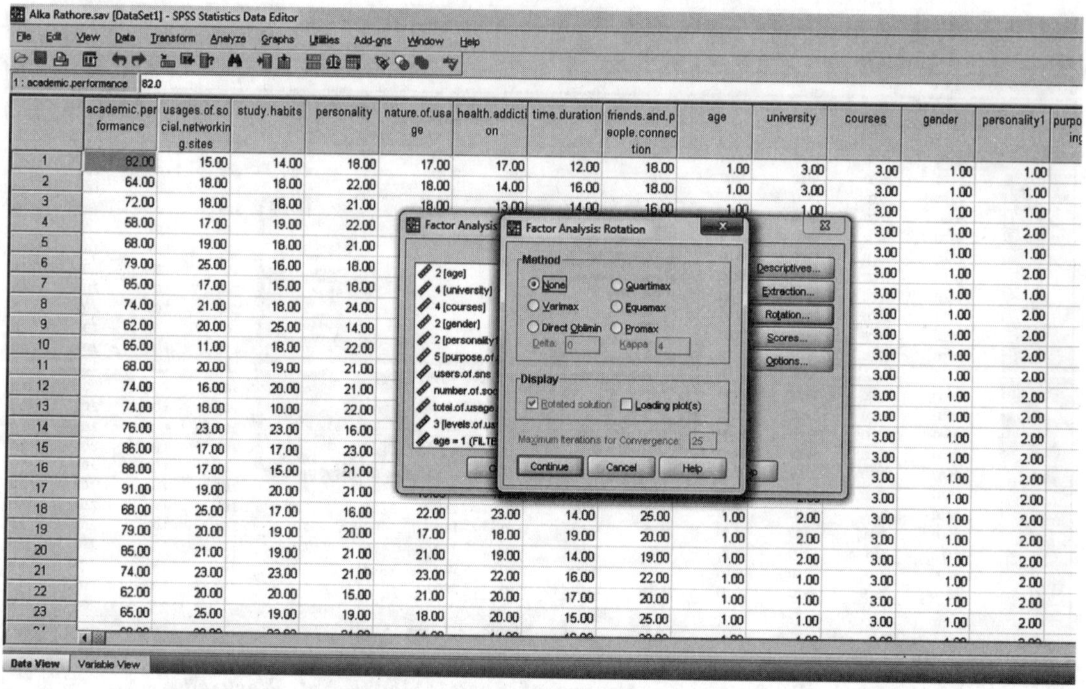

486. Under "**Method**" highlight "**Varimax**" to get the following screen.

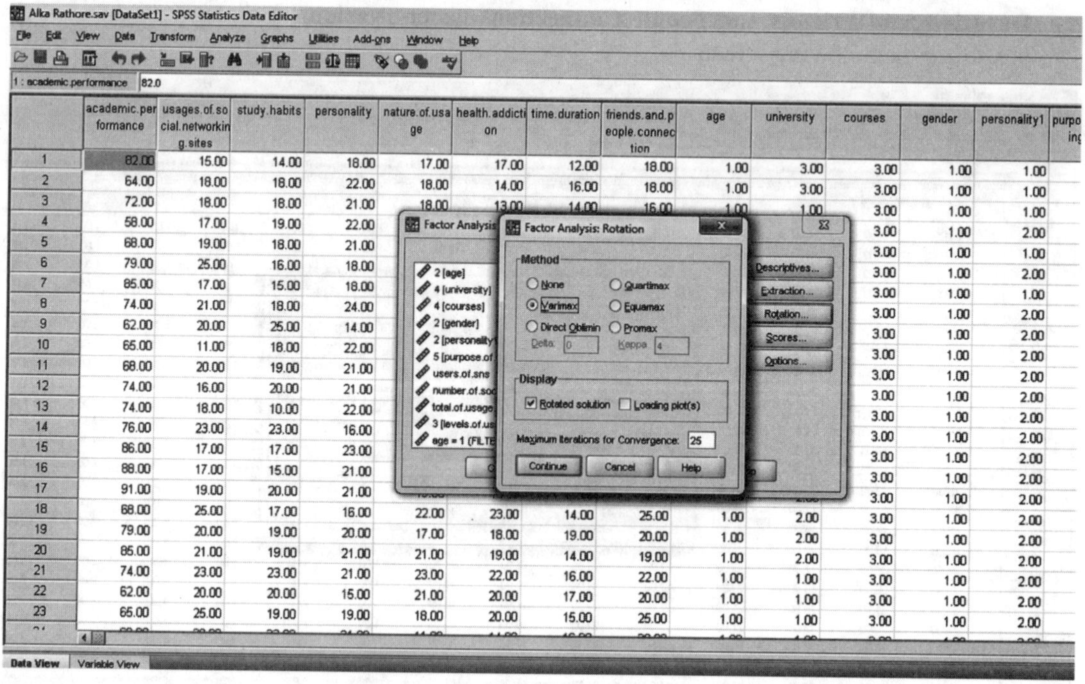

487. Click on "**Continue**" icon to get the following screen.

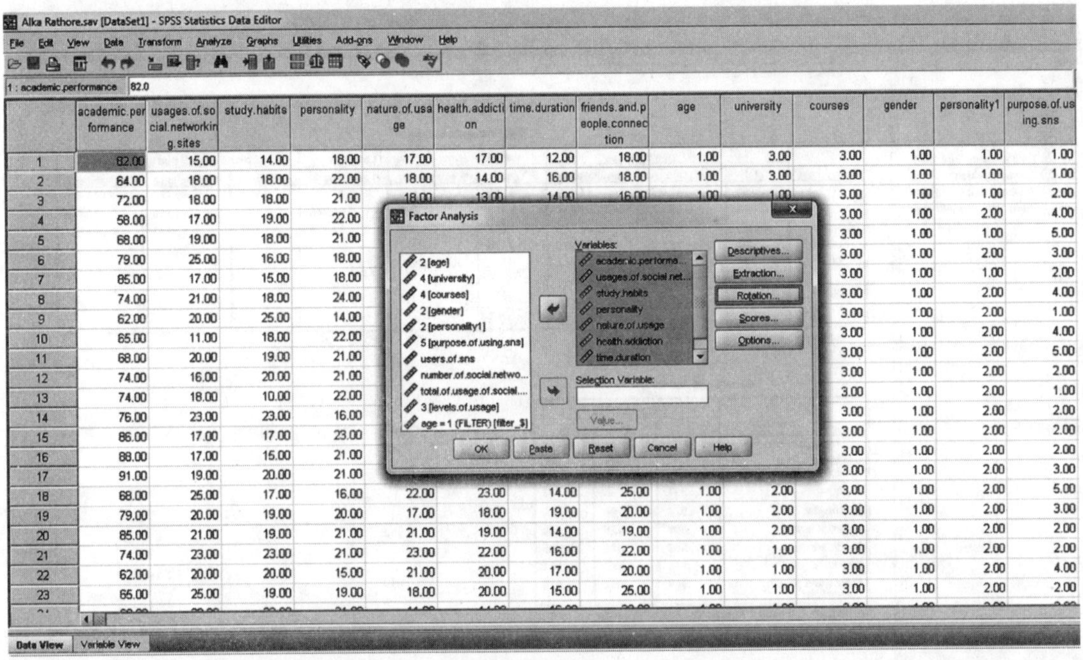

488. Click on "**OK**" to get the following outputs of "**Factor Analysis**".

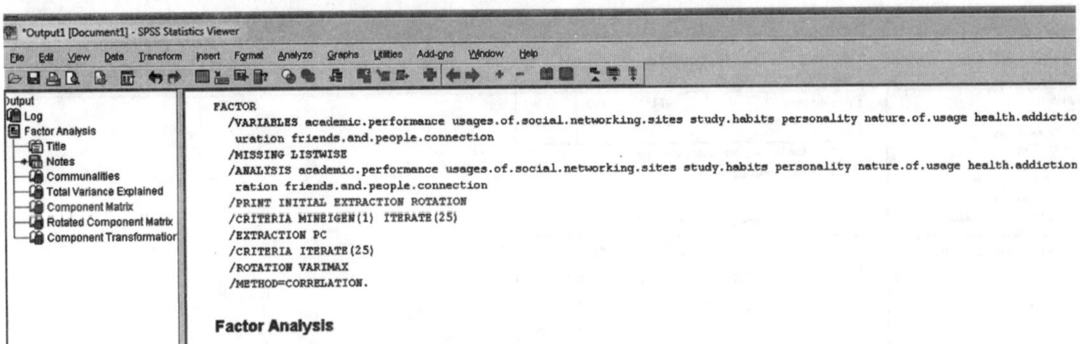

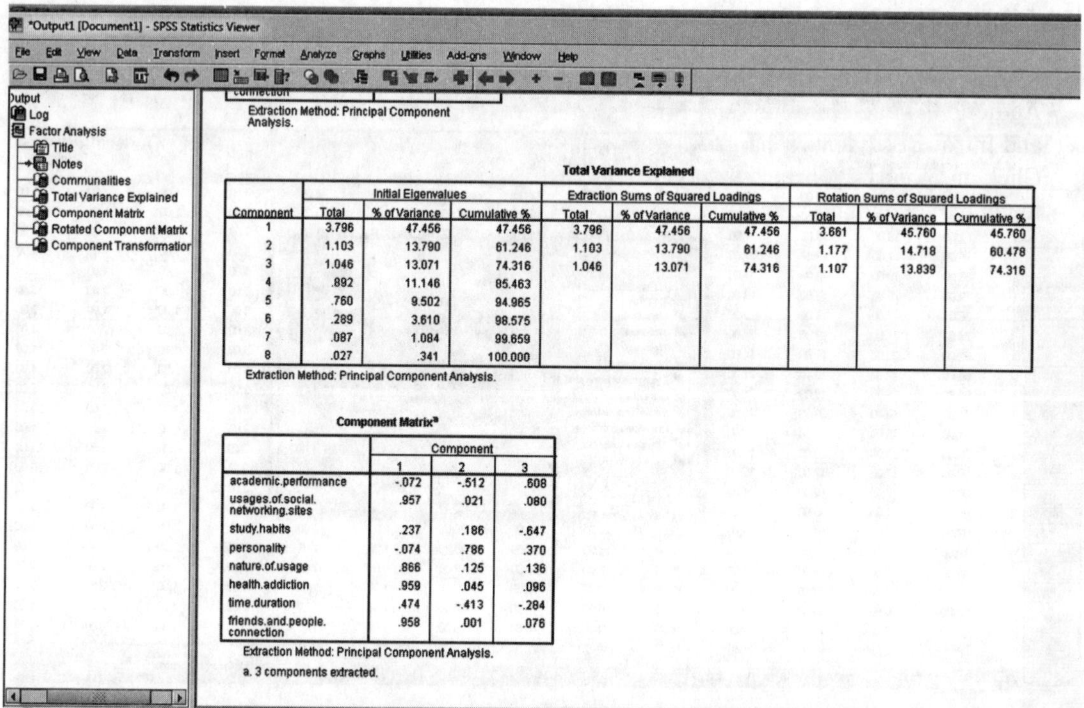

Extraction Method: Principal Component Analysis.

Total Variance Explained

Component	Initial Eigenvalues			Extraction Sums of Squared Loadings			Rotation Sums of Squared Loadings		
	Total	% of Variance	Cumulative %	Total	% of Variance	Cumulative %	Total	% of Variance	Cumulative %
1	3.796	47.456	47.456	3.796	47.456	47.456	3.661	45.760	45.760
2	1.103	13.790	61.246	1.103	13.790	61.246	1.177	14.718	60.478
3	1.046	13.071	74.316	1.046	13.071	74.316	1.107	13.839	74.316
4	.892	11.146	85.463						
5	.760	9.502	94.965						
6	.289	3.610	98.575						
7	.087	1.084	99.659						
8	.027	.341	100.000						

Extraction Method: Principal Component Analysis.

Component Matrix[a]

	Component		
	1	2	3
academic.performance	-.072	-.512	.608
usages.of.social.networking.sites	.957	.021	.080
study.habits	.237	.186	-.647
personality	-.074	.786	.370
nature.of.usage	.866	.125	.136
health.addiction	.959	.045	.096
time.duration	.474	-.413	-.284
friends.and.people.connection	.958	.001	.076

Extraction Method: Principal Component Analysis.

a. 3 components extracted.

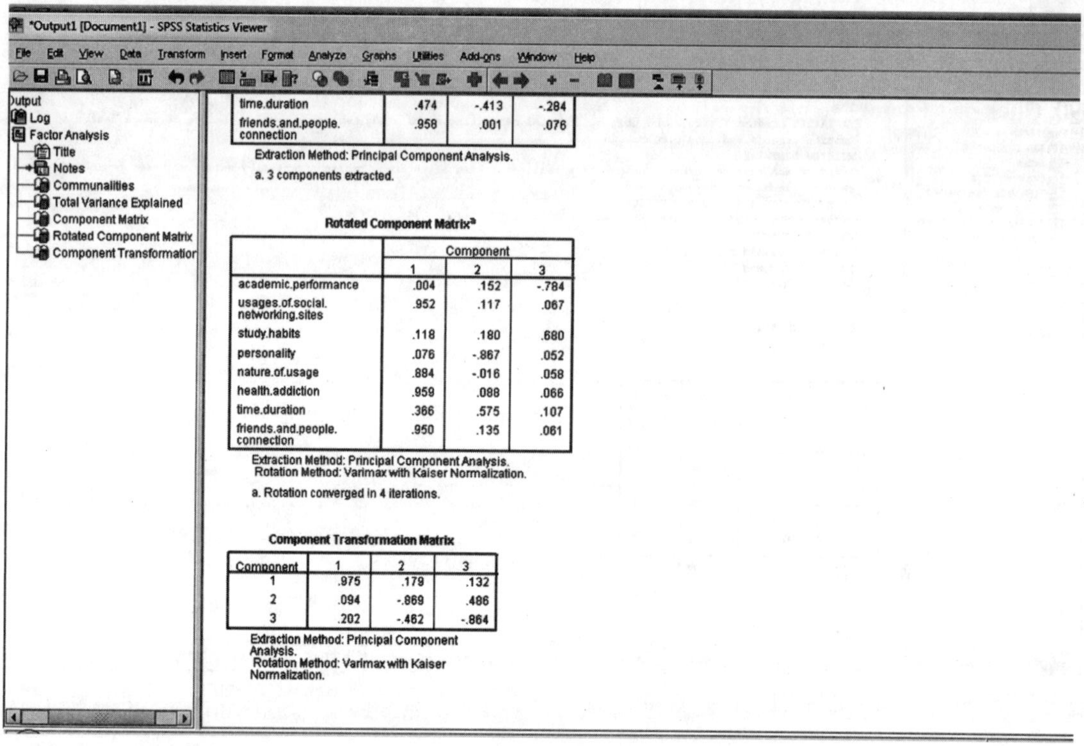

time.duration	.474	-.413	-.284
friends.and.people.connection	.958	.001	.076

Extraction Method: Principal Component Analysis.

a. 3 components extracted.

Rotated Component Matrix[a]

	Component		
	1	2	3
academic.performance	.004	.152	-.784
usages.of.social.networking.sites	.952	.117	.067
study.habits	.118	.180	.680
personality	.076	-.867	.052
nature.of.usage	.884	-.016	.058
health.addiction	.959	.088	.066
time.duration	.366	.575	.107
friends.and.people.connection	.950	.135	.061

Extraction Method: Principal Component Analysis.
Rotation Method: Varimax with Kaiser Normalization.

a. Rotation converged in 4 iterations.

Component Transformation Matrix

Component	1	2	3
1	.975	.179	.132
2	.094	-.869	.486
3	.202	-.462	-.864

Extraction Method: Principal Component Analysis.
Rotation Method: Varimax with Kaiser Normalization.

489. Let us consider the following objective of research.
To study factor structure underlying Academic Performance, Usages of Social Media Net Working sites, Study Habits, Personality, Nature of Usage, Health Addiction, Time Duration, and Friends and People Connection of Extrovert and Introvert students separately.
Click on "**Analysis**" bring curser on "**Dimension Reduction**" and to "**Factor**" to get the following screen.

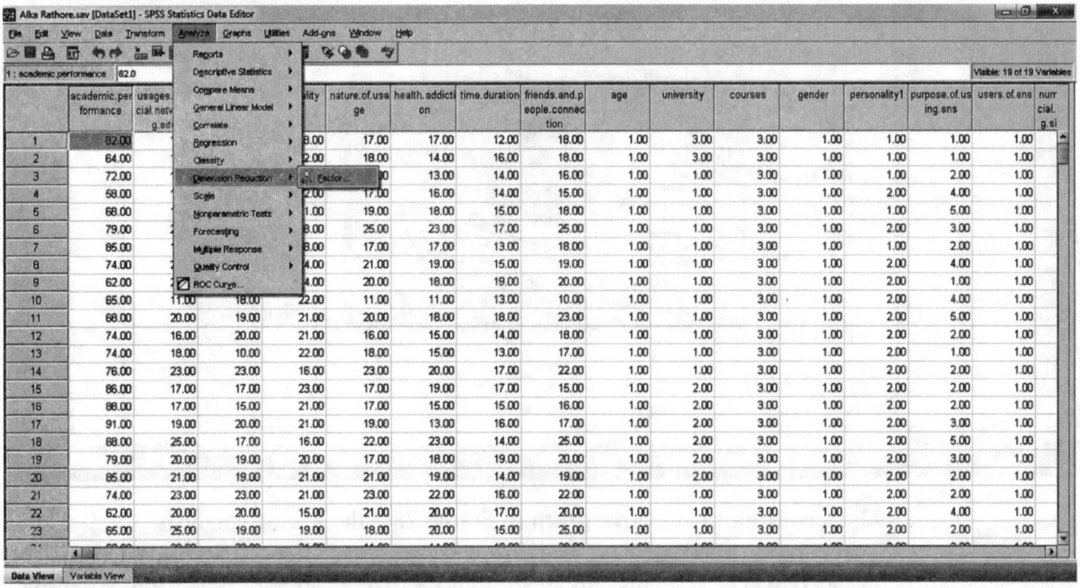

490. Click on "**Factor**" to get the following screen.

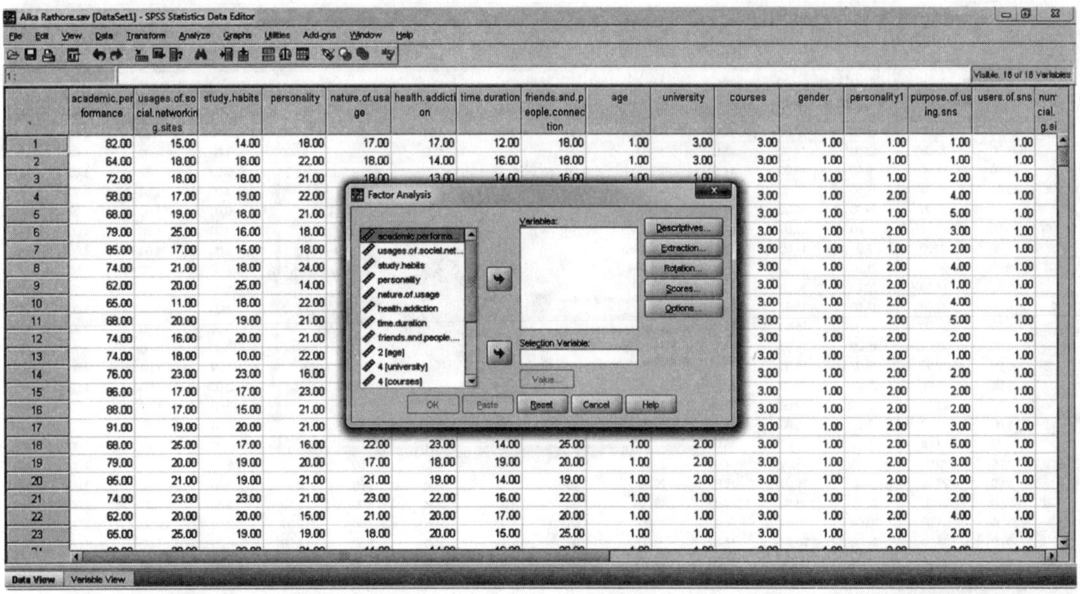

491. Shift "**Academic Performance, Usages of Social Media Net Working sites, Study Habits, Personality, Nature of Usage, Health Addiction, Time Duration, and Friends and People Connection**" under "**Variables**" dialog box to get the following screen.

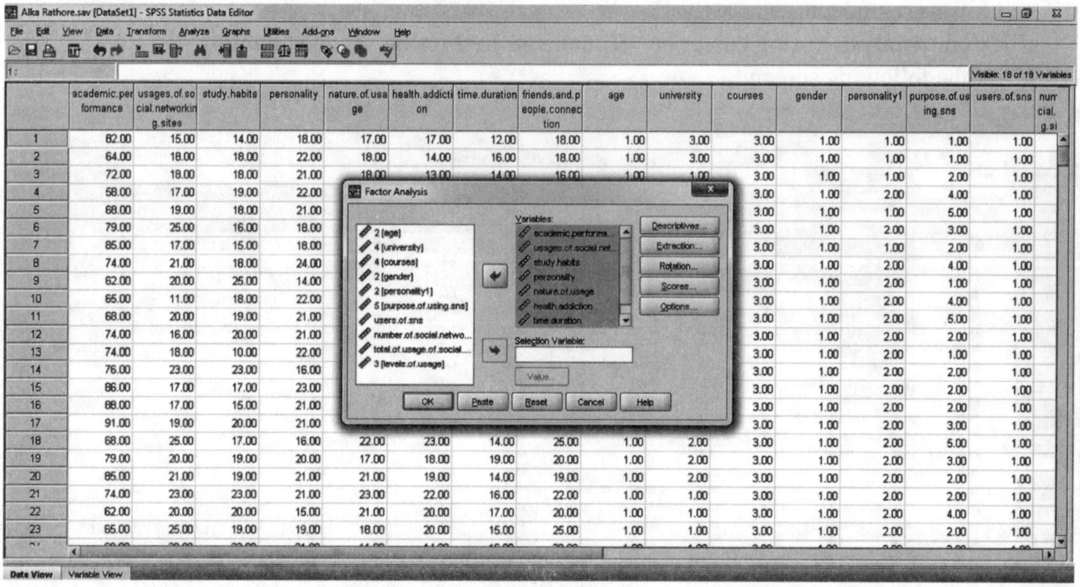

492. According to objective given in Frame 289, the Factor Analysis is to be done separately for Extrovert and Introvert students. Let us first do analysis for "**Extrovert**" students. So shift "**Personality 1**" under "**Selection Variable**" slot to get the following screen.

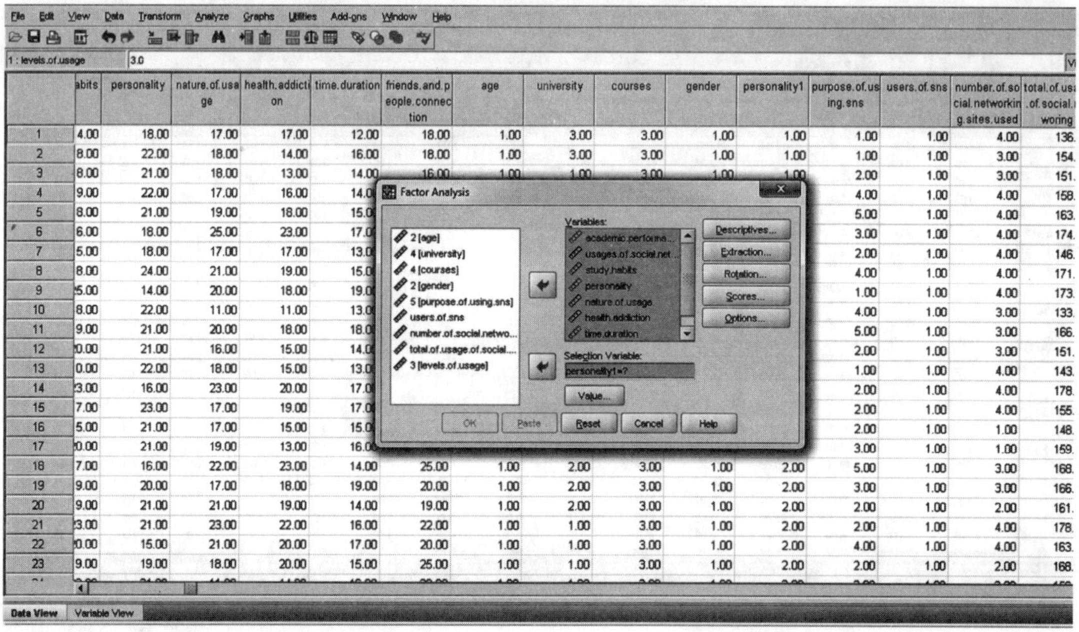

493. Click on "**Value**" to get the following screen.

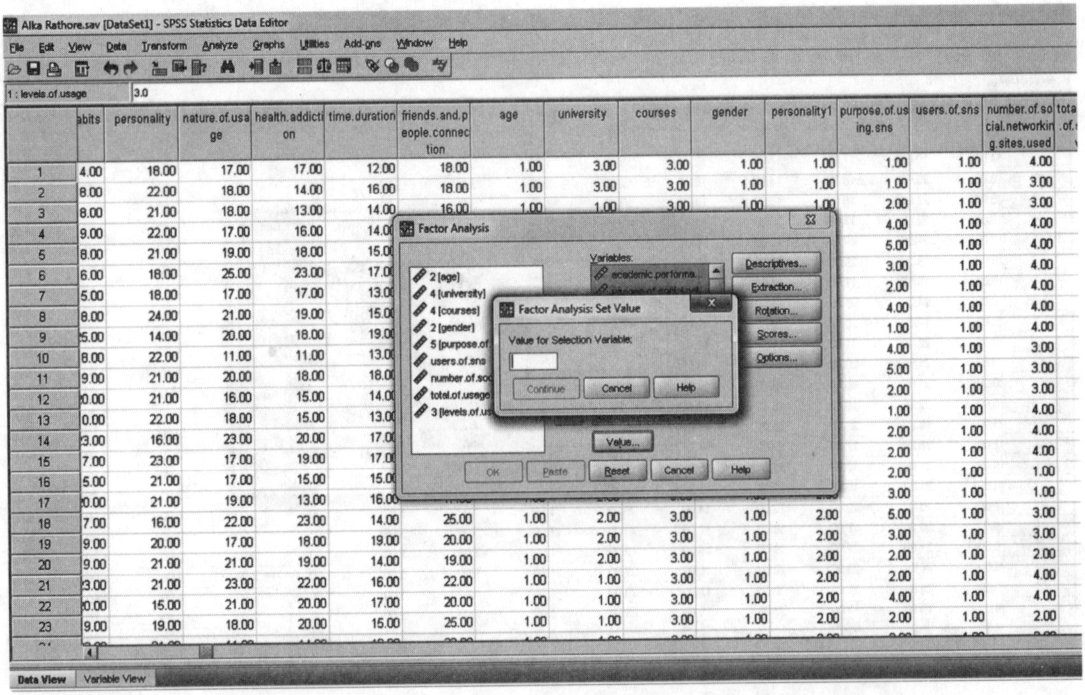

494. "**Extrovert**" is represented by "**1**" so type "**1**" under "**Value for selection Variable**" to get the following screen.

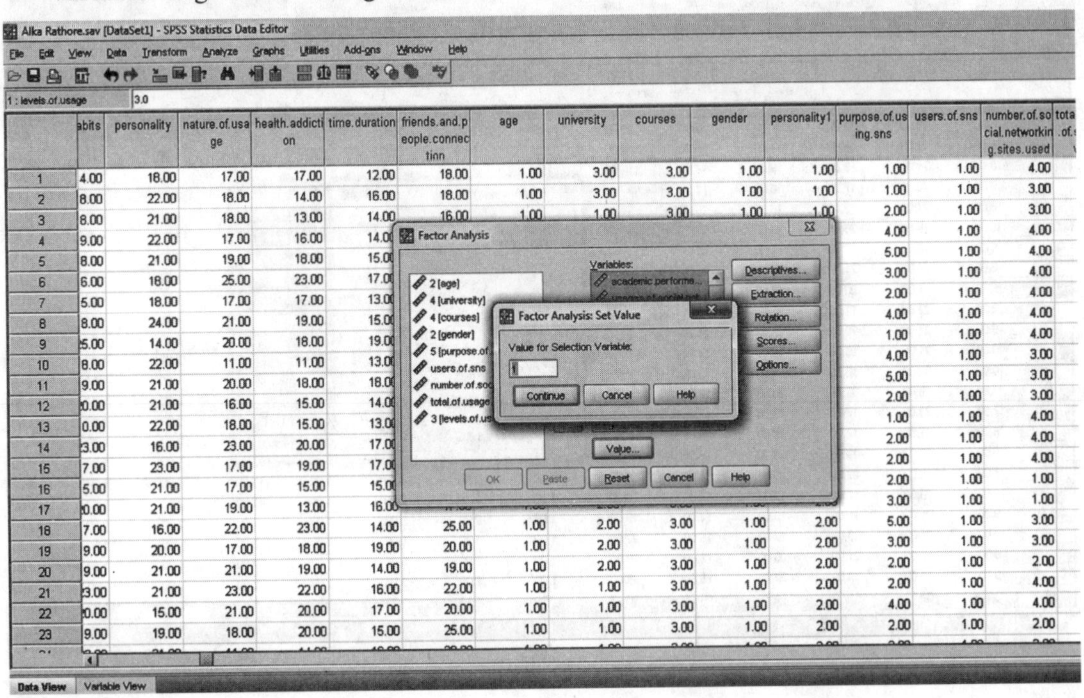

495. Click on "**Continue**" to get the following screen.

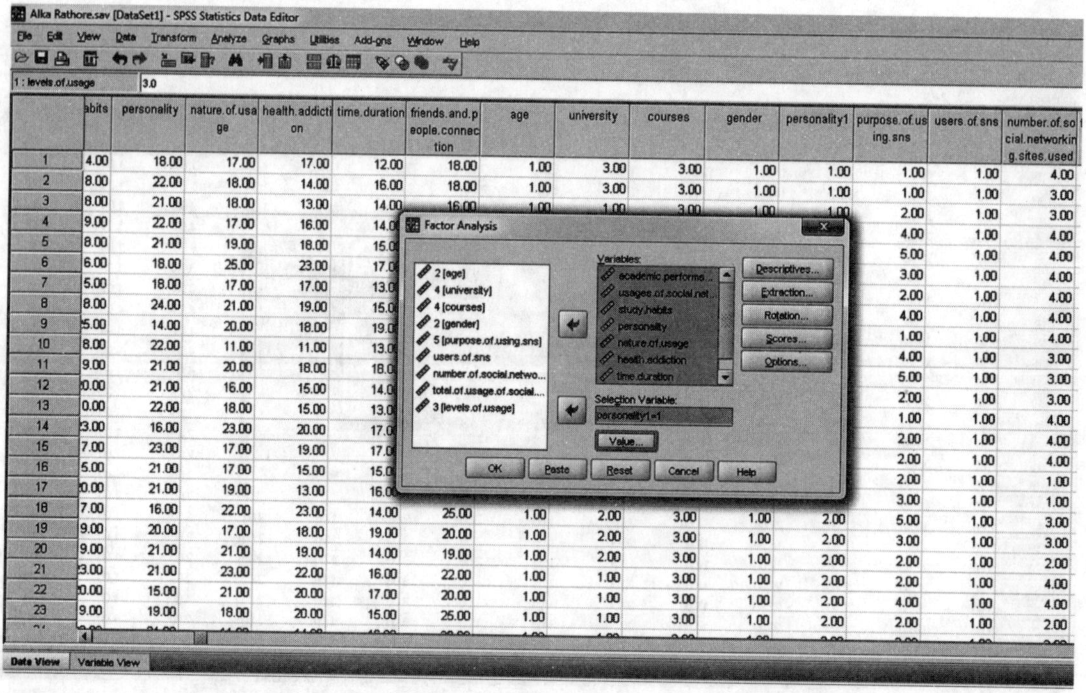

496. Click on "**Rotation**" icon to get the following screen.

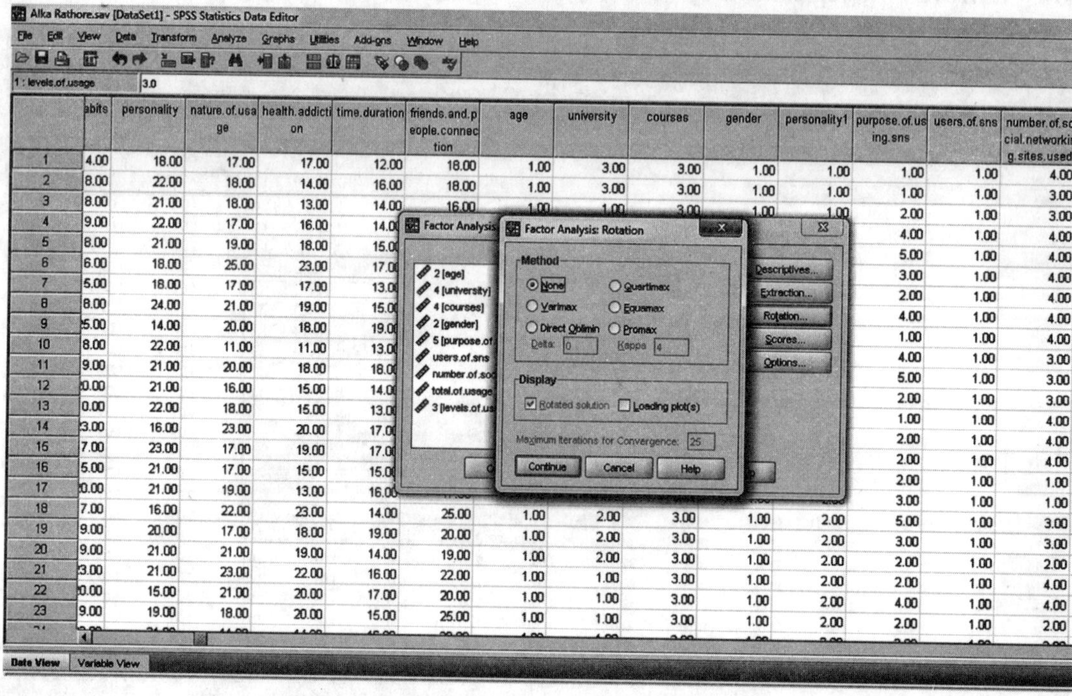

497. Under "**Method**" Click on "**Varimax**" to get the following screen.

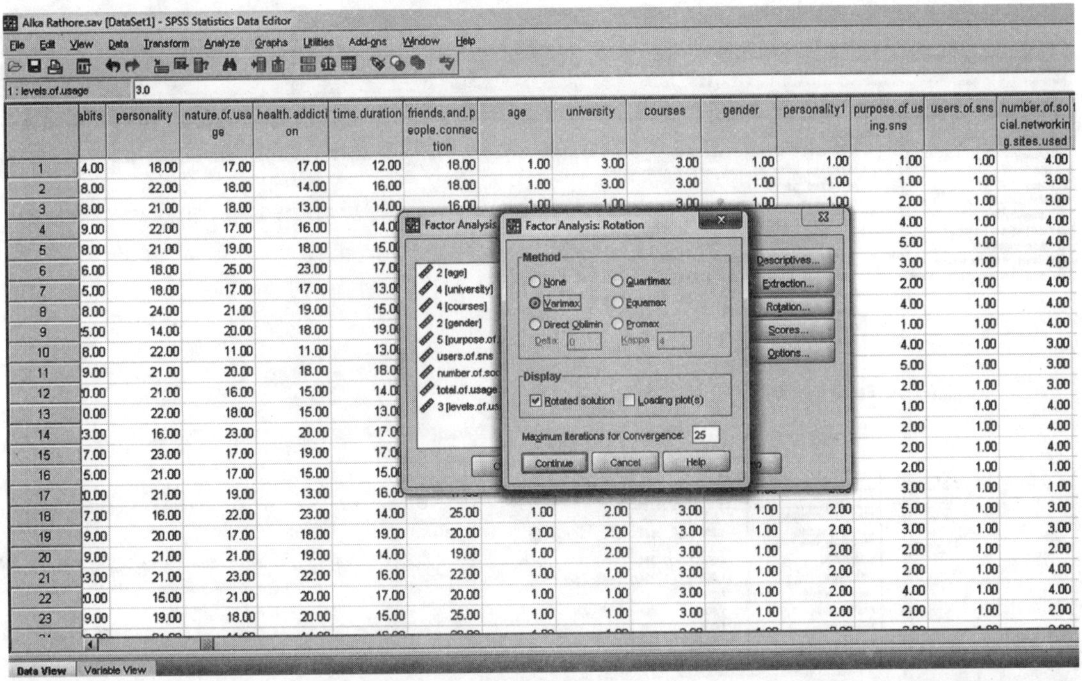

498. Click on "**Continue**" to get the following screen.

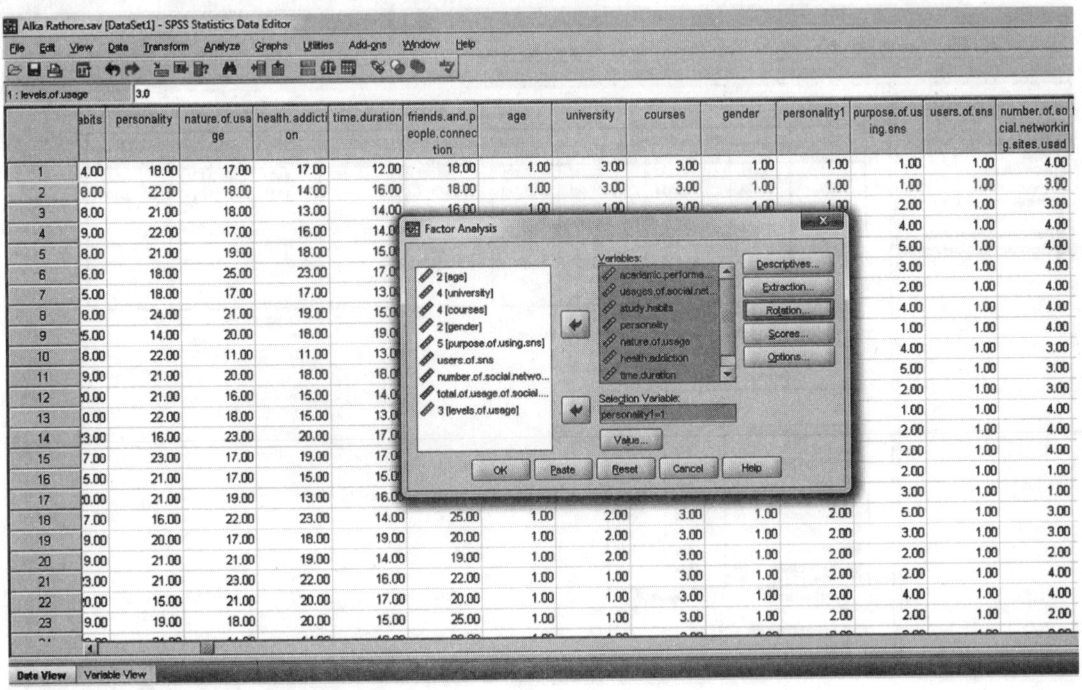

499. Click on "**OK**" to get the following outputs of Factor Analysis of Extrovert students.

```
FACTOR
  /VARIABLES academic.performance usages.of.social.networking.sites study.habits personality nature.of.usage health.addiction time.d
uration friends.and.people.connection
  /MISSING LISTWISE
  /ANALYSIS academic.performance usages.of.social.networking.sites study.habits personality nature.of.usage health.addiction time.du
ration friends.and.people.connection
  /SELECT=personality1(1)
  /PRINT INITIAL EXTRACTION ROTATION
  /CRITERIA MINEIGEN(1) ITERATE(25)
  /EXTRACTION PC
  /CRITERIA ITERATE(25)
  /ROTATION VARIMAX
  /METHOD=CORRELATION.
```

Factor Analysis

[DataSet1] D:\Documents\Alka Rathore.sav

Communalities[a]

	Initial	Extraction
academic.performance	1.000	.605
usages.of.social.networking.sites	1.000	.898
study.habits	1.000	.271
personality	1.000	.304
nature.of.usage	1.000	.691
health.addiction	1.000	.891
time.duration	1.000	.237
friends.and.people.connection	1.000	.903

Extraction Method: Principal Component Analysis.

Total Variance Explained[a]

Component	Initial Eigenvalues			Extraction Sums of Squared Loadings			Rotation Sums of Squared Loadings		
	Total	% of Variance	Cumulative %	Total	% of Variance	Cumulative %	Total	% of Variance	Cumulative %
1	3.671	45.887	45.887	3.671	45.887	45.887	3.660	45.753	45.753
2	1.129	14.114	60.001	1.129	14.114	60.001	1.140	14.248	60.001
3	.981	12.268	72.269						
4	.941	11.763	84.032						
5	.787	9.839	93.871						
6	.367	4.588	98.459						
7	.094	1.176	99.635						
8	.029	.365	100.000						

Extraction Method: Principal Component Analysis.

a. Only cases for which 2 = Introvert are used in the analysis phase.

Component Matrix[a,b]

	Component 1	Component 2
academic.performance	-.010	.778
usages.of.social.networking.sites	.947	.002
study.habits	.397	-.337
personality	-.081	-.545
nature.of.usage	.825	-.101
health.addiction	.944	.028
time.duration	.369	.318
friends.and.people.connection	.949	.036

Extraction Method: Principal Component Analysis.

a. 2 components extracted.

b. Only cases for which 2 = Introvert are used in the analysis phase.

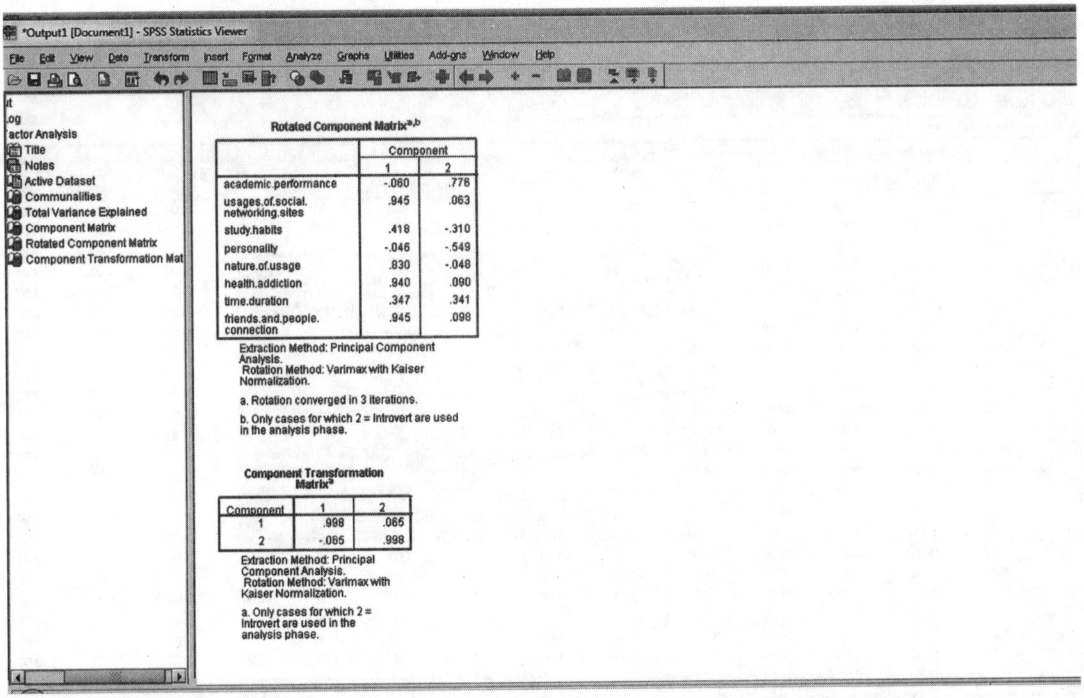

500. For doing analysis for "**Introvert**" students, click on "**Value**" to get the following screen.

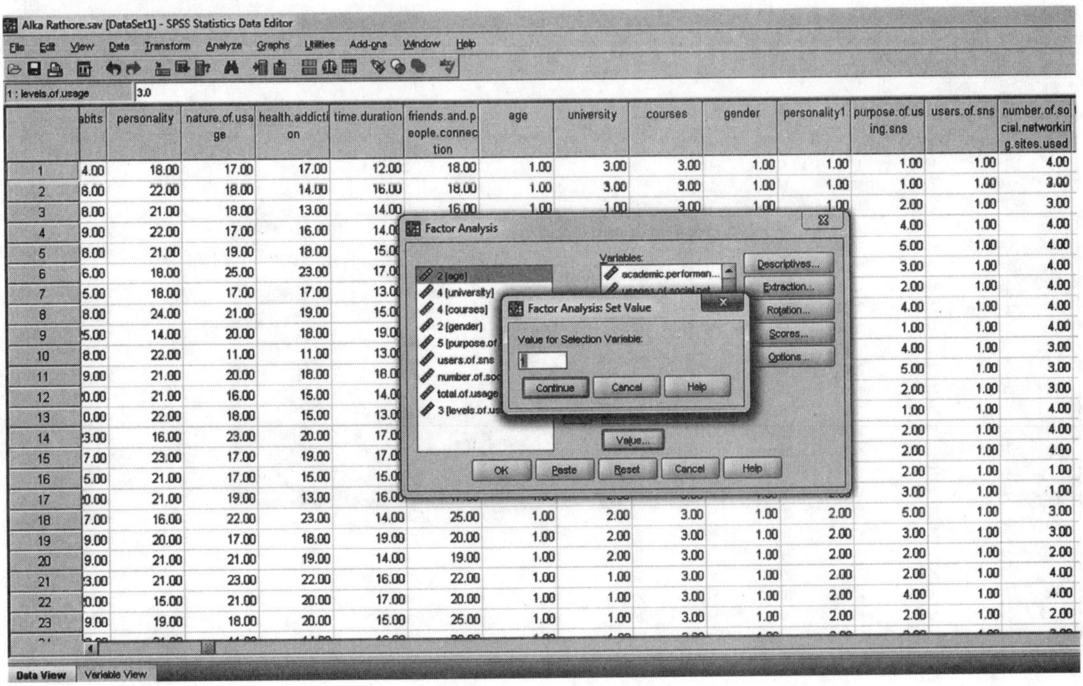

501. Type "**2**" under "**Value for Selection Variable**" to get the following screen.

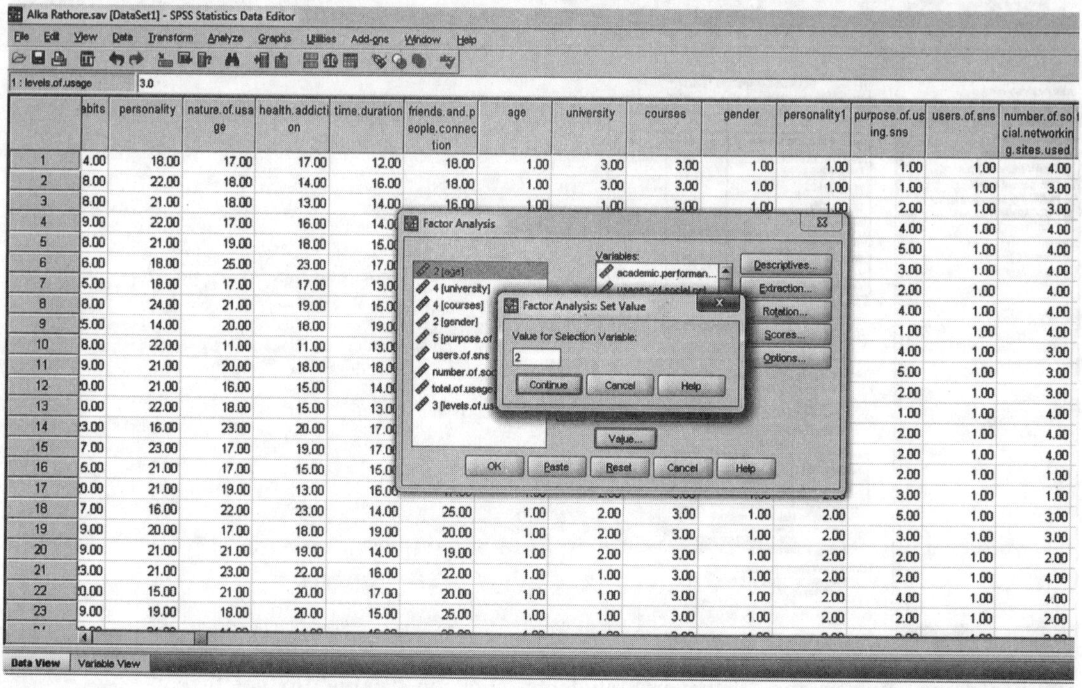

502. Click on "**Continue**" icon to get the following screen.

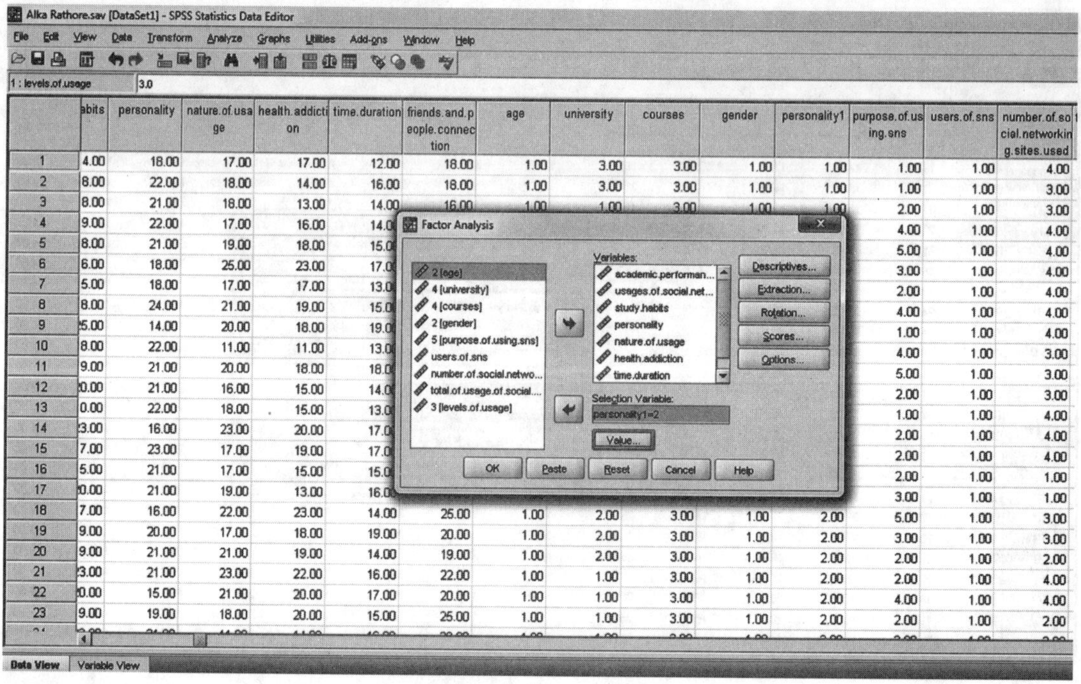

503. Click on "**OK**" to get the following Outputs of Factor Analysis of Introvert students.

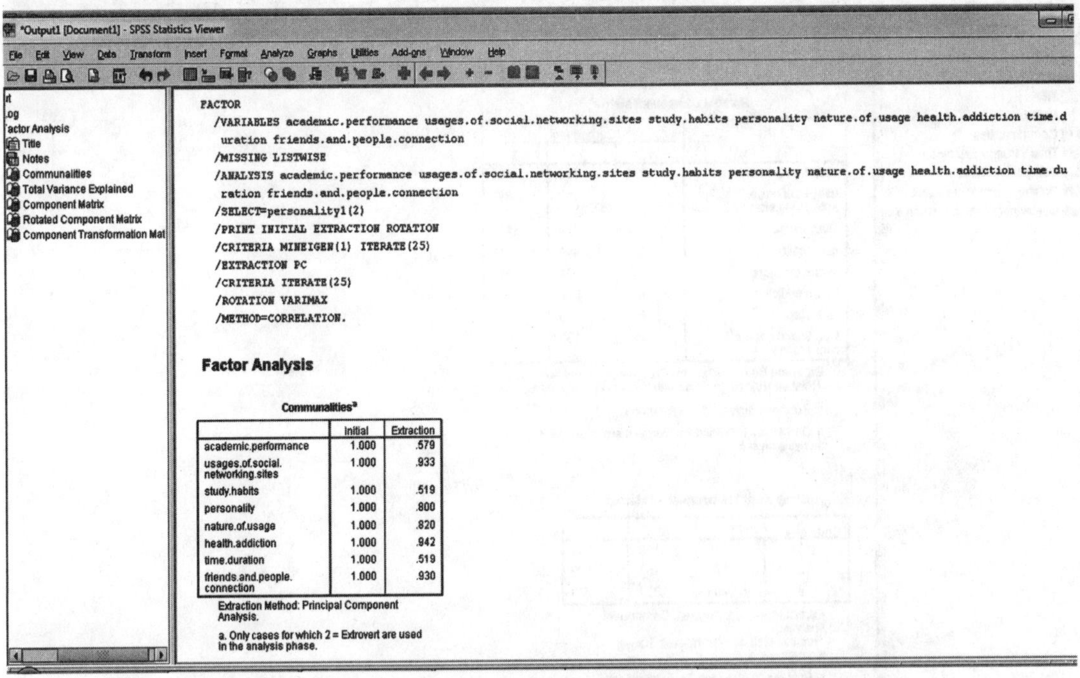

*Output1 [Document1] - SPSS Statistics Viewer

Output outline: Log; Factor Analysis; Title; Notes; Communalities; Total Variance Explained; Component Matrix; Rotated Component Matrix; Component Transformation Mat

```
FACTOR
  /VARIABLES academic.performance usages.of.social.networking.sites study.habits personality nature.of.usage health.addiction time.d
   uration friends.and.people.connection
  /MISSING LISTWISE
  /ANALYSIS academic.performance usages.of.social.networking.sites study.habits personality nature.of.usage health.addiction time.du
   ration friends.and.people.connection
  /SELECT=personality1(2)
  /PRINT INITIAL EXTRACTION ROTATION
  /CRITERIA MINEIGEN(1) ITERATE(25)
  /EXTRACTION PC
  /CRITERIA ITERATE(25)
  /ROTATION VARIMAX
  /METHOD=CORRELATION.
```

Factor Analysis

Communalities[a]

	Initial	Extraction
academic.performance	1.000	.579
usages.of.social.networking.sites	1.000	.933
study.habits	1.000	.519
personality	1.000	.800
nature.of.usage	1.000	.820
health.addiction	1.000	.942
time.duration	1.000	.519
friends.and.people.connection	1.000	.930

Extraction Method: Principal Component Analysis.

a. Only cases for which 2 = Extrovert are used in the analysis phase.

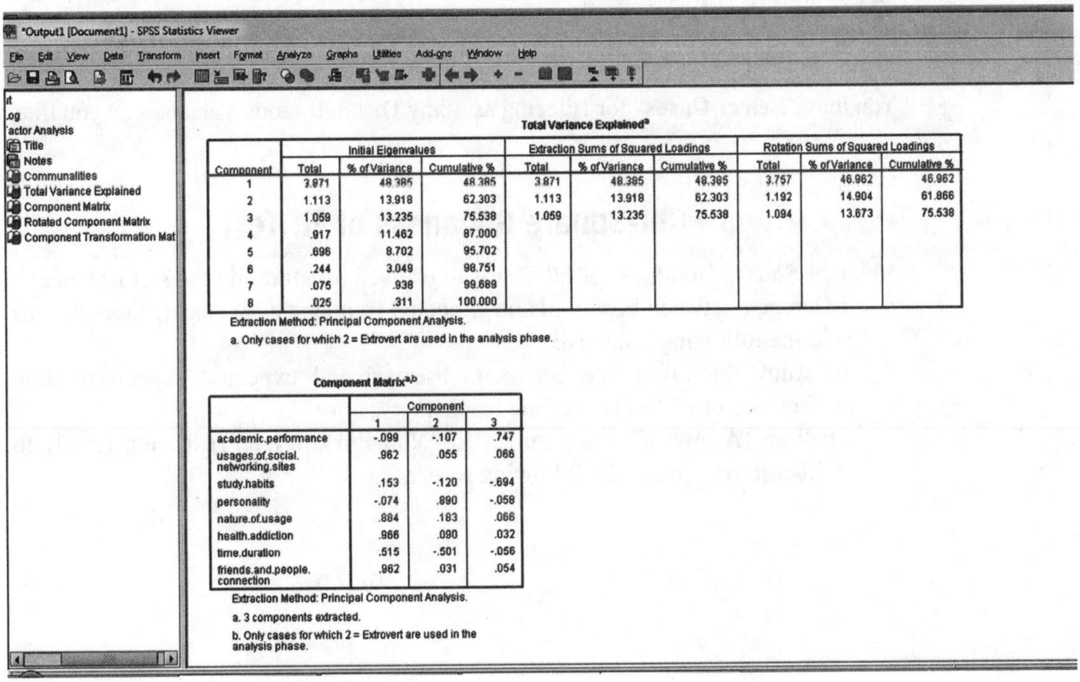

*Output1 [Document1] - SPSS Statistics Viewer

Total Variance Explained[a]

Component	Initial Eigenvalues			Extraction Sums of Squared Loadings			Rotation Sums of Squared Loadings		
	Total	% of Variance	Cumulative %	Total	% of Variance	Cumulative %	Total	% of Variance	Cumulative %
1	3.871	48.385	48.385	3.871	48.385	48.385	3.757	46.962	46.962
2	1.113	13.918	62.303	1.113	13.918	62.303	1.192	14.904	61.866
3	1.059	13.235	75.538	1.059	13.235	75.538	1.094	13.673	75.538
4	.917	11.462	87.000						
5	.696	8.702	95.702						
6	.244	3.049	98.751						
7	.075	.938	99.689						
8	.025	.311	100.000						

Extraction Method: Principal Component Analysis.

a. Only cases for which 2 = Extrovert are used in the analysis phase.

Component Matrix[a,b]

	Component		
	1	2	3
academic.performance	-.099	-.107	.747
usages.of.social.networking.sites	.962	.055	.066
study.habits	.153	-.120	-.694
personality	-.074	.890	-.058
nature.of.usage	.884	.183	.066
health.addiction	.966	.090	.032
time.duration	.515	-.501	-.056
friends.and.people.connection	.962	.031	.054

Extraction Method: Principal Component Analysis.

a. 3 components extracted.

b. Only cases for which 2 = Extrovert are used in the analysis phase.

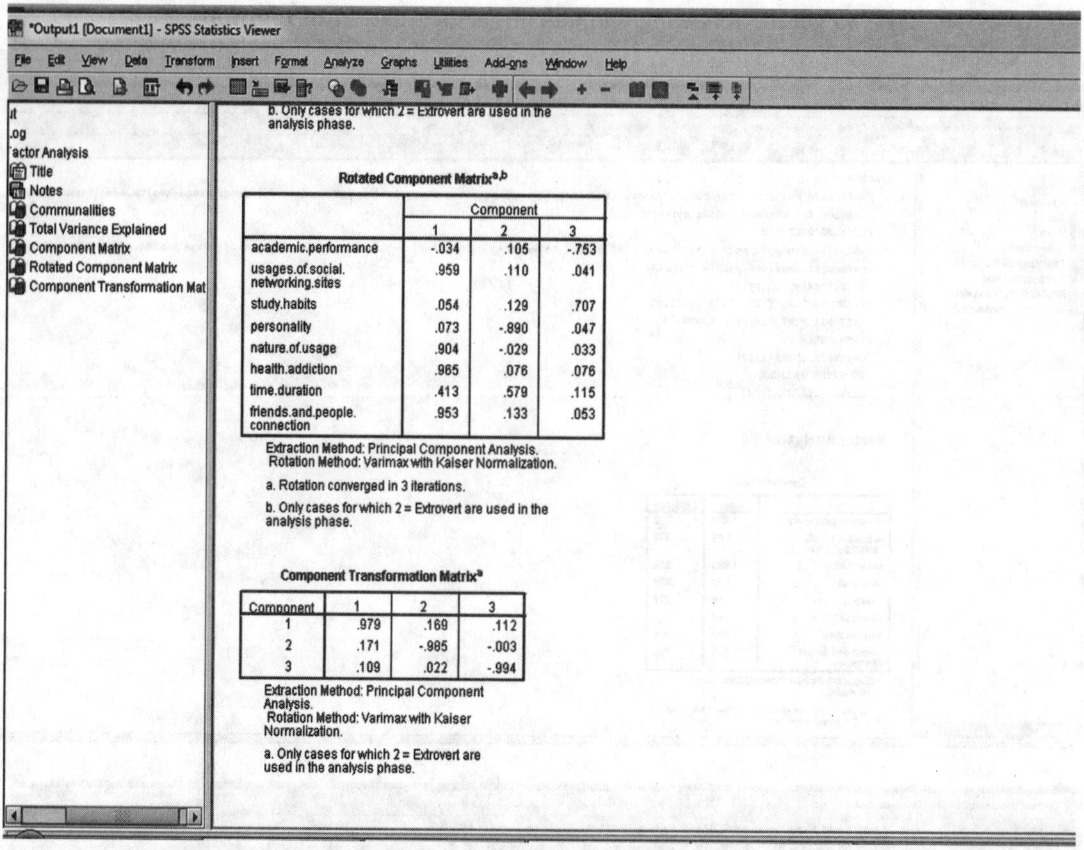

Rotated Component Matrix[a,b]

	Component		
	1	2	3
academic.performance	-.034	.105	-.753
usages.of.social.networking.sites	.959	.110	.041
study.habits	.054	.129	.707
personality	.073	-.890	.047
nature.of.usage	.904	-.029	.033
health.addiction	.965	.076	.076
time.duration	.413	.579	.115
friends.and.people.connection	.953	.133	.053

Extraction Method: Principal Component Analysis.
Rotation Method: Varimax with Kaiser Normalization.

a. Rotation converged in 3 iterations.

b. Only cases for which 2 = Extrovert are used in the analysis phase.

Component Transformation Matrix[a]

Component	1	2	3
1	.979	.169	.112
2	.171	-.985	-.003
3	.109	.022	-.994

Extraction Method: Principal Component Analysis.
Rotation Method: Varimax with Kaiser Normalization.

a. Only cases for which 2 = Extrovert are used in the analysis phase.

You may "**Select Cases**" for filtering as many Discontinuous Variables as you like.

Chi-Square Goodness of Fit Test

504. Chi-Square Goodness of Fit Test is to be used for studying the significance of difference between observed and expected frequencies or occurrences. Let us take the following objective.

To study the difference between observed and expected vegetarian food preferences of Male and Female teachers.

Click on "**Analysis**", bring curser to "**Non-Parametric Test**" and finally to "**Chi-Square**" to get the following screen.

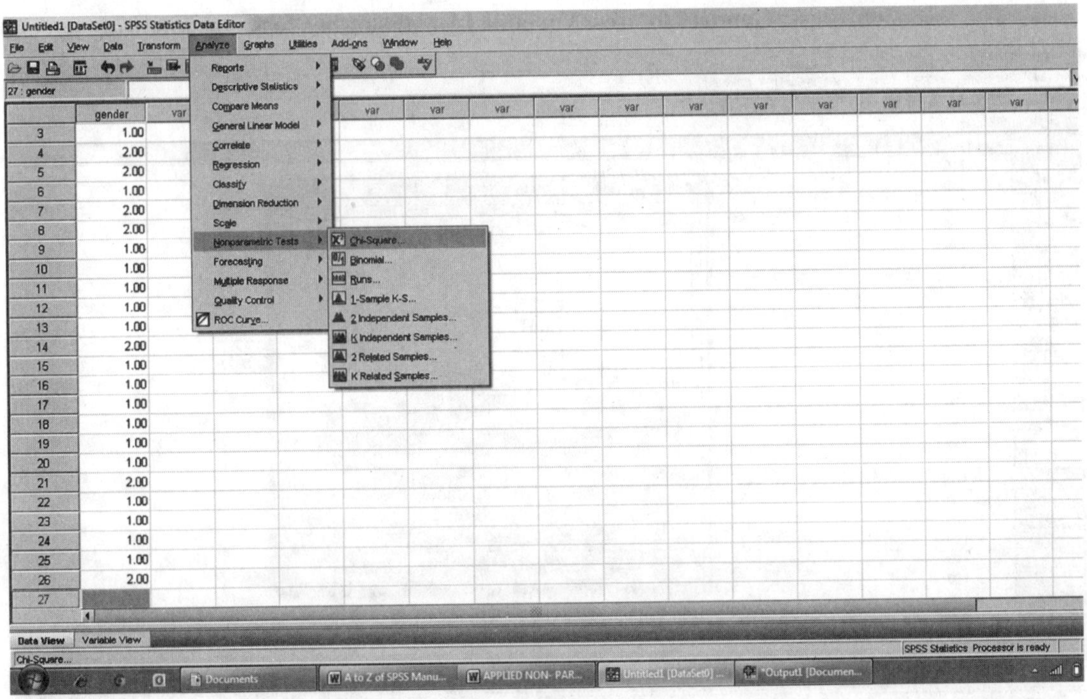

505. Click on "**Chi-Square**" to get the following screen.

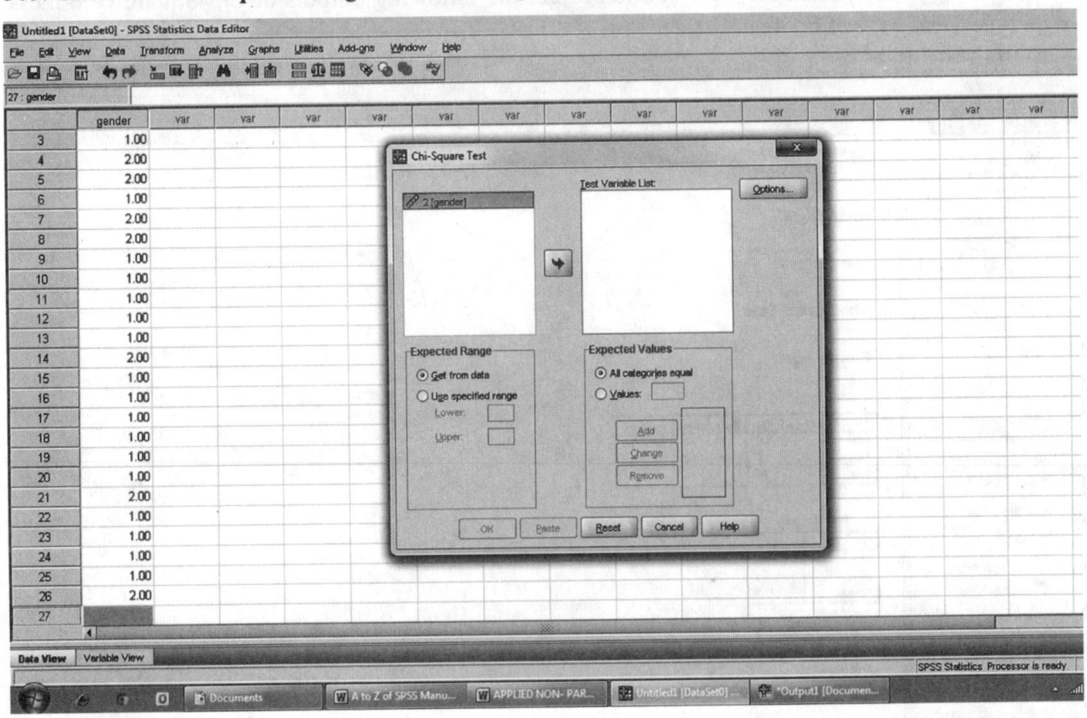

506. Shift "**Gender**" to "**Test Variable List**" dialog box to get the following screen.

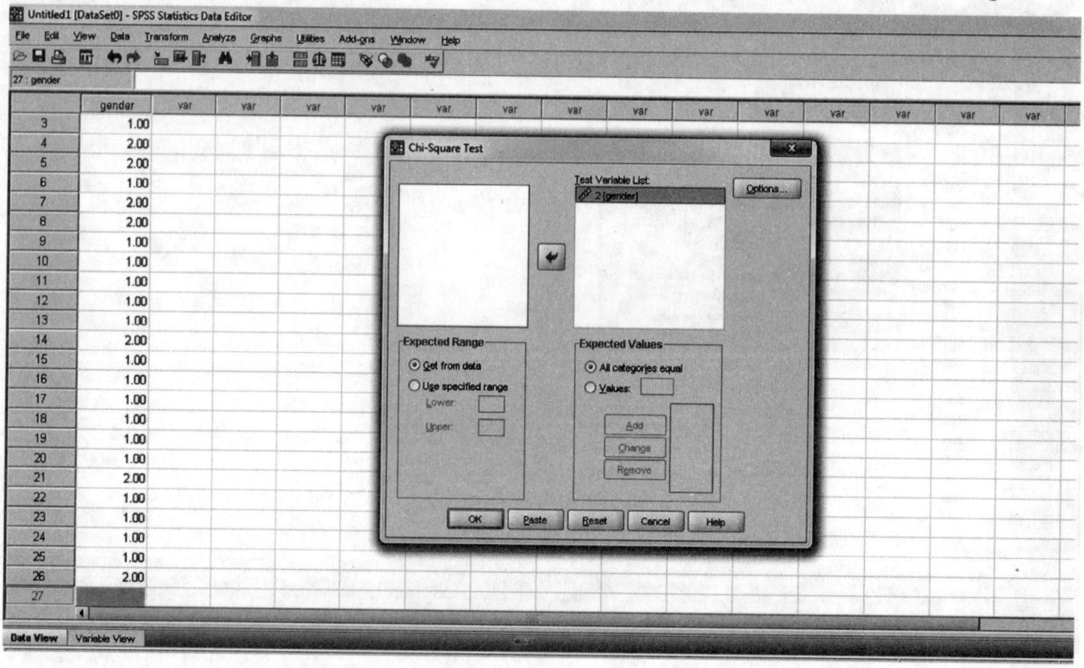

507. Click on "**OK**" button to get the following outputs of Chi-Square Goodness of Fit Test.

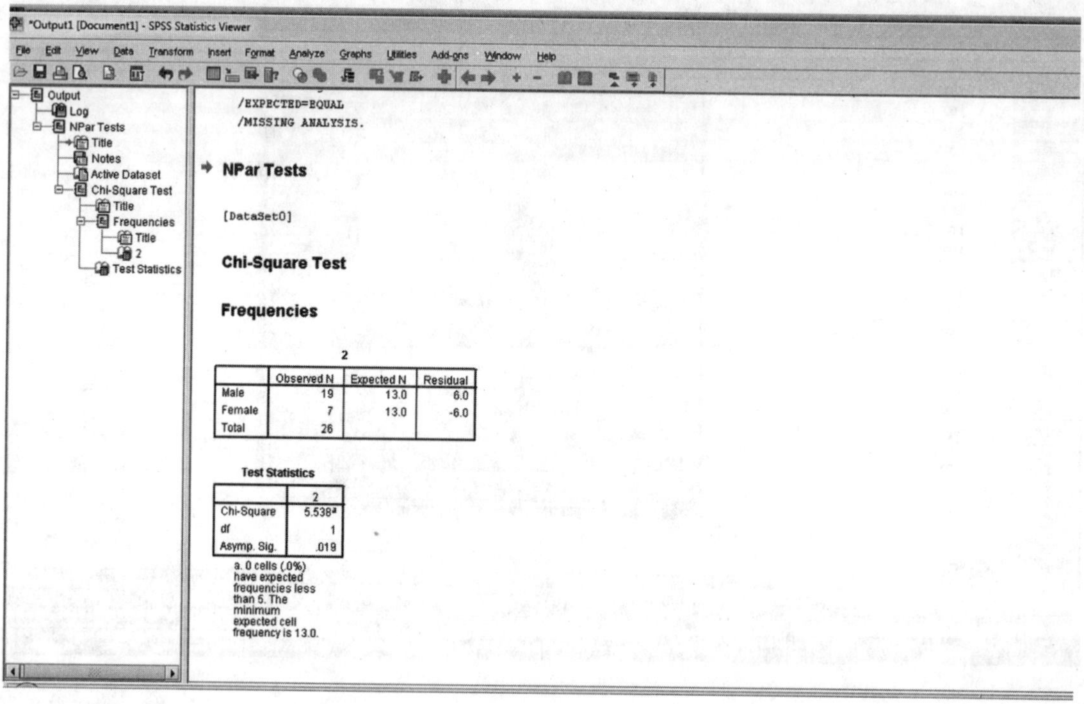

508. Chi-Square Test can also be used for studying the association between two discontinuous variables. Each discontinuous variable must have two or more labels or categories. Let us take the following objective.

To study the association between Gender and Reaction toward Online Teaching of Teachers.

Click on "**Analyse**", bring curser to "**Descriptive Statistics**" and then to "**Crosstabs**" to get the following screen.

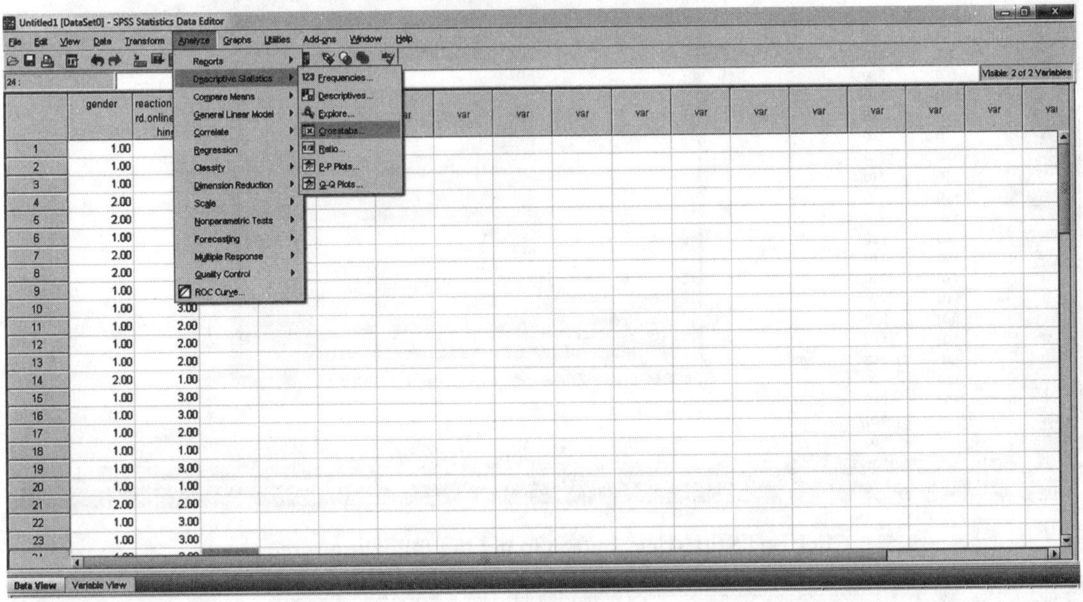

509. Click on "**Crosstabs**" to get the following screen.

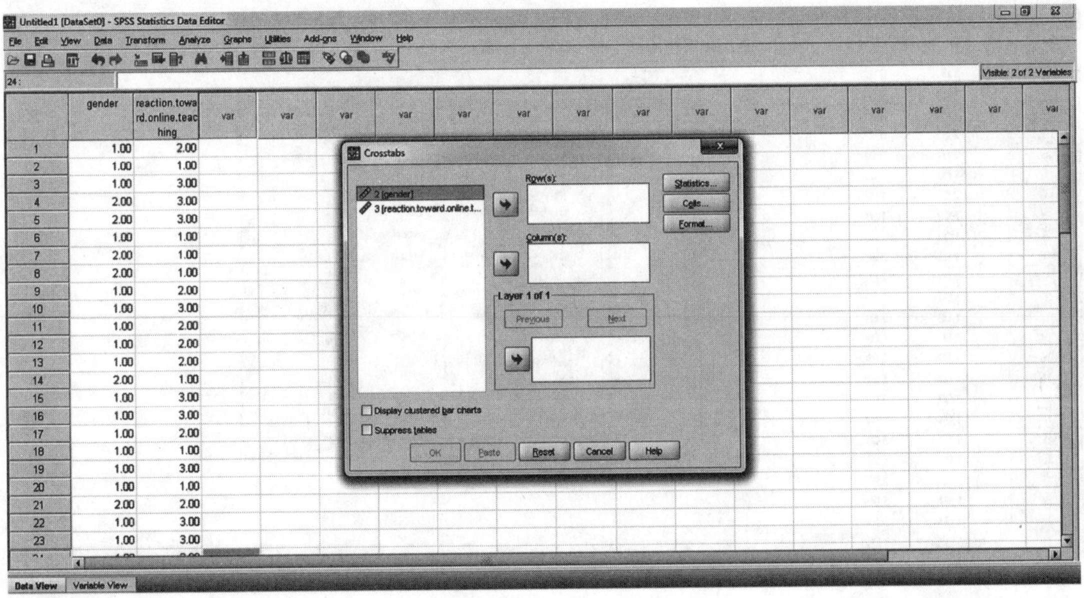

510. Shift "**Gender**" variable to "**Row(s)**" slot and "**Reaction towards Online Teaching**" variable to "**Column(s)**" slot to get the following screen.

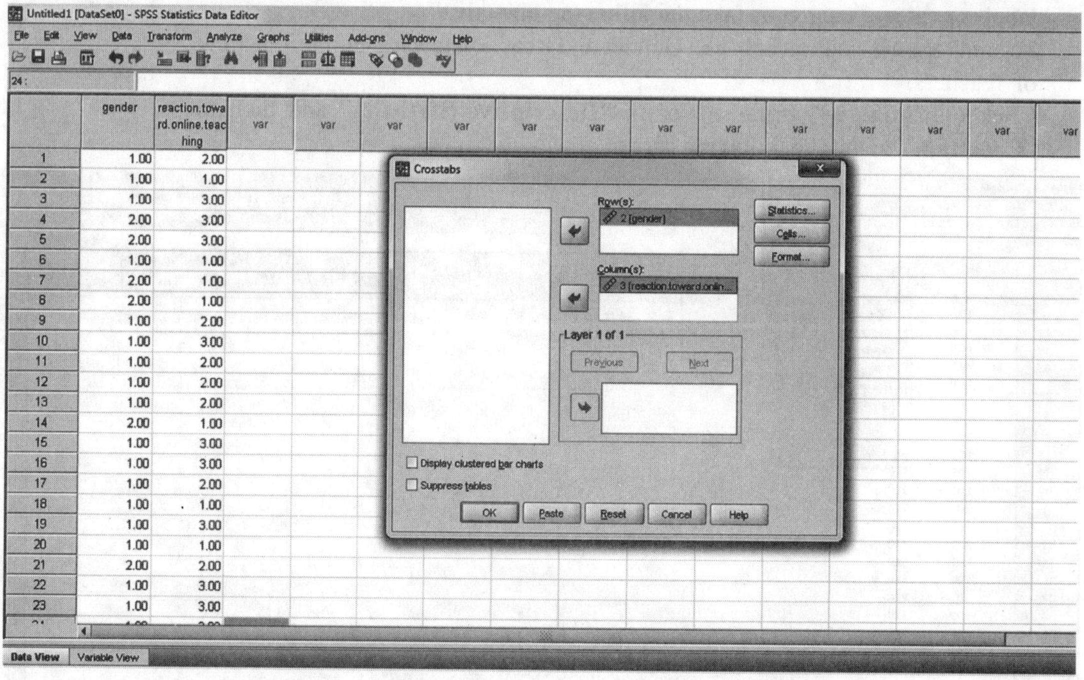

511. Click on "**Statistics**" button to get the following screen.

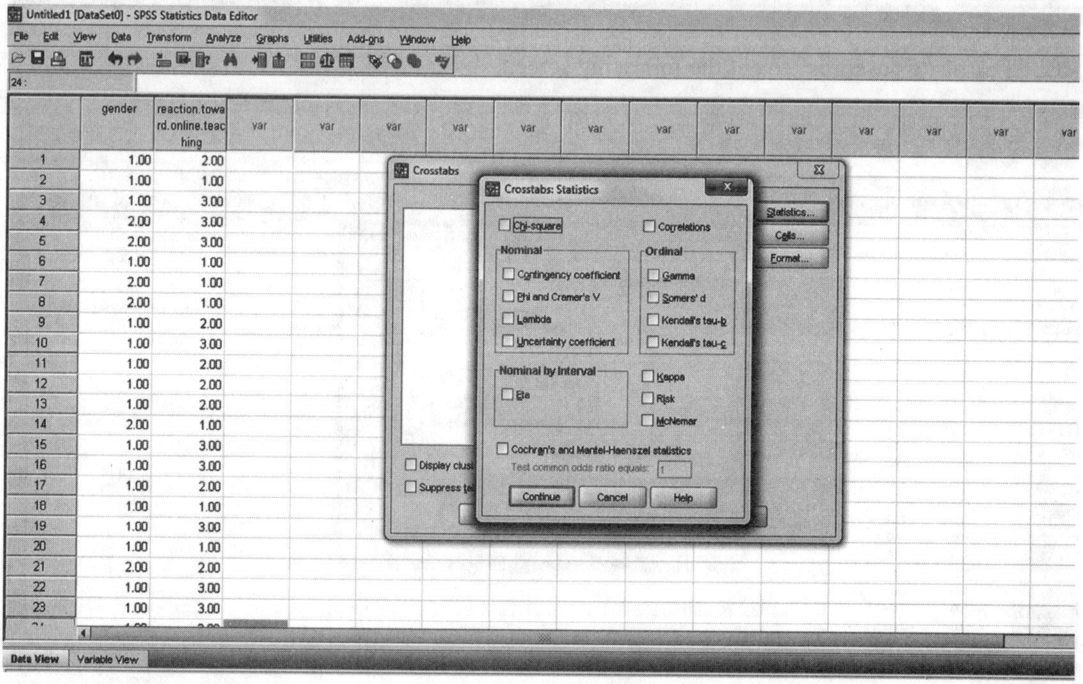

512. Highlight “**Chi-Square**” to get the following screen.

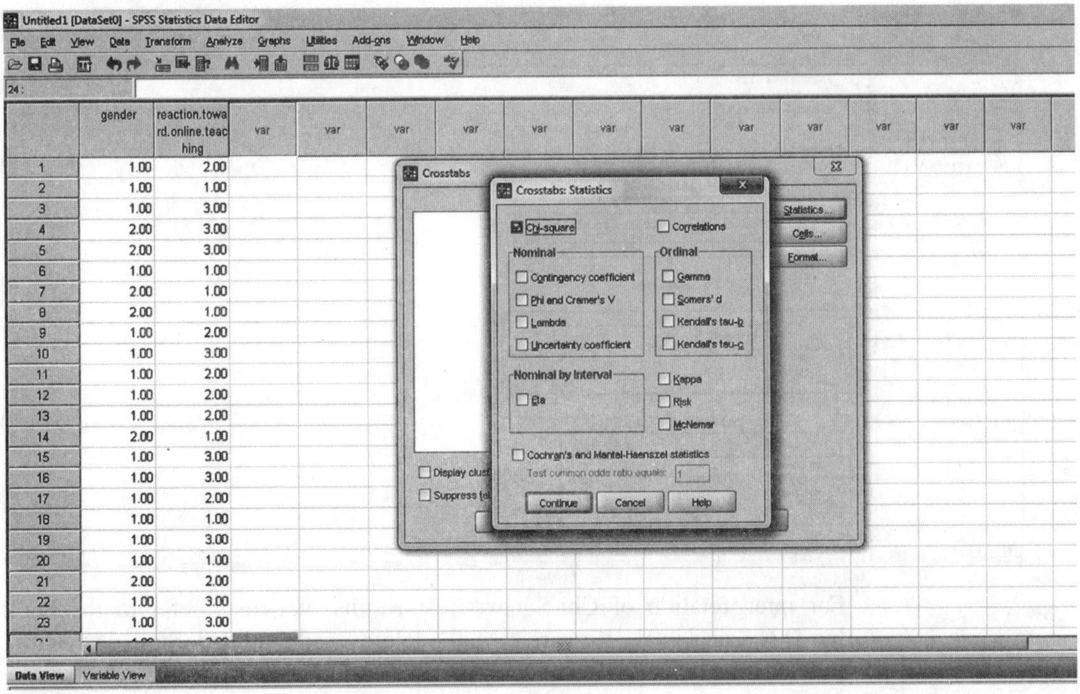

513. Click on “**Continue**” button to get the following screen.

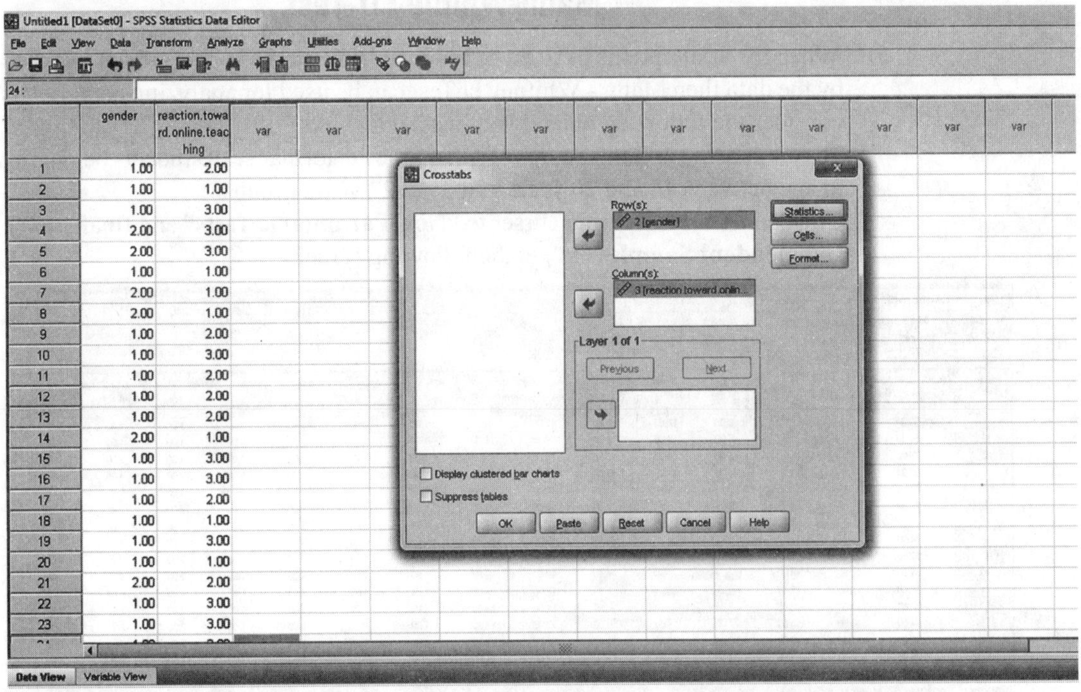

514. Click on "**OK**" button to get the following Outputs of Chi-Square Test.

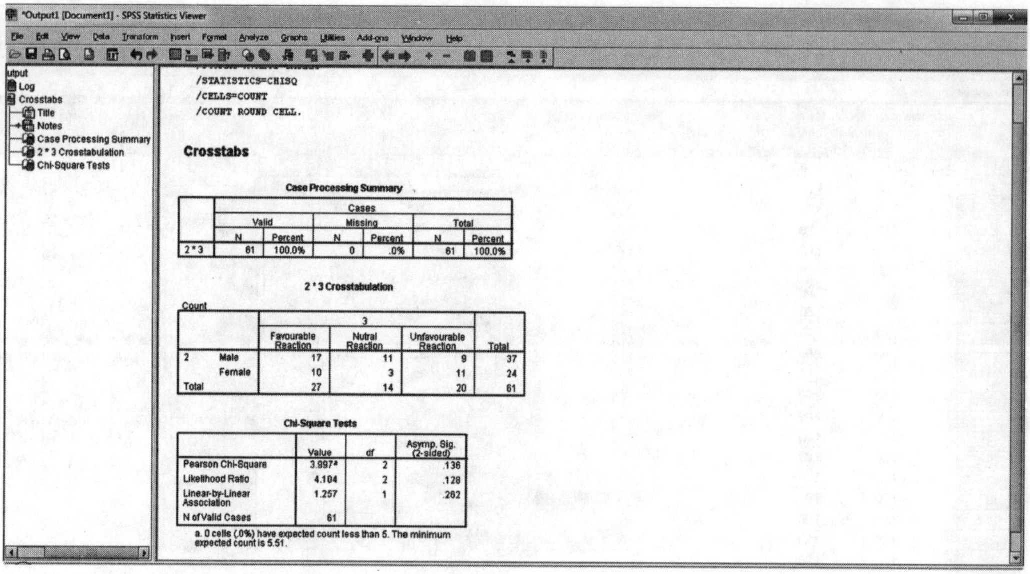

For interpretation of Chi-Square Test results, you may refer to the book by D.N.Sansanwal, Research Methodology and Applied Statistic, Shipra Publishers, Delhi, 2020.

Mann-Whitney U-Test

515. When the assumptions of t-Test or Independent Samples t-Test are not satisfied by the data then Mann - Whitney U-Test can be used for analyzing data. Let us consider the following objective of research.

To compare mean Rank Scores of Academic Performance of students belonging to age between 18 and 20 years and 21 & 22 years groups.

Click on "**Analyse**", bring curser to "**Non-Parametric Tests**" and finally to "**2 Independent Samples**" to get the following screen.

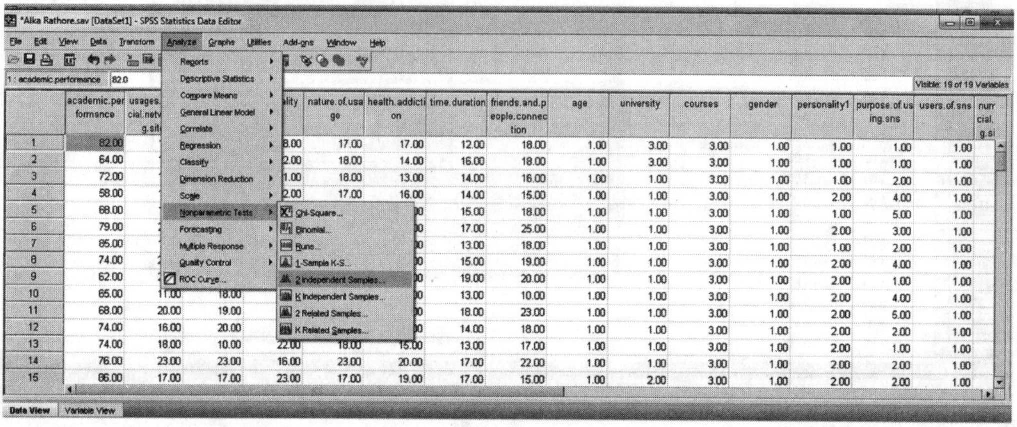

516. Click on "**2 Independent Samples**" icon to get the following screen.

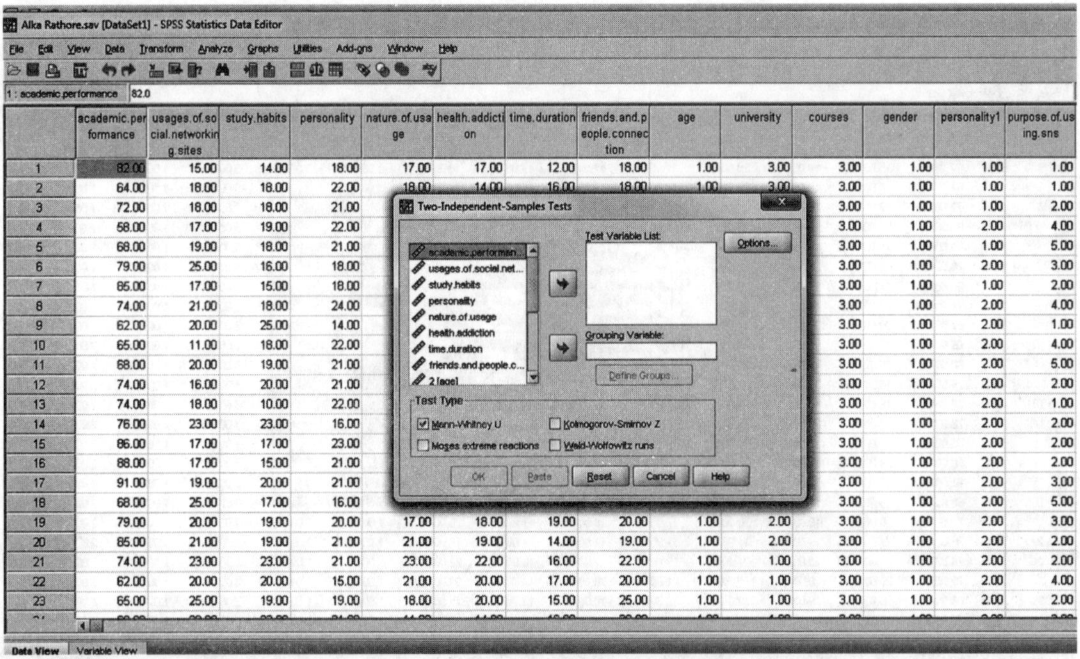

517. Shift "**Academic Performance**" to "**Test Variable List**" slot and "**Age**" to "**Grouping Variable**" slot to get the following screen.

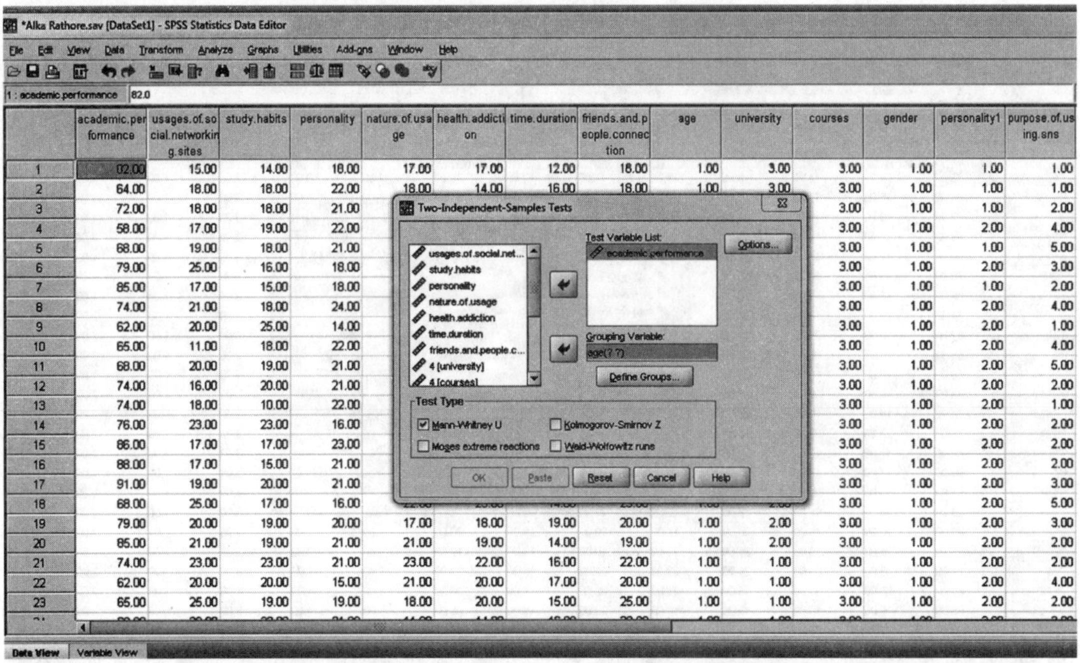

518. Click on "**Define Groups**" icon to get the following screen.

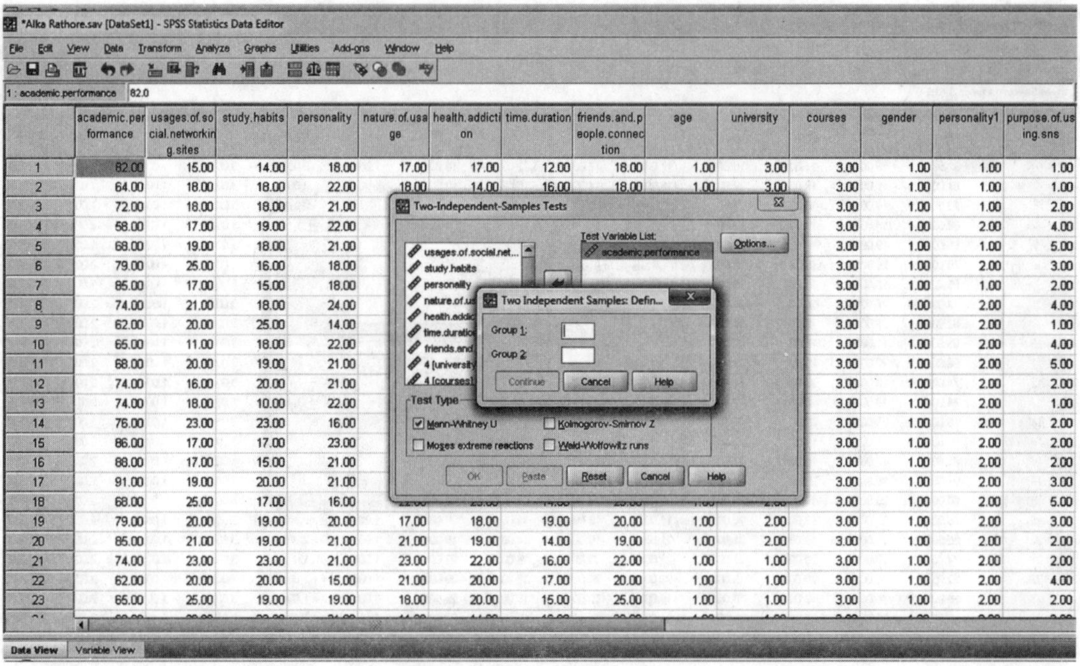

519. You have coded **Male as 1** and **Female as 2** so in the slot of "**Group 1**" you may type "**1**" and in slot of "**Group 2**" type "**2**" to get the following screen.

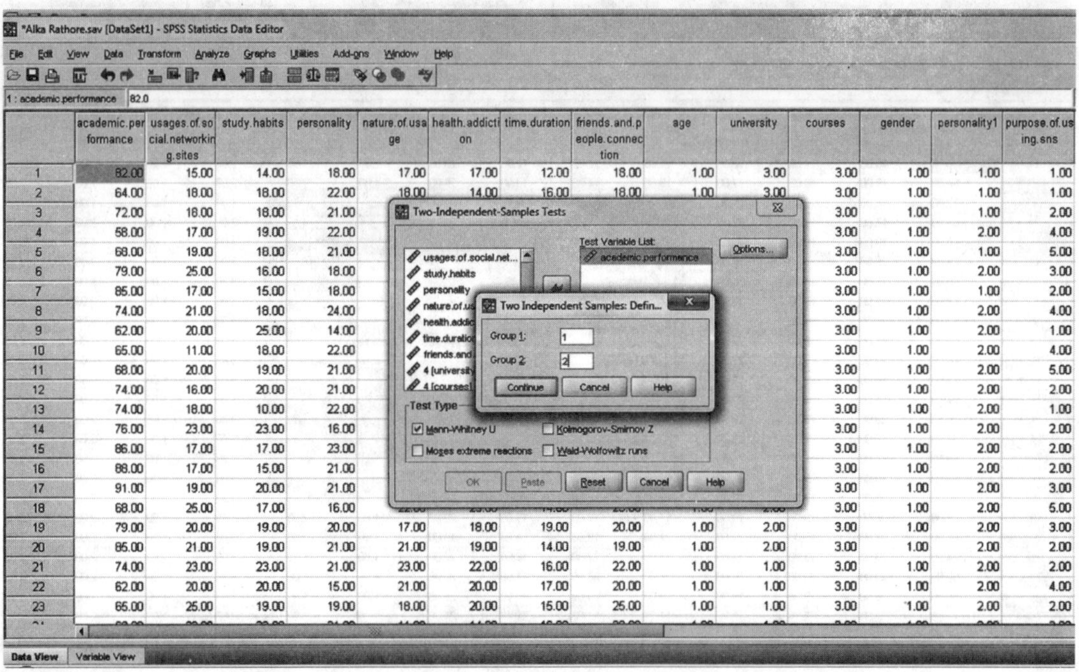

520. Click on "**Continue**" button to get the following screen.

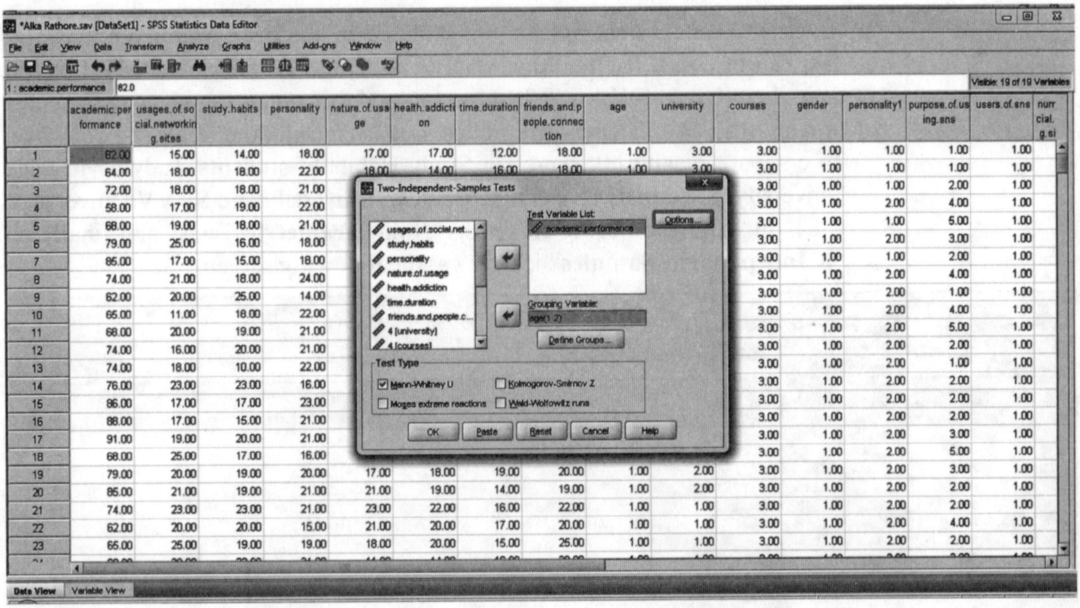

521. Under "**Test Type**" "**Mann – Whitney U**" is already highlighted, so click on "**OK**" to get the following Outputs of Mann – Whitney U – Test.

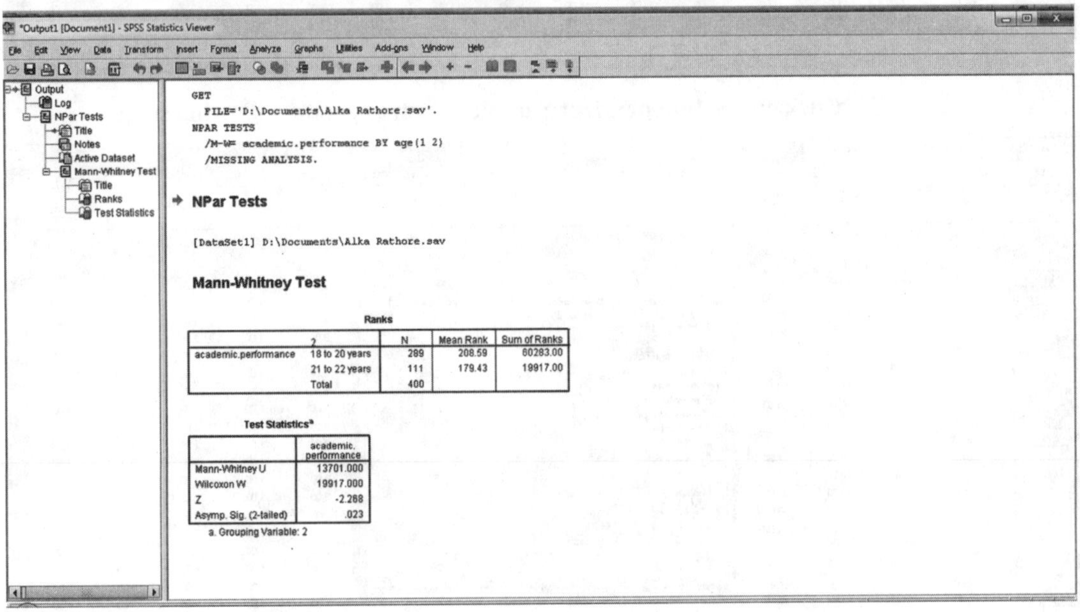

For interpretation of Mann-Whitney U - Test results, you may refer to the book by D.N.Sansanwal, Research Methodology and Applied Statistic, Shipra Publishers, Delhi, 2020.

Kruskal-Wallis H Test

522. In case t-Test assumptions are not satisfied by the data, Mann-Whitney U – Test can be used. If One Way ANOVA assumptions are not satisfied by the data, then Kruskal-Wallis H Test can be used for comparing mean rank scores of more than two independent groups. Let us consider the following objective. To compare mean rank scores of Study Habits of students studying in Sage University, Symbiosis University, Medicap University and SVVV University. Click on "**Analyse**", bring curser on "**Non-Parametric Tests**" and finally on "**K Independent Samples**" icon to get the following screen.

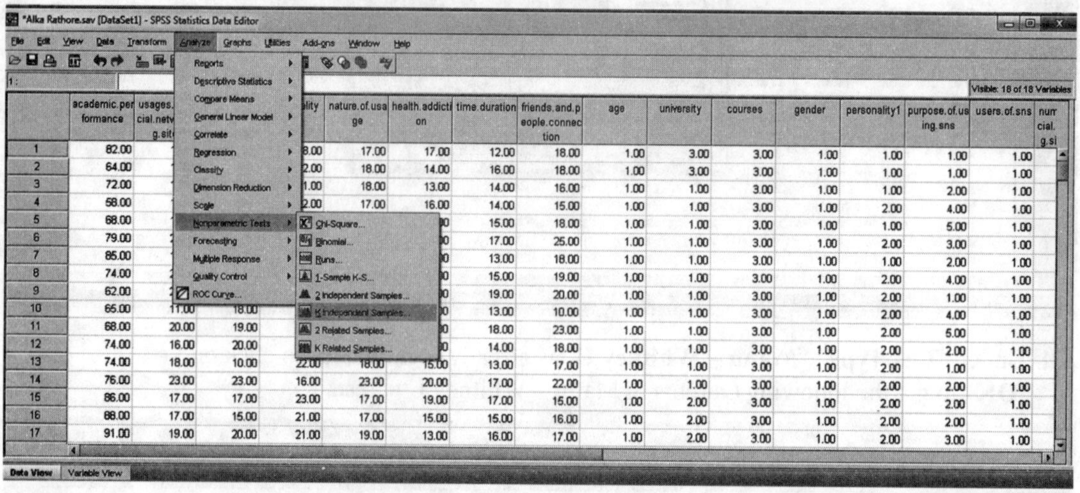

523. Click on "**K Independent Samples**" icon to get the following screen.

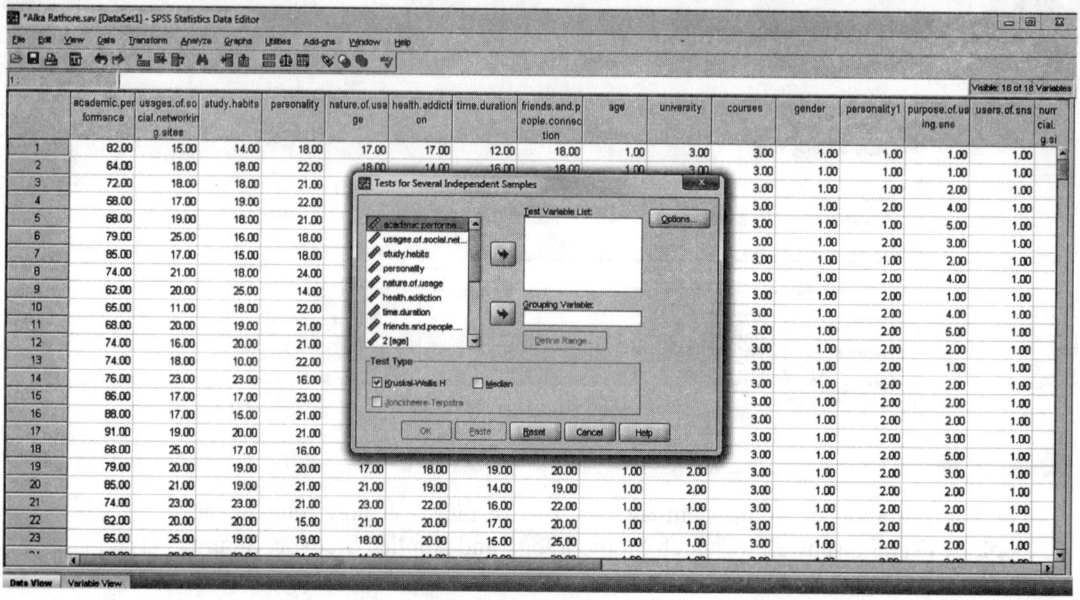

524. Shift "**Study Habits**" variable to "**Test Variable List**" slot and "**University**" variable to "**Grouping Variable**" slot to get the following screen.

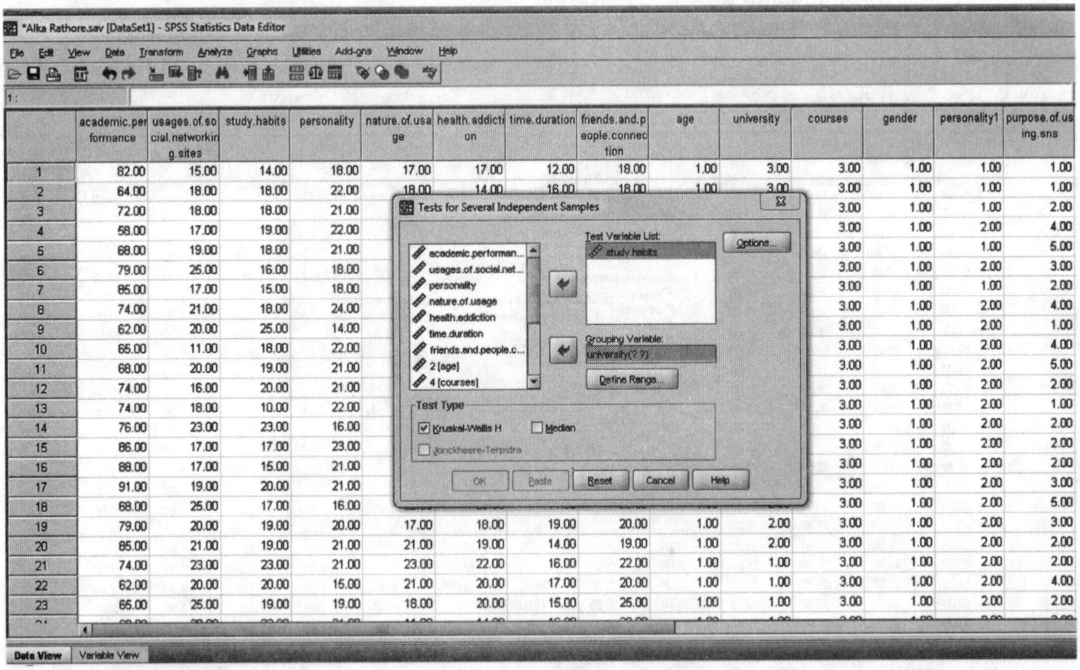

525. Click on "**Define Range**" icon to get the following screen.

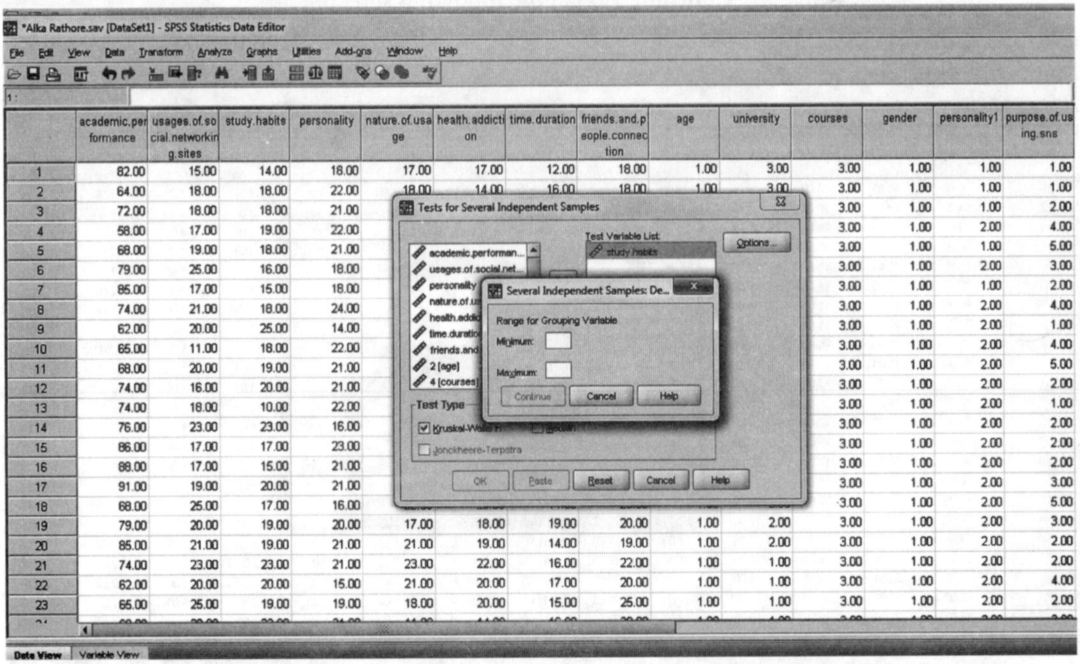

526. In this example "**Minimum**" code is "**1**" and "**Maximum**" code is "**4**", so under "**Minimum**" slot enter "**1**" and in "**Maximum**" slot enter "**4**" to get following screen.

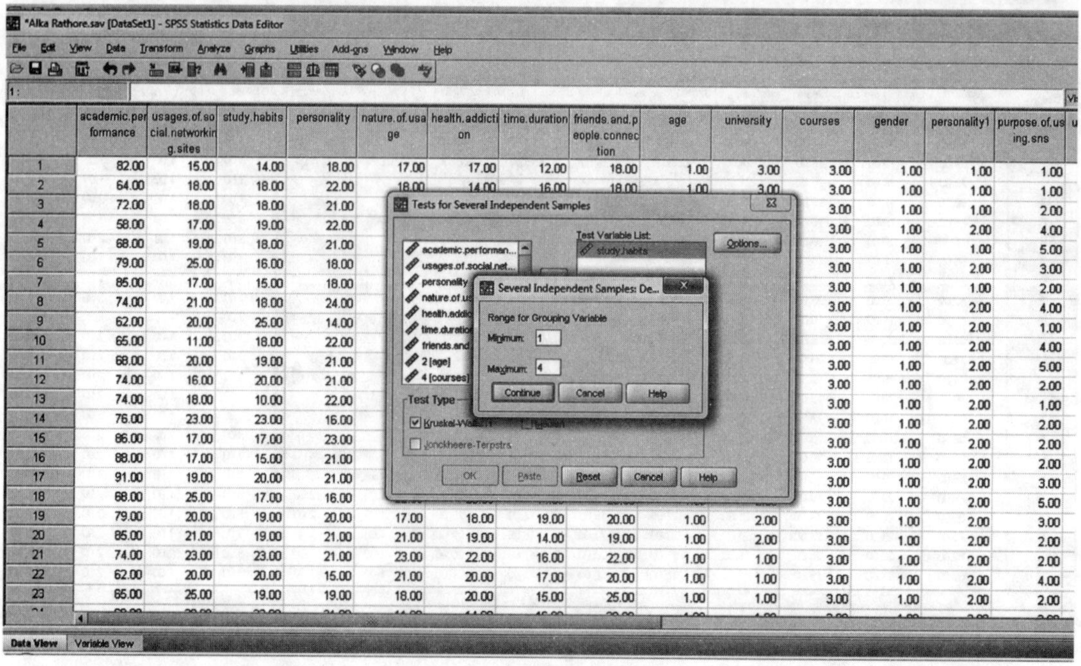

527. Click on "**Continue**" to get the following screen.

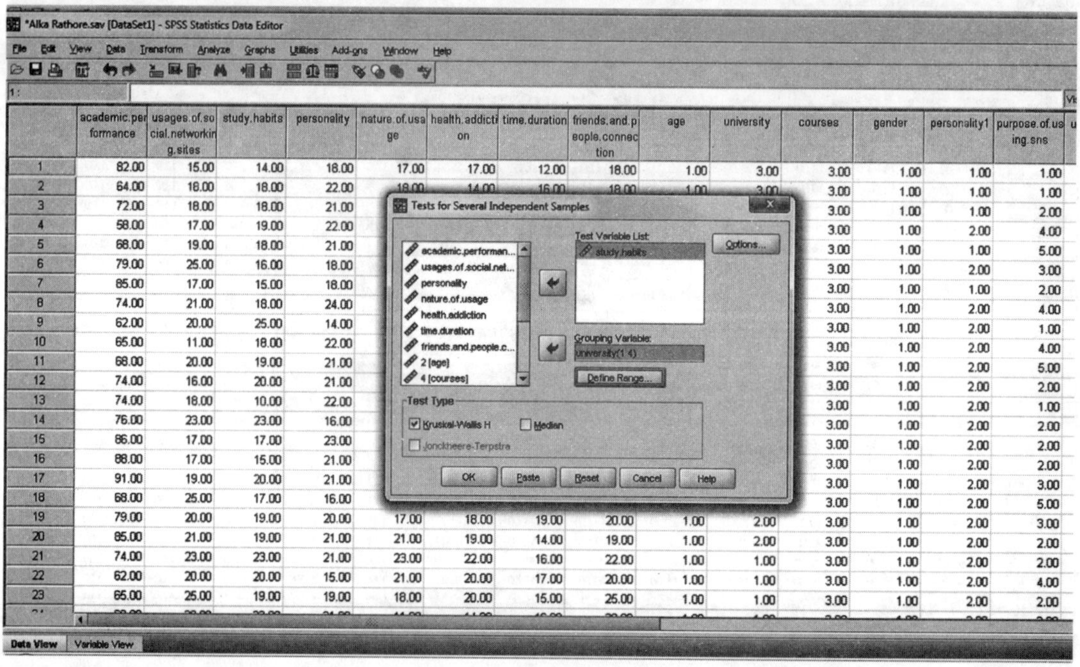

528. Click on "**OK**" to get the following Outputs of Kruskal-Wallis Test.

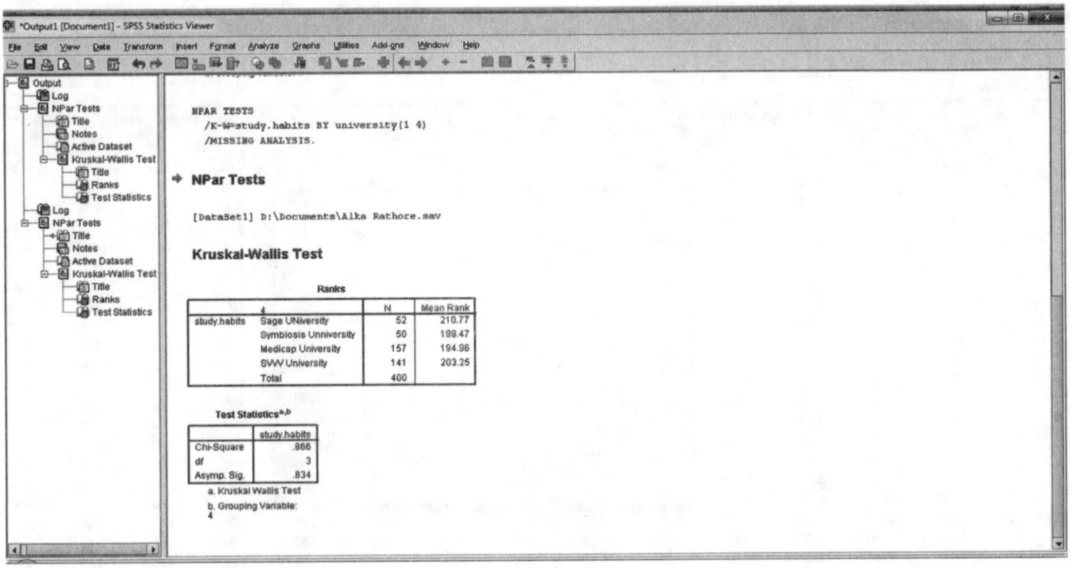

Median Test

529. Median Test is a special case of Pearson's Chi-square Test. It is a Non-Parametric Statistics used to test the null hypothesis that the medians of the population from two or more samples drawn are identical. Let us take the following objective of research

To compare median scores of Personality of students belonging to Architecture, Engineering, Law and Management.

Click on "**Analyse**" icon, bring curser to "**Non-Parametric Test**" icon and then to "**K Independent Samples**" icon to get the following screen.

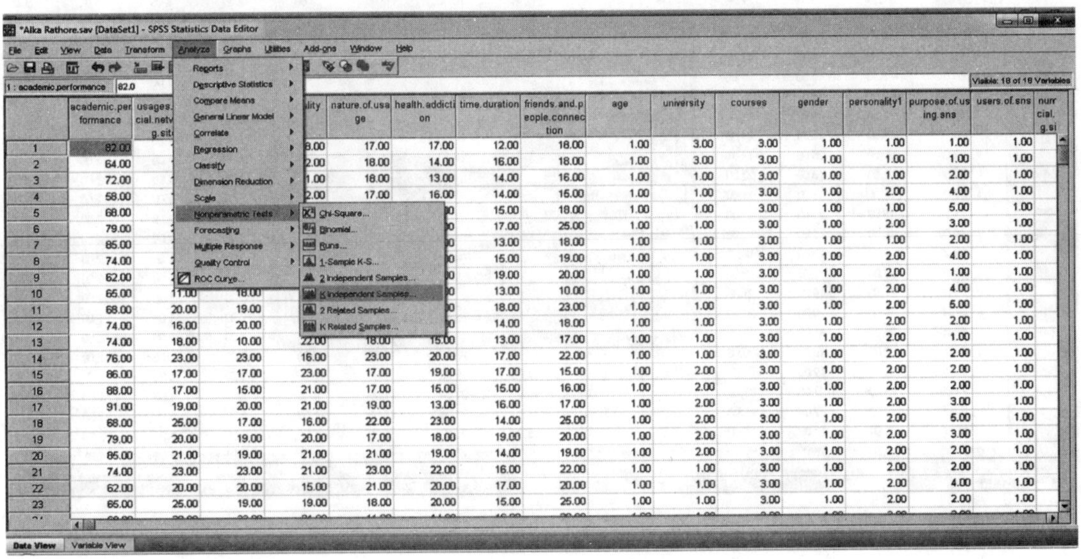

530. Click on "**K Independent Samples**" to get the following screen.

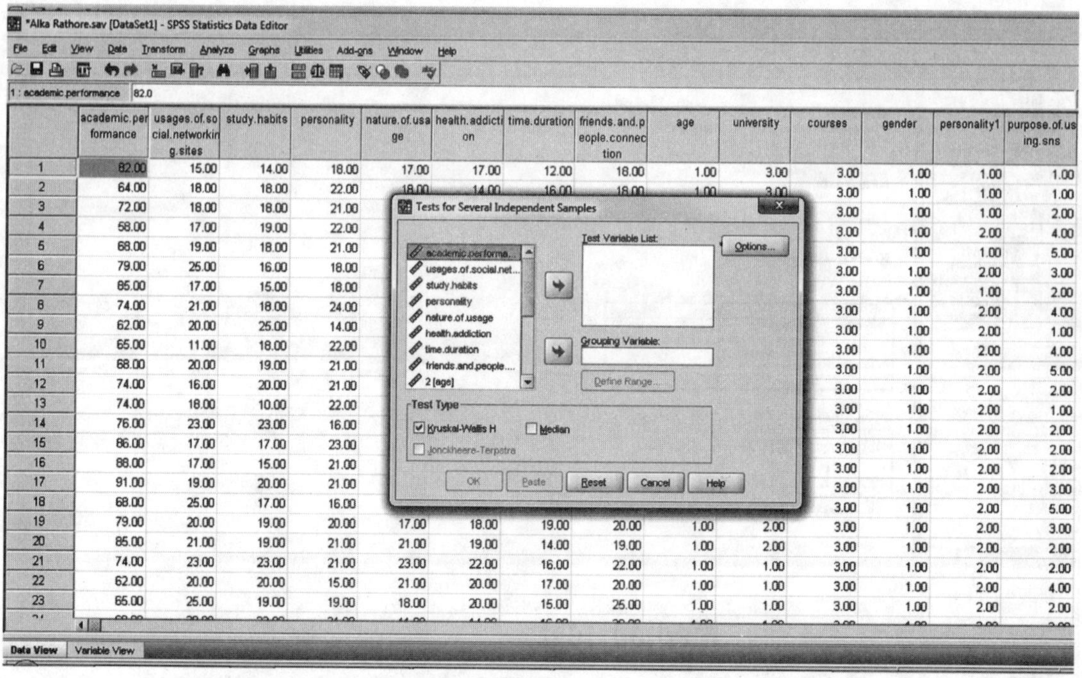

531. Shift "**Personality**" to "**Test Variable List**" dialog box and "**Courses**" to "**Grouping Variable**" slot to get the following screen.

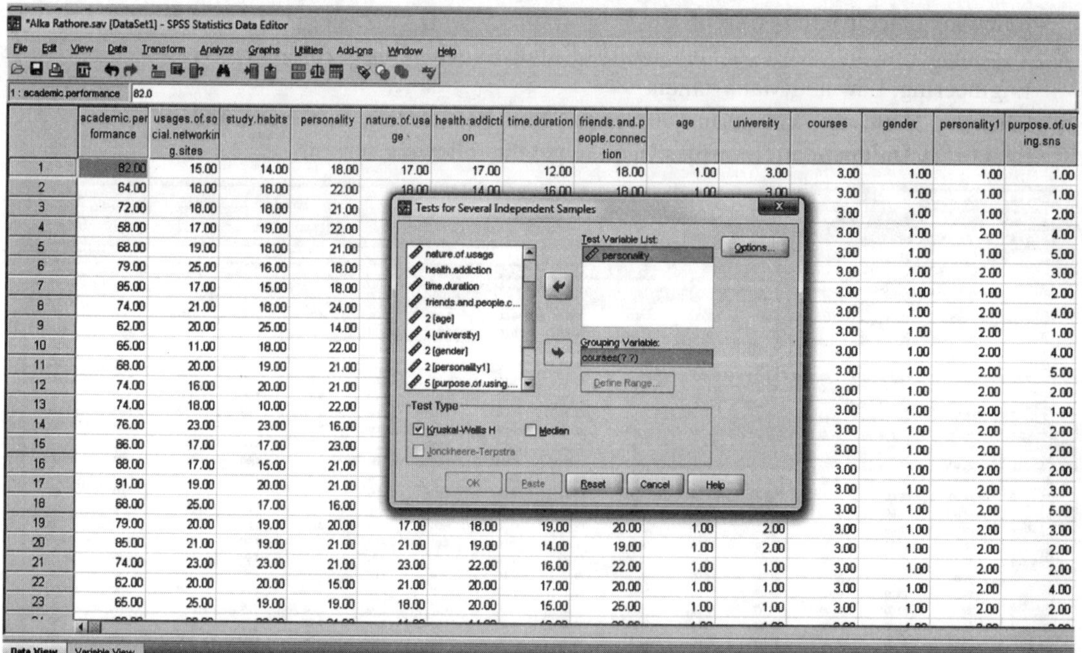

532. It is evident from objective given in Frame 529 that there are four courses, namely, Architecture, Engineering, Law and Management and have been coded as "1", "2", "3" and "4". Click on "**Grouping Variable**" slot to get the following screen.

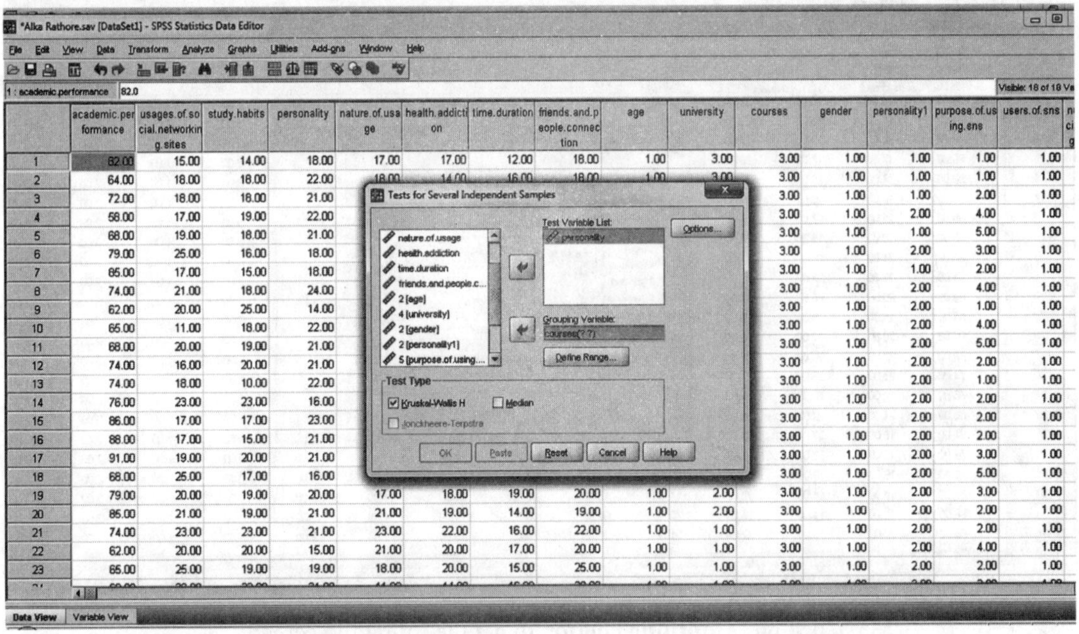

533. Now "**Define Range**" button is active. Click on "**Define Range**" button to get the following screen.

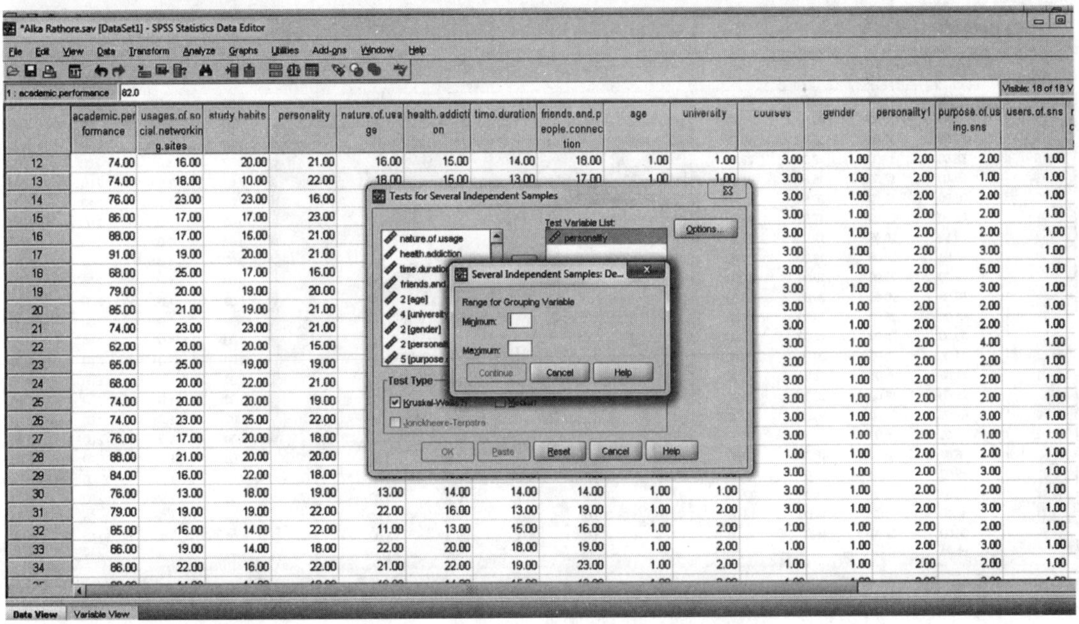

534. Grouping Variable ranges from 1 to 4. Under "**Minimum**" slot type "**1**" and under "**Maximum**" slot type "**4**" to get the following screen.

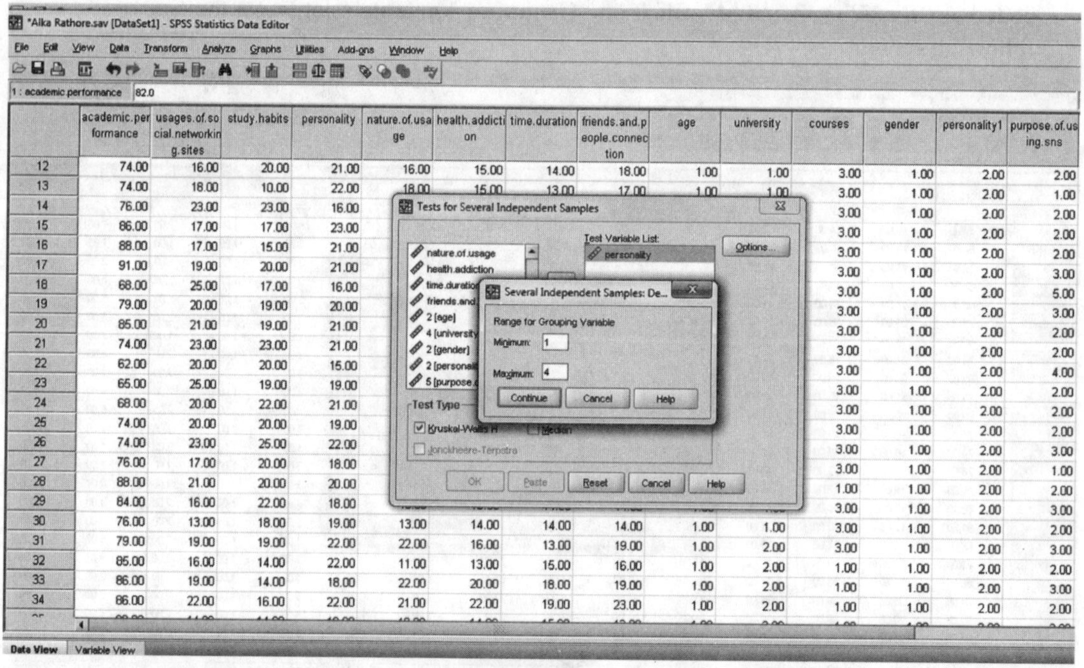

535. Click on "**Continue**" button to get the following screen.

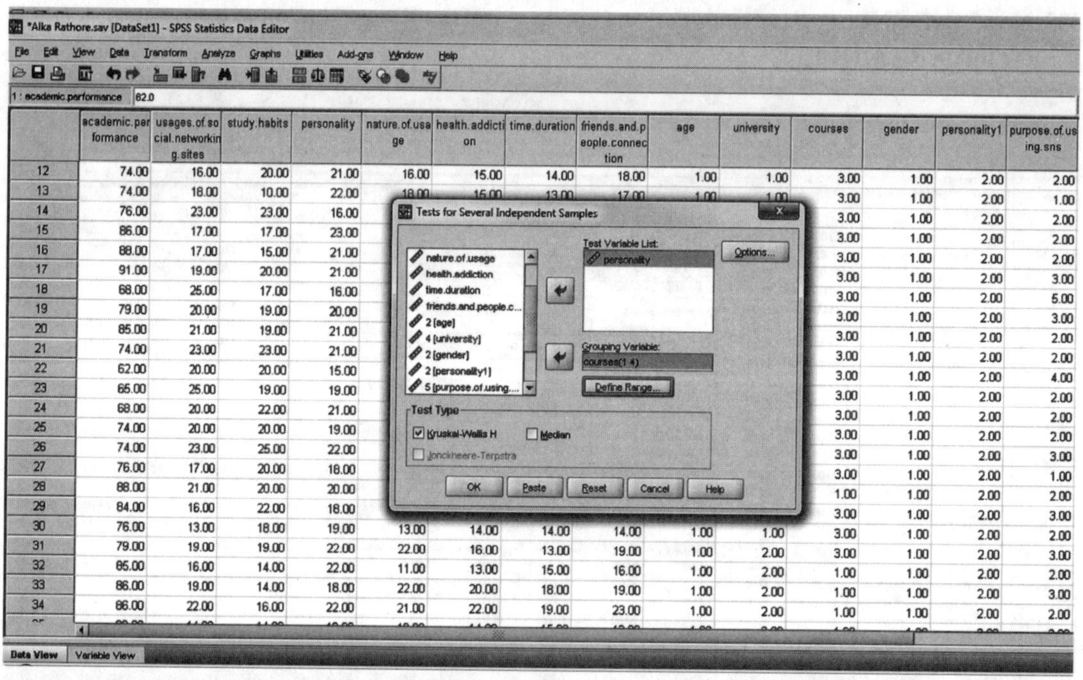

536. In the present case the data are to be analsyed with the help of "**Median Test**" so highlight "**Median**" only to get the following screen.

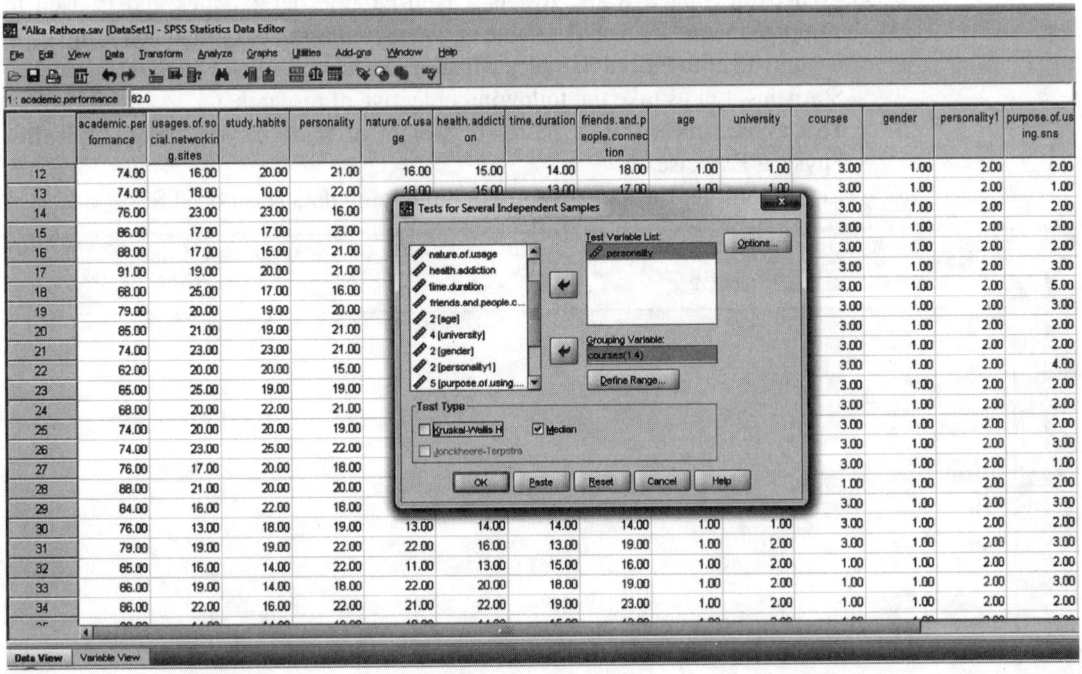

537. Click on "**OK**" to get the following Outputs of Median Test.

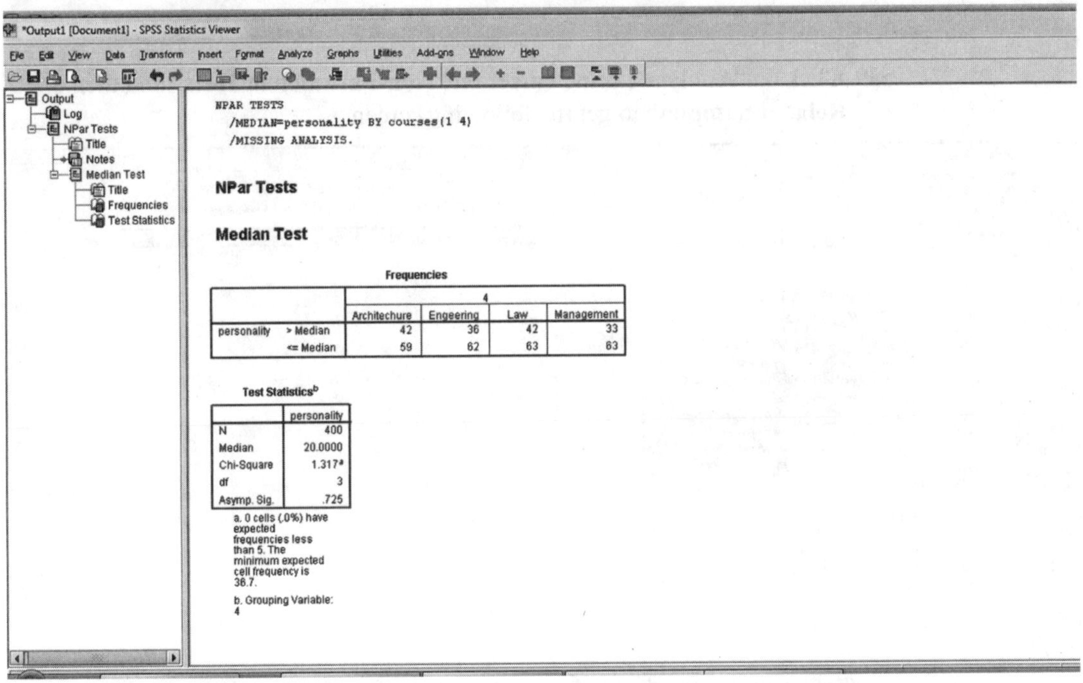


```
NPAR TESTS
  /MEDIAN=personality BY courses(1 4)
  /MISSING ANALYSIS.
```

NPar Tests

Median Test

Frequencies

		4			
		Architechure	Engeering	Law	Management
personality	> Median	42	36	42	33
	<= Median	59	62	63	63

Test Statistics[b]

	personality
N	400
Median	20.0000
Chi-Square	1.317[a]
df	3
Asymp. Sig.	.725

a. 0 cells (.0%) have expected frequencies less than 5. The minimum expected cell frequency is 38.7.

b. Grouping Variable: 4

Wilcoxon Singed Rank Test

538. Wilcoxon Singed Rank Test is a Non-Parametric statistics and is used to compare mean ranks of a variable of two paired samples or matched samples. It is equivalent to Paired Samples t-Test or Correlated t-Test which is Parametric Statistics. Let us take the following objective of research.

To compare mean ranks scores of weight of Male players before and after Physical Exercises

Let us consider the data given in the following data sheet of SPSS.

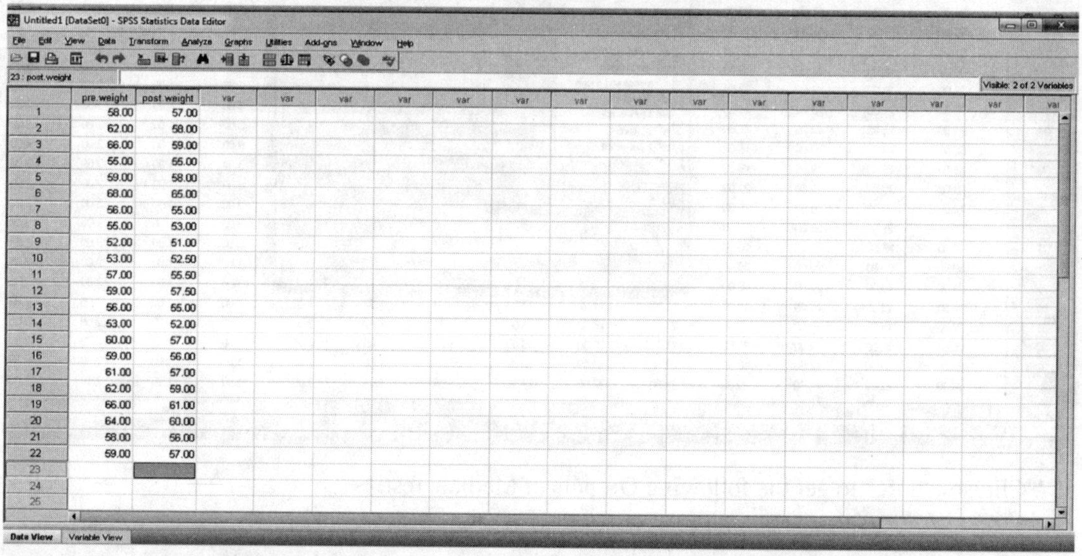

	pre.weight	post.weight
1	58.00	57.00
2	62.00	58.00
3	66.00	59.00
4	55.00	55.00
5	59.00	58.00
6	68.00	65.00
7	56.00	55.00
8	55.00	53.00
9	52.00	51.00
10	53.00	52.50
11	57.00	55.50
12	59.00	57.50
13	56.00	55.00
14	53.00	52.00
15	60.00	57.00
16	59.00	56.00
17	61.00	57.00
18	62.00	59.00
19	66.00	61.00
20	64.00	60.00
21	58.00	56.00
22	59.00	57.00

539. Click on "**Analyse**", bring curser on "**Non-Parametric Tests**" and then on "**2 Related Samples**" to get the following screen.

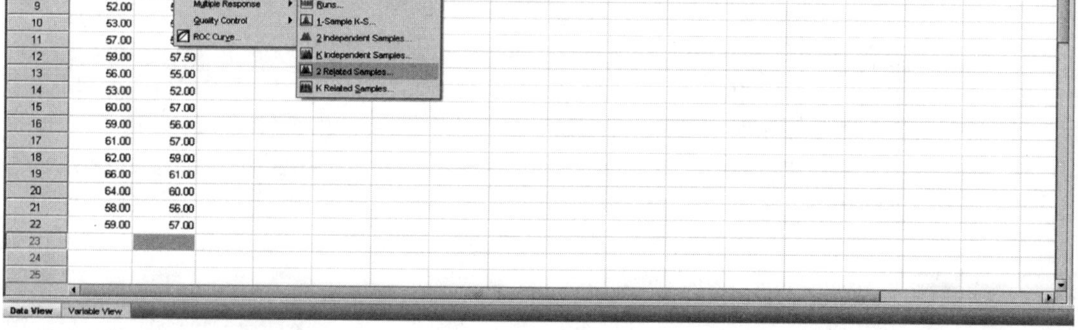

540. Click on "**2 Related Samples**" to get the following screen.

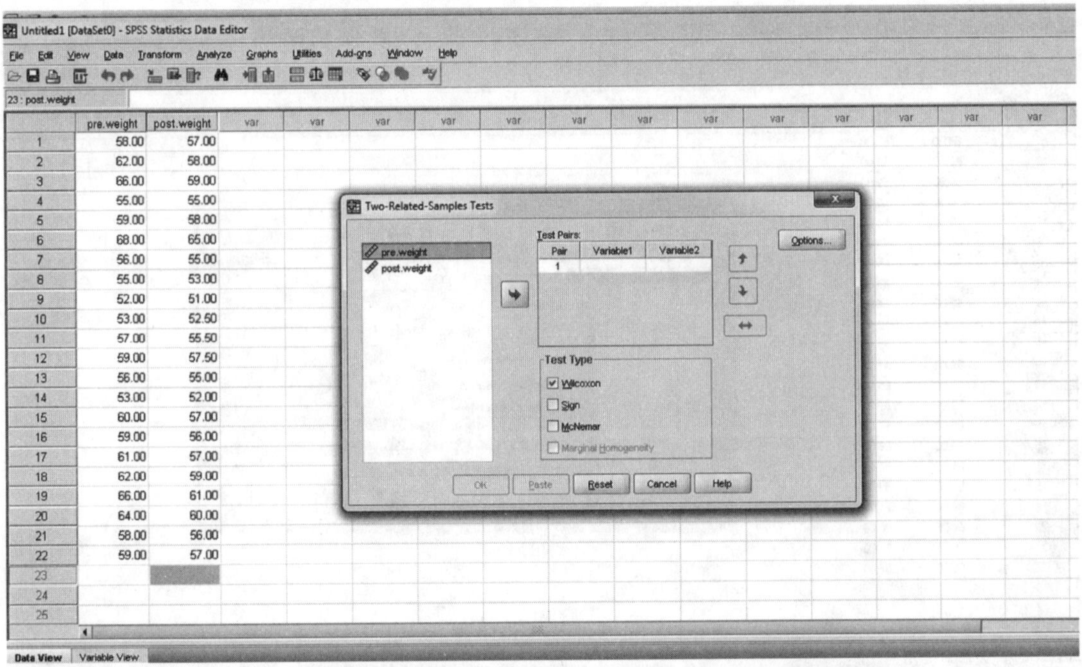

541. Shift "**Pre- Weight**" and "**Post-Weight**" in any order under "**Test Pairs**" slots. Suppose "**Pre- Weight**" is shifted under "**Variable 1**" and "**Post- Weight**" under "**Variable 2**" to get the following screen.

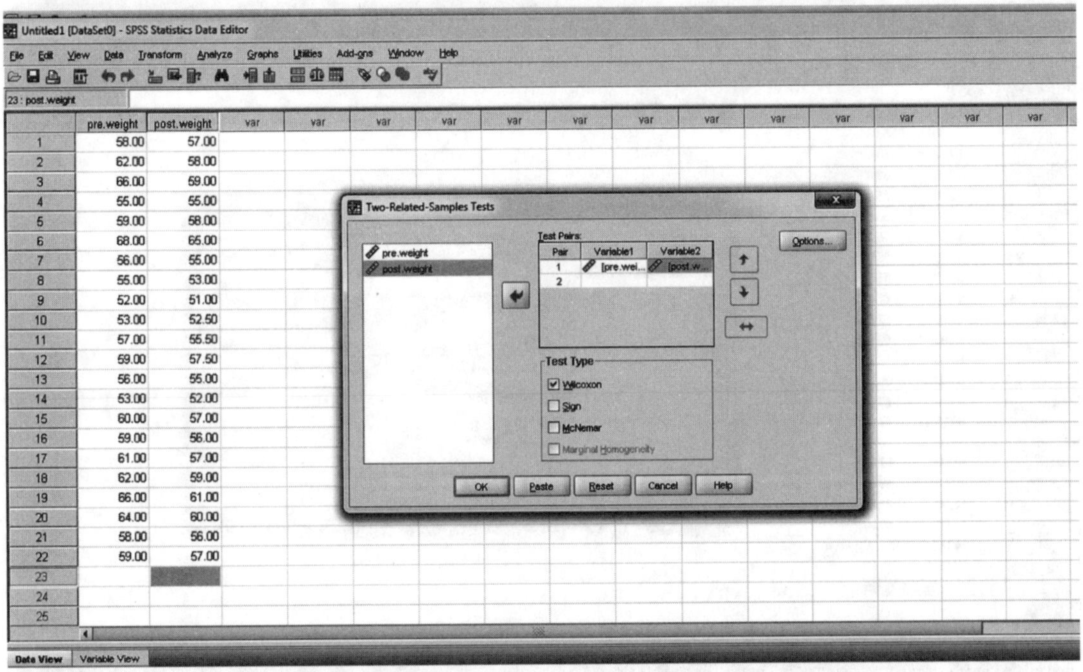

542. Click on "**Options**" to get the following screen.

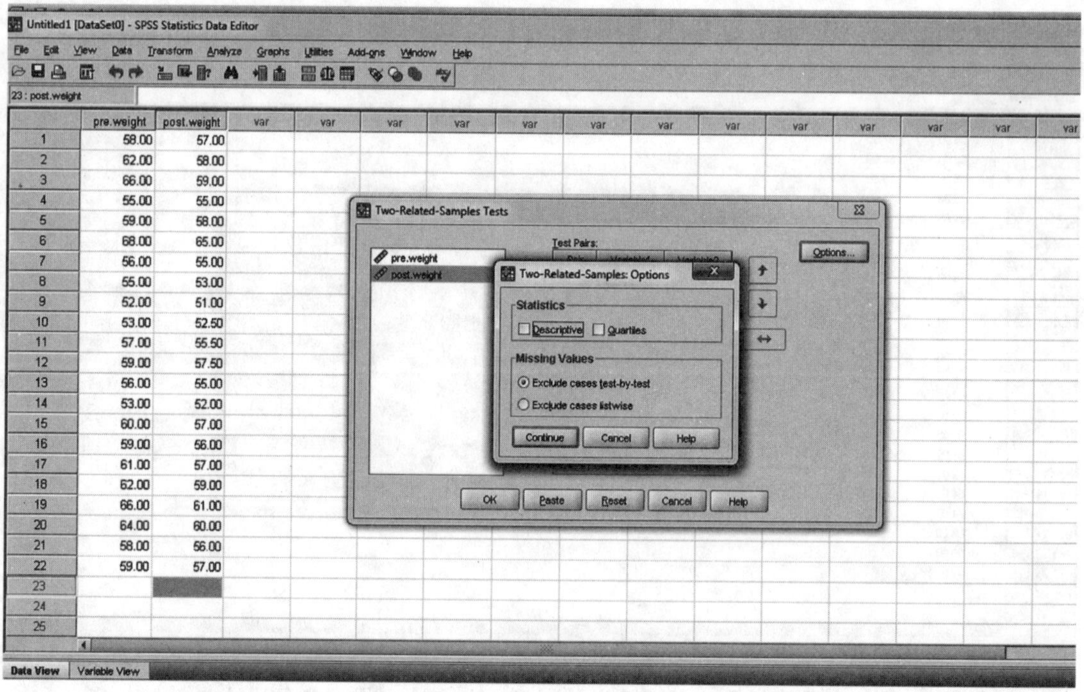

543. In case you want to compute "**Statistics**" you may click on appropriate options provided under it, else you may click on "**Continue**" to get the following screen.

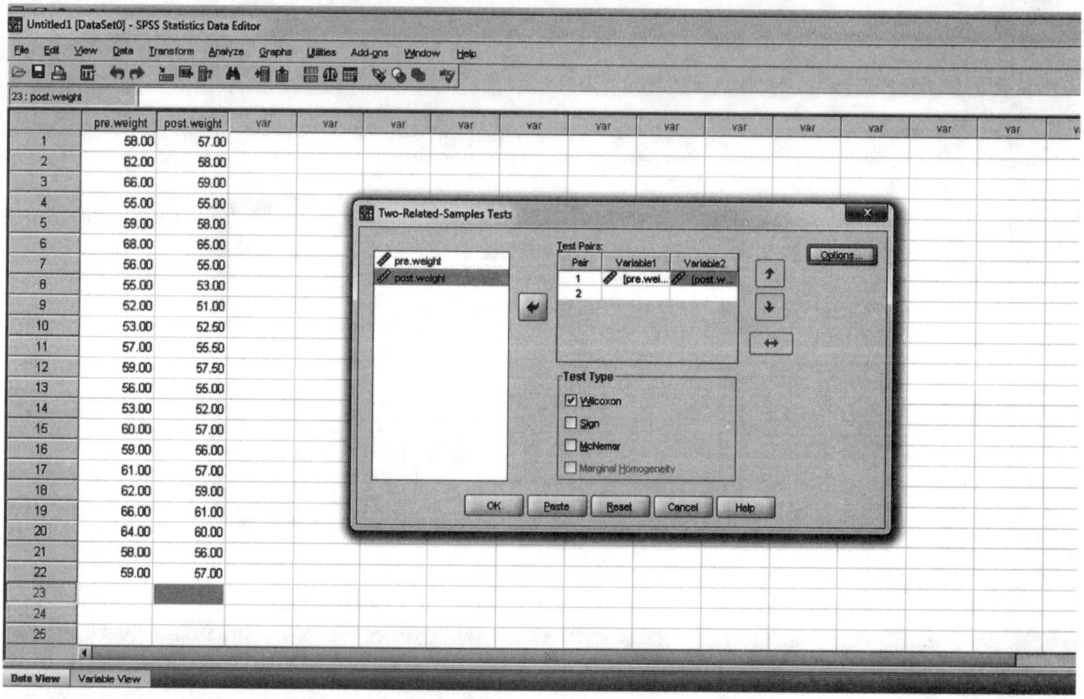

544. Under "**Test Type**" "**Wilcoxon**" is already highlighted. Click on "**OK**" to get the following outputs of Wilcoxon Singed Rank Test.

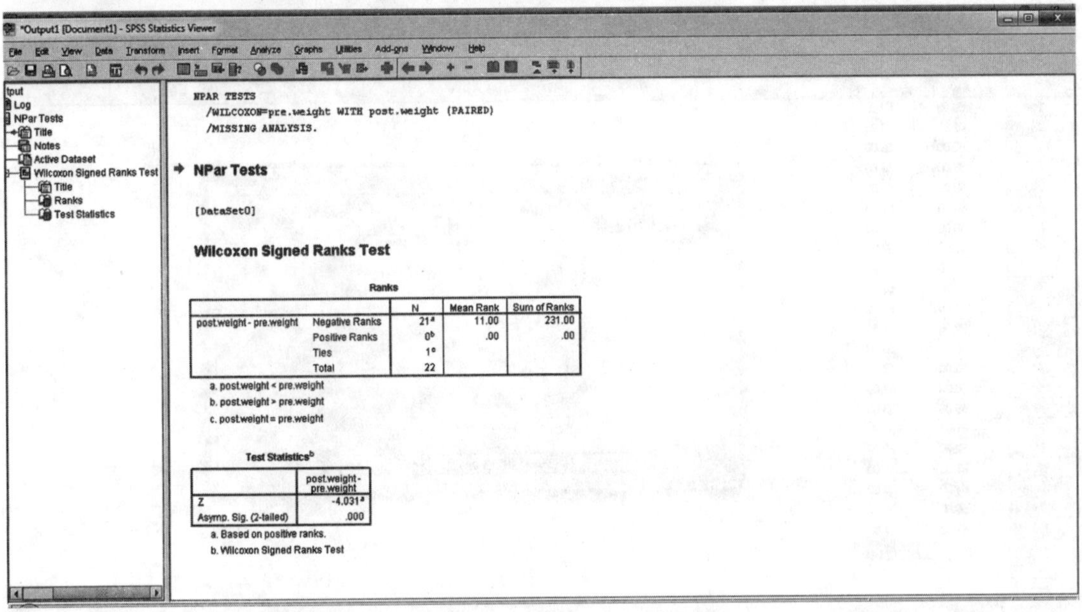

Sign Test

545. Sign Test is a Non-Parametric Statistics. It can be used in place of Paired Samples t-Test or One Sample t-Test. Let us consider the following objective.
To compare mean ranks scores of weight of Male players before and after Physical Exercises
Click on "**Analyse**", bring curser to "**Non-Parametric Test**" and then to "**2 Related Samples**" to get the following screen.

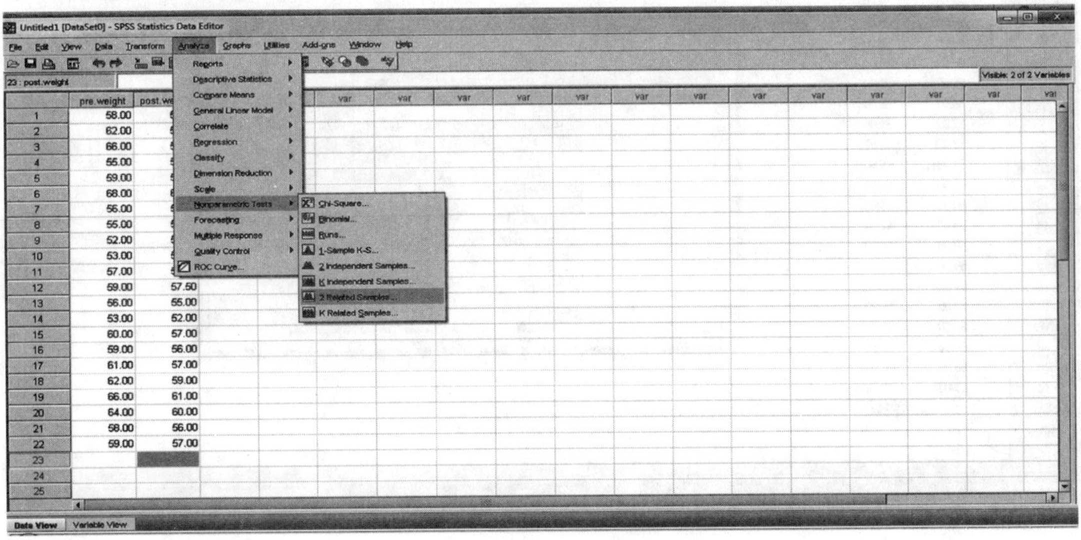

546. Click on "**2 Related Samples**" icon to get the following screen.

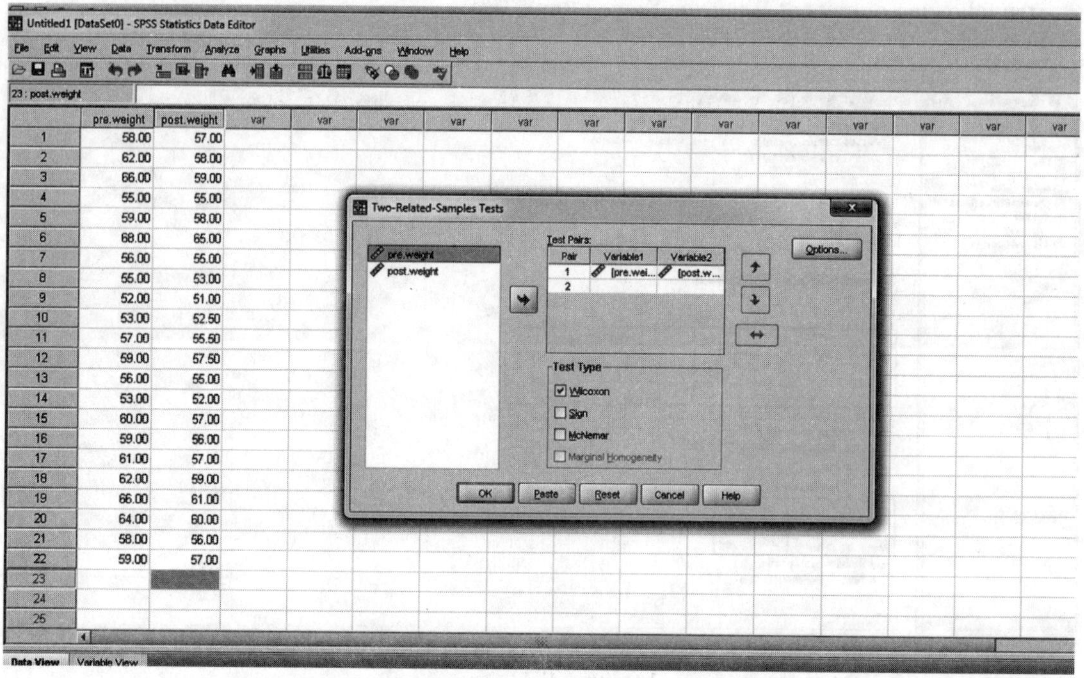

547. You want to analyse data with the help of "**Sign**" test so deactivate "**Wilcoxon**" and activate "**Sign**" to get the following screen.

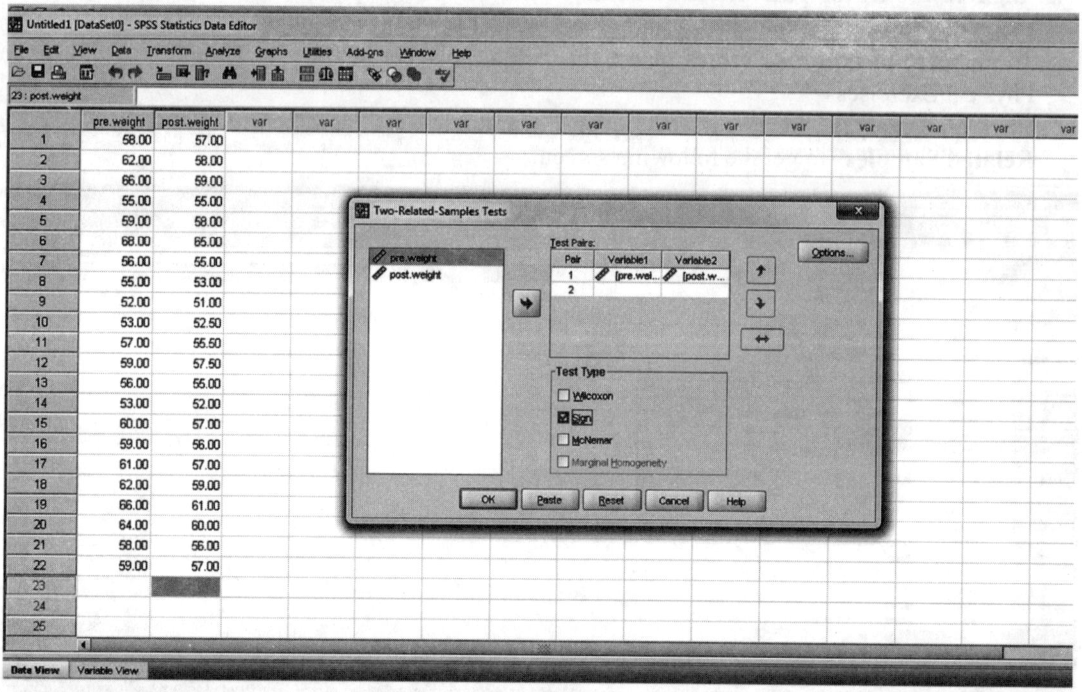

548. Click on "**OK**" to get the following outputs of Sign Test.

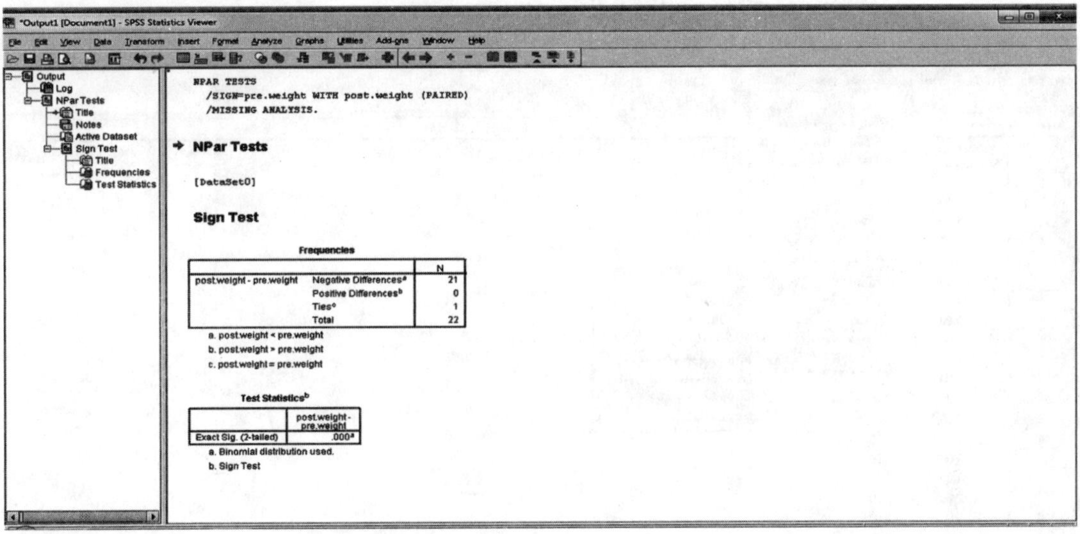

Frequencies

		N
post.weight - pre.weight	Negative Differences[a]	21
	Positive Differences[b]	0
	Ties[c]	1
	Total	22

a. post.weight < pre.weight
b. post.weight > pre.weight
c. post.weight = pre.weight

Test Statistics[b]

	post.weight - pre.weight
Exact Sig. (2-tailed)	.000[a]

a. Binomial distribution used.
b. Sign Test

McNemar Test

549. McNemar Test is a Non-Parametric Test used on Paired nominal data. It is applied to a 2 X 2 Contingency Table with a dichotomous trait or characteristics with matched pairs of subjects, to determine whether the row and column marginal frequencies are equal. It has been named after Quinn McNemar who introduced it in 1947. The data must be on Nominal Scale. Let us consider the following objective.

To study association between Video intervention and Status of smoking by Male students.

Let us consider the data as given in the following SPSS data sheet.

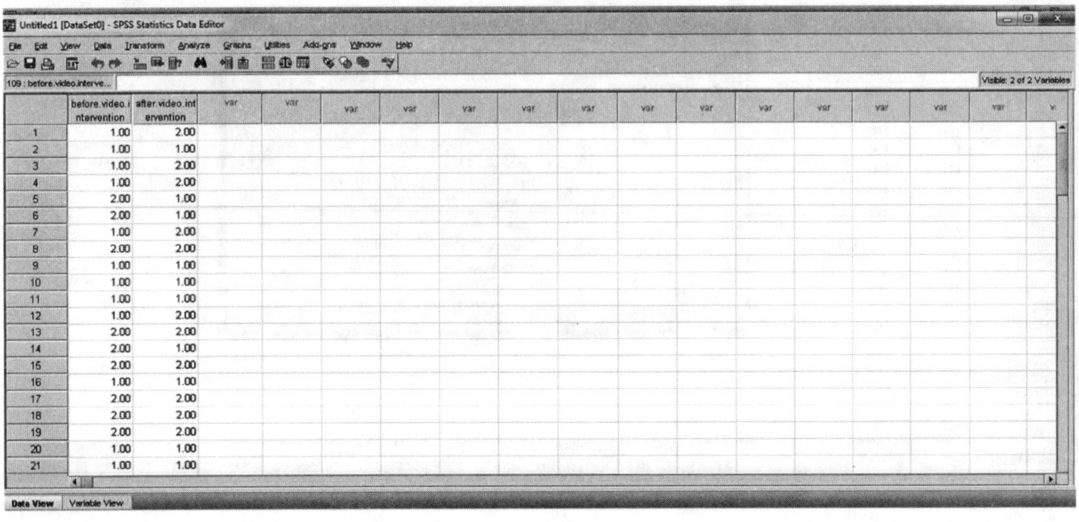

	before.video.intervention	after.video.intervention
1	1.00	2.00
2	1.00	1.00
3	1.00	2.00
4	1.00	2.00
5	2.00	1.00
6	2.00	1.00
7	1.00	2.00
8	2.00	2.00
9	1.00	1.00
10	1.00	1.00
11	1.00	1.00
12	1.00	2.00
13	2.00	2.00
14	2.00	1.00
15	2.00	2.00
16	1.00	1.00
17	2.00	2.00
18	2.00	2.00
19	2.00	2.00
20	1.00	1.00
21	1.00	1.00

550. Click on "**Analyse**", bring curser to "**Non-parametric Test**" and to "**2 Related Samples**" to get the following screen.

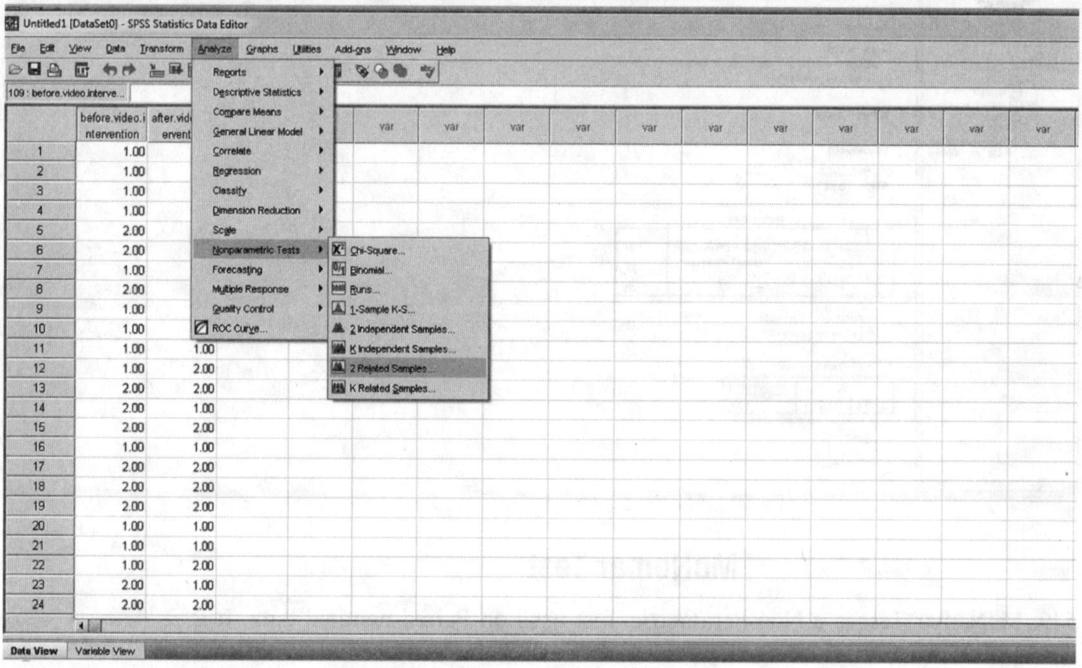

551. Click on "**2 Related Samples**" to get the following screen.

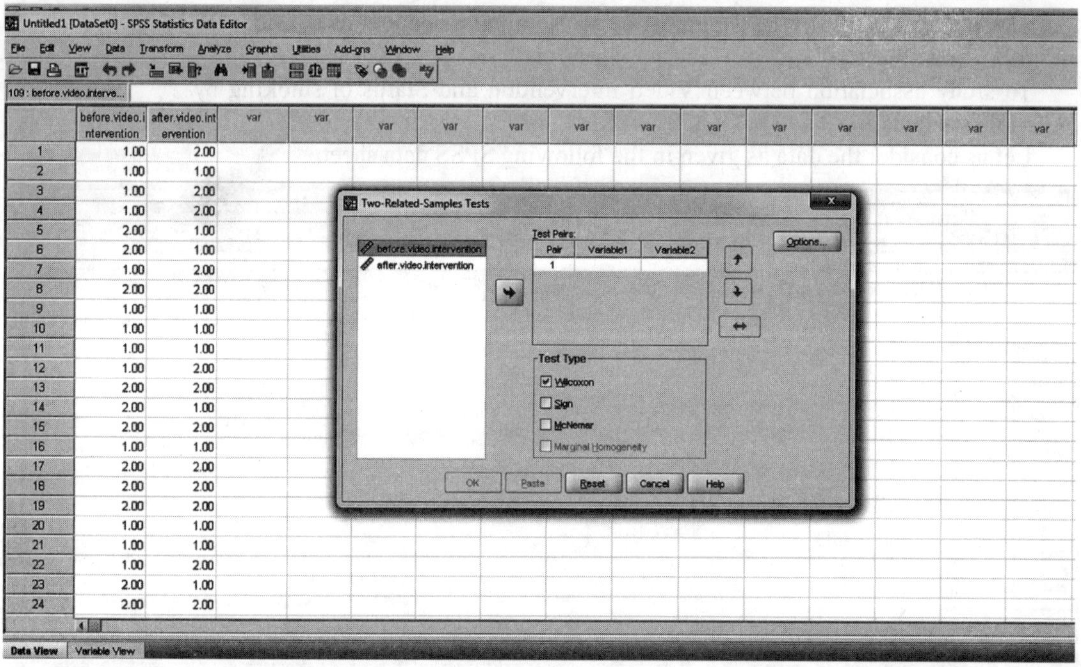

552. Shift "**before video intervention**" and "**after video intervention**" variables to "**Test Pairs**" under "**Variable 1**" and "**Variable 2**"

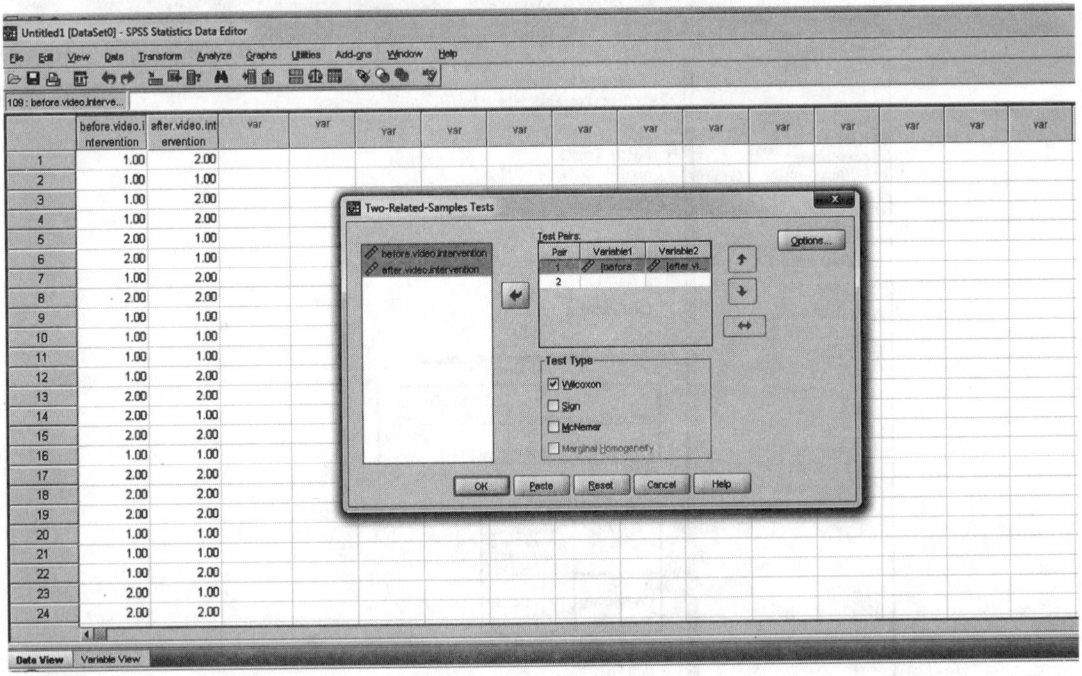

553. Highlight "**McNemar**" to get the following screen.

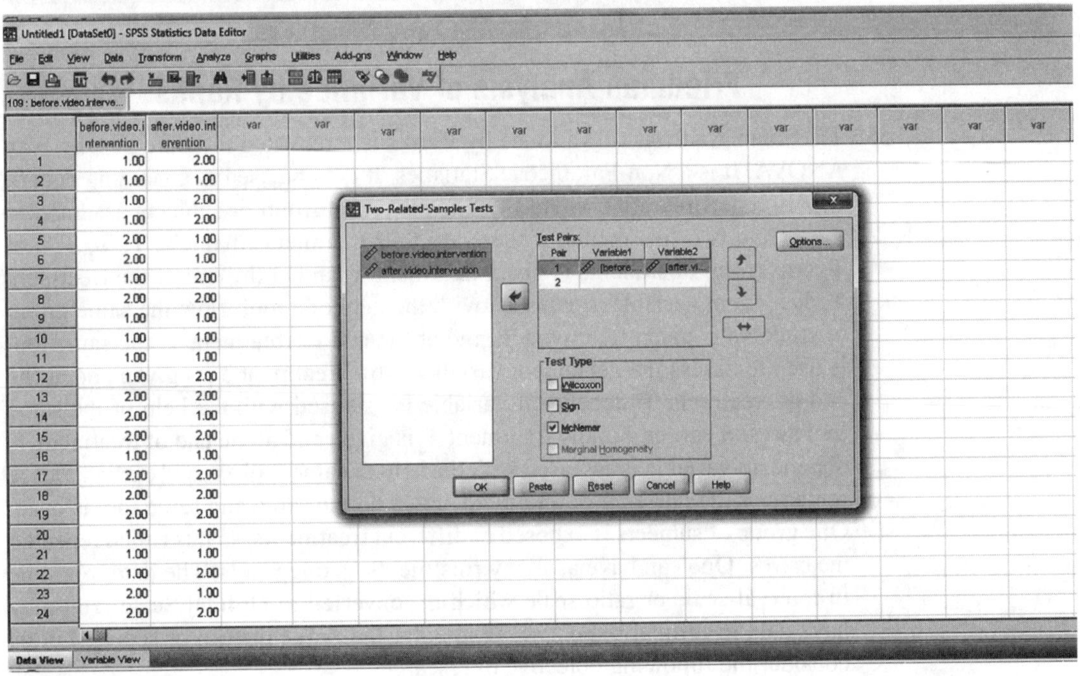

554. Click on "**OK**" to get the following outputs of McNemar Test.

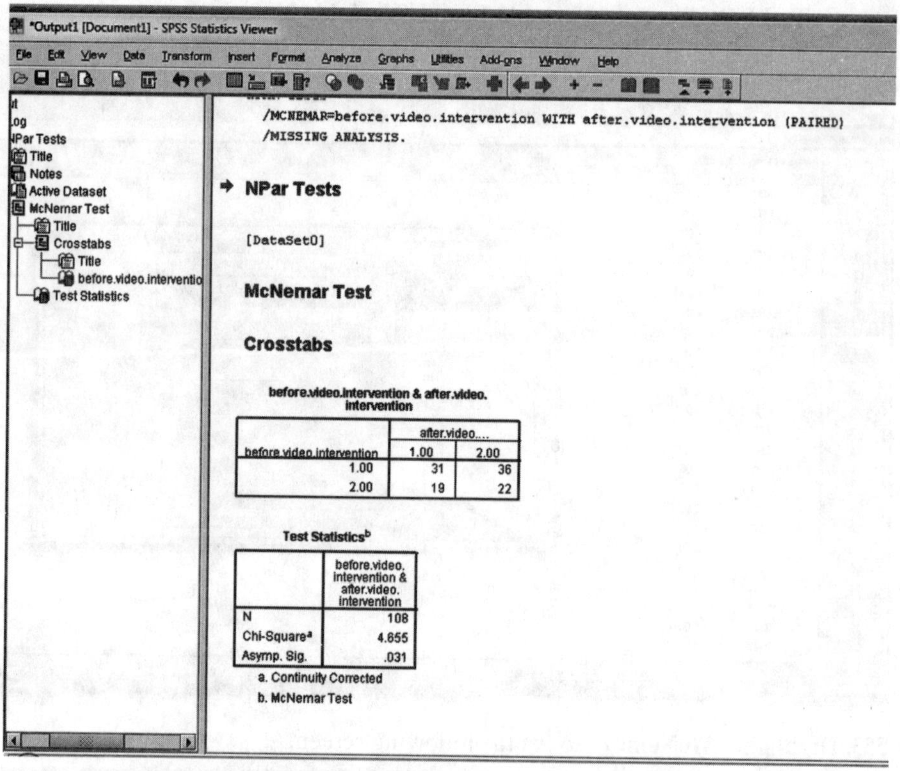

Friedman Analysis of Variance by Ranks

555. Friedman Analysis of Variance by Ranks is a repeated measure of One Way ANOVA. It is a Non-Parametric Statistics. It is to be used in analyzing data of experimental research where there is only one group of subjects assigned to more than two treatments. If there are four treatments, namely, $\mathbf{T_1, T_2, T_3}$ **and** $\mathbf{T_4}$, one group of students is given treatment $\mathbf{T_1}$ and at the end of the treatment $\mathbf{T_1}$ dependent variable is assessed with the help of a tool. Now the same group of students is given treatment $\mathbf{T_2}$ and at the end of treatment $\mathbf{T_2}$ the same tool is used to assess the dependent variable. Now treatment $\mathbf{T_3}$ is given and at the end of treatment $\mathbf{T_3}$ dependent variable is assessed with the help of the same tool as used earlier. Finally treatment $\mathbf{T_4}$ is given and at the end of treatment $\mathbf{T_4}$ dependent variable is assessed with the help of same tool as used earlier. Please remember the duration of treatments must be the same and same tool is used. One group of subjects is exposed to different treatments, so it is called repeated measures. One can have as many treatments as one wants. The data might be in interval scale or ratio scale which is converted to Ordinal Scale. You may have data in ordinal scale also. If so enter the ranks instead of scores. Let us consider the following objective of research.

To compare mean rank scores of Achievement in Physics of students taught through Lecture Method, Discussion Method and Online Teaching.
In SPSS first go to "**Variable View**" and enter name of each "**Treatment**" as shown in the following screen.

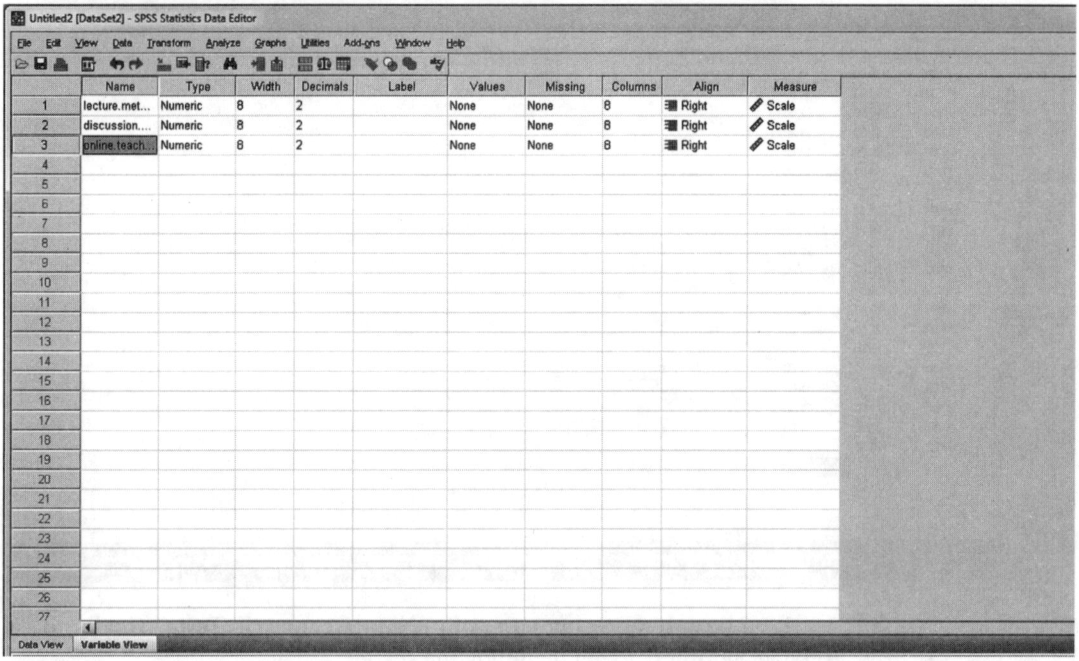

556. Click on "**Data View**" icon to get the following screen.

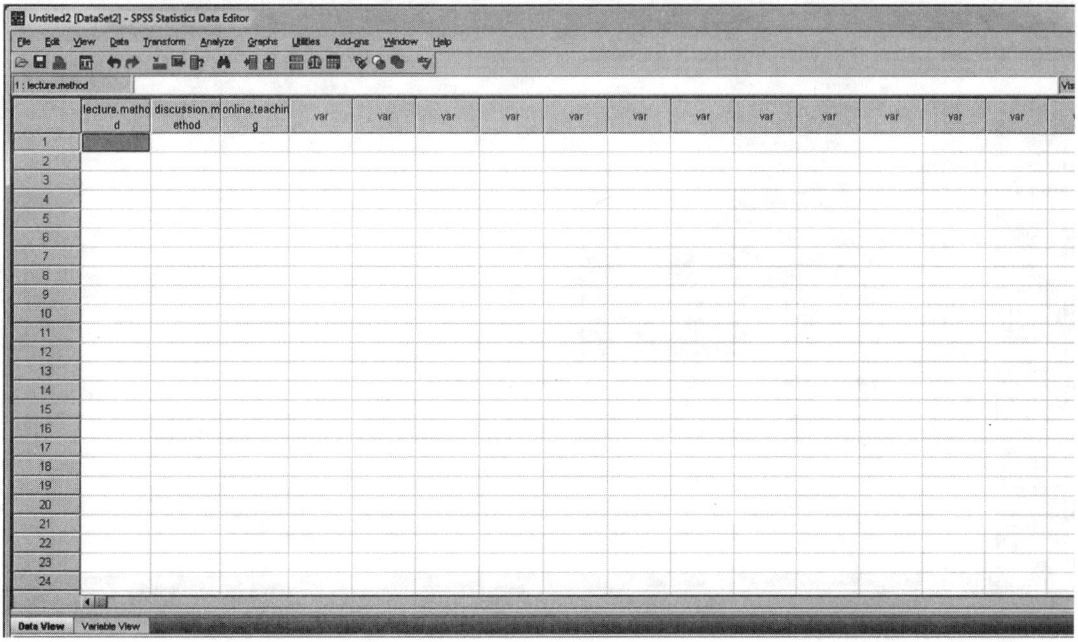

557. Enter the data of "**Achievement in Physics**" of students to get the following screen.

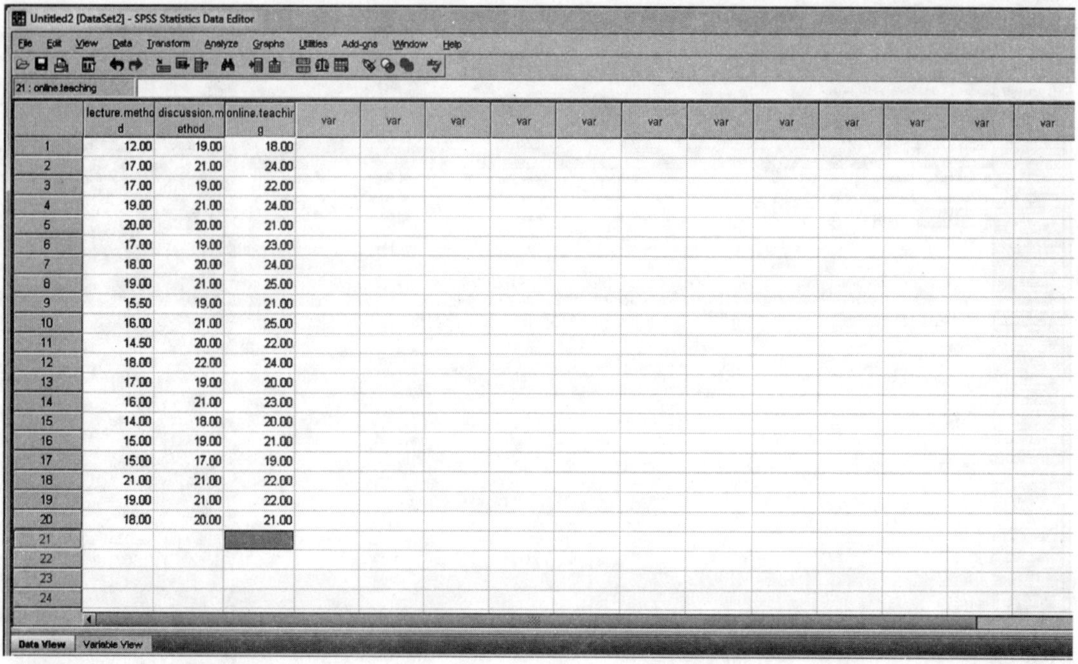

558. Click on "**Analyse**", bring curser to "**Non-parametric Tests**" finally to "**K Related Samples**" to get the following screen.

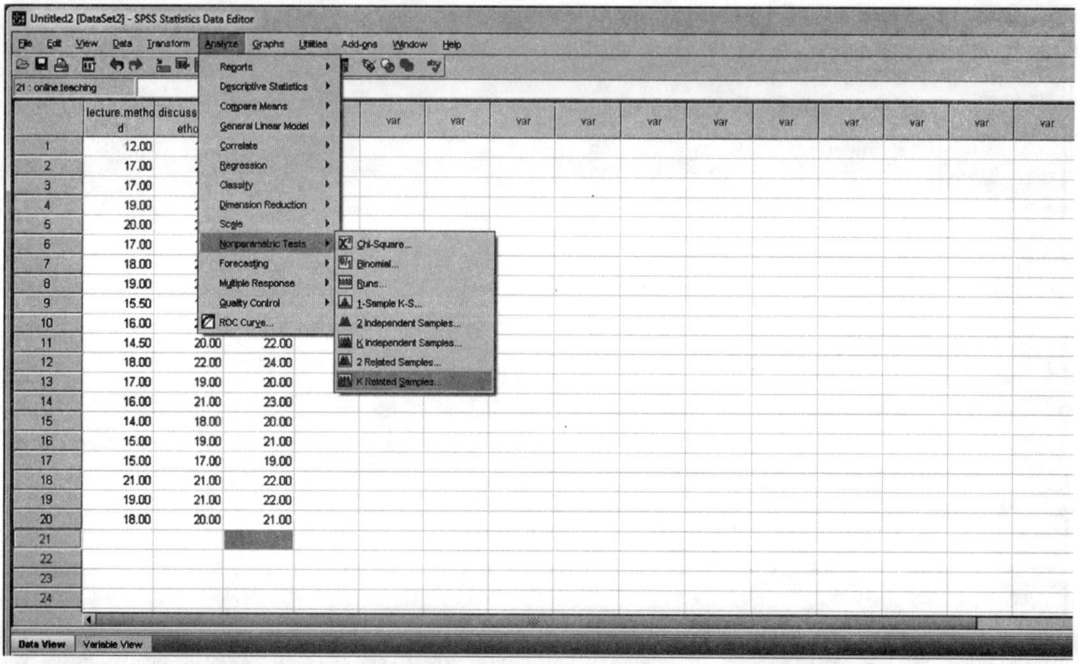

559. Click on "**K Related Samples**" to get the following screen.

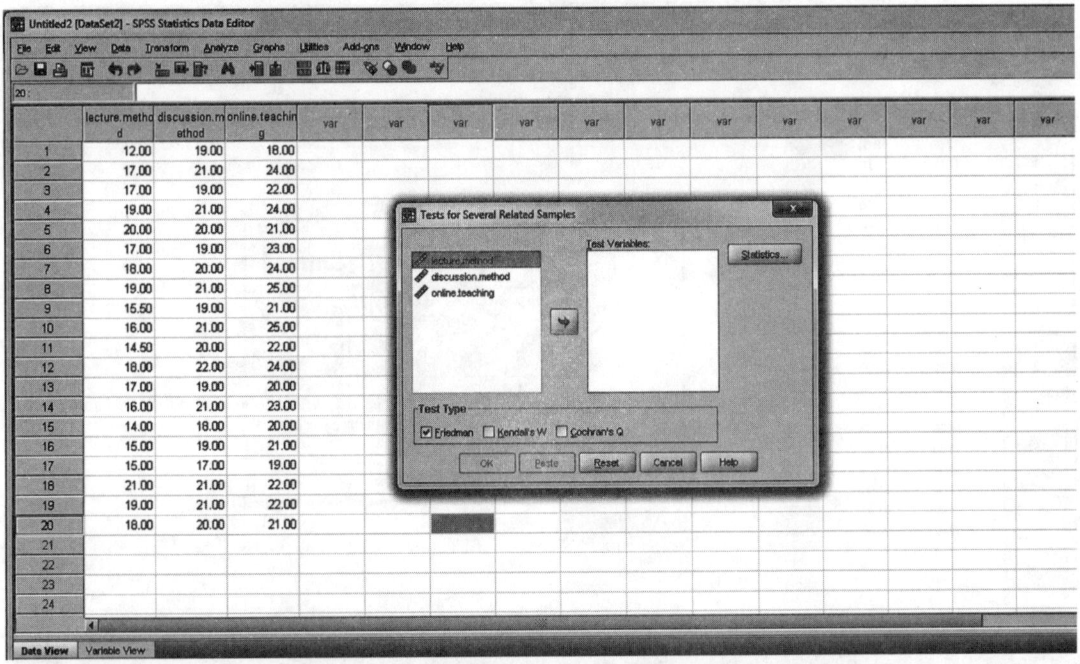

560. Shift each Treatment to the right hand side dialogue box to get the following screen.

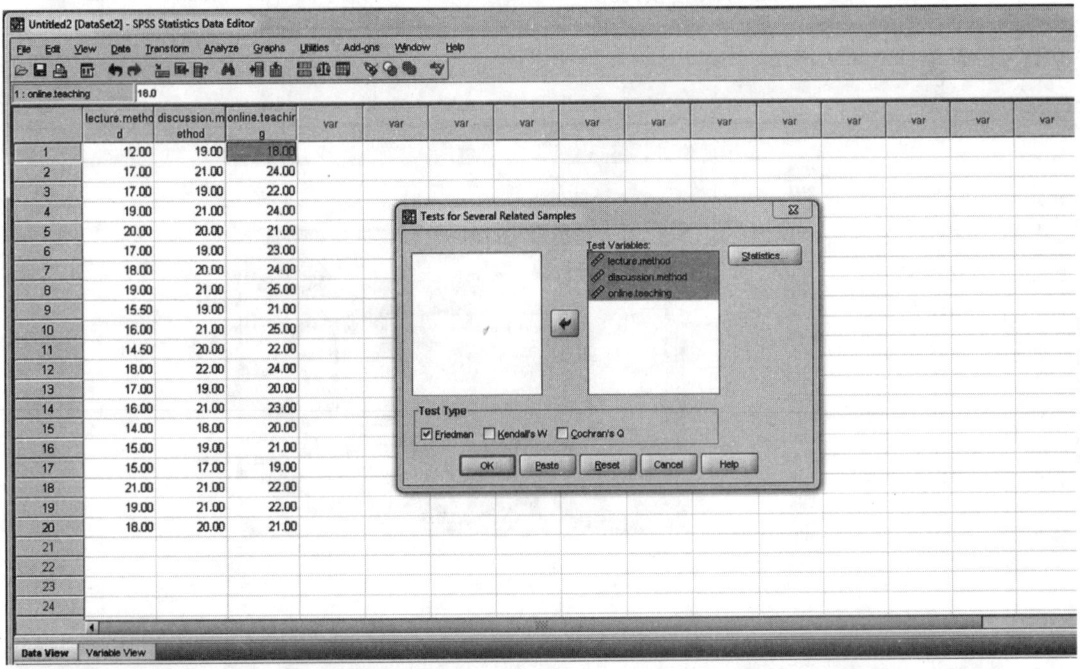

561. Click on "**Statistics**" icon to get the following screen.

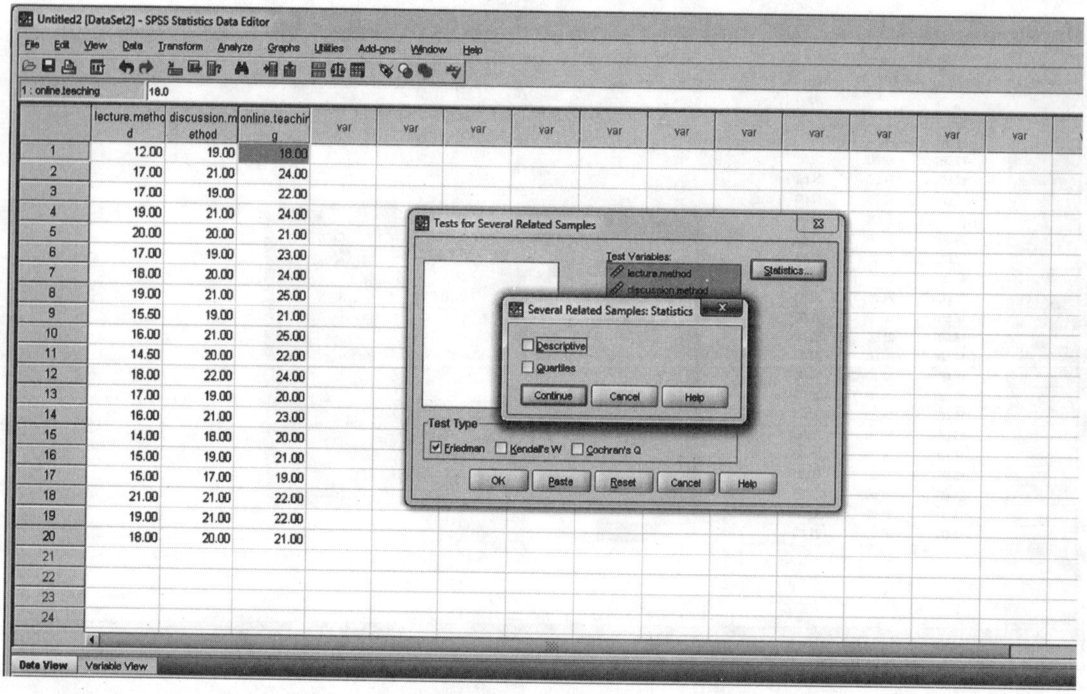

562. In case you want to compute descriptive statistics, click on "**Descriptive**" to get the following screen.

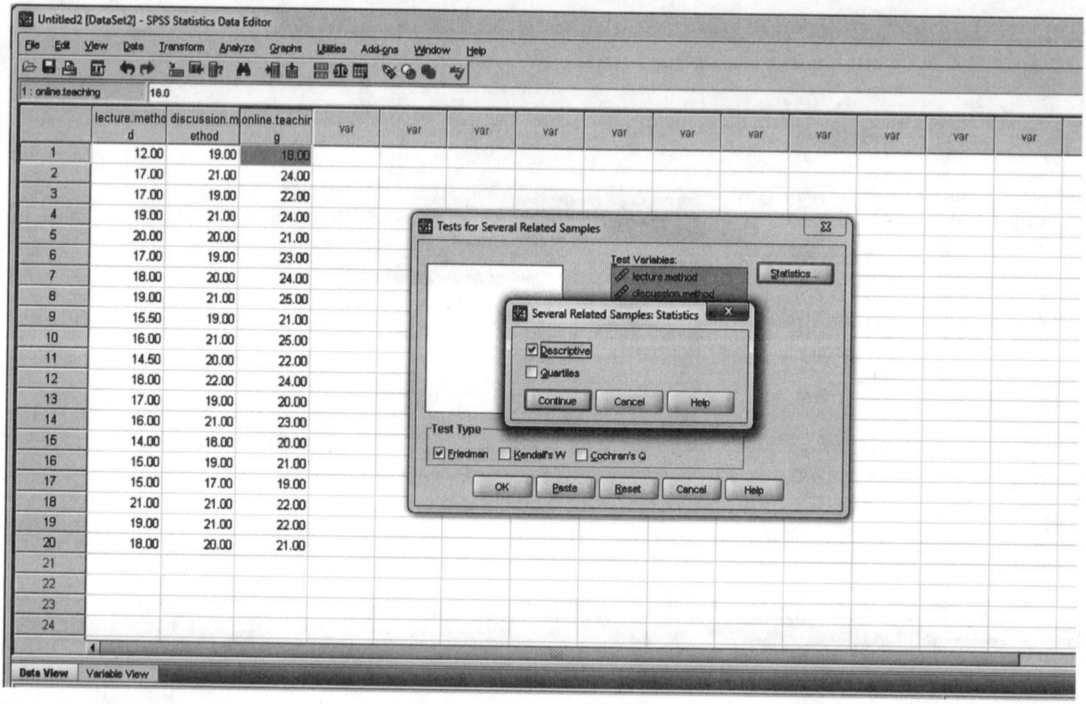

563. Click on "**Continue**" to get the following screen.

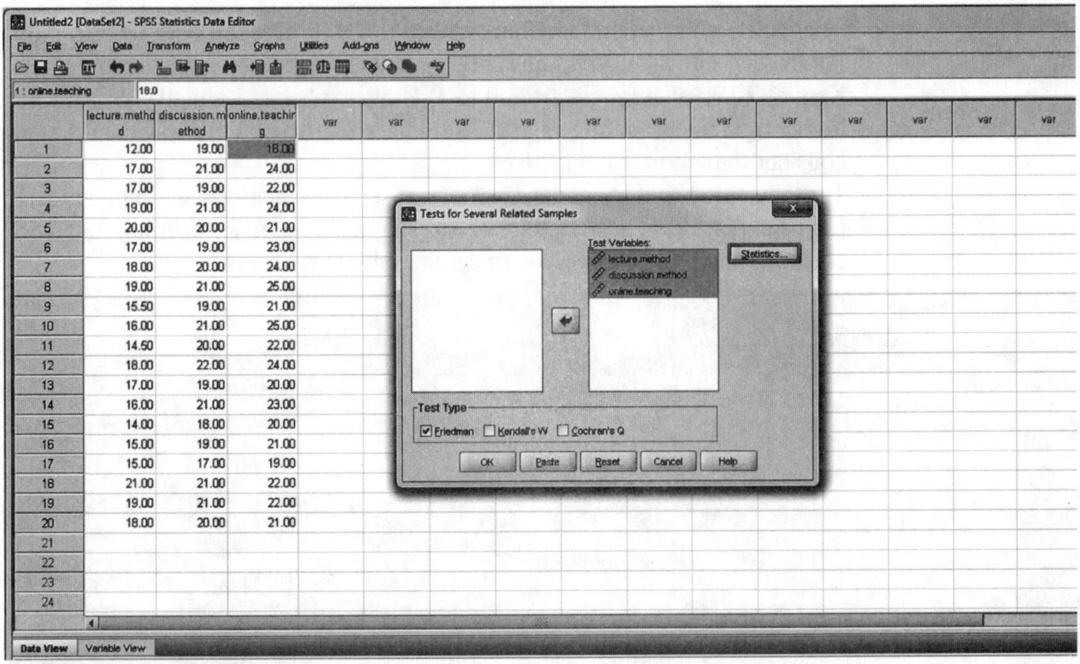

	lecture.method	discussion.method	online.teaching
1	12.00	19.00	18.00
2	17.00	21.00	24.00
3	17.00	19.00	22.00
4	19.00	21.00	24.00
5	20.00	20.00	21.00
6	17.00	19.00	23.00
7	18.00	20.00	24.00
8	19.00	21.00	25.00
9	15.50	19.00	21.00
10	16.00	21.00	25.00
11	14.50	20.00	22.00
12	18.00	22.00	24.00
13	17.00	19.00	20.00
14	16.00	21.00	23.00
15	14.00	18.00	20.00
16	15.00	19.00	21.00
17	15.00	17.00	19.00
18	21.00	21.00	22.00
19	19.00	21.00	22.00
20	18.00	20.00	21.00

564. Under "**Test Type**" three options are given and "**Friedman**" is already highlighted so click on "**OK**" to get the following outputs of Friedman Analysis of Variance by Ranks.

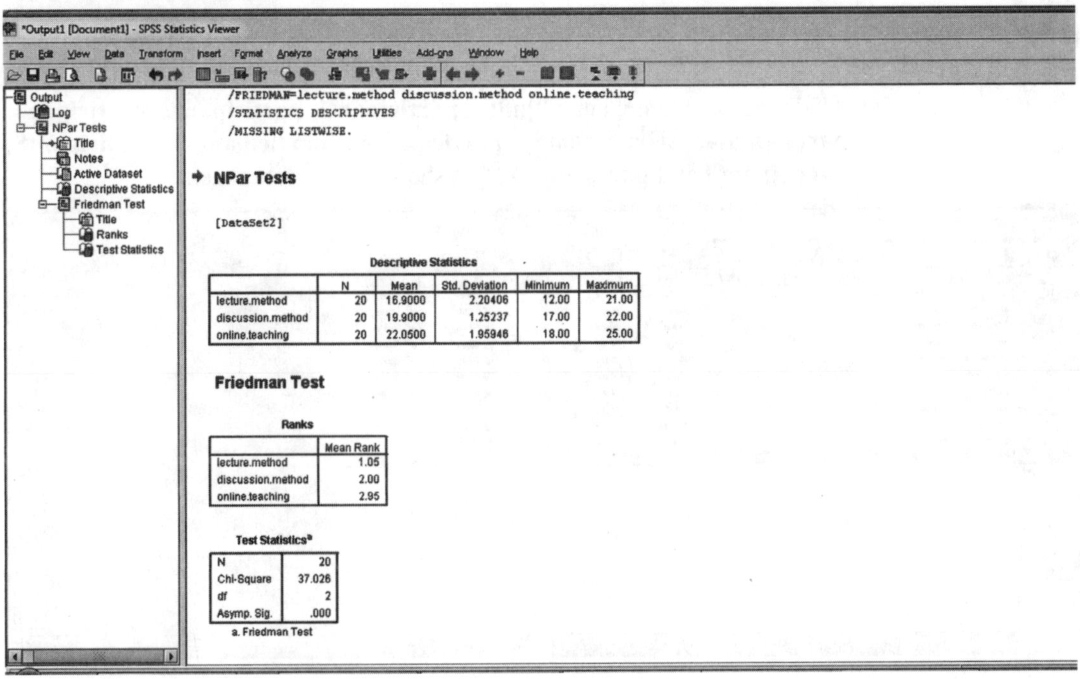

Descriptive Statistics

	N	Mean	Std. Deviation	Minimum	Maximum
lecture.method	20	16.9000	2.20406	12.00	21.00
discussion.method	20	19.9000	1.25237	17.00	22.00
online.teaching	20	22.0500	1.95946	18.00	25.00

Ranks

	Mean Rank
lecture.method	1.05
discussion.method	2.00
online.teaching	2.95

Test Statistics[a]

N	20
Chi-Square	37.026
df	2
Asymp. Sig.	.000

a. Friedman Test

Kendall's Coefficient of Concordance (W) or Kendall's W

565. Kendall's Coefficient of Concordance (W) or Kendall's W is the Non-Parametric statistical technique used for assessing the agreement among raters. Kendall's W value ranges from 0 to 1. Higher value of Kendall's W indicates higher agreement among raters. The data must be on Ordinal Scale. Let us consider the following objective.
To study agreement about the adequacy of science teaching aids among judges.
Let us understand the procedure of entering the data. After opening the SPSS, click on "**Variable View**" icon to get the following screen.

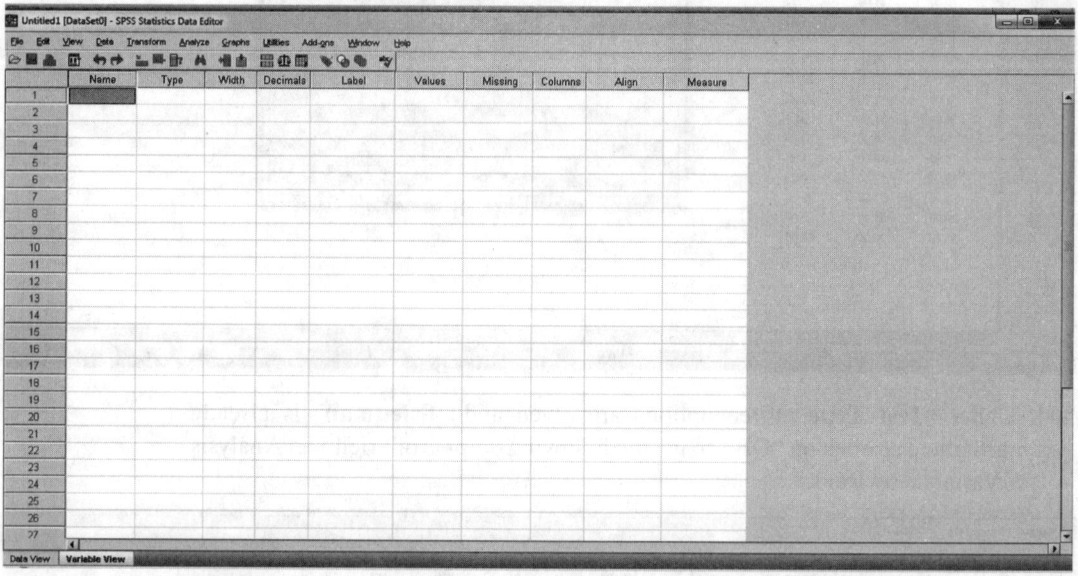

566. Under name column, enter "**judge, participant1, participant2, participan3, participant4, participant5, participant6, participant7, participant8, participant9 and participant10**" as shown in the data sheet.

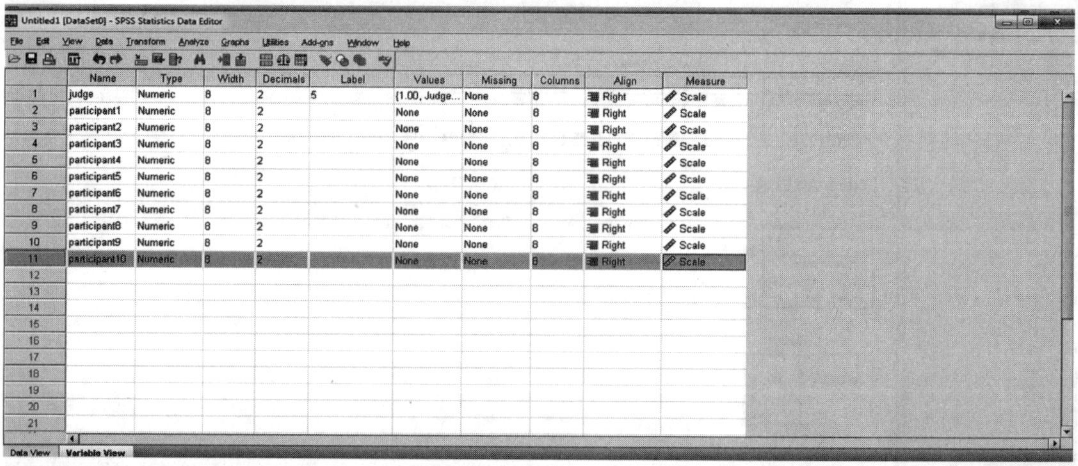

567. Now click on "Data View" to get the following screen.

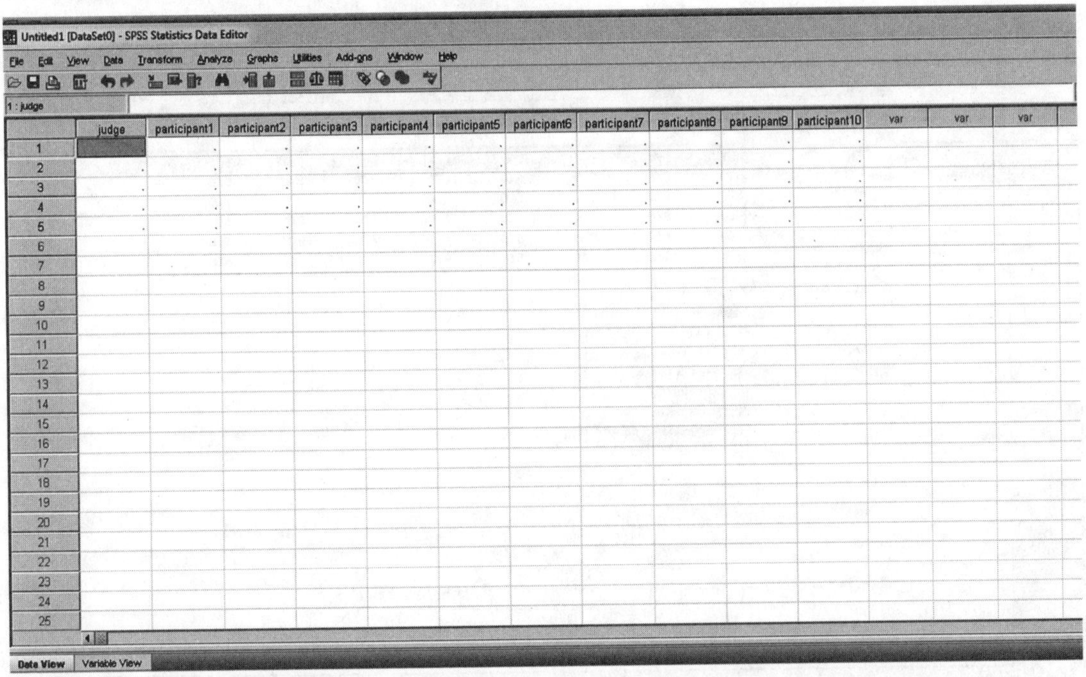

568. Suppose there are five judges and 10 participants. Each judge rated the adequacy of science teaching aids of each participant on a ten point scale. Score of 1 indicates low adequacy and score of 10 indicates highest adequacy. The data are given in the following SPSS data sheet.

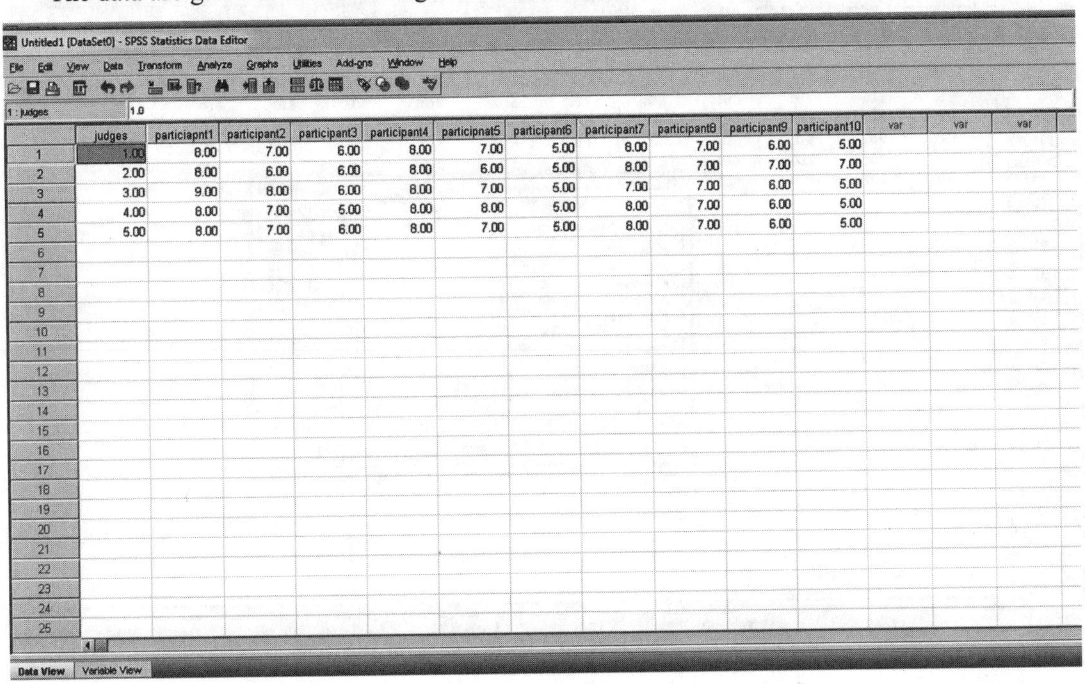

Untitled1 [DataSet0] - SPSS Statistics Data Editor

	judges	particiapnt1	participant2	participant3	participant4	participnat5	participant6	participant7	participant8	participant9	participant10
1	1.00	8.00	7.00	6.00	8.00	7.00	5.00	8.00	7.00	6.00	5.00
2	2.00	8.00	6.00	6.00	8.00	6.00	5.00	8.00	7.00	7.00	7.00
3	3.00	9.00	8.00	6.00	8.00	7.00	5.00	7.00	7.00	6.00	5.00
4	4.00	8.00	7.00	5.00	8.00	8.00	5.00	8.00	7.00	6.00	5.00
5	5.00	8.00	7.00	6.00	8.00	7.00	5.00	8.00	7.00	6.00	5.00

569. Click on "**Analyse**", bring curser to "**Non-parametric Test**" and finally to "**K Related Samples**" to get the following screen.

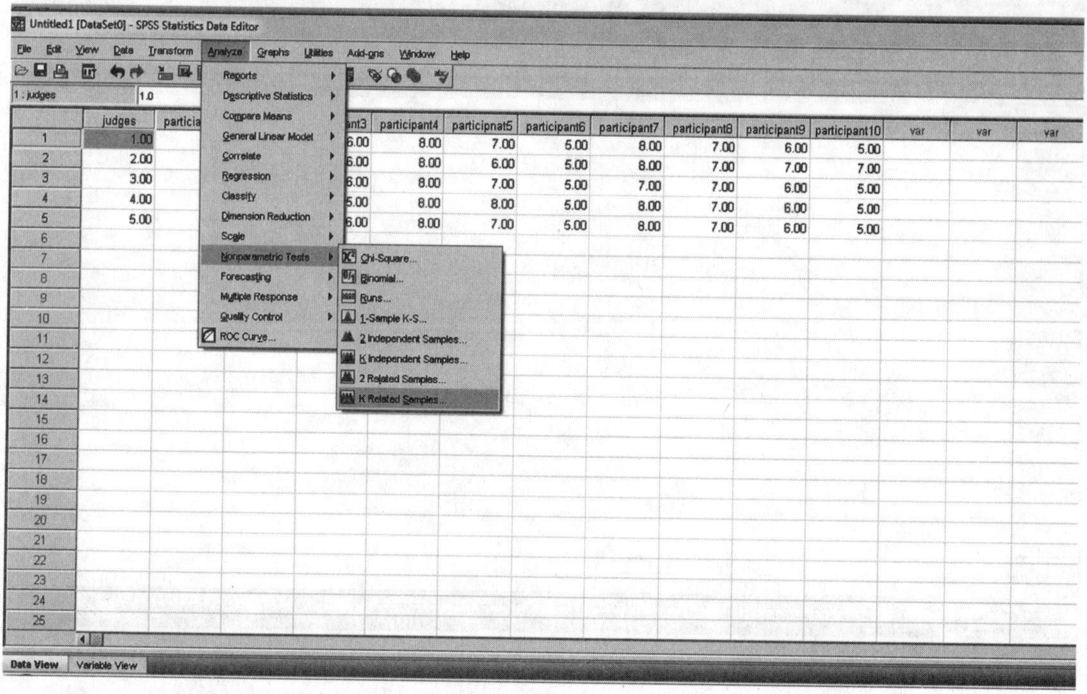

570. Click on "**K Related Samples**" to get the following screen.

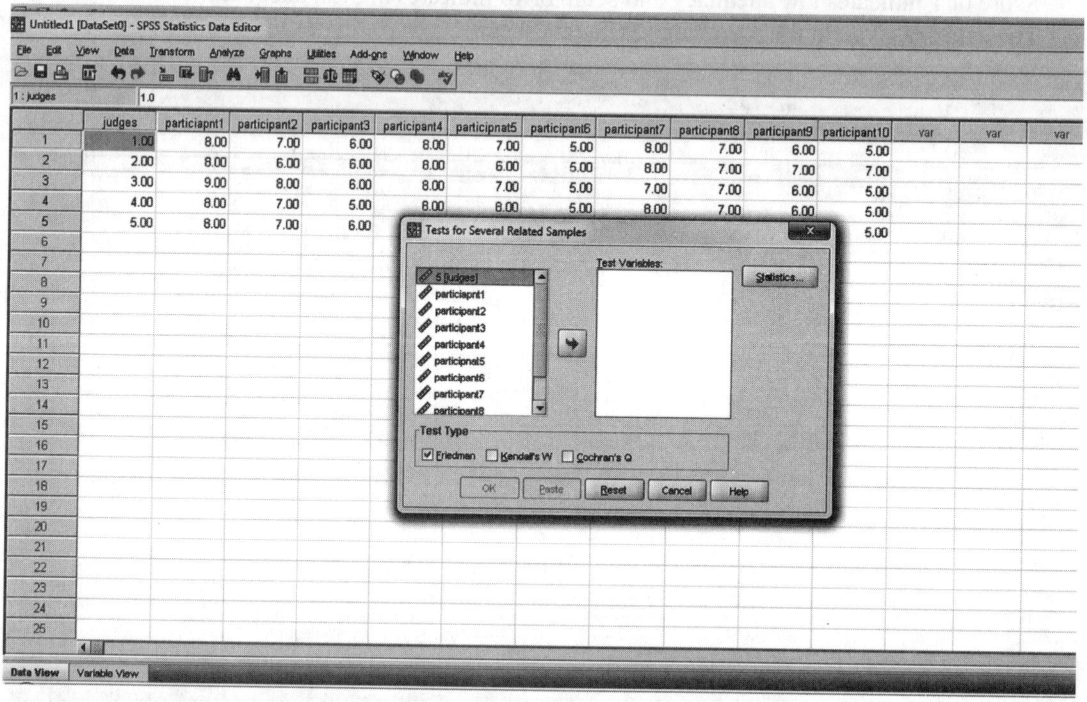

571. There were ten participants. Shift all "**Participants**" to the "**Test Variables**" dialog box to get the following screen.

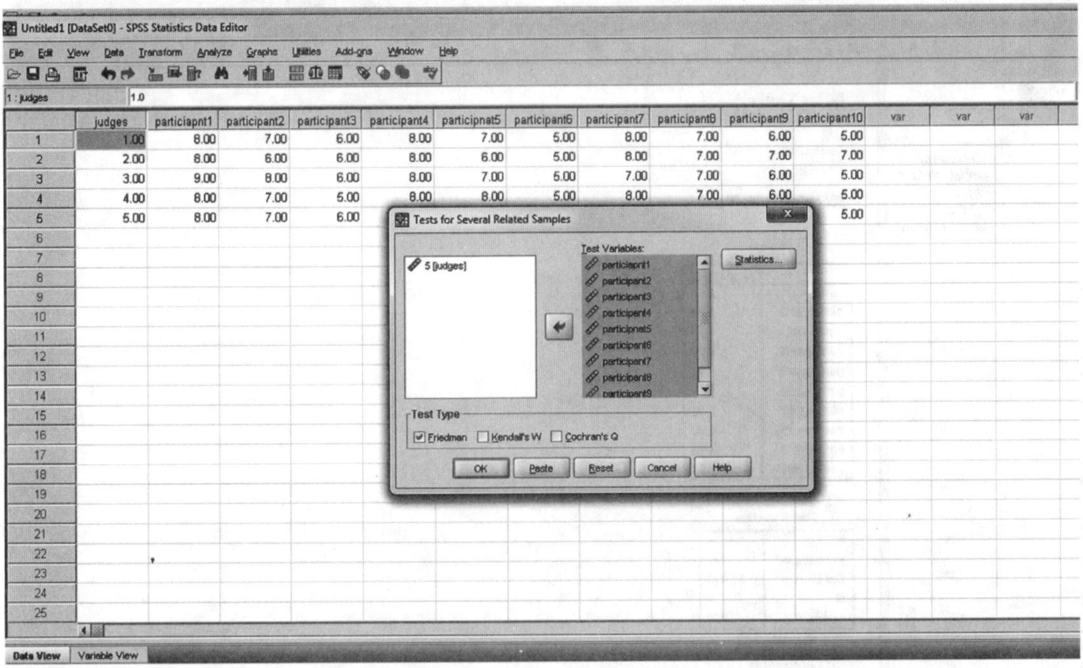

572. Deactivate Friedman and activate only "**Kendall's W**" to get the following screen.

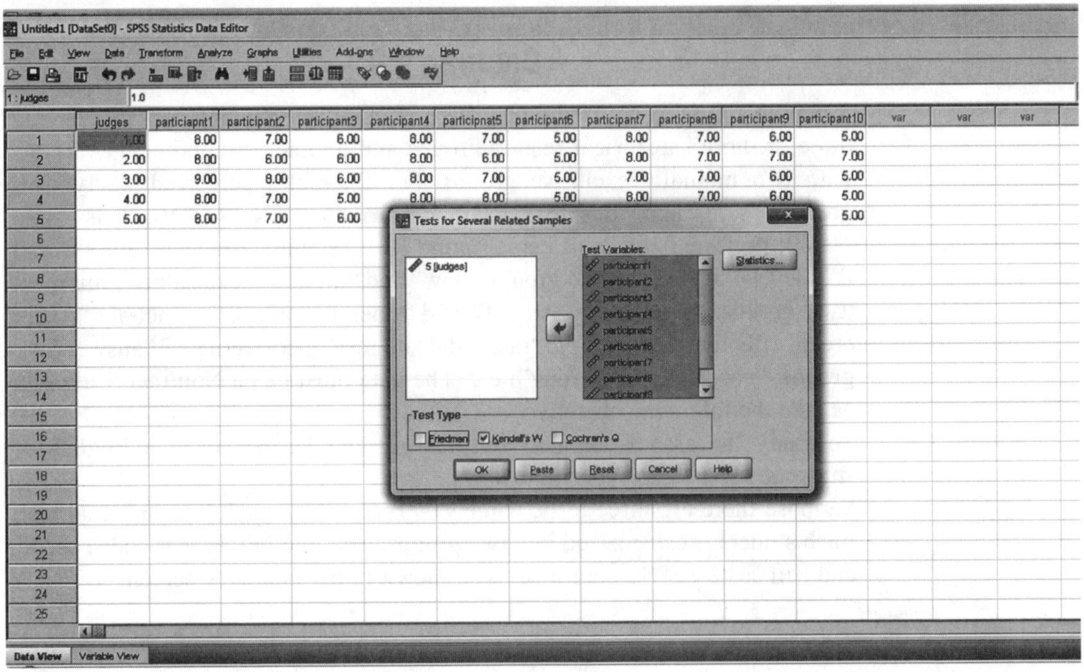

573. Click on "**OK**" to get the following outputs of Kendall's W.

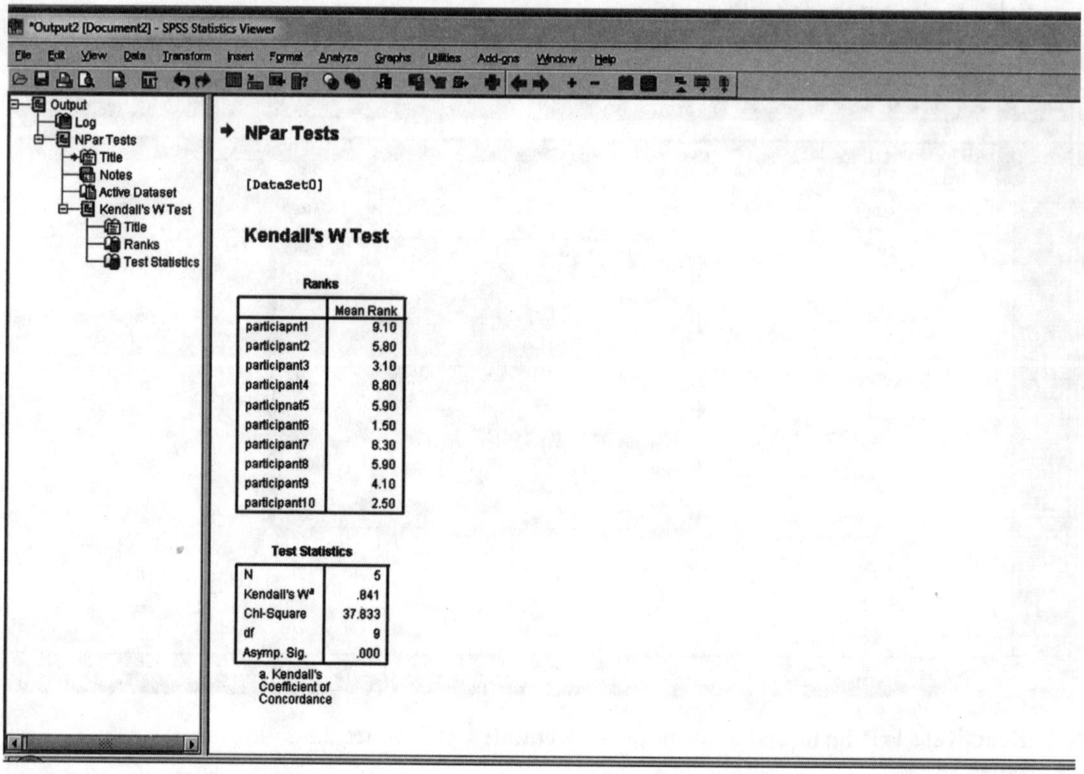

Cochran's Q

574. Cochran's Q is to be used when there is one discontinuous variable having three or more categorical related groups and another discontinuous variable with two mutually exclusive groups. For Examples perceived safety (two groups: "safe" and "unsafe"); exam performance (two groups: "pass" and "fail"); preferred choice of cereal brand (two groups: "Brand A" and "Brand B"); level of tiredness (two groups: "low" and "high"); use of safety equipment (two groups: "uses safety helmet" and "does not use safety helmet"); skin cream effective (two groups: "rash" and "no rash"); correctness of answer (two groups: "correct" and "wrong") etc. The data must be on Nominal Scale. Let us take the following objective.

To study the association between Testing and Performance in English of students.

Suppose there are three tests, namely, surprise test, mock test and final test. Each student is categorized into two groups: pass and fail. Pass is coded as "**1**" and Fail as "**2**". SPSS data sheet is as shown in the following screen.

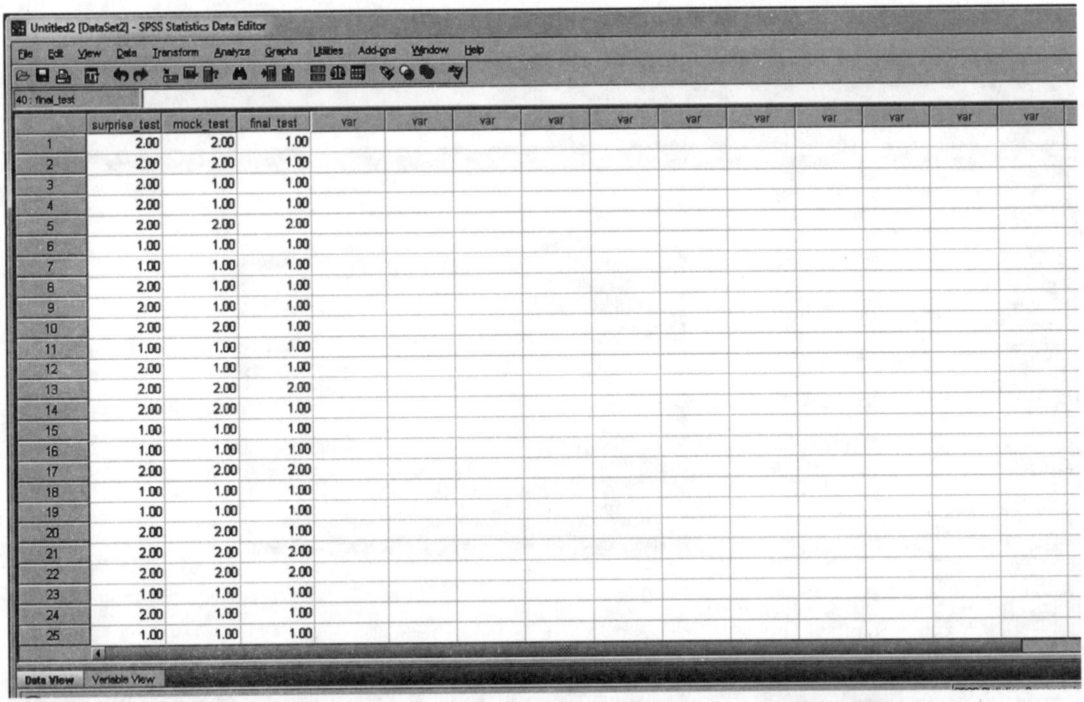

575. Click on "**Analyse**", bring curser to "**Non-Parametric Test**" and finally to "**K Related Samples**" to get the following screen.

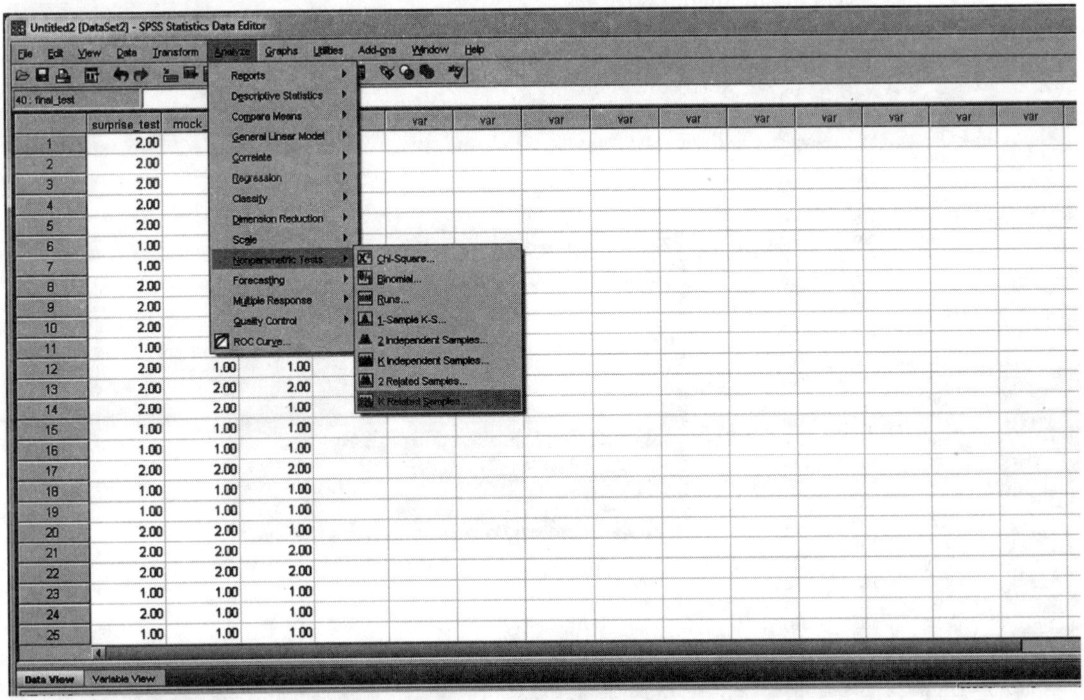

576. Click on "**K Related Samples**" to get the following screen.

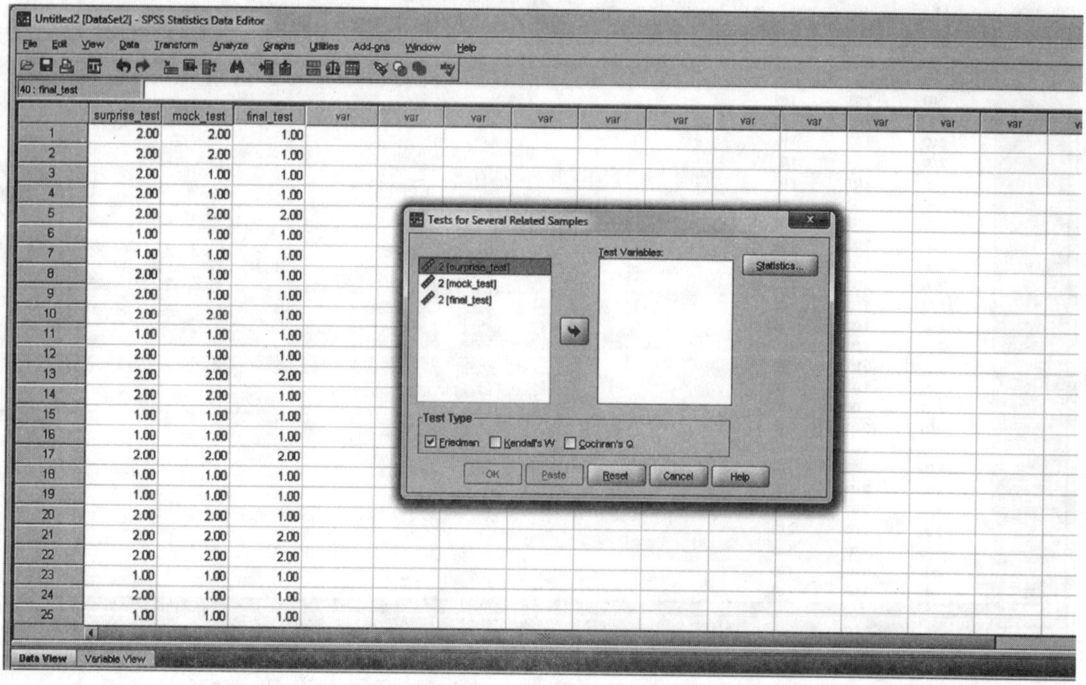

577. Shift all variables from right hand side dialog box to "**Test Variable**" slot to get the following screen.

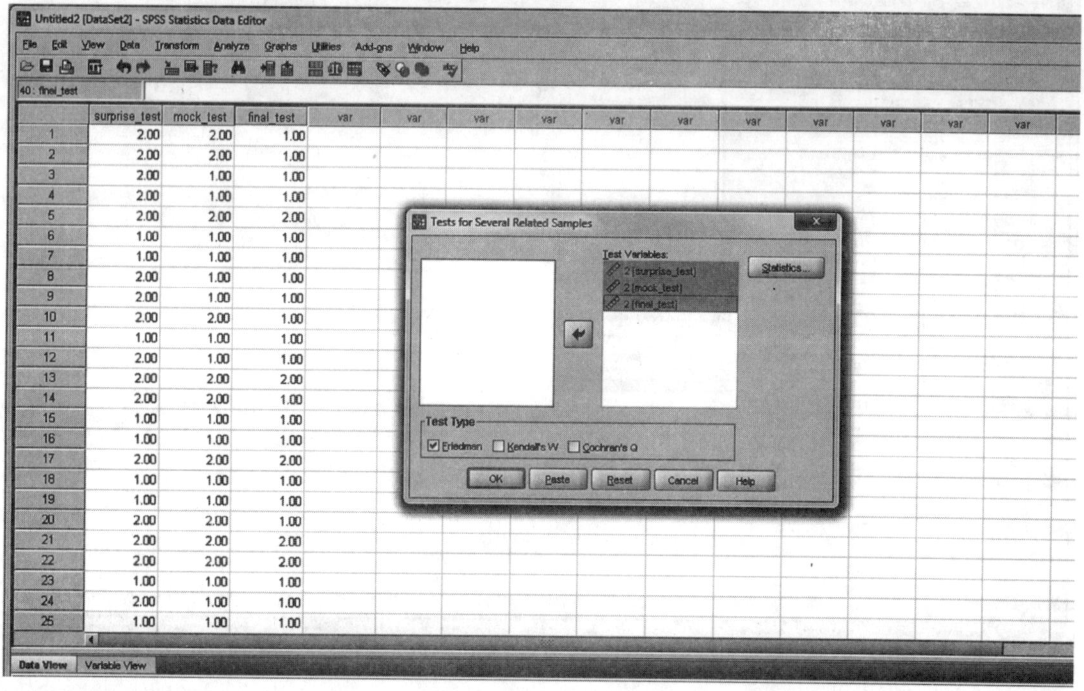

578. Deactivate Friedman and activate only "**Cochran's Q**" to get the following screen.

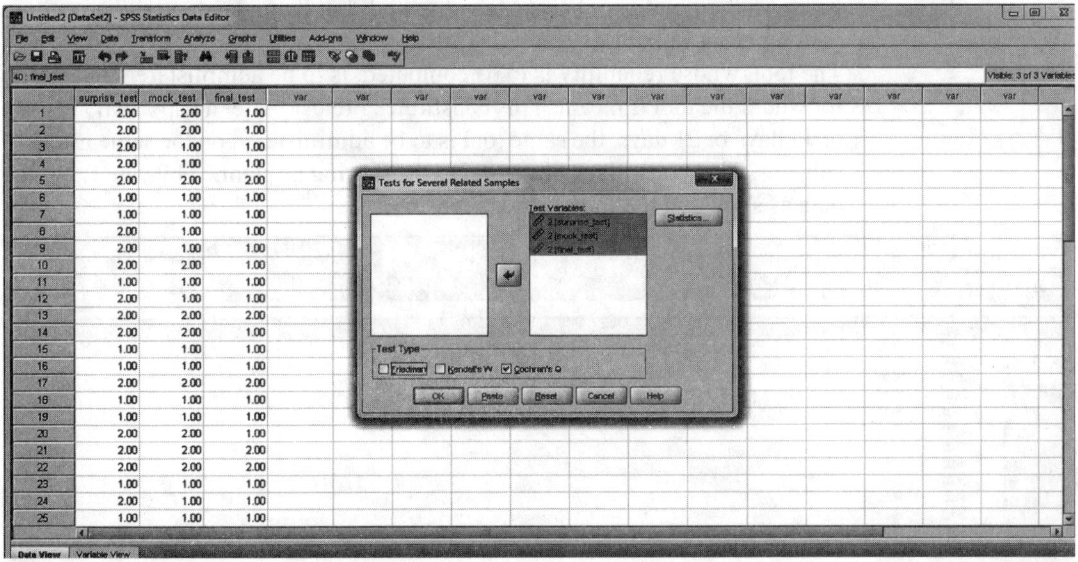

579. Click on "**OK**" to get the following outputs of Cochran's Q Test.

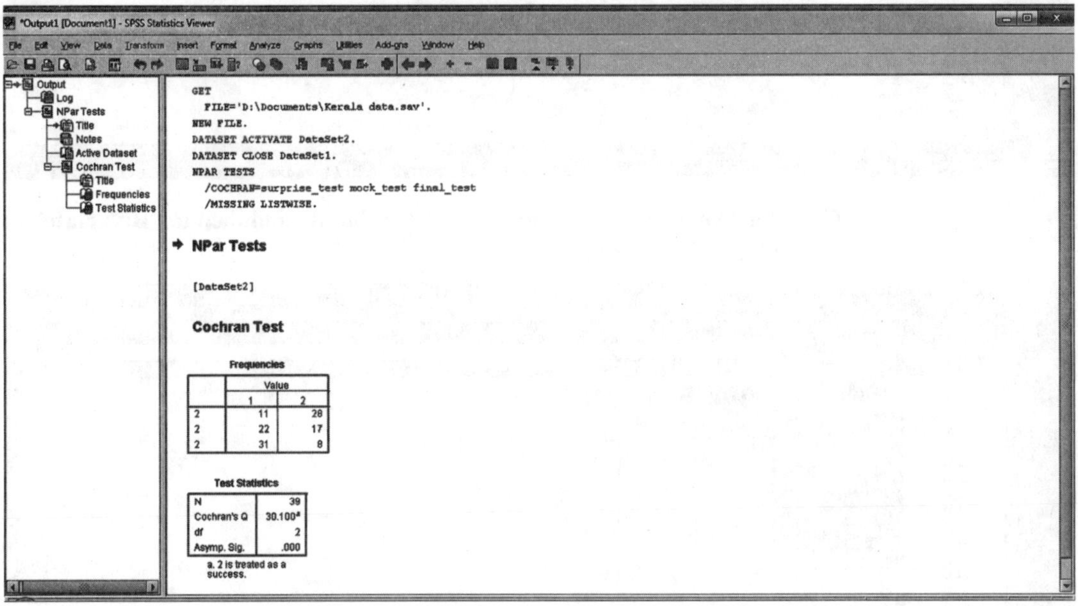

Test-Retest Method of Reliability

580. You know that Test, Scale and Inventory can be standardized but Interview Schedule, Observation Schedule and Questionnaire cannot be standardized. So reliability coefficient can be computed only for Test, Scale and Inventory.

There are different Methods of Reliability. SPSS can be used for establishing Reliability through the use of Test-Retest Method, Split-half Method, Parallel Form Method and Cronback Alpha Method. Let us understand the procedure of computing Reliability through Test-Retest Method.

The tool, whose reliability is to be computed, is to be administered on a group for whom the tool is meant. This constitutes Pretest. After a gap of say, 10 days or 15 days or 21 days, the same tool is to be administered on the same group of subjects. This constitutes Posttest. Do the scoring as planned by you. Enter the data as shown in the following screen.

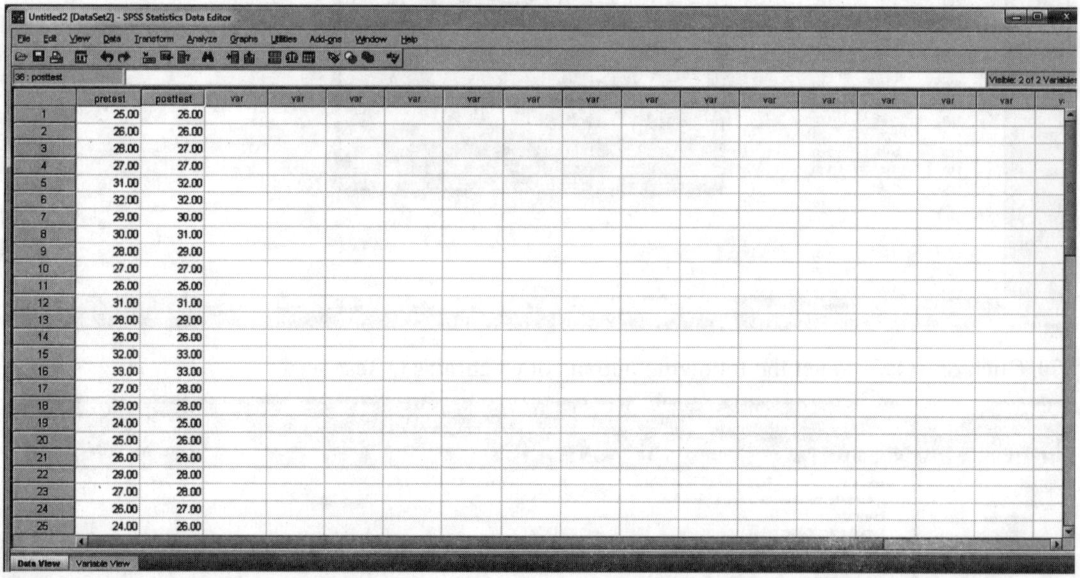

581. Click on "**Analyse**", bring curser to "**Correlated**" and then to "**Bivariate**" to get the following screen.

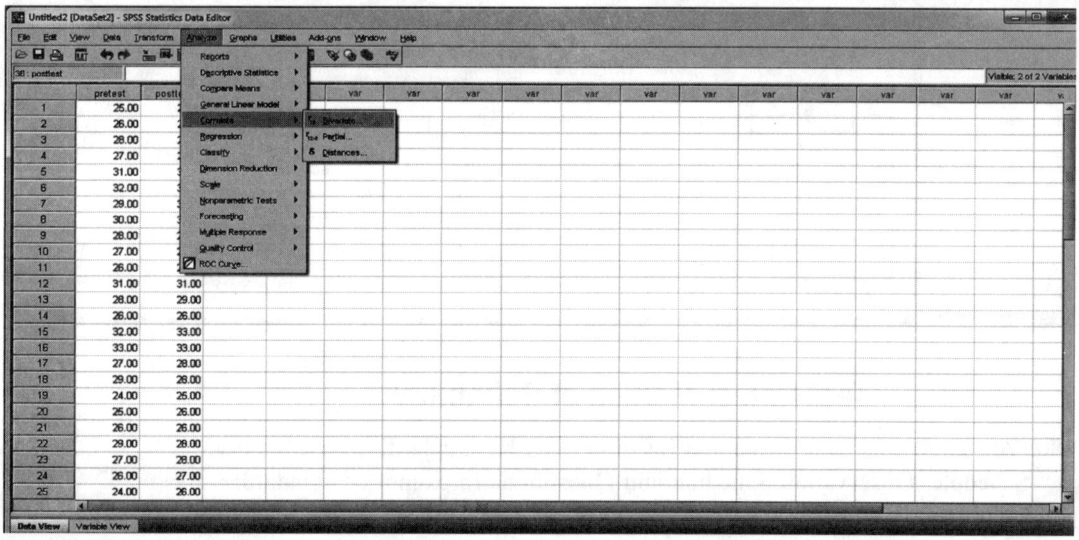

582. Click on "**Bivariate**" to get the following screen.

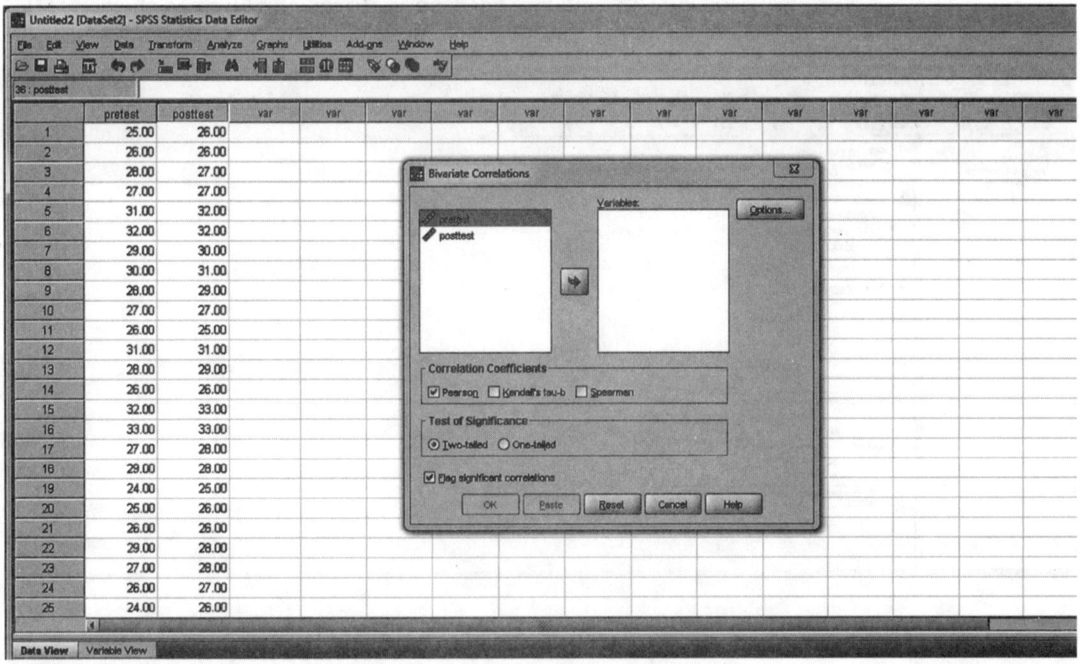

583. Shift both "**Pretest**" and "**Posttest**" under "**Variables**" box to get the following screen.

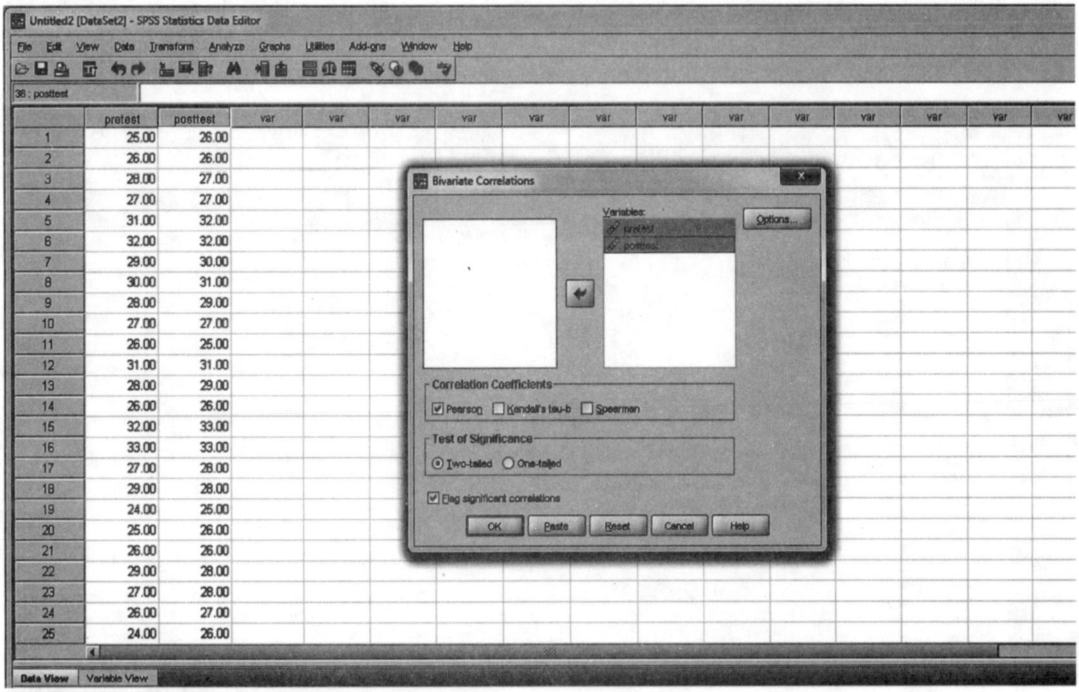

584. Here correlation is computed between Pretest and Posttest by using Pearson Product Moment Correlation. "**Pearson**" is already highlighted click on "**OK**" to get the output of Test-Retest Reliability Coefficient.

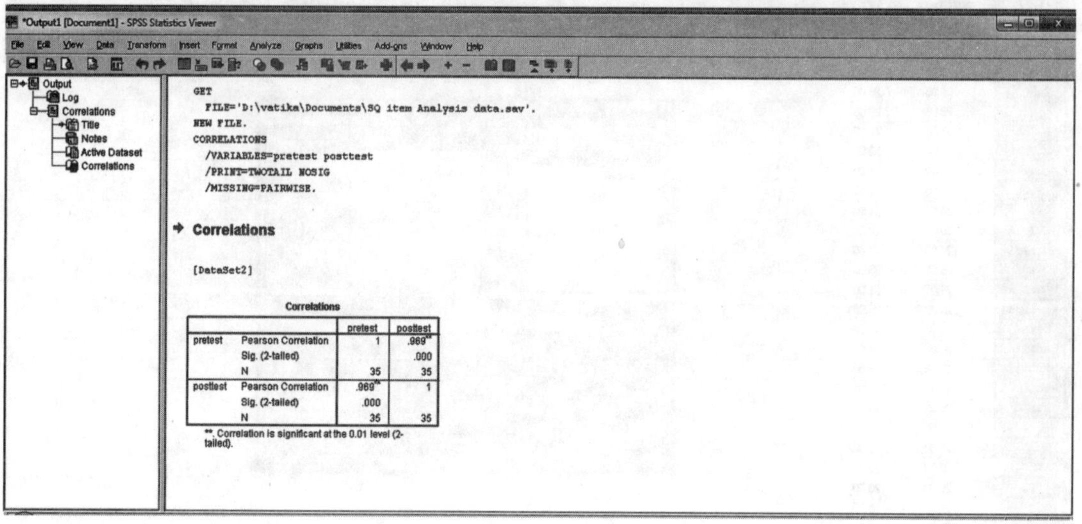

Split-Half Method of Reliability

585. Split-Half Method can be used for establishing Reliability of Test, Scale as well as Inventory. Suppose you administered an Achievement in Physics Test to class XII students. Suppose there are 40 items. You have computed total scores for odd items as well as even items. Scores are entered in the SPSS data sheet as shown in the following screen.

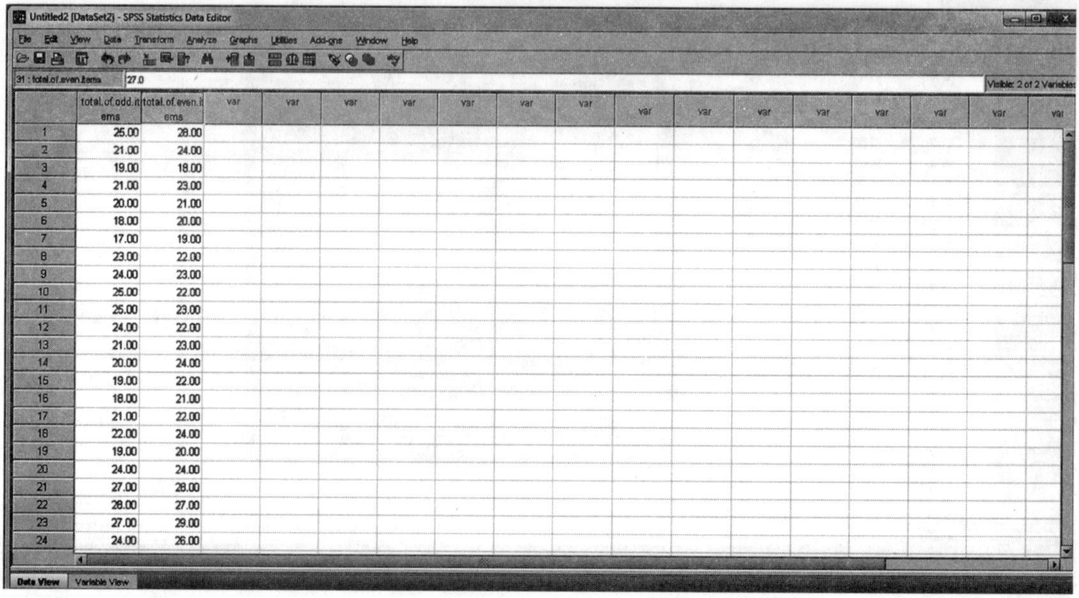

586. Click on "**Analyse**", bring curser to "**Scale**" and finally to "**Reliability Analysis**" to get the following screen.

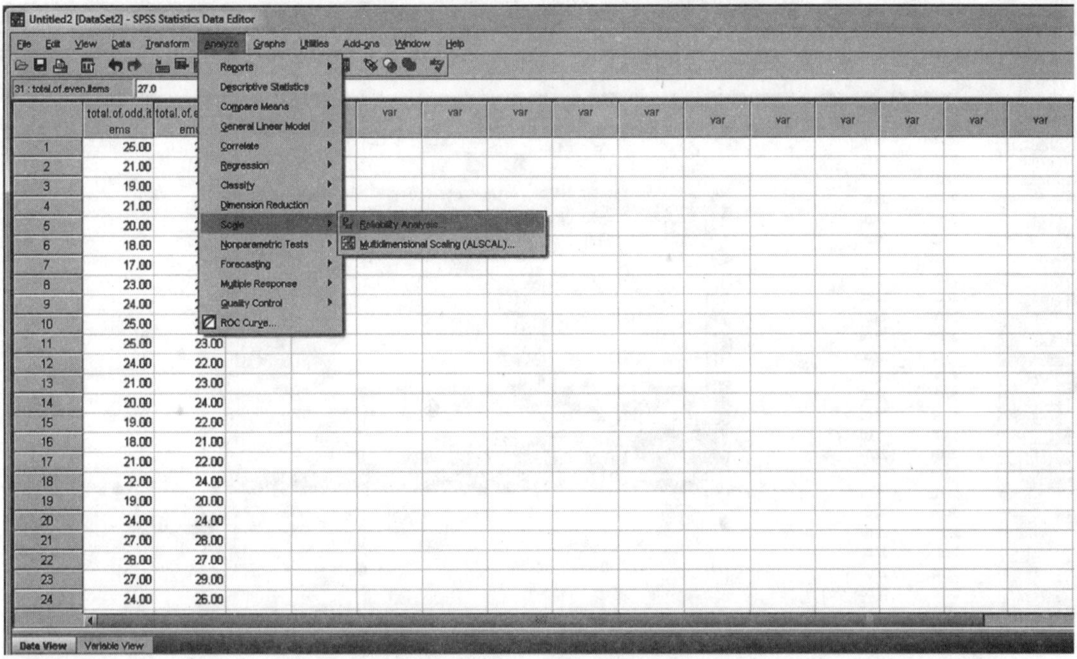

587. Click on "**Reliability Analysis"** icon to get the following screen.

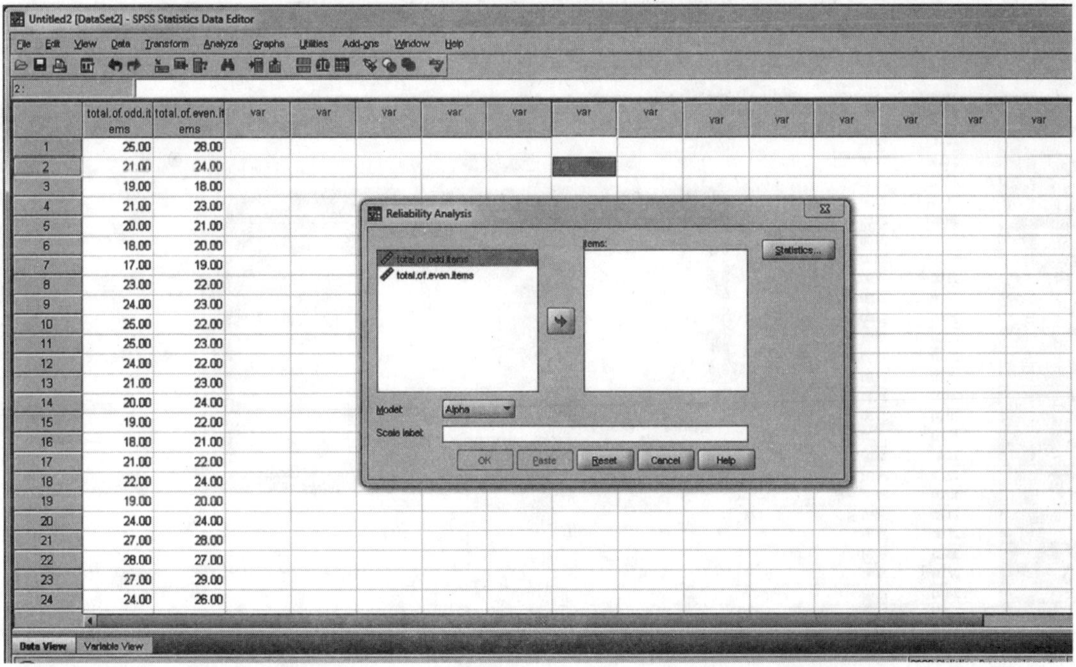

588. Shift both "**total of odd items**" and "**total of even items**" to the right hand side dialog box under "**Items**" to get the following screen.

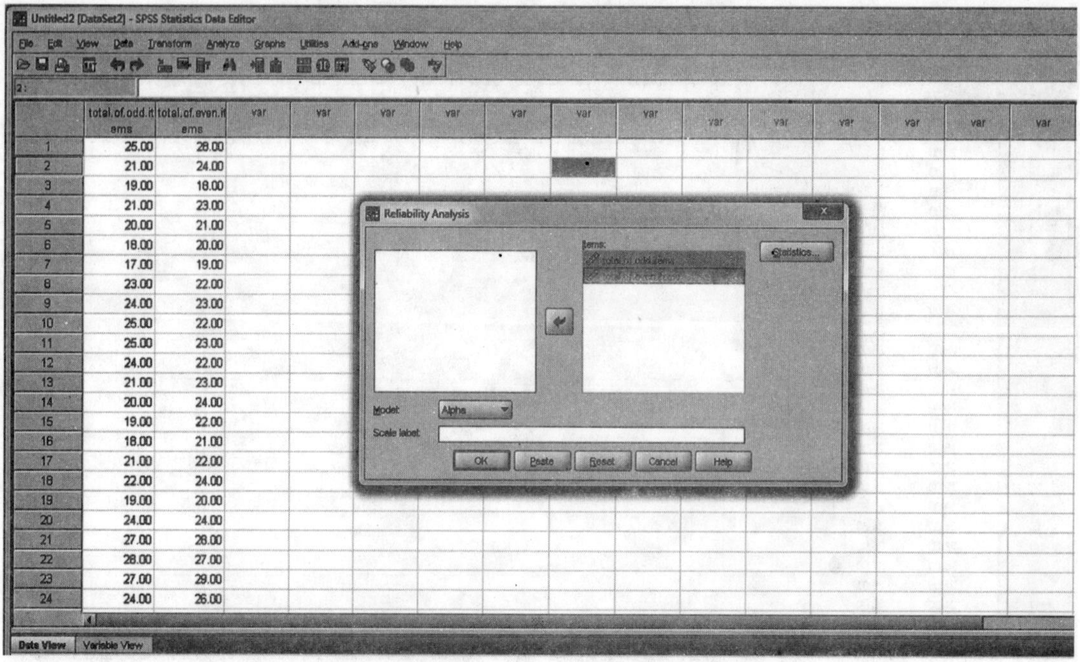

589. Click on "**Model: Alpha**" to get the following screen.

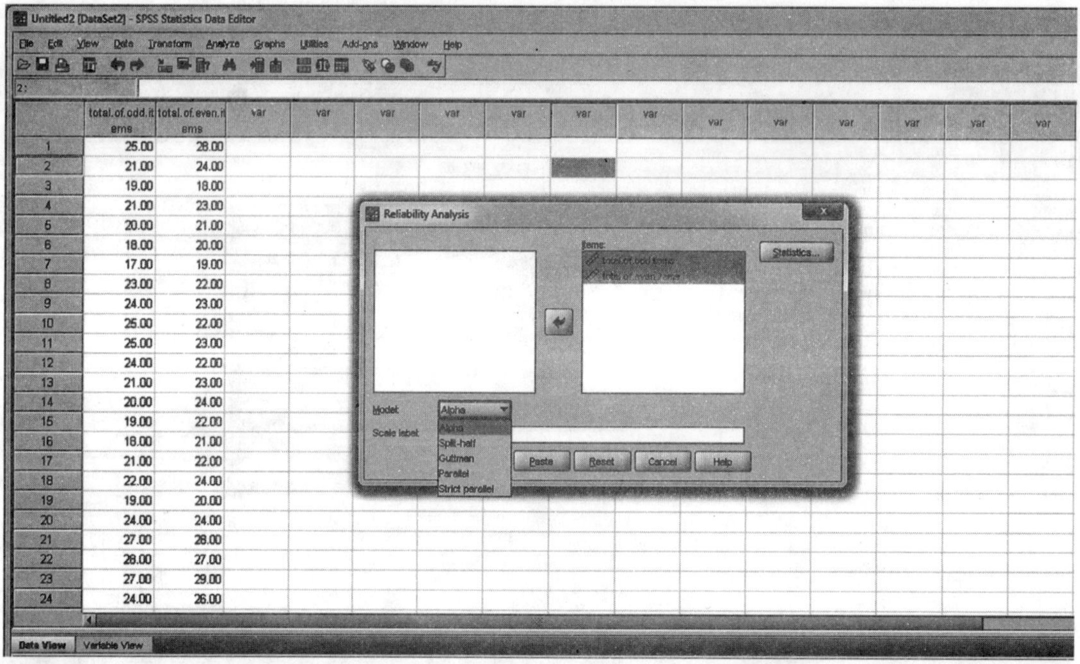

590. Click on "**Split-half**" to get the following screen.

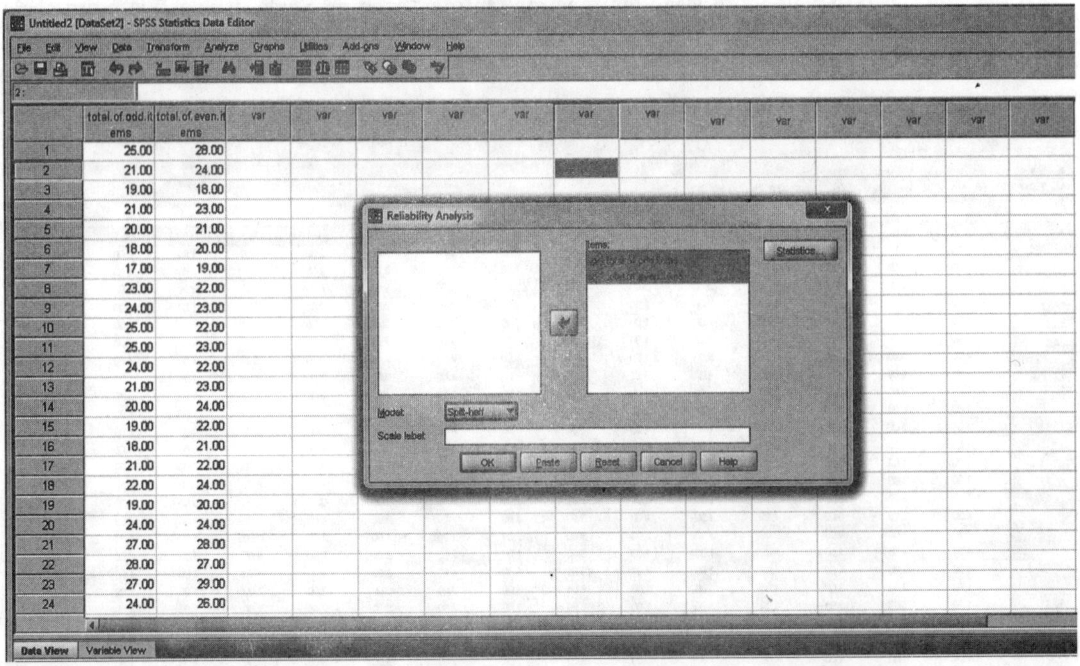

591. Click on "**OK**" to get the following outputs of Split-half Reliability coefficient.

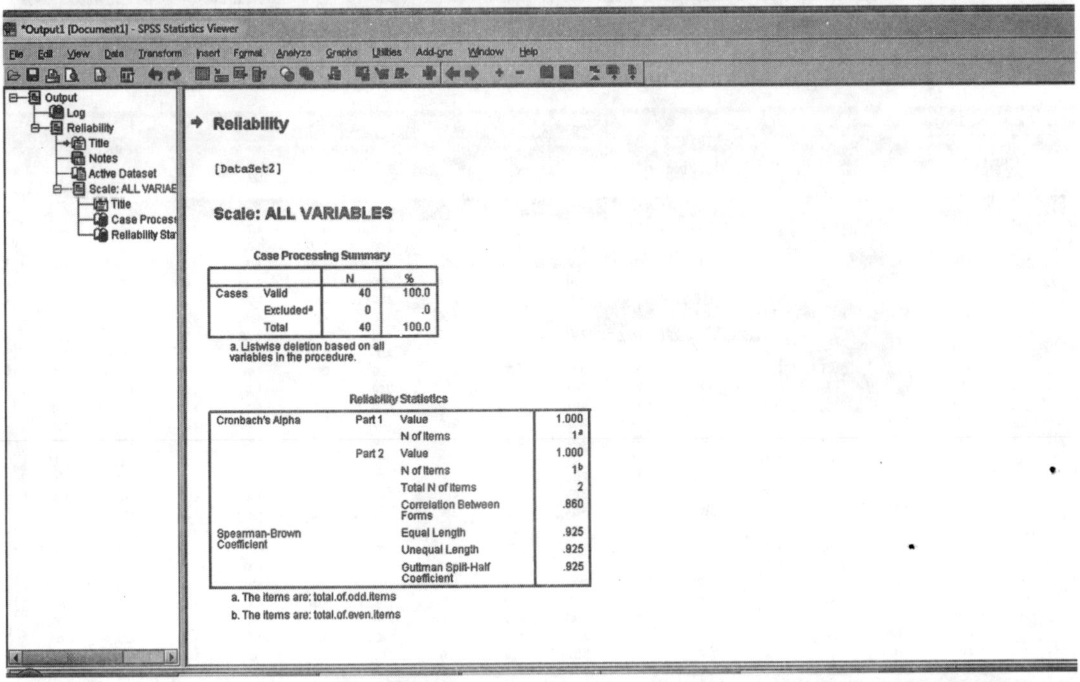

592. Suppose you want to study the Reaction towards Online Teaching. So you developed a Reaction towards Online Teaching Scale. It is a five point scale and written 34 items. It has been administered on 372 teachers and scoring it done. Item wise data have been entered in the SPSS sheet as shown in the following screen.

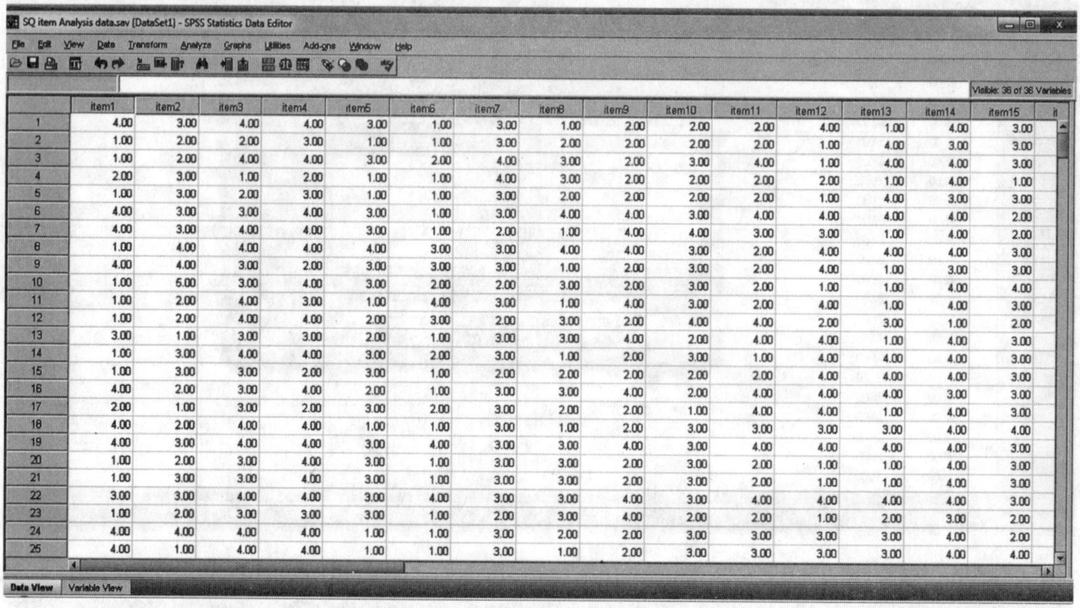

593. Click on "**Analyse**", bring curser to "**Scale**" and then to "**Reliability Analysis**" to get the following screen.

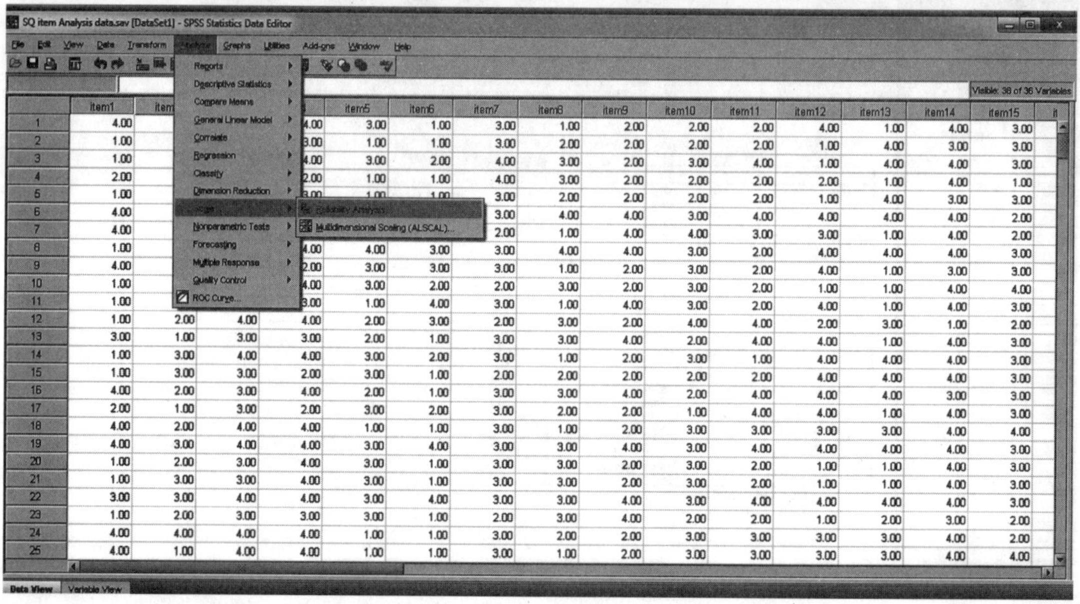

594. Click on "**Reliability Analysis**" to get the following screen.

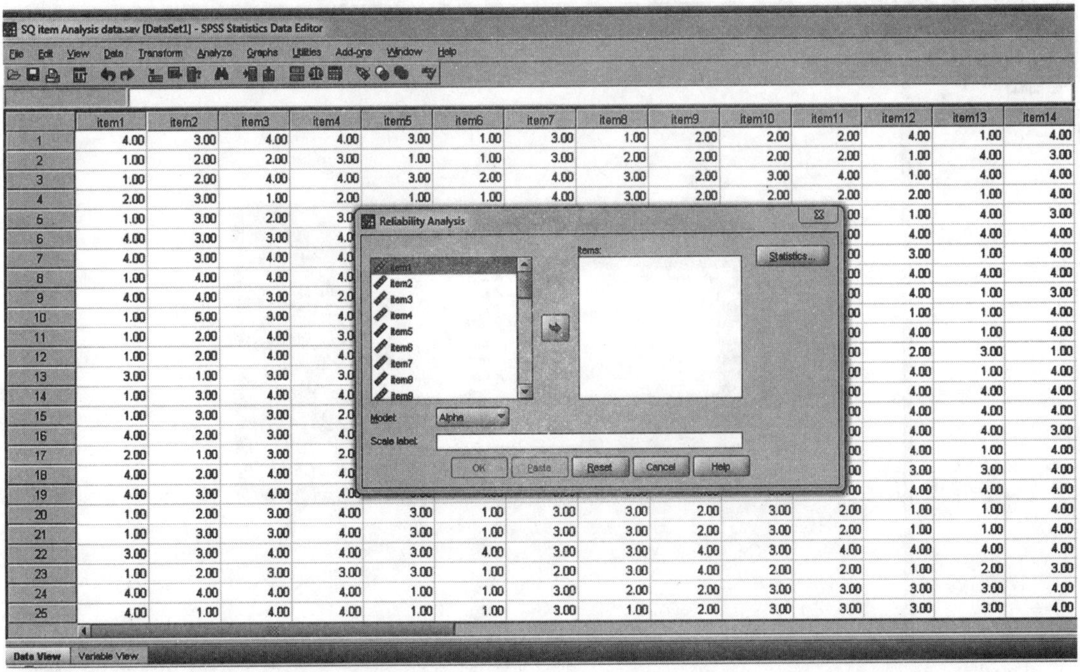

595. Shift all 34 items from left hand side to the right hand side dialog box to get the following screen.

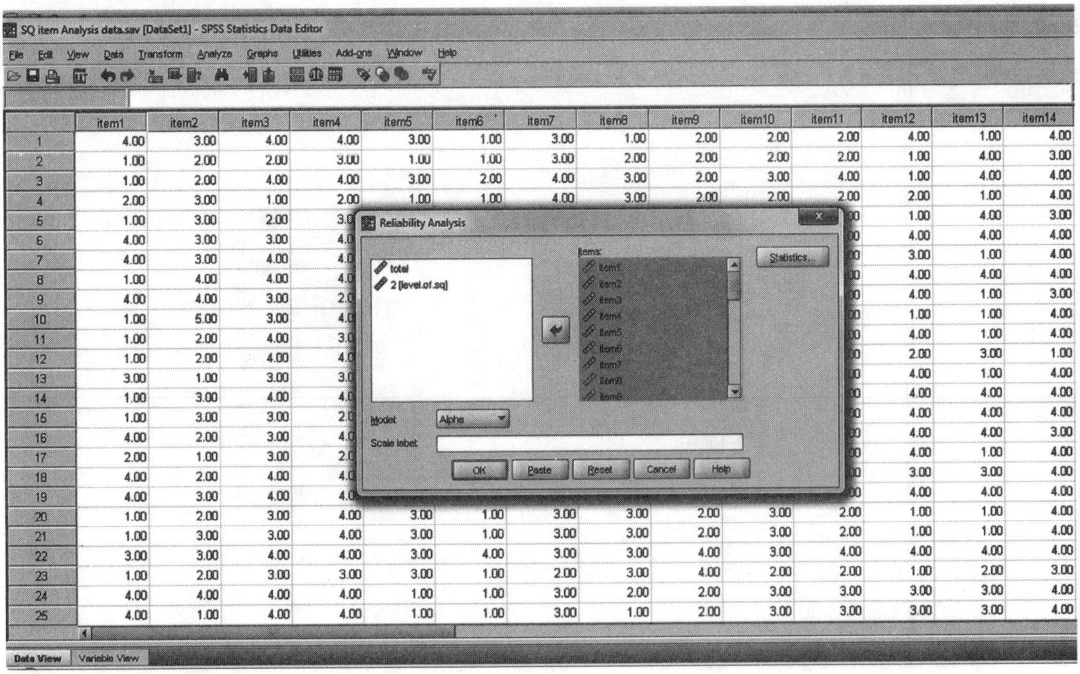

596. Click on "**Model: Alpha**" to get the following screen.

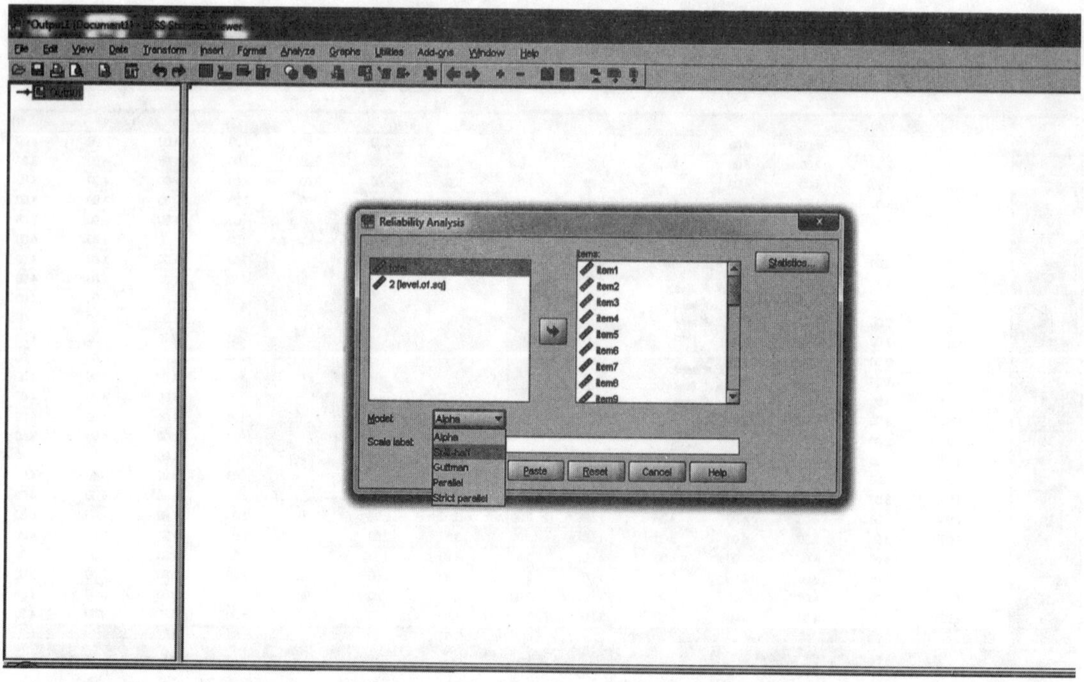

597. You want to compute Split-Half Reliability Coefficient so click on "**Split-half**" to get the following screen.

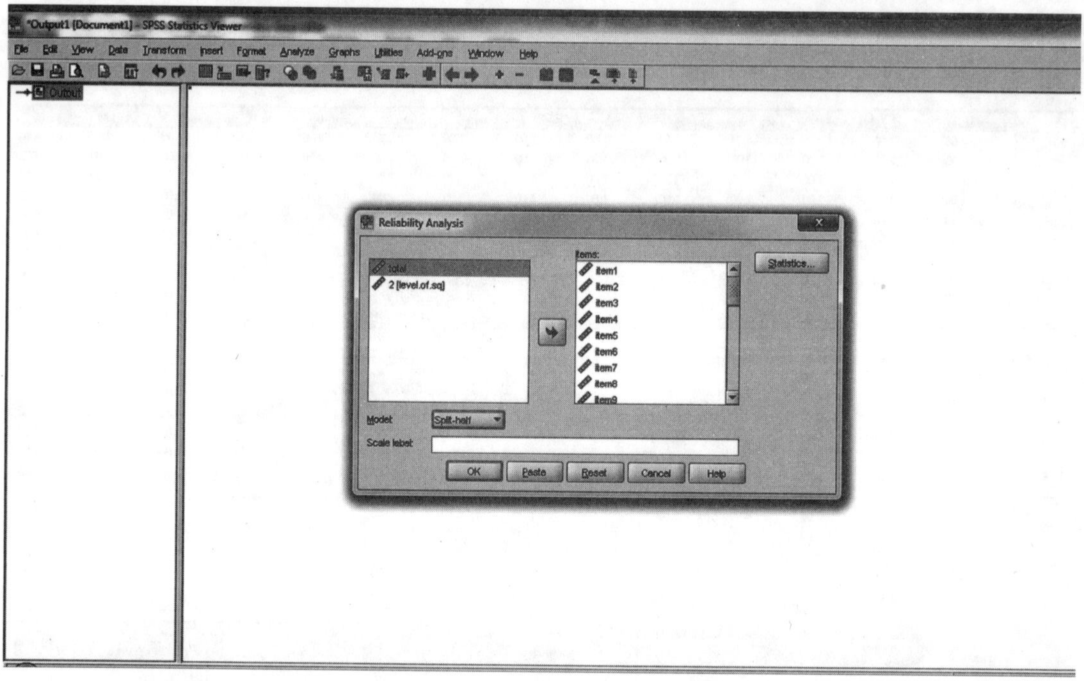

598. Click on "**OK**" to get the following outputs of Split-Half Reliability Coefficient.

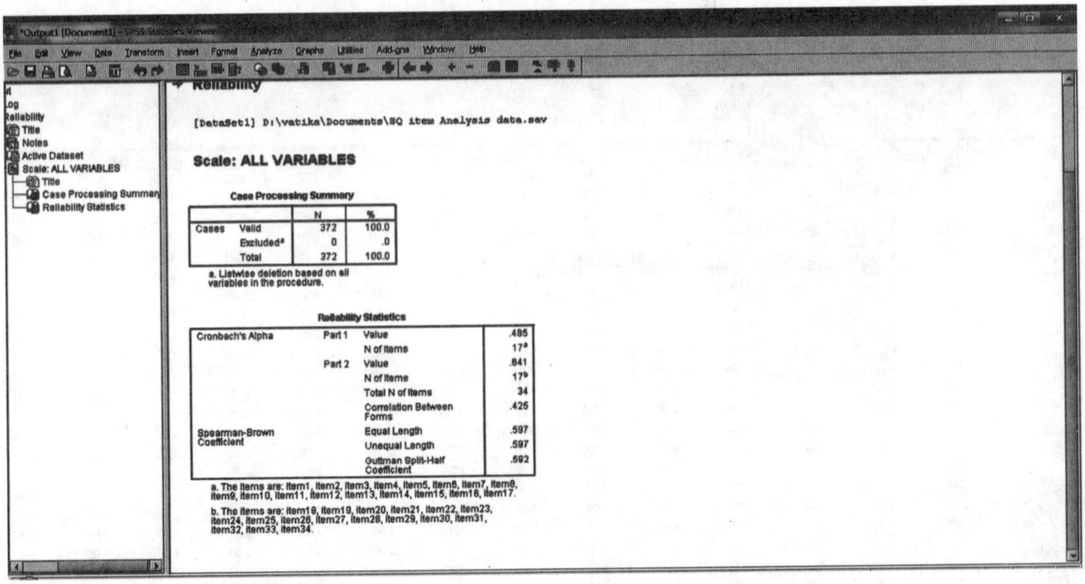

The outputs given in frame 598 have the "**Cronbach's Alpha**" as well as "**Spearman-Brown coefficient**". "**Spearman-Brown coefficient**" indicates the Split-half Reliability Coefficient.

Cronback's Alpha Method of Reliability

599. Cronback's Alpha Method is used for establishing Reliability of Scale only. It cannot be used for Test as well as Inventory. Suppose there are 34 items having five point Scale. The data are entered as shown in the following screen.

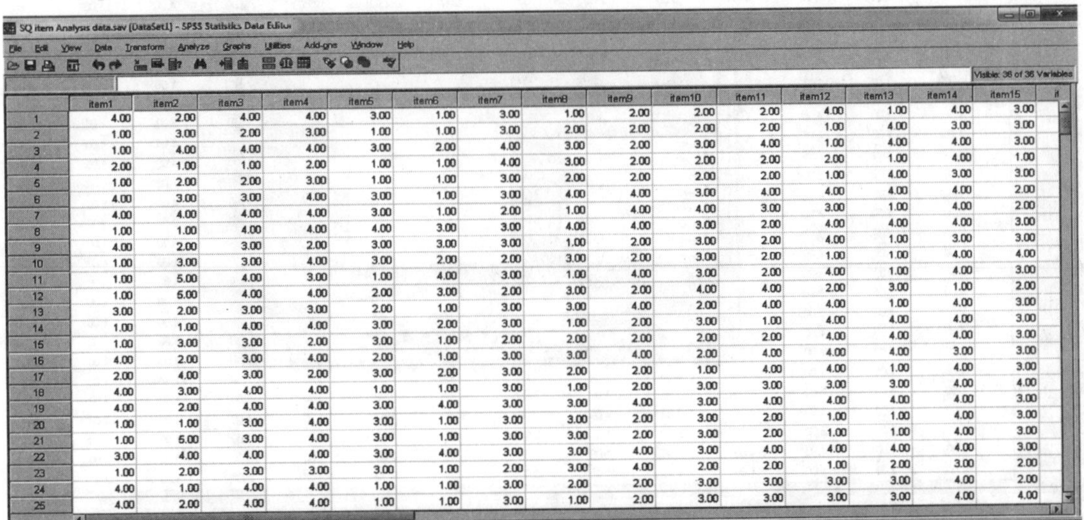

600. Click on "**Analyse**", bring curser to "**Scale**" and then to "**Reliability Analyse**" to get the following screen.

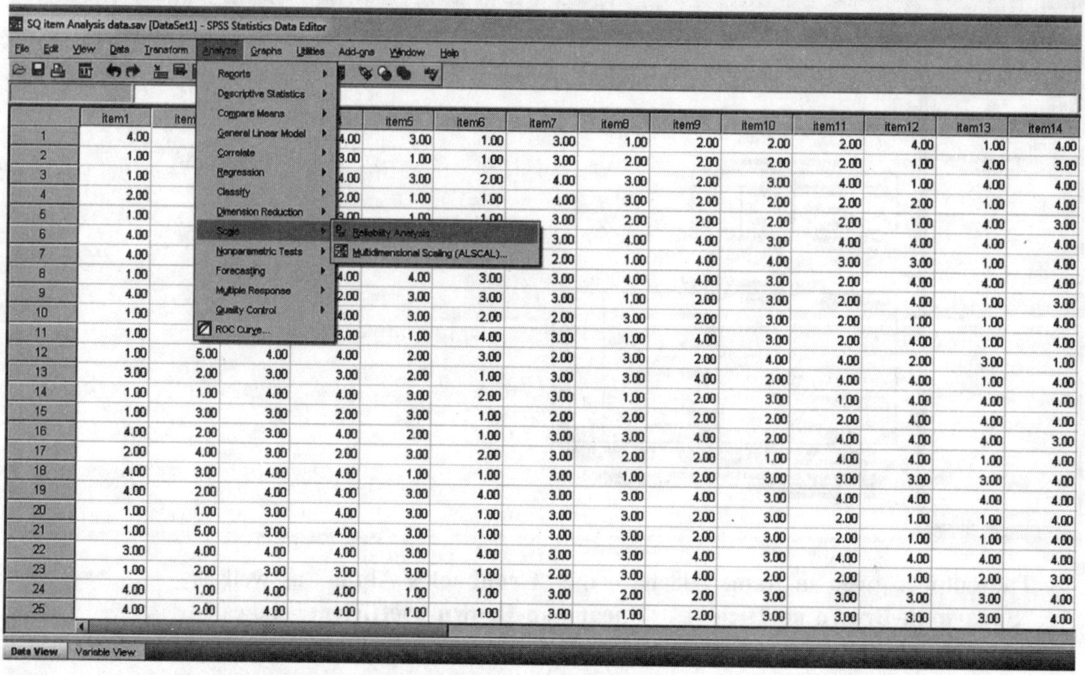

601. Click on "**Reliability Analyse**" to get the following screen.

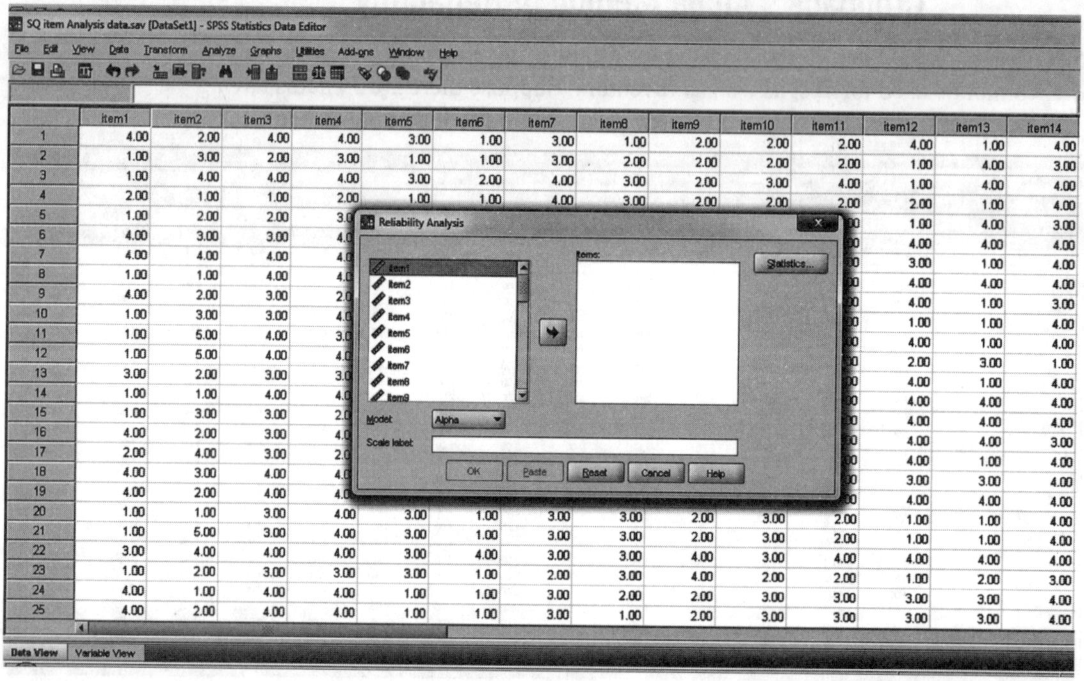

602. Shift all 34 items under "**Items**" dialog box to get the following screen.

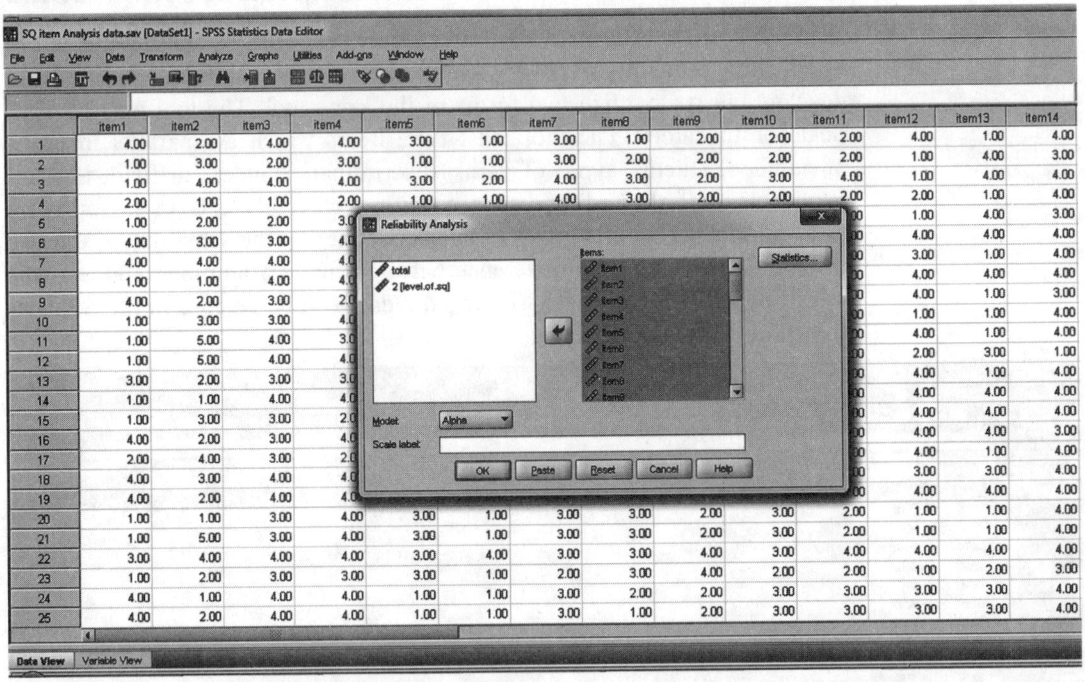

603. Under "**Model: Alpha**" is already active. Click on "**OK**" to get the following Cronbach's Alpaha Reliability Coefficient.

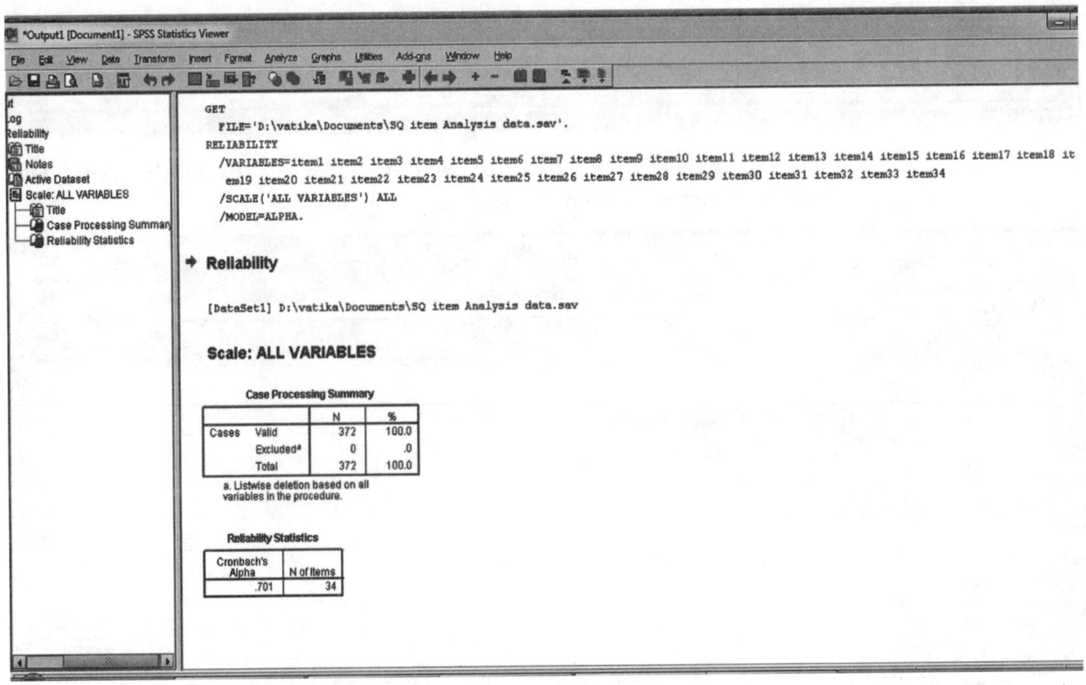

Parallel Form or Alternative Form or Equivalent Form Method

604. Parallel Form or Alternative Form or Equivalent Form is another method of establishing reliability. It is very useful method when the researcher wants to develop and standardize two forms of the same tool. The tool may be Test, Scale or Inventory. The tool must have items which are parallel in terms of number of items, types of items, discrimination index, difficult index if applicable, time allowed for response writing, scoring, etc. Both the forms are to be administered on a group of subjects either on the same day or the two different days. The time difference between the two administrations at the most can be 24 hours. After scoring the data can be entered in the SPSS as shown in the following screen.

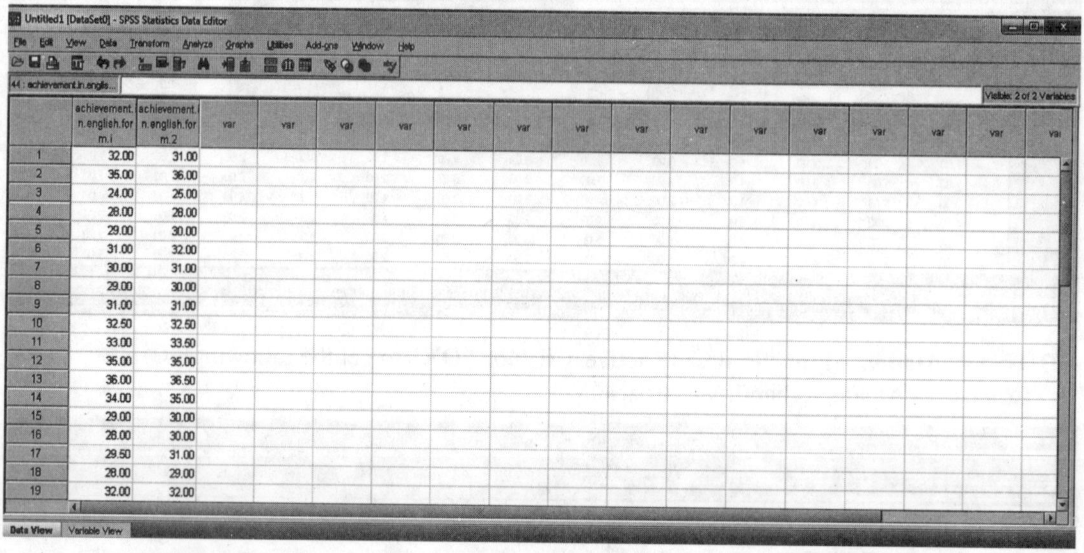

605. Click on "**Analyse**", bring curser to "**Scale**" and then to "**Reliability Analysis**" to get the following screen.

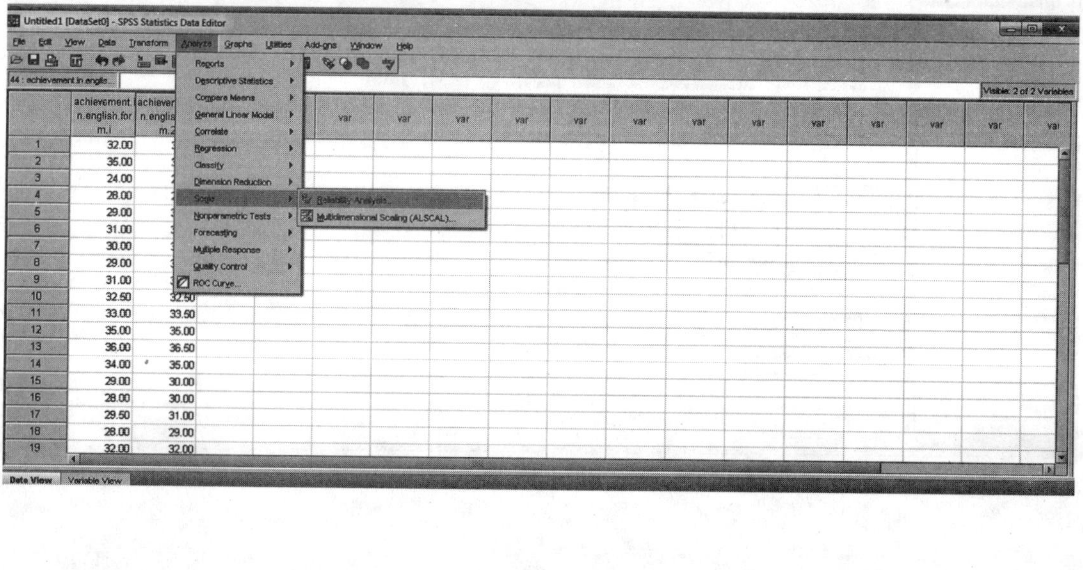

606. Click on "**Reliability Analysis**" icon to get the following screen.

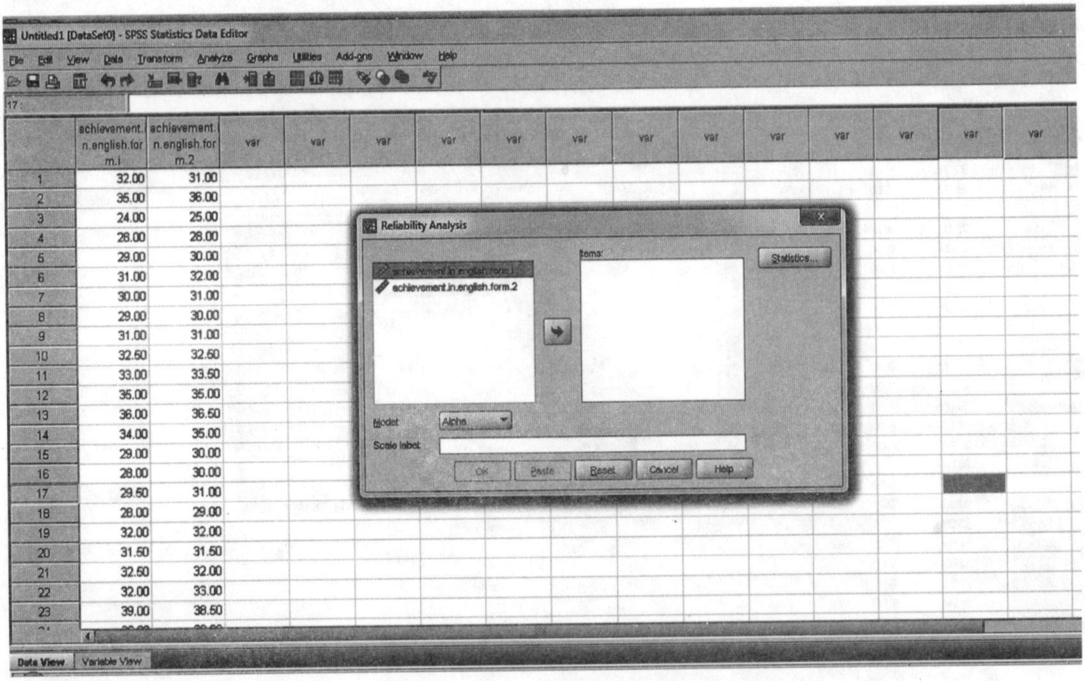

607. Shift both "**achievement in English form 1**" and "**achievement in English form 2**" to the right hand side dialog box as shown in the following screen.

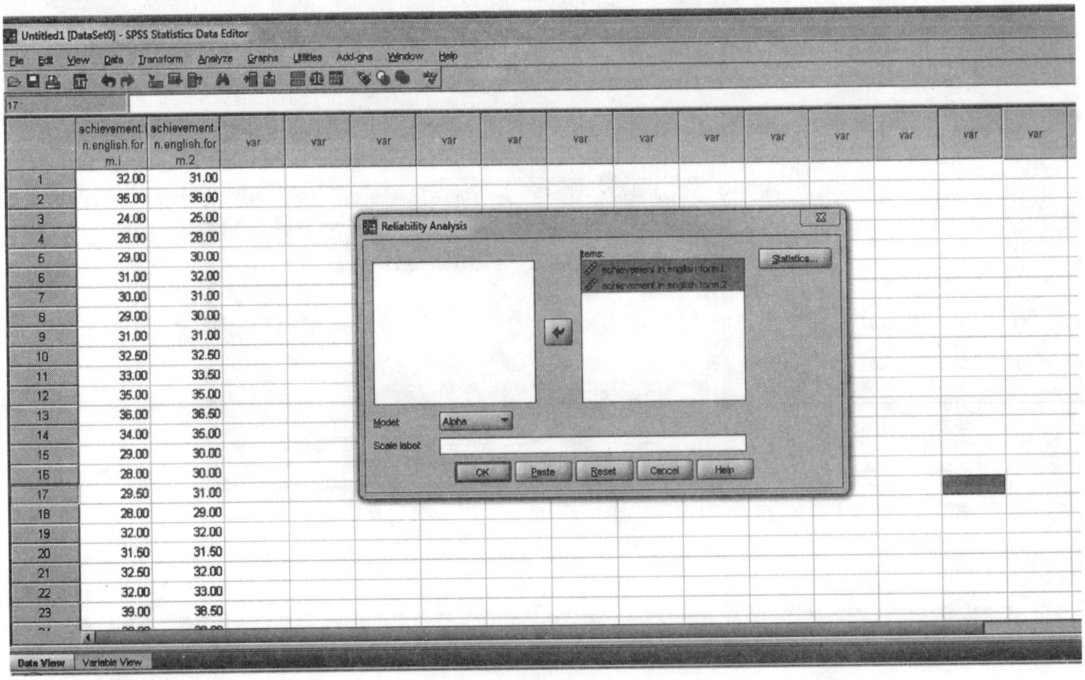

608. Click on "**Alpha**" under "**Model**" to get the following screen.

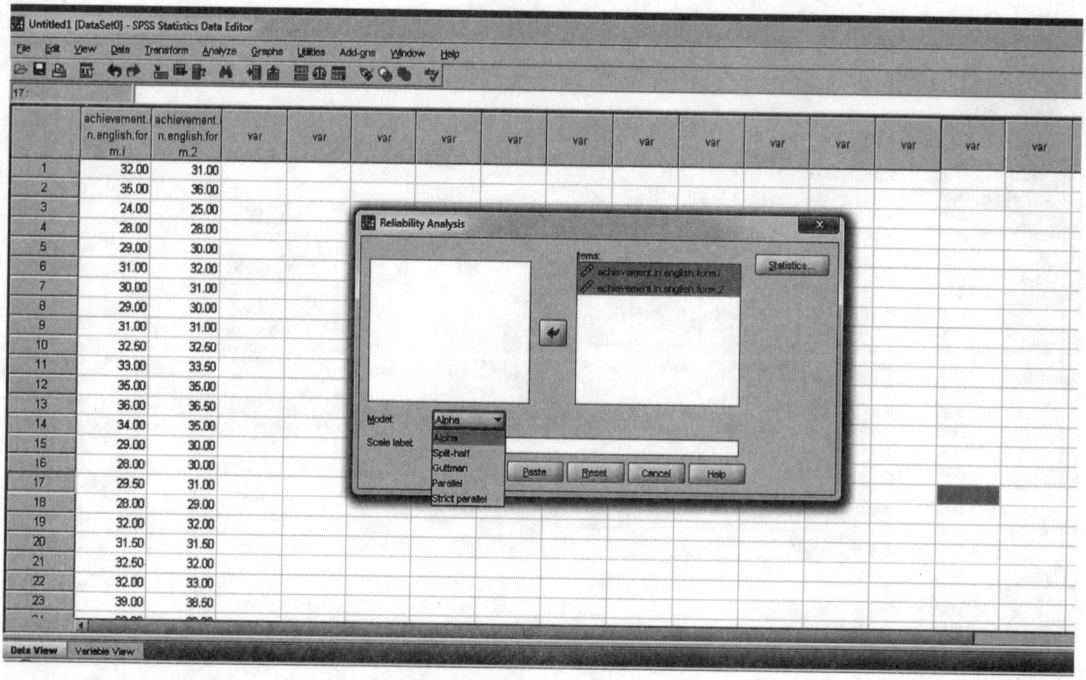

609. Click on "**Parallel**" to get the following screen.

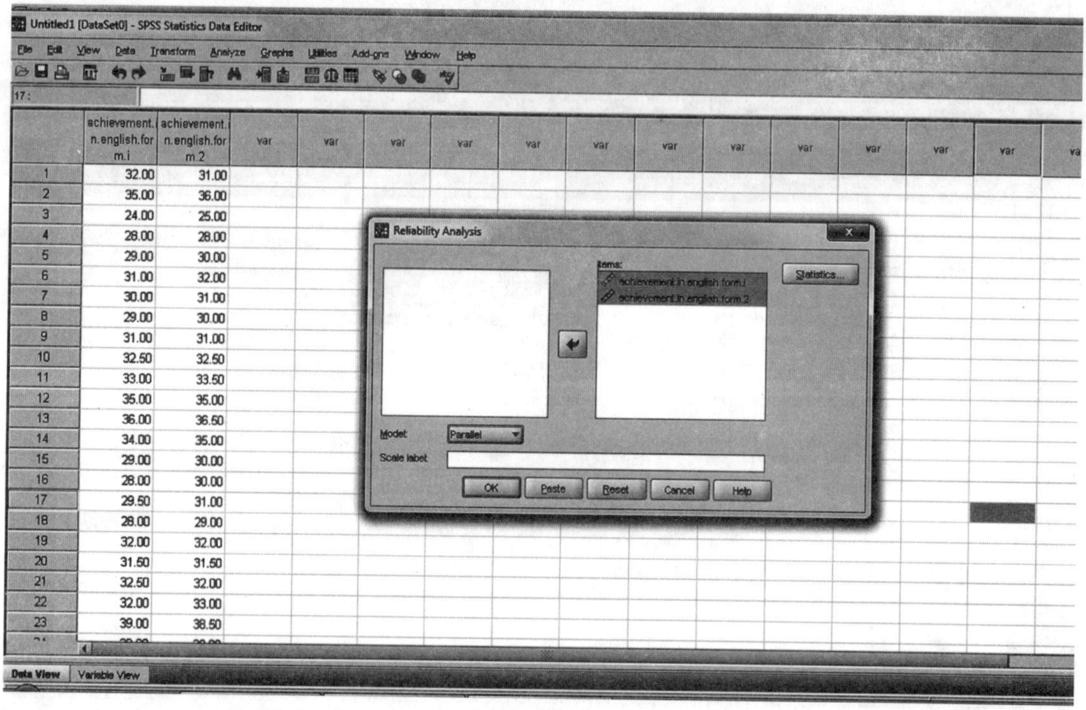

610. Click on "**OK**" to get the following outputs of Parallel Forms Reliability Coefficient.

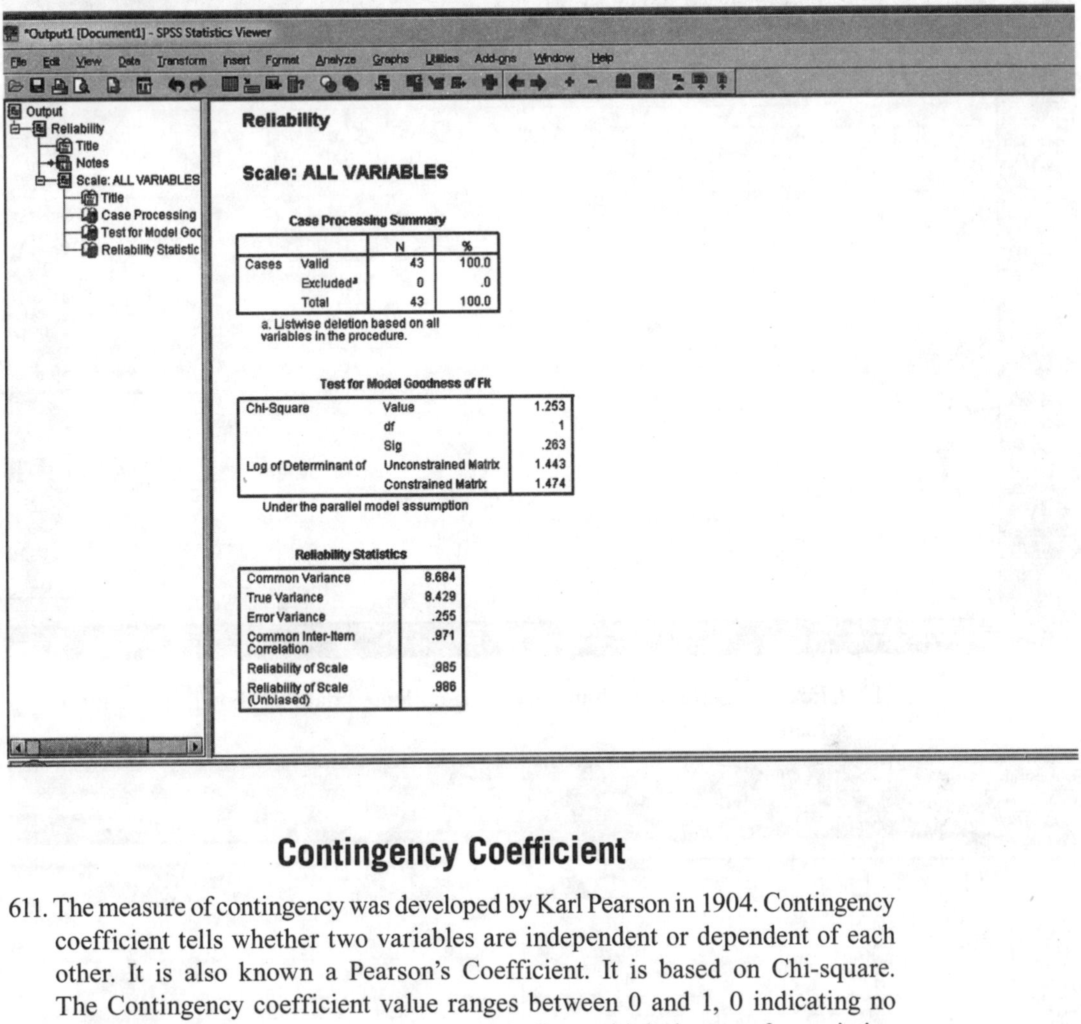

Reliability

Scale: ALL VARIABLES

Case Processing Summary

		N	%
Cases	Valid	43	100.0
	Excluded[a]	0	.0
	Total	43	100.0

a. Listwise deletion based on all variables in the procedure.

Test for Model Goodness of Fit

Chi-Square	Value	1.253
	df	1
	Sig	.263
Log of Determinant of	Unconstrained Matrix	1.443
	Constrained Matrix	1.474

Under the parallel model assumption

Reliability Statistics

Common Variance	8.684
True Variance	8.429
Error Variance	.255
Common Inter-Item Correlation	.971
Reliability of Scale	.985
Reliability of Scale (Unbiased)	.986

Contingency Coefficient

611. The measure of contingency was developed by Karl Pearson in 1904. Contingency coefficient tells whether two variables are independent or dependent of each other. It is also known a Pearson's Coefficient. It is based on Chi-square. The Contingency coefficient value ranges between 0 and 1, 0 indicating no association between two variables and 1 indicates high degree of association between two variables. The data are on Nominal Scale. Each variable should have three or more levels. Contingency coefficient is denoted by C. Let us consider the following objective.

To study association between Medium of Instruction and Subjects taught by Teachers.

Open SPSS and under "**Variable View**" icon enter the name of both the variables as shown in the following screen.

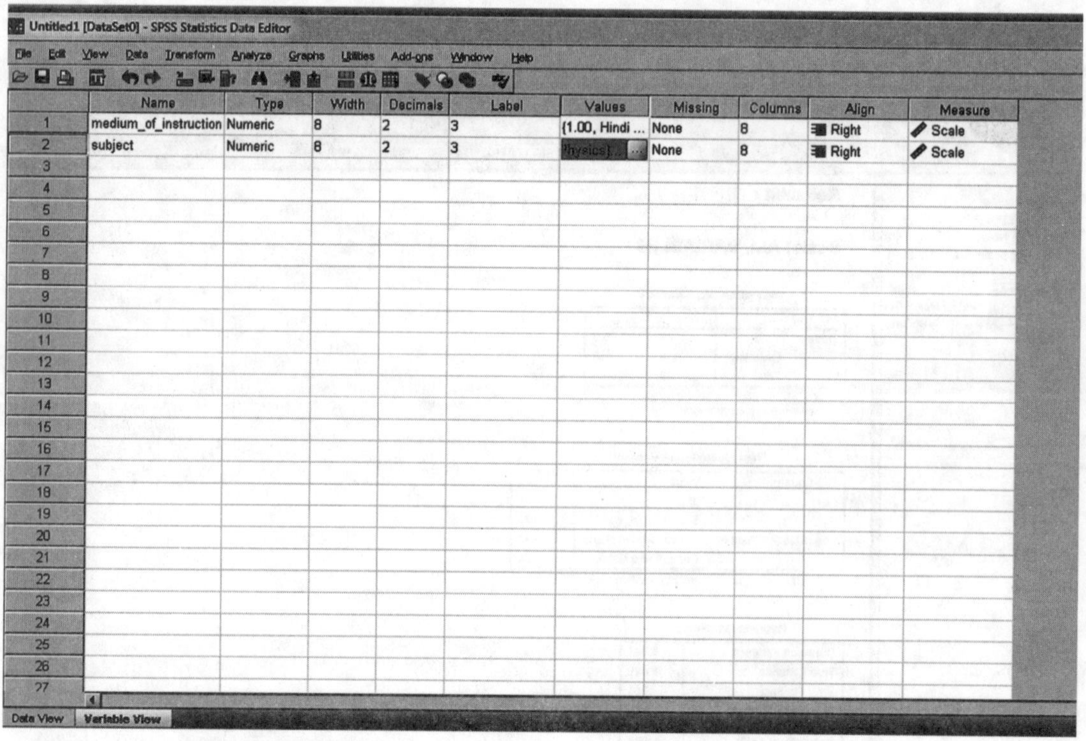

612. Click on "**Data View**" and enter the collected data as shown in the following screen.

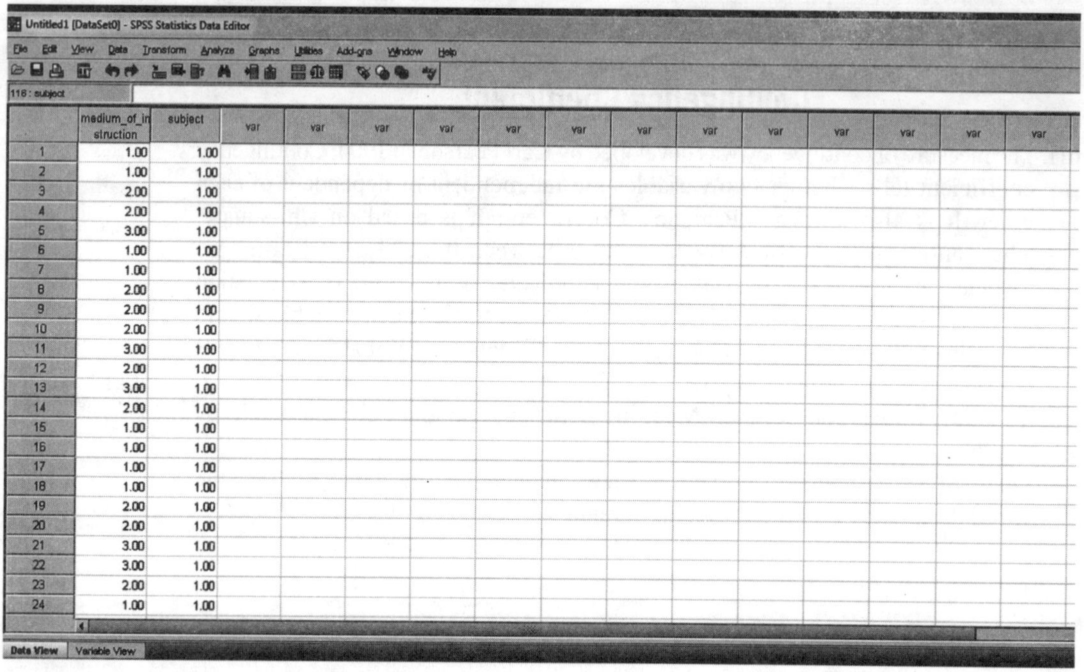

613. Click on "**Analyse**", bring curser to "**Descriptive Statistics**" and finally on "**Crosstab**" to get the following screen.

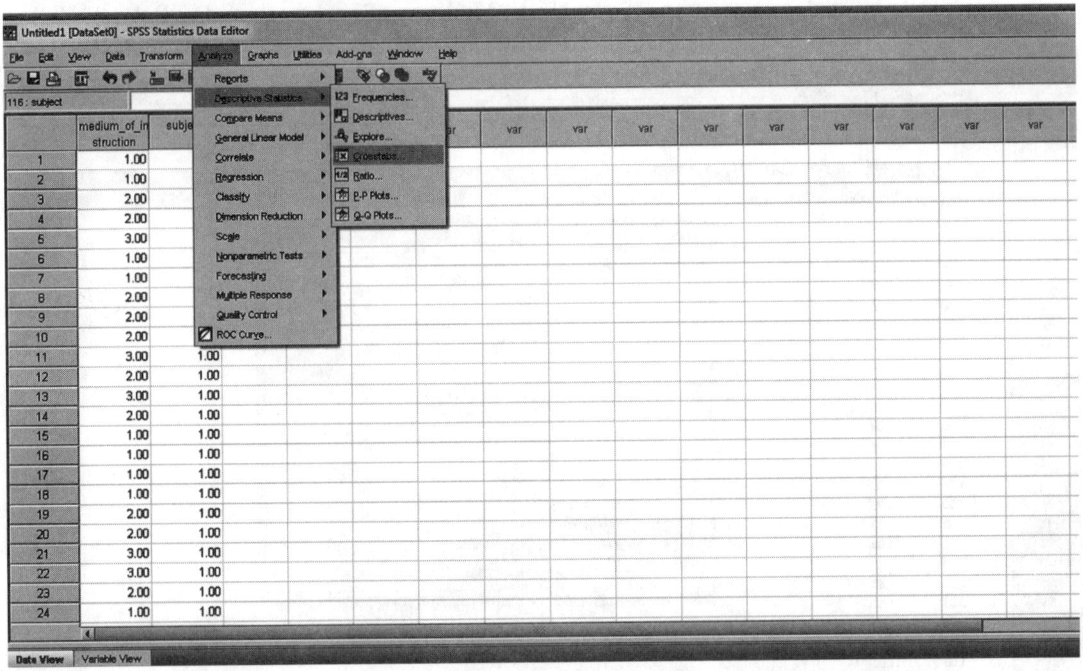

614. Click on "**Crosstab"** to get the following screen.

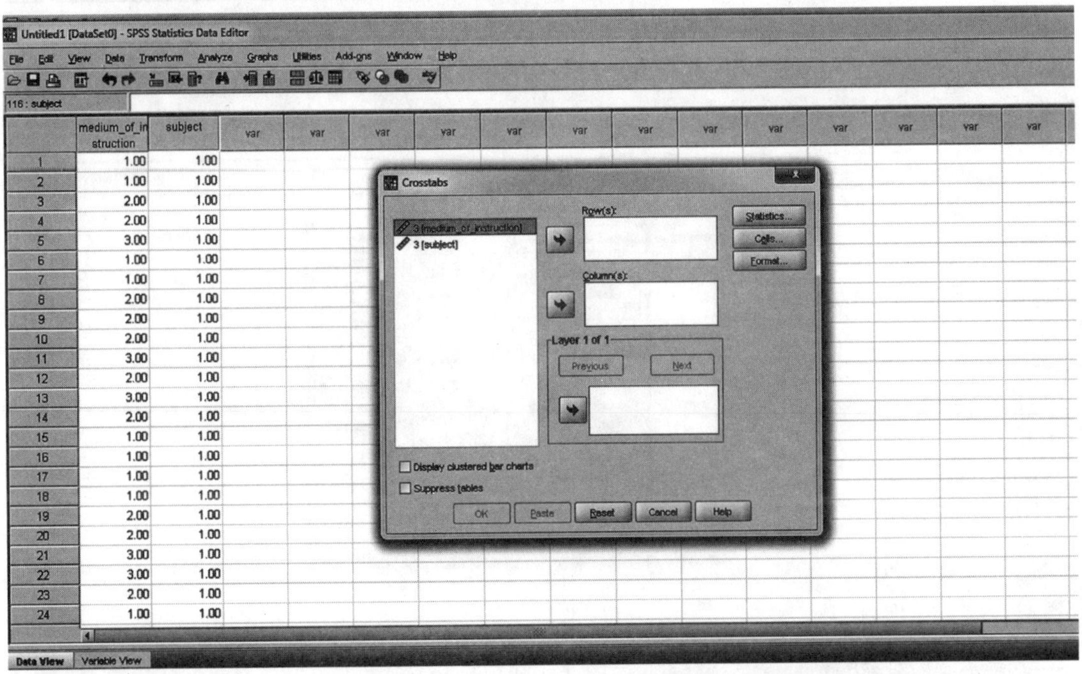

615. Medium of Instruction and Subjects are the two discontinuous variables. Shift any one variable to "**Row(s)**" dialog box and another variable to "**Colum(s)**" dialog box. Suppose you shift "**Medium of Instruction**" to "**Row(s)**" dialog box and "**Subjects**" to "**Colum(s)**" dialog box to get the following screen.

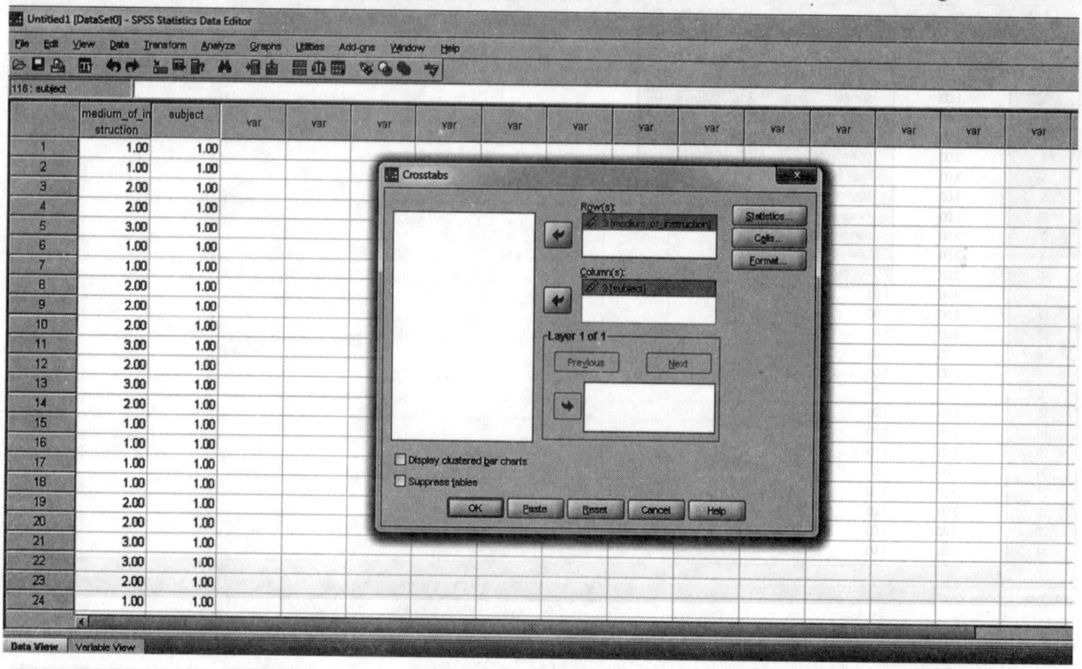

616. Click on "**Statistics**" button to get the following screen.

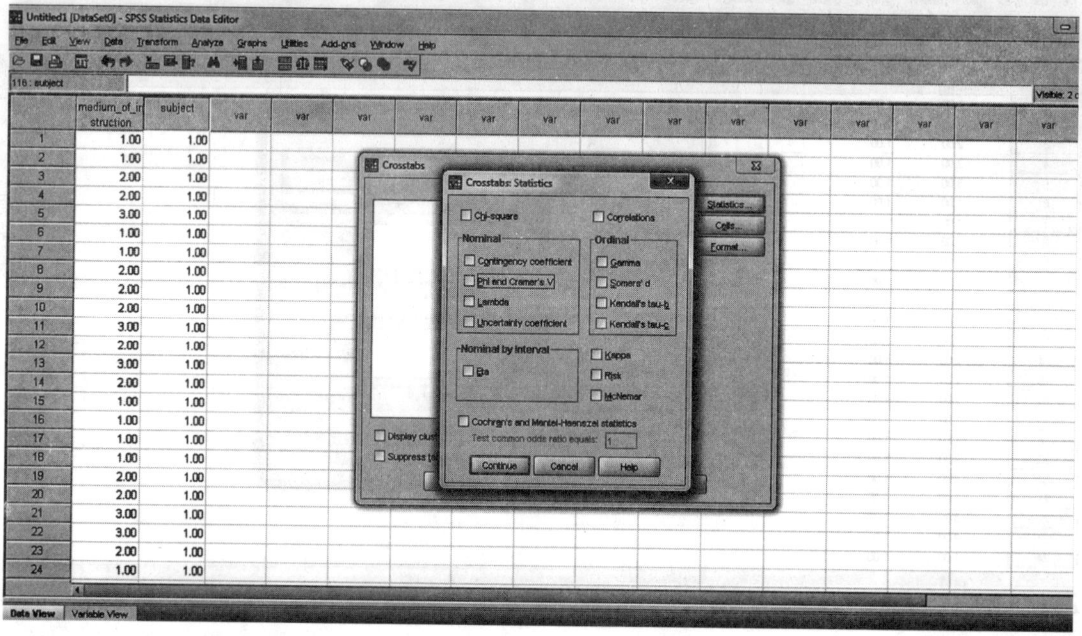

617. Under "**Normal**" highlight "**Contingency Coefficient**" to get the following screen.

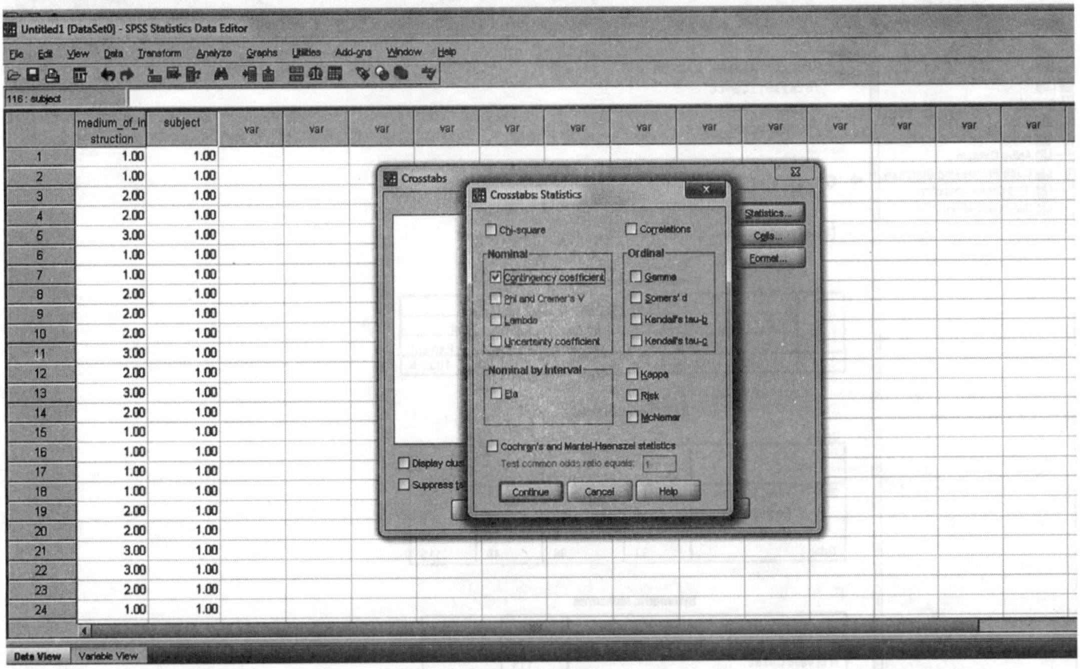

618. Click on "**Continue**" button to get the following screen.

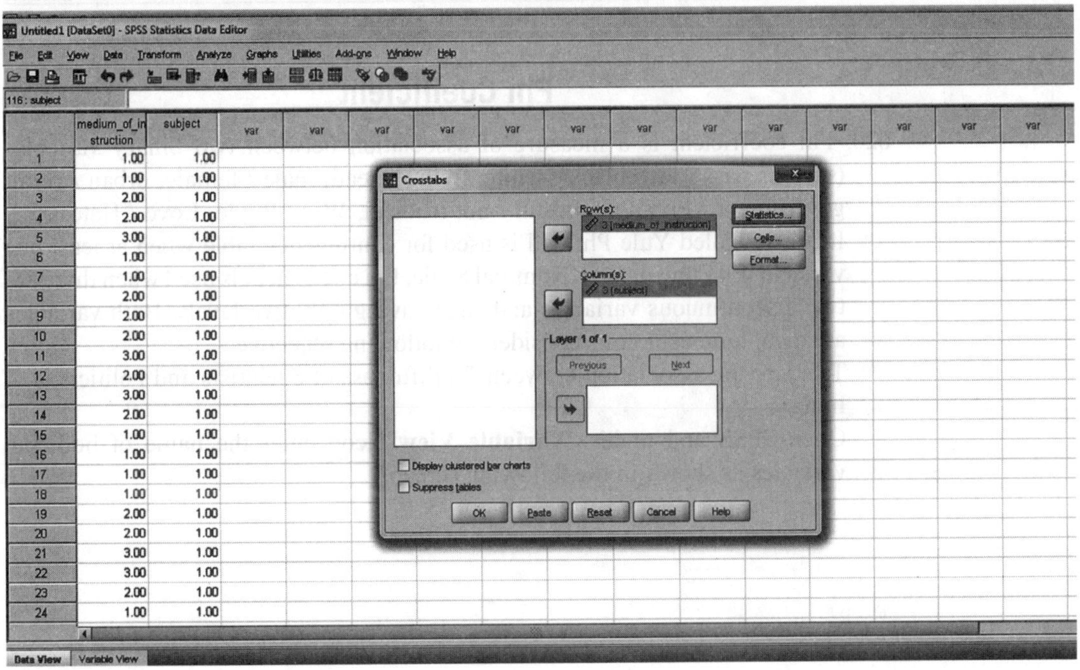

619. Click on "**OK**" button to get the following outputs of Contingency Coefficient.

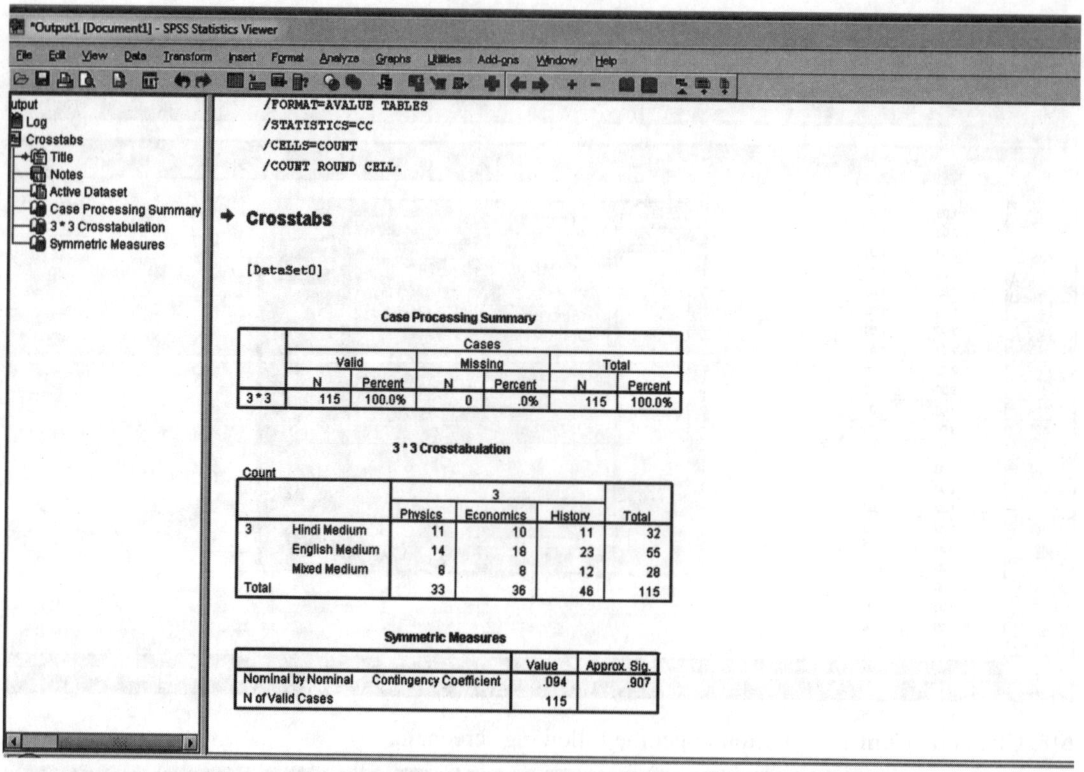

Case Processing Summary

	Cases					
	Valid		Missing		Total	
	N	Percent	N	Percent	N	Percent
3*3	115	100.0%	0	.0%	115	100.0%

3*3 Crosstabulation

Count

		3			Total
		Physics	Economics	History	
3	Hindi Medium	11	10	11	32
	English Medium	14	18	23	55
	Mixed Medium	8	8	12	28
Total		33	36	46	115

Symmetric Measures

		Value	Approx. Sig.
Nominal by Nominal	Contingency Coefficient	.094	.907
N of Valid Cases		115	

Phi Coefficient

620. Phi coefficient is a measure of association between two binary variables (such as pass / fail; black / white; living / dead; male / female; urban / rural; government / Private; truthful / not truthful, War / Peace, Love / Hate, etc.). It is also called Yule Phi and is used for contingency table when at least one variable is having data on Nominal Scale. Phi coefficient is used when there are two discontinuous variables and each having only two levels. Both variables are dichotomous. Let us consider the following objective.

To study the association between Truthfulness of Scientists and Politicians of India.

Open SPSS and under "**Variable View**" icon enter the name of both the variables as shown in the following screen.

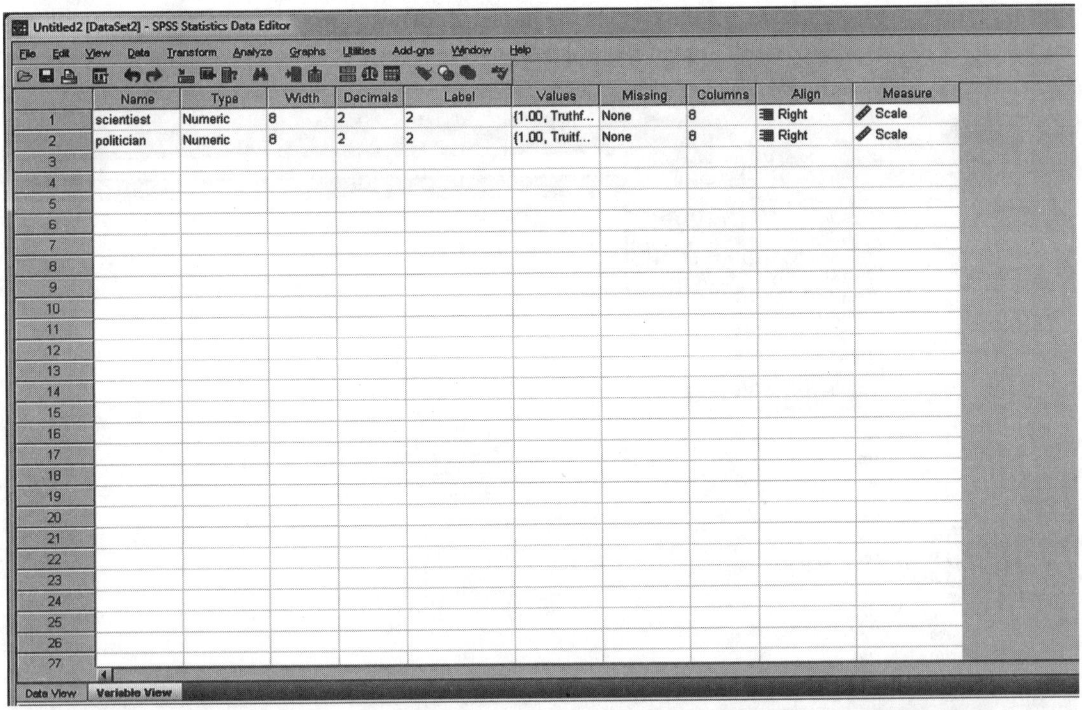

621. Click on “**Data View**” and enter the collected data as shown in the following screen.

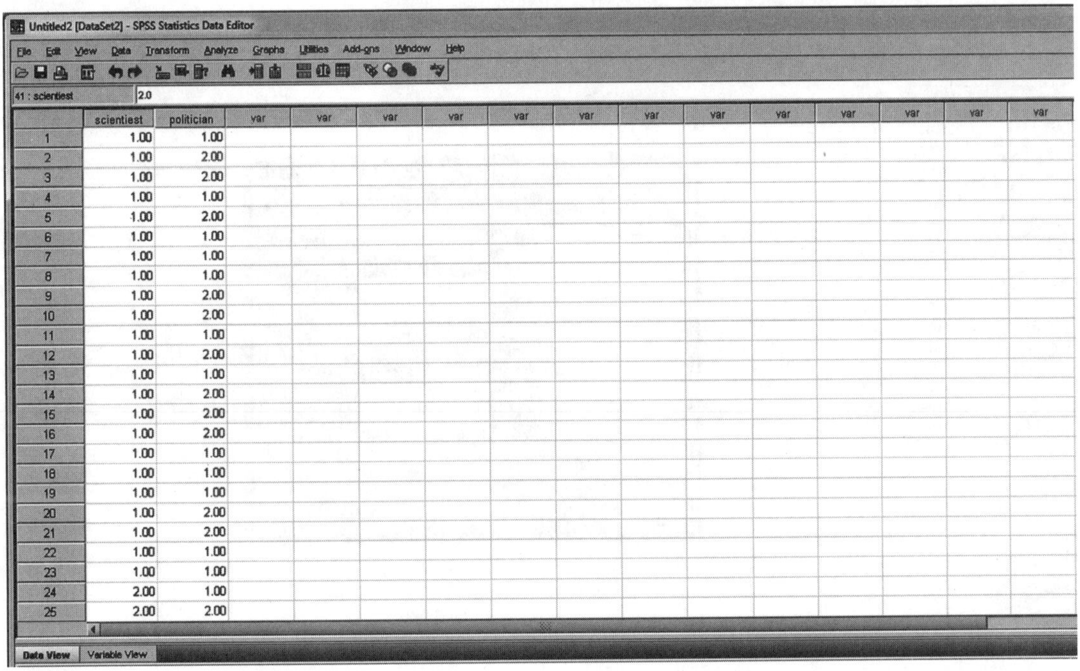

622. Click on "**Analyse**", bring curser to "**Descriptive Statistics**" and finally on "**Crosstab**" to get the following screen.

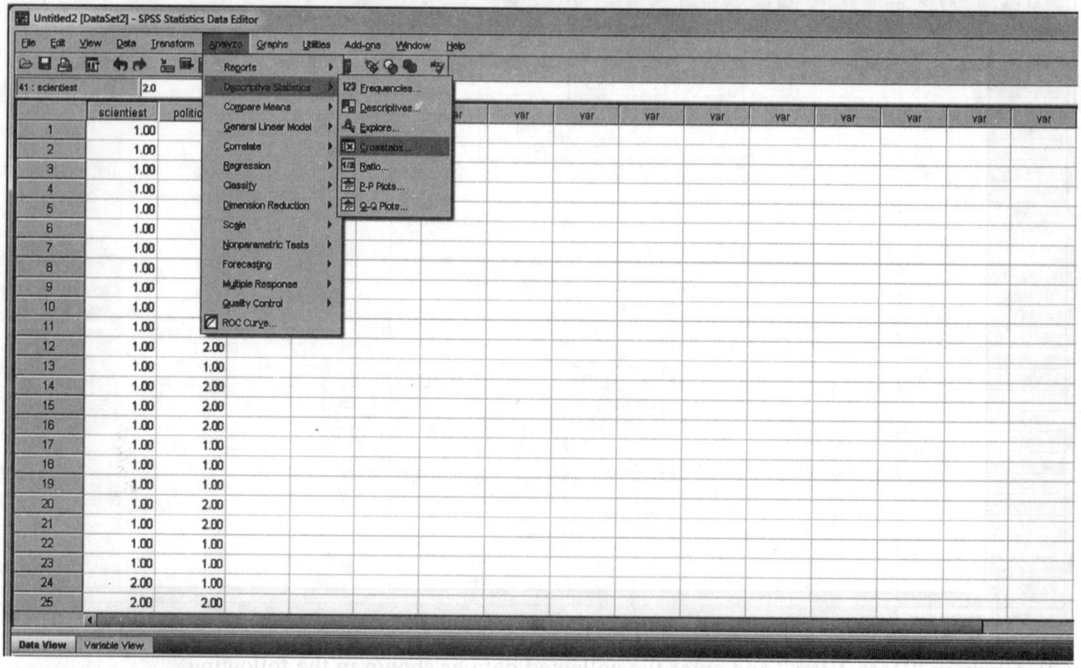

623. Click on "**Crosstab**" to get the following screen.

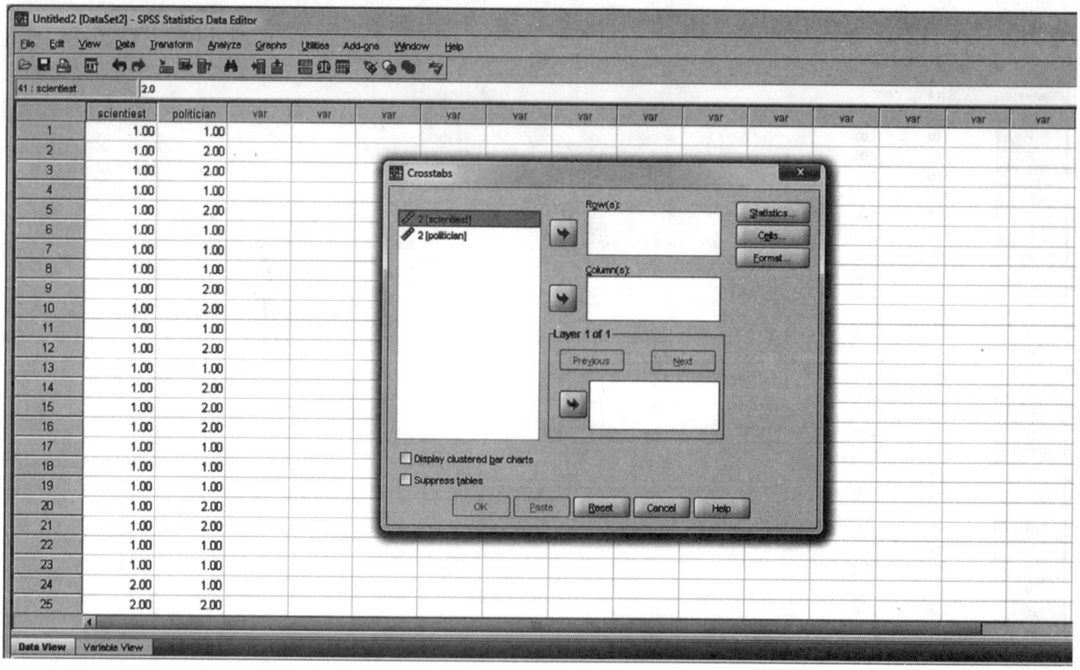

624. Shift any one variable in "**Row(s)**" dialog box and another in "**Column(s)**" dialog box. Suppose you shift "**Scientist**" in "**Row(s)**" dialog box and "**Politician**" in "**Column(s)**" dialog box to get the following screen.

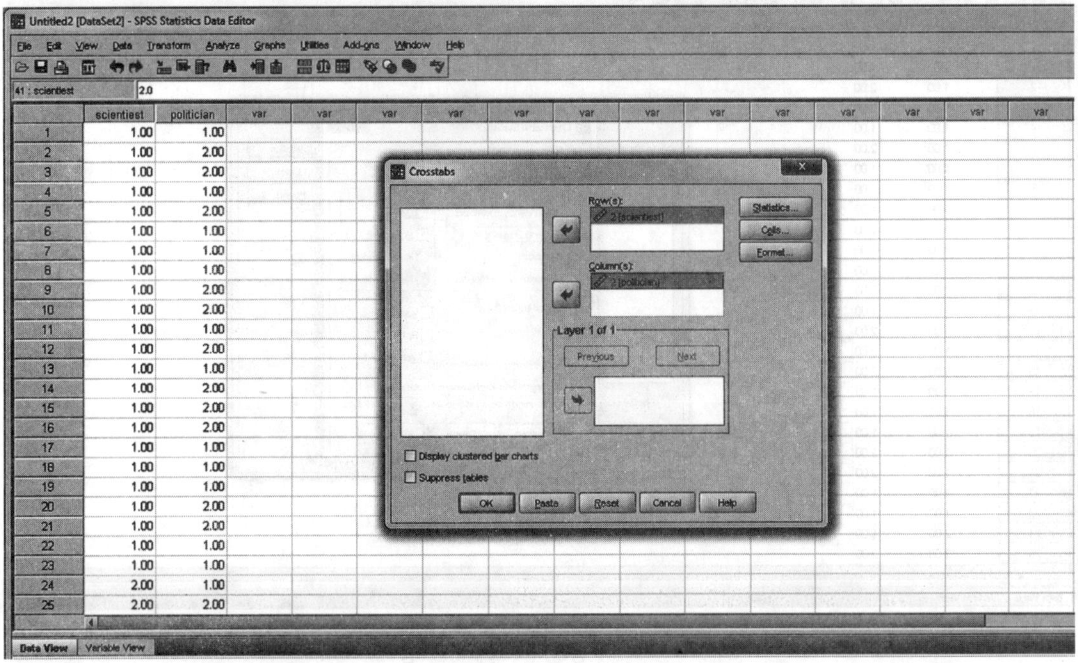

625. Click on "**Statistics**" button to get the following screen.

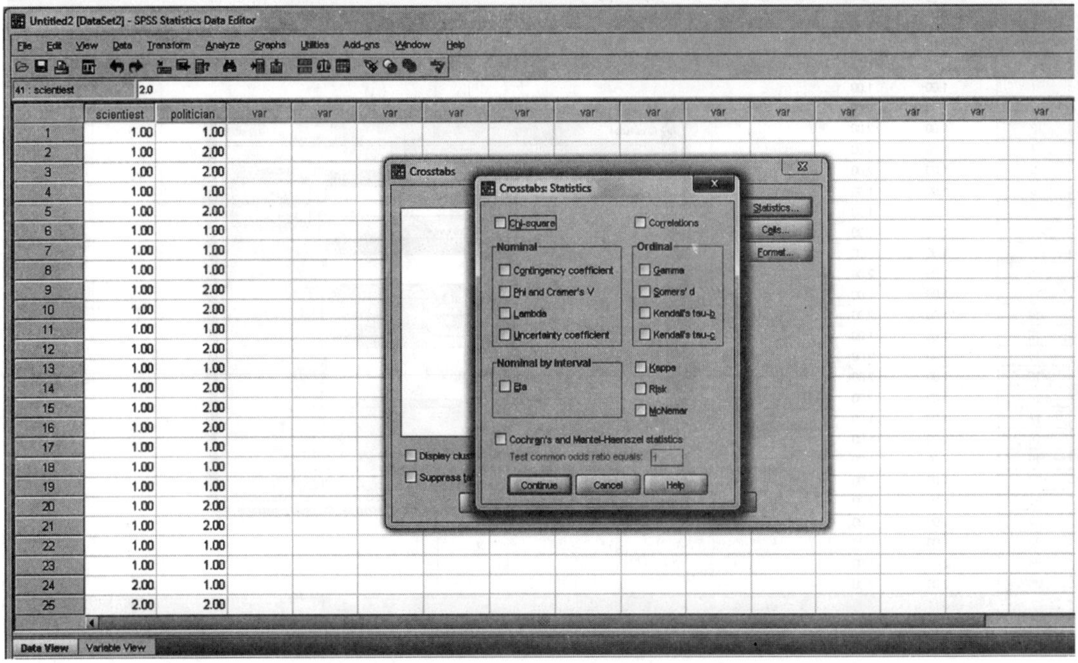

626. Highlight "**Phi and Cramer's V**" to get the following screen.

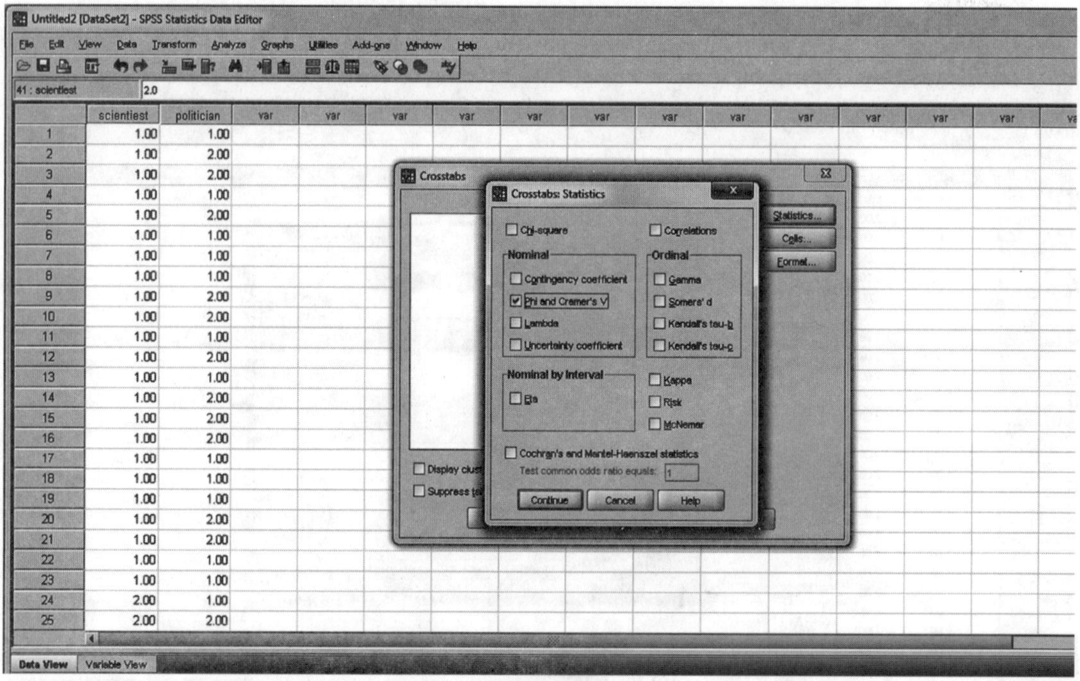

627. Click on "**Continue**" to get the following screen.

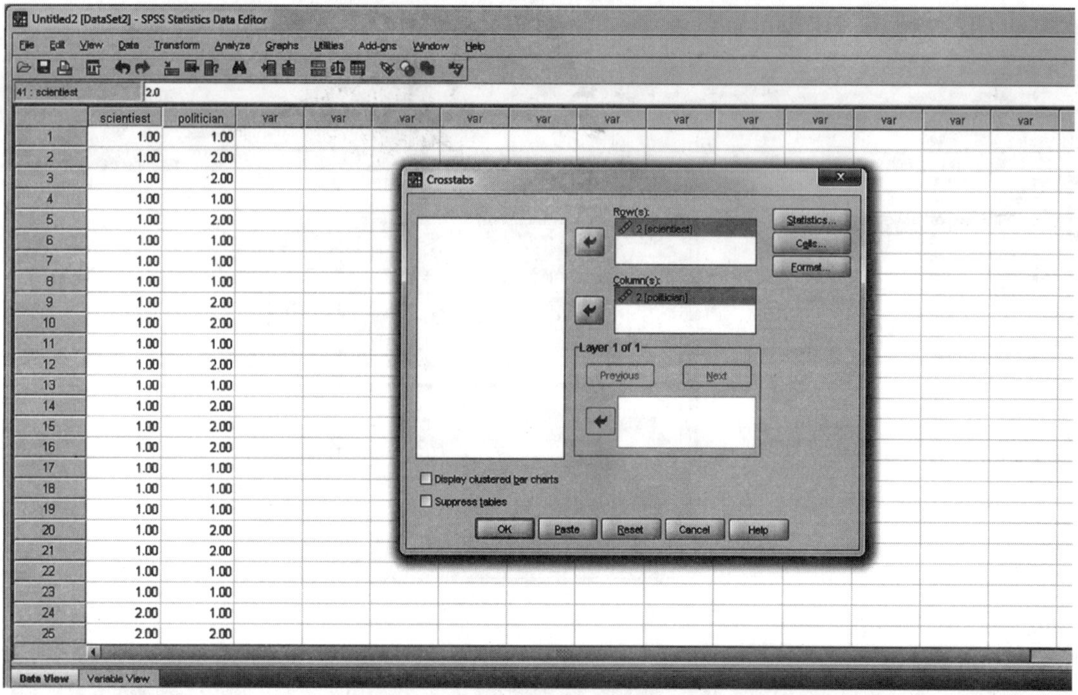

628. Click on "**OK**" to get the following outputs of Phi and Cramer's V.

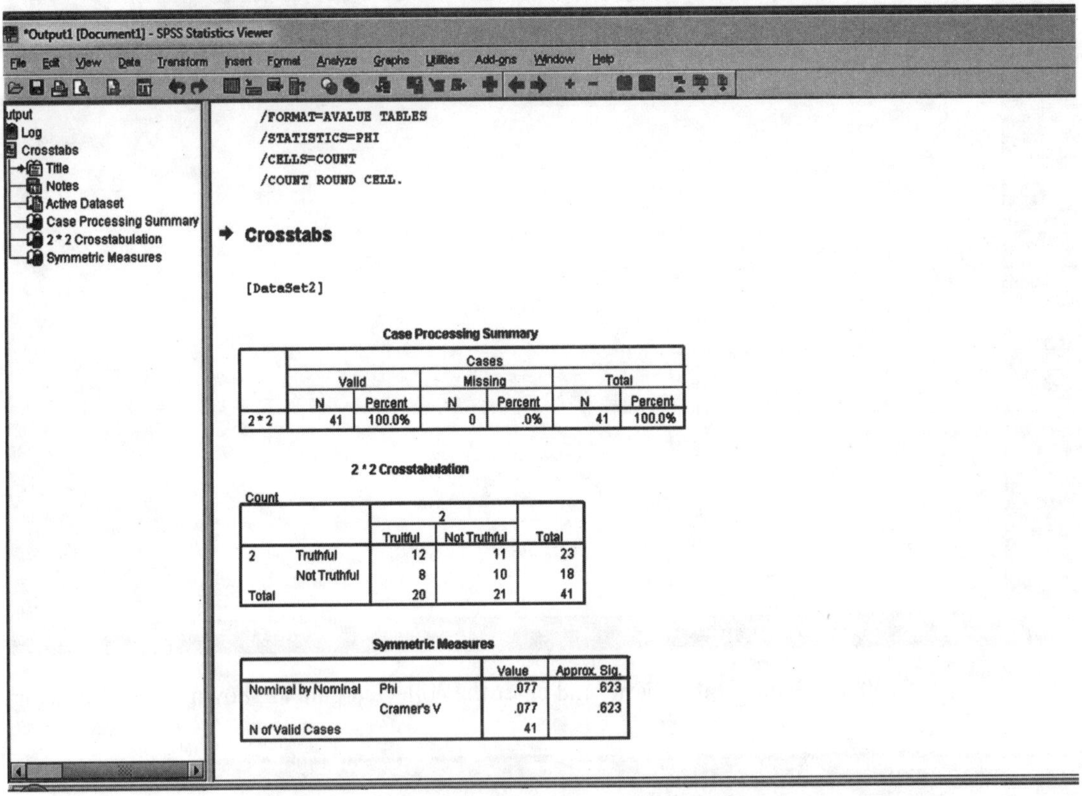

Case Processing Summary

	Cases					
	Valid		Missing		Total	
	N	Percent	N	Percent	N	Percent
2 * 2	41	100.0%	0	.0%	41	100.0%

2 * 2 Crosstabulation

Count

		2		
		Truitful	Not Truthful	Total
2	Truthful	12	11	23
	Not Truthful	8	10	18
Total		20	21	41

Symmetric Measures

		Value	Approx. Sig.
Nominal by Nominal	Phi	.077	.623
	Cramer's V	.077	.623
N of Valid Cases		41	

Cramer's V

629. Cramer's V was given by Harald Cramer in 1946. It is an effect size measurement for the Chi-square test of independence. It measures how strongly two categorical variables are associated. The data of both discontinuous variables must be on Nominal Scale. Its value ranges from 0 to 1. Let us consider the following Objective.

To study association between Happiness and Socio-economic Status of Teachers.

Open SPSS and under "**Variable View**" icon enter the name of both the variables as shown in the following screen.

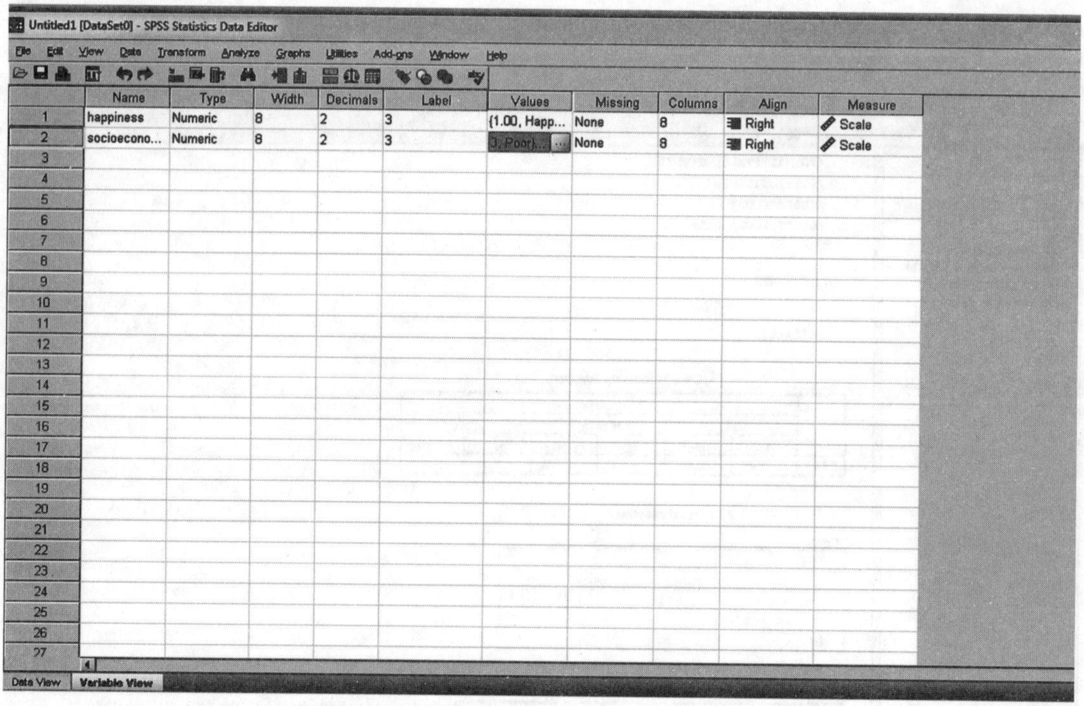

630. Click on "**Data View**" and enter the collected data as shown in the following screen.

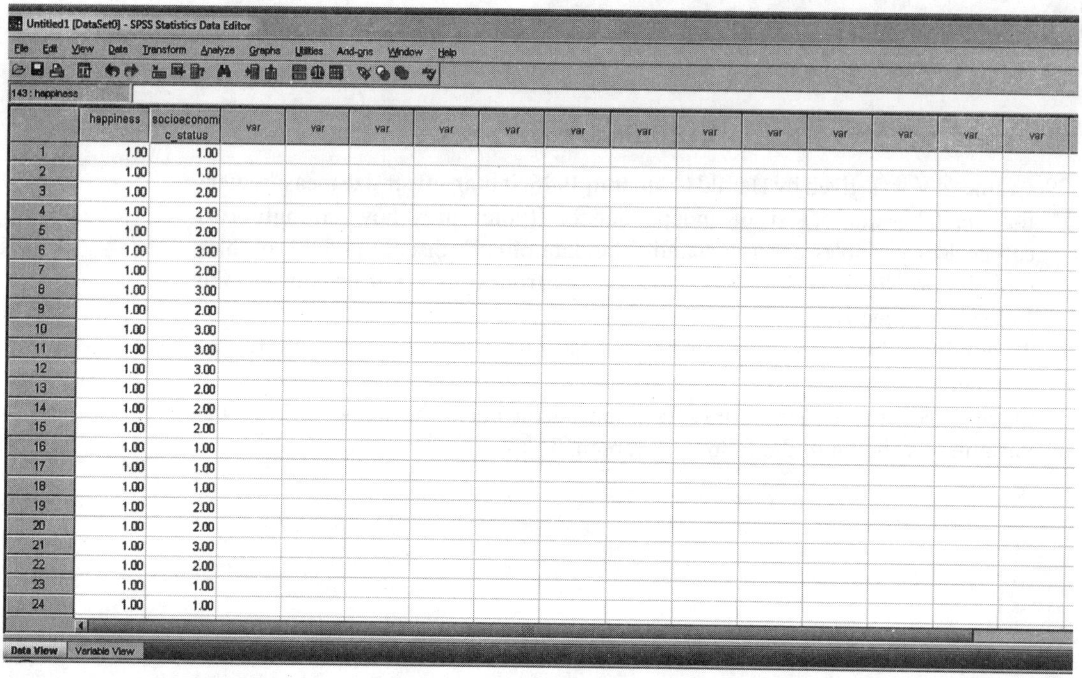

631. Click on "**Analyse**", bring curser to "**Descriptive Statistics**" and finally on "**Crosstab**" to get the following screen.

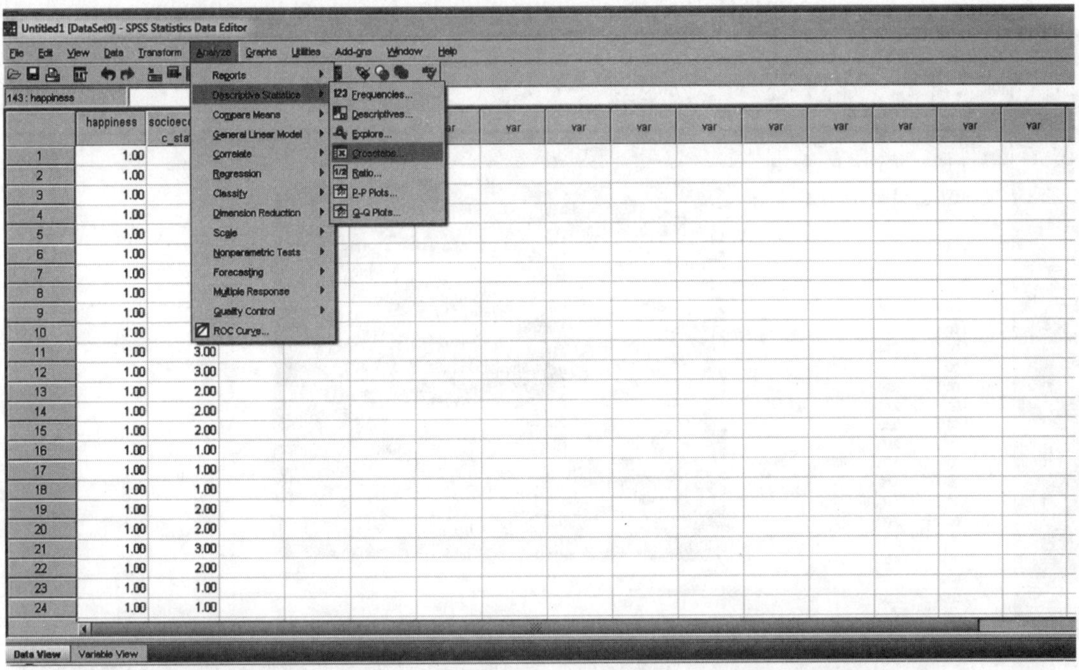

632. Click on "**Crosstab**" to get the following screen.

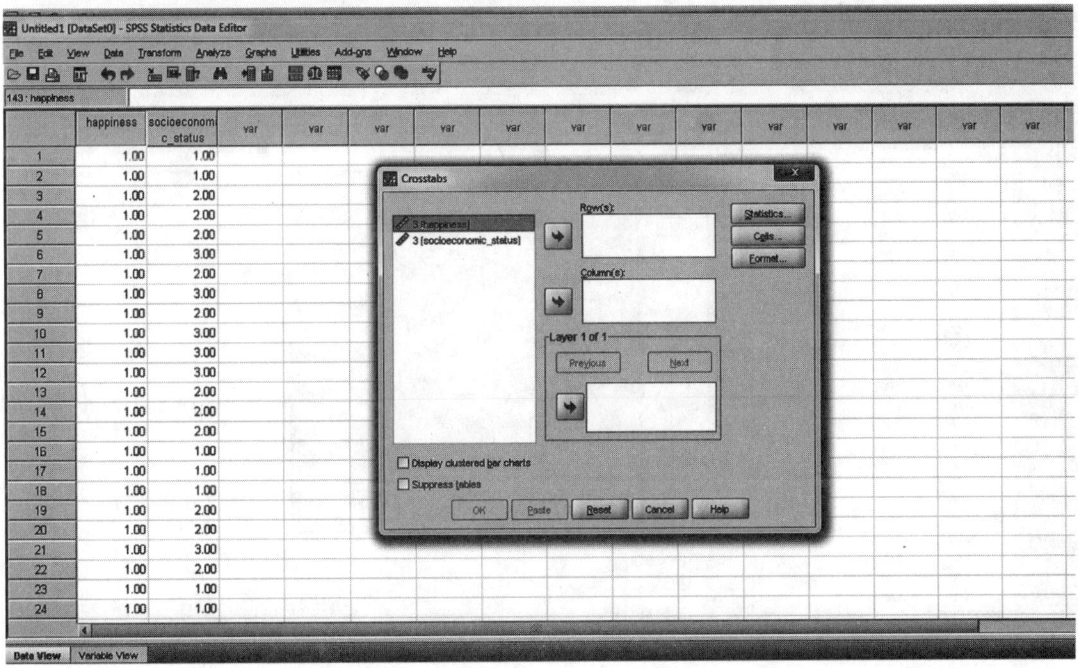

633. Shift any one variable in "**Row(s)**" dialog box and another in "**Column(s)**" dialog box. Suppose you shift "**happiness**" in "**Row(s)**" dialog box and "**Socio-economic status**" in "**Column(s)**" dialog box to get the following screen.

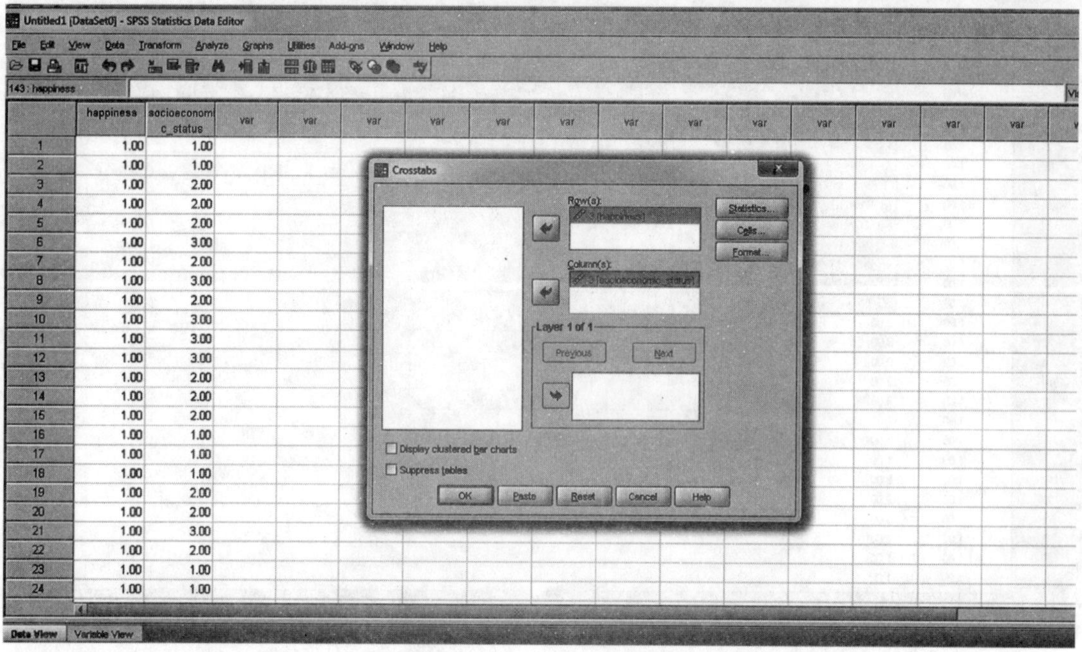

634. Click on "**Statistics**" button to get the following screen.

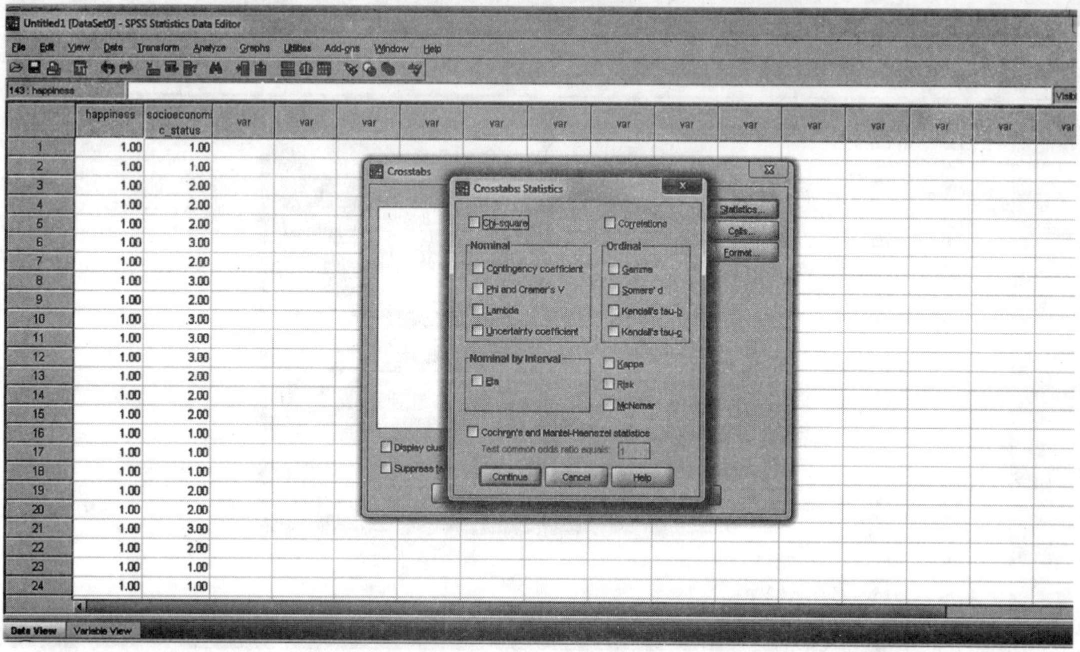

635. Highlight **"Phi and Cramer's V"** to get the following screen.

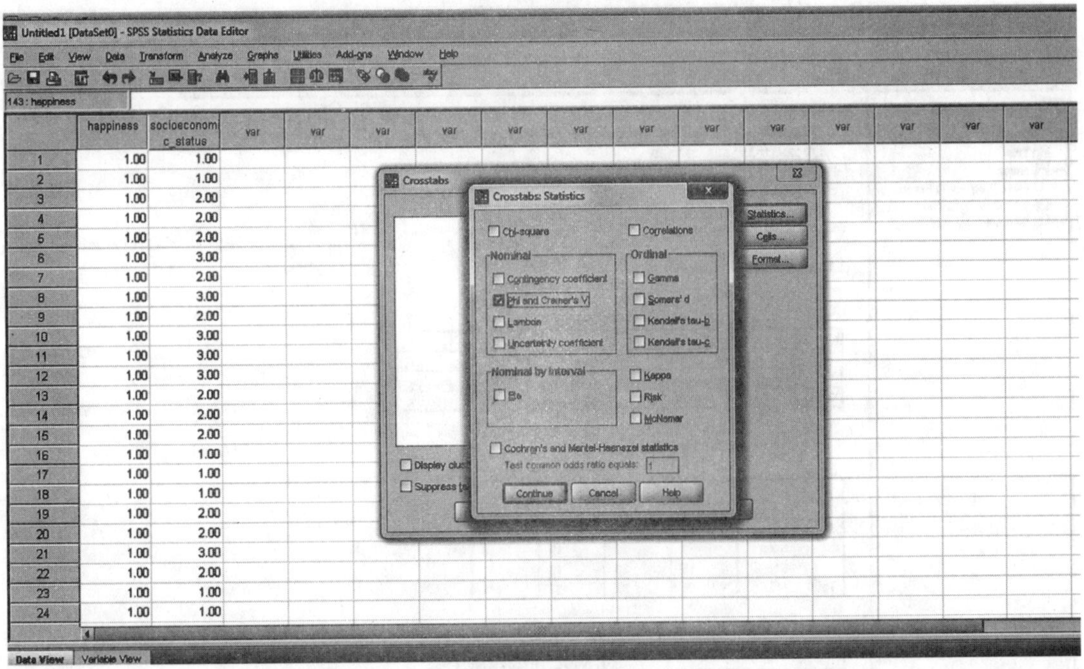

636. Click on **"Continue"** to get the following screen.

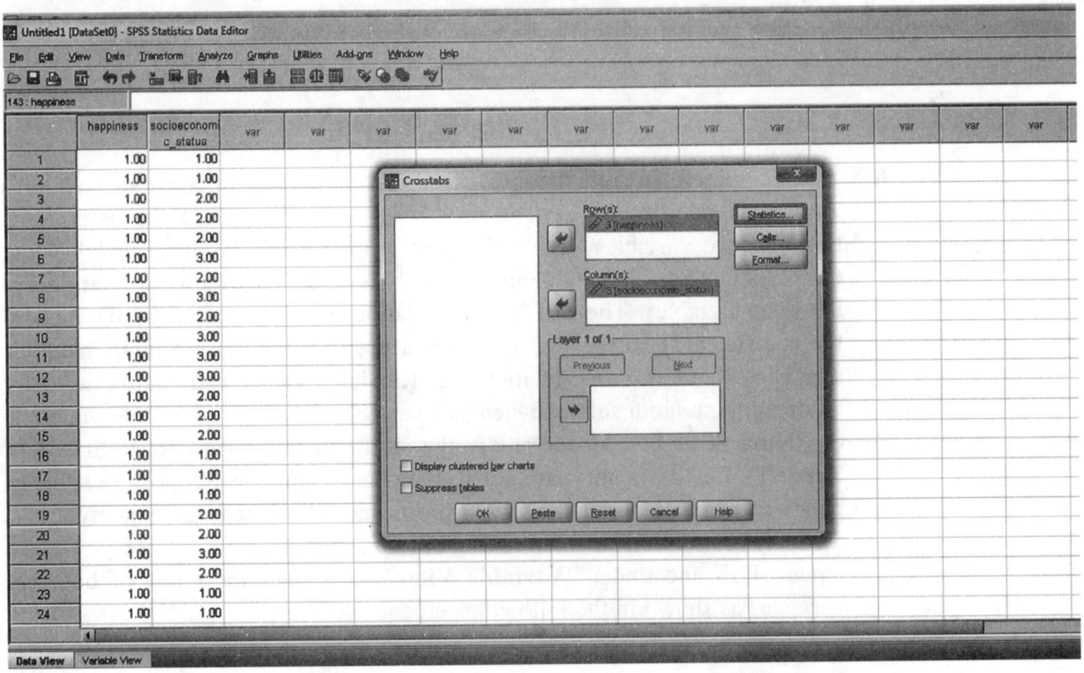

637. Click on "**OK**" to get the following outputs of Phi and Cramer's V.

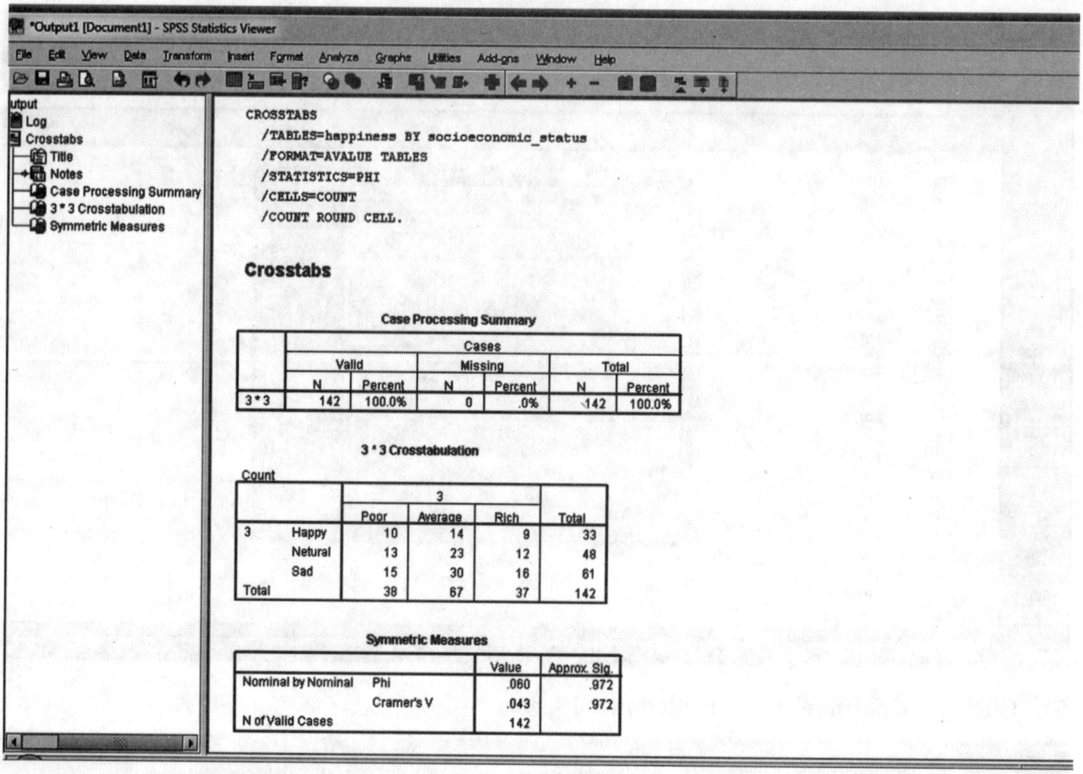

Kendall's Tau- c

638. Kendall Rank Correlation coefficient is commonly referred to Kendall's Tau- c (Kendall's Tau Coefficient). It is used to compute the association between two variables having data on Ordinal Scale. As the Kendall Rank Correlation coefficient value moves towards zero, it shows weak relationship between variables. The direction of relationship is indicated by the sign of the coefficient. Positive sign indicates a positive relationship while negative sign indicates a negative relationship. Kendall's Tau- c can also be used for studying the relationship between two variables having data on Interval Scale or Ration Scale but do not satisfy the assumptions of Parametric Statistics. Kendall's Tau- c is a non-parametric statistical technique. Suppose 18 subjects handwritings is to be rated by two experts and following is the objective.
To study association between raking of two experts.
Open SPSS and under "**Variable View**" icon enter the name of both the variables as shown in the following screen.

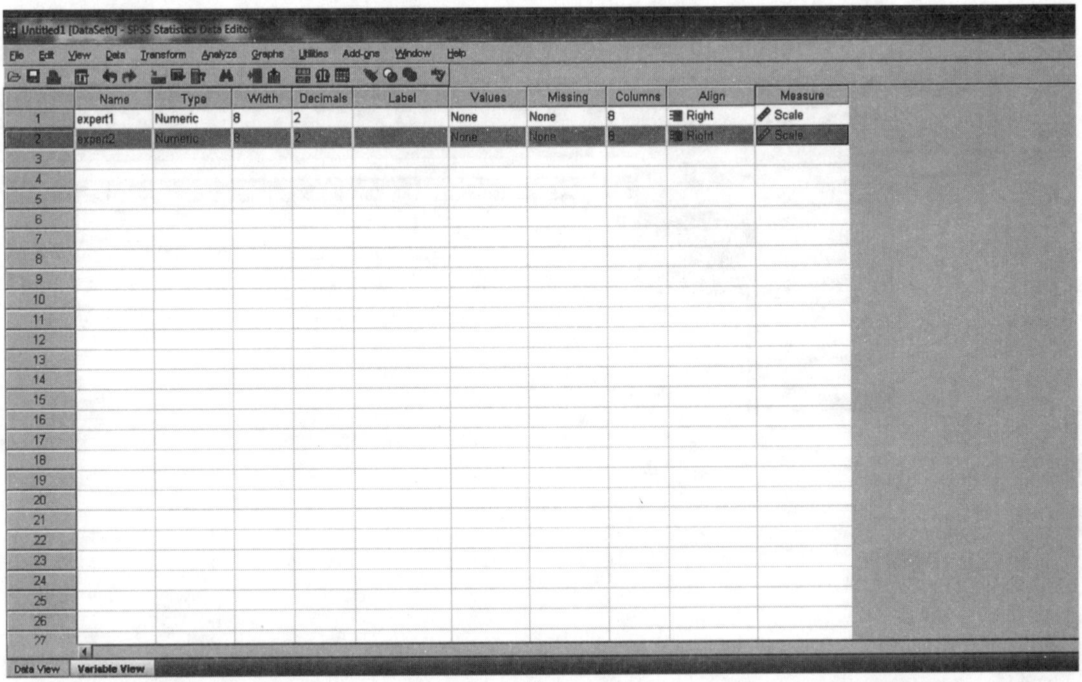

639. Click on "**Data View**" and enter the collected data as shown in the following screen.

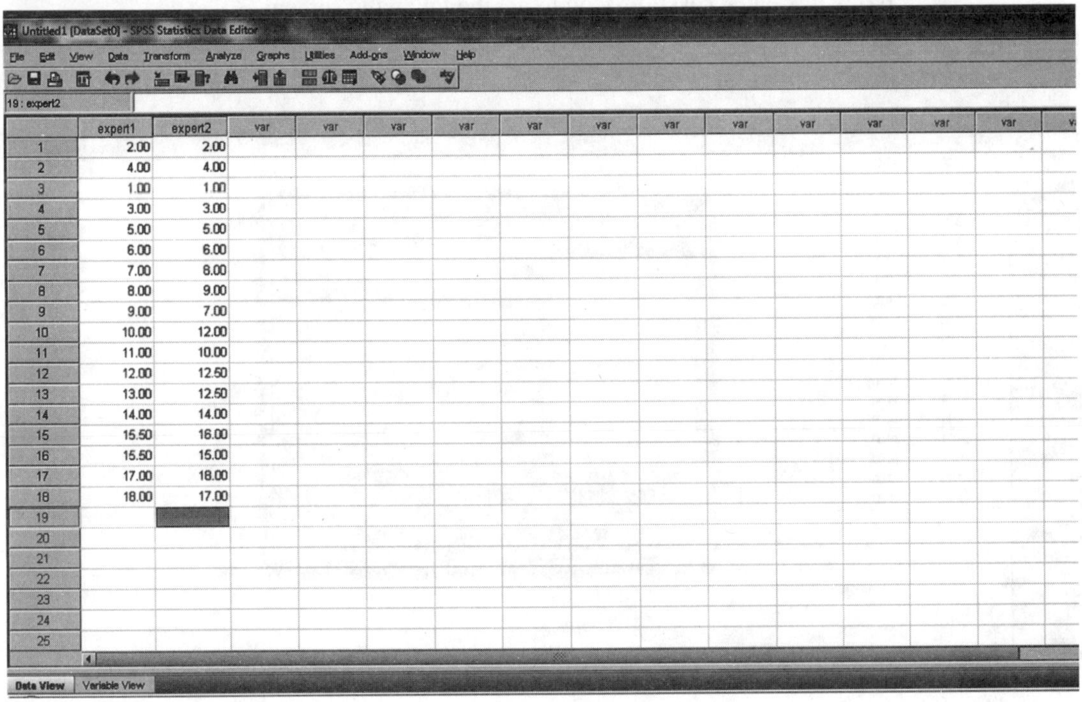

640. Click on "**Analyse**", bring curser to "**Descriptive Statistics**" and finally on "**Crosstab**" to get the following screen.

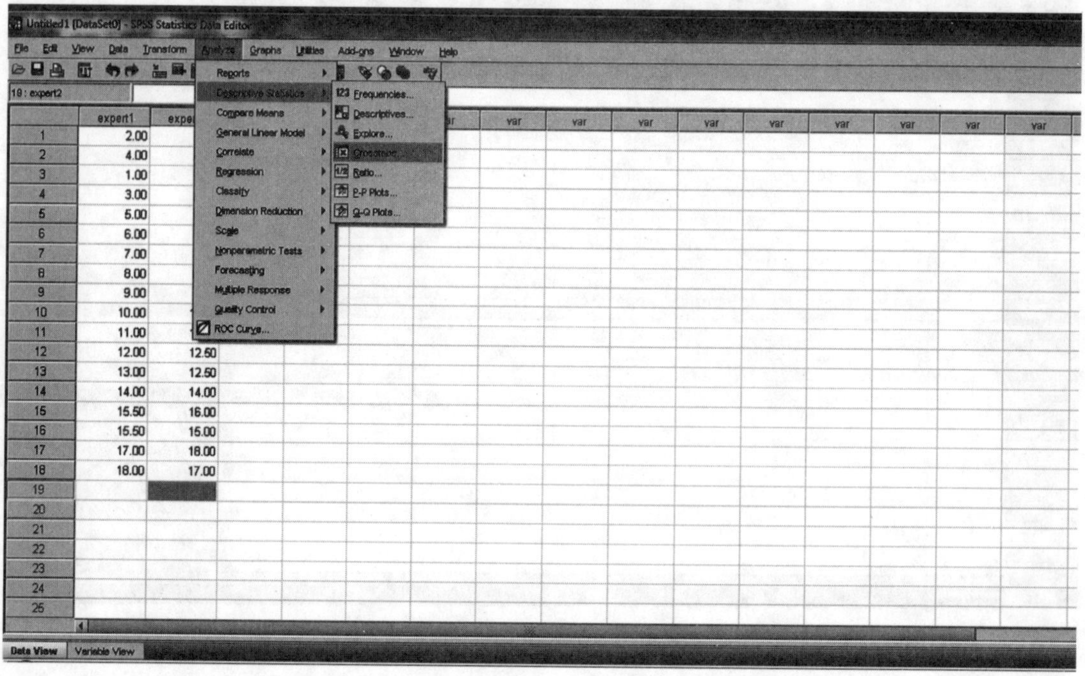

641. Click on "**Crosstab**" icon to get the following screen.

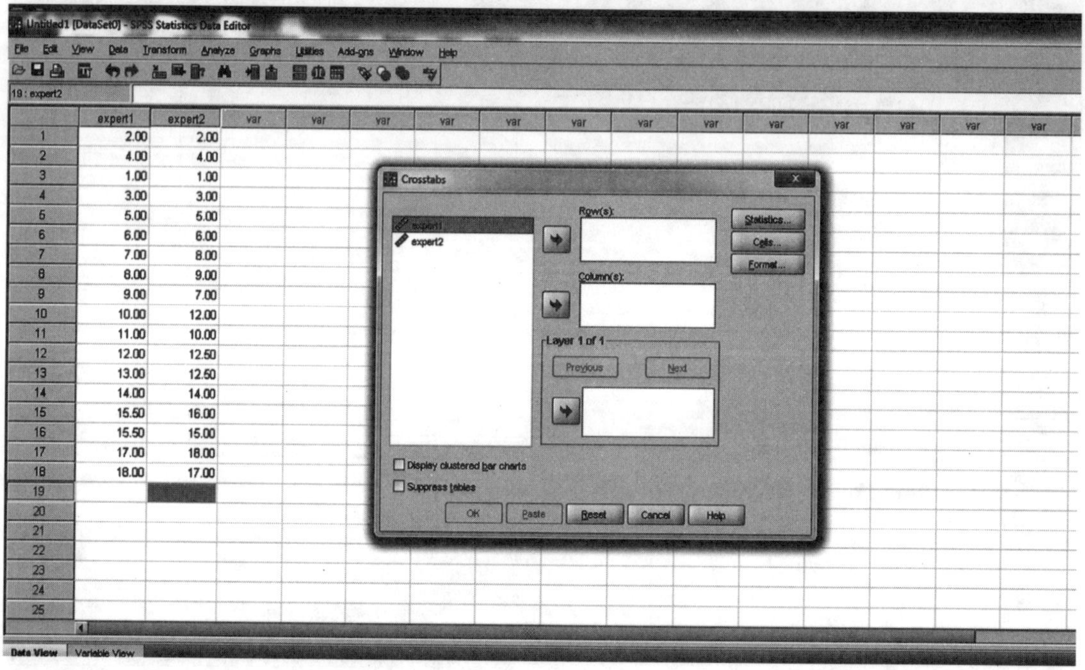

642. Shift "**expert1**" to the "**Row(s)**" dialog box and "**expert2**" to the "**Colum(s)**" dialog box to get the following screen.

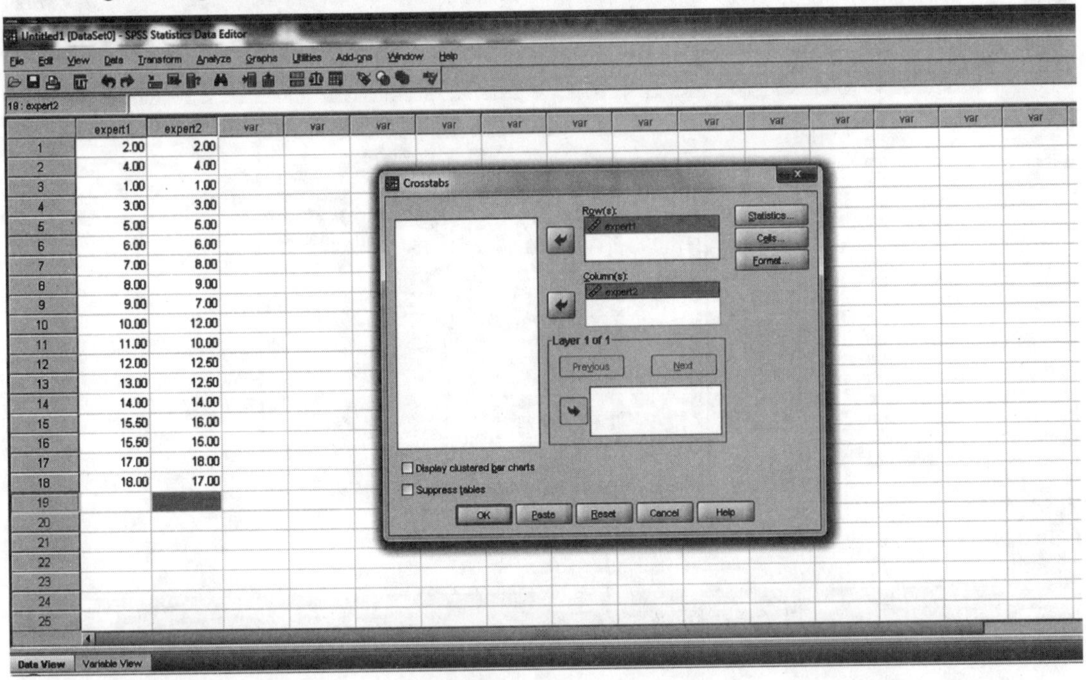

643. Click on "**Statistics**" icon to get the following screen.

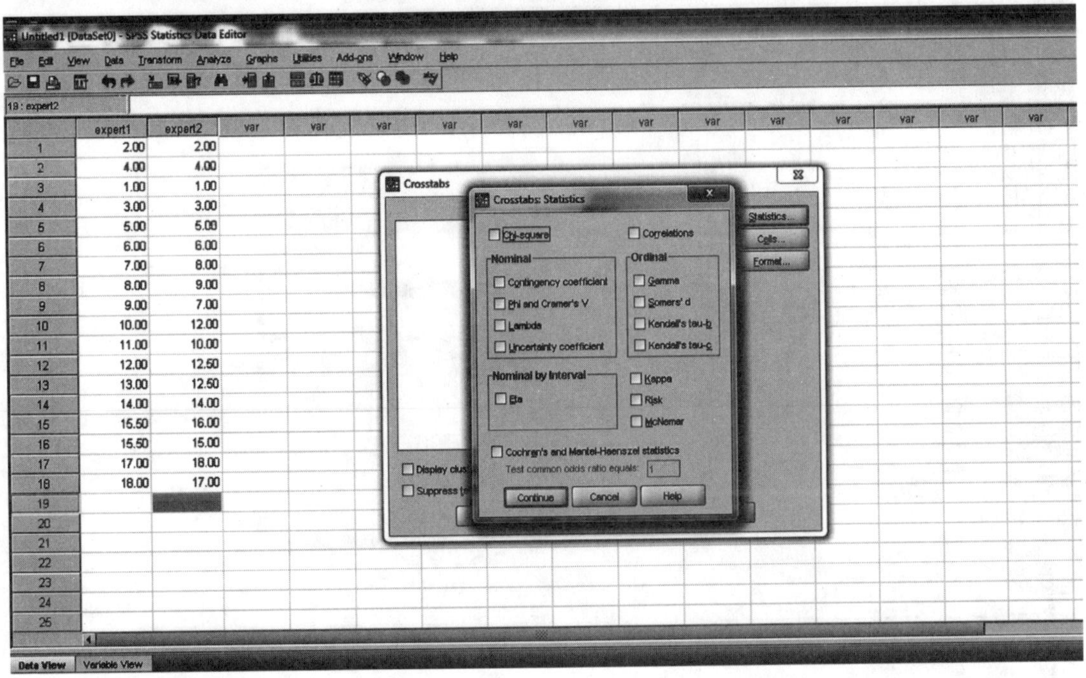

644. Highlight "**Kendall's Tau-c**" to get the following screen.

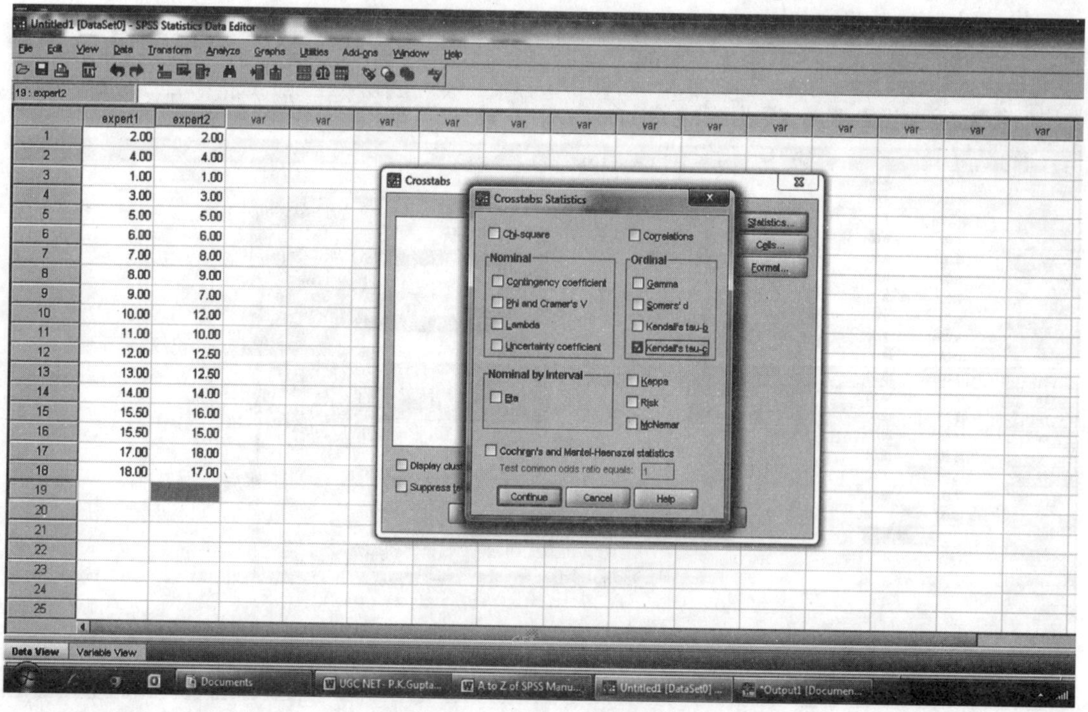

645. Click on "**Continue**" to get the following screen.

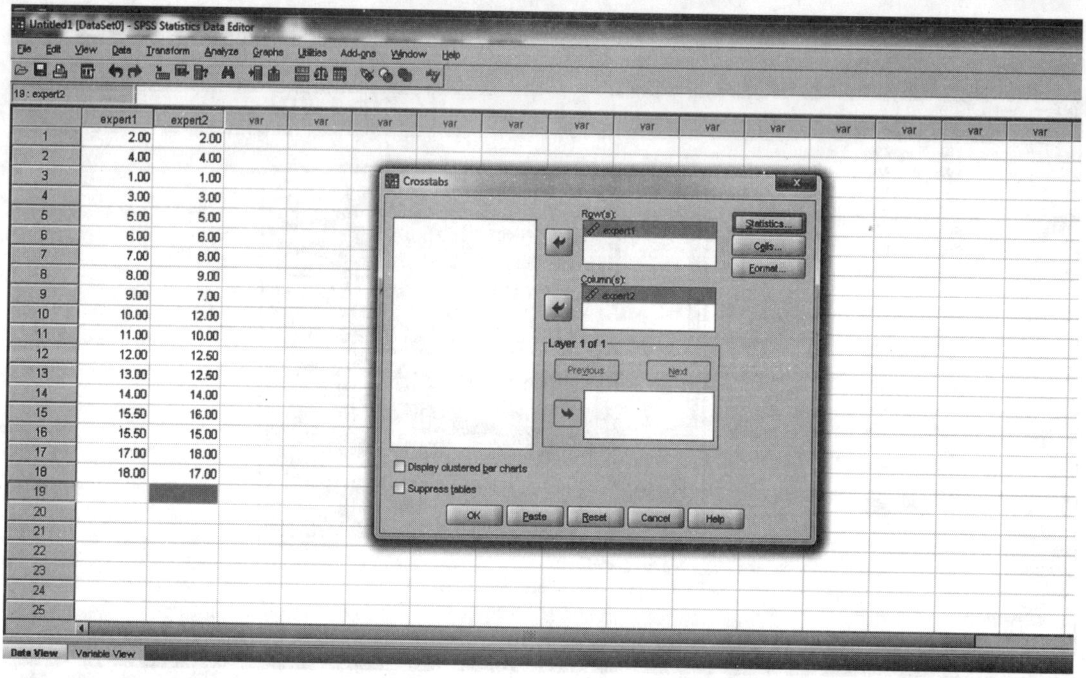

646. Click on "**OK**" to get the following output of Kendall's Tau-c.

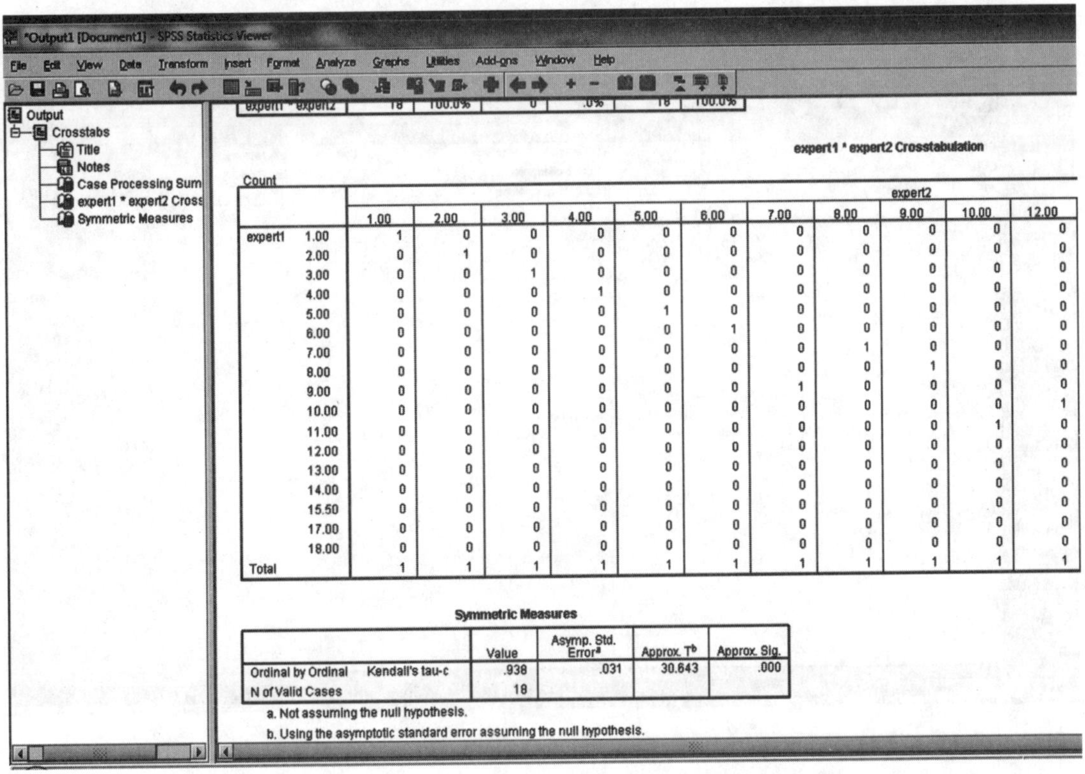

expert1 * expert2 Crosstabulation

Count

		expert2										
		1.00	2.00	3.00	4.00	5.00	6.00	7.00	8.00	9.00	10.00	12.00
expert1	1.00	1	0	0	0	0	0	0	0	0	0	0
	2.00	0	1	0	0	0	0	0	0	0	0	0
	3.00	0	0	1	0	0	0	0	0	0	0	0
	4.00	0	0	0	1	0	0	0	0	0	0	0
	5.00	0	0	0	0	1	0	0	0	0	0	0
	6.00	0	0	0	0	0	1	0	0	0	0	0
	7.00	0	0	0	0	0	0	0	1	0	0	0
	8.00	0	0	0	0	0	0	0	0	1	0	0
	9.00	0	0	0	0	0	0	1	0	0	0	0
	10.00	0	0	0	0	0	0	0	0	0	0	1
	11.00	0	0	0	0	0	0	0	0	0	1	0
	12.00	0	0	0	0	0	0	0	0	0	0	0
	13.00	0	0	0	0	0	0	0	0	0	0	0
	14.00	0	0	0	0	0	0	0	0	0	0	0
	15.50	0	0	0	0	0	0	0	0	0	0	0
	17.00	0	0	0	0	0	0	0	0	0	0	0
	18.00	0	0	0	0	0	0	0	0	0	0	0
Total		1	1	1	1	1	1	1	1	1	1	1

Symmetric Measures

		Value	Asymp. Std. Error[a]	Approx. T[b]	Approx. Sig.
Ordinal by Ordinal	Kendall's tau-c	.938	.031	30.643	.000
N of Valid Cases		18			

a. Not assuming the null hypothesis.

b. Using the asymptotic standard error assuming the null hypothesis.

Cochran's and Mantel-Haenszel Statistics

647. Cochran's and Mantel-Haenszel Statistics also known as Cochran's - Mantel-Haenszel Statistics. It is a Non-Parametric Statistics used to study the association between two categorical dichotomous variables after adjusting for or taking into account confounding variables. It is used for repeated test of independent. Suppose you have multiple 2 X 2 tables of independence and you have done the research multiple times or at multiple locations. The data may be either on Interval Scale or Ratio Scale but divided into two categories or classes. McNemar can be used only when there is 2 X 2 Contingency Table. On the other hand, Cochran's Mantel-Haenszel Statistics can handle analysis of multiple 2X2Xk tables from Stratified Samples. Let us take the following objective.

To study the association between Obesity and Cardio-vascular Disease (CVD) of people belonging to 31 to 35 Age, 36 to 40 Age and 41 to 45Age groups.

Open SPSS and under "**Variable View**" icon enter the names of all variables as shown in the following screen.

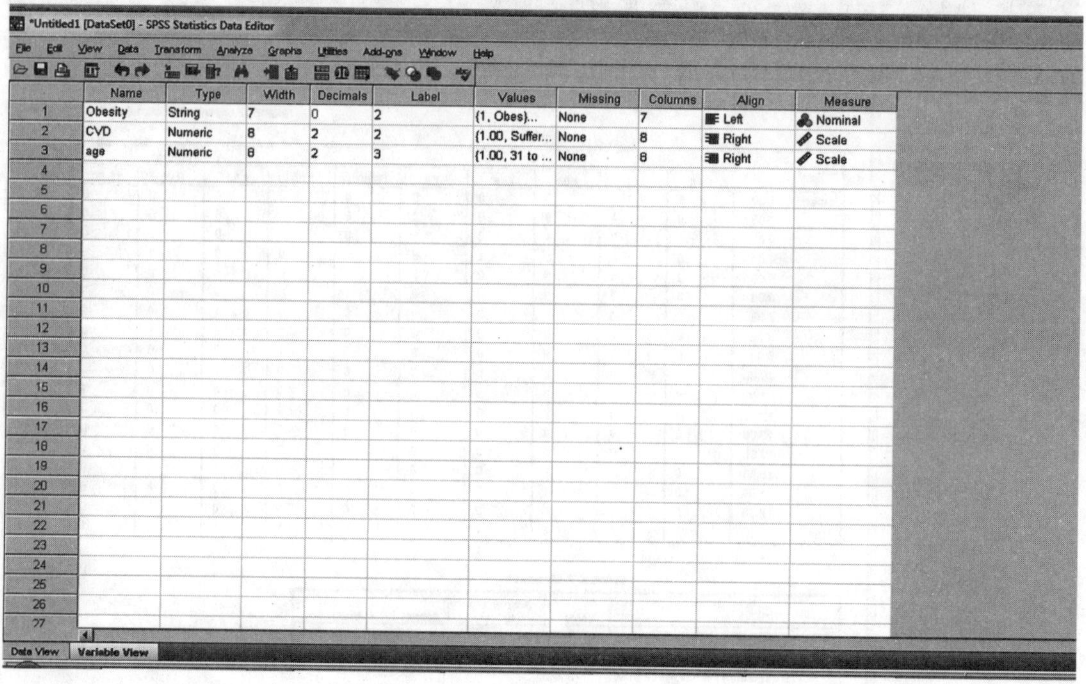

	Name	Type	Width	Decimals	Label	Values	Missing	Columns	Align	Measure
1	Obesity	String	7	0	2	{1, Obes}...	None	7	Left	Nominal
2	CVD	Numeric	8	2	2	{1.00, Suffer...	None	8	Right	Scale
3	age	Numeric	8	2	3	{1.00, 31 to ...	None	8	Right	Scale

648. Click on "**Data View**" and enter the collected data as shown in the following screen.

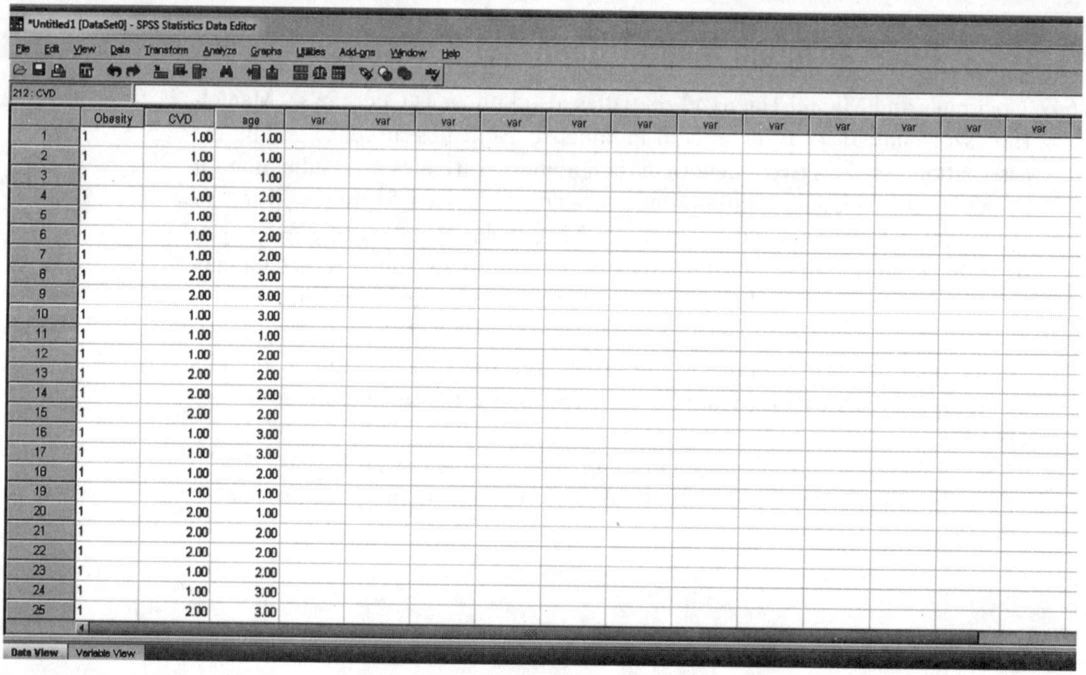

	Obesity	CVD	age	var	var	var	var	var	var	var	var	var	var	var	var
1	1	1.00	1.00												
2	1	1.00	1.00												
3	1	1.00	1.00												
4	1	1.00	2.00												
5	1	1.00	2.00												
6	1	1.00	2.00												
7	1	1.00	2.00												
8	1	2.00	3.00												
9	1	2.00	3.00												
10	1	1.00	3.00												
11	1	1.00	1.00												
12	1	1.00	2.00												
13	1	2.00	2.00												
14	1	2.00	2.00												
15	1	2.00	2.00												
16	1	1.00	3.00												
17	1	1.00	3.00												
18	1	1.00	2.00												
19	1	1.00	1.00												
20	1	2.00	1.00												
21	1	2.00	2.00												
22	1	2.00	2.00												
23	1	1.00	2.00												
24	1	1.00	3.00												
25	1	2.00	3.00												

649. Click on "**Analyse**", bring curser to "**Descriptive Statistics**" and finally on "**Crosstab**" to get the following screen.

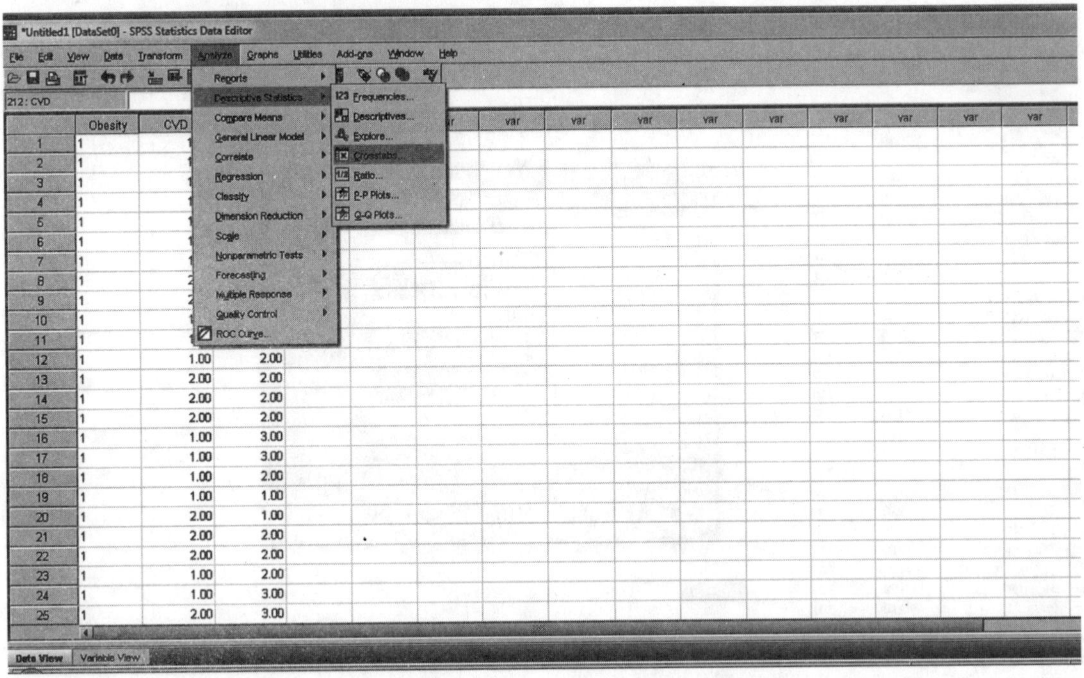

650. Click on "**Crosstabs**" to get the following screen.

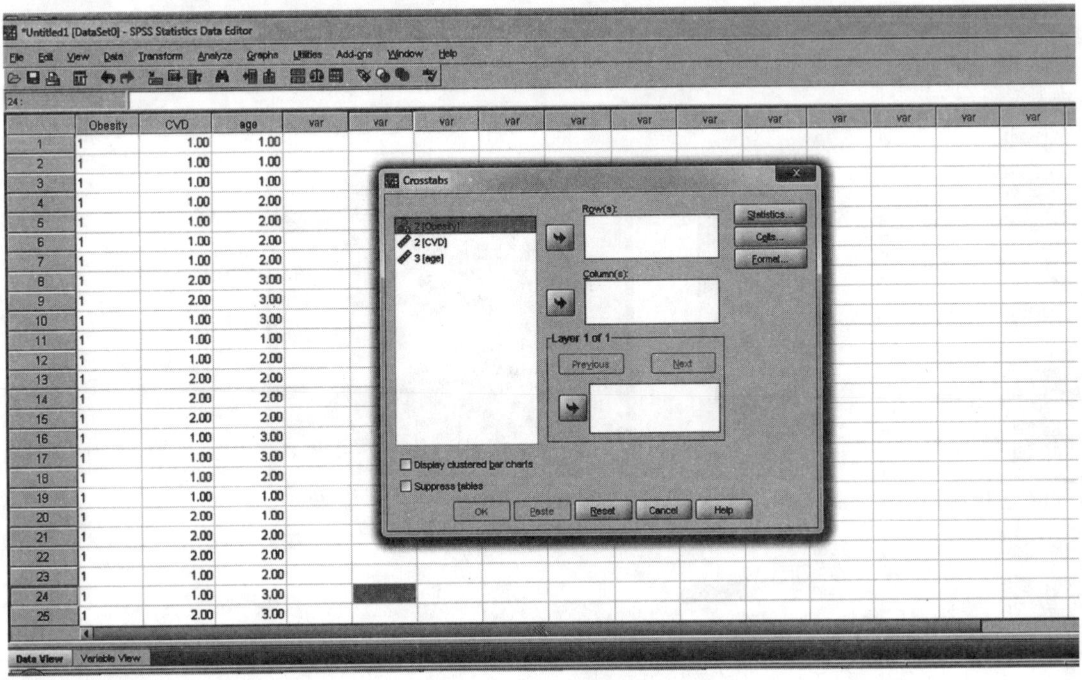

651. Shift "**Obesity**" to "**Rows**", "**CVD"** to "**Columns**" and "**Age**" to "**Layer 1 of 1**" dialog boxes to get the following screen.

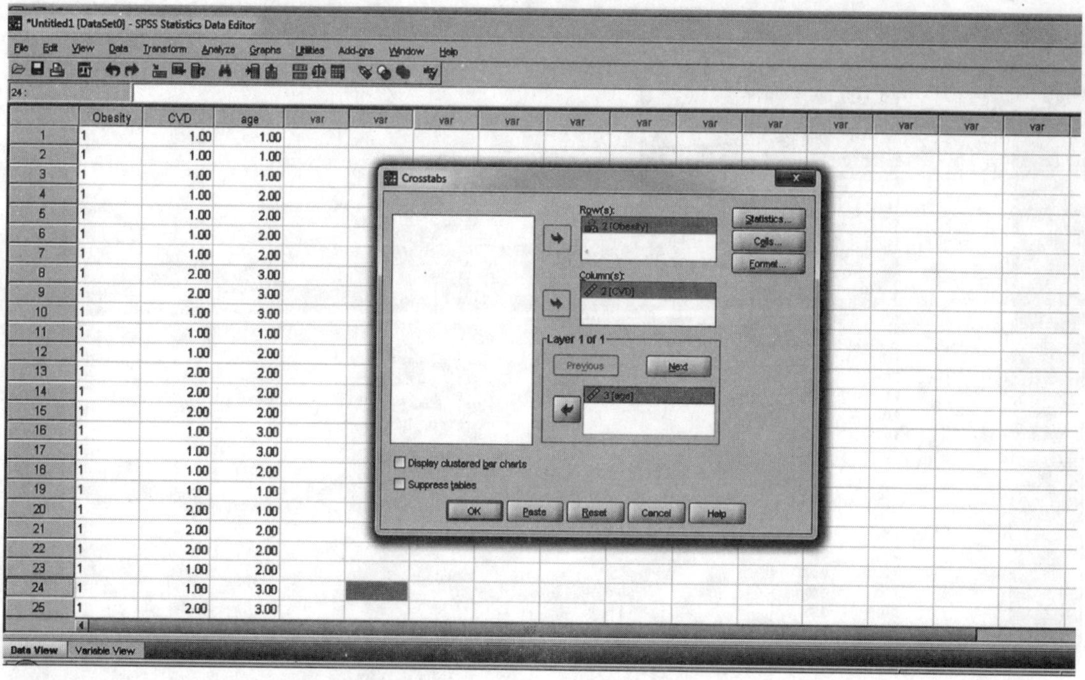

652. Click on "**Statistics**" to get the following screen.

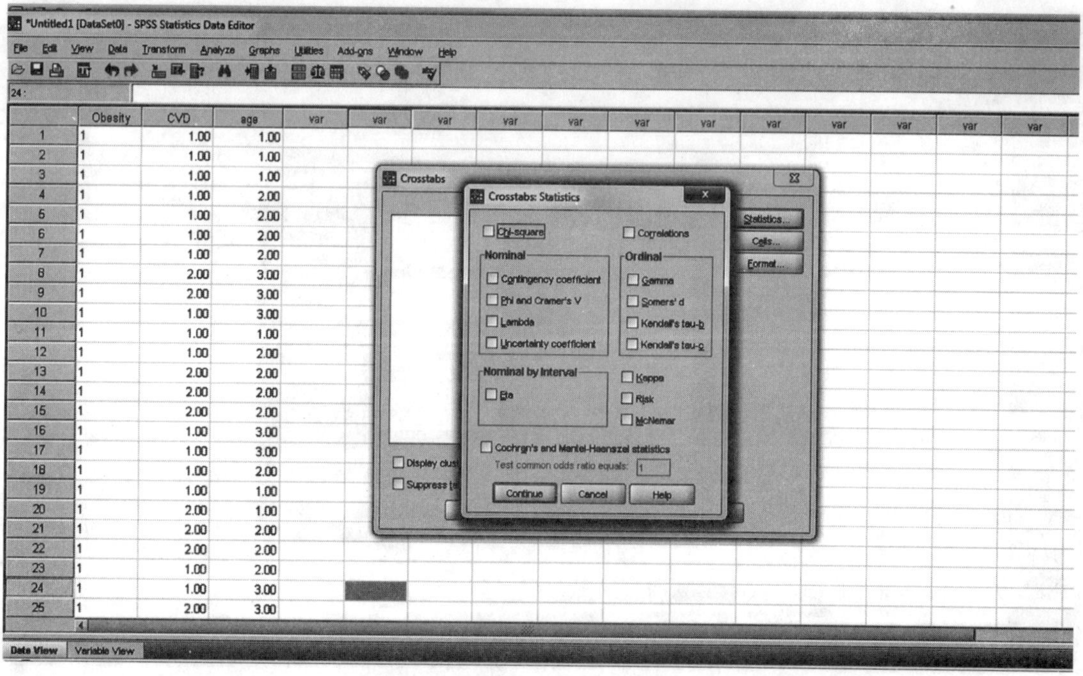

653. Highlight "**Cochran's and Mantel-Haenszel Statistics**" to get the following screen.

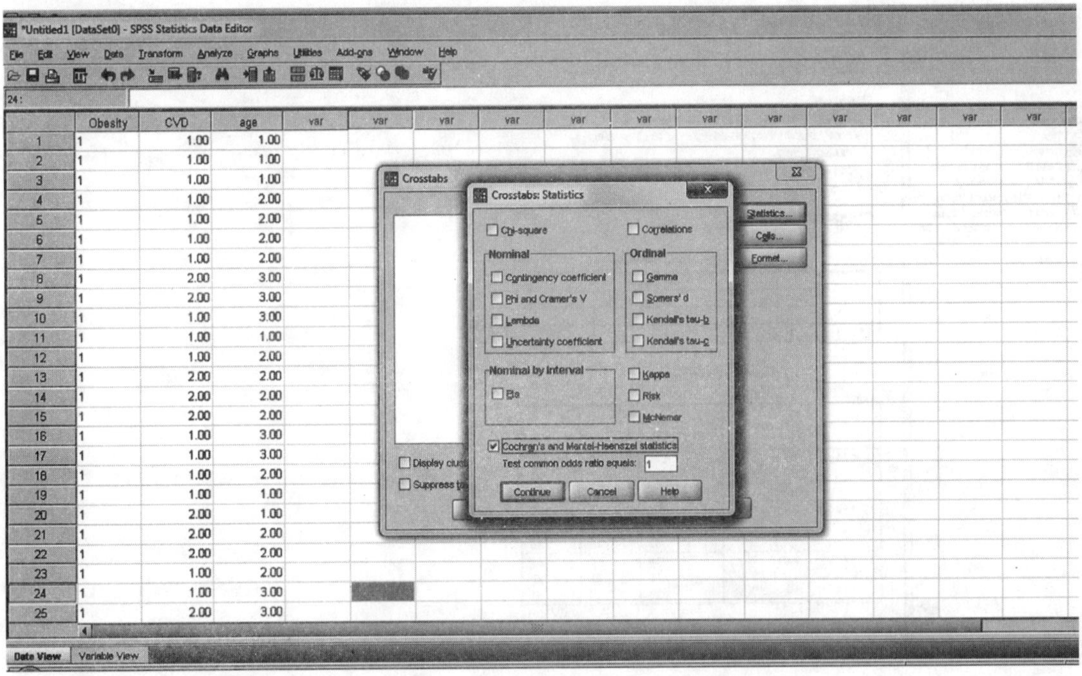

654. Click on "**Continue**" to get the following screen.

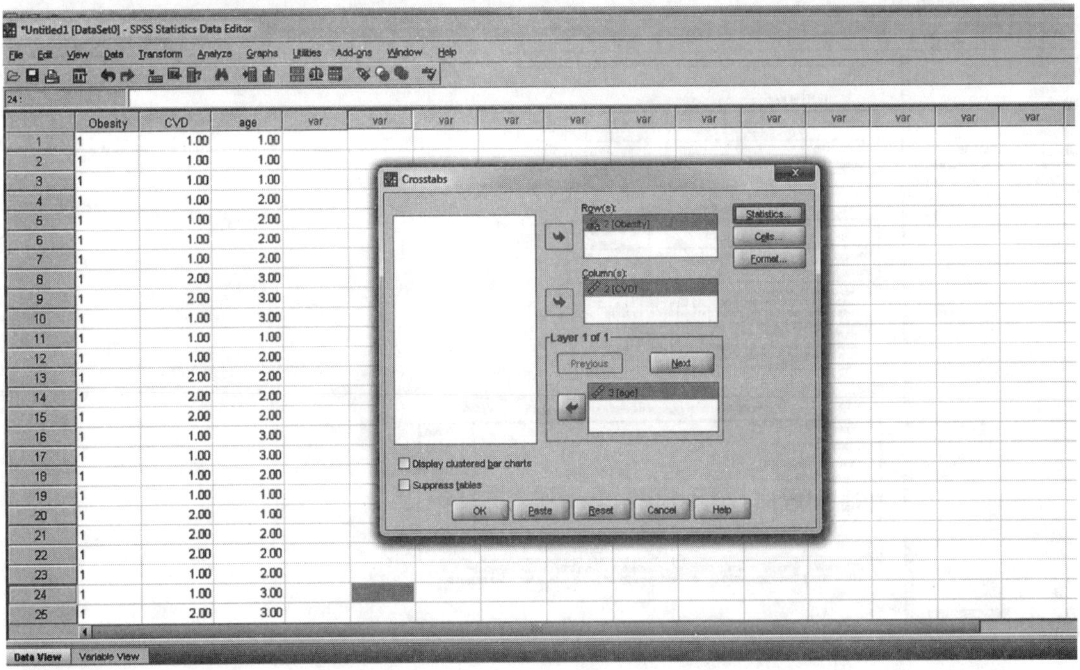

655. Click on "**OK**" to get the following outputs of Cochran's and Mantel-Haenszel Statistics.

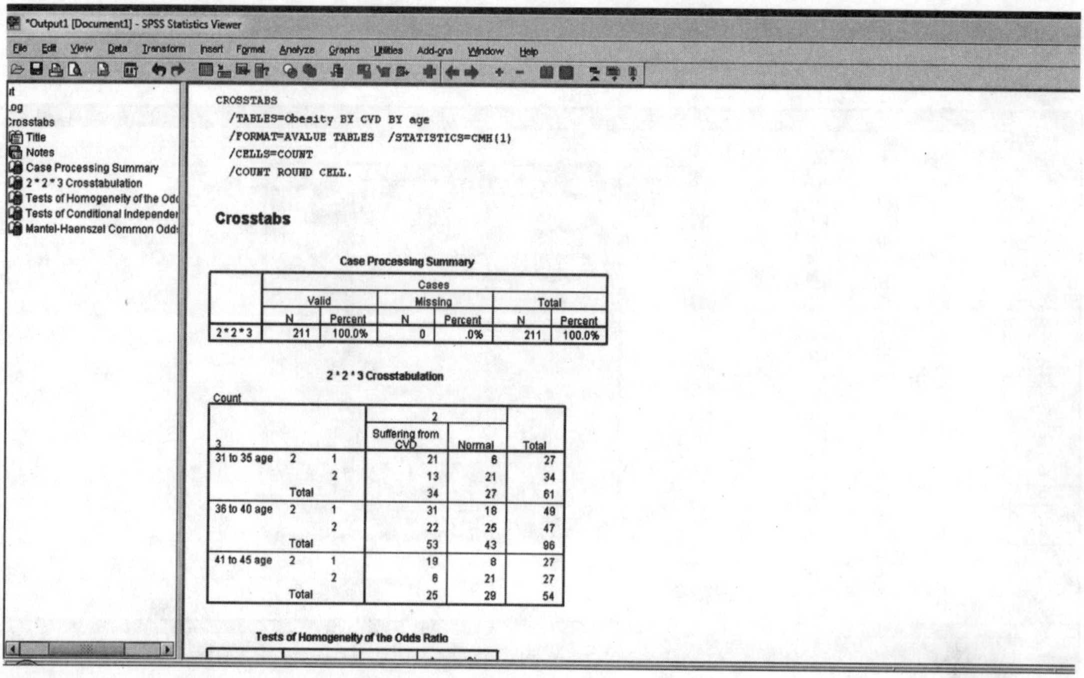


```
CROSSTABS
  /TABLES=Obesity BY CVD BY age
  /FORMAT=AVALUE TABLES  /STATISTICS=CMH(1)
  /CELLS=COUNT
  /COUNT ROUND CELL.
```

Crosstabs

Case Processing Summary

	Cases					
	Valid		Missing		Total	
	N	Percent	N	Percent	N	Percent
2*2*3	211	100.0%	0	.0%	211	100.0%

2*2*3 Crosstabulation

Count

3			2: Suffering from CVD	2: Normal	Total
31 to 35 age	2	1	21	6	27
		2	13	21	34
	Total		34	27	61
36 to 40 age	2	1	31	18	49
		2	22	25	47
	Total		53	43	96
41 to 45 age	2	1	19	8	27
		2	6	21	27
	Total		25	29	54

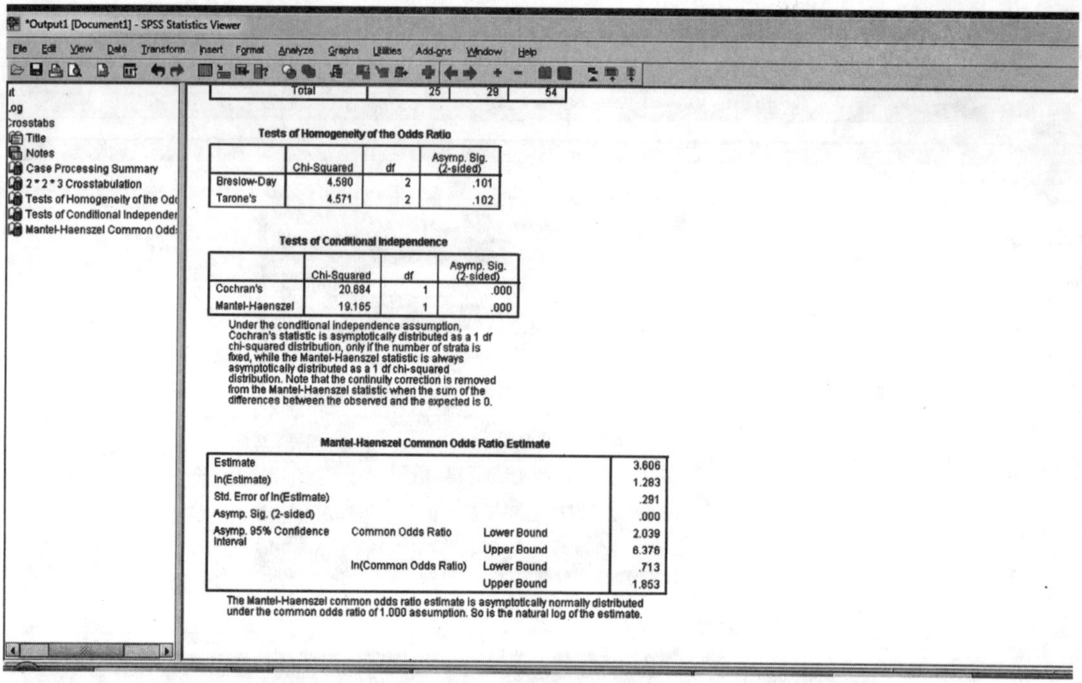

Tests of Homogeneity of the Odds Ratio

	Chi-Squared	df	Asymp. Sig. (2-sided)
Breslow-Day	4.580	2	.101
Tarone's	4.571	2	.102

Tests of Conditional Independence

	Chi-Squared	df	Asymp. Sig. (2-sided)
Cochran's	20.684	1	.000
Mantel-Haenszel	19.165	1	.000

Under the conditional independence assumption, Cochran's statistic is asymptotically distributed as a 1 df chi-squared distribution, only if the number of strata is fixed, while the Mantel-Haenszel statistic is always asymptotically distributed as a 1 df chi-squared distribution. Note that the continuity correction is removed from the Mantel-Haenszel statistic when the sum of the differences between the observed and the expected is 0.

Mantel-Haenszel Common Odds Ratio Estimate

Estimate			3.606
ln(Estimate)			1.283
Std. Error of ln(Estimate)			.291
Asymp. Sig. (2-sided)			.000
Asymp. 95% Confidence Interval	Common Odds Ratio	Lower Bound	2.039
		Upper Bound	6.376
	ln(Common Odds Ratio)	Lower Bound	.713
		Upper Bound	1.853

The Mantel-Haenszel common odds ratio estimate is asymptotically normally distributed under the common odds ratio of 1.000 assumption. So is the natural log of the estimate.